Elizabeth Madden

The Anglo-Saxon
Literature Handbook

Blackwell Literature Handbooks

This new series offers the student thorough and lively introductions to literary periods, movements, and, in some instances, authors and genres, from Anglo-Saxon to the Postmodern. Each volume is written by a leading specialist to be invitingly accessible and informative. Chapters are devoted to the coverage of cultural context, the provision of brief but detailed biographical essays on the authors concerned, critical coverage of key works, and surveys of themes and topics, together with bibliographies of selected further reading. Students new to a period of study or to a period genre will discover all they need to know to orientate and ground themselves in their studies, in volumes that are as stimulating to read as they are convenient to use.

Published

The Science Fiction Handbook
M. Keith Booker and
Anne-Marie Thomas

The Seventeenth-Century Literature Handbook
Marshall Grossman

The Twentieth-Century American Fiction Handbook
Christopher MacGowan

The British and Irish Short Story Handbook
David Malcolm

The Crime Fiction Handbook
Peter Messent

The Literary Theory Handbook,
second edition
Gregory Castle

The Anglo-Saxon Literature Handbook
Mark C. Amodio

The Anglo-Saxon Literature Handbook

Mark C. Amodio

WILEY-BLACKWELL

A John Wiley & Sons, Ltd., Publication

This edition first published 2014
© 2014 Mark C. Amodio

Blackwell Publishing was acquired by John Wiley & Sons in February 2007. Blackwell's publishing program has been merged with Wiley's global Scientific, Technical, and Medical business to form Wiley-Blackwell.

Registered Office
John Wiley & Sons, Ltd, The Atrium, Southern Gate, Chichester, West Sussex, PO19 8SQ, UK

Editorial Offices
350 Main Street, Malden, MA 02148-5020, USA
9600 Garsington Road, Oxford, OX4 2DQ, UK
The Atrium, Southern Gate, Chichester, West Sussex, PO19 8SQ, UK

For details of our global editorial offices, for customer services, and for information about how to apply for permission to reuse the copyright material in this book please see our website at www.wiley.com/wiley-blackwell.

The right of Mark C. Amodio to be identified as the author of this work has been asserted in accordance with the UK Copyright, Designs and Patents Act 1988.

All rights reserved. No part of this publication may be reproduced, stored in a retrieval system, or transmitted, in any form or by any means, electronic, mechanical, photocopying, recording or otherwise, except as permitted by the UK Copyright, Designs and Patents Act 1988, without the prior permission of the publisher.

Wiley also publishes its books in a variety of electronic formats. Some content that appears in print may not be available in electronic books.

Designations used by companies to distinguish their products are often claimed as trademarks. All brand names and product names used in this book are trade names, service marks, trademarks or registered trademarks of their respective owners. The publisher is not associated with any product or vendor mentioned in this book. This publication is designed to provide accurate and authoritative information in regard to the subject matter covered. It is sold on the understanding that the publisher is not engaged in rendering professional services. If professional advice or other expert assistance is required, the services of a competent professional should be sought.

Library of Congress Cataloging-in-Publication Data

Amodio, Mark.
The Anglo-Saxon literature handbook / Mark C. Amodio.
     pages cm
  Includes bibliographical references and index.
  ISBN 978-0-631-22697-0 (cloth) – ISBN 978-0-631-22698-7 (pbk.)   1. English literature–Old English, ca. 450-1100–History and criticism–Handbooks, manuals, etc.   2. Civilization, Anglo-Saxon.   I. Title.
  PR173.A46 2014
  829'.09–dc23
                                        2012050143

A catalogue record for this book is available from the British Library.

Cover image: Detail from miniature of St. Luke, from The Lindisfarne Gospels, 710–721. © The British Library Board, MS Cotton Nero D. IV, f.137v
Cover design by Richard Boxall Design Associates
Part opening images: Anglo-Saxon carved stone © Marbury / Shutterstock

Set in 10/13pt Sabon by SPi Publisher Services, Pondicherry, India
Printed in Singapore by Ho Printing Singapore Pte Ltd

1   2014

For Min and Luc,
heorðgeneatas

and

To the memory of John Miles Foley,
bocere 7 freond

Contents

Preface

In the preface to his translation of Pope Gregory the Great's *Pastoral Care*, King Alfred the Great famously remarked of Anglo-Saxon England's intellectual forebears that 'mon mæg giet gesion hiora swæð' (Sweet, 4.15–16) [one can yet see their footprints] in the texts they produced. The same can be said of the varied and extensive written records that survive from the Anglo-Saxon period, and in keeping with the general aim of the series of which it is a part, this *Handbook* attempts to provide a broad overview both of the many textual 'footprints' the Anglo-Saxons have bequeathed us and of the culture that produced them. Far from attempting to offer the 'last word' on any of the texts or topics it covers, this volume rather offers any number of 'first words' that will, in conjunction with the suggested further readings, provide readers with the means to undertake more detailed and specialized enquiries than can be offered here. The suggested further readings have been drawn for the most part from studies that have appeared in the last fifteen or so years, although on occasion some older pieces have been included as well.

The Anglo-Saxon era, which stretches roughly from the middle of the fifth century to the end of the eleventh has the distinction of being not only the longest single period in English literary history, but one of the most inaccessible ones as well. As the textual remains of the period eloquently testify, the Anglo-Saxon literary tradition was rich, vibrant, and especially complex. Its complexity stems, in part, from its dual nature since the Anglo-Saxon literary tradition was not a single, unified entity, but was rather comprised of two parallel branches in which texts were produced in, respectively, Latin and the vernacular. That Anglo-Saxon authors produced a significant body of Latin literature is not surprising since Latin was the *lingua franca* of the educated medieval West and England was throughout the early Middle Ages an important centre of learning. What is unusual, though, is that alongside the Anglo-Latin tradition another one emerges in which authors write in their native tongue, known as Old English (OE), and produce a voluminous, broad, and important body of work. While we will on occasion gesture towards the Anglo-Latin tradition and some of its texts, this *Handbook*'s focus will be primarily upon the tradition of vernacular writing in early medieval England, a tradition that comes to rival the Latin tradition in terms of its scope and importance.

Even though the language in which vernacular texts were produced in Anglo-Saxon England is the direct ancestor of Modern English (NE), it is sufficiently different from the language as spoken today that it must be learned like a foreign language. Whereas NE speakers are for the most part able to read Middle English (ME) texts with little or no special training, especially when the texts are presented in glossed editions, the grammar, syntax, and lexicon (or word-stock) of OE render Anglo-Saxon literature in its original form all but impenetrable without special training. However, the availability of many reliable and accurate modern translations means that contemporary students can have easy access to virtually all the poetry that was written in Anglo-Saxon England and to a large portion of the period's prose texts as well. But since translation is at best an imperfect art given what is necessarily lost in shifting a text from its native expressive economy to another, translators frequently have little choice but to mask or otherwise alter important, often crucial, aspects of Anglo-Saxon texts as they strive to produce the polished and idiomatic NE renderings their intended audiences expect. Since presenting translations absent the original text creates a false sense of familiarity while further eliding the original's inherent otherness, or alterity, this *Handbook* cites all vernacular Anglo-Saxon texts first in the original OE and then in NE translations. Because they attempt to preserve and reproduce, as far as is possible, the rhythm, feel, and word order of the OE, these translations can at times be somewhat unidiomatic. If there is a virtue to such translations, it is that in approximating some of the expressive patterns the Anglo-Saxons themselves employed they open a window onto the thought patterns of those who produced them. The potential insights thus to be gained may well offset the minor distraction of having to contend with translations that are not always wholly idiomatic. Keeping the original language quotations in close proximity to their modern translations also affords non-specialist readers the opportunity to discover and further contemplate some of the very many minor and major connections that remain between OE and NE, connections that would remain hidden were only NE translations supplied. For example, not only does the compound 'handbook' in the title of this volume descend directly from OE 'handboc', but the nature of the texts to which this term refers has remained largely unchanged from the Anglo-Saxon period to the present day, as we can see in Byrhtferth's explanation that the text he is writing in the early eleventh century on the computus is an 'enchiridion (þæt ys manualis on Lyden ond hondboc on Englisc)' (Baker and Lapidge, 120.248–49) [enchiridion (that is manual in Latin and handbook in English)].

Aside from the language that both connects OE to and separates it from NE, contemporary readers of Anglo-Saxon literature must not only contend with its profound alterity, but they must also keep in mind that the narrative strategies we habitually rely on to interpret literature can provide only limited (sometimes very limited) access to the world of Anglo-Saxon literature. To take but one example, were contemporary readers to approach Anglo-Saxon literature as if it were the product of authors whose compositional habits closely mirror those of contemporary authors, and were they further to assume that Anglo-Saxon authors possessed anything like the awareness modern authors possess (of their authority, cultural situation, etc.), they would find themselves asking questions that would be, at best, impertinent, and arriving at interpretations that run the risk of being highly skewed. The interpretive strategies of contemporary readers especially need to be recalibrated when reading Anglo-Saxon poetry because it is articulated via the lexical, metrical, and narrative pathways of a specialized expressive economy. Rooted in an earlier, oral and performative tradition, this expressive economy is no more limiting or restrictive to Anglo-Saxon authors than the grammatical and syntactic rules that govern NE are to contemporary ones. Some texts may be more grounded than others in the earlier oral tradition and so may preserve, for example, more of the performative features associated with oral texts, but they are not oral texts: what we have inherited from the Anglo-Saxons is the written record of a literate, entexted tradition very similar to the one in which texts continue to be produced and received today.

Part 1 of this *Handbook* contextualizes the literary remains of Anglo-Saxon England by providing brief sketches of the period's political, ecclesiastical, intellectual, linguistic, and literary histories before touching upon the interconnected and interdependent oral and literate traditions in which Anglo-Saxon literature emerges. Part 2 is organized along a roughly chronological line that starts with King Alfred the Great and concludes with Ælfric of Eynsham, and it focuses on the varied and extensive prose records that have survived from the period, many of which can be confidently dated because they were produced by historical figures. Because the poems that survive from Anglo-Saxon England are, with a few notable exceptions, very difficult to date, after beginning with the poem that is generally accepted as being one of the earliest examples of OE poetry, Cædmon's *Hymn*, Part 3 subsequently discusses the poetic records in the context of the manuscripts in which they are found, concluding finally with *Durham*, a demonstrably late OE poem. Throughout, the poems are discussed in the order in which they appear in their manuscripts. Parts 2 and 3 cover as much of Anglo-Saxon literature as possible, but considerations of space precluded the discussion of a number of texts. Parts 4 and 5 offer brief sketches, respectively, of some of the major critical approaches that have been taken to Anglo-Saxon literature and of some of the major themes that that have so far been identified in it. Neither of the final parts strives to be exhaustively comprehensive, but are necessarily selective in their coverage.

Acknowledgments

It is a pleasure to acknowledge the personal, institutional, and professional debts I have incurred while writing this book. Among my colleagues at Vassar College, I am particularly grateful to Frank Bergon, Eve D'Ambra, Beth Darlington, Don Foster, Ann Imbrie (*in memoriam*), Lisa Paravisini-Gebert, Dan Peck, and Paul Russell for their friendship and support. I owe a special debt of gratitude to Eamon Grennan, who heard, often at great length, about each stage of this project over the course of many an evening – and many a pint – at our local.

Thanks are due to Ron Sharp for generously supporting my research during his tenure as Dean of the Faculty, and to the Vassar College Committee on Research for its support. Much of this book was written during leaves, and I am grateful to Vassar College for making them possible. This project could not have been completed without the assistance of the staff in the Vassar College Interlibrary Loan and Acquisitions offices. Despite the at times no doubt overwhelming volume of my requests, everything was located and delivered more quickly than one would think humanly possible.

The bibliography stands as a partial acknowledgment of my debt not just to the scholars cited within it, but to all those whose work has helped inform my understanding of Anglo-Saxon literature. I owe more personal thanks to the following: Leslie Arnovick, Benjamin Bagby, Holly Bergon, Bob Bjork, Rob Brown, Tom Cable, Robert DeMaria, Jr., Antonette DiPaolo Healey, Bashir El-Beshti (*in memoriam*), Anne-Marie Foley, Lori Garner, Tom Hall, Joe Harris, John Hill, Tom Hill, Nick Howe (*in memoriam*), Ted Irving (*in memoriam*), Kevin Kiernan, Stacy Klein, Heather Maring, Michael Matto, John McBratney, J.K. 'Monk' McDonough, Sandy McEachern, Steve Mitchell, Kim Montgomery, Joe Nagy, Randall Nakayama (*in memoriam*), Alexandra Hennessey Olsen, Karl Reichl, Paul Remley, Jackie Rubio, Andrew Scheil, Vinni Genovese Schek, Mike Schoenfeldt, Paul Szarmach,

Pat Wallace, and Jan Ziolkowski. I am most especially grateful to the late Alain Renoir, who first as a teacher and then for many years as a friend, taught me not only about about medieval literature, but also about so much else.

Over the years I have had the good fortune to work with a number of very talented student assistants, and it is with pleasure that I thank Jaji Crocker, and Amanda Jameson for all their help during this project's early stages. I am also very grateful to Molly Bronstein and Julia Chang for their sharp eyes and keen attention to detail during the stages leading to its publication, and to Madeleine P. Amodio for all her careful work preparing the indices.

Katherine O'Brien O'Keeffe, Joel T. Rosenthal, and Samantha Zacher generously read portions of this book at its earliest stages, and I am grateful to them for their insightful and helpful comments. I am especially grateful to Andy Orchard for reading the manuscript in draft and for offering many incisive suggestions that helped me rethink and substantially improve it. That I did not follow all his suggestions is my fault, not his. While these readers saved me from any number of minor missteps as well as from some major ones, they are in no way responsible for any infelicities of thought or expression. All errors that remain within these pages are wholly mine.

I have have been fortunate to work with editors at Wiley-Blackwell who are not just extremely talented professionals, but who possess patience that even saints would envy. Emma Bennett, publisher for literature, social sciences, and humanities, and the project editor Ben Thatcher helped guide this project to completion with unfailing grace and good humour. I am also grateful to Andrew McNeillie for offering me this project while he was at the press.

I have always enjoyed the unwavering support of my parents, Theresa and Anthony, and I am grateful to them for all that they have given and continue to give me.

As the depth of my gratitude to Gena Andryshak cannot adequately be expressed, I must settle here simply for thanking her for daily bringing me much peace and joy.

This book is dedicated to my children, Min and Luc, who grace my life in innumerable ways, and to the memory of John Miles Foley, the likes of whom will not pass this way again.

Poughkeepsie, New York
21 October 2012

Note on the Text

The punctuation and capitalization of original-language quotations have, where necessary, been silently altered to align them with contemporary practices. Additionally, abbreviations and contractions have been silently expanded and macrons have been silently dropped throughout.

List of Abbreviations

ACMRS	Arizona Center for Medieval and Renaissance Studies
ASE	*Anglo-Saxon England*
ASPR	Anglo-Saxon Poetic Records
BL	British Library
BJRL	*Bulletin of the John Rylands University Library of Manchester*
CCCC	Cambridge, Corpus Christi College
CSASE	Cambridge Studies in Anglo-Saxon England
CUL	Cambridge University Library
ELN	*English Language Notes*
EEMF	Early English Manuscripts in Facsimile
EETS	Early English Text Society
EHR	*English Historical Review*
ES	*English Studies*
LSE	*Leeds Studies in English*
ME	Middle English
MÆ	*Medium Ævum*
MGH	Monumenta Germaniae Historica
ME	Modern English
MP	*Modern Philology*
MRTS	Medieval and Renaissance Texts and Studies
NM	*Neuphilologische Mitteilungen*
NQ	*Notes and Queries*
OE	Old English
PQ	*Philological Quarterly*
SN	*Studia Neophilologica*
SP	*Studies in Philology*

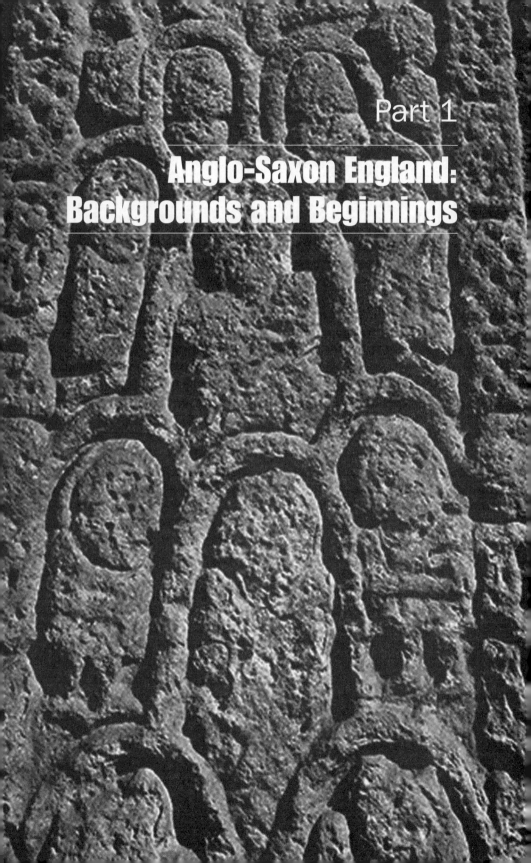

Part 1

Anglo-Saxon England: Backgrounds and Beginnings

Political History

The beginnings of Anglo-Saxon England are generally traced to 449 CE, the year in which, according to Bede's *Historia ecclesiastica gentis Anglorum* [*Ecclesiastical History of the English People*], the Germanic warrior brothers Hengist and Horsa led their troops across the English Channel. During the preceding four centuries, Britain had been under Roman control but in the face of growing threats to their homeland, the Romans withdrew the last of their troops from the island in 410. Soon after the Romans departed, the native Britons came under renewed attack from several northern tribes, which although unnamed are generally believed to have been the Picts and the Scots. The Britons appealed for help to the Roman forces in Gaul but when their request was refused, they mounted their own defence and successfully repulsed the invaders. Near the middle of the fifth century, Britain was again attacked from the north, and the Britons once again sought help from the continent, this time from several tribes. Bede tells us that among those who responded were members of 'three very powerful Germanic tribes' (Colgrave and Mynors, 51), the Angles, Saxons, and Jutes, but other tribes, including the Frisians and the Franks, came over as well. The Germanic tribes fought successfully in the service of King Vortigern and helped quell the problems besetting Britain from the north, but the mercenaries from the continent were soon to pose a problem in themselves when their leader Hengist led a revolt against Vortigern, setting in motion the process by which the long-established culture of the indigenous Britons came to be supplanted by that of the Anglo-Saxon invaders Vortigern had invited to the island.

Although the end result was the same – Britain was once again ruled by foreign forces – the invasion undertaken by the continental tribes during what is commonly known as the Age of Migration was of a very different

The Anglo-Saxon Literature Handbook, First Edition. Mark C. Amodio.
© 2014 Mark C. Amodio. Published 2014 by John Wiley & Sons, Ltd.

sort from that of the Romans several centuries earlier. During the centuries of Roman occupation, Britain remained an important and valuable colonial outpost, but it always remained precisely that: an outlying occupied territory, one they abandoned in the early fifth century. The Romans left behind many physical reminders of their occupation, any number of which remain visible to this day, but not much else because throughout the period of Roman rule, Roman and British culture remained largely separate, with the former ultimately having little impact on the latter.

Unlike the Romans, the early Germanic mercenary tribes did not simply conquer and subjugate Britain: they forever changed the island's cultural, linguistic, and political contours by driving the native inhabitants to what will later become Wales and Ireland in the west and northwest, and by bringing their families over from the continent to settle in England's more hospitable climate. The island is invaded twice more during the Anglo-Saxon period, first by the Vikings beginning in the late eighth century, and then most dramatically by the Normans (themselves descendants of northern tribes, as their name reveals) in the eleventh. One important difference between the invasion by the Germanic tribes and the two that follow is that the continental invaders of the fifth century did not so much intermix with the native peoples as simply displace them and their culture. This displacement did not come about, so far as can be determined, either because of a single, decisive event or as the result of a policy, but was rather the culmination of the very diffuse and undirected occupation of the island by the Germanic tribes. An OE word, *wealh* [foreigner; slave, servant], that comes down to NE as 'Welsh', suggests the degree to which the Germanic tribes not only displaced, but literally and figuratively marginalized the island's indigenous Celtic peoples, for as the meanings of *wealh* reveal, the Britons come to be seen as strangers in their native land by the Germanic invaders. So complete was the displacement of the native Britons that very few traces of their language survived into the Anglo-Saxon period, and those that did are largely confined to a few scattered place names. Nor do many traces of the indigenous culture survive, although one of England's most revered heroes, King Arthur, is British.

The political contours of Anglo-Saxon England are established in the early part of the period with the creation of the Heptarchy, which was comprised of the kingdoms of Northumbria, Mercia, East Anglia, Essex, Wessex, Sussex, and Kent. Power is initially concentrated in Northumbria, which by the late sixth century is the political and cultural centre of England, but over the course of the following centuries, the power base in the island shifts several times. Following the period of Northumbrian supremacy in the seventh century, the seat of power shifts south to Mercia in the eighth century, before settling, and remaining, in the island's southernmost region, Sussex, from the ninth century onward. Northumbria begins its rise to prominence during the reign of Æthelfrith (c. 593–616), and thanks largely to the efforts of Benedict Biscop (c. 628–89), who in 673 or 674 established the monastery at Monkwearmouth and in 685 established another monastery nearby at Jarrow, Northumbria came to house what may well have been the richest collection of books in Anglo-Saxon England. Located upon isolated sea coasts and so greatly removed from the distractions of secular life, these monasteries, as well as that of Lindisfarne to the north, were to become important centres of intellectual life throughout the eighth century. From the priory at Lindisfarne located on Holy Island off the coast of Northumbria comes the Lindisfarne Gospels, arguably one the most beautiful illuminated manuscripts to survive from the period.

The fortunes of Northumbria were to change forever in 678 when the Northumbrian king Ecgfrith lost a decisive battle against the Mercians near Trent. For a period of nearly fifty years after this battle no one kingdom established its supremacy over the others, but this was to change in 716 with the ascension in Mercia first of Æthelbald and then of Offa, who combined ruled not only Mercia but all the lands to the south for a period of nearly eighty years. The reigns of Æthelbald and Offa are noteworthy not simply for their length, but because by expanding their reach through the absorption of once-independent kingdoms, they helped pave the way for the political unification of the country that was to be the legacy of the southern kingdoms in the ninth century. Although the title *bretwalda* [ruler of Britain], which the Anglo-Saxon Chronicle (see Part 2) rather inaccurately bestows upon Ceawlin of Wessex (560–93), Æthelbert of Kent (d. 616), Edwin of Northumbria (616–33), and several other early kings, is never applied to Æthelbald, a charter of 736 aptly labels him 'rex Britanniae' [king of Britain]. Following Æthelbald's murder by a member of his own retinue in 757, Offa ascended the Mercian throne and successfully continued the program of expansion and consolidation begun under Æthelbald: precisely how Offa came to power following the civil war that followed Æthelbald's murder is not clear, but what is clear is that he not only re-established Mercian supremacy but extended it to include the southern kingdoms of Kent, Essex, and Sussex. In addition to his domestic accomplishments, which included the building of the period's most significant earthwork, Offa's Dyke, the unification of much of southern England, and the establishment of a system of coinage used throughout the country with the exception of Northumbria, Offa was active in continental affairs as well. He considered himself to be the equal of the great Carolingian king, Charlemagne, and in a gesture that reveals much about the Frankish ruler's perception of the Mercian king, Charlemagne proposed the marriage of his son Charles to one of Offa's daughters.

Following Offa's death in 796, Coenwulf ascended to the Mercian throne and for a time succeeded in maintaining Mercian power in the south, but following his death in 821, Mercia's fortunes begin a precipitous decline and by 829 the entire kingdom of Mercia comes under the domination of the West Saxon Ecgberht. Because Ecgberht was also acknowledged as overlord by the Northumbrians, for the first time in its history the lineaments of an England unified under a single ruler can be traced: earlier kings had claimed for themselves authority over the entire country, but it is only with the rise of the West Saxon dynasty at the beginning of the ninth century that such a claim accurately begins to reflect the political reality. Ecgberht's power does not extend far beyond the borders of his kingdom for nearly twenty years, but when he does directly challenge the Mercians, he does so as a king nearly as powerful as Offa.

The West Saxon dynasty of which Ecgberht was part would rise to a position of unrivalled power in England during the late eighth and early ninth centuries, but it was also during this period that England was for the first time in several centuries faced with a powerful external threat: that of the Vikings. Beginning with the sacking of the monastery at Lindisfarne in 793, an event dramatically recounted in the Anglo-Saxon Chronicle, the Vikings were to play a critically important role in shaping the history of England throughout the remainder of the Anglo-Saxon period. In plundering many monasteries during their raids of the eighth and ninth centuries, the Vikings struck a severe blow to the very heart of secular and ecclesiastical learning in England because even though the monastic communities were small and isolated, they were nevertheless early Anglo-Saxon England's most important intellectual and cultural centres.

As devastating as the attacks in the late eighth and early ninth century were, they were for the most part isolated raids conducted by men who afterwards returned to their homeland with their newly acquired treasures. But in the latter half of the ninth century, the nature and purpose of the Viking raids would change with the arrival in East Anglia in 865 of what the Anglo-Saxon Chronicle calls the 'micel here' [great army] of Vikings Several things set this group apart from the raiding parties that had been sporadically harrying English coastal settlements and monasteries over the preceding seventy or so years. Even allowing for some typical exaggeration in the reporting of its size, the 'micel here' was by far the largest group to land on the island, and it appears to have been composed of members of a number of different Scandinavian tribes. The aim and tactics of these Vikings differed sharply from those of the earlier raiders as well: the great army came prepared for a long, land-based campaign in England and began to proceed systematically through the country, heading first to Northumbria and then to East Anglia. In short, where their predecessors had engaged in what we may consider smash-grab-and-run skirmishes, the great army of 865 arrived as invaders who did not just strip England of its wealth, but occupied it.

The Danes' policy of controlling the lands they harried by installing English kings sympathetic to them met with mixed success: they were unable to do so in the powerful kingdom of Wessex and the king they established in Northumbria in 867, Egbert, was forced into exile in 872 and replaced by another Englishman, Ricsige, who remained independent for several years. In Mercia, the Danish invaders met with more success: they established Ceolwulf as king in 874, with the understanding that he would turn the land over to them when they asked for it. After fighting throughout the country as a single unit for nearly a decade, the great army split into two units, with Halfdan turning his attention to the North, and Guthrum seeking, unsuccessfully, to extend Danish control into Wessex before occupying East Anglia. The army was never to reunite. Guthrum's defeat in Wessex came at the hands of Alfred the Great, who also re-established English control over London in 886 and who came to be seen, in the words of the Anglo-Saxon Chronicle, as the 'cyning ofer eall Ongelcyn butan ðæm dæle þe under Dena onwalde wæs' [king over all the English race except that portion who were under Danish power]. What the chronicler fails to note is that the area under Danish control, known as the Danelaw, encompassed not only the entirety of East Anglia, but stretched from the eastern half of Anglo-Saxon Mercia as far north as Northumbria, as far south as the Thames, and as far east as Watling Street.

Following Alfred's death in 899, his son Edward the Elder embarked, along with his wife, Æthelflæd, upon a series of campaigns in which they succeeded in reasserting English rule throughout the Danelaw. Edward's military success reached its height in 920, four years before his death, when the king of the Scots, the Danish ruler of York, and the ruler of English Northumbria all submitted to his authority, thus securing Edward's position as the most powerful man in the entire land. Within several years of Edward's death, his son Æthelstan had pushed the borders established by his father some eighty miles north, so that the kingdom of England now encompassed not only the city of York but all of Lancashire and Westmorland. The first period of the Danish invasions comes to a close with the expulsion in 954 of Eric Bloodaxe, who in 947 had been named king of York.

Although the Vikings both those living in England and those voyaging from and then returning to Scandinavia, remained a constant threat throughout the first eighty years of the tenth century, the nature and scope of their threat did not approach that of their late-ninth-century predecessors and, as a result, England enjoyed a period of relative peace under the powerful Alfredian West Saxon dynasty. This peace was, however, to be shattered beginning in 980 by the second wave of Viking attacks. Whereas the first wave of Danish invasions resulted in the Danes ruling a large portion of England, the second wave, which like the first began with a series of attacks led by small raiding parties that plundered and departed before meeting anything other than local resistance, culminated in 1013 with King Æthelræd's flight to Normandy and the acceptance by the English of a Dane, Swein Forkbeard, as King of England. Following Swein's death a few months after his accession, Æthelræd regrouped and returned to England where he drove Swein's son Cnut from England and regained the throne. In 1016, Cnut returned with a formidable army and soon gained control over most of the country, including Wessex. While preparing for the defence of London in 1016, Æthelræd died, and his son Edmund Ironside was accepted as king by the English. Over the course of the next few months, Edmund raised a spirited but unsuccessful defence against Cnut, whose rule the English had by then already widely accepted. An agreement between Cnut and Edmund that same year set the amount that Edmund would have to pay Cnut's army to secure peace and also divided the country, giving control of Wessex to Edmund and of the rest of the country to Cnut. Following Edmund's death in November 1016, England was to be ruled by Danish kings until 1042, when once again a member of the West Saxon royal line, Edward the Confessor, came to power following the death of Cnut's son Harthacnut.

Cnut's reign (1016–35) was marked both by political stability and economic prosperity. It is during this period that England became, along with Denmark and Norway, part of a northern empire briefly ruled by Cnut. Yet even before Cnut's death, his grip on Norway had begun to weaken, and, following his death, internal and external forces would soon loosen forever the Danish hold on the throne of England. Pressure on the Danish throne kept Harthacnut, Cnut's legitimate son by Emma (Æthelræd's second wife), from immediately claiming the English throne following his father's death, and during the unsettled time that followed, Cnut's illegitimate son Harold was made regent before eventually being elected king. Harold's death from an illness in 1040 allowed Harthacnut to claim his English inheritance without bloodshed but his time on the throne was short: in 1042 he died unexpectedly while attending the wedding feast of one of his father's retainers. Harthacnut's half-brother, Edward the Confessor, the elder of Æthelræd and Emma's two sons, was elected king in London in 1042 and in him the West Saxon dynasty of Edward the Elder and Alfred the Great once again returned to power. But while Edward's birthright to the throne was universally acknowledged, the powerful earls who accepted him as king, including the Englishmen Godwine (d. 1053), Earl of Wessex, and Leofric (d. 1057), Earl of Mercia, as well as the Dane Siward (d. 1055), Earl of Northumbria, had all come to power under Cnut and so had no strong connection to or even affection for the West Saxon dynasty. Following Edward's death in early 1066, the English throne passed to Earl Godwine's son Harold. In the latter part of Edward's reign, Harold had risen to become Edward's most powerful subject and following his repulsion of King Gruffydd of Wales in 1063 (the Welsh had begun attacking England in 1055), he became more powerful than any other of Edward's subjects.

Although not a descendant of any English royal line, Harold was chosen over Edward's nephew, Edgar the Ætheling, but his reign was to be short, extending only from 6 January to 14 October 1066. During this period he successfully repelled a threat from Norway but then succumbed to one from Normandy. Harold's trouble began in May when his brother Tostig, the exiled earl of Northumbria, returned with an armed force and occupied Sandwich. His fleet of perhaps sixty ships sailed to the Humber, but there he suffered a defeat that caused him to retreat to Scotland, where he awaited the arrival of the Norwegian claimant to the throne, Harold of Norway. The Norwegians were victorious at the battle of Fulford on 20 September, but fell just five days later to Harold Godwinson's forces at the battle of Stamford Bridge, in which both Harold of Norway and Tostig were killed. So complete was the English victory that only twenty-four of the Norwegian's fleet of 300 ships were required to carry the survivors back to Norway. Harold's victory was to be short-lived, though, as within days of his victory in the northeast, William of Normandy set sail for England to exercise what is seen by many as his thin claim on the English crown, a claim grounded in his being the great-nephew of Queen Emma, sister of the Norman Duke Richard II. Following the landing of William and his forces in Pevensey in the southwest on 28 September, Harold headed south with all dispatch, his troops covering the 190 miles from York to London in nine days. While he arrived at the city with a force that was considerably larger than the one with which he had faced Harold of Norway, it was comprised chiefly of his own retinue and those of his brothers, Gyrth and Leofwine, as well as the men who had joined him on the marches to the north or south and those men who lived close enough to London to receive his messages in time; Harold moved from the north with such dispatch that there was simply no time for the forces of the distant shires to be effectively mustered. The Norman forces that awaited them in the south might not have equalled the English numbers, but they were well trained and well rested. At the Battle of Hastings on 14 October 1066, commemorated most famously in the Bayeux Tapestry, the English were routed and Harold and his brothers killed. With the ascent of William to the throne, England is ruled once again by a continental invader with strong ties to the north, for the Normans are themselves descendants of Scandinavian warriors who unsuccessfully attacked western Europe in the late ninth century. William's accession to the English throne on 25 December 1066 is generally accepted as marking the close of the Anglo-Saxon period.

Ecclesiastical History

Although Christianity is present in England during the centuries of Roman rule, it virtually disappears in the nearly two centuries that elapse between the withdrawal of the last Roman troops early in the fifth century and the arrival of Christian missionaries near the end of the sixth. There seems to have been no attempt by the surviving Romano-British clergy to convert the Germanic invaders and, as a result, Christianity plays, at best, a marginal role in Dark Age Britain. The continental tribes that spread slowly over England were pagan but little is known about the specifics of their religious practices. Although the Germanic tribes brought with them a system of writing, the runic futhorc, theirs was not a culture given to producing written records as the futhorc was employed chiefly to carve brief inscriptions, mostly in wood, but ones in stone and bone survive as well. What we know of Anglo-Saxon paganism comes chiefly from sources that must be approached cautiously as they were produced not by unbiased observers but by writers who filtered their observations through the lens of their own Christianity and who were actively engaged in promoting a Christian agenda.

The Christians' ability to adapt their practices may be one of the chief reasons Christianity spread so successfully throughout the island. Rather than forcing upon the pagan tribes a wholly alien set of beliefs, and more importantly, practices, the Christians worked to redirect the energies of the pagans away from their old gods to the new one. For example, the name of a continental Saxon fertility goddess, Eostre, comes to be used for a major festival in the Christian liturgical year, Easter, a festival that also celebrates life, and by extension, fertility. Similarly, in a strategy that probably did not originate with Pope Gregory the Great but was famously articulated by him, the Christian missionaries in England were instructed not to destroy

The Anglo-Saxon Literature Handbook, First Edition. Mark C. Amodio.
© 2014 Mark C. Amodio. Published 2014 by John Wiley & Sons, Ltd.

pagan places of worship, but to consecrate them for Christian purposes. There may not seem to be much difference between putting an existing place of worship to a new purpose and simply destroying it and erecting a new one in the same (or nearby) place, but through Gregory's strategy of re-direction the pagans were able to maintain physical continuity with their past practices: the focus of their devotions may have changed from the pagan idols to newly imported Christian ones, but the places in which they expressed their devotion did not.

The history of Christianity in the Anglo-Saxon period divides roughly into three phases: the first begins in 597 with the arrival on the island of Thanet in Kent of a group of some forty missionaries sent from Rome by Gregory's order and led by Augustine; the second begins with the dissolution of the monasteries, especially in Northumbria and the eastern half of Mercia, following the onset of the Viking attacks in the late eighth century; and the third begins with Alfred the Great's establishment at Athelney near Winchester of the first new monastic community in a generation and culminates in the reformation of the tenth century spearheaded by Dunstan.

Just as the political development of the country depended, especially in the sixth and seventh centuries, on the might and success of the various individual kings who ruled the different sections of the country, so, too, did the process of conversion: when the missionaries were in an area ruled by a king amenable to the teachings of either the Roman missions in the south or the Celtic ones in the north, the process of conversion would go far more smoothly than it would were the king hostile to or uninterested in their teachings, as was the early-seventh-century ruler Rædwald in the south. Although the conversion did not proceed without setbacks and although some areas, notably Sussex, resisted, the missionaries were ultimately successful in their endeavours, and Christianity, from roughly the mid seventh century onward, became securely established as the dominant religion of Anglo-Saxon England.

According to Pope Gregory's plan, England was to be divided into northern and southern ecclesiastical provinces, each overseen by an archbishop at, respectively, York and London. The provinces themselves were further to be divided into dioceses presided over by bishops who were often members of the aristocracy and who, moreover, derived considerable wealth and power from their ecclesiastical positions. From the earliest days, ecclesiastical and secular power often went hand in hand: many monasteries were founded and presided over by wealthy noblemen (and occasionally noblewomen) and those men who attained the rank of bishop enjoyed significant economic benefits.

The same period that witnessed the establishment of Gregory's episcopal system also witnessed the growth of the monastic system. As an organizing principle for monastic communities, the rule of St Benedict was favoured from early on, and while it provided the foundation for the rules of many monasteries, during this period it did not have the influence on monastic life and thought that it would come to have during the reformation of the tenth century. This was because in the early part of the Anglo-Saxon period the founder of a monastery was responsible for articulating the rule by which the monks in the community were to live. Some monasteries, such as that founded at Monkwearmouth by Benedict Biscop, came to be important centres of learning, but others, most of which have left no traces behind, were more modest sites where monks devoted themselves to work, contemplation, and prayer.

In 669, Theodore arrived in England and assumed the archbishopric of Canterbury, a position he held for twenty-one years, and it is to him that the Anglo-Saxon Church owes the structural organization and unity of focus that were to be so important for its ultimate success. Shortly after his arrival, he began filling vacant sees and creating new ones, and he was the first Anglo-Saxon archbishop to travel to Northumbria. In the late seventh century, the spread of Christianity was greatly aided by Theodore, who increased the number of dioceses and brought them firmly into the ambit of Canterbury's authority. This same period also witnesses a sharp increase in the number of monastic communities: numbering a dozen or so in the mid seventh century, by the time of the first wave of Viking assaults there were more than 200.

By the early eighth century, the Church in England had become stable and well enough established that some clerics began turning their attention outward, specifically to the pagan tribes on the continent. Two of the first and most important Anglo-Saxon clerics to go abroad on missions to the continent were Willibrord, a Northumbrian who was sent to Frisia in 690, and Boniface, a learned monk and member of a wealthy Southumbrian family, who, in 718–19, received permission from the pope to preach in Germany. Both these men were to prove instrumental in bringing the principles of English ecclesiastical organization to the continent, where they spent virtually all their remaining days. Willibrord died in 739 in the monastery he had founded between 704 and 706 at Echternach and Boniface was killed in Frisia in 754 when he was nearly eighty.

The Viking invasions of the late eighth century proved particularly disruptive to the Church's development. Because monasteries were intended to be sites where their communities could remove themselves from the cares and concerns of the world – the better to devote themselves to religious and intellectual matters –, many, including those at Monkwearmouth, Jarrow, and Lindisfarne, were situated in harsh and remote locales along the northeastern coast. Their locations, and in some cases their large libraries, certainly made them ideal locations for study and contemplation, but their locations and lack of defences also made them easy and accessible targets for the ships of raiders that began harrying England near the end of the eighth century.

As did the continental invaders of the fifth century, the Danes who began to settle in England in the ninth century reacted to Christianity in varied ways: some accepted it and converted while others seemed to have tolerated its presence while maintaining their pagan practices. Throughout the period of the Danish incursions, the Church, even in the lands that never came under direct Danish control, was severely distressed. The destruction of the monasteries had a predictable effect on monastic life, which nearly disappears. So depleted are the monastic ranks that when Alfred the Great established a monastery at Athelney, he had to invite foreign monks to live in it. By the mid tenth century, however, monasticism was again flowering. Under the direction of Æthelwold and with the approval of Dunstan and King Edgar, the *Regularis Concordia* [Agreement concerning the Rule] was produced, a document that was to direct the course of Anglo-Saxon monasticism throughout the remainder of the period and beyond, and was to provide it with a uniformity of practice that it had hitherto lacked. Although the Norman Conquest was drastically to alter the racial make-up of the English Church's leaders, the tenets of the Benedictine reform survived it intact and continued to influence the English Church in the centuries to follow.

Intellectual History

Although for the purposes of this brief and necessarily selective overview we have so far discussed the period's ecclesiastical history in isolation from its intellectual history, the two were closely intertwined throughout the period. The missionaries who came to England during the Anglo-Saxon period reintroduced not just Christian doctrine to the island but also the Roman alphabet. In bringing with them their well-established literate practices and habits of mind, they laid the foundation for the literate revolution that would, over the course of the Middle Ages, sweep through and radically transform the island.

The culture of the Germanic invaders may have been largely a non-literate one, but neither it nor that of the British could be classified as primary oral cultures, ones, that is, in which literacy is wholly unknown. Even during the darkest period following the departure of the Romans, literacy remained present on the island, if only in a limited fashion, for the early Germanic invaders brought with them the runic alphabet, the futhorc. Its origins are obscure, but it may have derived from the Roman alphabet in the first or second century CE, and it was used in the early Middle Ages by a number of tribes in the Germanic world. Deriving its name from the first six of its runes, the futhorc was not an alphabet that lent itself to anything more than short inscriptions that were most often carved into the surfaces of sticks and stones. The meaning of *run* in OE, 'mystery, secret', reveals much about the limited extent to which members of the tribes were trained in runes, for perhaps the best way to keep a secret during the Anglo-Saxon period was to write it down.

That the British clergy possessed considerable literate skills and a sound command of Latin is evidenced in the surviving works of Gildas – whose sixth-century *De excidio Britanniæ* [*Concerning the Fall of Britain*] remains

The Anglo-Saxon Literature Handbook, First Edition. Mark C. Amodio.
© 2014 Mark C. Amodio. Published 2014 by John Wiley & Sons, Ltd.

one of the most important contemporary accounts of post-Roman British history – as well as, among others, the early theologians Pelagius, and Faustus of Riez. The literate clerics who remained on the island seem to have had little impact on the culture of the invaders in part because they and their culture were in full retreat throughout the period; although the designation given to the period during which the continental tribes arrived on the island, the Age of Migration, chiefly describes the movements of the Germanic tribes westward across the Channel and then across the island, it applies equally well to the British, who similarly moved, or rather were pushed, west, to what would become Wales and Ireland. That the invaders were either hostile to or simply uninterested in the literate clergy did not do much to help matters. But even following the arrival of the Augustinian mission, bringing literacy to the pagan Anglo-Saxons was not high on the agenda of the Roman and Celtic missionaries; in fact, for reasons too complicated to explore here, literacy was to remain firmly entrenched in the hand of the Church throughout the entirety of the Anglo-Saxon period and for much of the ensuing Middle English period as well. Until the ninth century, we have very little evidence that any but ecclesiasts and their students had access to the technology of literacy, and when King Alfred the Great's biographer, Asser, reports on the king's ability to read and write – and perhaps even compose vernacular poetry – it establishes him as something of an anomaly because throughout the English Middle Ages literacy tended to be limited to the clerical class, one that was initially ecclesiastical but that comes over time to include members of the laity as well, as the primarily secular connotation of the modern English word *clerk* reveals.

Because literacy remained concentrated almost exclusively in religious houses and communities throughout the period, some of the diocesan centres and monasteries that were created during the first stage of England's conversion became important intellectual, as well as devotional, centres. The school at Canterbury established by Theodore and Hadrian offered instruction not just in Latin, but in Greek, and in addition to religious subjects, it offered instruction in a wide range of secular ones as well. The greatest student to emerge from this school during this period was Aldhelm (d. 709 or 710), who was born into the royal line of Wessex and who became Abbot of Malmesbury and in 706 Bishop of Sherborne. Little is known of the details of Aldhelm's lineage or early life. He appears to have studied at the school in Canterbury when he was around thirty and his earlier education may have been conducted under the direction of Irish scholars at Malmesbury, although the possibility has recently been raised that he spent some time during his youth on Iona. He is credited by William of Malmesbury, in a famous section of his early-twelfth-century *Gesta pontificum anglorum* [Deeds of the Bishops of England], with the composition and public performance of vernacular verse, but so far no vernacular poetry extant from Anglo-Saxon England can be confidently attributed to Aldhelm. He did, however, leave behind an extensive and varied body of Anglo-Latin writings in prose and verse, works that have survived in a large number of manuscripts. He favoured in all his writings what has come to be labelled the 'hermeneutic style', one that was highly ornamental and relied heavily, and perhaps excessively, on obscure, often arcane vocabulary – especially Greek words – as well as on a broad array of metrical and rhetorical features. While some modern commentators have faulted Aldhelm for his style, the anonymous Anglo-Saxon translator of Bede's *Ecclesiastical History* has nothing but praise for it, writing that it is composed 'on wordum hluttor and scinende' (Miller, 448) [in words clear and shining].

In the north, the monastery at Monkwearmouth housed one of the first great libraries in England. Endowed with the books its founder, Benedict Biscop, collected on the several journeys he took to Rome during his lifetime, this library would prove to be an invaluable resource to Anglo-Saxon England's greatest scholar, the Venerable Bede (d. 735), a Northumbrian who lived most of his life in the twin monastic communities of Monkwearmouth (founded *c.* 673) and Jarrow (founded *c.* 681). What we know of Bede's life comes largely from the biographical information he appends to his *Ecclesiastical History*, which he completed in 731. Within a generation of its completion, the *EH* had become one of the most influential books in the western Christian world. More than 150 copies of it survive, the earliest of which, the Moore Bede (CUL Kk. 5. 16) and the St Petersburg (formerly Leningrad) Bede (St Petersburg, Russian National Library Lat. Q. v. I. 18), date to within a decade of Bede's death. Both manuscripts were written in Northumbria and may have been produced within the same monastic communities of which Bede was part. Bede entered the monastery of Monkwearmouth in 680 at the age of seven as an oblate and was sent the following year to its sister house at Jarrow, where he was to spend the rest of his years. He was ordained a deacon at nineteen and in his thirtieth year achieved the priesthood. Writing, he tells us, in his fifty-ninth year, he lists in the appendix to the *EH* the many books he authored, among which are numerous Biblical commentaries, a history of his monastery's abbots, *De natura rerum* [*On the Nature of Things*], *De temporibus* and *De temporibus ratione*, respectively elementary and more technical manuals of chronology, as well as works on orthography and poetic metre. Bede, who wrote in Latin, also authored several verse works, including a book of hymns and a book of epigraphs. A single piece of vernacular verse, *Bede's Death Song*, has been attributed to him, although whether he authored it remains an open question.

Later in the eighth century, under the direction first of Ecgberht and then Ælberht, the school of York, one heavily influenced by Bede, rose to prominence. After becoming archbishop in 767, Ælberht left his student Alcuin in charge of the school, and over the next fifteen years Alcuin not only further enriched and expanded the already large library at York, but he attracted many students to the school and came to be known as the foremost scholar of his generation. It is not clear whether he was a deacon, a priest, a monk, or a member of the secular clergy, but in 781 he was invited by Charlemagne to become the head of his palace school, and, aside from a few brief visits to England, Alcuin spent the rest of his life abroad, dying on the continent in 804. Alcuin's writings include a verse history of the saints of York, treatises on, among other things, grammar, orthography, and rhetoric, but he is perhaps best known for the crucial role he and his students played in bringing English learning to the continent, where it was to have a profound impact on the development of Carolingian thought and literature.

Beginning with King Alfred the Great's victory over Guthrum in 878 and followed by his capture of London in 886, a period of relative stability descended upon the Kingdom of Wessex, the sole English kingdom not to fall under direct Viking rule, and it is during the period of peace following Guthrum's ascension to the East Anglian throne in 879 that English intellectual life undergoes something of a revival, one in which Alfred figures prominently. Not only did he establish a monastery at Athelney and a community for nuns at Shaftesbury, the first religious communities to be established in at least a generation, but he, like Charlemagne, also sponsored and encouraged extra-ordinary intellectual achievements by establishing a community of scholars, which included figures from Mercia, Wales, and the continent, at his court. While Alfred continued to view Latin as an essential component of the education of any boy who aspired to an ecclesiastical position, he also believed that the state of learning had greatly decayed in England since the age of Bede and, as a result, he established a programme of translating texts into the vernacular because as he, perhaps with some exaggeration, notes in the preface to his translation of Gregory the Great's *Regula pastoralis* [*Pastoral Care*], few south of the Humber can translate a letter from Latin into English. Although Alfred's aim was chiefly to revive Latin learning in England and re-establish England's importance as an intellectual centre, he provided a great impetus to the development of vernacular writing in England. Alfred himself may have participated in this programme as translator of Gregory's *Pastoral Care*, and Boethius's *Consolation of Philosophy*, and Augustine's *Soliloquies* have long been attributed to him. And if we are to believe Alfred's biographer Asser, the king from an early age showed a keen interest in vernacular poetry and also became an accomplished composer of it, although none survives.

Ælfric, Abbot of Eynsham and Wulfstan, Archbishop of York, two of Anglo-Saxon England's greatest prose writers, lived and wrote at the end of the tenth and beginning of the eleventh century. Ælfric wrote prolifically on a wide array of ecclesiastical and secular subjects, producing homilies, sermons, a collection of saints' lives, a grammar, and translations of Latin texts. Although the size of Wulfstan's corpus does not approach that of Ælfric's, Wulfstan also wrote on a range of subjects and produced, among other things, at least twenty-one homilies. He also helped write the legal codes of two kings, Æthelræd and Cnut.

Linguistic History

The language spoken throughout the Anglo-Saxon period is known as Old English (OE). OE belongs to the Germanic family of Indo-European languages, a group comprised of North Germanic, East Germanic, and West Germanic. North Germanic includes the ancestors of the present-day Scandinavian languages, most notably Old Norse (ON). Although a great number of runic inscriptions survive in this part of the Germanic world from early in the Middle Ages, ON texts do not begin to appear until the twelfth and thirteenth centuries. The East Germanic branch contains Gothic, in which only some portions of Bishop Ulfila's late-fourth-century translation of the Gospels and Pauline epistles survive. The West Germanic branch includes not just OE, but Old High German, Old Saxon, and Old Frisian.

Although OE is the direct ancestor of Modern English (NE), over the past thousand years the language has gone through so many radical changes in its syntax, lexicon, pronunciation, orthography, and spelling that the connections between OE and NE are often difficult to see. OE is an inflected language: in it grammatical information is carried by endings attached to nouns, pronouns, and adjectives. In contrast, in NE a word's placement in a sentence signals its grammatical function. For example, the OE word *guma* 'man' in the following phrase, *guma rād mearh* [the man rode a horse] would remain the subject even if we were to reorder the elements as follows: *mearh rād guma*, which rendered in NE would result in the following: 'a horse rode the man'. Unlike the NE word *man*, which maintains the same form whether it is used as a singular subject or direct (or indirect) object, when *guma* is used as anything other than the singular subject, it will take one of several endings, depending on whether it is used,

The Anglo-Saxon Literature Handbook, First Edition. Mark C. Amodio.
© 2014 Mark C. Amodio. Published 2014 by John Wiley & Sons, Ltd.

say, as a singular direct or indirect object (*guman*) or as a genitive (possessive) plural (*gumena*) or plural indirect object (*gumum*).

The OE inflectional system virtually collapses during the Middle English (ME) period, but traces of it survive to the present day, as can be seen in the NE noun *hound* which does not always keep the same form but takes -*s* in the plural (*hounds*) or -'*s* in the possessive singular (*hound's*). In both instances, these forms are survivals of OE inflectional endings, specifically the plural ending of the subject and direct object cases (known respectively as the nominative and accusative) and of the singular possessive case (known as the genitive) of the largest group of nouns in OE, the masculine strong declension, to which some 35 per cent of all OE nouns belong.

Even though OE is an inflected language, it shares some characteristics with the word-order-dependent syntax of NE. This is especially true of OE prose where the SVO (subject–verb–object) word order that characterizes NE syntax frequently occurs. For example, in the following clauses from the beginning of Wulfstan's *Sermo Lupi ad Anglos* [Sermon of the Wolf to the English], 'ðeos worold is on ofste, and hit nealæcð þam ende' (Whitelock, *Homilies of Wulfstan*, 267.1), the word order is the same as it is in the NE rendering: 'this world is in haste and it draws near to the end'. Many OE sentences do not follow NE word order, but as the sentence 'Þa heortas on nettum ic gefeng' from Ælfric's *Colloquy* reveals, Ælfric maintains the SV word order common to NE declarative statements even though he places the direct object to the left of the verb. A translation that maintains the original word order would read: 'Those harts in nets I caught'. OE poets exploit the opportunities OE's synthetic syntax offers them more fully than do prose writers, but even they employ a number of patterns typical of analytic syntax, including placing subjects before their verbs.

As do most inflected languages, OE distinguishes cases, numbers, and genders for its nouns, pronouns, and adjectives. It is generally recognized as having five cases – the nominative (subject), accusative (direct object), genitive (possessive), dative (indirect object), and instrumental – although the distinction between the dative and instrumental has already begun to collapse partially in some instances (certain classes of masculine nouns, for example) and wholly in others (feminine nouns) by the time the written records begin to appear. With the exception of the instrumental, which in NE can only be expressed in prepositional phrases (the OE instrumental, *sweorde*, can only be rendered in NE as 'with a sword'; 'by a sword', etc.), NE syntax preserves all the OE cases, and even, as we saw above, some OE inflectional endings. OE grammar marks, as does NE grammar, both the singular and the plural, but OE also marks grammatical gender – masculine, feminine, and neuter –, something that NE does not. Grammatical gender can sometimes reflect natural gender, as it does in the feminine noun *hlæfdige* 'lady', but it does not necessarily have to do so: *wif* 'wife' is a neuter noun. Grammatical gender is an important component of OE syntax because the principle of grammatical concord demands that nouns and the adjectives that modify them and the pronouns that refer to them all agree in number, case, and gender.

OE has two main classes of verbs, the strong, in which verbs mark their past tense by means of an internal vocalic alternation, as in OE *hladan* 'to load', *hlōd*, 'I/he/she loaded', and the weak, in which changes in tense are signalled by the addition of a *-d* or *-t* as in OE *fremman* 'to perform', *fremede* 'I/she/he performed'. These same classes survive in NE syntax, as we can see in the strong verb *sing, sang* and the weak *open, opened*. As English evolved, many verbs that had previously been strong migrated to the weak class, as is the case with NE *help, helped* and *melt, melted*, which in OE were strong: *helpan, healp*, and *meltan, mealt*. All new verbs that come into the language follow the weak model: *telephoned, googled*, etc.

During the Anglo-Saxon period, the English word-stock, or lexicon, was made up primarily of native Germanic words. Although some words of British, Latin, and even French origin come to be incorporated into the OE word-stock, they do so only to a very limited extent. The waves of invasions that washed over England beginning in the ninth century had a far-ranging impact on the development of the English lexicon because first the Vikings and later the Normans who invaded England also settled there and mixed, culturally and linguistically, with the native English population. One of the reasons North Germanic words entered easily into English is that the dialects of the Viking raiders and settlers and those of the English were to some extent mutually intelligible. For example, when the Vikings arrived, they brought with them the Old Norse (ON) word *skyrta* 'shirt', which was closely related to the OE word for the same item of clothing, *scyrte*, although the two terms had different pronunciations, with the ON word's initial consonant cluster being pronounced /sk/ as in NE *skirt* and the OE word's initial consonant cluster being pronounced /sh/ as in NE *shirt*. Both these terms have survived in NE, but in many instances, a foreign word displaces a native one, as in the following sets of words, in each of which only the second, ON term, survives in NE: *welkin, skÿ* [sky]; *seax, knifr* [knife]; *niman, taka* [take] and *fel, skinn* [skin].

The influence of the North Germanic dialects extended as well to a type of words, the function words, that are usually immune from foreign influence. It is one thing to adopt a foreign term for something one's culture lacks or to adopt and/or adapt a foreign term's meaning to a native lexeme, both of which frequently occur when cultures and languages collide, but it is something entirely different to substitute a foreign term for a native function word because function words are a small and closed class of words (including articles, prepositions, conjunctions, and pronouns) that have no meaning on their own and exist only to express grammatical relationships. But for some reason, the native OE forms of the third person plural pronouns, *hie* [they], *him* [them], and *hira* [their], are replaced by the ON forms, *þeir* [they], *þeim* [them], and *þeira* [their]. Of the OE third person plural pronouns, only the form *him* survives in the contracted form *'em* found in a phrase such as 'Go get 'em'.

While a number of Scandinavian loanwords appear to have come into English via the early Viking raiders, the largest percentage date from the early eleventh century, a time when the Scandinavian presence on the island extended beyond the borders of the Danelaw as for nearly thirty years Danish kings occupied the English throne. When another foreign-born ruler, the Norman William, comes to power later in the same century, the English lexicon undergoes yet more changes, although this time of far greater magnitude. The French lexemes recorded in the vernacular written records of Anglo-Saxon England amount to little more than a scattered handful, but during the Middle English period, some 10,000 words of French origin enter the English word-stock.

OE had four main dialects: Northumbrian and Mercian (which are known as the Anglian dialects), Kentish, and West Saxon. The extant records of the first three dialects are very sparse. Our knowledge of Northumbrian derives chiefly from the versions of Cædmon's *Hymn* that survive in two eighth-century manuscripts of Bede's *Ecclesiastical History* (the St Petersburg Bede and the Moore Bede), the early manuscript versions of Bede's *Death Song* and the *Leiden Riddle*, and some runic inscriptions, the most important of which are those found on the Ruthwell Cross and the Franks Casket. Mercian survives mostly in a large collection of charters of Mercian kings, but it appears also in the glosses to the *Vespasian Psalter*, the *Blickling Homilies*, and in the *Epinal Glossary* as well as scattered other places. Kentish survives from the eighth century in names that appear in Latin charters, in a few ninth-century charters, and in the *Kentish Psalm* and *Kentish Hymn*. The early records of West Saxon are also rather sparse, but this changes in the final decade or so of Alfred's reign when West Saxon scribes begin to produce large numbers of texts.

Literary History

When we speak of Anglo-Saxon England's literary history, we are, in reality, speaking of twinned, intersecting *histories*: the Anglo-Latin (which encompasses the Latin prose and poetry produced on the island by native Anglo-Saxons) and the Anglo-Saxon (which encompasses the vernacular prose and poetry produced on the island by native Anglo-Saxons). Of the two, the written records of the former, which first appear in the seventh century, pre-date by several centuries those of the latter, the earliest of which date from the ninth century and which do not begin to appear in any real quantity until the tenth. Latin was the language of learning and learned discourse on both religious and secular topics throughout the Middle Ages, and, given England's position as an early medieval intellectual centre, it is not surprising that a rich, varied, and important tradition of writing in Latin took root and blossomed there. The literate Latin tradition within which these Anglo-Latin authors worked played an important role in shaping the tradition of vernacular letters that developed in England, one that is in so many ways modelled on the Latin tradition, but the details of just how and, perhaps more importantly, why the vernacular came to be put to the purposes to which it was put in Anglo-Saxon England remain unknown.

Although Anglo-Saxon vernacular literary history's origin may be lost in the mists of time, we can with some certainty single out King Alfred the Great as one of the key figures, and perhaps the key figure, in its development. His military and political successes helped establish a period of relative stability, but England in the ninth century did not enjoy a golden era of peace and prosperity: the threat of the Vikings remained acute and the possibility of renewed hostilities was always present. In some ways, the Vikings may have helped spark the English literary tradition since the great centres of

The Anglo-Saxon Literature Handbook, First Edition. Mark C. Amodio.
© 2014 Mark C. Amodio. Published 2014 by John Wiley & Sons, Ltd.

Latin learning in Anglo-Saxon England, the monastic communities that sprung up along the isolated, physically remote northeastern coast, were also the first to fall under the relentless attacks that began in the eighth century, attacks so devastating that they led to the virtual dissolution of the monasteries. With monks and scribes either falling under Viking swords or being displaced from their monasteries (the monks of Lindisfarne had to abandon their monastery in the face of the raids, and they carried the bones of St Cuthbert with them until they returned to the island of Lindisfarne some twelve years later), Latin learning declined precipitously. In the famous preface that he attached to his translation of Pope Gregory the Great's *Pastoral Care*, Alfred paints a dismal picture of the state of learning in late ninth-century England: 'Swæ clæne hio wæs oðfeallenu on Angelcynne ðæt swiðe feawa wæron behionan Humbre ðe hiora ðeninga cuðen understondan on Englisc, oððe furðum an ærendgewrit of Lædene on Englisc areccan; ond ic wene ðætte noht monige begiondan Humbre næren' (Sweet, 2) [So completely was it (i.e. learning) decayed among the English that very few of them on this side of the Humber could understand their divine service in English or even translate a letter from Latin into English; and I expect that there were not many beyond the Humber (who could do so)]. Given our great temporal and cultural remove, we cannot, of course, determine whether the state of learning was truly as decayed as Alfred claims (and the fact that his rhetoric has been echoed by others over the centuries suggests that it might not have been), but Latin learning did suffer greatly, and for a long time following the advent of the Vikings. As a means of addressing this problem, Alfred set out to revive learning in England by bringing scholars to his court, including the Welsh monk Asser, later Bishop of St David's (and the king's biographer), Wærferth, the bishop of Worcester, the Mercian Plegmund, Archbishop of Canterbury, Æthelstan, and Werwulf, and from Gaul Grimbald, Dean of the New Minster at Winchester and John the Old Saxon. The reputation of this group of scholars may not have rivalled that of the scholars in Charlemagne's court, but the men Alfred assembled nevertheless played an important role in the revival of learning in England that began in the last decade of Alfred's reign.

Because Alfred desired to make available to the growing number of Englishmen with little or no Latin those books he considered to be the 'nidbeðyrfesta sien eallum monnum to witanne' (Sweet, 6) [most necessary for all men to know], he is widely credited with advancing the state of vernacular letters and, moreover, several translations are attributed to him, although the evidence of his authorship remains inconclusive. Although he is rightly credited with being the father of English prose, we need to keep in mind that Alfred was perhaps less driven by a desire to establish English in its own right as a language of intellectual discourse and more concerned with stemming the decline of learning in England. For Alfred, the decision to translate essential texts such as Gregory's *Pastoral Care* and Bede's *Ecclesiastical History* may have been motivated more by practical than political concerns.

While we may never be able to uncover the reasons the Anglo-Saxons turn to the vernacular to express sophisticated intellectual thought on a wide variety of ecclesiastical and secular matters, something that happens in no other early medieval culture, all of which employ Latin exclusively for such discourse, those who employed it created a rich, varied, and large body of prose and poetic writings. But before we turn to consider these writings in more detail in Parts 2 and 3 of this book, we will conclude this brief survey of the backgrounds and beginnings of Anglo-Saxon literature by considering the two traditions, the oral and the literate, that helped shape its contours.

Traditions: Oral and Literate

Just as the Anglo-Latin and Anglo-Saxon literary traditions had long been thought to be separate, largely parallel ones, so, too, have the English oral and literate traditions long been considered discrete, mutually exclusive entities. The dichotomy between the oral and literate traditions was believed to be so absolute that any contact between the two traditions inevitably signalled the demise of the former. Oral poets were thought to be unlettered singers who (re-)composed poems in the moment of performance using only traditional, pre-formed blocks (groups of words or phrases, say, or even larger thematic and narrative units). Believed to be virtual prisoners of their traditional ways of speaking, they were thought to do little more than reassemble, perhaps in slightly different ways, the material they inherited from their tradition. Oral poets were not credited with any artistic impulse and, as a result, it was the structure of the verbal art they produced, not its aesthetics, that attracted the most critical attention. In contrast, literate poets, because they composed privately and in writing and not publicly during performance were thought to be completely removed from the oral tradition. A far more nuanced sense of the complex relationship between orality and literacy has recently emerged, one that acknowledges interconnected and interdependent cultural forces, not conflicting ones.

It is important to keep this point in mind when reading the literary remains of Anglo-Saxon England because even though all of it was produced by literate authors, many of whom were able to read and write Latin as well as English, the larger society of which they were a part remained far more fully attuned to the oral than to the literate world. Until well beyond the close of the Middle Ages, the vast majority of the island's population remained non-literates whose experience of texts was aural,

The Anglo-Saxon Literature Handbook, First Edition. Mark C. Amodio.
© 2014 Mark C. Amodio. Published 2014 by John Wiley & Sons, Ltd.

not ocular; that is, they heard texts read aloud to them and did not read them privately to themselves.

The oral tradition has only a limited effect on the prose works that survive from the period, but the ways in which texts are committed to the surface of manuscripts, their *mise-en-page*, reveals a great deal about the orality of the culture within which they were inscribed. OE prose manuscripts are undeniably anchored to the world of letters and writing but they stand in much closer proximity to the world of orality than contemporary texts do. There is much about an Anglo-Saxon prose manuscript page that looks familiar to our contemporary eyes: the area in which the text is to be presented is frequently marked by lines scratched into the surface of the parchment or vellum, and the writing itself moves from the left to right margins and from the top of the page to the bottom. Some of the letters might look unusual (ſ, ƿ, ꞅ [NE *s, r, f*] and others are no longer part of the English alphabet [þ, ð], but many are instantly recognizable even at the distance of a thousand years or so (τ, m, a). What primarily separates the manuscript page from a contemporary one such as the one you are currently reading is the manuscript page's much lower degree of visual information. Among other things, in Anglo-Saxon manuscripts, words are divided and combined with far more flexibility than they can currently be and punctuation is less consistent and tends to be more expressive than grammatical in function.

The manner in which poetic texts were presented is even more instructive since throughout the Anglo-Saxon period poetry displays none of the specialized characteristics of presentation we have come to associate with poems on the printed page, but is always written out in just the way prose texts are: both fill the available space on the page in continuous strings of words. It is not until the early post-Conquest period that Anglo-Saxon poetic texts come to be presented in the specialized form that they maintain to this day: one line of verse per manuscript line with a caesura between half lines and significant blank space at the end of each line. Specialized conventions for presenting poetry in writing are found in manuscripts dating to antiquity, but they are not applied to English poetic texts until after the close of the Anglo-Saxon period, something that, again, suggests that English was more closely associated with the world of orality than literacy.

While the *mise-en-page* of Anglo-Saxon manuscripts reveals the still developing state of Anglo-Saxon textuality, Anglo-Saxon poetry displays its deep indebtedness to the oral tradition in many ways, including its metrics and its formulaic verbal expressions, themes, and story patterns. To compose poetry in Anglo-Saxon England required poets to engage the expressive economy of Anglo-Saxon oral poetics, a specialized register, or way of speaking, that developed first as a way of assisting poets who composed during performance to do so fluently and expediently. Having a readily available assortment of formulaic half-lines to introduce, say, direct speech, such as 'Beowulf maþelode' [Beowulf spoke] or 'weard maþelode' [the guard spoke], or epithets such as 'helm Scyldinga' [protector of the Scyldings] or 'glædman Hroþgar' [gracious Hrothgar] allows such a poet (one who composes during performance) to meet the demands of his tradition's metrics and keep his narrative progressing while he crafts its subsequent lines. Larger traditional themes and type-scenes work in very much the same way: they block out the narrative's broad contours for the poet and so assist him in shaping the work of verbal art.

In contemplating the complicated medieval oral–literate nexus from which all Anglo-Saxon literature emerges, we need to understand that the oral poetics evidenced everywhere in the poetry's highly formulaic diction, its singular, four-beat, alliterative metrics, and its traditional themes and story-patterns, is not so closely linked to performance as is the oral poetics of other traditions in which the creation of verbal art takes place only during public performance. Anglo-Saxon poets necessarily engage their tradition's oral poetics, but for the most part they do so privately and non-performatively. This is especially true for Anglo-Saxon prose writers, whose practices very closely mirror those that continue to prevail today and whose texts show as high a degree of intertextuality as do modern ones. For Anglo-Saxon poets, who also composed pen-in-hand, the situation is similar but somewhat different because in order to articulate poetry in Anglo-Saxon England, poets had to engage the specialized expressive economy that is medieval English oral poetics. From a contemporary perspective, this sounds limiting, but for Anglo-Saxon poets, who as we will see in Part 3 use their tradition's expressive economy to produce a corpus of great variety, it was no more constricting than the rules of contemporary grammar and syntax are for us.

A Note on Dating Anglo-Saxon Texts

Except in isolated instances, dating the literary remains of Anglo-Saxon England is, at best, a rather imprecise science. When we can attach an author's name securely to one or more prose texts, as with the works of Ælfric, or Alfred's preface to his translation of Gregory the Great's *Pastoral Care*, we can confidently locate the composition of the work within the author's lifetime, but even then we are often unable to date individual works with any real precision. Further complicating matters is that most of the manuscripts containing Anglo-Saxon verse and prose texts are not autograph manuscripts (that is they are not texts written in the author's hand) but are scribal productions that are often copies of copies and so stand at several removes from the original text. In the process of being copied, changes large and small were frequently introduced, either consciously or unconsciously, so while we must take it on faith that the texts as they survive accurately reflect what their authors wrote, there is finally no way to be certain that what appears on the page is entirely the author's. Since they were working under physical conditions that were frequently trying, scribes understandably made a variety of mechanical mistakes when copying. There was also little concern for preserving the dialectal features of any given text and scribes routinely filtered the text they were copying through their own dialect, silently and permanently replacing the distinctive dialectal features of the original with those of their own. This practice, and the concentration of power in the south of the island, helped West Saxon become the island's de facto standard written language throughout the tenth and eleventh centuries. Finally, when reading any Anglo-Saxon text, we must keep in mind that the scribes were not simply mere copyists, but that many of them may well have recomposed parts of the texts they copied.

The Anglo-Saxon Literature Handbook, First Edition. Mark C. Amodio.
© 2014 Mark C. Amodio. Published 2014 by John Wiley & Sons, Ltd.

Assigning even a rough chronology for the surviving poetic texts is a task that verges on the impossible for several reasons. First of all, the date of a poem's composition and the date at which it was physically encoded onto the surface of a manuscript page are not necessarily one and the same, but may be separated by as much as several hundred years if a poem had circulated orally, as many of them are thought to have done, before being committed to writing. Additionally, the several manuscripts that contain the majority of the poetic texts that survive from the period each dates from *c.* 1000, so the physical evidence itself offers scant assistance in determining which poems might be earlier or later than others. There have been some attempts to establish dates for texts using linguistic criteria but, again, the evidence often does not provide clear answers in large part because in addition to dating from roughly the same period, they all may have been produced in the same geographical area and they were all written using the specialized poetic register, one that preserved a rich variety of dialectal (and perhaps rare or even obsolete) forms in the same way that the specialized register of Greek epic, the Homeric *Kunstsprache*, preserved many archaisms. The Anglo-Saxon poetic texts contain a variety of dialectal forms, but we cannot, finally, confidently determine that a given poem was, say, 'originally' Anglian based on the presence of some decidedly Anglian features; rather, about all we can say is that a given poem written in the West Saxon dialect preserves certain features associated with the Anglian dialect. The Anglian forms may certainly indicate the Anglian origin of the text being copied, but they could just as well be derived either from the poetry's specialized register – its expressive economy –, or they could be part of the scribe's idiolect.

Even the few names that we can associate with Anglo-Saxon poets prove to be of little help in matters of dating. The names Deor and Widsith probably do not refer to actual poets, but respectively, to 'the dear one' who reveals to us in the eponymously titled poem *Deor* that he apparently lost his position at a court to another poet, and to the 'widely travelled one' in whose voice the eponymously titled poem *Widsið* is purportedly spoken. We know somewhat more about the cowherd-turned-poet Cædmon, but, as we will see in Part 2, the information Bede supplies about him in the *Ecclesiastical History* needs to be approached cautiously, as does the evidence offered by the one vernacular poem attributed to Bede, *Bede's Death Song*. The only other name of an Anglo-Saxon poet that we know is that of Cynewulf, who 'signs' four poems using the runes that spell his name (see Part 3, *Fates of the Apostles*, *Elene*, *Ascension*, and *Juliana*). But even though several of these signatures appear in the prayers for the author that conclude the poems and even though there are very good stylistic and grammatical reasons for attributing these four poems to a single author, about that author himself we know virtually nothing except that his name was 'Cynewulf'.

Because the historical record helps establish a chronology for Anglo-Saxon prose texts, we will consider first the earliest of those texts and then proceed to the later ones. When we turn to the poetry, however, we will of necessity adopt a different approach, one that does not depend on chronology but rather considers the poems in their manuscript context.

Further Reading

Baker, Peter S. *Introduction to Old English*. 2003. 3rd edn. Oxford: Wiley-Blackwell, 2012.

Barlow, Frank. *The English Church 1000–1066: A History of the Later Anglo-Saxon Church*. 1963. 2nd edn. London: Longman, 1979.

Blair, Peter Hunter. *An Introduction to Anglo-Saxon England*. 1956. 3rd edn. Cambridge: Cambridge University Press, 2003.

Blair, Peter Hunter. *The World of Bede*. New York: St Martin's, 1971.

Campbell, James. *The Anglo-Saxon State*. 2000. Rpt. London: Hambledon Continuum, 2003.

Campbell, James, Eric John, and Patrick Wormald, eds. *The Anglo-Saxons*. 1982. Rpt. London: Penguin, 1991.

Carver, Martin. *Sutton Hoo: Burial Ground of Kings?* Philadelphia: University of Pennsylvania Press, 1998.

Hamerow, Helena, David Alban Hinton, and Sally Crawford, eds. *The Oxford Handbook of Anglo-Saxon Archaeology*. Oxford: Oxford University Press, 2011.

Hill, David. *An Atlas of Anglo-Saxon England*. 1981. 2nd edn. Oxford: Blackwell, 2002.

Keynes, Simon. 'The cult of King Alfred the Great'. *ASE* 28 (1999): 225–356.

Lapidge, Michael. 'The career of Aldhelm'. *ASE* 36 (2007): 15–69.

Lapidge, Michael, John Blair, Simon Keynes, and Donald Scragg, eds. *The Blackwell Encyclopaedia of Anglo-Saxon England*. 1999. Rpt. Oxford: Blackwell, 2004.

Mayr-Harting, Henry. *The Coming of Christianity to Anglo-Saxon England*. 1972. 3rd edn. University Park: Pennsylvania State University Press, 1991.

Mitchell, Bruce, and Fred C. Robinson, eds. 1982. *A Guide to Old English*. 8th edn. Oxford: Wiley-Blackwell, 2012.

Pelteret, David, ed. *Anglo-Saxon History: Basic Readings*. Basic Readings in Anglo-Saxon England 6. New York: Garland, 2000.

Pratt, David. *The Political Thought of King Alfred the Great*. Cambridge: Cambridge University Press, 2010.

Rumble, Alexander, ed. *Leaders of the Anglo-Saxon Church: From Bede to Stigland*. Woodbridge: Boydell Press, 2012.

Smyth, Alfred P. *King Alfred the Great*. Oxford: Oxford University Press, 1995.

Stenton, F.M. *Anglo-Saxon England*. 1943. 3rd edn. 1971. Reissue Oxford: Oxford University Press, 2001.

Yorke, Barbara. *The Conversion of Britain: Religion, Politics, and Society in Britain c. 600–800*. New York: Pearson/Longman, 2006.

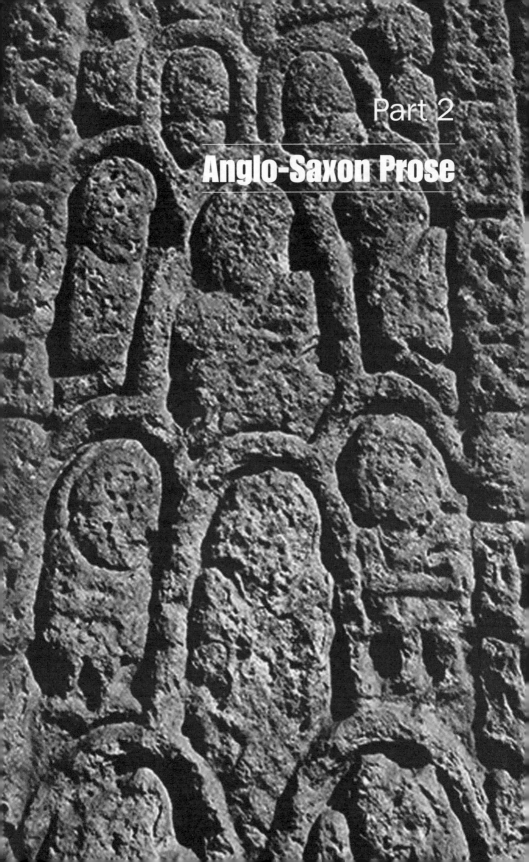

Part 2

Anglo-Saxon Prose

The Writings of King Alfred the Great

King Alfred the Great (b. 847/848, d. 899) is often considered the 'father of English prose' because it was during the last decade of his reign that he provided the impetus for the Anglo-Saxons to turn to the vernacular as the vehicle for legal, ecclesiastical, medical, historical, philosophical, and theological writings. As part of his plan to revive religious and secular learning in an England that had not only been ravaged by years of Viking attacks but in which increasingly large numbers of Viking invaders had begun to settle, Alfred brought English, Welsh, and continental scholars to his court. He did more, however, than just place a royal stamp upon this revival; he played an active role in it by translating several texts and by composing original prefaces to some of them, prefaces that may preserve the voice of the king himself. Although Alfred is widely acknowledged to have translated the texts generally attributed to him, his role in producing any of them cannot be established, and we are similarly unable to know with any certainty whether the translations are entirely his or if he was aided by some of the learned members of his court, all of whom would have had much more extensive training in Latin than the king, who acquired Latin only fairly late in his life, at the age of thirty-nine.

Thanks to the biography of the Welsh cleric and scholar Asser, one of the men Alfred brought to his court, we have considerably more information available to us about Alfred's life than we do for any other Anglo-Saxon king. Although we should not blindly accept as truth everything Asser relates, the picture his *Life* paints of a man who highly valued learning is entirely consonant with what we know of the figure who sought to revive learning in England and in so doing helped place the vernacular English literary tradition on secure

The Anglo-Saxon Literature Handbook, First Edition. Mark C. Amodio.
© 2014 Mark C. Amodio. Published 2014 by John Wiley & Sons, Ltd.

footing. Although at times the *Life* shades decidedly towards hagiography, its depiction of Alfred as a man who was deeply concerned with the state of ecclesiastical and lay learning in England is strongly supported by the extant writings attributed to the king and by what we know of his programme to revive learning in England by making essential books available in the vernacular.

While the attribution of any writing to Alfred is by no means certain or universally accepted, he is generally accepted as having been the translator of, or primary translator of, four works: Pope Gregory the Great's *Regula Pastoralis* [*Pastoral Care*], Boethius's *De Consolatione Philosophiae* [*Consolation of Philosophy*], St Augustine's *Soliloquia* [*Soliloquies*], and the initial fifty psalms of the Psalter. Additionally, he is credited with having been the sole author of the prefaces attached to his translations of the *Pastoral Care*, the *Consolation*, and the Laws of Alfred. The preface to the *Soliloquies*, which wants its beginning, is generally considered to be his, as is the prose preface attached to two of the surviving versions of Bishop Werferth's translation of Pope Gregory's *Dialogues*.

Further Reading

Bately, Janet M. 'The Alfredian canon revisited: one hundred years on'. In *Alfred the Great: Papers from the Eleventh-Centenary Conference*, ed. Timothy Reuter, 107–20. Burlington: Ashgate, 2003.

Bately, Janet M. 'Did King Alfred actually translate anything? The integrity of the Alfredian canon revisited'. *MÆ* 78, (2009): 189–215.

Bately, Janet M. 'Old English prose before and during the reign of King Alfred'. *ASE* 17 (1988): 93–138.

Godden, Malcolm. 'Did King Alfred write anything?' *MÆ* 76 (2007): 1–23.

Pratt, David. 'Problems of authorship and audience in the writings of Alfred the Great'. In *Lay Intellectuals in the Carolingian World*, ed. Patrick Wormald and Janet L. Nelson, 162–91. Cambridge: Cambridge University Press, 2007.

King Alfred's Translation of Pope Gregory the Great's *Pastoral Care*

Survives in four manuscripts: Oxford, Bodleian Library, Hatton 20; London, BL, Cotton Tiberius B.xi (both of which are dated to Alfred's lifetime); London, BL, Cotton Tiberius B.ii (tenth century); and CUL Ii.2.4 (late eleventh century). Both Cotton MSS suffered heavy damage in the Ashburnham House fire of 1731. Tiberius B. xi. was so severely damaged that we would know its text only as a fragment were it not for the transcript Franciscus Junius made in the seventeenth century.

Although we are unable to establish any sort of precise chronology for Alfred's works, both the style and the content of his preface to the *Pastoral Care* suggest that it is among the earliest of them. The preface contains many of the direct and unadorned statements that we have come to regard as hallmarks of Alfred's style, and the king's voice stands forth clearly and consistently, as in the following: 'Her mon mæg giet gesion ... swæð' (Sweet, 4.15–16) [Here one may still see ... the path] of England's learned forefathers and 'Ac ic ða sona eft me selfum andwyrde, and cwæð: "Hie ne wendon þætte æfre menn sceoldon swa reccelease weorðan and sio lar swa oðfeallan"' (Sweet, 4.22–23) [But I then soon once more answered myself and said: 'They did not think that men would ever be so careless, and that learning would so decline']. However, at times the preface's syntax and grammar become unidiomatic and even strained, as in the following sentence, one well known to beginning OE students: 'Forþam ic ðe bebeode ðæt ðu do swa ic gelife ðæt ðu wille, ðæt ðu ðe þissa woruldðinga to ðæm geæmettige swa ðu oftost mæge, ðæt ðu ðone wisdom þe ðe God sealde ðær ðær ðu hine befæstan mæge, befæste' (Sweet, 4.1–4). Many translators quite understandably opt to render this and other of Alfred's more convoluted sentences idiomatically, as Michael Swanton does: 'And therefore I command you to do, as I believe you wish, that you disengage yourself as often as you can from the affairs of this world, so that you can apply the wisdom which God has given you wherever you are able to apply it' (Swanton, 31). A more literal translation of the same sentence reads 'And therefore I command you that you do as I believe that you desire, that you from these worldly affairs should free yourself as often as you are able to, so that the wisdom that God gave you, there where you are able to apply it, you should apply it.' This and the other sentences that are modelled more closely on Latin than OE syntax are grammatically correct, if unidiomatic, and suggest that Alfred is seeking to elevate his vernacular composition by modelling it upon Latin discourse, a discourse that had been, until the late ninth century, the sole avenue for serious, written intellectual expression. From our perspective, it is hard to understand how radical a departure from centuries of tradition writing in the vernacular was in the ninth century: until the end of the century, the vernacular had been used in only very limited ways for such things as law codes, cartularies, wills, and land grants. When Alfred and his circle begin to translate texts into and to compose texts in the vernacular, they do so under the long shadow of the Latin tradition and, further, they do so without the benefit of having any vernacular models to follow, unless, that is, we accept the existence of a now-lost group of Mercian texts, as some do.

But the occasionally Latinate syntax and grammar of the preface are not the only clues that it may be one of Alfred's earliest works: his looking back to a past, more accomplished Golden Age, his ruminations on the present, greatly decayed state of ecclesiastical and secular learning in England, his outlining of a specific and ambitious programme to revive it, his explanation of the principles that guided his translation, and his desire to have his translation widely disseminated throughout the kingdom further suggest its position among the first works he produced. The *handboc* [handbook] Asser tells us Alfred always carried on his person and which he consulted whenever and wherever he could is lost to us, but in the preface to the *Pastoral Care* Alfred has left behind another, perhaps even more valuable *handboc*, one that does nothing less than outline in the king's own voice the purpose of and plan for his revival of learning.

The preface to the *Pastoral Care* begins with a warm greeting from Alfred to the bishop into whose care the manuscript was given. In the Hatton manuscript, the bishop is identified as 'Wærferð', Bishop of Worcester, and the book's destination is indicated in large letters on the first page: 'ÐEOS BOC SCEAL TO WIOGORA CEASTRE' [This book must go to Worcester] (Ker, *Pastoral Care*, 1ʳ) while in CUL Ii.2.4 the bishop is identified as Wulfsige, Bishop of Sherborne. From the transcription Franciscus Junius made of a note appended to a copy that survives now only as charred fragments, London, BL, Cotton Tiberius B.xi, we know that in addition to Wærferth and Wulfsige, Archbishop Plegmund and Bishop Swithulf of Rochester were also recipients. In Tiberius B. xi the first line reads 'ÆLFRED kyning hateþ gretan ... his wordum loflice and freondlice' (Sweet, xiii) [King Alfred greets ... with loving and friendly words]. What the manuscript lacuna here represented by ellipsis reveals is that its recipient had yet to be determined at the time of its production, something that strongly suggests that Alfred's desire that a copy of his translation of the *Pastoral Care* be sent 'to ælcum biscepstole on minum rice' (Sweet, 6.24–25) [to every bishopric in my kingdom] was put into action. While the surviving evidence suggests that his ambitious plan was only partially realized, what is perhaps more important than the number of copies that were produced and circulated is that Alfred did more than ruminate upon his plan to revive learning; he took concrete steps to enact it.

Keenly aware that England was once the intellectual centre of Western Europe and mindful of 'hu man utanbordes wisdom and lare hider on lond sohte' (Sweet, 2.10–11) [how men from abroad sought in this land wisdom and teaching], Alfred uses the preface to lament the decayed state of Latin learning in his kingdom; at the time of his accession to the throne, there were, he tells us, few people in England 'þe hiora ðenunga cuðen understandan on Englisc, oððe furðum an ærendgewrit of Lædene on Englisc areccan' (Sweet, 2.14–15) [who could understand their divine service in English, or translate a letter from Latin into English]. The surviving evidence is not sufficient enough to allow us to determine the degree to which this statement reflects the actual state of learning in late-ninth-century England or how much it exaggerates it; after all, similar comments about the glories of the recent past and the decrepitude of the present are found throughout English literary history, from Alfred to the present day. The king does not exaggerate, however, when he observes that while once 'þa cirican giond eall Angelkynn stodon maðma ond boca gefylda' [the churches throughout the whole of England stood filled with treasures and books], now they are 'forheregod ... and forbærned' (Sweet, 4.9–10) [all ravaged ... and destroyed by fire]. His regret over the destruction of the monasteries is acute, but rather than simply bemoaning the decay of learning in England, he puts forth a solution that is revolutionary because it will make Latin learning available to a much wider audience and practical because he realizes that if he is going to succeed in making available to the English those 'bec, ða þe nidbeðyrfesta sien eallum monnum to witanne' (Sweet, 6.7) [books, the ones which are most needful for all men to know], they are going to have to be translated into the vernacular, the language 'we ealle gecnawan mægen' (Sweet, 6.8) [we can all understand].

From what Asser tells us of the king's early life, Alfred apparently learned to read English as a youth but only acquired the ability to read Latin towards the end of his life. If this is so, and there is little reason to doubt it, Alfred's plan reflects the reality of his own educational experience and the reality of schooling in the late ninth century, a period in which instruction could be more easily offered in the vernacular than in Latin. Alfred envisions that 'gif we þa stilnesse habbað' [if we have peace], all 'sio gioguð þe nu is on Angel kynne friora monna' [the free-born youth now in England] who have the means to do so will devote themselves to the study of English 'oð ðone first þe hie wel cunnen Englisc gewrit arædan' (Sweet, 6.7–12) [until the time that they readily know how to construe English writing], with the study of Latin being reserved for those destined for higher clerical office. Perhaps wishing to forestall criticism of his plan for putting the vernacular to a use to which it had not previously been put, Alfred situates it within historical precedent: the Greeks first translated the Hebrew laws into their own language and the Romans subsequently did the same with Greek texts.

Although he elsewhere only speaks generally of the help he receives, Alfred closes the preface by explicitly noting that four members of his circle, Plegmund, Asser, Grimbold, and John assisted him. How much or even what sort of help these scholars gave the king cannot be determined since he credits them with helping him learn Gregory's text after which he then translated it into English as he 'forstod and ... andgitfullicost areccean mæhte' (Sweet, 6.23–24) [understood ... and might most intelligibly set it forth]. Perhaps betraying a certain lack of confidence, he also notes that he translates 'hwilum word be worde, hwilum ondgit of andgite' (Sweet, 6.19–20) [at times word for word, at times sense for sense] just as he was taught.

We do not know if the *Pastoral Care* was the first text Alfred chose to translate, but he could not have chosen a more appropriate one upon which to initiate his plan for reviving learning in England. Gregory was one of the most influential ecclesiasts in the early Western medieval world, and Bede and Alcuin are among those who urged that the *Pastoral Care* be read. A metrical preface not attributed to Alfred follows the prose preface and in it the book itself claims that no less of a figure than Augustine brought it with him to England at the behest of Pope Gregory. Although written expressly to aid bishops in their pastoral duties, much of Gregory's text can easily be transposed to a secular key, speaking as it does directly and profitably to lay rulers as well.

The Latin *Pastoral Care* is usually divided into four parts in its surviving manuscripts: the first section is an extended meditation on what drives men to seek (or refuse) positions of power and on how those desires must be examined from a variety of perspectives before they are acted upon; the second ponders the qualities that an ideal ruler must possess; the third, and by far longest, section details at great length how the bishops should treat the diverse needs of the people in their care; and the short, concluding section warns those in power against the dangers of pride. For the most part, Alfred follows the structure and substance of Gregory's text, omitting little but occasionally fleshing out some of what he perceived to be Gregory's more opaque or obscure examples, perhaps with an eye towards making them more comprehensible to his Anglo-Saxon audience. To the same end, Alfred does not attempt to replicate Gregory's Latin syntax, but renders the Latin text in idiomatic OE, often replacing a syntactically complex Latin construction with a series of shorter and more direct OE ones. Alfred also does not break his text into sections as Gregory does, preferring instead to present it in a single series of chapters that are numbered from I to LXV. Alfred provides a list of all the chapter headings before the translation proper begins and so offers what may well be the first table of contents found in a vernacular text. His motivation for adding the list of chapter heads is unclear, but he may have done so in an attempt to make the text accessible to as wide an audience as possible, some of whom would be far more proficient readers than others.

The following two chapter heads and some representative sentences from them provide a good sense of both the text's focus and tone:

I. Ðætte unlærede ne dyrren underfon lareowdom (Sweet, 8.17) [That unlearned men should not dare undertake teaching].

Forðon þe nan cræft nis to læronne ðæm ðe hine ær geornlice ne leornode, forhwon beoð æfre swæ ðriste ða ungelæredan ðæt hi underfon ða heorde ðæs lareowdomes, ðonne se cræft ðæs lareowdomes bið cræft ealra cræfta? Hwa nat þæt ða wunda ðæs modes bioð digelran ðonne ða wunda ðæs lichoman? (Sweet, 24.14–19) [Because no discipline can be taught by him who had not earlier eagerly learned it, why are the unlearned ever so confident that they are able to undertake the care of teaching, when the discipline of teaching is the discipline of all disciplines? Who does not know that the wounds of the mind are more hidden than wounds of the body?]

X. Hwelc se beon sceal þe to reccendome cuman sceall (Sweet, 60.5) [What type of man must he be who is to rule?]

Ne sceal he noht unalyfedes don, ac ðæt þætte oðre men unaliefedes doð he sceal wepan swæ swæ his agne scylde, hiora untrymnesse he sceal ðrowian on his heortan, and ðæs godes his nihstena he sceal fagenian swæ swæ his agnes. His weorc sculon ðæs wierðe beon þæt him oðre men onhyrien. (Sweet 60.15–19) [He must not do anything illicit, but he must lament the illicit deeds that other men do as if they were his own crimes; he must suffer their infirmities in his heart, and he must rejoice in the good of his neighbors as if it were his own. His works must be worthy so that other men emulate him.]

Gregory's text may have appealed so greatly to Alfred not just because it contains sagacious, detailed, and pragmatic advice for bishops that could be easily applied to secular rulers but because it often seems directly to address the circumstances of the king's life: he ascended the throne, as Asser informs us, 'almost unwillingly' (Keynes and Lapidge, 81), just as Gregory counsels a good ruler ought to do: 'Ðonne he oferstæled bið ... þæt he oðrum mæg nyt bion on ðæm þe him mon ðonne bebeodeð, mid his mode he hit sceal fleon and ðeah for hiersumnesse he hit sceal underfon' (Sweet, 46.16–19) [When he is convinced ... that he may be useful to others in that which is charged to him, he should flee it in his spirit, and yet out of obedience he must accept it]. In summing up the attributes of an ideal ruler, Gregory effectively holds a mirror up to Alfred, a devout Christian, a successful warrior, and a king who cared deeply about improving the education of both laymen and the clergy: 'His weorc sculon ðæs wierðe beon þæt him oðre menn onhyrien. He sceal tilian swæ to libbenne swa he mæge ða adrugodan heortan geðwænan mid ðæm flowendan yðum his lare. He sceal geleornian þæt he gewunige to singallecum gebedum' (Sweet 60.18–21) [His works must be worthy so that other men will emulate him. He must strive to live so he may wash the withered hearts with the flowing waves of his teaching. He must learn that must accustom himself to perpetual prayers]. Chapter XXXVI, 'Ðætte on oþre wisan sint to manianne ða halan, on oðre ða unhalan' (Sweet, 246, 4–5) [That the healthy are to be admonished in one way, the unhealthy in another way], must have held a special resonance for Alfred, who Asser reports, from the age of twenty 'has been plagued continually with the savage attacks of some unknown disease, such that he does not have even a single hour of peace in which he does not either suffer from the disease itself or else, gloomily dreading it, is not driven almost to despair' (Keynes and Lapidge, 101). Alfred, who ascended the throne at an especially crucial and turbulent moment in English history and who managed to push back the Viking invaders and establish a fragile peace, might have found Gregory's text an important source of practical advice, consolation, and edification.

Further Reading

Clement, Richard W. 'The production of the *Pastoral Care*: King Alfred and his helpers'. In *Studies in Earlier Old English Prose*, ed. Paul E. Szarmach, 129–52. Albany: State University of New York Press, 1986.

O'Brien O'Keeffe, Katherine. 'Inside, outside, conduct and judgment: King Alfred reads the *Regula Pastoralis*'. In *'Un serto di fiori in man recando': Scritti in onore di Maria Amalia D'Aronco*, ed. Silvana Serafin and Patrizia Lendinara, 333–45. 2 vols. Undine: Forum, 2007.

Schreiber, Carolyn. *King Alfred's Old English Translation of Pope Gregory the Great's 'Regula Pastoralis' and Its Cultural Context*. Münchener Universitätsschriften 25. Bern: Peter Lang, 2002.

Shippey, Thomas A. 'Wealth and wisdom in King Alfred's *Preface* to the Old English *Pastoral Care*'. EHR 94 (1979): 346–55.

Szarmach, Paul E. 'The meaning of Alfred's *Preface* to the *Pastoral Care*'. Mediaevalia 6 (1982 for 1980): 57–86.

Alfred's Translation of Boethius's *Consolation of Philosophy*

Survives in two MSS: London, BL, Cotton Otho A.vi, fols 1–129 and Oxford, Bodleian Library, Bodley 180 (2079). Cotton Otho A.vi, which is dated to the tenth century, was badly damaged in a fire at Ashburnham

House, then the repository of the Anglo-Saxon manuscripts that would form the basis of the collection currently housed in the British Library, in October of 1731. Bodley 180 is dated to the late eleventh or early/mid twelfth century. Cotton Otho follows the Latin prosimetric model and contains alternating sections of verse and prose (see Part 3). Bodley 180 (2079), in contrast, renders the text, metres included, entirely in prose. In the late seventeenth century, Franciscus Junius transcribed Bodley 180 in what is now Oxford, Bodleian Library, MS Junius 12 (*Sum. Cat.* 5124). Junius separately transcribed the metres from Cotton Otho onto separate sheets of paper, which were at some point pasted into the volume near the relevant prose sections. A fragment, since lost, of a single leaf from another manuscript was diplomatically transcribed by A.S. Napier in the late nineteenth century.

It is impossible to establish with any certainty the chronology of the works attributed to King Alfred the Great, but he is generally thought to have translated Boethius's *De consolatione philosophiae* [*The Consolation of Philosophy*] after translating the *Pastoral Care*. As is the case with the *Pastoral Care*, a preface has been added to the *Consolation*, but since there is reason to think that Alfred may not be the author of the preface, we must approach the evidence it offers cautiously. Shorter and less elaborate than the preface to the *Pastoral Care*, the *Consolation*'s preface does not mention Alfred's programme to revive learning in England, it does not attempt to justify having translated Boethius's Latin text into the vernacular, it does not credit anyone but the king himself for the translation, and, finally, it takes a retrospective view of Alfred's reign that suggests it was written following his death. The *Consolation*'s preface uses the same language used in the preface to the *Pastoral Care* to inform us that Alfred at times translates literally and at others more idiomatically, but whereas in the preface to the *Pastoral Care* Alfred places this within the contexts of his intellectual training and limitations, the author of the *Consolation*'s preface tells us Alfred does so 'for þam mistlicum and manigfealdum woruldbisgum þe hine oft ægðer ge on mode ge on lichoman bisgodan' (Godden and Irvine, I.239, 4–6) [on account of the various and manifold worldly troubles that often afflicted him either in the mind or the body].

Although the *Consolation*'s preface reasserts the translation strategy Alfred articulates in his preface to Gregory, in his translation of the *Consolation* Alfred departs from the Latin original in ways that he rarely, if ever, does in the *Pastoral Care*. In the *Pastoral Care*, Alfred clarifies some of Gregory's Biblical allusions and often uses OE doublets to render a single

Latin term, but on the whole he remains fairly faithful to the original in that his additions and deletions are all relatively minor. While adhering closely to the Latin text's substance, he reorders and simplifies Gregory's sentences almost as a matter of course. In the OE *Consolation*, in contrast, we discover a translator who departs from his original text so freely and so frequently that he should be considered more a reviser, or even perhaps a co-author, than just a translator. Among other things, while Alfred retains the dialogue structure of the Latin text, he changes its participants from Boethius and Lady Philosophy to Wisdom, Reason, and Mind. In the version preserved in Bodley 180 (2079), he makes several significant formal alterations as well, rendering Boethius's originally prosimetrical text entirely in prose and opting to present his text in chapters (an unnumbered table of which immediately follows the preface) rather than follow the Latin original's division into five books (although the conclusion of Books II and III and the beginning of Books III and IV are noted, respectively, at the ends of Chapters 21 and 35). The version in Cotton Otho A.vi reflects the structure of the Latin and, according to the OE prose preface found in Bodley 180, Alfred composed not just the prose sections but the verses as well: when he 'þas boc hæfde geleornode and of Lædene to Engliscum spelle gewende, þa geworhte he hi eft to leoðe swa swa heo nu gedon is' (Godden and Irvine, I.239.7–9) [this book had learned and from Latin into English discourse had turned it, then he made it again into song just as it is now done]. The attribution of the verses to Alfred, however, is a complicated and problematic issue, and it seems unlikely that he authored them.

In both versions, Alfred omits a good deal of the Latin original, including the many autobiographical passages that are so integral to the early books of the Latin text and virtually all of the dense and difficult Book V. He seems to have drawn from earlier Latin commentaries upon the *Consolation*, although the extent of his borrowings and the identity of the sources from which he drew remain matters of some dispute. Alfred adds explicitly Christian references, and he also explains, sometimes in considerable detail, many of Boethius's mythological, historical, and geographical references. He may have added many of these to aid his contemporary audience's comprehension of the matter being presented to them, as when he notes at the end of Chapter 21 that 'Se Boetius wæs oðre naman gehaten Seuerinus; se wæs heretoga Romana' (Godden and Irvine, I.286.49–50) [Boethius was called by another name, Severinus; he was a consul of the Romans], but others might be best categorized as digressions in which he dilates upon a wide range of topics not found in the Latin text, including the nature of earth, water, air, and fire (OE Godden and Irvine, I.316–18; trans. II.52–53) and a king's 'andweorc ond his tol to ricsianne' (Godden and Irvine, I.277.11–12) [raw material and his tools for governing]. It is also in these additions that Alfred's voice seems to emerge most clearly, as when he closes his discussion of how he wished that he 'unfracodlice and gerisenlice mihte steoran and reccan þone anweald þe me befæst wæs' (Godden and Irvine, I.277.6–8) [might honourably and fittingly steer and direct the absolute power that was entrusted to me] with the following well-known comment: 'Þat is nu hraþost to secganne þæt ic wilnode weorðfullice to libbane þa hwile þe ic lifede, and æfter minum life þam monnum to læfanne þe æfter me wæren min gemynd on godum weorccum' (Godden and Irvine, I.278.26–28) [That is now to say in short that I desired to live worthily the time that I lived, and after my life to leave to the men who were to come after me my remembrance in good works].

Although Boethius is believed to have been a Christian, the Latin *Consolation* contains no explicit articulation of Christian doctrine: it does not cite any Christian authorities – even in those instances when it seems to be drawing upon them –, and it does not mention by name Christ or indeed any other figure from the Christian tradition. The devoutly Christian Alfred remedies this by adding explicit references to Christ and his father as well as to such Old Testament figures as Noah and Nimrod. These Christian additions, many of which he may have imported into his translation from the commentaries upon which he drew, sometimes occur in digressions, as with the mention of the devil found in a brief aside on the opposing natures of good and evil in Chapter 16 (OE Godden and Irvine, I.275; trans. II.25) or they are used to amplify and make more doctrinally explicit one of Boethius's points, as in the discussion of power and its relation to the 'hehst god' [highest good], in Latin the 'summum bonum', that is so central to Boethius's philosophical thought. After presenting Boethius's view in Chapter 36 that 'se fulla anweald to tellanne to þam hehstum godum, forþam ægðer ge se anweald ge þa oðru god and þa cræftas þe we longe ær nemdon sindon fæste on þam hehstan gode' (Godden and Irvine, I.344.201–203) [the full power is to be reckoned the highest form of good, for not only power, but also the other kinds of good, and the virtues we long since named, are firmly fixed in the highest good], Alfred redirects it in order to give it an explicitly Christian colouring: 'Swa swa ælces huses wah bið fæst ægþer ge on þære flore ge on þam hrofe, swa bið ælc god on Gode fæst, forþam he is ælces godes ægþer ge hrof ge flor' (Godden and Irvine, I.344–45.203–206) [Just as each house's wall is securely set both on the floor and in the roof, so is each good securely set in God, because he is both each good's roof and floor].

Alfred not only adds material to clarify and Christianize Boethius's text, he also compresses or simply deletes much of it, as we can see in his treatment of Boethius's Book V. In the Latin text, Book V is the culmination of the carefully plotted journey upon which Lady Philosophy has been slowly leading Boethius. After helping him move beyond the immediate – and ultimately insignificant – temporal matters which preoccupy him in the first few books (among which are his loss of power and status, his exile, and his imminent execution) to a greater comprehension of such larger and more important issues as the nature of good and evil and the varied and necessary roles they play in this world's grand design, Lady Philosophy tries in Book V to help him understand the most important issue of all: the way in which human free will works within the divinely ordered structure of the universe, a structure in which Fate and Providence are central powers. To help Boethius grasp this difficult concept, she explains that since God exists in the eternal present, he is able to see all possible actions without in any way determining them. In the Alfredian text, Wisdom takes a very different approach throughout the work's final sections. Rather than seeking to elevate Mind to the point where he is able to ponder something that lies on the very edge of human understanding, he attempts to explain eternity by contrasting the transitory nature of this world with what he labels the two types of eternity: that which has a beginning but no end (angels and men's souls, according to Wisdom) and that which has neither beginning nor end (God). He does not delve further into these issues because, as he says, 'Gif wit þæt eall sculon asmeagan, þonne cume wit late to ende þisse bec oððe næfre' (Goddon and Irvine, I.381.20–21) [If we two must all that scrutinize, then must we come late to the end of this book or never]. Compare this to Lady Philosophy's rather different approach to the same issue in the Latin *Consolation*:

> You may still wonder, however, whether God's knowledge is changed by your decisions so that when you wish now one thing, now another, the divine knowledge undergoes corresponding changes. This is not the case. For divine Providence anticipates every future action and converts it to its own present knowledge. It does not change, as you imagine, foreknowing this or that in succession, but in a single instant, without being changed itself, anticipates and grasps your changes. God has this present comprehension and immediate vision of all things not from the outcome of future events, but from the simplicity of his own nature.
>
> (Green, 119)

As even these two brief examples makes clear, Alfred does not so much simplify Boethius's subject matter in Book V as replace it with material that is both more limited in scope and more doctrinal in nature. We finally can do little more than speculate as to whether Alfred deviates from Boethius's text because he found himself out of his intellectual depth when he came to Book V, or because he followed Gregory's advice in the antepenultimate chapter of the *Pastoral Care* and wished to avoid overtaxing the minds of his readers by putting before them such lofty, abstract, and challenging subject matter.

Further Reading

Bately, Janet M. 'Boethius and King Alfred'. In *Platonism and the English Imagination*, ed. Anna Baldwin and Sarah Hutton, 38–44. Cambridge: Cambridge University Press, 1994.

Bolton, Whitney F. 'How Boethian is Alfred's *Boethius*?' In *Studies in Earlier Old English Prose*, ed. Paul E. Szarmach, 153–68. Albany: State University of New York Press, 1986.

Discenza, Nicole Guenther. *The King's English: Strategies of Translation in the Old English 'Boethius'*. Albany: State University of New York Press, 2005.

Godden, Malcolm, and Susan Irvine, eds. 'Introduction'. *The Old English Boethius: An Edition of the Old English Versions of Boethius's 'De Consolatione Philosophiae'*. Oxford: Oxford University Press, 2009.

Szarmach, Paul E. 'Alfred's *Boethius* and the four cardinal virtues'. In *Alfred the Wise: Studies in Honour of Janet Bately on the Occasion of Her Sixty-Fifth Birthday*, ed. Jane Roberts, Janet L. Nelson, and Malcolm Godden, 223–35. Cambridge: D.S. Brewer, 1997.

King Alfred's Translation of St Augustine's *Soliloquies*

Survives in a mid-twelfth-century MS, London, BL, Cotton Vitellius A.xv, fols 4–93.

The *Soliloquia* [*Soliloquies*] of St Augustine, Bishop of Hippo and one of the towering figures of the late antique Church, is a dense, cryptic rumination in the form of a dialogue between Augustine and Reason pertaining to matters of the soul, knowledge, and being. Over the course of the dialogue, Augustine considers such weighty and complex matters as 'the faculties of the soul through which God is known' (I.vi); 'those things which are necessary to know God' (I.viii); 'the manner in which the soul is known' (I.xv); and 'whether a body truly exists' (II.xviii). Although its subject matter is of great importance in Christian thought, in both its tone and outlook the *Soliloquies* is, like Boethius's Latin *Consolation*, a far more overtly philosophical than theological work. As does Lady Philosophy, Reason relies almost exclusively on scholastic logic, not

Christian doctrine to make his points, as illustrated by his proof of the soul's immortality:

> Every branch of learning is in the soul as in a subject. If, therefore, learning endures forever, then the soul must endure forever. But learning is truth, and, as reason showed in the beginning of this book, truth abides forever. Therefore, the soul endures forever, and if it died, we would not call it the soul. Consequently, only he can reasonably deny the immortality of the soul who proves that some point in the above reasoning was granted illogically.
>
> (Gilligan, 123)

The manner in which Alfred treats the *Soliloquies* is very much of a piece with his handling of Gregory's *Pastoral Care* and Boethius's *Consolation of Philosophy*: as he does to Gregory's text, he adds a preface; he deviates freely and frequently from his source text, contracting (and in the *Soliloquies* simply excising) many of the original's more difficult or abstruse points and expanding upon and clarifying others for an audience far different from that of Augustine's intended one. As he does throughout the *Consolation*, Alfred also draws out in many places the Christian implications of Augustine's original Latin text and he further grounds many of his additions firmly in Christian doctrine.

The preface to the only extant copy of Alfred's translation begins abruptly, and probably defectively, with its unidentified first-person speaker employing the metaphor of constructing a house out of the forest of wisdom to explain his compositional practices: 'Gaderode me þonne kigclas and stuþansceaftas' (Carnicelli, 47.1) [I gathered then for myself thick sticks and posts]. Because he did not seek to bring 'ealne þane wude ham' (Carnicelli, 47.5) [all the wood home], Alfred encourages his readers each to journey to the woods and select what seems most proper to them so that each of them may 'manig ænlic hus settan' (Carnicelli, 47.10) [many a unique house build]. The raw materials he gathers, both for the concrete project of creating his text and for the abstract one of building a 'house' of doctrinal knowledge in which to pass one's time on earth, are, he tells us, the works of Augustine, Gregory, and Jerome, and the dwelling he erects out of the various pieces of their writings mirrors the everlasting house of true knowledge that awaits us after death, one that like its transitory counterpart is under the direct authority of God, the 'weliga gifola' (Carnicelli, 48.10) [rich bounteous one]. The preface to the *Soliloquies* is not as ambitious in its scope or as rich in its detail as is the preface to the *Pastoral Care*, but in inviting its readers to discover and explore for themselves the sources out of which it was formed and in encouraging them to construct for themselves their own edifices, it recalls the unattributed quotation found at the end of Asser's eighty-eighth chapter which explains that 'The just man builds on modest foundations and gradually proceeds to greater things' (Keynes and Lapidge, 100).

Although it remains faithful to the broad outlines of Augustine's text, the first book of Alfred's translation amounts to a somewhat loose rendering of the Latin text, one that we should view more as an adaptation of the original than a literal translation of it. The looseness of the translation may be a sign that Alfred simply could not always penetrate the philosophical logic of the original, as seems to be the case when Reason turns to mathematical reasoning to explain how we know God. In the Latin original, Reason first asks Augustine if he 'at least know[s] what a line is in geometry?' (Gilligan, 23). After receiving Augustine's assurance that he does in fact know this, Reason asks him if he knows 'that ball which they call a sphere ... ... as [he] know[s] a line?' (Gilligan, 23). He continues by asking if the line and the sphere 'seem to you to be one and the same thing, or is there some difference between them?' (Gilligan, 25) before moving on to his conclusion: 'Thus you know a line as you know a sphere even though a line is not like a sphere. Therefore, tell me whether it would be enough for you to know God as you know this geometric sphere, that is, to have no doubt about God as you have none about it' (Gilligan, 27). Alfred follows Augustine's lead in having his Reason draw upon mathematics as a way of explaining the ways in which man's 'inner' and 'outer senses' know God. Alfred explicitly mentions 'þone creft þe we hatað geometrica' (Carnicelli, 60.15) [the discipline we call geometry] and he retains the ideas of the sphere, which he concretizes as a 'þoðere oðþe on æpple oððe on æge atefred' (Carnicelli, 60.16) [a ball, or an apple, or a painted egg], and that of the line, both of which are fundamental to Augustine's explanation. But unlike Augustine who explores the geometric properties of lines and spheres as a means of illuminating 'not what you know like to God, but what you know as you desire to know God' (Gilligan, 27), Alfred instead embarks upon a discussion of how lines and spheres help us 'ongytan þises roðores ymbehwirft and þara tungla færeld' (Carnicelli, 60.17–18) [to understand the orbit of the sky and the movement of the stars]. Augustine's abstract line becomes in Alfred's hands an actual line painted on the equally concrete painted ball 'þe þu on leornedost ymbe þises rodores hwyrft' (Carnicelli, 61.8) [from which you learned about the movement of the sky]. Alfred opts not to adhere to Augustine's logical argument that the ultimate difference 'lies in the things known, not in the manner of knowing them' (Gilligan, 27) and instead argues from a homiletic, if typically homely, perspective that faith must be the key to perception: 'for þam þingum is ðearf þæt þu rihte hawie mid modes æagum to gode, swa rihte swa swa scipes ancer streng byð aþenæd on gerihte fram þam scype to þam ancræ; and gefastna þa eagan þines modes on gode swa se ancer byd gefastnoð on ðære eorðan' (Carnicelli, 61.23–25–62.1) [for those things it is necessary that you look with your mind's eyes to God, as rightly as the ship's anchor cord is stretched properly from the ship to the anchor; and fasten the eyes of your mind on God as the anchor is fastened on the earth].

Alfred's veering off here from the complex arguments Augustine articulates may reveal the degree to which he simply fails to comprehend, here and in numerous other places, some individual parts, or even whole portions, of Augustine's text. Given the state of education in England in the late ninth century even among the most learned, it is perhaps understandable that Alfred and his circle on occasion fail fully to comprehend texts that grow out of very different rhetorical traditions and are composed by authors with far more extensive rhetorical and philosophical training. However, we must also remain alive to the possibility that the changes Alfred makes in some instances result from his having consciously rejected Augustine's positions, either because he found them unacceptable (as is certainly the case when he revises Augustine's claim that only the good will see God in the afterlife to read that *both* the good and the bad will be able to do so) or because he felt that his audience, which was not well trained in Latin rhetoric, was not suitably equipped to grasp the finer aspects of the saint's points.

We must be careful, however, not to let the many omissions and points of confusion evident in Alfred's translation dominate our perception of it; rather we ought to keep in mind that all three of the possibilities outlined above (misunderstanding, conscious rejection, desire to make the text accessible) come into play at various points in the translation, and to varying degrees. For example, Book II of the OE translation moves much further afield from Augustine's topic than does Book I and it contains material that seems to derive from several sources (an Augustinian epistle, Boethius's *Consolation*, and Gregory's *Dialogues*), although the allusive nature of the discussion in Book II and the heavy damage the surviving manuscript has sustained makes it difficult, if not impossible, finally to tell which sources inform which sections of the translation.

But even when he departs from Augustine's text, Alfred nonetheless remains faithful to its project, something that his major additions to Book II and the entirety of the brief Book III bear out, despite the discussion's occasionally lapsing into near incoherence. Augustine left the *Soliloquies* incomplete, stopping after he wrote the first two books and never returning to it. Alfred concludes his additions to (or to be more precise, recreation of) Book II with a sentiment that not only echoes one of the most important ones Augustine makes in Book I but that explicitly recalls in the word 'gegadrad' [gathered] the metaphor that is foundational to his preface: 'Nu ic gehyre þæt min sawel is æcu and a lifað, and eall þæt min mod and min gescadwisnesse goodra crefta gegadrad, þæt mot þa simle habban. And ic gehere æac þæt min gewit is æce' (Carnicelli, 91.21–24) [Now I hear that my soul is eternal and ever lives, and that all that my mind and my reason gathered of good virtues it must always have. And I hear also that my intellect is eternal]. In continuing 'Ac me lyste gyt witan be ðam gewitte þæt ic ær acsode: hweðer hyt æfter þæs lichaman gedale and þare sawle weoxe þe wanede, þe hyt swa on stæle stode, þe hyt swa dyde swa hyt ær dæð on þisse weorulde – oðre hwile weoxe, oðre hwile wanode' (Carnicelli, 91.24–27) [But I desire yet to know about the intellect what I earlier asked: whether it, after the separation of the body and soul, will wax or wane, or will it thus stand in place, as it did earlier in this world: at one time wax, at another wane], Alfred introduces the topic of Book III, one raised but never explored by Augustine. The short and at times confused Book III does not, of course, establish Alfred as Augustine's intellectual peer, especially since its argument rests securely upon scriptural authority and not philosophical speculation, but it is an admirable attempt to bring Augustine's daunting text to a satis-factory close and it remains important in its own right as a piece of writing and thinking that may well be original to Alfred (and his advisors).

Further Reading

Gatch, Milton McC. 'King Alfred's version of Augustine's *Soliloquia*: some sugges-tions on its rationale and unity'. In *Old English Prose: Basic Readings*, ed. Paul E. Szarmach, with the assistance of Deborah A. Oosterhouse, 199–236. Basic Readings in Anglo-Saxon England 5. New York: Garland, 2000.

Godden, Malcolm. 'Text and eschatology in Book III of the Old English *Soliloquies*'. *Anglia* 121 (2003): 177–209.

Heuchan, Valerie. 'God's co-workers and powerful tools: a study of the sources of Alfred's building metaphor in his Old English translation of Augustine's *Soliloquies*'. *NQ* ns 54 (2007): 1–11.

Hitch, Susan. 'Alfred's cræft: imagery in Alfred's version of Augustine's *Soliloquies*'. *Journal of the Department of English* (University of Calcutta) 22 (1986–87): 130–47.

King Alfred's Translations of the Prose Psalms of the Paris Psalter

Prose translations of psalms are found in two MSS dated to the mid eleventh century: Paris, Bibliothèque nationale de France, Fonds latin 8824 (fols 1–65ᵛ), a manuscript apparently owned at one point by John, Duke of Berry, and known as the Paris Psalter, and in fragments in London, BL, MS Cotton Vitellius E.xviii.

In Asser's *Life of King Alfred*, Alfred emerges as an extremely thoughtful, self-reflective ruler who, having 'taken over the helm of his kingdom, ...

alone, sustained by divine assistance, struggled like an excellent pilot to guide his ship laden with much wealth to the desired and safe haven of his homeland, even though all his sailors were virtually exhausted' (Keynes and Lapidge, 101). We know from the preface to the *Pastoral Care* and from the other translations attributed to Alfred that he was keenly concerned with the state of ecclesiastical and lay learning in England, but he was also a devout Christian, for as we learn from Asser, Alfred 'was also in the invariable habit of listening daily to divine services and Mass, and of participating in certain psalms and prayers and in the day-time and night-time offices, and, at night-time, ... of going (without his household knowing) to various churches in order to pray' (Keynes and Lapidge, 91).

Alfred's devout nature is important because it is largely upon it, as well as some stylistic and circumstantial evidence, that the translation of the Prose Psalms in the Paris Psalter is attributed to him: there is nothing in the surviving manuscript of the Prose Psalms to indicate Alfred's role in their production. It contains no preface in which he identifies himself nor does it have a colophon, such as the one found in the *Soliloquies*, that attributes it to him: 'Hær endiað þa cwidas þe Ælfred kining alæs of þære bec þe we hatað on ...' (Carnicelli, 97.17) [Here ends the sayings which King Alfred selected from the book we call in ...]. Alfred may have translated the psalms from a Latin text of the Roman Psalter, and the Paris Psalter presents the Latin and OE texts on alternating pages. As is true of Alfred in general, at times he renders the Latin fairly closely and at other times he adds material of an exegetical nature to them. Beyond their appeal as devotional texts, there is reason to think that the psalms may have had a special attraction and perhaps immediacy for Alfred, a king whose entire reign was conducted under the threat of foreign invasion, since in many of the Prose Psalms King David laments the great oppression he and his people suffered at the hands of foreign forces. In these psalms, King David also stresses the necessity of turning to God and trusting to his help in the face of present and pressing woes, a theme that runs so consistently through all of Alfred's translations that it may have had a particular resonance for him as well. Additionally, the psalms fit quite comfortably into his programme of making essential texts available to his subjects in the vernacular, and as the most strictly doctrinal of his works, his translation of the psalms complements the other, more philosophical texts he chose to translate.

With the exception of Psalm 1, all the Prose Psalms are preceded by brief introductions in which Alfred – again perhaps with an eye towards his programme of educational reform – provides some historical context for the psalm and then suggests several different levels of interpretation for it. As we can see in his introduction to Psalm 10:

Ðysne teoþan sealm Dauid sang þa he wæs adrifen on þæt westen fram Sawle þam cynge, þa his geferan hine lærdon þæt he hine þær hydde swa þer spearuwa; and swa ylce þa rihtwisan þe hine singað, hi seofiað be heora feondum, ægðer ge gesewenlicum ge ungesewenlicum; and swa dyde Crist be Iudeum þa he þysne sealm sang.

(O'Neill, *King Alfred's Old English Prose Translations*, 109–10)

[This tenth psalm David sang when he was driven out into the desert by Saul the king, when his companions instructed him that he hide himself there like a sparrow; and just as those same righteous men who themselves sing, they complain of their enemies, both the visible and the invisible; and so did Christ about the Jews when he sang this psalm.]

The subject matter of the psalms and their tone must have resonated powerfully for Alfred, who may have be drawn to the parallels between the specific trials he faced and those of David. Just as David is driven into the desert, so, too, had Alfred been forced to hide from the Vikings in the forests of Wessex that lay to the west of Selwood. The introduction to Psalm 13 sounds another typically Alfredian note, this one concerning the current decayed state of religion and learning:

Ða Dauid þisne þretteoðan sealm sang, þa seofode he to Drihtne on þam sealme þæt æfre on his dagum sceolde gewurðan swa lytle treowa, and swa lytle wisdom wære on worulde; and swa deð ælc rihtwis man þe hine nu singð, he seofað þæt ylce be his tidum; and swa dyde Crist be Iudeum; and Ezechias be Rapsace, Assyria cyninge.

(O'Neill, *King Alfred's Old English Prose Translations*, 112)

[When David this thirteenth psalm sang, then he complained to the lord in the psalm that ever in his day there should be so little assurance of good faith and that there should be so little wisdom in the world; and so does each righteous man who now sings it, he complains similarly about his times; and so did Christ about the Jews, and Ezechial about Raspaces, the Assyrian king.]

And in the introduction to Psalm 15,

Þone fifteoðan sealm Dauid sang be his earfoðum, ægðer ge modes ge lichaman; and eft swa ilce Ezechias hine sang be his mettrumnesse, wilnode him to Gode sumre frofre; and swa deð ælc rihtwis man þe hine singð on his earfoðum; and swa dyde Crist þa he hine sang.

(O'Neill, *King Alfred's Old English Prose Translations*, 114)

[David sang the fifteenth psalm about his afflictions, both of the mind and the body; and just as Ezechial himself sang similarly about his infirmity, he desired for himself some consolation from God; and so does each righteous man who sings it in his distress; and so did Christ when he himself sang], it is not difficult to hear echoes of the very similar types of afflictions that plagued Alfred, who suffered from severe and still undetermined physical ailments throughout his life.

The twelfth-century chronicler William of Malmesbury asserts that Alfred translated just the first fifty psalms because his death interrupted the project, and while this claim cannot be verified, if the Prose Psalms are in fact the final pieces of writing Alfred produced before his death, they are a fitting tribute to a man who strove to provide his kingdom with political stability and his people with the tools they needed to pursue knowledge and the path of righteousness.

Further Reading

Bately, Janet M. 'Lexical evidence for the authorship of the prose psalms in the Paris Psalter'. *ASE* 10 (1982): 69–95.

O'Neill, Patrick P. 'The Old English introductions to the prose psalms of the Paris Psalter: sources, structure, and composition'. *SP* 78 (1981): 20–38.

King Alfred's Preface to Wærferth's Translation of Pope Gregory's *Dialogues*

Survives in CCCC, 322 and Oxford, Bodleian Library, Hatton 76.

Perhaps the most important aspect of the preface King Alfred added to Bishop Wærferth's translation of Pope Gregory's *Dialogues* is the possible evidence it offers regarding Alfred's commissioning of other translations, which may have been intended for either, or both, his personal use and for wider distribution in accordance with the programme to revive learning in England that he details more fully in his preface to Gregory's *Pastoral Care*. In the brief preface to the *Dialogues*, written in the king's own voice and beginning 'Ic Ælfred geofendum Criste mid cynehades mærnysse geweorðod' [I, Alfred, through the gift of Christ honoured with the distinction of kingship], Alfred reveals that he 'sohte and wilnade to minum getreowum freondum, þæt hi me of Godes bocum be haligra manna þeawum and wundrum awriten þas æfterfylgendan lare, þæt ic þurh þa mynegunge and lufe gescyrped on minum mode betwih þas eorðlican gedrefednesse hwilum gehicge þa heofonlican' (Hecht, 1) [sought and asked for from his true friends that they for me should write down from God's books concerning the customs and wonders of holy men so that I through the exhortations and love they contain might at times amidst earthly vexations think about the heavenly]. Even though it is generally thought that Wærferth produced his translation for Alfred's personal use, the metrical preface – which is not attributed to Alfred – that replaces Alfred's prose preface in the only other extant manuscript of the *Dialogues*, London, BL, Cotton Otho C.i Vol. II, witnesses that the text also circulated, perhaps as part of Alfred's programme of educational reform and revival. The metrical preface, which is spoken by the book itself, informs us that Bishop Wulfsige, who preceded Asser as Bishop of Sherborne, received the exemplar from which his copy was made directly from King Alfred.

The *Vercelli Homilies*

Exist in the unique manuscript, Vercelli, Biblioteca Capitolare, CXVII, which is wanting some leaves but is otherwise well preserved.

The manuscript designated as Vercelli, Biblioteca Capitolare, CXVII, is more familiarly known as the Vercelli Book. Produced by a single scribe at some point in the second half of the tenth century, it is perhaps best known for the six pieces of OE Christian poetry it contains (see Part 3), including two of the four poems that bear the runic signature of Cynewulf, but it also houses what is generally agreed to be the earliest collection of homiletic prose writings to survive from the period, predating those of the *Blickling Homilies*. The twenty-three prose pieces in the manuscript are gathered together into four groups and are collectively referred to as the *Vercelli Homilies* (*VH*) even though only a few of them are truly homiletic: several, including IV, VII, VIII, and IX, are sermons on rather general topics, while others (XVIII and XXIII) are saints' lives or are largely eschatological (including II, IV, and XI). Still others are religious narratives largely devoid of homiletic content (XVIII and XXIII). The collection is truly miscellaneous and does not follow (nor attempt to follow) the liturgical calendar, even to the loose extent that the *Blickling Homilies* do, and the principle of selection, if there was one, that led the scribe to copy and compile the *VH* is now lost to us. There are some stylistic and thematic similarities evident among the prose pieces in the Vercelli Book and when we further consider the manuscript's contents as a whole, it seems to have been created as a collection of pious prose and poetic writings; beyond this, we know little regarding how, when, where, and why it was assembled and whether it was meant

The Anglo-Saxon Literature Handbook, First Edition. Mark C. Amodio.
© 2014 Mark C. Amodio. Published 2014 by John Wiley & Sons, Ltd.

chiefly to be used by a private reader or to be read aloud to a listening audience.

The individual homilies, five of which (V, and XI–XIV) bear headings in the manuscript, were written by different authors, but the linguistic and stylistic features of XIX, XX, and XXI strongly suggest that one author was responsible for producing them. While some of the pieces may have been written close to the date at which the manuscript was compiled, a number of others appear to have been composed much earlier. The *VH* draw upon a wide and varied range of Latin source materials, including writings by Gregory the Great, Paulinus of Aquileia, and Caesarius of Arles, among others. In some instances, the authors translate their sources closely, if selectively (e.g., I and III), and in others (e.g., V and XXII) they draw freely from one or more identifiable sources. The sources for Homily II and Homily VII have recently been identified, but that of XII has yet to be uncovered.

Despite having been produced by a number of authors separated by as much as a generation or more, the *VH* share a number of similarities. The exegesis they contain is usually articulated in a direct and uncomplicated fashion, as in V when we are told that we should pay tribute to God in 'in þrim wisum' [three ways], 'þæt is on wordum and on geþohtum and on dædum' (Scragg, *Vercelli Homilies*, 116.92) [that is in words and in thoughts and in deeds] or in XI when the author mentions the 'gastlice blacernas' [spiritual lanterns] the Lord has 'geæld' [kindled], and then asks, and immediately answers, the question 'Hwæt syndon þa blacernas þe us hafað ure dryhten forgifen to anlyhtanne ða dimnesse mancynnes ungetre-owennesse?' (Scragg, *Vercelli Homilies*, 221.13–15) [What are these lanterns that our lord has given us to illuminate the darkness of mankind's faithlessness?].

As a group, the homilies in *VH* reveal a certain degree of stylistic sophistication and many of them are extremely effective pieces of writing. Their authors habitually compress their source material with great skill and they also characteristically reshape their sources, frequently with considerable deftness. For example, in Homily XIII, one of several that contain passages in which souls address their dead bodies, the author elects to dramatize the *ubi sunt* motif by having bones in a grave directly address the audience. While not reaching the level of rhetorical or narrative sophistication of, say, *Blickling Homilies* X, another homily that employs the motif of talking bones, the passage in *VH* XIII nevertheless has considerable power: 'Beheald me and sceawa mine ban and ondræd þe þinne fyrenlust and þine gytsunge. Þæt ðu eart nu, þæt ic wæs io; þæt ic eom nu, þæt ðu wiorðest eft. ... Geseoh ðu me in duste formolsnodne, and þurh þæt forlæt ðu þinne þone yfelan lust' (Scragg, *Vercelli Homilies*, 235.27–32) [Behold me and look upon my bones and be afraid of your sinful pleasures and your inordinate desire. What you are now, that I was formally; what I am now, that you will become again ... Look upon me in the dust crumbled, and through that abandon you your evil pleasure].

Homily X, which has no heading in the manuscript, exemplifies the Vercelli Book's homiletic writings. Largely eschatological in focus, as are several others, it is based in part – and rather loosely – on several sources, chiefly Latin texts by Paulinus of Aquilea, Isidore of Seville, and pseudo-Augustine. The careful, didactic style of the homilist is evidenced in the groups of doublets and triplets he employs early on: 'Þæt heahfæderas bod-edon and cyðdon, þæt witegan witegedon and heredon, þæt sealmscopas sungon and sædon, þæt se wolde of ðam rice cuman and of ðam cynestole and of ðam þrymrice hyder on þas eorðan' (Scragg, *Vercelli Homilies*, 196.11–13) [That the patriarchs announced and proclaimed, that the prophets prophesied and praised, that the psalmists sang and said, that he would come from that kingdom and that royal seat and from that realm of glory hither to this earth]. There follows in short order a list of what those who love God should avoid:

> Ne syn we to gifre, ne to frece ne to fyrenlusteorne, ne to æfestige ne to inwitfulle, ne to tælende ne to twyspræce, ne morðor to fremmanne ne aðas to swerianne ne niðas to hæbbenne ne leasunga to secganne ne þeofða to beganganne ne wirignessa to fyligenne ne heafodlice leahtras; ne lufien we ne scincræftas, ne herien we ne galdorsangas; ne unriht lyblac ne onginnen we.
> (Scragg, *Vercelli Homilies*, 198.45–51)
>
> [We are not to be too greedy, neither too dangerous nor too eager to enage in sexual sin, neither too envious nor too crafty, neither too censorious nor too hypocritical, neither murder to perform nor oaths to swear, neither to have enmities nor speak lies, neither thefts to practice nor blasphemies to follow nor capital sins; we are not to love sorceries, nor should we praise incantations; nor should we practice evil sorcery.]

The rhetoric and the grammar employed here are not nearly so complex as they will be in the works of later homilists, but there is, nevertheless, a certain elegant simplicity to the language of Homily X and many other of the *VH* that allows them to continue resonating in the present day. The simple and lovely image that brings Homily X's extended, if elsewhere rather standard, articulation of the *ubi sunt* motif to a close, aptly illustrates this: 'Swa læne is sio oferlufu eorðan gestreona, emne hit bið gelice rena scurum, þonne he of heofenum swiðost dreoseð and eft hraðe eal toglideð – bið fæger weder and beorht sunne' (Scragg, *Vercelli Homilies*, 211.241–44) [So transitory is excessive love of the treasures of the earth: it is exactly like rain showers when they from the heavens fall hardest and again quickly all vanish: then there is fair weather and bright sunshine].

The language the Vercelli homilists employ may be simple, but the minds responsible for creating the homilies are sophisticated and learned. The author of Homily X, for example, draws his disparate sources together with considerable finesse and provides the homily with a complex, multi-part structure. He begins by reminding his audience of the importance of the 'ælmihtiges dryhtnes godspelle' [almighty lord's gospel] and of how it serves 'to bysene and to lare' (Scragg, *Vercelli Homilies*, 196.1–3) [for an example and for a lesson], continues through such topics as the Incarnation, the Last Judgement, and the transitoriness of earthly life and possessions, and concludes by pointing the path to salvation in a series of neatly balanced contrasts: 'For þam iorðlicum ic sylle þa heofonlican, for þyssum hwilendlicum þa ecan, for þyssum lænan life þæt unlæne, for þyssum uncorenan life þæt gecorene, for þyssum earmlican life þæt eadige' (Scragg, *Vercelli Homilies*, 212.254–56) [for the earthly I will give the heavenly, for the transitory the eternal, for this transitory life the eternal, for this unselected life the chosen, for this wretched life the blessed]. Homily II, a hortatory, eschatological piece, begins by cataloguing some of the many fearful events that will occur at the final reckoning before turning to the reasons that the faithful should 'ne ondrædaþ þone toweardan ege domes dæges' (Scragg, *Vercelli Homilies*, 56.36–37) [not fear the approaching day of judgement]. This is a standard treatment of the topic, but the author's use of the phrase 'on þæm dæge' (Scragg, *Vercelli Homilies*, 56) [on that day] reveals his rhetorical sophistication because he repeats it several times when detailing the terrors of Judgement Day and employs it also to introduce as well the joys the chosen will experience 'on þam dæge'. While eschatological homilies commonly begin by stressing the imminence of Judgement Day, the author of Homily II discusses its terrors and joys without any reference to when it will occur, choosing instead to defer this information until his conclusion, when he suddenly and dramatically reveals that 'he us swiðe to nealæceð' (Scragg, *Vercelli Homilies*, 64.108) [it truly approaches us].

The simplicity of presentation and straightforward explications, including the usually careful translation of Latin sources, that so characterize the *VH* suggest that their intended audience may have been largely comprised of laymen, but the fact that Latin citations are on occasion left untranslated may point to a more learned audience. In Homily V, we see both approaches in close proximity to each other: after quoting from 'se eadega Paulus' [the blessed Paul] in Latin and immediately translating the saint's words into the vernacular, the homilist offers an unattributed and untranslated piece of scripture a few sentences later: 'Gaudete et exultate quia nomina uestra scripta sunt in celis' (Scragg, *Vercelli Homilies*, 116.103–104) [Rejoice and exult because your name is written in the sky]. Although we cannot be sure just what audience the *VH* were intended for and whether the manuscript itself was meant for private devotional reading or for use in a public, preaching context, some of the homilies, including II and XXI, seem well suited to oral delivery and may have been read aloud to a listening clerical, monastic, or lay audience. Homily II, which also is used in the second half of XXI, reveals its aural orientation in several ways: much of its prose is alliterative, it relies heavily on repetition and variation, it contains passages that conform sufficiently closely to the metrical principles of Anglo-Saxon verse to be labelled 'embedded poetry', and, it is punctuated frequently by the interjectory phrase 'La, hwæt' [Lo, listen!], a device that not only connects the homily to the world of Anglo-Saxon oral poetics but that also allows the author to heighten its emotional pitch and add a certain amount of rhetorical flourish to his discussion.

Generally confining themselves to spiritual matters, the homilists of the Vercelli Book do not often allow contemporary matters to creep into their writings, but on occasion they do, as in Homily XI's comments on the disorders of its day: 'Nu syndon þa Godes cyrican bereafode and þa wiofeda toworpene þurh hæðenra manna gehresp and gestrodu, and þa weallas syndon tobrocene and toslitene and þa godcundan hadas syndon gewanode for hyra sylfra gewyrhtum and geearnungum' (Scragg, *Vercelli Homilies*, 225.90–93) [Now are God's churches ravaged and the altars overthrown through the plundering and thefts of heathen men, and the walls are destroyed and broken asunder and the holy orders are diminished on account of their own works and deserts]. But while this passage recalls those in which Ælfric and especially Wulfstan will point to the contemporary, real-world ills besetting their country, whether the Vercelli author is doing something similar or is merely invoking the trope of ecclesiastical and social decay and disorder in which heathens typically – and generically – figure prominently, remains unclear.

Further Reading

Dockray-Miller, Mary. 'Female devotion and the Vercelli Book'. *PQ* 83 (2004): 337–54.

Scragg, Donald G. 'The significance of the Vercelli Book among Anglo-Saxon vernacular writings'. In *Vercelli tra Oriente ed Occidente tra Tarda Antichita e Medioevo*, ed. Vittoria Dolcetti Corazza, 35–43. Vercelli: Edizioni dell'Orso, 1997.

Szarmach, Paul E. 'The Vercelli Homilies: style and structure'. In *The Old English Homily and its Backgrounds*, ed. Paul E. Szarmach and Bernard F. Huppé, 241–67. Albany: State University of New York Press, 1978.

Szarmach, Paul E. 'The Vercelli prose and Anglo-Saxon literary history'. In *New Readings in the Vercelli Book*, ed. Samantha Zacher and Andy Orchard, 12–40. Toronto Anglo-Saxon Series 4. Toronto: University of Toronto Press, 2009.

Zacher, Samantha. 'Locating the Vercelli Homilies: their place in the book, and the book in its place'. In her *Preaching the Converted: The Style and Rhetoric of the Vercelli Book Homilies*, 3–29. Toronto Anglo-Saxon Series 1. Toronto: University of Toronto Press, 2009.

The *Blickling Homilies*

Survive uniquely in Princeton University Library, Scheide Collection, MS 71, a manuscript that wants its beginning and end and that lacks internal leaves and possibly whole quires.

The *Blickling Homilies (BH)* is a collection of eighteen homilies, sermons, and saints' lives, one of which is fragmentary, that survive in a defective manuscript that dates to the tenth or eleventh century. As is always the case with the manuscript records from Anglo-Saxon England, we cannot know with any certainty if the age of the manuscript in which the homilies are preserved accurately reflects anything other than the particular point in time at which they were copied into their present form. Homily XI refers explicitly to 'þys geare' [this year] of 'nigon hund wintra and lxxi' (Morris, 119) [nine hundred winters and seventy-one], but we have no way of determining if this reference is original to the homily or is a later, scribal addition to it. The language and syntax of the *BH* suggest a relatively early date of composition and the homilies may originally have been composed as early as the late ninth century. Unlike the *Vercelli Homilies*, which are truly miscellaneous, the sermons and homilies of the Blickling collection correspond to certain Sundays and feast days in the liturgical calendar, including Palm Sunday (VI), Easter Sunday (VII), and Holy Thursday (XI).

Although *BH* is a far less comprehensive collection than the later homilaries of Ælfric, and although we cannot determine precisely what the organizing principle of the collection is, it does offer commentary on a number of important ecclesiastical events, including several of the Sundays in Lent, Easter, and the Ascension. In addition, the collection includes lives

The Anglo-Saxon Literature Handbook, First Edition. Mark C. Amodio.
© 2014 Mark C. Amodio. Published 2014 by John Wiley & Sons, Ltd.

of saints whose feasts were widely celebrated in the Middle Ages. The sources for the homilies are many and varied, and for several remain undiscovered. Some of the homilies, including Quadragesima, remain very close to their Latin originals (in this instance one of Gregory's homilies) and stand almost as literal translations while others, including Quadragesima I, depart so freely and frequently from their source (in this instance another of Gregory's homilies) that they should, at best, be considered a loose adaptation of the original rather than a translation of it. In still others the homilist combines material from a number of different sources. As we might expect, the way in which the sources are handled in the individual texts shows considerable variation as well, something that may indicate that the collection is a compilation of pieces by different authors and is not the product of a single authorial sensibility.

The homilies can be grouped roughly into those that are hortatory and eschatological and those that are exegetical and didactic. The former attempt to elicit an emotional response from their reading or listening audience by stressing the proximity of the 'end of days' and by dwelling on the transitory nature of life on this earth as well as the present, greatly decayed state of the world, as the following from Homily X illustrates:

> Magon we þonne nu geseon and oncnawan and swiþe gearelice ongeotan þæt þisses middangeardes ende swiþe neah is, and manige frecnessa æteowde and manna wohdæda and wonessa swiþe gemonigfealdode; and we fram dæge to oþrum geaxiað ungecyndelico witu and ungecynelice deaþas geond þeodland to mannum cumene, and we oft ongytaþ þæt ariseþ þeod wiþ þeode, and ungelimplico gefeoht on wolicum dædum; ... swa we eac geaxiað mislice adla on manegum stowum middangeardes, and hungras wexende.
>
> (Morris, 107/109)

> [May we then now see and know and very readily understand that the end of this world is very near, and many physical dangers have appeared and the wicked deeds and depravities of men are greatly multiplied; and we from one day to another hear of unnatural torments and unnatural deaths that have come upon men throughout the land, and we often perceive that nation rises against nation, and unhappy wars brought about by perverse deeds; ... so we also hear of various diseases in many parts of the world, and increasing famines.]

In several of these homilies, the authors of *BH* employ, with great effectiveness, the *ubi sunt qui nos ante fuerent* [where are those who were before us] motif to drive home that men must live their lives virtuously as a means of attaining the bliss of heaven, and that doing so requires them to focus not on the mutable, material aspects of this world, but on the larger, eternal ones that await the righteous in the afterlife.

Homily X contains an especially full and vibrant treatment of the *ubi sunt* motif, one that begins by explicitly treating the transitory nature of the human body:

> hwæt biþ hit la elles buton flæsc seoððan se ecea dæl ofbiþ, þæt is seo sawl? Hwæt biþ la elles seo laf buton wyrma mete? Hwær beoþ þonne his welan and his wista? Hwær beoð þonne his wlencea and his anmedlan? Hwær beoþ þonne his idlan gescyrplan? Hwær beoþ ðonne þa glengeas and þa mycclan gegyrelan þe he þone lichoman ær mid frætwode? Hwær cumaþ þonne his willan and his fyrenlustas ðe he her on worlde beeode? Hwæt he þonne sceal mid his saule anre Gode ælmihtigum riht agyldan, ealles þæs þe he her on worlde to wommum gefremede.

> (Morris, 111/113)

> [lo, what is it else but flesh once the eternal part – that is the soul – departs? Lo, what else is the remnant but the food of worms? Where then are his wealth and his feasts? Where then are his pride and arrogance? Where then are his vain garments? Where then are the ornaments and the expensive clothing with which he earlier adorned his body? Where come then his desires and his sinful pleasures that he here in the world pursued? Indeed, then he must alone repay to God what is proper, for all that he here in the world sinfully performed.]

Later in X, the homilist returns to the *ubi sunt* motif but this time adds greatly to its affective dynamics by articulating it not in his voice, as above, but by the bones of a dead man: 'Forhwon come þu hider us to sceawig-enne? Nu þu miht her geseon moldan dæl and wyrmes lafe, þær þu ær gesawe godweb mid golde gefagod. Sceawa þær nu dust and dryge ban, þær þær þu ær gesawe æfter flæsclicre gecynde fægre leomu on to seonne' (Morris, 113) [Why have you come hither to look at us? Now you may see here a portion of dust and the leavings of worms, where you earlier saw a fine cloth adorned with gold. See there now dust and dry bones, there where you earlier saw man's nature after the flesh, fair limbs to look upon].

Although the end of days is a recurrent topic in *BH*, and although in Homily XI it is revealed that all but one of the events heralding the world's demise has already passed, the homilist does not attempt to fix the date of the world's destruction but rather employs the topos as a way of remind-ing his audience both of the inevitable end that awaits all men and of the ever present need to be ready for the final judgement when it does arrive. To this end, the homilist continually stresses the necessity of private devo-tion and the importance of selfless public service, and as does King Alfred, he emphasizes the obligation leaders have to govern honestly and faithfully.

Those homilies that attempt to reach their audience through channels more intellectual than emotional often seem to be less successful than the more dramatic and powerful eschatological ones, and their authors reveal themselves to be a careful and focused, if at times somewhat plodding, thinkers. Homily VI, Palm Sunday, is typical of the exegetical writing in *BH*. It begins with a brief explanation of why palms are associated with the Sunday before Easter, a narrative presented with clarity if not much inspiration: after raising Lazarus from the dead, Christ is met by 'Iudea folce' [the Jewish people] who 'bæron hie him togeanes blowende palmtwigu, forþon þe hit wæs Iudisc þeaw, þonne heora ciningas hæfdon sige geworht on heora feondum, and hie wæron eft ham hweorfende, þonne eodan hie him togeanes mid blowendum palmtwigum, heora siges to wyorþmyndum. Wel þæt gedafenode þæt Drihten swa dyde on þa gelicnesse; forþon þe he wæs wuldres cyning. Þysne dæg hie nemdon siges dæg' (Morris, 67) [carry towards him flourishing palm branches, because it was a Jewish custom when their kings had gained victory over their enemies and they were again returning homeward, then they went to them with flourishing palm branches, their victory to honour. It is very fitting that our lord did so in that likeness because he was the king of glory. This day they named victory's day].

Although their exegetical writings do not reach the intellectual or spiritual heights of later homilists, the authors of *BH* prove themselves on occasion to be rather adept at writing narrative, as Homily XVI (Morris XVII) bears out. The homily opens with a lively account of a recalcitrant bull who refuses to be driven by a herdsman and instead decides to abide 'on þæt westen ... to sumes scræfes dura' [in that wasteland ... at the door of a certain cave]. Outraged at the bull's actions, the wealthy man who owns it journeys to where it is and shoots a poisoned arrow at the bull. But just after he looses it, 'swiðe mycel windes blæd' (Morris, 199) [a very great blast of wind] springs up that redirects the arrow back at the shooter, who dies after being struck by it. This same homily also contains what is probably the best-known passage in the entire collection, a description of a watery locale very reminiscent of Grendel's mother's mere in *Beowulf*: above the water there is 'sumne harne stan; and wæron norð of ðæm stane awexene swiðe hrimige bearwas, and ðær wæron þystro-genipo, and under þæm stane wæs niccra eardung and wearga ... and þæt wæter wæs sweart under þæm clife neoðan' (Morris, 209/211) [a hoary stone; and north of the stone were woods thickly covered with hoar-frost, and there were dark mists and under the stone was the dwelling place of water monsters and malignant beings ... and the water was black beneath the cliff]. While there are certainly some lexical and thematic correspondences between the homily and the poem, they are not very extensive and as is often the case with Anglo-Saxon literature, it is very difficult, if not impossible, to determine whether either author knew and was influenced by the work of the other or even, for that matter, whether the description derived from traditional Anglo-Saxon thematics (in which case it would be part of each author's shared inheritance), or if it was independently created by each author. What is important about these descriptions is that they share, on some level and through some undetermined means, similar thematics, something that happens only rarely in Anglo-Saxon literature because for the most part the specialized expressive economy of poetry remains distinct from the expressive economy found in the prose.

We can illustrate this point by briefly comparing the treatment St Andrew's mission to Mermedonia receives in *BH* with its treatment in the Anglo-Saxon poem, *Andreas*. Although the prose and poetic narratives of Andrew's rescue of the imprisoned Matthew from the cannibalistic Mermedonians are very similar, they diverge sharply on the level of thematics. To take but one example, when Andrew arrives at the gate of the prison in the prose text, he prays 'on his heortan' [in his heart] and 'raðe hio wæron deade' (Morris, 237) [immediately they (the seven guards) were dead]. In the poem, the narrative remains the same – Andrew arrives at the prison's gate and discovers guards, who shortly die –, but not the thematics through which it is articulated. The death of the guards receives scant notice in the prose version and while they die just as suddenly and, we might add, just as inexplicably in the poem as they do in the prose, in the poem their death is apparently violent. They do not simply drop down dead (as the prose text implies they do) but rather seem to have been torn limb from limb: 'Deaðres forfeng / hæleð heorodreorige' (995b–996a) [Sudden death seized the gory warriors] who 'deaðwang rudon' (1003b) [stained with blood the field of death]. The bloodshed that marks the guards' demise in the poem occurs not simply because the poet wished to shock or titillate his audience, but because it is an important element in the traditional thematics upon which the poet draws, a thematics grounded in the specialized expressive economy that was the shared inheritance of all Anglo-Saxon poets.

Further Reading

Aronstam, Robin Ann. 'The *Blickling Homilies*: a reflection of popular Anglo-Saxon belief'. In *Law, Church, and Society: Essays in Honor of Stephan Kuttner*, ed. Kenneth Pennington and Robert Somerville, 271–80. Philadelphia: University of Pennsylvania Press, 1977.

Clayton, Mary. 'Homilaries and preaching in Anglo-Saxon England'. *Peritia* 4 (1985): 207–42.

Jeffrey, J. Elizabeth. *Blickling Spirituality and the Old English Vernacular Homily: A Textual Analysis*. Studies in Mediaeval Literature 1. Lewiston: Edwin Mellen Press, 1989.

The Anglo-Saxon Chronicle

Survives in six manuscripts: CCCC 173, the Parker MS (known as the A version); London, BL, Cotton Tiberius A.vi (B); London, BL, Cotton Tiberius B.i (C); London, BL, Tiberius B.iv (D); Oxford, Bodleian Library, Laud Misc. 636 (E); London, BL, Cotton Domitian viii (F). Another version, that in London, BL, Cotton Otho B.xi (G), a manuscript of which we now have only fragments following the Ashburnham House fire of 1731, survives in a sixteenth-century transcript. Entries for the years 1113–14 survive in a fragment, London, BL, Cotton Domitian ix., fol. 9 (H).

The Anglo-Saxon Chronicle, the compilation of which was begun in the latter part of the ninth century, is one of the most important and most remarkable documents to survive from Anglo-Saxon England. Its origins are unclear; although it may have been based on a Latin model, it probably evolved from the marginal notations that were frequently added to the tables used to determine the date of Easter. Covering the period from 60 BCE to 1154 CE, it reports on events in a series of generally brief, annalistic entries that are characterized by their national focus, their brevity, and their objectivity. For its pre-ninth-century entries, the Chronicle draws upon several sources, among which are Bede's *Ecclesiastical History* (from which it cites 449 as the year in which Hengist and his brother Horsa arrived in England with their troops), and it may have utilized genealogies (one of which serves as a sort of preface to the earliest version of the Chronicle) and lists of kings for information on the early history of the West Saxon kingdom. But from the ninth century onward, the Chronicle ceases to rely on an external source or sources for its information and instead becomes an

The Anglo-Saxon Literature Handbook, First Edition. Mark C. Amodio.
© 2014 Mark C. Amodio. Published 2014 by John Wiley & Sons, Ltd.

independent account of events, some of which the compiler(s) may either have witnessed themselves or came to know through second- or third-hand accounts. But whether the compiler(s) drew upon their own experiences or relied chiefly on the living memory of others, the Chronicle remains an unrivalled source of information, one from which a great deal of what we know of Anglo-Saxon England's history derives.

Unlike the *Orosius*, another ninth-century text with a historical focus, the Chronicle does not systematically seek to place the events it records into a Christian framework, or indeed, into any larger political, religious, or moral framework. Accordingly, its entries are generally devoid of ecclesiastical or political commentary and instead frequently amount to little more than terse recitations of some significant event or events that occurred in a given year, as in the following examples from the C-text:

> 485 Her Ælle gefeaht wið Wealum neh Mearcredesburnan stæðe (O'Brien O'Keeffe, *Anglo-Saxon Chronicle*, 30) [Here Ælle fought against the Welsh near the bank of Mearcredesburna]

> 607 Her Ceolulf feaht wið Suþseaxe (O'Brien O'Keeffe, *Anglo-Saxon Chronicle*, 36) [Here Ceolwulf fought against the South Saxons]

> 995 Her on þissum geare æteowde cometa se steorra, and Sigeric arcebisceiop forðferde (O'Brien O'Keeffe, *Anglo-Saxon Chronicle*, 87) [Here in this year became visible the star comet, and archbishop Sigeric passed away]

> 1030 Her wæs Olaf cing ofslagen on Norwegon of his agenum folce and wæs syððan halig; and þæs geres ær ðæm forferde Hacun se dohtiga eorl on sæ (O'Brien O'Keeffe, *Anglo-Saxon Chronicle*, 105) [Here was King Olaf slain in Norway by his own people and he was afterwards made holy; and earlier in this year Jarl Hakon the Good passed away at sea]

Even events of great moment, ones that forever changed the cultural landscape of Anglo-Saxon England, such as the sacking of Lindisfarne in 793, the arrival of the 'micel hæðen here' [great heathen army] in 866, or the Norman Conquest of 1066, are presented with considerable restraint:

> 793 vi idus Ianuarii earmlice heðenra manna hergung adiligode Godes cyrican in Lindisfarenaee þurh reaflac and mansleht and Sicga forðferde ... (Irvine, *Anglo-Saxon Chronicle*, 85) [on 8 January the ravages of heathen men wretchedly destroyed God's church at Lindisfarne through plunder and slaughter and Sicga passed away ...]

> 866 And þy ilcan geare com mycel hæðen here on Angelcynnes land and wintersetle namon æt Eastenglum and þær gehorsade wurdon, and hi heom wið frið genamon (Irvine, *Anglo-Saxon Chronicle*, 48) [And that same year came a great heathen army here into the land of the English and

took winter-quarters among the East-Angles where they were supplied with
horses and made peace with them]

For ease of reference the Chronicle is frequently discussed as if it were a
unified, monolithic text, *the* Chronicle, but it would be more accurate to
describe it as a series of interconnected texts, produced in different parts of
the country by a variety of anonymous, perhaps monastic, annalists over the
course of several centuries. Because the annalists who produced the surviving versions of the Chronicle (and in some cases the scribes who later copied
them) remain silent on the crucial matters of authorship, place of origin,
and date of composition, we must rely on internal evidence to answer the
questions of when and where the versions of the Chronicle were initiated
and/or continued, and even that evidence is partial and often less clear than
we might wish. We cannot know for certain, but the A-text – which is
generally accepted as the oldest version – may have been produced in the
West Saxon kingdom in the late ninth century before circulating to other
parts of the country and serving as the basis for the other related, but in
many ways independent, versions that have survived.

The Chronicle is intended to serve as a national record of sorts, but it
nevertheless includes a great many details that reveal the compilers' local
interests, details that help identify the sections of the country in which each
version was compiled. To cite but a few examples, the A-text is prefaced by
a genealogy of the West Saxon royal line from Woden down to Alfred, it
refers familarly to Winchester, it has throughout a strong focus on West
Saxon affairs, and it includes important details concerning Alfred's campaigns against the Vikings. The D- and E-texts, because their early entries
contain much material of a northern nature, some of which derives from the
work of the great northern cleric and scholar Bede, together form what is
known as the northern recension of the Chronicle. The F-text, which is
known as the Domitian Bilingual, contains entries in Latin and English and
appears to be based on E. There is no way of knowing whether the extant
versions and fragments that we have represent all or only some of the
Chronicles produced in the Anglo-Saxon period.

Although the entries in the Chronicle are frequently as terse, annalistic,
and objective as the ones for 485, 607, 995, and 1030 cited earlier, some are
more discursive than others and in many the voices and concerns of the
compilers emerge, sometimes subtly and sometimes with startling clarity.
Even in the rather laconic and objective annal for 793 cited above, the compiler's distress at the sacking of the monastery at Lindisfarne, although
muted, is clearly evident, and in the annal for 866 cited above, the word
'hæðen' [heathen] is an equally clear sign of the compiler's opprobrium. The

political leanings of the compilers also rise to the surface on occasion. In the E-text, for example, the entry for 1048 [1051] betrays a strong sympathy for Earl Godwine in the dispute that erupts when the king's brother-in-law and count of Boulogne, Eustace, and his men arrive in Dover, while the D-text's version offers a very different reading of the events.

The annal for 755, which is common to all the major versions, goes well beyond many of the Chronicle's entries in offering a detailed description of the unhappy events that led to the resolution of a long-standing conflict between the West Saxon king Cynewulf and the nobleman Cyneheard, whose brother, Sigeberht, Cynewulf had many years earlier driven from the throne. Instead of following the model used to report the deaths of many other notable figures, 'this year X passed away', the entry offers a richly detailed narrative of the events that precipitate the king's death. Cyneheard and his men surprise the king when he is visiting his mistress and slay him. The men who accompanied the king to his rendezvous, and who apparently remained at a discreet distance from the chamber in which the assignation was to take place, are alerted by the mistress's outcry and hurry to the spot where the king lies dead. Cyneheard offers Cynewulf's men 'feoh and feorh' (Irvine, *Anglo-Saxon Chronicle*, 38) [money and life] but each of them, including a British hostage with no social or tribal affiliation to Cynewulf, refuse and all but the hostage, who 'swyðe gewundod wæs' (Irvine, *Anglo-Saxon Chronicle*, 38) [was severely wounded], are killed. The next morning, a troop of the slain king's men arrive and refuse the 'feos and landes' [money and land] he promises them on the condition that 'heo him þæs rices uðon' [they grant the kingdom to him]. His offers refused, Cyneheard, in a desperate attempt to stave off an imminent attack, reveals that among his allies are kinsmen of the king's men. These men are offered safe passage by Cynewulf's troop, but as the king's retainers did the preceding day, they disdain to follow the slayer of their lord and the episode ends with all but one man of Cyneheard's being killed. The narrative of this event is valuable for the brief glimpses it gives into Anglo-Saxon daily life and also because it remains the fullest and most important (if highly idealized) contemporary prose articulation of the bonds of loyalty upon which are founded the idea of the comitatus [war-band], an important component of the Anglo-Saxon heroic code. By choosing to die alongside their respective lords rather than accept the offered settlements, the two groups of retainers underscore the importance of the bond of loyalty by which a leader and his men were inextricably linked.

Many of the Chronicle's entries for the tenth and eleventh centuries are lengthy, opinionated, and discursive, but at different places and in different ways, the various versions of the Chronicle always remain chronicles, and they always reflect the interests and concerns of their compilers. Perhaps the clearest illustration of this is the treatment the watershed year 1066 receives in the A-, C-, D-, and E-texts. The latter three differ to some degree in their perspectives, with the C-text notably implying a certain legitimacy to William's claim, but they all accord this year's events very full, and sometimes quite biased, treatment. D paints perhaps the darkest picture of this year, and concludes by poignantly noting that the Normans 'worhton castelas wide geond þas þeode, and earm folc swencte, and a syððan hit yflade swiðe. Wurðe god se end þonne God wylle' (Cubbin, 81) [built castles widely throughout this nation and afflicted the people and ever afterwards it grew very bad. The end will be good when God wills it]. In contrast, A has only the following to say about the year in which the entire fabric of life in England was rent: 'Her forðferde Eaduuard king, and Harold eorl feng to ðam rice and heold hit xl wucena and ænne dæg, and her com Willelm and gewann Ængla land. And her on ðison geare barn Cristes cyrce. And her atiwede cometa' (Bately, *Anglo-Saxon Chronicle*, 83) [Here passed away King Edward and Earl Harold succeeded to the kingdom and held it forty weeks and one day, and here came William and won England by fighting. And in this year Christ Church burned and a comet appeared].

The Chronicle also contains what may be some of the latest poems to survive from the period. In the A-, B-, C-, and D-texts, the entries for 937, 942, 973, 975, 1036, and 1065 all conform to the metrical principles that govern the articulation of Anglo-Saxon verse, and they all further engage the specialized linguistic and thematic registers that are essential constituents of the period's vernacular verse. The topics of these poems range from a stirring account of an English victory that took place in the town of Brunanburh, to a poem commemorating the capture of the five boroughs, to several commemorating the deaths of kings.

Further Reading

Bredehoft, Thomas A. *Textual Histories: Readings in the Anglo-Saxon Chronicle*. Toronto: University of Toronto Press, 2001.

Clark, Cecily. 'The narrative mode of the Anglo-Saxon Chronicle before the Conquest'. In *England before the Conquest: Studies in Primary Sources Presented to Dorothy Whitelock*, ed. Peter Clemoes and Kathleen Hughes, 215–35. Cambridge: Cambridge University Press, 1971.

Sheppard, Alice. *Families of the King: Writing Identity in the 'Anglo-Saxon Chronicle'*. Toronto Old English Series 12. Toronto: University of Toronto Press, 2004.

Stafford, Pauline. 'The Anglo-Saxon Chronicles, identity and the making of England'. *Haskins Society Journal* 19 (2007): 28–50.

Stodnick, Jacqueline. 'What (and where) is the *Anglo-Saxon Chronicle* about?: spatial history.' *BJRL* 86.2 (2004): 87–104.

The OE Version of Paulus Orosius's *Historiarium adversum Paganos Libri Septem* (Seven Books of History against the Pagans)

Survives in four manuscripts: London, BL, Additional 47967, the Lauerdale or Tollemache Orosius; London, BL, Cotton Tiberius B.i.; Oxford, Bodleian Library, Eng. Hist. e. 49 (30481), a fragment; Vatican City, Biblioteca Apostolica, Reg. Lat. 497, fol. 71. The first is dated to the tenth century, the second to the middle of the eleventh, and the final two to the latter part of the eleventh century.

Paulus Orosius was an Iberian priest who lived during the late fourth and early fifth centuries. Sometime in the early fifth century, he fled Spain to escape the barbarians and came to Hippo in northern Africa. He wrote the *Historiarium adversum Paganos* at the prompting of St Augustine not only to defend Christianity from the charge that the calamities that had been visited upon Rome, including its sacking by the Visigoth Alaric I in 410, resulted from the Romans' rejection of paganism and their adoption of Christianity, but also to provide a universal and decidedly Christian history of the world from the creation of mankind to the present day (the text was completed in 417–18 CE, or by the means of reckoning employed throughout the text, 1168 years after Rome had been built).

The Anglo-Saxon Literature Handbook, First Edition. Mark C. Amodio.
© 2014 Mark C. Amodio. Published 2014 by John Wiley & Sons, Ltd.

The OE translation of the *Historiarium* was composed sometime near the end of the ninth century and is oftentimes referred to simply as the *Orosius*, following the practice of the unknown scribe who wrote the words 'Her onginneð seo boc þe man Orosius nemeað' (Bately, *Old English Orosius*, 1) [Here begins the book that one calls Orosius] in the Cotton manuscript. It is also known alternatively and more descriptively as the *World History*. Far more a paraphrase than a close translation, the *Orosius* compresses the Latin *Historiarium*'s seven books into six, and its more than 230 chapters into ninety-eight sections of varying lengths. The compression becomes especially notable towards the end of the OE work where many of the entries cease to be discursive and full and become far more annalistic in nature, as for example, in VI.xvii, which is cited here in its entirety: 'Æfter þæm Romeburg getimbred wæs dcccc wintra and lxx, feng Marcus Aurelius to Romana onwalde and hiene hæfde iiii ger. Hiene ofslogon eac his agene men and his modor mid' (Bately, *Old English Orosius*, 142.20–23) [Nine-hundred and seventy winters after Rome was built, Marcus Aurelius came to power among the Romans and he had it four years. His own men slew him, and his mother with him]. The annalistic nature of some the *Orosius*'s entries may explain why in Cotton Tiberius it is followed by the Anglo-Saxon Chronicle, a text which evidences some similarity in phrasing to that of the *Orosius*.

The OE translator excises much of Orosius's philosophical and theological thought and while he remains faithful throughout to the original's view of Rome's central place within the Christian scheme as the earthly kingdom that will pave the way to the celestial one, the OE text is far less polemical than the Latin original. Whereas Orosius gives himself over to speculation, as he does at the beginning of several books, on such things as the nature of Christianity, its relationship to paganism, or the stubbornness of those pagans who hold Christianity in contempt, the OE translator prefers to highlight the work's theme by offering more direct and less philosophical statements and exhortations such as when he suggests that the 'cristendomes wiþerflitan' [opponents of Christianity] may 'hiora spræce gemetgian ... gif hie gemunan willað hiora ieldrena unclænnessa and heora wolgewinna and hiora monigfealdan unsibbe and hiora unmiltsunge þe hie to gode hæfdon ge eac him selfum betweonum, ðæt hie nane mildheortnesse þurhteon ne mehtan, ær þæm him seo bot of ðæm cristendome com þe hie nu swiþost tælað' (Bately, *Old English Orosius*, 38. 25–30) [moderate their speech ... if they will recall the impurity of their ancestors and their pestilential conflicts and their many enmities and the pitilessness that they had to God and also between themselves, that they no mercy performed nor might, before the deliverance of Christianity came to them, which they now especially revile]. But because the OE translator omits Orosius's introduction, the work's moral theme is not explicitly articulated until I.viii:

> Ic wolde nu, cwæð Orosius, þæt me ða geandwrydan þa þe secgað þæt þeos world sy nu wyrse on ðysan cristendome þonne hio ær on þæm hæþenscype wære, þonne hi swylc geblot and swylc morð donde wæron swylc her ær beforan sæde. Hwær is nu on ænigan cristendome betuh him sylfum þæt mon him þurfe swilc ondrædan, þæt hine mon ænigum godum blote? Oððe hwær syndon ure godas þe swylcra mana gyrnen swilce hiora wæron?
>
> (Bately, *Old English Orosius*, 27.11–17)

> [I wish now, says Orosius, that they would answer me, the ones who say that this world is now worse in this Christianity than it was earlier in that paganism, when they were making sacrifices and committing murders, as here was said earlier. Where is now in any part of Christendom between themselves that a man need to dread such, that one will sacrifice him to any gods? Or where are our gods who yearn for such wickednesses such as those were?]

From its opening sentence, which reads in part 'Ure ieldran ealne þisne ymbhwyrft þises middangeardes, cwæþ Orosius, swa swa Oceanus utan ymbligeþ, þone mon garsæcg hateð, on þreo todældon ...' (Bately, *Old English Orosius*, 8.11–13) [Our ancestors divided in three all the extent of this earth, said Orosius, just as Oceanus, which one calls the ocean, surrounds it from without ...], through the early chapters of Book I, the *Orosius* reads like a secular, not ecclesiastical work, one in which world history will be recounted in some detail but not put within any moral, didactic framework. For example, he mentions in I.ii the wars waged for decades by the Assyrian king Ninus, wars that his queen Semiramis continued after his death, and concludes only that 'Sio gitsung þa and þa gewin wæron grimlicran þonne hy nu syn, for ðon hy hyre nane bysene ær ne cuðan swa men nu witon, ac on bilwitnesse hyra lif alyfdon' (Bately, *Old English Orosius*, 22.16–18) [Avarice and wars were more cruel than they are now, because they did not for themselves have any examples as men now do, but in ignorance of evil lived their lives]. He follows this by recounting Semiramis's famously lustful appetite, and while he does not hesitate to label her actions – which include incest and sleeping with, and then murdering, many noblemen – lewd and sinful, he nevertheless refrains from judging them from the perspective of Christian morality and instead concludes his discussion by stating that because 'hio hyre firenluste fulgan ne moste butan manna bysmrunge, hio gesette ofer eall hyre rice þæt nan forbyrd nære æt geligere betwuh nanre sibbe' (Bately, *Old English Orosius*, 22.26–28) [she could not engage wholly in her lustful desires without the censure of men, she decreed over all her kingdom that there be no restriction on illicit intercourse between any kindred].

As Anglo-Saxon translators typically do, the author of the OE *Orosius* departs quite often and quite freely from his original, and he also recasts many of the original's details using terms that would be familiar to his contemporary Anglo-Saxon audience, such as when he describes the Vestal virgin Caparronia who commits adultery and is hanged for her sin as a 'goda nunne' [a nun of the gods] (Bately, *Old English Orosius*, 88.5), or when he uses such familiar terms as *beot* [vow], *sciphere* [ship army], *scipfierd* [ship army], *scop* [poet], *scopleoþ* [poet's song; poem], and *truma* [troop] to render the original's Latin terms. Other additions seek to clarify practices and terms that might have puzzled an Anglo-Saxon audience, as when the translator explains in some detail the meaning of the word *triumphan* [triumph], a word not recorded in OE outside of the nineteen times it appears in the *Orosius*. What follows amounts to less than half of the *Orosius*'s explanation:

> Þæt hie triumphan heton, þæt wæs þonne hie hwelc folc mid gefeohte ofercumen hæfdon, þonne wæs heora þeaw þæt sceoldon ealle hiera senatus cuman ongean heora consulas æfter þæm gefeohte, siex mila from ðære byrig, mid crætwæne mid golde and mid gimstanum gefrætwedum ...
>
> (Bately, *Old English Orosius*, 42.1–5)
>
> [What they call a triumph, that was when they some people in war had overcome, then it was their custom that all their senators should come meet their consuls after the battle, six miles from the city with a triumphal chariot adorned with gold and gemstones ...]

As Alfred does in Books II and III of his translation of Augustine's *Soliloquies*, the translator of the OE *Orosius* often silently adds material not found in the Latin original. For example, he adds the names of two magicians, 'Geames and Mambres' (Bately, *Old English Orosius*, 26.20–21), who assure the Pharaoh and the other Egyptians who are pursuing Moses and his people that it is safe to follow them across the path God had opened up in the Red Sea. He also excises material just as freely and just as silently, as when he presents the murder of Julius Caesar in a brusquely economical fashion: 'þa eallum þæm senatum ofþyncendum and þæm consulum þæt he heora ealdan gesetnessa tobrecan wolde, ahleopan þa ealle and hiene mid heora metseacsum ofsticedon inne on heora gemotærne. Þara wunda wæs xxvii' (Bately, *Old English Orosius*, 129.32–35) [Then all the senate and the consuls were offended that he would break their old laws, and they all leapt up and stabbed him with their daggers in their senate-house. The number of wounds was twenty-seven]. The Latin text, in contrast, dwells more fully on this event and the conspirators who brought it about and further stresses the civil discord that breaks out in the assasination's aftermath, something the

OE translator fails to mention. Finally, in an attempt to validate the authority of much of the material he adds to his text (whether of his own creation
or drawn from the sources and commentaries upon which he relied), the OE
translator frequently attributes it to the author of the original, invariably
using the phrase 'cwæð Orosius' [Orosius says] or its variants, just as the
post-Conquest *Proverbs of Alfred*, a very popular poetic compilation of
wise sayings attributed to the king, uses 'Þus queð Alfred' [Thus says Alfred]
as an authenticating device throughout.

The entire first chapter of Book I of the *Orosius* is devoted to a detailed
rehearsal of world geography, and while the information presented contains
any number of inaccuracies, not all of its geographical information is mistaken, as we can see from the following description of Spain: 'Ispania land is
þryscyte and eall mid fleote utan ymbhæfd, ge eac binnan ymbhæfd ofer ða
land ægþer ge of þæm garsecge ge of ðam Wendelsæ' (Bately, *Old English
Orosius*, 19.1–3) [Spain is a triangular land and is surrounded on the outside
with estuaries, and also the land within is surrounded either by the ocean or
the Mediterranean]. The sources upon which the OE translator relied for his
additions to Orosius's world geography have yet to be uncovered, but he
likely worked from a number of classical and contemporary texts and commentaries, and may even have consulted a *mappus mundi*. In what are perhaps the best-known sections of the entire *Orosius*, the OE translator
supplements his source's geographical information with what purport to be
contemporary eye-witness accounts of the seamen Ohthere and Wulfstan of
their respective journeys to northern and central Europe. While these additions are important both as ninth-century travel narratives (each mentions
some of the strange cultural practices of the peoples in the lands they visit,
something that the *Wonders of the East* will do at much greater length) and
for the details they offer about distant lands and peoples (from Ohthere we
learn upon which islands dwelt the 'Engle, ær hi hider on land coman'
[Bately, *Old English Orosius*, 16] [Angles before they came hither to this
land]), they also help us fix the date of the *Orosius*'s translation to the
period between the time Alfred ascended the throne in 871 and his death in
899 since Ohthere, who was apparently a Norwegian, gave his report
directly to 'his hlaforde, Alfrede cyninge' (Bately, *Old English Orosius*,
13.29) [his lord, King Alfred] during a visit to England. Wulfstan's name
seems to indicate that he was an Englishman, but we cannot be certain of
this. Although the *Orosius* does not state that Wulfstan related his tale per-
sonally to the king, there is some, if admittedly slim, evidence that suggests
the OE translator may have been among the audience who heard Wulfstan
tell his tale: in presenting Wulfstan's narrative, the translator quickly drops
the third-person pronouns he uses at the story's outset – 'Weonoðland him

wæs on steorbord' [the territory of the Wends was on *his* starboard side (emphasis added)] – in favour of the first-person-plural pronoun Wulfstan himself would have used – 'and þonne Burgenda land wæs us on bæcbord' (Bately, *Old English Orosius*, 16.23 and 25–26) [and then Bornholm was on *our* portside' (emphasis added)] in recounting his travels.

The long-held attribution of the *Orosius* – along with a number of the other extant OE translations – to Alfred no longer has any currency. The narratives of Ohthere and Wulfstan place the *Orosius* within the orbit of Alfred and his circle of scholars, but we remain unable to determine whether it was produced at Winchester or elsewhere. However, as a work more historical than theological or philosophical in focus, the *Orosius* well complements the other texts foundational to the Alfredian programme.

Further Reading

Bately, Janet M. 'The classical additions in the Old English *Orosius*'. In *England before the Conquest: Studies in Primary Sources Presented to Dorothy Whitelock*, ed. Peter Clemoes and Kathleen Hughes, 237–51. Cambridge: Cambridge University Press, 1971.

Liggins, Elizabeth M. 'The authorship of the Old English *Orosius*'. *Anglia* 88 (1970): 290–322.

VanderBilt, Deborah. 'Translation and orality in the Old English *Orosius*'. *OT* 13 (1998): 377–97.

Bede's *Ecclesiastical History of the English People*

OE translation survives in four Anglo-Saxon manuscripts: Oxford, Bodleian Library, Tanner 10; CCCC 41; Oxford, Corpus Christi College, 279; and CUL, Kk. 3. 18. Fragments of it survive in London, BL, Cotton Otho B.xi (which sustained heavy damage in the Ashburnham House fire of 1731), and three passages have also been written on fol. 100 of London, BL, Cotton Domitian A.ix.

The Venerable Bede (673–735), author of the monumental *Historia ecclesiastica gentum anglorum* [*Ecclesiastical History of the English People*, hereafter *EH*], is one of the towering figures of the Anglo-Saxon period, and his writings did much to shape the contours of intellectual life throughout the period and beyond. A Northumbrian cleric, he tells us in the concluding chapter of the *EH* that he was born on land owned by the twin monastic communities at Monkwearmouth and Jarrow where, when he 'wæs seofanwintre, þa wæs [he] mid gimene minra maga seald to fedanne and to lærenne þam arwyrþan abbude Benedicte and Ceolferþe æfter þon' (Miller, 480.25–28) [was seven years old, [he] was given with the care of my kinsmen to be brought up and instructed by the esteemed abbot Benedict and then afterwards by Ceolfrith]. A list he appends to the *EH*, a work he completed in 731 just four years before his death, provides a good sense of the scope and number of his writings. Far too long to cite in its entirety, the list includes the *EH* and all the other works Bede wrote from the time he entered the priesthood until his fifty-ninth year. The following represents just a small portion of the more than thirty works it contains: four books 'on fruman Genesis oð Isaces

The Anglo-Saxon Literature Handbook, First Edition. Mark C. Amodio.
© 2014 Mark C. Amodio. Published 2014 by John Wiley & Sons, Ltd.

gebyrd and aworpenesse Ismahelis' (Miller, 482.11–12) [on the beginning of Genesis to the birth of Isaac and the casting out of Ishmael]; 'Þæs halgan fæder lif and muneces somed and bisceopes Sce Cuþbertes ærest eroico metere and æfter fæce gerædeword ic awrat' (Miller, 484.13–14) [the life of the holy father and monk, the bishop St Cuthbert I first wrote in heroic metre and after a time in plain words]; 'Be gecynde wisana and be tydum sindrie bec' (Miller, 484.25) [on the nature of things and on time sundry books]; 'Boc de orthographia mid stæfræwe endebyrdnesse tosceadene' (Miller, 484.27) [a book on orthography arranged by the order of the alphabet]' and 'Boc de metrica arte, and oþere to þisse geþydde be schemati- bus and tropes boc' (Miller, 484.28–29) [a book on the art of metre, and another book joined to this on forms and tropes]. Of all his texts, the *EH* is the most important and most influential, something we can gauge both by the impact it had (and continues to have) on later writers and thinkers and by the fact that more than 150 copies of it are extant from the Middle Ages. This figure is all the more impressive when we recall that the vast majority of the texts produced in Anglo-Saxon England, in Latin or the ver- nacular, survive in unique copies. At least four manuscripts of the *EH* date from the eighth century, including two, CUL Kk. 5.16 (known as the Moore Bede and dated to 737) and St Petersburg, Russian National Library, Lat. Q.v.I.18 (dated to 747), that were produced in Northumbria shortly after his death, perhaps by scribes who resided in the same monastic community in which Bede passed his life. From the time of Ælfric of Eynsham (who explicitly attributes it to Alfred's pen in a homily written for 12 March [*CH II*]) to the middle of the last century, the OE translation of Bede was widely considered to be Alfred's, but is now considered the work of an anonymous translator.

In the preface he added to the *EH* after its completion, Bede reveals that he undertook the project at the behest of King Ceolwulf and that his pur- pose in writing it was chiefly didactic: as he tells the king, 'For þinre ðearfe and for þinre ðeode ic þis awrat' (Miller, 2.12) [for your need and for that of your people I wrote this]. To edify (and perhaps also entertain) his audi- ence, Bede liberally employs a variety of genres, including dream visions and more frequently, miracle stories, some of which he allows to occupy entire chapters or series of chapters, as is the case when he devotes Chapters 9–13 of Book II to the recitation of some of the many miracles of healing associ- ated with King Oswald following his death. In addition to articulating his reasons for undertaking the *EH*, Bede also devotes a considerable portion of the preface to detailing the sources upon which he relied in compiling his text so that the king and the book's other readers should 'ðy læs tweoge hwæðer þis soð sy' (Miller, 2.14) [the less doubt whether this is true]. Not only does he name his sources in the preface, throughout his work he cites them carefully and rigorously, something that sets him apart from most medieval authors. In the preface he reveals that he drew primarily upon three types of sources: the written record ('gewritum' [Miller, 2.21–22] [written texts]), oral tradition ('ealdra manna sægenum' [Miller, 2.22] [the spoken traditions of old men]), and finally, those reports that he 'ongitan mihte þurh swiðe getreowra manna gesægene' (Miller, 4.31–32) [might percieve through the speech of very trusty men].

Bede is often cited as being one of the medieval world's first historians and the *EH* continues to this day to be a valuable source of information regarding the complex and competing forces out of which English culture was forged in the early Anglo-Saxon period. In the first book, Bede sketches the history of Roman Britain, a history that stresses the political and moral decline of the native Britons following the departure of the Romans and their subsequent abandonment of Christianity. He details the arrival of the Germanic tribes and their displacement of the Britons who had invited them to England in the first place, and he also treats the arrival of the Augustinian mission, which Bede reports met with a hospitable reception from the pagan King Æthelbert. Although he eventually converts, the king chooses at the time of the mission's arrival not to 'forlæten þa wisan, þe we longre tide mid ealle Ongolþeode heoldon' (Miller, 60.3–4) [abandon those things which we for a longer time with all the English race have held]. But despite his desire to cling to his traditional beliefs, beliefs which Bede does not here or elsewhere present in any detail, Æthelbert helps pave the way for the spread of Christianity by permitting the missionaries to convert 'ealle ða þe ge mægen þurh eowre lare to eowres geleafan æfæstnisse geðeode' (Miller, 60.10–11) [through your teaching to your pious beliefs all those of the people you can], perhaps because his wife Bertha was Christian. Book I also contains what is probably Bede's best known and most important addition to the sources he relied upon for the early history of England, his identification of the 'þrim folcum ðam strangestan Germanie' [three of the strongest German tribes] who arrived in the fifth century as 'of Seaxum and of Angle and of Geatum' (Miller, 52.2–4) [of the Saxons, Angles, and Jutes]. Book II begins with a chapter on the death of Pope Gregory, one of early medieval Christendom's most important figures, and one who, moreover, occupies an especially important position in English ecclesiastical history since it was he who sent Augustine and his band of missionaries to England in the late sixth century. Books II and III are devoted chiefly to the progress enjoyed and setbacks suffered by the missions of Augustine and others as they work to spread Christianity throughout the island. Book IV recounts the arrival of Theodore who not only helped strengthen the

Church's footing on the island but who also greatly refined its organization. As he travels throughout the country, Theodore not only consecrates bishops 'in gelimplecum stowum' [in suitable places] but, moreover, 'þa þing, þe he unfulfremed gemette, mid heora fultume he ða rehte and bette' (Miller, 260.1–2) [those things, which he found flawed, he corrected and bettered with their help]. In Book V, the English Church not only finally brings the Celtic Church to conform to the Roman dating of Easter, but it becomes so secure and well established that it sends missions abroad to continental Germany.

Bede's overarching aim in the *EH* is to establish the foundational and unifying role the Roman Church played in knitting the disparate Germanic tribes into a single, unified English people and he never strays far from this topic, whether he's relating the more than fifty miracle stories found in the *EH*, many of which cluster around a single figure, such as Cuthbert or King Oswald; whether he's detailing the political fortunes (and misfortunes) of the parade of pagan and Christian kings who appear in his pages; whether he's raising one of his recurrent themes, the controversy that arose between the Celtic and Roman Churches over the dating of Easter; or whether he's relating the famous story of Pope Gregory and the beautiful Anglian slaves he comes upon in a Roman market. For Bede, charting the development of the English Church is crucial not just to his conversion narrative but also to his argument concerning the central role the Church played in unifying the English.

The OE translation of the *EH* dates to some point in the late ninth century. As is true of the other extant Anglo-Saxon prose texts, the OE translation of the *EH* is written in the standard West Saxon literary dialect, what we may almost think of as the de facto 'house style' of the scribes who laboured in the scriptorium at Winchester, but a number of the text's linguistic features seem to point to its having been composed originally in the Anglian dialect and, as a result, it may have originated not in Wessex, but rather in Mercia.

As is typical of Anglo-Saxon translators, the one responsible for the OE version of the *EH* remains fairly faithful to the Latin original, but he also takes liberties with his source text as he frequently condenses or simply (and silently) fails to include material contained in the source. He notably omits the texts of the sometimes lengthy letters of Gregory to Augustine, Brunhild, Vergilius, Mellitus, and Æthelbert that Bede includes. The translator also excises the poems Bede includes without any comment or any indication that he has done so. He greatly compresses the biography of Gregory, one that makes much of the pope's voluminous written output and explicitly mentions the names of several of his works, including the *Pastoral Care* and the *Dialogues*, both of which were translated by the Alfredian circle, perhaps even by Alfred himself. But for the most part, the translator of the OE *EH* renders his Latin source with care and fidelity and occasionally with great stylistic success. The alterations he makes to the text are often restrained and logical, and they further reveal him to have a sharp sense not just of his souce text but of his target audience. His treatment of the story in V.ii in which Bishop John of Hexham miraculously bestows the power of speech upon a young man who has been dumb from birth is typical of the translator's approach to his source.

In the Latin text, Bede explicitly articulates the steps John takes to cure the afflicted young man and reports that John commanded the young man to 'Dicito ... aliquod uerbum; dicito *gae*, quod est lingua Anglorum uerbum adfirmandi et consentiendi, id es etiam' [Say some word ... say *gæ*, which in English is the word of assent and agreement, that is, yes] (Colgrave and Mynors, 458/459). The OE translator faithfully follows the actions the bishop takes (taking hold of the young man's chin and making the sign of the cross) but simplifies the command John gives to 'Cweð hwelc hwugu word; cweð nu gee' (Miller, 388.28–29) [Say some word; say now yes], because the explanation of the word *gæ* that Bede includes would be unnecessary for an English-speaking audience. The OE translator makes one further noteworthy change in his source, one that seeks to clarify several points that might have been puzzling to his audience. In describing the cured young man, who is so joyful about being able to speak that 'he never ceased [talking] all that day and night', Bede likens him to 'the man who had long been lame, who, when healed by the Apostles Peter and John, stood up, leapt and walked ...' (Colgrave and Mynors, 459). Again, the OE translator is faithful to his source and employs Bede's analogy when he says that the young man was 'on gelicnisse þæs monnes, þe longe halt wæs and swa geboren of his modor hrife' [in the likeness of a man who long was lame and was born thus from his mother's womb], but before completing the analogy and invoking the image of the once-lame man literally jumping for joy, the OE translator pauses to twice clarify the word *halt* (which has the same form in OE and NE) by explaining that since he was lame, 'his eldran beran scoldan and he gan ne meahte' (Miller, 390.6–8) [his parents must carry him and he could not walk]. Finally, whereas Bede remains silent on the Biblical source of the story upon which his analogy rests, the OE translator alludes directly to it by adding the phrase 'cwið seo boc' (Miller, 390.8–9) [says the book] to his account.

Another example of the subtle way the translator reshapes, we may be tempted to say edits, his Latin source for his contemporary English audience occurs in one of the most famous passages of the *EH*, the one in Book IV in which Bede relates the story of the illiterate cowherd Cædmon who, after having a vision during his sleep one night, suddenly acquires the ability to compose vernacular verse.

Bede tells us that in response to the command to 'sing me hwæthwugu' [sing me something] Cædmon receives from a spectral visitor one evening after leaving a 'gebeorscipe' [feast at which (alcoholic) drink is served], the obliging (terrified?) cowherd sings 'verses which he had never heard before in praise of God the Creator' (Colgrave and Mynors, 417). Bede elects not to present Cædmon's verses in the vernacular and although he elsewhere includes poetry in the *EH*, in this instance he gives us what he labels 'the general sense' in Latin of the cowherd's vernacular composition. In case his readers might have missed it the first time, Bede then repeats that what he has provided 'is the sense but not the order of words [Cædmon] sang as he slept' and he further reveals that he offers the paraphrase because 'it is not possible to translate verse, however well composed, literally from one language to another without some loss of beauty and dignity' (Colgrave and Mynors, 417).

As the Latin text does, the OE text presents Cædmon as being unwilling (or unable) to participate in the ritual production of song in which all who attend the 'gebeorscipe' engage. The OE version also follows the Latin text's account of the cowherd's dream and apparently miraculous acquistion of the power to create vernacular verse, with a notable exception: the OE translator silently excises the framing comments in which Bede stresses that he presents a paraphrase of Cædmon's vernacular poem. He follows Bede's Latin text in informing us that Cædmon 'ongon ... sona singan in herenesse Godes Scyppendes þa fers and þa word he næfre gehyrde' (Miller, 344.3–4) [began soon ... to sing, in praise of God the creator, those verses and words which he had never heard], but the OE translator deviates from his source by adding not only that the singing took place 'be hearpan' [with a harp] but also that what follows is the 'endebyrdnesse' (Miller, 344.5) [order] of Cædmon's words. In contrast to Bede, the OE translator leads us to believe that what follows the command Cædmon receives in his dream is the poem itself and *not* a paraphrase.

When Cædmon's gift becomes known to Hild, abbess of the monastery at Whitby, she brings him before herself and the scholars in her monastic community so that they 'might all examine him and decide upon the nature and origin of the gift of which he spoke' (Colgrave and Mynors, 417). The divine source of his gift quickly becomes 'clear to all of them' and they then set him a second task: they 'read to him a passage of sacred history or doctrine, bidding him make a song out of it, if he could, in metrical form'. Cædmon dutifully departs and on 'returning the next morning he repeated the passage he had been given, which he had put into excellent verse'

(Colgrave and Mynors, 419). So pleased is Hild with Cædmon's newly acquired gift that she convinces him to renounce his secular life and take monastic vows, and he spends the rest of his life as an honoured brother to whom others read lessons in divine history which he then memorizes and ruminates upon, 'like some clean animal chewing his cud', before turning them into the 'most melodious [vernacular] verse' (Colgrave and Mynors, 419). Bede goes into considerable detail about Cædmon's subsequent poetic productions and while he never offers even a paraphrase of them, we learn that Cædmon sings of divine history and 'of many other of the stories taken from the sacred Scriptures' as well as of 'the terrors of future judgement, the horrors of the pains of hell, and the joys of the heavenly kingdom' (Colgrave and Mynors, 419). Bede's account, however, remains rather fuzzy on some important details: Cædmon's teachers become his 'audience' but beyond this Bede is silent and so we are left to wonder how Cædmon's orally composed and delivered poems were preserved, if indeed they were. When Cædmon's story is first introduced, we learn that 'By his songs the minds of many were often inspired to despise the world and to long for the heavenly life' (Colgrave and Mynors, 415), from which we may surmise that the audience for his songs was not limited to the members of his monastic community but included many outside it as well. However, a number of questions remain: did the monks send Cædmon forth into the surrounding community so that he could spread the word of God through his vernacular adaptations of stories from divine history? As native English speakers themselves, did the residents of the monastery view Cædmon's transpositions of divine history into vernacular verse as edifying and/or entertaining in and of themselves? Did they see his 'gift' as a valuable tool in their continuous efforts to bring the word of God to those who could not understand Latin? On these matters, and many more, Bede remains silent.

The OE translator includes many of the details outlined above, but he makes, along the way, the following small, yet significant, addition: 'And his song and his leoð wæron swa wynsumu to gehyranne, þætte seolfan þa his lareowas æt his muðe wreoton and leornodon' (Miller, 346.3–5) [And his song and his verses were so pleasant to hear that his teachers themselves wrote the words from his mouth and learned them]. Bede informs us that Cædmon's teachers become his audience, but in the hands of the OE translator, the scholars in the monastic community at Whitby are not just passive recipients (and appreciators) of Cædmon's skill; they actively engage in the vernacular oral tradition within which Cædmon has both his feet so firmly planted. What the translator means by the phrase 'and learned them' is by no means clear: did they memorize his poetic creations for their own pleasure? Did they memorize them so that they could use them as conversion tools? Did they perhaps learn the craft of oral composition from him? Bede carefully establishes Cædmon as the font of Christian vernacular verse when he informs us that 'It is true that after him other Englishmen attempted to compose religious poems, but none could compare with him' (Colgrave and Mynors, 415). While the vagaries of this statement keep us from being certain, it is possible that some of the learned brothers of the monastery at Whitby were among those who emulated Cædmon's vernacular compositions, since, according to the OE translator, the literate members of the monastery at Whitby did more than simply inscribe Cædmon's oral, vernacular discourse onto the page: they became his students as well.

As is true of the Anglo-Saxon Chronicle and perhaps even the *Orosius*, the OE *EH* may well have been undertaken outside the ambit of the late-ninth-century Alfredian revival, but if this is so, its status as one those 'bec, ða þe nidbeðyrfesta sien eallum monnum to witanne' (Sweet, 6.7) [books, the ones which are most needful for all men to know] ensured it a spot within the Alfredian programme. One of the manuscripts, CUL, Kk. 3.18, includes after Bede's preface a genealogy of the West Saxon dynasty from its fifth-century founders Cerdic and Cyneric down to Alfred, something that may evidence that this copy of the *EH* was produced during Alfred's reign. While this may be the case, we must also consider that whoever added the genealogy did so in order explicitly to link the translation of the *EH* to Alfred and his circle. Since the beginning of the text is taken by some to be defective in several of the other manuscripts, Tanner 10, Oxford, Corpus Christi College, 279, and the severely damaged Cotton Otho B.xi, and since the genealogy does not appear in the complete CCCC 41, it is impossible for us to determine whether it owes its appearance in CUL, Kk. 3.18 to the impulse of a single copyist or if it was systematically added to the other versions at the time of their copying as well.

Further Reading

Chenard, Marianne Malo. 'King Oswald's holy hands: metonymy and the making of a saint in Bede's *Ecclesiastical History*'. *Exemplaria* 17 (2005): 33–56.

Discenza, Nicole Guenther. 'The Old English *Bede* and the construction of Anglo-Saxon authority'. *ASE* 31 (2002): 69–80.

Harris, Stephen J. *Race and Ethnicity in Anglo-Saxon Literature*. Medieval History and Culture 24. New York: Routledge, 2003.

Higham, N.J. *(Re-)reading Bede: the 'Ecclesiastical History' in Context*. New York: Routledge, 2006.

Molyneaux, George. 'The *Old English Bede*: English ideology or Christian instruction?' *EHR* 124 (2009): 1289–1323.

Rosenthal, Joel T. 'Bede's *Ecclesiastical History*: numbers, hard data, and longevity'. In *Intertexts: Studies in Anglo-Saxon Culture Presented to Paul E. Szarmach*, ed. Virginia Blanton and Helene Scheck, 91–102. MRTS 334. Arizona Studies in the Middle Ages and the Renaissance 24. Tempe: ACMRS, 2008.

Rosenthal, Joel T. 'Bede's use of miracles in *The Ecclesiastical History*'. *Traditio* 31 (1975): 328–35.

Rowley, Sharon M. *The Old English Version of Bede's Historia Ecclesiastica*. London: D.S. Brewer, 2011.

Szarmach, Paul E. 'The "poetic turn of mind" of the translator of the OE *Bede*'. In *Anglo-Saxons: Studies Presented to Cyril Roy Hart*, ed. Simon Keynes and Alfred P. Smyth, 54–68. Dublin: Four Courts Press, 2006.

Wallace-Hadrill, J.M. *Bede's Ecclesiastical History of the English People: A Historical Commentary*. Oxford: Clarendon Press, 1988.

Apollonius of Tyre

Survives in a single, defective version in CCCC 201.

The story of Apollonius of Tyre, a prince who flees his homeland in order to escape being put to death by a tyrannical king who wishes to keep secret his incestuous relationship with his daughter, was extremely popular from Antiquity (it survives in more than fifty Latin manuscripts and the tale may originally have been a Greek romance, although no Greek versions of it survive), until the Middle Ages (where, for example, a version in English comprises more than half of Book 8 of John Gower's fourteenth-century *Confessio Amantis* [Peck, ll. 271–2008]), and into the Renaissance (Shakespeare's *Pericles, Prince of Tyre* draws upon Gower's version and Laurence Twine's late-sixteenth-century one). No single source for the OE version has yet been discovered, but virtually all of its narrative particulars can be matched with the details contained in one or another of the Latin versions of the *Historia Apollonii regis Tyri* found in a group of manuscripts known to have originated in England. There is a lacuna in the unique OE text where several folios of CCCC 201, the manuscript containing it, have gone missing, but since it adheres closely to the surviving Latin versions, they provide us with a fairly accurate sense of what might have been in the missing OE narrative.

As is generally true of Anglo-Saxon translators, the one responsible for the *Apollonius* transposes some of his source's details to a native key, so that, for example, Apollonius, who in the Latin is introduced as 'adolescens Tyrius princeps patriae ... nomine Apollonius' (Goolden, 5.22–3) [a young leader of Tyre ... named Apollonius] becomes an 'ealdorman' [nobleman] who is, further, 'swiðe welig and snotor' (Goolden, 4) [very wealthy

The Anglo-Saxon Literature Handbook, First Edition. Mark C. Amodio.
© 2014 Mark C. Amodio. Published 2014 by John Wiley & Sons, Ltd.

and wise]. The translator at times clarifies some classical figures for his contemporary audience, as when he adds that Apollo, whose name he has just cited, is 'hæðenra God' (Goolden, 26.11) [the heathens' God]. In other instances he simply adapts ancient Greek terms and practices with remarkable ease and fluency. The 'puerum nudum' (Goolden, 19.22) [naked boy] who runs through the town inviting all men to engage in sporting contests becomes 'ænne nacodne cnapan' (Goolden, 18.26) [a naked boy] and the place where the games will take place, the 'gymnasium' (Goolden, 19.25), becomes the 'bæðstede' (Goolden, 18.30) [bath-house], a word attested only two other times in OE. Elsewhere he translates the Latin 'naufrago' [shipwrecked; ruined] with 'forlidenum', a word found only fifteen times in all of OE, and only one time outside of *Apollonius*. The translator also does not attempt to model his language on Latin grammar or syntax, but typically renders the adventures of the hero in OE that is lively, idiomatic, and stylistically successful.

The single extant version of the OE *Apollonius* survives in a manuscript that dates to the middle of the eleventh century, making it one of the latest pieces to survive from the period. *Apollonius* is also the only example of a genre that becomes very popular in post-Conquest England, the romance, to come down to us from Anglo-Saxon England. At least a century separates it from the earliest Middle English romances, including the the mid-twelfth-century *King Horn*.

As a hero, Apollonius himself has considerably more in common with the figures who follow him in English literary history than with those who precede him. When he arrives in Pentapolis after swimming an indeterminate distance following the shipwreck, he not only 'sarlice' [sorely] addresses the old fisherman he meets upon the shore, but he several times requests that the fisherman 'Gemiltsa me' [Show mercy to me], because even though he is 'nacodum, [and] forlidenum' [naked (and) shipwrecked] he is 'na of earmlicum birdum geborenum' (Goolden, 18.5–6) [not born of a base woman]. It is hard to imagine, for example, either Beowulf or Breca, warriors who in their youths engage in a contest on (or perhaps in) the sea, behaving similarly when, after being driven apart by fierce weather, they wash up upon the respective shores they reach. The tears that 'him feollon … of ðam eagum' (Goolden, 24.14) [fell from his eyes] after he relates his story to Arcestrate, and the blush that turns his face 'eal areodode' (Goolden, 32.30) [all red] when he finally finally realizes that he is the object of Arcestrate's affections, further distinguish Apollonius from other Anglo-Saxon heroes.

Arcestrate, in contrast, fits more comfortably into the patterns of female behaviour preserved in Anglo-Saxon literature in that she is self-assured and knows (and reveals, if indirectly at first) her desires, but her authority is limited to the domestic sphere (she urges her father to protect the newly enriched Apollonius by keeping him close by, and close to her; she engineers Apollonius's appointment as her tutor, again so she can be near him; and finally, she reveals to her father that she wishes to marry Apollonius and not any of the three suitors who have been pursuing her) and to the religious sphere (after washing up on the shore of Ephseus, she becomes a priestess of Diana's temple). Even though she eventually sits on the throne beside Apollonius for many years, there is no indication that she ever wields political power of the type, say, that Wealtheow memorably claims to possess in *Beowulf* (1216–31) or the martial prowess that Judith possesses. In many ways, it is as difficult to place Arcestrate alongside such heroines as Judith, Juliana, and Elene as it is to put Apollonius in the company of Byrhtnoth, Beowulf, or Andreas.

But if the characters in *Apollonius* do not seem as elevated as their heroic forebears, they do seem more human. The despair of Antiochus's daughter following her rape by her father, the practical advice her female servant offers her, Antiochus's fear of exposure following Apollonius's solving the riddle, Apollonius's consulting books when he returns home to see if he did, in fact, correctly interpret the king's riddle, Arcestrate's inability to sleep for love of Apollonius, and her father's chiding her for bringing Apollonius to tears by asking about his former state are but a few of the many instances in which *Apollonius*'s characters show a greater range of emotion and greater psychological depth than are encountered in Anglo-Saxon literature. The narrative itself also moves on several occasions into territory not elsewhere explored by Anglo-Saxon authors, such as when it depicts a moment of light comedy and a scene in which a woman plays music and performs a song (or perhaps a poem). The comic moment involves the three suitors who have been seeking Arcestrate's hand, and while it is an admittedly small moment in the narrative and in English literary history, its presence is worth noting, given the rarity of comic moments in Anglo-Saxon literature. After learning from Arcestrate that she is in love with a shipwrecked man and not knowing to whom she refers, her father Arcestrates asks the suitors 'Hwilc eower is forliden?' (Goolden, 32.20) [Which of you has been shipwrecked?] Readily seizing the opportunity before him, one of the three responds 'Ic eom forliden' (Goolden, 32.21) [I am shipwrecked] but one of his fellows immediately calls him on this false claim saying 'Swiga þu; ... Mid me þu boccræft leornodest and ðu næfre buton þare ceastre geate fram me ne come. Hwar gefore ðu forlidennesse?' (Goolden, 32.22–24) [Shut up .... You studied with me and acquired book-learning and you never outside the gate of this city have gone without me. Where did you suffer shipwreck?]. After deducing the correct answer to his own question, Arcestrates quietly, and wittily, informs the three suitors that 'Soð is þæt ic eow ær sæde þæt ge ne comon on gedafenlicre tide mynre dohtor to biddanne' (Goolden, 34.7–8) [What I earlier said to you is true, that you have not come to ask for my daughter at a good time], since the king had decided to give Apollonius his daughter.

The second, and final, moment from *Apollonius* that we will consider involves the performance of a song by a *scop* [poet; shaper]. In *Beowulf*, *scops* step forward at several points in the narrative to perform, in one instance singing a song of more than 100 lines, and several poems, *Deor* and *Widsið*, even present themselves as the record of a *scop*'s direct discourse. *Scops* also appear in the prose, but only rarely, and Bede's story of the cowherd Cædmon in the *EH* is the fullest presentation of scopic activity to survive in either verse or prose. The situation in *Apollonius* is unusual, though, because when Arcestrates calls for a harp to be brought forth and a song to be sung to relieve Apollonius of the pain the memory of his now vanished good fortune causes him, the *scop* who performs is not a man, but Arcestrate, his daughter. Her moment in the spotlight is, however, brief: the song she sings is not reported either directly or indirectly, but we do learn first from the narrator that 'heo mid winsumum sange gemængde þare hearpan sweg' (Goolden, 24.27–28) [she blended the sound of the harp with a pleasant song] and second that '[ð]a ongunnon ealle þa men hi herian on hyre swegcræft' (Goolden, 24.28–29) [then all those men (who heard her performance) began to praise her music-making]. She does not receive universal praise though, as Apollonius, who does not join the chorus of males praising her but 'ana swigode' (24.29) [alone was silent] remarks about her 'swegcræft' that 'heo næfð hine na wel geleornod' [she has not well learned it]. Arcestrates then orders the harp be given to Apollonius, who retires briefly in order to clothe himself (as a singer?) and 'sette ænne cynehelm upon his heafod' (Goolden, 26.7–8) [set a wreath on his head], before returning to perform first one song and then a number of them 'þe þam folce ungecnawen wæs and ungewunelic, and heom eallum þearle licode ælc þara þinga ðe he forð teah' (26.17–19) [that were unknown and unusual to the people and all of them were very much pleased by all the things he brought forth].

Because this episode is not the OE translator's addition but derives from the source text (or texts) he consulted, we cannot put too much weight on either its depiction of female scopic activity or the haste with and degree to which this very rare moment of female performance is corrected, improved upon, and ultimately eclipsed by a male's performance, a performance praised 'micelre stæfne' [with a great voice]. Apollonius goes to great lengths to trump Arcestrate's performance, donning what may be special garb (which she does not do), and after performing once to the harp, he puts it down and plays other, unspecified instruments and produces 'fela fægera þinga þar' (26.17) [there many fair things]. We can only regret that the extant literature from Anglo-Saxon England does not preserve more moments of female scopic activity.

Further Reading

Heyworth, Melanie. 'Apollonius of Tyre in its manuscript context: an issue of marriage'. PQ 86 (2007): 1–26.

Ogawa, Hiroshi. 'Stylistic features of the Old English Apollonius of Tyre'. Poetica (Tokyo) 34 (1991): 57–74.

Riedinger, Anita R. 'The Englishing of Arcestrate: woman in Apollonius of Tyre'. In New Readings on Women in Old English Literature, ed. Helen Damico and Alexandra Hennessey Olsen, 292–306. Bloomington: Indiana University Press, 1990.

The Old English Martyrology

Incomplete versions survive in five tenth- and eleventh-century manuscripts. Two, London, BL, Cotton Julius A.x and CCCC 196, contain fairly full versions and the other three, London, BL, Additional 23211, London, BL, Additional 40165 A.2, and CCCC 41, contain only fragments.

The *Old English Martyrology* is an 'historical' or 'narrative' collection of more than 225 entries recounting the lives or passions of a broad array of Roman, continental, and English saints. Although the *OEM* is generally believed to have been compiled during the ninth century, there seems to be no direct link between it and the Alfredian revival of learning, and the *OEM* may pre-date Alfred's programme. Bede is credited with creating the genre of 'historical' martyrology in his *Martyrologium*, and while it is certainly possible that the compiler of the *OEM* knew of and perhaps even at times drew directly from Bede's text, his own work shows only a relatively minor debt to the earlier one. The compiler of the *OEM* did not depend upon any one text, but drew widely, judiciously, and intelligently from a varied group of Latin texts, and he proves himself to be generally an accurate and careful translator. Even though he relies heavily on his sources, the martyrologist only rarely names the authors or the texts from which he draws. Among the very short list of authors he cites we find Bede and Gregory, and the few named texts include Bede's *Ecclesiastical History* and Aldhelm's *De virginitate* [*About Virginity*].

We do not know for sure where the *OEM* was compiled, but since the English saints it mentions are almost exclusively from the northern kingdoms of Mercia and Northumbria, he may have been a northerner. The martyrologist also directly names the Northumbrian Bede and his

The Anglo-Saxon Literature Handbook, First Edition. Mark C. Amodio.
© 2014 Mark C. Amodio. Published 2014 by John Wiley & Sons, Ltd.

Ecclesiastical History several times, as in the entry for St Chad (2 March): 'þæs wundor ond life Beda se leornere wrat on Angelcynnes bocum' (Herzfeld, 32.15–16) [of this miracle and life the learned Bede wrote in his books of the English] but elsewhere he mentions only the *EH*, sometimes by its Latin title, 'historia Anglorum' (Herzfeld, 86.25). Whether this establishes the compiler as a northerner, though, is far from certain since Bede's book was known throughout the island.

The narratives contained in the *OEM* tend to be brief: the shortest ones, including those of St Sylvester (31 December), St Anteros (3 January), and St Pega (9 January), are only a few sentences while the lengthiest ones, such as those of St Christophorus (28 April), St Cecilia (22 November), and St Lucia (13 December), can run to a page or so, but none are very long. The narratives are not just brief, but they are sometimes quite allusive, as is the case with the entry for Sts Sisinnius, Martyrius, and Alexander (29 May), which reads in its entirety as follows: 'On þone nygan ond twentegðan dæg þæs monðes bið þara halegra martyra tid sancti Sisinni ond sancti Martyri ond sancti Alexandri, þa þrowedan wuldorfæstne martyrdom for Criste' (Herzfeld, 88) [On the twenty-ninth day of the month is the time of the commemoration of St Sisinnius and St Martyrius and St Alexander, who suffered a glorious martyrdom for Christ]. Elsewhere, all we are told of St Symphorosa (18 July) is that she suffers martyrdom with her seven sons and that 'æt þara lichoman gewurdon monegu heofonlico wundru' (Herzfeld, 122) [at their bodies many heavenly wonders occurred].

The martyrologist rarely dwells on (or even provides) many details of a saint's life or passion, and even the somewhat longer entries are marked by their narrative economy. For example, he needs just three sentences to introduce St Marcus and St Marcellinus (18 June), explain that they were brothers and Christians, and reveal that the Emperor Diocletian condemned them to death because they refused to sacrifice to pagan gods. When the saints begin to contemplate worshipping the idols, the martyrologist simply relates how St Sebastian learned of this and 'ongan he him secgan hu lytel ond hu scomlic þæs mannes lif bið her on worolde, ond hu long ond hu ondrysnlic þæt ece wite bið, on hu wuldorlic seo ece eadignes bið, oð þæt him seo heorte eft to Criste gecerde, ond hi þa gecyston hi ond þa wæron for Criste gemartyrad' (Herzfeld, 98.13–17) [began to say to them how little and how shameful the life of man is here in the world, and how long and how terrible eternal punishment will be, and how glorious eternal happiness will be, until their hearts again turned to Christ, and they kissed and then were martyred for Christ]. On occasion the martyrologist will offer more, rather than less detail, but even in such cases he never becomes truly expansive. Consider for example the entry for St Milus (15 November), where we learn not just of the saint's death at the hands of two brothers, but of a prophecy the saint makes before he dies: 'to morgen to þysse tyde yncer ægðer ofslyhð oðerne on þysse ylcan stowe ond hundas licciað eower blod ond fugelas fretað incer flæsc ond yncer wif beoð on anum dæge wudewan' (Herzfeld, 206.6–8) [in the morning at this time each of you will kill the other in this same place and dogs will lick up your blood and birds will eat your flesh and both your wives will be widows on the same day]. Instead of being told that events transpired as the dying saint predicted, we get in this instance what amounts to an unusally detailed account: 'Þa gelamp þæt hig hunte-don on mergen on þære ylcan stowe: þa geearn sum hynd betweox þam gebroðrum, ond hig sceoton hyra strælas on two healfa tosomne; ond þa becom þæs yldran stræl on þæs gingran ynnoð, ond þæs gingran stræl on þæs yldran breost, ond hig wæron sona deade on þære ylcan stowe þe hig ær þone godes man slogon' (Herzfeld, 206.8–14) [then it befell that they hunted in the morning on that same spot: then ran a certain doe between those brothers, and they shot their arrows on both sides together; and then went the elder's arrow into the younger's stomach, and the younger's arrow went into the elder's breast, and they were soon dead upon the same spot where they earlier slew the man of God].

The brevity and allusiveness that characterize even the lengthier of the *OEM*'s entries may hold the key to its purpose because they strongly suggest that its target audience would already have known the full stories to which the *OEM* refers only in passing. Unlike the far more expansive and directed lives and passions that Ælfric of Eynsham and Bishop Wulfstan will com-pose in the late tenth and early eleventh century, texts meant in part to be read aloud as part of the liturgy to both learned and unlearned audiences that frequently contain lengthy and detailed explications, the entries in the *OEM* are telegraphic and may have been intended primarily to serve as *aides-memoire* for the learned ecclesiastical readers and listeners who may have comprised its target audience. In this way, the *OEM* might have functioned as a sort of quick reference guide, both for personal devotional purposes and for homilists.

Further Reading

Cross, J.E. 'On the library of the Old English martyrologist'. In *Learning and Literature in Anglo-Saxon England: Studies Presented to Peter Clemoes on the Occasion of his Sixty-fifth Birthday*, ed. Michael Lapidge and Helmut Gneuss, 227–49. Cambridge: Cambridge University Press, 1981.

Kotzor, Günter. 'The Latin tradition of martyrologies and the *Old English Martyrology*'. In *Studies in Earlier Old English Prose*, ed. Paul E. Szarmach, 301–33. Albany: State University of New York Press, 1986.

Rauer, Christine, 'Usage of the *Old English Martyrology*'. *Foundations of Learning: The Transfer of Encyclopaedic Knowledge in the Early Middle Ages*, ed. Rolf H. Bremmer, Jr. and Kees Dekker, 125–46. Storehouses of Wholesome Learning 1. Dudley: Peeters, 2007.

The Life of St Guthlac

Unique copy survives in an eleventh-century MS, London, BL, Cotton Vespasian, D.xxi, fols 18–40ᵛ.

The OE *Life of St Guthlac* is a fairly faithful translation of the eighth-century Latin *Vita sancti Guthlaci* written by the monk Felix. We know nothing of Felix's life and no other work attributed to him survives, but since he tells us that he wrote the *Vita* at the request of the East Anglian King Ælfwald, we can at least tentatively locate both the date (*c.* 713–49) and the place (East Anglia) of its composition. Regarding the date and location of the OE translation, we find ourselves in much less certain territory: that sections four and five serve as the basis of Vercelli Homily XXIII raises the possibility that it was composed in the late ninth or early tenth century but of this we cannot be certain. The linguistic evidence of the only complete version of the OE prose *Life* suggests that it is a copy of an originally Anglian text, but, again, this cannot be absolutely determined.

Of Guthlac's early life, we know only what Felix relates: Guthlac was born during the reign of Æthelred of Mercia (*c.* 675–704) and was the son of Penwald, a prosperous Mercian who was 'þæs yldestan and þæs æþelstan cynnes, þe Iclingas wæron genemnede' (Gonser, 104.3–4) [of the oldest and most noble race, who were named Iclings] and the noblewoman Tette. By fifteen Guthlac was the leader of a war-band and he enjoyed a successful martial career until, at twenty-four, he renounced arms and was granted admission to the monastery at Repton. After two years, he forsook the monastic community and retreated to the remote and inhospitable island of Crowland, where he lived an ascetic, eremetic life. As Felix records, though, the inaccessibility of the fen in which Guthlac passed the final fifteen years

The Anglo-Saxon Literature Handbook, First Edition. Mark C. Amodio.
© 2014 Mark C. Amodio. Published 2014 by John Wiley & Sons, Ltd.

of his life and the hardships entailed in getting there did not prevent a veritable flood of people in need of spiritual and/or physical help from seeking out the holy hermit. Guthlac died in the fens south of Lincolnshire in 714.

As does the Latin *Vita*, the OE prose *Life*, which survives in a collection of biblical translations and other writings of Ælfric of Eynsham, offers us a fairly complete, if at times sketchy account of the saint's early life, touching on his birth into a noble Mercian family, his early successes as a warrior, his renunciation of the martial life, and his taking of holy orders. The latter part of the saint's life receives the most attention, as the *Life* relates in detail the saint's struggles against the various demons and devils that tempt and torment him. The *Life* concludes not with Guthlac's death, but with the transportation of his miraculously preserved remains a year after his initial interment and with two brief chapters, one in which Guthlac posthumously aids King Æthelbald and one in which a subject of Æthelbald's has his sight restored when he visits Guthlac's tomb.

Judging from the evidence of the manuscript record, Guthlac was a popular figure in Anglo-Saxon England: Felix's *Vita* survives in some twelve manuscripts dating from the ninth to the early-fourteenth centuries and, in addition to the two OE prose treatments of his life, two OE poems, *Guthlac A* and *Guthlac B* (see Part 3), are devoted to him as well. The reason for Guthlac's popularity remains unknown, but his life's trajectory may well have held considerable appeal. As a youth he seemed destined for holy orders, or some similarly devout life because 'se scima gastlicre beorhtnysse swa swyðe scinende, þæt eall þa men, þe hine gesawon, on him geseon mihton þa þing þe him towearde wæron' (Gonser, 108.29–31) [the splendour of spiritual brightness shone so much in him, that all men who looked upon him might see in him all those things which were to happen to him]. But as he grew into young manhood, he came to reflect more and more on the 'strangan dæda þara iumanna and þara woruldfrumena' (Gonser, 108.33–34) [strong deeds of the men of old times and of the world's great men] and soon decided to engage in martial life by taking up arms himself and gathering a 'miccle scole and wered his geþoftena and hys efenhæfdlingas' (Gonser, 108.36) [great band and troop of his comrades and his equals] with which he 'wræc ... his æfþancas on his feondum, and heora burh bærnde, and heora tunas oferhergode; and he wide geond eorþan menigfeald wæl felde, and sloh, and of mannum heora æhta nam' (Gonser, 108.38–41) [wreaked ... his disdain on his enemies, and burned their stronghold and ravaged their villages; and he widely over the land made much carnage, and seized their possessions from men]. After a few years and after many battlefield successes, he reflects one night on the 'ealdan kyningas' (Gonser, 109.52) [kings of old] in whose footsteps he was following, and on how those kings suffered 'þurh earmlicne deað and þurh sarlicne utgang þæs manfullan lifes, þe þas woruld forleton' (Gonser, 109.53–54) [through a wretched death and a painful departure from this evil life when they abandoned this world]. He further thinks about how quickly and completely the great wealth they worked so hard to acquire vanished, and, perhaps most importantly, he 'geseah his agen lif dæghwamlice to þam ende efstan and scyndan' (Gonser, 109.56–57) [saw his own life daily hasten and hurry to that end]. The following morning he announces to his troop that they need to find another leader, and he renounces not just his martial career, but his entire former life: 'he þas woruld forseah, ac swilce hys yldrena gestreon and his eard and þa sylfan his heafodgemacan, þæt he þæt eall forlet' (Gonser, 110.73–75) [he scornfully rejected the world, and likewise the riches of his parents and his home and his own companions, so that he abandoned it all]. In so turning from a life of active engagement in worldly affairs to one of solitary contemplation of God and his divine plan, Guthlac follows a path taken by many other Anglo-Saxons, including the two Mercian kings, Æthelred and Cœnred, under whose rule Guthlac lived most of his life.

Further Reading

Downey, Sarah. 'Too much of too little: Guthlac and the temptation of excessive fasting'. *Traditio* 63 (2008): 89–127.

Roberts, Jane. '*Guthlac A*: sources and source hunting'. In *Medieval English Studies Presented to George Kane*, ed. Edward Donald Kennedy, Ronald Watson, and Joseph S. Wittig, 1–18. Suffolk: D.S. Brewer, 1988.

Waugh, Robin. 'The blindness curse and nonmiracles in the Old English prose *Life of Saint Guthlac*'. MP 106 (2009): 399–426.

The Wonders of the East, The Letter of Alexander to Aristotle, and The Life of St Christopher

Wonders of the East survives in London, BL, Cotton Vitellius A.xv, fols 98ᵛ–106ᵛ and London, BL, Cotton Tiberius B.v., fols 78ᵛ–87ʳ; *The Letter of Alexander* and the *Life of St Christopher* survive uniquely in Vitellius A.xv, on, respectively, fols 107ʳ–131ᵛ and fols 94ʳ–98ʳ.

The *Wonders of the East* is a translation of a Latin text, *De rebus in Oriente mirabilibus,* that presents itself as a letter from King Pharasmanes of Iberia to the Emperor Hadrian. Three separate versions of this text survive in the Anglo-Saxon manuscript records, one in OE (in Vitellius A.xv), one in which a section in Latin is followed by an oftentimes loose OE translation (in Tiberius B.v), and one in Latin (in Oxford, Bodleian Library, Bodley 614). The similarities between the Latin versions in Tiberius B.v and Bodley 614 suggest that they descend from a common source but the vernacular versions are independent of each other. All three texts of the *Wonders* are illuminated, with the Tiberius B.v and Bodley 614 versions again showing considerable similarity: they each contain thirty-seven illuminations, while Vitellius A. xv contains twenty-nine. The survival of *Wonders* in two languages and in multiple, carefully and fully illuminated versions suggests the popularity of the travel narrative, a genre with roots that reach back to Antiquity.

The narrative of the *Wonders* amounts to a straightforward catalogue of the many people and places, always marvellous and often dangerous, that the writer claims to have encountered in his travels. Among some of its more

The Anglo-Saxon Literature Handbook, First Edition. Mark C. Amodio.
© 2014 Mark C. Amodio. Published 2014 by John Wiley & Sons, Ltd.

memorable creatures are: two-headed snakes whose 'eagan scinað nihtes swa leohte swa blacern' (Orchard, *Pride and Prodigies*, 186 §5) [eyes shine at night as brightly as candles]; the Blemmyae, 'menn akende butan heafdum, þa habbaþ on heora breostum heora eagan and muð. Hi syndan eahta fota lange and eahta fota brade' (Orchard, *Pride and Prodigies*, 192 §15) [men born without heads who have in their breasts their eyes and mouth. They are eight feet tall and eight feet wide]; women 'ða habbað beardas swa side oð heora breost' (Orchard, *Pride and Prodigies*, 198 §26) [who have beards as long as their breast] and wear horse hides; 'æmættan swa micle swa hundas' [ants as large as dogs] that 'delfað gold up of eorðan' (Orchard, *Pride and Prodigies*, 190 §9) [dig gold up from the earth]; strange, cannibalistic men; and fowl that burst into flames when someone seizes them. In most instances the narrative amounts to little more than a brief description of these and other wonders. For example, the men with fan-like ears wrap themselves up in their ears at night, lift them as they run from any visitors who approach, and in so doing seem to fly (they also sweat blood as they run). Elsewhere we hear of the Donestre, a race of men who have the power to speak to visitors in their native languages and do so in order to capture and devour the visitors, 'ealne butan his heafde and þonne sittað and wepað ofer ðam heafde' (Orchard, *Pride and Prodigies*, 196 §20) [all but his head and then they sit and weep over the head]. On occasion, the author will offer a more detailed account, as he does in the section where we learn of giant ants that live by the side of a river, have feet like those of locusts, are coloured red and black, and dig gold from before nightfall until the fifth hour of the day. Bold men who wish to seize the ants' gold take with them male camels and females with their foals. They tether the foals and cross the river with the males and females. The men load the females with the gold the ants have dug up, mount them, and ride away, forsaking the males. When the ants return, they fall upon and devour the male camels that have been left behind, apparently for this purpose, while the men and gold-laden females cross the river so quickly that it seems to men 'þæt hi fleogende syn' (Orchard, *Pride and Prodigies*, 190 §9) [that they are flying].

The illuminations for the most part faithfully represent the creatures and places described in the text, and in some instances offer important supplemental information. The illuminations that accompany the passage about the giant ants, for example, show the ants attacking and eating the abandoned male camels, something not spelled out in the text, which cryptically reports only that the ants 'abiscode beoð' (Orchard, *Pride and Prodigies*, 190 §9) [are busied] with the male camels. The *mise-en-page* of both Tiberius and Bodley reveals that the text and illuminations were taken into account while the manuscripts were being laid out as the illuminations are set off from the surrounding text by frames of various colours, some of which are used to dramatic effect. For example, the heads of the two-headed, fifteen-foot man found in Tiberius on folio 81^r extend into the upper edge of the frame and the rather pensive-looking Blemmyae depicted on Tiberius folio 82^r and Vitellius folio 102^v has, in Tiberius, his hands wrapped around both the left and right sides of his frame while his prehensile toes grasp the bottom of the frame.

In addition to the *Wonders of the East*, Cotton Vitellius A.xv also contains two other narratives which we will here briefly consider: one, the *Letter of Alexander to Aristotle*, is another narrative in which an author reports on the marvels he encounters travelling in the east, and the other, the *Life of St Christopher*, is not a catalogue of wonders but focuses on the death of a saint who, being a dog-headed giant, is certainly exotic. The *Letter of Alexander* immediately follows the *Wonders* and, like *Wonders* and *Christopher*, is written by the same scribe who copied the first 1939 lines of *Beowulf*. Although the Anglo-Saxon translator at times expands and/or compresses his source material, and although there are instances where he apparently misunderstands his source, the *Letter* is a rather close translation of a Latin text, *Epistola Alexandri ad Aristotelem*, that details the king's military expedition to India. While it contains extended accounts of battles with the many strange beasts (including multitudes of various coloured serpents, some of which are horned) that attack them, and while it also touches on his encounters with some strange people (among whom are a hairy race of men and women whose only garments are animal pelts), the narrative of the OE *Letter*, like its Latin original, is on the whole more fully grounded in realistic detail than is the *Wonders*. In addition to being attacked by fantastic creatures, Alexander's army is also beset by more recognizable beasts during their travels, as when they travel through the night in search of potable water, a journey during which they are constantly harried by 'leon ond beran ond tigris ond pardus ond wulfas' (*Orchard, Pride and Prodigies*, 234 §16) [lions and bears and tigers and leopards and wolves].

And in some ways, the *Letter* can lay claim to being unusually realistic. For example, knowing that they are travelling through dangerous territory, Alexander commands his men to march in their battle-dress, even though no threat is anywhere apparent, despite the hardship this causes them (they are travelling in extreme heat, do not have sufficient potable water with them, and each soldier also carries his own share of the booty they have acquired on what has been a very successful military mission). The extreme heat oppresses Alexander as well and he reports that 'we wurdon earfoðlice mid þurste geswencte and gewæcte' (Orchard, *Pride and Prodigies*, 230 §12) [we were terribly oppressed and afflicted with thirst]. His servant, who like everyone is very 'þursti' [thirsty], discovers some water in a hollow stone, fills his helmet with it, and offers it to Alexander because he cares more about the king's health than his own. When he brings the helmet of water to the king, the king first orders all his troops to be gathered and then 'beforan heora ealra onsyne niðer ageat, þy læs ic drunce ond þone minne þegn þyrste and minne here and ealne þe mid me wæs' (Orchard, *Pride and Prodigies*, 230 §12) [in sight of them all pours it out, lest I should drink and my officer and my army and all who were with me should be thirsty]. He then publicly commends the generosity of his servant before resuming the march.

The *Letter* concludes simply and effectively with a passage in which Alexander informs his 'leofa magister' [dear master] that he is not so much distressed by the approaching end of his life as he is by the knowledge that he 'læs mærðo gefremed hæfde þonne min willa wære' (Orchard, *Pride and Prodigies*, 252 §41) [had performed less glory than was my desire]. Alexander's explanation of why he has written the letter, namely so that 'ecelice min gemynd stonde and hleouige oðrum eorðcyningum to bysne' (Orchard, *Pride and Prodigies*, 252 §41) [my memory should stand eternally and tower over other earth kings as an example], opens a small but perhaps telling window on the period's oral–literate matrix by revealing the author's trust in the power of the written word to preserve Alexander's memory.

The *Life of St Christopher*, which precedes both the *Wonders* and Alexander's *Letter* in the codex, was damaged in the Ashburnham House fire; it lacks one or more leaves at its beginning and the margins of the text are severely damaged. London, BL, Cotton Otho B.x contained a now lost version of the saint's passion, and versions survive in several of the extant manuscripts of the *Old English Martyrology*. Although the source of the OE *Christopher* has yet to be discovered, the acephalic text preserved in Cotton Vitellius A.xv faithfully follows the narrative contours of Christopher's fatal but successful mission to an unnamed city ruled over by King Dagnus as it is preserved in a number of Latin texts. The version of the saint's passion found in Vitellius A. xv opens in the midst of Christopher's refusal to submit to Dagnus, a refusal that leads to his being tortured and eventually martyred. After several days of being tortured, the saint predicts his death on the following day and also teaches the king how to restore his sight, which he had lost when, following his taunting of Christopher, 'twa flana' [two arrowheads] from the great many that were shot at Christopher all day but do not harm the saint thanks to God's intervention suddenly 'scuton on þas cyninges eagan' (Fulk, 6) [suddenly shot into the king's eyes]. Christopher promises that if the king mixes some of Christopher's blood with the 'eorðan lam þe ic on gemartyrod wæs' (Fulk, 8) [clay of the earth on which I was martyred], smears it on his eyes and 'gelyfst on God of ealre heortan' (Fulk, 8) [believes in God with all your heart], his sight will be restored. After the saint is martyred the next day, the king follows the instructions he was given and upon the restoration of his sight he 'cigde micelre stemne, ond he cwæð beforan eallum þam folce, "Wuldorfæst ys ond micel Cristenra manna God, þæs wuldor-geworces nane mennisce searwa ofercuman ne magon"' (Fulk, 10) [cried out with a great voice, and he said before all the people, 'The God of Christian men is secure in glory and great, whose glorious works no human contrivances can overcome']. The king not only embraces the faith, but commands that none of his people henceforth should do anything 'ongean þæs heofonlican Godes willan þe Cristoforus beeode' (Fulk, 10) [against the will of the heavenly God that Christopher worshipped].

The incomplete state of *Christopher* prevents us from knowing whether its Christopher is a cynocephalus [dog-head], but the widespread nature of this stem of Christopher's myth and some other evidence suggest that he probably is. His counterparts in the other OE narratives are cynocephali, and there are several textual clues in the Vitellius version that point to his extraordinary physicality and perhaps even his fearsomeness, traits characteristic of cyno-cephali: the saint is bound by the king's decree to a bench equal to his height, which the author informs us is 'twelf fæðma lang' (Fulk, 2) [the length of twelve cubits], and the king, in asking Christopher how long he will try to convert his people calls the saint the 'wyrresta wild-deor' (Fulk, 4) [worst wild beast].

Since those who gathered the surviving Anglo-Saxon texts into the various codices which house them rarely, if ever, offer any insight into the thought processes behind their compilations, we can only speculate as to why certain texts are grouped together. Sometimes the principle of organi-zation, if there had been one, is so obscure as to defy categorization, but in other cases we may be able to get a glimpse of it. To this end, *Christopher*, Alexander's *Letter*, the *Wonders*, and *Beowulf* (and perhaps even *Judith*) may have been put into the same codex because they all deal (to greater or lesser extent) with fantastic events, often set in exotic locales. Perhaps more importantly, these disparate texts were grouped together because their narratives all contain monsters, or, in the case of St Christopher and *Judith*'s Holofernes, humans with exaggerated, perhaps monstrous, characteristics.

Further Reading

Austin, Greta. 'Marvelous people or marvelous races? Race and the Anglo-Saxon *Wonders of the East*'. In *Marvels, Monsters and Miracles: Studies in the Medieval and Early Modern Imaginations*, ed. Timothy S. Jones and David A. Sprunger, 25–51. Studies in Medieval Culture 42. Kalamazoo: Medieval Institute Publications, 2002.

Friedman, John Block. 'The marvels-of-the-east tradition in Anglo-Saxon art'. In *Sources of Anglo-Saxon Culture*, ed. Paul E. Szarmach with the assistance of Virginia Darrow Oggins, 319–41. Studies in Medieval Culture 20. Kalamazoo: Medieval Institute Publications, 1986.

Kim, Susan M. '"If one who is loved is not present, a letter may be embraced instead": Death and the *Letter of Alexander to Aristotle*'. *JEGP* 109 (2010): 33–51.

Lionarons, Joyce Tally. 'From monster to martyr: the Old English legend of Saint Christopher'. In *Marvels, Monsters and Miracles: Studies in the Medieval and Early Modern Imaginations*, ed. Timothy S. Jones and David A. Sprunger, 167–82. Studies in Medieval Culture 42. Kalamazoo: Medieval Institute Publications, 2002.

McFadden, Brian. 'The social context of narrative disruption in *The Letter of Alexander to Aristotle*'. *ASE* 30 (2001): 91–114.

Mittman, Asa Simon. 'Part II: *The Marvels of the East* over three centuries and a millennium'. In his *Maps and Monsters in Medieval England*, 66–114. Studies in Medieval History and Culture. New York: Routledge, 2006.

Orchard, Andy. 'The Alexander-legend in Anglo-Saxon England'. In his *Pride and Prodigies: Studies in the Monsters of the 'Beowulf' Manuscript*, 116–39. 1985. Rev. edn. Toronto: University of Toronto Press, 1995.

Bald's Leechbook and Leechbook III

Survives in a mid tenth century manuscript, London, BL, Royal 12.D.xvii.

Bald's Leechbook (*BL*), or book of remedies, stands as the most complete and most extensive compilation of medical writing to have survived from Anglo-Saxon England, the only early medieval European culture to have produced vernacular medical texts. *BL* is a handbook comprised of two parts, each of which begins with a numbered list of the various illnesses and remedies that will be treated, sometimes perfunctorily, sometimes in considerable detail, in each part. The second book of *Bald's Leechbook* concludes with a Latin colophon that identifies Bald as the owner of the book and Cild as the scribe who wrote or compiled it. Immediately following this is a separate, independent book of remedies, known as *Leechbook III*, copied by the same scribe who wrote *BL*. Both texts have survived relatively intact: part II of *BL* is missing several folios after folio 104^v and the final two remedies from *L III* are wanting owing to the loss of a manuscript leaf.

Part I of *BL* is devoted largely to the treatment of external ailments and wounds such as 'Læcedomas wið toþwærce and gif wyrm toþ ete and toþsealfa, eft wið þam uferan toþ ece and wið þam niþerran' (Cockayne, 2.4) [Remedies for tooth ache, and if a worm should eat the tooth, and tooth salves, again for the upper tooth ache and for the lower] and 'Læcedomas wiþ wede hundes slite and wið hundes dolge' (Cockayne, 2.14) [Remedies for a mad dog's bite and for a hound's bite]. Part II, in contrast, chiefly focuses on treatments for 'eallum innoþa mettrymnessum' (Cockayne, 2.158) [all internal illnesses], including ones for 'lifre swyle' (Cockayne, 2.160) [swelling of the liver] and 'ablawunge and aheardunge þæs blodes on þam

The Anglo-Saxon Literature Handbook, First Edition. Mark C. Amodio.
© 2014 Mark C. Amodio. Published 2014 by John Wiley & Sons, Ltd.

milte' (Cockayne, 2.168) [distension and hardening of the blood in the spleen]. *Leechbook III*, which is much shorter than either part of *BL*, includes remedies for both internal and external ailments. Native plants, and others of more exotic origins, are called for in many of the remedies, but animal products, both human and non-human, also form part of the pharmacopia of the Anglo-Saxon healer (OE 'læc'). Christian and non-Christian magical elements, including amulets, charms, spells, incantations, benedictions, and rituals involving either or both actions and words (sometimes in writing, sometimes spoken) also figure in a number of remedies.

No single source has yet been identified for either text, but *BL* draws widely upon a number of medical treatises from the ancient world, including those of Alexander of Tralles, a Byzantine physician who taught and practised in Rome in the late fifth century, and Paul of Aegina. The compiler (or compilers) of *BL* would likely have known these and other sources through extracts contained in Latin compilations of medical knowledge. *Leechbook III*, in contrast, does not rely upon written sources to the extent that *BL* does; rather it stands as a more haphazardly collected array of medical remedies and recipes, many of which are thought to be of insular rather than continental or Mediterranean origin because they rely on the native plants and herbs that would have been available to Anglo-Saxon healers. Although *Leechbook III* has a higher concentration of native remedies than *BL*, *BL* nonetheless also includes many remedies not found in any source, ones that therefore may well derive from what may have been a long-standing and widespread tradition of folk medicine in the early Germanic world.

Whereas *Leechbook III* tends generally to focus solely on the remedy to the illness being discussed, *BL* will at times delve into symptoms and even root causes. To take but one example, after listing a number of ways to treat 'heafod ece' [headache], the author turns both to the 'tacnu þære adle' [the signs of this ailment] and to its causes, which in this case are traced to 'yfelne wætan' (Cockayne, 2.20) [evil humor]. Both texts not only frequently include detailed instructions on the preparation of their remedies, but on their applications as well, which run from the practical and prosaic ('gebeat lege on' [lay it on the bite]) to the esoteric: 'asleah v scearpan ane on þam bite and feower ymbutan weorp mid sticcan swigende ofer wænweg' (Cockayne, 2.144) [make five scarifications, one on the bite and four around it with a stick; throw the stick silently over a cart road].

Both texts focus on the practical aspects of treating human maladies, but both also contain a number in which incantations of a religious or secular nature figure prominently, as we can see in the consecutively presented remedies for 'ælfadle' [elf-disease] and 'wæter alfadle' [water elf-disease], a disease that remains unidentified. Among the longest of the remedies in *Leechbook III*, that for 'ælfadle' begins simply by listing the ingredients, which include bishop's wort, fennel, and woody nightshade, that must be bound up in a cloth that one must 'gedyp on font wætre gehalgodum' (Cockayne, 2.344) [dip in consecrated font water]. What follows, however, is a set of instructions as complex as the concoction's recipe is simple. Among its many steps are the following: three specific masses need to be sung over the concoction; the patient needs to be treated in the morning and the night; on 'þunres æfen' [Thursday evening] after the sun has set the healer must sing the 'benedicite and pater noster and letanian' (Cockayne, 2.346) [Benedicite and Pater Noster, and a litany] over the concoction before sticking his knife in it and going away. The remedy for 'ælfsogeþa' which is in the same section as that for 'ælfadle', includes specific Latin phrases that must be written ('Writ þis gewrit' [write this writing]) as well the Latin that needs to be sung over both the writing and a drink that has been prepared for the patient: 'Sing þis ofer þam drence and þam gewrit: deus omnipotens, pater domini nostri Iesu Cristi ...' (Cockayne, 2.348). The following section offers a remedy for a related malady, 'wæter ælfadl' and it, too, relies heavily on incantations, but of a wholly secular, not religious nature: in place of Christian, Latin phrases and prayers, this remedy utilizes several vernacular charms, including the one with which it concludes: 'eorþe þe on bere eallum hire mihtum and mægenum' (Cockayne, 2.352) [may the earth support you with all her might and strength]. The degree to which Anglo-Saxon medicine relied on magic remains an open question; as we can see from the two cited above, remedies can include some sort of Christian or secular spell, incantation, or charm, and while these latter have understandably received a great deal of attention, Anglo-Saxon medicine relied on the whole more on the rational than the magical.

Although the remedies contained in these books may be grounded in what seemed to the Anglo-Saxons to be rational observations, we may wonder at their efficacy, since a number of them, including those that call for dung to be used as an ingredient in poultices for open wounds, seem unlikely to produce the desired healing result. It may well prove to be impossible to judge the effectiveness of most of the remedies that have come down to us from Anglo-Saxon England, in part because we are often left to guess at such crucial components of them as ingredients and measurements, but some of them may nevertheless have proved useful in treating illnesses and injuries. Even their magical elements may have served a positive purpose by reassuring patients that all available healing powers were being brought to bear on their problems. And, finally, some of the remedies contain advice that one imagines might easily win the endorsement of physicians today, such as the injunction to pregnant women that they should not 'beor drince ... ne druncen gedrince ... ne on horse to swiðe ride' (Cockayne, 2.330) [drink beer ... nor drink until they become drunk ... nor ride very much on a horse].

BL appears to be either the work of a learned, sophisticated medical practitioner who had access to one or more manuscripts that contained Latin versions (or extracts) of important post-classical medical texts, or it was drawn up at the request or under the supervision of such a person. Whereas *Lacnunga*, another vernacular medical text extant from Anglo-Saxon England notable for its preservation of some half-dozen metrical charms, is a rather undirected collection of remedies, *BL* and, to a lesser degree, *Leechbook III* stand as carefully organized and thorough catalogues of various ailments and their remedies. Despite the enormous gulf between Anglo-Saxon medical practices and those of our day, the author of *Leechbook III* sounds a note in the remedy for 'cancre' [ulcerous sore] that may resonate with contemporary practitioners when, with perhaps a certain resignation, he acknowledges the limits of his healing power: 'gif þu mid þys ne meaht gelacnian ne meaht þu him æfre naht' (Cockayne, 2.328) [if you with this are unable to heal him, you won't afterwards be able to do anything at all for him].

Further Reading

Buck, R.A. 'Women and language in the Anglo-Saxon *Leechbooks*'. *Women and Language* 23 (2000): 41–50.

Cameron, M.L. *Anglo-Saxon Medicine*. CSASE 7. Cambridge: Cambridge University Press, 1993.

Jolly, Karen. 'Cross-referencing Anglo-Saxon liturgy and remedies: the sign of the cross as ritual protection'. In *The Liturgy of the Late Anglo-Saxon Church*, ed. Helen Gittos and M. Bradford Bedingfield, 213–43. Woodbridge: Boydell Press, 2005.

Nokes, Richard Scott. 'The several compilers of Bald's *Leechbook*'. ASE 33 (2004): 51–76.

The Writings of Wulfstan, Archbishop of York

Wulfstan's writings date to the late eleventh century and survive in numerous manuscripts, some of which have sections or additions that may be in his hand. The four most important manuscripts of his homilies, the writings for which he is best known, are: CCCC 419; CCCC 201; Oxford, Bodleian Library, Hatton 113; and Oxford, Bodleian Library, 343 (2406). The *Institutes of Polity* survives in three manuscripts: London, BL, Cotton Nero A.i; CCCC 201B; and Oxford, Bodleian Library, Junius 121.

About the early life of Wulfstan (d. 1023), we know little; nothing is known for sure about the circumstances of his birth in the latter part of the tenth century, about the training he received, or about the positions he held before he was appointed Bishop of London in 996, but from the scattered evidence of some charters and wills it seems likely that he came from a prominent family of Mercian descent. In 1002, he was appointed Archbishop of York and Bishop of Worcester and held both sees in plurality until 1016. The period in which Wulfstan lived was especially tumultuous: in the late tenth century, fierce and frequent attacks by the Vikings resume, and throughout this period the English suffer a string of military defeats, including one that occurs in 991 and is memorably recounted in *The Battle of Maldon* (see Part 3).

Wulfstan is known to us today chiefly as the author of more than twenty vernacular homilies and sermons (one of which survives in three different versions and several of which he outlines in Latin before developing in English) as well as four wholly Latin ones (several of which he translated

The Anglo-Saxon Literature Handbook, First Edition. Mark C. Amodio.
© 2014 Mark C. Amodio. Published 2014 by John Wiley & Sons, Ltd.

into the vernacular), but he also wrote on secular and legal matters. He seems to have had a hand in drafting and/or recording the later laws associated with Æthelred's reign as well as those of Cnut, and he is also credited with having written two works, the *Canons of Edgar*, which sets forth canon law and appears to be intended for use by the secular clergy when they gathered in triennial synods, and the *Institutes of Polity*, in which he details behavioural codes to be followed by all ranks of ecclesiasts and laity. Scattered passages in other homiletic texts also recall Wulfstan's highly individualized style and may either witness his direct contributions to these homilies or may be the work of his imitators. Several entries in the D-version of the Anglo-Saxon Chronicle (those for 959 and 975), one of the two versions of the Chronicle that comprise its so-called northern recension, have also been attributed to his pen.

Unlike his contemporary, Ælfric of Eynsham, who lived a life of quiet seclusion and into whose writings contemporary social or political matters creep only on rare occasions – and even then only in a very modulated manner –, Wulfstan's ecclesiastical positions kept him very much in the public eye, and throughout his career he remained attuned to the political and social situations of his day. As an advisor both to Æthelred II and Cnut he also came to occupy positions of some political importance. His lengthy residence in the northern city of York, in which there had long been a strong Danish presence, may have made him especially aware of the threat posed to English Christianity by the Danes, many of whom held to their pagan beliefs and practices after settling in England. In his extant writings, he frequently took it upon himself to address not only the wickedness of the Danes, but the more general and very widespread decay and disorder he saw all about him in English society, in both ecclesiastical and laic circles. In the *Institutes*, for example, he warns against greedy priests who 'læccað of manna begeatum ... hwæt hi gefon magan eall swa gyfre hremnas of holde doð' (Thorpe, *Ancient Laws*, 2.328) [take of men's belongings ... all that they are able to seize just as the voracious ravens do from a carcass] and further reminds earls that 'þeofas and þeod-sceaðan hi scylan hatian and ryperas and reaferas hi sculan hynan butan hy geswican' (Thorpe, *Ancient Laws*, 2.320) [thieves and criminals who harm the community they must hate and plunderers and reavers they must humble unless they desist]. His convictions that he was living in the 'end of days' and that the apocalyptic calamities that were everywhere befalling the English were divinely sent punishments for their sinful behaviour permeate virtually all his extant writings, lending them an urgency and power that still resonates nearly a millennium after their composition.

Wulfstan's canon has been established through his use of a pen name and through the stylistics of his prose. Beginning shortly after his appointment as Bishop of London and continuing until the end of his life, Wulfstan identifies himself in some of his writings using the name Lupus [Wolf], a name that he also uses regularly as his signature. His prose style, which does not earn him universal praise among contemporary scholars, is nevertheless highly distinctive. He frequently deploys favourite expressions, including 'leofstan men' [beloved men] and 'us is mycel þearf' [to us there is great need], he relies heavily on doublets to stress his points, and he further likes to link doublets alliteratively in short, two-stress phrases tied together with the conjunction 'and'. The following sentence from his homily on 2 Mark [*Secundum Marcum*] not only sounds one of Wulfstan's recurrent themes, the imminent end of the world, but also illustrates a number of his style's characteristic features: 'Eac sceal aspringan wide and side sacu and clacu, hol and hete and rypera reaflac, here and hunger, bryne and blodgyte and styrnlice styrunga, stric and steorfa and fela ungelimpa' (Bethurum, 140.102–04) [There also will arise far and wide strife and harm, slander and hatred and plundering by robbers, ravaging and famine, and burning and bloodshed and harsh tumult, plague and pestilence and many misfortunes]. His point is driven forcefully home not only because he lists some of the woes that he sees gathering on the near horizon, but because he utilizes a number of rhetorical devices, including, as here, alliteration, a two-beat stress pattern, and internal and end rhyme to tie the components of his utterance into a sharply focused and tightly unified whole. Wulfstan is also fond, perhaps overly so, of using intensifiers such as 'georne' [eagerly], 'eal' [entirely], 'eala' [alas], 'oft' [often], 'gelome' [frequently], 'anrædlice' [resolutely], 'rihte' [properly], 'to swyþe' [too much], 'hraðost' [most quickly], and 'ealles to wide' [all too widely] to heighten his writing's rhetoric.

However one judges Wulfstan's stylistic proclivities and idiosyncracies, his vernacular writings remain remarkably vibrant even at our great cultural and temporal remove. That they were apparently written for oral delivery (or at least with oral delivery in mind) and were aimed at a general, not learned, audience may help explain the lack of learned references in his writings which for the most part aim to resonate emotionally, not intellectually, with his intended listening audience. When he does cite a phrase or sentence in Latin, he almost always immediately translates it into English, as he does at the beginning of the *Gifts of the Holy Spirit* [*De Septiformi Spiritu*]: 'Þa seofonfealdan gyfa synd þus genamode: *sapienta* on Leden, þæt is wisdom on Englisc; *intellectus* on Leden, andgyt on Englisc ...' (Bethurum, 185.21–22) [The sevenfold gifts are named thus: *sapientia* in Latin, that is wisdom in English; *intellectus* in Latin, understanding in English ...]. Elsewhere he ensures that his audience will not miss the point of the Latin citations by carefully paraphrasing them in the vernacular, on occasion going so far as he does in *Concerning Divine Warning* [*Be Godcundre Warnunge*]: 'And se þe ne cunne þæt Leden understandan, hlyste nu on Englisc be suman dæle hwæt þæt Leden cwede' (Bethurum, 252.42–44) [And he who cannot understand that Latin, listen now in English to part of what that Latin said].

Wulfstan's homilies and sermons are generally divided into four categories: eschatological ones in which he finds in the contemporary world ample signs that point to the Antichrist's imminent arrival; ones addressed to clerics and laity that focus on matters of the Christian faith, such as baptism, the creed, and confirmation in which he strives, in keeping with the general aims of the Benedictine reformation, to regularize ecclesiastical practices; ones that are episcopal in nature and set out to explain the duties of a bishop or archbishop; and, finally, ones addressed to the entire populace focusing on the political and spiritual decay that he saw everywhere about him in eleventh-century England. This last group of homilies includes one of the most famous pieces of Anglo-Saxon prose, the *Sermon of the Wolf to the English when the Danes most greatly persecuted them which was in the year 1014 from the Incarnation of our lord, Jesus Christ* [*Sermo Lupi ad Anglos quando Dani maxime persecuti sunt eos, quod fuit anno millesimo XIIII ab incarnatione domini nostri Iesu Cristi*].

The *Sermon of the Wolf* displays Wulfstan's considerable rhetorical skills to good effect. He begins with one of his favourite pastoral openings, 'Leofan men' (Bethurum, 267.7) [Beloved men], but follows this by immediately establishing the near fever-pitch tone in which he will couch the entirety of the sermon: 'gecnawað þæt soð is: ðeos worold is on ofste, and hit nealæcð þam ende, þy hit is on worolde aa swa leng swa wyrse' (Bethurum, 267.7–9) [know that this is the truth: this world is in haste and it draws near to the end; and therefore it is in the world ever the worse the longer the world exists]. What follows this fiery opening is not a detached, intellectual, abstract meditation on the evils of the world but a focused, specific listing of many of the ills that plague Wulfstan's contemporary world in language that is at times brutally frank: at one point he takes to task men who pool their resources to buy a woman and with her 'fylþe adreogað, an after anum and ælc æfter oðrum, hundum gelicost' [perform fornication one after another and each after the other, most like dogs] before selling her 'of lande feondum to gewealde' (Bethurum, 270.88–90) [out of the land and into the control of enemies]. In this sermon, Wulfstan stresses that the evils he cautions against are not on the horizon, but are present all around him, and he argues that steps must be taken immediately if the country is to avoid the terrible fate towards which it is rushing headlong.

Perhaps because he lived for many years in the north among Danish settlers who had not entirely (if at all) foregone their heathen practices, Wulfstan stresses in the sermon the degree to which 'Godes þeowas syndan mæðe and munde gewelhwær bedælde' (Bethurum, 268.33–34) [God's servants are deprived everywhere of honour and protection], a situation that is all the more appalling to him because 'gedwolgodan þenan ne dear man misbeodan on ænige wisan mid hæðenum leodum' (Bethurum, 268.34–35) [the servants of false gods one dare not offend in any manner among the heathen people]. The evils he sees are not limited to ecclesiastical ones, but are rampant in the secular sphere as well: 'her syn on lande ungetrywþa micle for Gode and for worolde, and eac her syn on earde on mistlice wisan hlfordswican manege' (Bethurum, 270.71–73) [here in this land there are many breaches of good faith towards God and the world, and also here are in this place in various manners many a traitor to his lord]. He paints an equally bleak picture of the social order's wider decay by informing us that 'wydewan syndan fornydde on unriht to ceorle' [widows are compelled wrongfully to take a husband] and that 'earme men syndan beswicene and hreowlice besyrwde and ut of þysan earde wide gesealde, swiðe unforworhte, fremdum to gewealde' (Bethurum, 268.42–45) [wretched men are ensnared and grievously tricked and out of this place are widely sold, completely innocent, into the power of foreigners]. Even children suffer by being 'geþeowode þurh wælhreowe unlaga' (Bethurum, 269.46) [enslaved through cruel laws].

Elsewhere in the sermon, Wulfstan resorts to one of his favourite rhetorical practices and offers what amounts to a veritable litany of abuses in a series of two-beat phrases that, in the original, are further linked through alliteration:

ac wearð þes þeodscipe, swa hit þincan mæg, swyþe forsyngod þurh mænigfealde synna and þurh fela misdæda: þurh morðdæda and þurh mandæda, þurh gitsunga and þurh gifernessa, þurh stala and þurh strudunga, þurh mannsylena and þurh hæþene unsida, þurh swicdomas and þurh searacræftas, þurh lahbrycas and þurh æwswicas, þurh mægræssas and þurh manslyhtas, þurh hadbrycas and þurh æwbrycas, þurh siblegeru and þurh mistlice forligru.

(Bethurum, 272.131–38)

[but this nation has become, so it may seem, completely sinful through manifold sins and through many misdeeds: through deadly sins and through evil deeds, through covetousness and greediness, through stealing and pillaging, through wrongfully selling men into slavery and through vicious heathen customs, through frauds and through cunning arts, through violations of the law and through acts of deception, through attacks of kinsmen upon kinsmen and through murders, through injuries done to those in holy orders and through adulteries, through incests and through a variety of fornications.]

This is but one of several such passages in the sermon in which he provides a detailed and sometimes lengthy list of the evil practices of both the Danish raiders and the English themselves, lists perhaps meant both to overwhelm and alarm his audience.

Wulfstan bluntly attributes the social disorder and evil misfortunes that have befallen the English, especially the renewal of the Viking attacks in the late-tenth and early-eleventh centuries, to the sinful behaviour of the English. Near the sermon's conclusion he parallels the contemporary situation in Anglo-Saxon England with that of the Britons just before *they* were conquered by the Germanic tribes in the fifth and sixth centuries. He invokes the figure of Gildas, a British priest and historian of the sixth century who, like Wulfstan, lived and wrote during a time of great social and political upheaval and who, also like Wulfstan, saw the conquest of his sinful people by foreign invaders as divine retribution. To drive home his point regarding the bleak fate that awaits the English should they continue on their current course, Wulfstan reveals that the sinfulness of the Anglo-Saxons outstrips even that of the Britons: 'wyrsan dæda we witan mid Englum þonne we mid Bryttan ahwar gehyrdan' (Bethurum, 274–75.187–89) [we know of worse deeds among the English than we have ever heard of among the Britons]. The sermon ends with Wulfstan's hopes that the English will defend themselves against the 'weallendan bryne hellewites' [raging fire of hell-torment] and so will earn for themselves 'þa mærða and þa myrða þe God hæfð gegearwod þam þe his willan on worolde gewyrcað' [those glories and those joys that God has prepared for those who work his will in the world], but his final words are perhaps his most affecting: eschewing the heightened rhetoric and dire tone that are so characteristic of this sermon, he suddenly switches gears and finishes with a simple, plaintive wish, 'God ure helpe, amen' (Bethurum, 275.199–202) [God help us, amen], a wish that sums up how bleak things appeared to him and one that continues to resonate across the many centuries that separate him from us.

Further Reading

Barrow, Julia and Nicholas Brooks, eds. *St. Wulfstan and His World*. Burlington Ashgate, 2005.

Gatch, Milton McC. *Preaching and Theology in Anglo-Saxon England: Ælfric and Wulfstan*. Toronto: University of Toronto Press, 1977.

Godden, Malcolm. 'Apocalypse and invasion in late Anglo-Saxon England'. In *From Anglo-Saxon to Early Middle English: Studies Presented to E.G. Stanley*, ed. Malcolm Godden, Douglas Gray, and Terry Hoad, 130–62. Oxford: Clarendon Press, 1994.

Orchard, Andy. 'Wulfstan as reader, writer, and rewriter'. In *The Old English Homily: Precedent, Practice, and Appropriation*, ed. Aaron J. Kleist, 157–82. Studies in the Early Middle Ages 17. Turnhout: Brepols, 2007.

Townend, Matthew, ed. *Wulfstan, Archbishop of York: The Proceedings of the Second Alcuin Conference*. Studies in the Early Middle Ages 10. Turnhout: Brepols, 2004.

Wilcox, Jonathan. 'The wolf on the shepherds: Wulfstan, bishops, and the context of the *Sermo Lupi ad Anglos*'. In *Old English Prose: Basic Readings*, ed. Paul E. Szarmach, with the assistance of Deborah A. Oosterhouse, 395–418. Basic Readings in Anglo-Saxon England 5. New York: Garland, 2000.

The Writings of Ælfric of Eynsham

Ælfric's writings survive in numerous Anglo-Saxon manuscripts and manuscript fragments and they continued to be widely copied in the post-Conquest period and beyond. CUL Gg.3.28 preserves the entirety of the first series of the *Catholic Homilies*, and is the only manuscript that preserves the Latin and OE prefaces to both series of *Catholic Homilies*. Other manuscripts that have a complete or nearly complete version of *CH I* include London, BL, Royal 7 C. xii, London, BL, Cotton Vitellius C.v, CCCC 188, and Oxford, Bodleian, Bodley 340 and Bodley 342 (2404–5). The second series of the *CH* survives complete in one manuscript, CUL Gg.3.28, and partially in two, Bodely 340 and Bodley 342 (2404–5), that contain, respectively, thirty-three and twenty-five of the second series's fifty-two homilies. The *Lives of the Saints* survives in nine manuscripts, only one of which, London, BL, Cotton Julius, E.vii, is complete. Of the remaining eight manuscripts, five contain eleven or less of Cotton Julius's forty-nine lives, two contain eighteen or nineteen, and one, London, BL, Cotton Vitellius D.xvii, contains twenty-six. The *Colloquy on the Occupations* survives in Latin in four manuscripts, one of which, London, BL, Cotton Tiberius A.iii, contains OE interlinear glosses.

Ælfric of Eynsham (*c.* 950 – *c.* 1010), who describes himself as a 'munuc and mæssepreost' (Clemoes, *CH I*, 174.44) [monk and mass-priest] and 'alumnus Aðelwoldi, benevoli et venerabilis presulis' [student of the benevolent and venerable prelate Æthelwold] (Wilcox, *Ælfric's Prefaces*, 107; trans. 127), lived from roughly the middle of the tenth century until sometime in the second decade of the eleventh. A man whose great scholarly learning

The Anglo-Saxon Literature Handbook, First Edition. Mark C. Amodio.
© 2014 Mark C. Amodio. Published 2014 by John Wiley & Sons, Ltd.

was matched by his deep devotion to the Church, he may well have been the most learned man in late Anglo-Saxon England, and he was the most prolific of the authors whose works are extant. Although he lived and wrote during a time of great social flux and in a period in which the Vikings renewed their widespread attacks on England, he lived a rather quiet life and did not, as did his contemporary Wulfstan, turn his attention to the problems facing his nation or work to advance a political agenda. A product of the second generation of the Benedictine reform, he wrote a number of Latin and vernacular works, including *De Temporibus Anni*, a very free adaptation of Bede's discourse on the computation of Easter, long a disputed topic in the Middle Ages; a Latin rule known as the *Letter to the Monks of Eynsham*; a Latin life of St Æthelwold, under whom he studied in Winchester; a grammar which he explicitly notes is intended for 'inscientiburs puerulis, non senibus' (Wilcox, *Ælfric's Prefaces*, 114; trans. 130) [ignorant boys, not for their elders] in which he uses the vernacular to explain basic concepts of Latin grammar in his typically clear, straightforward, and teacherly manner ('Littera is stæf on englisc' [*Littera* is 'letter' in English]); a Latin–English glossary; summaries of several Old Testament books, including Genesis, Joshua, and Judith; pastoral letters, including ones to Bishop Wulfsige and to Bishop Wulfstan, which he wrote at the request of each bishop; and a *Colloquy on the Occupations* that aims to teach Anglo-Saxon school boys a wide range of basic, practical vocabulary and that continues to serve a very similar function today, although with something of a twist, as we will see below. Although he often wrote in Latin, Ælfric's most important works are in the vernacular, including the first and second series of *Catholic Homilies* (CH), his *Lives of the Saints* (LS), and a number of other homilies and sermons (some of which are revisions of earlier ones and others of which are new compositions) that were not included in *CH I*, *CH II*, or *LS*. A number of his vernacular letters, including his translations of some he had written in Latin to Wulfstan – produced at Wulfstan's request – , and several to noble laymen, also survive.

As is often the case with figures who lived in Anglo-Saxon England, we know little about the details of Ælfric's life, especially his youth. From his own testimony, we know that he was educated at Æthelwold's school at Winchester, one of the intellectual centres of the Benedictine Reform, and that in the late 980s, by which point he was already a priest, he was sent to the monastery at Cerne Abbas in Dorset by Ælfheah, Bishop of Winchester. Ælfric was made abbot of the monastery, and in addition to instructing the monastic community there in the principles of the Benedictine Reform, he took charge of its school for boys. It was at Cerne Abbas where he was to write the works that earned him his reputation as one of his day's foremost ecclesiastical thinkers, and a manuscript probably produced there, London, BL, Royal 7. C. xii, preserves marginal corrections and cancellations that are apparently in Ælfric's hand. Ælfric's influence can be detected in many of the anonymous homilies that have survived from the period and his reputation was such that other bishops, including Wulfstan (who rewrote one [*De Falsis Dies*]), sought his advice and requested copies of his texts for their own use. And from what Ælfric tells us in the prefaces to *LS*, laymen did so as well. In 1005, Ælfric became abbot of a newly founded monastery at Eynsham, where he remained until his death, the date of which is not recorded but is generally believed to have occurred some time in the second decade of the eleventh century.

At some point in his career, Ælfric composed homilies and saints' lives, but it is not clear whether he wrote these first for use in his own preaching and then adapted them for general circulation, or whether he composed them for general circulation. He compiled the *LS* at the request of the ealdorman Æthelwerd, as he states in that work's prefaces, but satisfying a patron's request was not his sole motivation for undertaking the task of translation: the impetus for producing the vernacular versions of *CH I* and *II*, which he wrote before *LS*, seems to have been wholly his. He was moved to write his texts in English to make them widely accessible, both to the congregations who would hear them and to the priests with no Latin who would read them aloud in the church, because he had seen and 'gehyrde mycel gedwyld on manegum Engliscum bocum ðe ungelærede menn ðurh heora bilewitnysse to micclum wisdome tealdon' [heard great errors in many English books which unlearned men through their ignorance hold to be great wisdom] and because 'me ofhreow þæt hi ne cuðon ne næfdon ða godspellican lare on heora gewritum buton ðam mannum anum ðe þæt Leden cuðon and buton þam bocum ðe Ælfred cyning snoterlice awende of Ledene on Englisc' (Clemoes, 174.53–55) [it grieved him that they neither knew nor had the teaching of the Gospels in their writings except for those men alone who knew Latin and except for those books that King Alfred wisely translated from Latin into English]. Although we don't know if Ælfric knew or had access to the preface Alfred added to his translation of Gregory the Great's *Pastoral Care*, his early training in Winchester may well have exposed him to it and to the philosophy upon which the Alfredian revival of learning was founded. Ælfric's decision to compose his homilies in the vernacular is also entirely consonant with not only the programme of education Alfred articulated some hundred years earlier but with Ælfric's own abiding interest in the moral education and edification of the English, to whom he desires to bring 'þurh tungan oððe þurh gewritu ða godspellican soðfæstnysse, þe he sylf gecwæð and eft halgum lareowum onwreah' (Wilcox, *Ælfric's Prefaces*, 110.78–80) [through tongue or through writings the truth of the Gospels which [God] himself spoke and afterwards disclosed to holy teachers], for, as he says elsewhere in the preface, 'menn behofiað godre lare swiðost on þisum timan þe is geendung þyssere worulde' (Clemoes, 174.57–59) [men require good teaching, most especially at this time, which is the ending of this world].

Ælfric is not just the most prolific writer to have lived in late Anglo-Saxon England (and if we limit ourselves to considering only vernacular writings, we can remove the qualifier 'late' and assert that he is the most prolific author who lived during the period), but he is also the period's greatest prose writer. His command of Latin was masterful and he raises English prose to heights that it was not to reach again until long after his death. As is true of many of the period's prose texts, Ælfric's are highly intertextual: he acknowledges and works closely with a wide array of sources, including works by 'Augustinum Yipponensem, Hieronimum, Bedam, Gregorium, Smaragdum, et aliquando Hægmonem' (Clemoes, 173.15–16) [Augustine of Hippo, Jerome, Bede, Gregory, Smaragdus, and sometimes Haymo], among others. Ælfric does not slavishly follow his source texts, but rather turns them to his own purposes as he synthesizes, simplifies, and distills them. He offers an astute and accurate commentary on his role as translator in the Latin preface to *CH I* where he acknowledges that he has 'not translated word for word throughout but in accordance with the sense; guarding, nevertheless, most diligently against deceptive errors so that we might not be found to have been led astray by any heresy or darkened by fallacy' (Wilcox, *Ælfric's Prefaces*, 127), a point he will reiterate in very similar language in the Latin preface to *LS* – and omit from the OE prefaces to these works. Ælfric's skill as a translator/composer leads him to create discourses that are well unified – even when their substance is being taken from several different, and sometimes difficult or simply esoteric sources – and that are written in language that is remarkably fluid, straightforward, and clear, language that, in short, played a large role in making his subject matter accessible to his intended, non-learned audience.

In its measured thoughtfulness and careful and clear expositions, Ælfric's prose gives us a good sense of what sort of preacher and teacher he may have been. In the Latin preface to *CH I*, Ælfric tells us he decided to translate his texts 'into the language to which we are accustomed for the edification of the simple who know only this language, either through reading or hearing it read; and for that reason we could not use obscure words, just plain English, by which it may more easily reach to the heart of the readers or listeners to the benefit of their souls, because they are unable to be instructed in a language other than the one to which they were born'

(Wilcox, *Ælfric's Prefaces*, 127). And in the Latin preface to *LS*, he explicitly articulates the philosophy that guides his translations: he is not, he informs us, 'able in this translation always to translate word for word but, rather, we have taken care to translate diligently according to the sense, as we find it in Holy Scripture, in such simple and clear phrases as will profit our listeners' (Wilcox, *Ælfric's Prefaces*, 131). Ælfric may employ the vernacular because he wishes to reach a wider audience than he could were his works only to be read, silently or aloud, in Latin, but he remains keenly aware of his intended audience's limitations and so carefully regulates just how much material, especially regarding the lives of saints, he puts into the vernacular 'ne forte despectui habeantur margarite Christi' [lest, perhaps, the pearls of Christ be held in disrespect] (Wilcox, *Ælfric's Prefaces*, 119; trans. 131) by readers or listeners who come to them without the necessary training, and who cannot therefore situate them in their proper ecclesiastical and philosophical contexts. As he says in the Latin preface to *CH I*, he realizes that he is writing for 'the simple' [simplicibus] and that 'laymen are not able to take in all they hear, even from the mouths of the learned' (Wilcox, *Ælfric's Prefaces*, 127).

Writing for an unlearned audience, however, has some attendant risks, as Ælfric himself seems to be aware for he finds it necessary almost to defend his vernacular translations, which make it possible for the less learned to negotiate ecclesiastical matters without the direct involvement of a cleric, by noting that they were requested of him not only by Æthelwerd and Æthelmer, but by 'multorum fidelium' [many of the faithful] (Skeat, I, 4.30–31). He is also careful to note, as he does in the homily on the assumption of the virgin Mary in *CH II*, that he does not stray far from his sources and that he is aware that if he should 'mare secgað be ðisum symbeldæge þonne we on ðam halgum bocum rædað þe ðurh Godes dihte gesette wæron, ðonne beo we ðam dwolmannum gelice, þe be heora agenum dihte, oððe be swefnum, fela lease gesetnyssa awriton' (Godden, *Ælfric's Catholic Homilies: The Second Series*, 259.119–23) [say more about this feast-day than we read in the holy books that have been composed by the inspiration of God, then should we be like unto those heretics, who from their imagination, or from dreams, have recorded many false traditions]. Ælfric knows that even though 'þa geleaffullan lareowas Augustinus, Hieronimus, Gregorius and gehwilce oðre, þurh heora wisdom, hi towurpon' [faithful teachers, Augustine, Jerome, Gregory, and many others through their wisdom ... have rejected] such 'dwollican bec' [heretical books], they nevertheless exist 'ægðer ge on Leden ge on Englisc' (Godden, *Ælfric's Catholic Homilies: The Second Series*, 259.125–26) [both in Latin and in English]. What troubles Ælfric the most about this is that he knows 'hi rædað ungerade menn'

(Godden, *Ælfric's Catholic Homilies: The Second Series*, 259.126) [ignorant men read them].

Over the course of his career, Ælfric develops a distinctive prose style, one that incorporates rhythms and two-beat stress patterns that often recall (and are perhaps his loose adaptations of) the metrics of Anglo-Saxon verse. Although he utilizes alliteration to link stressed pairs of words, he does not frequently employ poetic syntax or word-order, and he does not often utilize words from the highly specialized lexicon of the poetry. Even though Ælfric's rhythmic prose does not very closely approximate the metrics of Anglo-Saxon poetry and even though he employs in his rhythmic passages neither the specialized vocabulary nor heightened diction that are the hallmarks of the period's vernacular poetry, some editors, including Skeat and Pope, lineate his writings as poetry as a way of highlighting its 'poetic' features. As was the practice throughout the period for all poetic and prose texts, though, Ælfric's are all written in *scriptio continua*, and so there is no formal distinction in the manuscripts between his rhythmic and non-rhythmic prose.

The following, in which the alliterating elements are italicized, is a representation of Ælfric's rhythmic prose as lineated by Skeat, taken from the *Life of Saint Agnes, Virgin*:

> *Agnes* him *andwyrde*, Se *ælmihtiga* herað
> swiðor *manna mod* þonne heora *mycclan* ylde.
>
> (Skeat, I, 176.110–11)

> [Agnes answered him, The Almighty listens to
> the minds of men rather than their great age.]

When we place this random selection alongside a sample of his non-rhythmic prose taken from *The Nativity of Our Lord Jesus Christ*, their differences emerge quite clearly:

> Be þæm cwæð se ædiga Iob: Þæs mannes wisdom is arfæstnys and soð ingehyd þæt heo yfel forbuge. Witodlice þæt is soþ wysdom, þæt man gewylnige þæt soðe lif on þam þe he æfre lybban mæg mid Gode on wuldre gif he hit on þyssere worulde ge-earnað.
>
> (*Skeat*, I, 24.235–39)

> [The blessed Job spoke about this: Man's wisdom is piety and to avoid evil is his true purpose. Certainly that is true wisdom, that a man wishes for that true life in which he ever may live with God in glory if in this world he earns it.]

Even in the non-rhythmic passage, however, elements of his rhythmic prose are present, including the short, two- and three-stress clauses with which it begins, the alliterative pairing of 'witodlice' and 'wysdom' within a single clause, and the alliteration of 'wuldre' and 'worulde' that stretches across a clausal boundary to rhetorically link 'glory' to 'world'. We find little or no rhythmic prose in *CH I* and only a small amount in *CH II*, but by the time Ælfric comes to write *LS* it has become almost his default compositional mode, although the reasons for this have yet to be uncovered. One possibility is that Ælfric, who was keenly aware that his sermons, homilies, and saints' lives were going to be received chiefly through the ears by listeners and not through the eyes by silent readers, turned to rhythmic prose as an aid to his texts' reception. Even though Ælfric came to embrace the stylistics of rhythmic prose, few others follow his lead: scattered sentences in this style appear in various places, but whether these are the work of conscious imitators or just random and unintentional turns of phrase cannot be determined.

Catholic Homilies

The *Catholic Homilies* that Ælfric wrote sometime after his arrival at Cerne Abbas are two sets of discourses that supplement the gospel readings on some of the principal saints' days celebrated in Anglo-Saxon England. Ælfric's purpose in writing the two series of *CH* is not entirely clear, but since, as he tells us in the vernacular preface to *CH II*, he wrote them in the 'Engliscum gereorde þam mannum to rædenne þe þæt Leden ne cunnon' (Godden, *Ælfric's Catholic Homilies: The Second Series*, 1.29–31) [English language, for those men to read who do not know Latin], he may well have viewed these discourses heuristically. What is clear is that in the two series of *CH* he strove to compile a foundational and orthodox body of work that preachers (and silent readers) could turn to for edification throughout the liturgical year. By beginning *CH I* with a discussion of the creation of the world and then turning to the nativity of Christ, he offers a basic, general outline of sacred history, specific moments of which he will then explore in greater length and greater detail in the various homilies, narratives of saints' lives (hagiographies), etymological explanations, and expositions of scriptural readings that follow, but precisely what his guiding principles of selection were remain difficult, if not impossible, to discern.

He writes *CH* in two books because, as he informs us in the vernacular preface to *CH II*, he 'ðohte þæt hit wære læsse æðryt to gehyrenne, gif man ða ane boc ræt on anes geares ymbryne, and ða oðre on ðam æftran geare'

(Godden, *Ælfric's Catholic Homilies: The Second Series*, 2.35–37) [thought that it would be less tedious to hear, if the one book were read in the course of one year, and the other in the year following]. The listeners in his target audience were laymen, the vast majority of whom experienced the world of letters through the ear and not the eyes. The readers were of two types: clerics (and educated laymen) who could read his discourses privately by themselves and priests with little or no Latin who would read them publicly after reciting the gospel as a way of explicating the sacred text for listening congregations.

The sheer size of the Ælfrician corpus makes it impossible to do more than simply gesture at a passage that typifies what and how Ælfric does what he routinely does. Of the many, sometimes lengthy, examples of his careful exposition found throughout *CH*, we will consider only a passage from the homily in *CH I*, XVIII, *On the Greater Litany*. After opening the homily by explaining that the Latin term 'letanie' means 'gebeddagas' (Clemoes, 317.2) [prayer-days], Ælfric briefly recounts the story of Jonah and the whale, passing quickly over Jonah's time in the whale and laying more stress on his role as a prophet sent to Nineveh. He then offers an exposition of a gospel passage which he cites in Latin and translates into the vernacular that affords him the opportunity to explain the concept of the Holy Trinity, a fundamental point of Church doctrine that Ælfric characteristically offers in simple, straightforward language, language, moreover, that can be easily recognized by speakers of Modern English: 'Se ælmihtiga fæder is God, and his sunu is ælmihtig God, and se halga gast is ælmihtig God; no þry godas, ac hi eall an ælmihtig God untodæledlic' (Clemoes, 319.65–67) [The almighty father is God, and his son is almighty God, and the holy ghost is almighty God; not three gods, but they all are one almighty God indivisible]. He also takes up the issue of faith and recounts several parables, including one in which Christ asks 'Hwilc fæder wile syllan his cylde stan gif hit him hlafes bitt? oððe nædran gif hit fisces bitt? oððe þone wyrm þrowend gif hit æges bit? (Clemoes, 320.98–99) [What kind of father would give his child a stone if it asks for bread? or a serpent if it asks for fish? or the creeping insect scorpion if it asks for an egg?]. Ælfric does not allow his listeners/readers to ponder these questions but immediately explains that 'God is ure fæder þurh his mildheortnysse, and se fisc getacnað geleafan and þæt æg þone halgan hiht, se hlaf þa soðan lufe' (Clemoes, 320.99–101) [God is our father through his mildheartedness, and the fish signifies faith, that egg holy hope, and the bread true love]. As is his general practice, Ælfric then clarifies his statements and makes explicit the points underlying his analogies, as he does, for example, with regard to the fish: 'Se fisc getacnað geleafan for ðon þe his gecynd is swa hyne swiðor þa yþa wealcað swa he strengra bið and swiðor batað. Swa eac se geleaffulla mann swa he swiðor bið geswenct for his geleafan, swa se geleafa strengra bið' (Clemoes 321.104–07) [The fish signifies belief because his nature is that the more the waves toss him the stronger he is and the more he strives. So also the faithful man, as he is the more harassed for his belief, the stronger is his faith]. Throughout the *CH*, Ælfric moves steadily and slowly through his discourses, setting out his argument's components with clarity and precision. Since his primary purpose is to edify his lay and monastic audiences, he frequently articulates his purpose for his listeners/readers, as he does in *The Nativity of St Paul the Apostle* when he announces 'We wyllað nu mid sumere scortre trahtnunge þas rædinge oferyrnan and geopenian gif heo hwæt digeles on hyre hæbbende sy' (Clemoes, 402.65–66) [We will now with a certain short explanation go over this reading and reveal what of hidden thought there may be in it].

Although he chiefly focuses on fundamental matters of Church doctrine, Ælfric does on occasion tackle issues that are thornier, as when he discusses the mysteries of the Eucharist in *A Sermon on the Sacrifice on Easter Day* (*CH II*, XV). Ælfric begins this sermon with a brief rehearsal of the flight of the chosen people from Egypt, and then with his characteristic clarity comments that 'Sume ðas race we habbað getrahtnod on oðre stowe, sume we willað nu geopenian, þæt þe belimpð to ðam halgan husle' (Godden, *Ælfric's Catholic Homilies: The Second Series*, 151.34–35) [Some of this narrative we have explained in another place, some we will now reveal, that which has to do with the holy Eucharist]. He moves deliberately from the actual sacrifice of lambs that God directed Moses and his people to undertake to a more immediately pressing point: what the sacrifice 'gastlice getacnige' (Godden, *Ælfric's Catholic Homilies: The Second Series*, 151.37) [should signify spiritually] for his contemporary audience. Instead of quoting Christ's instructions to the apostles to eat his flesh and drink his blood from the Latin gospel, Ælfric paraphrases them in the vernacular and explicates for his audience how their partaking of the Eucharist symbolically reenacts the chosen people's eating the flesh of the lamb and how Christ equated his body with 'se liflica hlaf ðe of heofonum astah' (Godden, *Ælfric's Catholic Homilies: The Second Series*, 152.73–74) [the living bread which from heaven descended].

All this leads Ælfric to his main point, the knotty problem of the transubstantiation of what men know to be bread into the divine body of Christ. Ælfric puts the matter before his listeners without any heightened rhetoric and, just as importantly, he employs familiar, easily comprehended terms, ones no doubt quite similar to what his audience may have used themselves when thinking about this matter or that they may have heard coming from the mouths of others: 'Nu smeadon gehwilce men oft, and gyt gelome smeagað, hu se hlaf þe bið of corne gegearcod and ðurh fyres hætan abacen, mage beon awend to Cristes lichaman; oððe þæt win, ðe bið of manegum berium awrungen, weorðe awend þurh ænigre bletsunge to Drihtnes blode?' (Godden, *Ælfric's Catholic Homilies: The Second Series*, 152.86–90) [Now have many men often investigated, and still frequently ponder how the loaf, which is prepared from grain, and baked through the heat of fire, can be turned into Christ's body; or the wine, which is squeezed out from many berries can be turned through any blessing into the Lord's blood?]. Ælfric begins his extended explication by recalling for his audience 'þæt sume ðing sind gecwedene be Criste þurh getacnunge, sume ðurh gewissum ðinge' [some things are said concerning Christ through a symbol, some through the real thing] and he continues saying that Christ 'is gecweden hlaf þurh getacnunge, and lamb, and leo, and gehu elles' (Godden, *Ælfric's Catholic Homilies: The Second Series*, 152.91–95) [is called bread through signfication, and lamb and lion and whatever else] before briefly explaining why Christ is called bread, lamb, and lion, among other things.

Throughout the ensuing exposition, one that differs from those he usually offers both in terms of the complexity of its subject matter and its length, Ælfric touches upon a number of difficult issues, including the role of priests in sanctifying and so enabling earthly bread's transubstantiation into the body of Christ, the fact that the hallowed bread retains all the physical characteristics it had before being blessed, and how, after being blessed, its new properties are invisibly and incorruptibly vested within it even though it remains physically unchanged. Perhaps because he realizes that he might have pushed his listeners and readers beyond the limits of their comprehension or because he might have led them to contemplate matters they were not sufficiently trained to contemplate, Ælfric chooses to conclude this portion of the homily by invoking the principle of faith necessary to move beyond the narrow limits of human understanding: 'Þeos gerynu is wedd and hiw; Cristes lichama is soðfæstnyss. Ðis wed we healdað gerynelice oð þæt we becumon to ðære soðfæstnysse, and ðonne bið þis wedd geendod' (Godden, *Ælfric's Catholic Homilies: The Second Series*, 154.153–55) [This mystery is a pledge and a symbol; Christ's body is truth. This pledge we hold as a mystery until we come to the truth, and then is this pledge ended]. He brings rhetorical closure to this section by returning to an earlier point and reminding his audience that the Eucharist is 'swa swa we ær cwædon, Cristes lichama and his blod, na lichamlice ac gastlice' (Godden, *Ælfric's Catholic Homilies: The Second Series*, 154.156–57) [as we said earlier, Christ's body and his blood, not bodily but spiritually], but he does not stop there. Perhaps aware that he *has* brought them into waters too deep for them, Ælfric, as he does on occasion elsewhere, drops all attempts at exposition and concludes on an uncharacteristically dogmatic note: 'Ne sceole ge smeagan hu hit gedon sy, ac healdan on eowerum geleafan þæt hit swa gedon sy' (Godden, *Ælfric's Catholic Homilies: The Second Series*, 154.157–58) [You should not ponder how it is done, but hold on to your belief that it is so done].

Lives of Saints

Sometime after completing the first and second series of the *CH*, Ælfric embarked upon a related project, his *Lives of the Saints*, another collection of discourses meant to be read in connection with specific feasts. But whereas in *CH* Ælfric leads his readers or listeners through the liturgical year by taking as his starting point the gospel readings used on specific feast days, in *LS* he does so by recounting the lives of Roman and English saints. *LS* also contains several longer pieces that seem designed not for oral recitation on the anniversaries they commemorate, but rather for private reading at any time in the year. As is the case with the two series of *CH*, throughout *LS* Ælfric freely condenses, combines, and generally reworks the many sources he employs, including some of his own earlier writings: in the *Life of St Martin*, he includes a revised version of a homily contained in *CH*. And as is also true of *CH*, his perspective throughout *LS* remains wholly and uncomplicatedly orthodox, and he utilizes once again the same 'usitatam Anglicam sermocinationem' [ordinary English language] (Wilcox, *Ælfric's Prefaces*, 119; trans. 131) that he employs to such good effect in *CH*.

In its Latin and OE prefaces, Ælfric distinguishes *LS* from the preceding volumes by stressing that he will focus on the saints whose lives are celebrated by the monastic community, not by the laity at large. But in terms of its stylistics (much of *LS* is written in his distinctive and idiosyncratic rhythmic prose) and its rhetoric (Ælfric is as careful and as thorough in his expositions as he is throughout *CH*), there are many points of continuity between the two works, and it may be profitably viewed as the third in his series of Catholic homilies. Although written for a very different audience in terms of their training and social position, Ælfric envisioned that *LS* would reach its monastic audience just as *CH* would: through the ears of those listening to it being read aloud rather than through the eyes of silent readers. Ælfric again reveals some anxiety about his translating the lives and passions of the saints into the vernacular. Adroitly attempting to forestall any potential criticism, Ælfric notes in the Latin preface – something that would be available only to suitably learned readers – that he does not plan to use the vernacular to 'plura ... scripturum hac lingua' [write more in this language] (Wilcox, *Ælfric's Prefaces*, 119; trans. 131) beyond *LS*, a promise he apparently keeps since no fourth series of his Catholic homilies is extant. In what may be a further effort to deflect criticism, he in the same preface later claims that he wrote *LS* at the urging of 'multorum fidelium' [many of the faithful] including two important laymen, 'Æþelwerdi ducis et Æðelmeri nostri' [ealdorman Æthelweard and ... our friend Æthelmer] (Wilcox, *Ælfric's Prefaces*, 120; trans. 131), both of whom he names in the opening sentence of the work's vernacular preface.

LS focuses on a broad array of important Roman and English figures and in writing it, as he tells us in its Latin preface, Ælfric employed several different types of hagiographic narrative. The majority are saints' lives, but he also includes a large number of passions, and a small number of narratives that are more akin to sermons in that they focus upon matters of general moral import, such as *Ash Wednesday* (XII), *Auguries* (XVII), and *The Holy Cross* (XXVII). Ælfric delights in recounting the pious acts in which saints engaged while alive, and he at times dwells at length on the many miracles attributed to them after their deaths, but, with his typically sharp sense of audience, he is nevertheless aware that focusing so intently on the saints may inadvertently result in his readers or listeners excessively venerating them. He feels so strongly about this that in the life of St Swithun, whose catalogue of miracles performed to the benefit of English men and women is one of the most extensive Ælfric recounts, he is moved to warn that 'we ne moton us gebiddan swa to godes halgum swa swa to gode sylfum forðan þe he is ana god ofer ealle þincg ac we sceolon biddan soðlice þa halgan þæt hi us þingion to þam þrym-wealdendum gode se þe is heora hlaford þæt he helpe us' (Skeat, I, 458.284–89) [we must not pray so to God's saints as to God himself because he alone is God over all things; but we should truly entreat the saints that they intercede for us with the glory-wielding God who is their lord so that he should help us].

Colloquy on the Occupations

Written in Latin, the *Colloquy* survives in four manuscripts: London, BL, Cotton Tiberius A.iii; Oxford, St John's College, 154; Antwerp, Plantin-Moretus Museum, 47; and London, BL, Additional 32246. Only in Tiberius A.iii is the Latin text accompanied by continuous, interlinear OE glosses.

Ælfric's *Colloquy on the Occupations* may well be the best known of all the texts that have survived from Anglo-Saxon England. It earns this distinction neither for its literary merit nor for its cultural and social significance, but rather because it continues to be used today in very much the same way it was intended to be used when it was composed in the late tenth or early eleventh century: as a classroom exercise. Taking the form of a dialogue between a master and his pupils, the *Colloquy* was created as a way to teach basic Latin vocabulary and grammar to schoolboys, probably pupils of the monastic school at Cerne Abbas that Ælfric directed. At some point after its composition, perhaps as early as the middle of the eleventh century, an unknown hand added continuous interlinear glosses in the vernacular to one of the four manuscripts in which the *Colloquy* survives, Tiberius A. iii, and it is the 'text' of these interlinear glosses that generations of beginning OE students have come to know, somewhat inaccurately, as Ælfric's *Colloquy on the Occupations* (calling it an OE interlinear gloss of Ælfric's Latin *Colloquy* would be a more accurate, if more cumbersome description). The author of the *Colloquy* does not identify himself, but the text was attributed to Ælfric by one of his pupils, Ælfric Bata, himself an author of Latin colloquies, and this attribution has long been accepted.

In the *Colloquy*, the master engages in short exchanges with labourers who represent a broad cross-section of Anglo-Saxon occupations and so, in addition to offering instruction in Latin, the *Colloquy* may also have served as a sort of social primer designed to teach young boys something about the occupations of the different types of men with whom they will eventually have to deal. The 'text' formed by the glosses found in Cotton Tiberius, A. iii, which, following convention, we will refer to as Ælfric's *Colloquy*, is clear and straightforward in its lexicon, grammar, and syntax. The purpose of the *Colloquy* is to offer basic language instruction by presenting uncomplicated questions and equally uncomplicated answers, and, as the following example reveals, it does so with a decided economy of purpose:

> Ic axie þe, hwæt sprycst þu? Hwæt hæfst þu weorkes?

> Ic eom geanwyrde monuc, and ic sincge ælce dæg seofon tida mid gebroþrum, and ic eom bysgod ... on sange, ac þeahhwæþere ic wolde betwenan leornian sprecan on leden gereorde.
> > (Garmonsway, 19.11–16)

> [I ask you, what do you say? What work do you have?

> I have taken my vows as a monk and I sing each day seven times with my bretheren, and I am occupied ... in singing, but nevertheless I wish in the meanwhile to learn to speak in the Latin language.]

Along with the monk, the *Colloquy* also includes a ploughman, a shepherd, an oxherd, a huntsman, a fisherman, a fowler, a merchant, a shoemaker, a salter, a baker, and a cook. All of them are questioned by the master and all of them give brief accounts of their jobs, and in several cases of the hardships that their professions entail. Although the dialogue in the *Colloquy* never reaches the level of realism found in the so-called Wakefield Master's *Second Shepherds' Pageant*, the *Colloquy* offers us an important window onto the details of the workers' lives. Ælfric may have heightened for dramatic effect the rhetoric of the ploughman's response to the master's query about the nature of his work, but in it he affords us a revealing, if brief, glimpse into the social dynamics of a world we continue to know little about, that of common men and women during the period:

> Eala, leof hlaford, þearle ic deorfe. Ic ga ut on dægræd þywende oxon to felda, and iugie hig to syl; nys hit swa stearc winter þæt ic durre lutian æt ham for ege hlafordes mines, ac geiukodon oxan, and gefæstnodon sceare and cultre mit þære syl, ælce dæg ic sceal erian fulne æcer oððe mare.
>
> (Garmonsway, 20.23–27)

> [Oh, dear lord, I work hard. I go out at dawn driving the oxen to the field, and I yoke them to the plough; for fear of my lord, there is no winter so hard that I dare lie hidden at home, but with the oxen yoked and the share attached and the coulter with the plough, each day I must plough a full acre or more.]

To the master's sympathetic comment, 'Hig! Hig! Micel gedeorf ys hyt' (Garmonsway, 21.34) [Alas! Alas! It is hard work], the ploughman replies tellingly: 'Geleof, micel gedeorf hit ys, forþam ic neom freoh' (Garmonsway, 21.35) [Sir, hard work it is because I am not free]. Perhaps to break the monotony of the master's string of 'who are you and what do you do?' questions, Ælfric has him interact a bit more dramatically with the cook, the necessity of whose craft he questions. The cook responds defensively, almost huffily, saying 'Gif ge me ut adrifaþ fram eowrum geferscype, ge etaþ wyrta eowre grene, and flæscmettas eowre hreawe' (Garmonsway, 37.194–95) [If you drive me out of your fellowship, you will eat your plants uncooked and your meat raw]. The master, unswayed by this threat, responds that 'We ne reccaþ ne he us neodþearf ys, forþam we sylfe magon seoþan þa þingc þe to seoþenne synd, and brædan þa þingc þe to brædene synd' (Garmonsway, 37.197–99) [We do not care nor is he necessary to us, because we ourselves can boil those things that are to be boiled and roast those things that are to be roasted]. Unable or perhaps unwilling to defend his craft to the monastic and certainly culinarily ascetic master, the cook shifts gears and points, albeit exaggeratedly, to the social disruption that would follow his expulsion: 'Gif ge forþy me fram adryfaþ, þæt ge þus don, þonne beo ge ealle þrælas, and nan eower ne biþ hlaford' (Garmonsway, 37.200–1) [If you therefore drive me away so that you can do thus, then will you all be thralls and none of you will be lord].

While the bulk of the *Colloquy* is given over to the answers of the workmen, members of several other classes, including skilled craftsmen such as blacksmiths, goldsmiths, and carpenters – who engage in a brief but spirited dispute concerning whose craft is the most beneficial to society – make appearances, as does a learned counsellor who mediates the skilled craftsmen's dispute. Appropriately, and amusingly enough, the *Colloquy* ends with an exchange between the master and one of his own pupils that concludes with the master indirectly offering us a glimpse into the behaviour of schoolboys in Anglo-Saxon England when he admonishes them, in language that will sound all too familiar to contemporary teachers (and students), 'healdan eow sylfe ænlice on ælcere stowe. Gaþ þeawlice þonne ge gehyran cyricean bellan, and gaþ into cyrcean, and abugaþ eadmodlice to halgum wefodom, and standaþ þeawlice, and singað anmodlice, and gebiddaþ for eowrum synnum, and gaþ ut butan hygeleaste to claustre oþþe to leorninga' (Garmonsway, 48–49.310–15) [to comport yourself decorously in every place. Go obediently when you hear the church bells and go into the church, and bow humbly to the holy altars and stand obediently and sing boldly and pray for your sins, and go out without fooling around to the cloister, or to learn].

Ælfric as Author

Unlike his contemporary Wulfstan, who was active in a very public fashion on the national level and who in his sermons and homilies frequently addressed the social turmoil that arose following the renewal of the Viking attacks in the late tenth and early eleventh centuries, Ælfric maintains a focus that is much more local: only rarely does he allow any current social troubles, or indeed, any real-world issues, to creep into his writings, preferring instead to keep them at arm's length. Ælfric maintains his focus so assiduously on enduring and important spiritual matters that were his writings our only source of information regarding England in the late tenth and early eleventh century, a very different, far less discordant, picture of the period would emerge.

Whereas Wulfstan uses the Viking attacks to contextualize his most famous sermon, the *Sermon of the Wolf to the English*, Ælfric mentions the events transpiring in the world only on a few occasions, and even then he does so with none of the urgent, frequently alarmist rhetoric Wulfstan habitually employs. For example, in the *Life of St Edmund* (LS, XXXIII), Ælfric presents the attacks that took place during the ninth century as follows: 'Hit gelamp ða æt nextan þæt þa Deniscan leode ferdon mid scip-here hergiende and sleande wide geond land swa swa heora gewuna is' (Skeat, II, 316.26–28) [Then it next happened that the Danish people journeyed with a naval force, ravaging and slaying widely throughout the land just as is their custom]. And later in the same passage, he reports the savage deeds of Hingwar, one of this Danish troop's leaders, in an almost matter-of-fact manner: 'se foresæda Hinguar færlice swa swa wulf on lande bestalcode and þa leode sloh weras and wif and þa ungewittigan cild and to bysmore tucode þa bilewitan Cristenan' (Skeat, II, 316.39–42) [the aforesaid Hingwar without warning, just like a wolf, moved stealthily on the land and slew the people, men and women and unreasoning children and shamefully afflicted the virtuous Christians].

In LS XIII, *The Prayer of Moses*, Ælfric makes it clear that his view of the Viking attacks accords with Wulfstan's when he asks 'Hu wæs hit ða siððan ða þa man towearp munuclif and Godes biggengas to bysmore hæfde buton þæt us com to cwealm and hunger and siððan hæðen here us hæfde to bysmre? (Skeat, I, 294.152–55) [How was it then when men overthrew the monastic life and held God's rituals in contempt but that pestilence and famine came to us and afterward the heathen army disgraced us?]. Ælfric is also aware of the immediacy of the Vikings' threat for after detailing some of the punishments that God promises Moses should the chosen people 'me forseoð and mine gesetnyssa awurpað' (Skeat, I, 294.163) [disdain me and cast off my laws], Ælfric notes 'Þus spræc God gefyrn be þam folce Israhel; hit is swa ðeah swa gedon swyðe neah mid us nu on niwum dagum and undigollice' (Skeat, I, 296.175–77) [Thus spoke God long ago about the people of Israel; it is nevertheless done very similarly with us now in recent days and openly]. Yet rather than ratcheting up his rhetoric at this point or dwelling on the horrible fate in store for the English, Ælfric simply counsels that 'We sceolan God wurðian mid soðre anrædnysse forþan þe he is ælmihtig God and he us to menn gesceop; nu do we swyðe wolice gif we ne wurðiað hine us sylfum to þearfe and urum sawlum to blisse' (Skeat, I, 296.178–81) [We must worship God with true constancy because he is almighty God and he created us as men; now we do very wrongly if we do not worship him for our own need and to the bliss of our souls]. And although Ælfric believes that 'Þes tima is enda-next and ende þyssere worulde' (Skeat, I, 304.294.) [This time is the last and the end of this world], he does not view the sinful behaviour of men and the dire consequences that await them through the lens of the Viking attacks, but always keeps his focus on larger matters. Ælfric was certainly neither unaware of nor unaffected by the Viking attacks, even though they figure only peripherally in his texts: writing in the Latin preface to *CH II*, he speaks with moving directness of how he was shaken by 'multis iniuriis infestium piratarum'

(Wilcox, *Ælfric's Prefaces*, 111; trans. 128) [the great injuries of the dangerous pirates] after completing *CH I* and of how he completed *CH II* 'dolente animo' [with a grieving mind] only because he had promised Archbishop Sigeric that he would write a second series of homiles. One explanation for why the Viking invasions play such a small part in Ælfric's writings may be that his piety enabled him to look past current troubles, no matter how pressing, and to focus on matters of more enduring spiritual and moral import.

Ælfric is an important figure in late Anglo-Saxon literary history not just because he was a prolific and talented writer, but because his writings and practices reveal a good deal about his authorial sensibilities. The many rhetorical techniques he uses, including rhyme, word-play, alliteration, classification, balance, repetition, and enumeration that he inherited from the expressive economies of Latin and the vernacular, and one, rhythmical prose, that he seems to have invented, reveal Ælfric to have been sharply attuned not just to the craft of writing but to the reception of his works by listeners and silent readers. This is also evident in the many direct addresses he makes to his audience, an audience he figures frequently as a listening one, and in his reliance on short clauses, many of which are marked by parallelism and controlled rhythm. There is evidence that Ælfric corrected some of his works and also returned to and revised some of them. His contemporaries may have done the same, but what is important about Ælfric's authorial practices is that we can do more than make conjectures regarding them; in the cancelled passages and the holographic marginal notes to himself and his scribes found in London, BL, Royal 7. C. xii we see evidence of his having rethought and reworked what might be early or draft copies of some homilies.

As an author, Ælfric further shows himself to be attuned to a number of practical matters: the length of many of his discourses suggests that he wrote them with oral recitation in mind, and his rhythmical prose may have developed as a way of further facilitating the oral delivery and aural reception of his writings. Ælfric was also aware of the needs – and limitations – of his readerly audience, and he also speaks candidly about the decisions he made while creating his texts, as, for example, in the *CH II* version of the *Life of Martin*: 'Ne mage we awritan ealle his wundra on ðisum scortan cwyde, mid cuðum gereorde, ac we wyllað secgan hu se soðfæsta gewat' (Godden, *Ælfric's Catholic Homilies: The Second Series*, 295.266–68) [We cannot write down all his miracles in this short treatise, with familiar language, but we will say how the righteous man departed]. He similarly frequently explains why he is not going on at greater length, as in the two following statements from, respectively, the *Writer's Apology* and *Palm*

Sunday: 'Fela fægere godspel we forlætað on ðisum gedihte: ða mæg awendan se ðe wile. Ne durre we ðas boc na miccle swiðor gelengan, ði læs ðe heo ungemetegod sy, and mannum æðryt þurh hire micelnysse astyrige' (Godden, *Ælfric's Catholic Homilies: The Second Series*, 297.1–4) [Many excellent gospels we have omitted in this piece of writing; he may translate them who wishes. We dare not lengthen this book much more, lest it should be immoderate, and through its size seem wearisome to men]; and 'Drihtnes ðrowunge we willað gedafenlice eow secgan on Engliscum gereorde, and ða gerynu samod; na swa ðeah to langsumlice' (Godden, *Ælfric's Catholic Homilies: The Second Series*, 137.1–3) [We will suitably say to you in the English language the suffering of the lord, together with the mysteries; not, however, too lengthily].

As we noted above, Ælfric not only leaves explicit instructions concerning the use to which *CH* is to be put, but he is also very concerned with the accurate transmission of his work, a topic to which he returns on several occasions. After admitting that some may find fault with his text 'because it is not word for word or is a shorter explication than one has in the books of the authorities – or because we do not proceed through all the gospels in the order in which ecclesiastical custom treats them', he urges anyone who finds fault with his work to 'make for himself a book with a better translation in whatever manner is pleasing to his understanding'. The only thing Ælfric asks is that the critic create his own work and 'not pervert our version' (Wilcox, *Ælfric's Prefaces*, 27). Similar sentiments, although much abbreviated, crop up in the lengthy OE preface to *CH I* and in the much shorter vernacular preface to *CH II*, where Ælfric asks transcribers of 'ðas boc' [this book] to copy carefully 'þe læs ðe we, þurh gymeleasum writerum, geleahtrode beon' (Godden, *Ælfric's Catholic Homilies: The Second Series*, 2.44–46) [lest we, through negligent writers, be rebuked].

Throughout his long and productive career, Ælfric remained first and foremost concerned with distilling and reshaping the orthodox teachings of the Church fathers so that they could reach a much wider audience than they would have had they not been translated into the vernacular. By using his considerable intellectual gifts not to ponder the esoteric mysteries of Church doctrine but rather to bring before the unlearned foundational matters of Christian thought in familiar terms and simple language, Ælfric remained true to his primary aim: revealing to his audience the spiritual truths that will help lead them to salvation. Unlike Chaucer's corrupt Pardoner, who cares not a bit if the souls of the people who purchase his worthless pardons 'goon a-blakeberyed!' [go blackberry picking] (Benson, *Riverside Chaucer*, VI [C] 405), Ælfric keeps the needs of his intended audiences's souls squarely in view at all times.

Further Reading

Gretsch, Mechthild. Ælfric and the Cult of the Saints in Late Anglo-Saxon England. CSASE 34. Cambridge: Cambridge University Press, 2005.

Harris, Stephen J. 'The liturgical context of Ælfric's homilies for rogation'. In The Old English Homily: Precedent, Practice, and Appropriation, ed. Aaron J. Kleist, 143–69. Studies in the Early Middle Ages 17. Turnhout: Brepols, 2007.

Magennis, Hugh. 'Ælfric and heroic literature'. In The Power of Words: Anglo-Saxon Studies Presented to Donald G. Scragg on his Seventieth Birthday, ed. Hugh Magennis and Jonathan Wilcox, 31–60. Morgantown: West Virginia University Press, 2006.

Magennis, Hugh. 'Warrior saints, warfare, and the hagiography of Ælfric of Eynsham'. Traditio 56 (2001): 27–51.

Magennis, Hugh, and Mary Swan, eds. A Companion to Ælfric. Brill's Companions to the Christian Tradition 18. Leiden: Brill, 2009.

Stanley, Eric G. 'Wulfstan and Ælfric: "The true difference between the Law and the Gospel"'. In Wulfstan, Archbishop of York: the Proceedings of the Second Alcuin Conference, ed. Matthew Townend, 429–41. Studies in the Early Middle Ages 10. Turnhout: Brepols, 2004.

Szarmach, Paul E. 'Ælfric revises: the lives of Martin and the idea of the author'. In Unlocking the Wordhord: Anglo-Saxon Studies in Memory of Edward B. Irving, Jr., ed. Mark C. Amodio and Katherine O'Brien O'Keeffe, 38–61. Toronto: University of Toronto Press, 2003.

Whatley, E. Gordon. 'Hagiography and violence: military men in Ælfric's Lives of Saints'. In Source of Wisdom: Old English and Early Medieval Latin Studies in Honour of Thomas D. Hill, ed. Charles D. Wright, Frederick M. Biggs, and Thomas N. Hall, 217–38. Toronto Old English Series 16. Toronto: University of Toronto Press, 2007.

Part 3

Anglo-Saxon Poetry

The Anglo-Saxon Poetic Tradition

When compared to the voluminous amounts of prose that survive, the poetic records of the Anglo-Saxons are rather modest: only some 30,000 lines of verse written in OE survive, with two poems, *Beowulf* and *Genesis*, accounting for more than 6,000 lines and the *Metrical Psalms* found in the Paris Psalter accounting for an additional 5,000 lines. The entire surviving corpus of vernacular Anglo-Saxon verse is thus roughly equivalent to the *Iliad* and *Odyssey* of Homer, and it is, further, dwarfed by the many thousands of lines of vernacular poetry that were produced in England during the post-Conquest period. Just how much of the vernacular poetry that was composed in Anglo-Saxon England was committed to the manuscript page and whether the surviving poetic records represent most of what was written down during the period or only a portion of it remain open questions.

Much of the poetry that has survived from the Anglo-Saxon period is housed in four late-tenth-century codices: the Vercelli Book (Vercelli, Biblioteca Capitolare, MS CXVII); London, BL Cotton Vitellius A.xv; Oxford, Bodleian Library, MS Junius II; and the Exeter Book (Exeter, Cathedral Library, Dean and Chapter MS 3501). Additionally, a considerable amount of vernacular verse is also found in two other manuscripts, Paris, Bibliothèque Nationale, MS 8824 (known as the Paris Psalter) and London, BL, Cotton Otho A.vi: the former contains metrical versions of 100 psalms, beginning with Psalm 51, and the latter the prose and metrical sections of the OE translation of Boethius's *The Consolation of Philosophy*, texts that together run to more than 5,000 lines. The remaining verse texts are scattered throughout the Anglo-Saxon manuscript records, where they are found sometimes singly, sometimes in small clusters, alongside prose texts in OE and Latin, and alongside Latin verse.

The Anglo-Saxon Literature Handbook, First Edition. Mark C. Amodio.
© 2014 Mark C. Amodio. Published 2014 by John Wiley & Sons, Ltd.

Not all of the extant OE verse survives in contemporary manuscripts; a few poems, including *The Fight at Finnsburh*, *The Battle of Maldon*, and *The Rune Poem*, survive only because transcripts were made before the manuscript leaves on which they appeared went missing (*Finnsburh*) or were destroyed in the Cottonian fire of 1731 (*Maldon, Rune Poem*). In a very few instances, OE verse survives entirely outside of the manuscript records: the Ruthwell Cross, a large stone monument in Dumfriesshire, Scotland, and the Brussels Cross, a wooden reliquary housed at the Cathedral of Saints Michel and Gudule, Brussels, both have vernacular poetry inscribed upon them. The latter has two lines of verse inscribed in the Roman alphabet while the former contains several sentences of *The Dream of the Rood* carved into its stone using the runic alphabet. The Franks Casket, a small box made of whale-bone, contains a few lines of Anglo-Saxon verse written in runes as well.

As is true of OE prose, OE poetry is not the product of any single, homogeneous tradition; rather it emerges from the complex interactions of several traditions, both native and imported, over the course of a number of centuries. When the Germanic tribes came to England in the middle of the fifth century, they brought with them from their continental homelands both a system of writing (the runic alphabet, or futhorc) and a system of metrics (one that was stress-based and alliterative). Although the runic alphabet was brought to England fairly early in the Anglo-Saxon period, it was to the Roman alphabet, supplemented by the addition of the runic characters ash (æ), thorn (þ), eth (ð), yogh (ȝ), and wynn (ƿ), that the Anglo-Saxons turned when they began to produce vernacular texts in the ninth century.

But while the futhorc was not used widely in England, even for inscriptions, the metrical system the Germanic tribes brought over from the continent was. One of the most striking features of the Anglo-Saxon poetic tradition is that its metrics remains stable, homogeneous, and singular throughout the entirety of the period. Although separated by nearly 400 years, the principles of versification that undergird what is generally accepted as the earliest piece of OE verse to survive in the written records, an early eighth-century version of Cædmon's *Hymn* written in the bottom margin of a Latin text of Bede's *Ecclesiastical History of the English People*, are also identifiable in *Durham*, a poem that dates from the early twelfth century and is generally regarded as one of the latest OE poems. As in all OE poetry, the verses cited below are knit together by alliteration or assonance (respectively the repetition of stressed initial consonants and the repetition of stressed initial vowels `1) and they follow one of five metrical stress patterns:

Nu sculon herigean heofonrices weard,
meotodes meahte and his modgeþanc.

(Cædmon's *Hymn*, 1–2)

Is ðeos burch breome geond Breotenrice,
steppa gestaðolad, stanas ymbutan
wundrum gewæxen.

(*Durham*, 1–3a)

Were we to look elsewhere throughout the OE poetic corpus, we would discover the same metrical principles at work: a heroic epic such as *Beowulf*, a riddle from the Exeter Book collection, or verses retelling the book of Genesis all conform to the same general metrical principles and patterns. Exceptions do exist, but hypermetric verses (lines which contain a considerably higher number of syllables than is found within an average line of verse) and the verses in the *Rhyming Poem* (in which internal and end-rhyme play an integral metrical role) still conform to the general principles of OE metre. And even though the OE metrical system is remarkably stable, towards the end of the period signs of change begin to appear. The causes of these changes are complex and lie outside the scope of the present discussion, but the impact the Norman Conquest of 1066 had on the culture, politics, and language of Anglo-Saxon England and the grammatical and syntactic changes that were already in progress prior to the Conquest were important contributing factors.

To our contemporary sensibilities, ones that have developed within and have been shaped by a tradition in which poets are able to articulate poetry following as many, or as few, formal constraints as they wish, the singular system under which Anglo-Saxon poets operated for several hundred years may seem decidedly restrictive. Why Anglo-Saxon poets employed such a singular metrics for as long as they did is yet another question to which there is no clear answer. Literate, bilingual poets would undoubtedly have been exposed to many of the various metrical patterns and styles in which Latin verse was composed, yet Latin models have only limited impact upon the vernacular poetic tradition. The practices Anglo-Saxon authors and scribes followed when physically encoding vernacular verse on the manuscript page are, like the metrics through which that verse was articulated, strikingly uniform throughout the period, and as is true of vernacular metrics, these practices show little, if any, evidence of having been influenced by the practices of Latin textual culture. From Antiquity onward, Latin verse was physically presented on the page in ways that distinguished it from prose. Scribes, who in some cases were the texts' authors as well, used a wide variety of formal techniques to mark Latin poetry visually as poetry, including, among other things, aligning the beginning of each successive line of poetry against the left-hand margin or leaving a space between the first and second letters of the first word in a line of poetry. They also placed each line of poetry on its own manuscript line, a practice that has continued down to the present day.

By way of contrast, OE verse and prose texts are physically encoded on the page via a single, unvarying system of presentation: they are written out continuously in lines that generally fill all the available space between the left and right margins, with no formal or visual cues distinguishing prose from verse. For reasons that remain unknown, the system of visual cues used in Latin textual culture was neither imported into nor adapted for Anglo-Saxon textual culture, even though many of the scribes who copied down vernacular poems also produced Latin verse and prose texts. Why Anglo-Saxon poets utilized only the uniform, autochthonous metrics they employed and why they (and/or the scribes who produced the manuscripts) opted not to follow the well-established practices of Latin literate culture when committing vernacular verse to the manuscript page are questions to which there are no simple answers. We can perhaps shed some light on this situation by briefly considering the complex and interconnected relationships a native language has to a foreign one and that orality has to literacy.

From the perspective of contemporary literates, the difference between employing Latin or OE as the language of a prose or poetic text seems negligible since we can recognize and readily acknowledge that both are excellent (and essentially equivalent) communicative technologies through which ideas of great subtlety and complexity could be, and often were, expressed in the early medieval period. But to the Anglo-Saxons, the two languages may have appeared to be markedly dissimilar. Latin remained the exclusive province of the educated class (a small percentage of the population), and further, in most western medieval cultures Latin was the sole vehicle for the transmission of secular and ecclesiastical knowledge. In contrast, even though the Anglo-Saxons eventually come to have considerable intercourse with continental cultures, their language does not spread beyond its insular home. Latin was spoken by the educated throughout the west, and at the dawn of the Middle Ages it had already enjoyed a long history as a written language. The roots of OE, in contrast, extend back only to the Age of Migration, the period following the departure of the Romans in which England came to be settled by members of various continental Germanic tribes. The origins of the language that we know as OE are lost to us in the mists of time that envelop Dark Age Britain, but the tribes that began journeying to the island sometime in the middle of the fifth century did not arrive speaking it; rather OE grew out of the various Germanic dialects that these tribes spoke and only gradually coalesced into the language we know today as OE.

We must rely entirely on conjecture when discussing the pre-history of OE because throughout the period of its formation and for a considerable time after it becomes established as a discrete language, OE remained primarily, and perhaps solely, a spoken language. The ramifications of this may be somewhat difficult for us to grasp since from very early in our cognitive development we are exposed to – and are expected to acquire – the practices and habits of mind associated with and valued by literate culture. In the Middle Ages, though, the situation was very different: for the vast majority of the population, language was always and only something that was spoken, not written. Non-literates were exposed to literate culture only indirectly, as they experienced written documents and texts exclusively through their ears (by hearing texts read aloud), not their eyes (by reading texts or composing and/or copying them themselves). Only a very small percentage of the population was able to participate directly in literate culture by reading and/or writing texts, but even for them the situation was complicated since the literate, textual culture which they were trained to negotiate was not that of their mother tongue but of Latin.

From our perspective, literate and oral culture seem far from equivalent because contemporary culture depends heavily upon, and so privileges, the former over the latter, and because our culture better understands (and so more highly values) the fixity that is a hallmark of literate culture than it does the ephemerality that characterizes oral culture. As members of a culture situated nearer the literate than the oral end of the oral–literate continuum, we are steeped in literate practices and habits of mind from very early childhood. As a result, we often view literacy as not only the best but as the *only* way to preserve and transmit the products of high, middle, and even low culture. Orality remains an essential component of our lives and we engage it daily in countless ways, but it no longer performs the work that it did when western culture was situated more towards the oral than the literate end of the oral–literate continuum. In the early Middle Ages, orality served the same communicative function that it continues to serve in contemporary culture, but it also functioned in ways that are sometimes difficult for literates to grasp. For example, throughout much of the medieval period, testimony delivered orally by an eye-witness to an event carried far more weight and was accepted much more readily by judges and jurors than was a disembodied, written statement that was read aloud in the witness's absence. While there are a great many differences between the oral–literate matrix of Anglo-Saxon England and that of contemporary western culture, one of the most important for our purposes is the presence in the former of a strong and very cohesive system for the production of verbal art, a system that descends directly from the medieval English oral tradition and that survives even after vernacular verse comes to be composed chiefly, and perhaps exclusively, by poets writing in private and not by singers composing orally during public performances.

Being responsible readers of any oral traditional verbal art requires that we avoid applying a cookie-cutter template to it and that we re-calibrate our interpretive strategies to bring them, so far as we possibly can, into alignment with the verbal art we wish to explore. If we were to apply the strategies that have developed for investigating texts produced in a literate culture to those very different 'texts' produced in an oral culture, we would be able to do little more than describe how one fails to resemble the other and we would, further, be able to offer readings that are either impertinent or misguided. To understand, say, the repeated epithets that are frequently attached to characters in Homeric epic, we need to be aware that even though to our literate sensibilities they may initially appear to be simply meaningless metrical fillers or clichés, they are instead integral components of the traditional oral poetics of Homeric epic. An epithet such as 'Podas ôkus' [swift-footed], one applied frequently to Achilleus, serves not only a clear metrical function within the Homeric decasyllabic line, but via the pathway of traditional referentiality the epithet also metonymically and economically summons the totality of Achilleus's character to the narrative surface every time it occurs. Similarly, in *Beowulf* we frequently find the phrase 'helm Scyldinga' [protector of the Scyldings] attached to the Danish King Hrothgar even though he has for twelve years been unable to protect his people from Grendel's nightly attacks on the hall Heorot. Considered from the perspective of a literate poetics, the epithet may strike us as ironic, praising as it does a king who sits powerlessly by while Grendel kills many Danes. However, the phrase 'protector of the Scyldings' draws meaning not just from the narrative moment in which it occurs, but also summons to the narrative present the entirety of Hrothgar's glorious heroic past. Interpreting the epithet requires that we be sensitive to how it functions on the surface of the narrative (as a potentially ironic comment), and that we also remain sensitive to its greater-than-narrative resonances since they complicate, and perhaps even cancel, any irony contemporary audiences might hear in the phrase.

The components of oral poetics – formulas (which fulfil metrical demands), traditional themes, and traditional story-patterns – provide the poet, who in oral cultures composes during performance, with structures as small as a word, phrase, or single line and as large as a story pattern. For example, a line such as 'Beowulf maþelode, bearn Ecþeowes' [Beowulf spoke, the son of Ecgtheow] offers a poet a 'ready-made' way of introducing direct speech that conforms to the demands of OE metrics. Similarly, the narrative elements that comprise a traditional theme such as the hero on the beach provide the poet with a narrative template which he then fleshes out in whatever way seems best to him by using some constellation of the numerous narrative details that comprise this particular theme's contours.

At some point in its history, England's culture was primarily oral and the verbal art produced in it was oral-traditional, but by the tenth century, the period during which the manuscripts that contain virtually all the surviving OE poetry were written, the island's culture had already shifted towards the literate pole of the oral–literate continuum. For the present purposes, what is of most import is not the steady rise of documentary culture during the centuries before the Norman Conquest of 1066, but rather the persistence of traditional oral features in OE poems, poems that found their way onto the manuscript page not from the tongue of a singer composing during public performance but from the pen of a poet composing privately and in writing. But even though English culture moves becomes ever more literate, the relationship between the oral and the literate continues to be marked by confluence, not divergence.

Keeping in mind that oral and literate ways of thinking are interconnected and mutually influential will be especially important once we turn to look more closely at the Anglo-Saxon poetic records because written OE poetry – which is by definition the only type of poetry to survive from the period – depends heavily upon oral poetics. What these features witness, however, is not the poems' proximity to orality or the oral tradition but rather the degree to which the process of composing written poetry in Anglo-Saxon England continued to be influenced by the practices that had developed in the centuries that preceded the rise of textual culture. Even though the mode of composition changes radically, the expressive economy within which poetry had long been articulated did not. OE poetry remains so uniform and so deeply indebted to traditional oral poetics long after the pen comes to supplant the tongue as the primary means of producing poetry because the specialized register of oral poetics is nothing less than a dedicated way of speaking – and thinking – poetry. Although it may be difficult for us to conceive given the degree to which our own culture leans toward the literate pole of the oral–literate continuum, in Anglo-Saxon England both oral singers and literate poets engaged the same specialized register when composing a poetic work, the only significant difference being that for the oral poet, the arena in which composition took place was necessarily performative, while for the literate poet it was non-performative.

The oral poetics through which poetry was expressed in Anglo-Saxon England was a highly deterministic system, but its 'grammar' is finally no more inhibiting or restrictive than is the grammar of Modern English or any other language: languages are communicative systems that require their users to adhere to certain rules, but within each system the expressive possibilities are limited only by the talents and abilities of each user. Contemporary poets might well chafe at the thought of having to use, for example, a single metrical system whenever they composed a poem, but in pre-Conquest England the singular, deterministic metrics of Anglo-Saxon oral poetics was a fundamental part of a system that enabled both poetic expression and its reception. Our contemporary perspective allows us to recognize that the four-beat, alliterative metrical system Anglo-Saxon poets invariably employed is just one type of the many metrical systems available to poets, but for the Anglo-Saxons the expression of poetry was inseparably intertwined with this singular, native metrics. The same holds true of the larger, narrative elements of traditional oral poetics; poets were not imprisoned by the traditional narrative structures they employed because, as is the case with the tradition itself, these structures were dynamic, flexible, and fluid tools for the expression of verbal art, ones that all poets altered, sometimes significantly, sometimes insignificantly, each time they used them. A brief consideration of one example – the theme of the beasts of battle that appears in *Beowulf* and elsewhere – will serve to illustrate this point.

In this well-attested theme, carrion-eating beasts hurry silently towards the scene of an imminent battle, eager to enjoy the feast that they know awaits them following the cessation of fighting. Although in *Beowulf* the theme conforms to the traditional pattern in many ways, it also differs significantly from the other surviving instances of it: only in *Beowulf* are the beasts and their expectations of feasting on corpses divorced from the martial context in which the theme generally, and logically, occurs, and only in *Beowulf* will one of the animals, the raven, 'fela reordian' (3025b) [speak of many things]. Do the unique aspects of the theme's instantiation in *Beowulf* – its use in a non-martial context and the report that the raven will speak about how it will 'æte speow' (3026b) [succeed at the eating] – render this occurrence more or less traditional than other occurrences of it? Additionally, should the *Beowulf*-poet's handling of the theme be seen as innovative or, conversely, does the theme as he presents it more closely reflect the ways that oral poets articulated it when it occurred in their oral, unrecorded poems? Compelling arguments in support of both views readily suggest themselves, but they cannot be resolved because the theme is a multiform and has no fixed, standard form against which all other instantiations can be measured. Although we may think that the *Beowulf*-poet's ascribing the raven the power of human speech is of a piece with the other evidence in the poem of his unique genius for altering, expanding, and enriching the traditional fabric out of which its narrative is woven, the opposite may in fact be true: his version of the theme of the beasts of battle may be the most traditional one to survive.

Just as we may never be able to discover why scribes and authors in the period did not follow the practices of Latin textual culture when they inscribed vernacular verse on the surface of the manuscript page, so, too, we may never fully understand why literate Anglo-Saxon poets continued to employ oral poetics so extensively throughout the period. A possible, if partial, answer lies in the highly specialized nature of the expressive economy of which oral poetics is an integral part. Although oral poetics developed in an oral and necessarily performative cultural matrix, it remains foundational to the articulation of verbal art once Anglo-Saxon England becomes more fully oriented towards literacy because it was – for both oral and literate poets – not just one of many different ways of voicing or penning poetry in the vernacular, but the *sole avenue* for doing so. Oral poetics is also a dedicated register for the transmission of traditional meaning, one that provided poets with a powerful and effective way of metonymically tapping into the associative webs of meaning positioned beyond the surface of traditional narratives. The close, perhaps symbiotic relationship that existed between the transmission of traditional meaning and that meaning's reception by its intended audience also played a significant role in the survival of Anglo-Saxon oral poetics. For such an audience, the specialized expressive economy which poets engaged when articulating poetry charted the very pathways along which traditional meaning was transmitted.

The Anglo-Saxons bequeathed us a complex, magnificent, and strikingly varied body of poetry, and it is to the extant written records of their verbal art that we now turn.

Further Reading

Amodio, Mark C. 'The medieval English oral–literate nexus'. In his *Writing the Oral Tradition: Oral Poetics and Literate Culture in Medieval England*, 1–32. Poetics of Orality and Literacy 1. Notre Dame: University of Notre Dame Press, 2004.

Foley, John Miles. 'From traditional poetics to traditional meaning'. In his *Immanent Art: From Structure to Meaning in Traditional Oral Epic*, 1–37. Bloomington: Indiana University Press, 1991.

Foley, John Miles. *Pathways of the Mind: Oral Tradition and the Internet*. Urbana: University of Illinois Press, 2012.

Foley, John Miles. 'The rhetorical persistence of traditional forms'. In his *The Singer of Tales in Performance*, 60–98. Bloomington: Indiana University Press, 1995.

O'Brien O'Keeffe, Katherine. 'Introduction'. In her *Visible Song: Transitional Literacy in Old English Verse*, 1–22. CSASE 4. Cambridge: Cambridge University Press, 1990.

Renoir, Alain. 'Oral–formulaic context and critical interpretation: general principles'. In his *A Key to Old Poems: The Oral–Formulaic Approach to the Interpretation of West-Germanic Verse*, 81–104. University Park: Pennsylvania University Press, 1988.

Stock, Brian. 'Orality, literacy, and the sense of the past'. In his *Listening for the Text: On the Uses of the Past*, 1–15. Parallax: Re-Visions of Culture and Society. Baltimore: Johns Hopkins University Press, 1990.

Cædmon's *Hymn*

Survives in seventeen manuscripts dating from the eighth to the fifteenth centuries. The earliest of these are CUL, Kk. 5. 16 (the Moore Bede), which is generally dated to 737 and St Petersburg, Russian National Library, Q. v. I. 18, which dates to the middle of the eighth century.

Although the dating of Anglo-Saxon poetry remains at best a very inexact science, the nine-line poem that has come to be known as Cædmon's *Hymn* is generally thought to be the earliest piece of vernacular poetry to have survived from Anglo-Saxon England. Two of the manuscripts that contain it, one in the Russian National Library and one in the Cambridge University Library, have been confidently dated to shortly after Bede's death in 735. These manuscripts are believed to have been produced at, respectively, the monastery at Jarrow where Bede spent most of his life, and at Jarrow's twin monastery, Monkwearmouth.

The *Hymn* is a simple, graceful, and lovely expression of devotion towards the Christian creator of the earth and mankind, as we can see from its opening lines: 'Nu sculon herigean heofonrices weard, / meotudes meahte' (1–2a) [Now we must praise the guardian of the heavenly kingdom, the might of the creator]. Although it contains elements of the Christian creation myth, it is not based upon the account of creation contained in Genesis or any other written source, as a comparion of the Vulgate's 'In the beginning God created heaven, and earth' (Genesis 1.1) with the *Hymn*'s 'He ærest sceop eorðan bearnum / heofon to hrofe' (5–6a) [He first created for the sons of earth heaven as a roof] makes clear. Its importance, however, extends far beyond the piety expressed in its nine lines: its shared lexicon and metrics reveal that both the dedicated register upon which Anglo-Saxon poets drew

The Anglo-Saxon Literature Handbook, First Edition. Mark C. Amodio.
© 2014 Mark C. Amodio. Published 2014 by John Wiley & Sons, Ltd.

when composing poetry and the singular metrical system within which they always articulated their compositions were already well established by the early eighth century, and its *mise-en-page* – the manner in which the poem is situated on the manuscript page – tells us much about the state of English as a written language at a time when it was being newly committed to the page. In addition, the poem's paratactic syntax and its style, especially its heavy reliance on variation (its nine lines contains eight phrases that refer to the Christian God, only one of which is repeated in the poem), remain important characteristics of vernacular poetry throughout the period. The *Hymn* is also important in other ways that space will not permit us to explore: it is one of the only poems from the period to survive in multiple versions, some of which are contained in manuscripts that date to the fifteenth century; it is one of the only poems to survive in more than one dialect; and it appears both in the Latin versions of Bede's *Ecclesiastical History of the English People* – where it is located in the margins in all but one fourteenth-century manuscript –, and in the five surviving manuscripts of the OE translation of the *EH* (see Part 2), where it is incorporated into the main text.

Although written some 200 years before most of the surviving OE poetry is committed to the page, Cædmon's *Hymn* is very much of a piece grammatically, stylistically, lexically, and metrically with the rest of the corpus. In fact, were we to place the *Hymn* alongside a demonstrably late poem such as *Durham*, we would discover that there is little that distinguishes the former as being from the early eighth century and the latter as being from the early twelfth century. As is true of the poetry that post-dates it, the *Hymn*'s language is highly formulaic, with most of its lexemes and many of its phrases well attested elsewhere in the Anglo-Saxon poetic records. For example, the phrase with which the poem ends, 'frea ælmihtig' [almighty lord], occurs an additional eighteen times in a wide variety of OE poems, and the closely related phrase 'frea mihtig' [mighty lord] occurs six times, meaning that of the eighty-six times in which *frea* appears in poetic texts, it is part of a formula with *ælmihtig/mihtig* fully twenty-four times. The *Hymn*'s metrics is the same native, stress-based, alliterative one through which all OE poetry is articulated.

Because the manuscript history of the *Hymn* is too complex to take up here, we will touch upon the poem's situation only in the two earliest ones, the St Petersburg and Moore manuscripts, both of which contain Latin versions of Bede's text and vernacular versions of Cædmon's nine-line song. In the former, the vernacular version of the poem is found on fol. 107^r, written apparently in the same hand responsible for copying the Latin text. In the Moore Bede, the poem appears at the top of fol. 128^v, where it is

written in a contemporary, but different hand from that of the text of the
EH. The Latin text of the *EH* and the annals are the product of the same
scribe, but the vernacular version of Cædmon's *Hymn* is written by another
contemporary hand. While the vernacular version of the *Hymn* was deemed
important enough to be included in these manuscripts of the *Historia*, the
ways in which it is presented indicates the lower status they accorded it.
In the Moore manuscript, it is squeezed in after several brief annalistic
entries in Latin before some brief memoranda on Northumbrian history. In
the St Petersburg manuscript the poem does not even have the status of
addendum that it has in the Moore Bede, but is rather a piece of marginalia
written outside the page's formally delineated area for text. In both
manuscripts, the vernacular poem is not formatted as poetry, but is rather
written out continuously as prose.

The sections of the manuscripts containing the Latin text of Cædmon's
Hymn similarly contain no formal, visual cues indicating the presence of
verse, but this is not surprising since, as Bede tells us, he reports only the
sense of Cædmon's song, not his exact words. Bede, in fact, goes rather out
of his way to stress this point, mentioning it both before and after presenting
what he claims is a Latin paraphrase of the verses Cædmon produced. Bede
prefaces the *Hymn* by saying 'this is the general sense' of what Cædmon
spoke. Following his paraphrase, Bede states further that 'This is the sense
but not the order of the words which he sang as he slept. For it is not
possible to translate verse, however well composed, literally from one
language to another without some loss of beauty and dignity' (Colgrave and
Mynors, 417). But despite his assertions to the contrary, Bede's Latin
paraphrase of Cædmon's *Hymn* is so closely related to the OE poem that we
simply cannot determine whether the Latin is a paraphrase of the OE, or if
the OE is a paraphrase of the Latin. If the OE is the original, then Bede
remains quite faithful to it in his 'translation/paraphrase', something that
may offer indirect evidence of Bede's continued engagement with his native
language and perhaps even with the larger native cultural world that lay
outside the monastery's walls. If the Latin is the original, those responsible
for the OE versions (the St Petersburg scribe and an early owner/reader of
the Moore Bede?) display a fidelity to the original's phraseology rarely
encountered in OE translations, which generally should perhaps be classified
as re-creations.

The *Hymn* appears in Book IV, chapter 24 of Bede's *EH*, where it is
embedded within the larger narrative of Cædmon, a cowherd who lived
near the monastery at Whitby during the time it was under the direction
of Abbess Hild. According to the OE translation of Bede's Latin text, a
translation that adds important details to its source (see Part 2), one night at

a 'geobeorscipe' (Miller, 342.21) [feast at which (alcoholic) drink is served], when it is decided that 'heo ealle scalde þurh endebyrdnesse be hearpan singan' (Miller, 342.21–22) [they all should in proper sequence sing to a harp], the middle-aged Cædmon gets up and goes home 'þonne he geseah þa hearpan him nealecan' (Miller, 342.22–23) [when he saw the harp approach him]. Once home he falls asleep and is visited in a dream by someone who calls him by his name and commands him to sing. Cædmon responds by prostesting that 'Ne con ic noht singan, and ic forþon of þeossum gebeorscipe uteode, and hider gewat, forþon ic naht singan ne cuðe' (Miller, 342.30–31) [I cannot sing, and because of that I went from the feast and came here, because I do not know how to sing]. The spectral visitor, however, insists that Cædmon sing and even supplies the subject for the cowherd's first composition: 'frumsceaft' (Miller, 344.2) [the beginning of the world]. In response to the visitor's command, Cædmon produces his nine-line hymn to the Creator, in verses, Bede stresses, that the cowherd had 'næfre gehyrde' (Miller, 344.4) [never heard]. Word of Cædmon's sudden acquisition of the gift of song spreads to the local reeve, who promptly brings Cædmon to the abbess, and before her and an assembly of learned men, he recites the *Hymn*. Upon deciding that Cædmon is the recipient of a divine gift, the learned men read to him 'sum halig spell and godcundre lare word' (Miller, 344.25) [a certain holy narrative and words of divine teaching] and bid him 'gif he meahte, þæt he in swinsunge leoþsonges þæt gehwyrfde' (Miller, 344.26–27) [if he is able, to turn them into the harmony of song]. The next morning the cowherd returns, having turned the passages into the 'betstan leoðe' (Miller, 344.28) [best verse]. Shortly thereafter Cædmon enters monastic life and spends the rest of his days creating, Bede tells us, songs based upon the passages of sacred history that are read to him, although nothing but his first song survives. His songs do not just please Hild and the learned members of the monastery at Whitby but are vehicles through which Cædmon attempts to further the Church's work of conversion since he desires through his songs to lead men 'from synna lufan and mandæda, and to lufan and to geornfulnesse awehte godra dæda' (Miller, 346.16–17) [from the love of sins and evil deeds, and to stir them to love and to desire to do good deeds].

The narrative that frames Cædmon's *Hymn* is important because it contains one of the only contemporary accounts of vernacular poetic activity to survive from Anglo-Saxon England, but we must bear in mind that Bede includes it because it serves his doctrinal, and not anthropological or historical, purpose. In other words, while the poem and its surrounding narrative may be profitably mined for information about the vernacular poetic tradition in the late seventh and early eighth centuries, the evidence Bede offers must be approached with care since his main purpose in citing the story of Cædmon was not to provide future generations with a snapshot of the native poetic tradition but to situate vernacular poetry within sacred history. The subject matter of Cædmon's productions is what is important to Bede, not the means through which that subject matter is disseminated. That he provides us with a tantalizing, if brief, glimpse of the native tradition is simply a happy accident.

Tempting as it may be to see Cædmon as an oral poet, we must always be cautious in crediting Bede, or any other Anglo-Saxon author, with depicting actual cultural praxes. His narrative may well be an accurate account of Cædmon's compositional practices, and if this is so, then Cædmon stands in the company of artists from numerous oral traditions who do in fact compose their texts in private before performing them orally in public. It is also possible that Cædmon may have composed in the moment of performance and that Bede, who simply may not have understood this process, may have placed Cædmon within a template that was familiar to him as a way of coming to terms with a tradition very different from the learned, literate one in which Bede and his audience operated. And we must also consider the possibility that the cowherd is not a historical figure, but is merely a creation of Bede's.

Further Reading

Holsinger, Bruce, 'The parable of Caedmon's *Hymn*: liturgical invention and literary tradition'. *JEGP* 106 (2007): 149–75.

Kiernan, Kevin. 'Reading Cædmon's "Hymn" with someone else's glosses'. *Representations* 32 (1990): 157–74.

Lord, Albert Bates. 'Cædmon revisited'. In *Heroic Poetry in the Anglo-Saxon Period: Studies in Honor of Jess B. Bessinger, Jr.*, ed. Helen Damico and John Leyerle, 121–37. Studies in Medieval Culture 32. Kalamazoo: Medieval Institute Publications, 1993.

O'Brien O'Keeffe, Katherine. 'Orality and the developing text of Cædmon's *Hymn*'. In her *Visible Song: Transitional Literacy in Old English Verse*, 23–46. CSASE 4. Cambridge: Cambridge University Press, 1990.

O'Donnell, Daniel P. *Cædmon's Hymn: A Multimedia Study, Edition, and Archive.* Cambridge: D.S. Brewer in association with SEENET and The Medieval Academy, 2005.

Orchard, Andy. 'Poetic inspiration and prosaic translation: the making of *Cædmon's Hymn*'. In *Studies in English Language and Literature. 'Doubt Wisely': Papers in Honour of E.G. Stanley*, ed. M.J. Toswell and E.M. Tyler, 402–22. London: Routledge, 1996.

Bede's *Death Song*

Survives in twenty-nine manuscripts dating from the ninth to the sixteenth centuries.

The topic of the five-line poem that has long been known as Bede's *Death Song* – the judgement of the soul following its departure from this world – is a common one in OE poetry. The poem survives in the text of a Latin letter from Cuthbert, a student of Bede's, to Cuthwin, in which Cuthbert relates the rather hagiographic details of Bede's death. There is not much evidence, compelling or otherwise, establishing Bede as the creator of the *Death Song*. In his letter, Cuthbert claims that Bede produced the poem 'In our own language, – for he was familiar with English poetry' (Colgrave and Mynor, 581), but whether he was repeating a snatch of vernacular verse that he recalled from elsewhere or composed the poem himself remains far from clear. And, of course, we must also consider the possibility that the whole account of Bede's death, including the song, is the creation of Cuthbert, in much the same way that Bede's account of the cowherd Cædmon's acquisition of the gift of song may have been Bede's creation. Cuthbert does not offer a Latin paraphrase of the poem, as Bede claims to do with Cædmon's *Hymn*, but rather presents the poem in the vernacular. By doing so, he underscores the diglossic nature of Anglo-Saxon culture in the period and reminds us of the influence and important place that the mother tongue continued to have even for someone such as Bede, one of the period's most important and prolific authors of Latin texts.

The Anglo-Saxon Literature Handbook, First Edition. Mark C. Amodio.
© 2014 Mark C. Amodio. Published 2014 by John Wiley & Sons, Ltd.

Further Reading

Chickering, Howell D., Jr. 'Some contexts for Bede's *Death-Song*'. *PMLA* 91 (1976): 91–100.
Reichardt, Paul F. 'Bede on death and a neglected Old English lyric'. *Kentucky Philological Review* 12 (1997): 55–60.

The Junius Manuscript

Containing four poems based on Christian material, *Genesis*, *Exodus*, *Daniel*, and *Christ and Satan*, the Junius Manuscript has generally been dated to the late tenth or early eleventh century, although some now place it as early as the middle of the tenth century. Junius 11 preserves an illuminated poem, *Genesis*, and the codex's layout suggests that other of its poems were meant to be illuminated as well, though for unknown reasons the plan suggested by the layout was never brought to fruition. The manuscript contains two types of illuminations: line drawings illustrating narrative moments and large, ornate, capitals formed out of the bodies of various types of creatures. There are nearly fifty illustrations for the first poem, *Genesis*, and the ornate, zoomorphic capitals are used through the first seventy-three pages of the manuscript, after which plainer capitals come to be used almost exclusively. Although numerous, the illustrations in Junius 11 represent only about one-third of the illuminations that had been planned for the manuscript because it contains nearly ninety spaces, including a number of full pages, that were left blank to accommodate drawings. Why the plan to illuminate the manuscript was abandoned after only a portion of the planned illustrations were added is a question that has yet to be answered.

Four different manuscript hands are found in Junius 11: the first three poems, which all follow the same layout, were written by a single scribe while the final poem, *Christ and Satan*, was produced by three different hands. *Genesis*, *Exodus*, and *Daniel* are all generally thought to have been conceived as a unified group, with *Christ and Satan* being added to the codex at a later date. That *Christ and Satan* does not follow the layout of the other three poems – it contains no blank spots for illuminations – further

The Anglo-Saxon Literature Handbook, First Edition. Mark C. Amodio.
© 2014 Mark C. Amodio. Published 2014 by John Wiley & Sons, Ltd.

suggests that it was not part of the manuscript's original plan. The scribe who produced the last section of *Christ and Satan* evidently saw the contents of the manuscript as falling into two distinct parts, something that is witnessed by the Latin phrase in small capitals that he added following the conclusion of the poem on p. 229: FINIT LIBER II AMEN [the end of Book II Amen].

Further Reading

Hall, J.R. 'The Old English epic of redemption: the theological unity of MS Junius 11'. In *The Poems of MS Junius 11: Basic Readings*, ed. Roy M. Liuzza, 20–68. Basic Readings in Anglo-Saxon England 8. New York: Routledge, 2002.

Genesis

Written in a single scribal hand, the poem survives in a unique and illuminated copy in Oxford, Bodleian Library, Junius 11, pp. 1–142. There are several lacunae in the text owing to the loss of an unknown number of leaves and folios.

The poem that we have come to know as *Genesis* is, at 2936 lines, one of the longest poems to have survived from the Anglo-Saxon period, but if we had all the leaves and folios now missing from the manuscript, the poem likely would have been even longer than *Beowulf*. *Genesis* does not cover all the chapters of the Biblical book but only treats, and selectively at that, material drawn from Chapters 1 to 22, before concluding – or perhaps breaking off due to loss – with the testing of Abraham and his sacrifice of a ram after an angelic voice stops him from slaying his son Isaac. Much of *Genesis* reads as a rather literal paraphrase of the Biblical episodes it draws upon, but as is typical of the other OE prose and poetic texts with identified sources, *Genesis* does not always follow the Biblical account but rather on occasion departs, sometimes quite freely, from its source as it amplifies certain episodes and condenses or elides others. Part of the poem, specifically lines 235 to 851, however, are very unlike the surrounding narrative because they are derived from an Old Saxon account of the temptation and fall of Adam and Eve that was translated into OE and interpolated into the narrative at some point. Because this section differs sharply in style and substance from the rest of the poem, it is designated *Genesis B*, and the main narrative is designated *Genesis A*, a practice we follow below.

Genesis A

Rather than beginning with the creation of the heavens and earth, as in the Biblical book, *Genesis A* opens with several verses praising the Creator which in turn are followed by a section of nearly 100 lines in which the poet first comments on the beauty and contentment of the angelic hosts before rehearsing, in brief, the fall of the rebel angels. While the *Genesis A*-poet makes it clear that the fallen angels are renegades who deserve the harshest of punishments for turning away from the 'siblufan' (24b) [love such as exists between kinsmen] God had shown them, he, like his descendant John Milton, nevertheless allows their defiance to resonate heroically, if briefly, as when they remain true to their desire for a kingdom independent of God's even after God in his anger promises that they will be cast into the hell he newly created for them, a place 'synnihte beseald, susle geinnod, / geondfolen fyre and færcyle, / rece and reade lege' (42–44a) [surrounded by perpetual night, filled with torments, filled with fire and intense cold, smoke and red flame]. But unlike the fallen angels of *Paradise Lost*, those of *Genesis A* are not fleshed out in very much detail or at any great length; it is only under the hand of the *Genesis B*-poet that the rebel angels acquire any complexity and appear as more fully realized characters.

The *Genesis A*-poet begins his close paraphrase of the Biblical book on line 112 with the assertion that 'her ærest gesceop ece drihten, / helm eallwihta, heofon and eorðan' [here first created, the eternal lord, the protector of all creation, heaven and earth]. Not all the lines in *Genesis A* follow the Biblical account as closely as these do, but in general the poet remains true to the Biblical narrative's details while articulating them within the homogeneous poetics that characterizes OE vernacular poetry, as he does when he describes Cain after his killing of Abel as a 'wineleas wrecca' (1051a) [a friendless exile]. An important component of the traditional and widespread topos of exile, this phrase would have resonated powerfully in the minds of the poem's readers and listeners. The poet elsewhere employs the highly formulaic diction bequeathed him by the vernacular tradition when he refers to Cham and Sem, the sons of Noah, as 'hæleð hygerofe' (1550a) [brave warriors]. The fullest instantiations of traditional thematics are found in the battle scenes that occur near the poem's conclusion. For example, Abraham and the three chieftains who pledge their troth to him are described as 'Rincas ... rofe' (2049a) [valiant warriors] who bear their shields boldly as they march to meet their enemies, who are described as 'hildewulfas' (2051a) [battle-wolves]. The narrative of

the ensuing encounter would not be out of place in any piece of OE secular
heroic poetry:

> Þa ic neðan gefrægn under nihtscuwan
> hæleð to hilde. Hlyn wearþ on wicum
> scylda and sceafta, sceotendra fyll,
> guðflana gegrind; gripon unfægre
> under sceat werum scearpe garas,
> and feonda feorh feollon ðicce,
> þær hlihende huðe feredon
> secgas and gesiððas.
>
> (2060–67a)

[Then I heard that under the cover of darkness the warriors ventured into
battle. The roar of battle resounded in the camps, of shields and shafts, the fall
of warriors, the grinding together of war-arrows; sharp spears horribly gripped
them under their clothes and the lives of enemies fell thickly where the warriors
and companions went, exulting in the booty.]

But while the poet of *Genesis A* articulates his verse via the pathway of
Anglo-Saxon oral poetics, he does not rely on the traditional thematics of
his native poetics to the degree that other OE poets do. With the exception
of the poem's several battle scenes, the poet does not invoke very fully any of the
many typical scenes or traditional thematic structures found throughout
the extant OE poetic corpus. For example, while Cain, as we saw above, is
described as a 'wretched exile', the remainder of the topos of exile, a powerful
and widely attested one, is left largely unarticulated. Similarly, in the section
on Noah, the narrative contains several of the key components of what is
known as the theme of the beasts of battle, but they do not coalesce into an
instantiation of this theme. A second occurrence of this theme is also very
underdeveloped, containing as it does only a mention of 'nefuglas' (2159b)
[birds of prey] who 'blodige sittað, / þeodherga wæle þicce gefylled' (2060b–61)
[sit bloody, with the corpses of the army lying thick on the ground].

Genesis B

Although the section of *Genesis* known as *Genesis B* is not based on a Latin
version of the Bible but on an Old Saxon poem, there is nothing in the way
it is encoded onto the pages of the manuscript that distinguishes it in any
way from the poem into which it was at some point interpolated. The
beginning of *Genesis B* is lost to another lacuna in the manuscript caused by
a missing leaf or leaves, but from the way the scribe marks its ending near the
right margin of line eight on page 41 (by a *punctus* similar to all the others

he places in the manuscript) before immediately resuming *Genesis A*, we can see that he treats the two narratives as a single entity. Why and when *Genesis A* was supplemented with material derived from an Old Saxon (OS) source remain, and are likely to remain, unanswered questions.

Even if we did not have the evidence of the formal features that establish the OS origins of *Genesis B*, there are many narrative signs within the poem that point both to its descent from a source very different from that of the surrounding narrative and to its also being the product of a poetic sensibility very different from that responsible for *Genesis A*. Whereas *Genesis A* on the whole rather closely paraphrases the material contained in the Bible, *Genesis B* departs frequently and sometimes quite markedly from the Biblical account. In addition, the characters in *Genesis B* are also far more fully realized than are their counterparts in *Genesis A*: when Adam and Eve appear in *Genesis A*, their speeches adhere closely to those in the Biblical account and are short and rather flat, unlike their speeches in *Genesis B*. Since *Genesis A* breaks off during the Creation and since the fallen angels only appear in *Genesis B* (the preface to *Genesis A* recapitulates the fall of the angels only in general terms), we do not have the luxury of comparing the ways the two narratives present them, but as is the case with Adam and Eve, the fallen angels of *Genesis B* are developed far more extensively than any of *Genesis A*'s characters.

Following a manuscript lacuna, this one between pages 12 and 13, the narrative of *Genesis B* begins in the middle of God's telling Adam and Eve that they should enjoy all the trees found in Paradise, with the exception of 'þone ænne beam' (235b) [that one tree], a tree that the poet will explicitly label a 'deaðbeam' [tree of death] when Eve brings its fruit to Adam. The poem then shifts to a rather lengthy and intriguing account of the angelic rebellion, casting it in terms of the bond between a lord and his servant, a bond critical to all aspects of Anglo-Saxon culture, and one upon which the structure of the comitatus [war-band] depended heavily. God creates the angels within a strictly hierarchal framework, setting them out in ten ranks and trusting that they will repay him for the gifts he gives them with the 'giongorscipe' (249a) [service] that is expected of the warriors in a comitatus. One angel, whose strength, beauty, and power is second only to God's finds such service onerous because he judges himself to be equal, if not superior, to God in many ways: his body is 'leoht and scene' (265b) [bright and shining] and it seems to him that he commands a host of warriors that is greater than God's. In his first direct speech in the poem, this angel announces that he has the power to create a more powerful throne (but it is not clear whether the comparand here is God's throne or the throne that God established for his second-in-command) and also reveals that he wants no longer to be subordinate to God, although for him this does not necessarily entail overthrowing God's rule. The angel asserts that he 'mæg wesan god swa he' (283b) [can be a god as he is] and, in what might be his most damning assertions, claims both that 'Nis me wihtæ þearf / herran to habbanne' (278b–79a) [there is no need at all for me to have a lord] and that he 'Ne wille ... leng his geongra wurþan' (291b) [will no ... longer be his servant]. The fallen angel's comrades are 'strange geneatas' (284a) [strong retainers], 'hæleþas heardmode' (285) [brave-minded warriors], and 'rofe rincas' (286a) [strong warriors] who must find the rebel angel's plan to establish another kingdom attractive since they all follow him willingly: 'Hie habbað me to hearran gecorene' (285b) [they have chosen me as their lord]. This plan is never effected, however, since once God hears of it, he moves swiftly and throws the rebel angel into hell, where he is turned into a devil along with all his companions. It is only when the rebel angel is firmly chained in hell that God renames him Satan, his heavenly name being never uttered in the poem. While this depiction of the fall of the angels remains true to the narrative's traditional doctrinal focus, it speaks as well directly to an important political and cultural matter because God, like an earthly lord, expects his gifts to be repaid with loyalty since the system upon which the idea of the comitatus depends is reciprocal: the lord gives gifts and the warriors pay him back by standing with him in his time of need.

Although it reflects the cultural concerns of the early Germanic world, the fall of the angels in *Genesis B* nevertheless remains close in many of its particulars to the narrative's traditional contours. In contrast, the narrative of Adam and Eve's fall in *Genesis B* is anything but traditional, and contains many unique, and at times startling, details. To begin, Satan does not tempt Adam and Eve directly, but because he is so thoroughly bound by chains in hell, a detail the illuminator depicts on page 20, he must seek a volunteer to undertake the mission for him. The devil who accepts the challenge prepares himself by donning a 'hæleðhelm' (444a) [helmet of concealment], which he can be seen wearing in the illumination on page 24. He relies on his strength to hold the fires at bay as he passes out of hell through what seems to be a hatch. Upon his arrival in Eden, the fiend transforms himself into a snake and, after plucking a fruit from 'þone deaðes beam' (491a) [the tree of death], first approaches Adam, not Eve. The rhetorical tack the demon takes is non-traditional as well: rather than extolling the virtues of the fruit, he begins by asking Adam if he lacks anything he desires. After claiming, perhaps truthfully enough, to have been in the divine presence 'nu fyrn ne' (498b) [not long ago], the demon reveals what Adam stands to gain from eating the fruit, but only after claiming that he offers the fruit because God commanded that he bring it to Adam. Adam rejects the demon's argument, confident that he 'wat hwæt he me self bebead' (535b) [knows what [God] himself commanded me] and, perhaps more importantly, because the messenger 'gelic ne bist / ænegum his engla þe ic ær geseah' (538b–39) [is not like any of his angels I have earlier seen].

In his temptation of Eve, the fallen angel once again adopts a rhetorical strategy that is both unique to *Genesis B* and that would have resonated powerfully with an Anglo-Saxon audience: rather than tempting Eve along the traditional lines (with the beauty of the fruit or with the powers that attend eating it), he urges her rather to consider eating it as a way of lessening the punishment she and Adam stand to receive for Adam's having disobeyed the 'new' divine injunction the fallen angel has just delivered. It is only after he reveals that she has the power to 'wite bewarigan' (563a) [protect from punishment] both herself and Adam that he turns to the fruit's bene-fits: not only will her vision clarify to the extent that she will be able to see what God sees, but she will also henceforth have his favour. The tempter also obliquely promises Eve power over Adam, telling her that she will be able to lead him and later he tells them that he will protect them by concealing Adam's 'yfel andwyrde' (573a) [evil response] from God. He concludes his temptation by acknowledging, truthfully enough, that he knows well the environs of heaven, that he himself had 'geornlice gode þegnode / ... / drihtne selfum' (585b–87a) [eagerly served God ... the lord himself], and, finally, that he 'ne eom ... deofle gelic' (587b) [is not ... like a devil]. This final com-ment of his may well just be a lie, but while the fallen angel assumes the shape of a snake when he speaks with Adam, it is not clear that he retains that shape when talking to Eve. Eve offers conflicting evidence regarding her interlocutor's appearance, and the text itself also admits the possibility that the fallen angel is not in the shape of a snake when he talks to her. Further complicating matters, the illustrator presents the fallen angel as both a snake and an angel during his tempation of Eve: of the five illustrations that accompany Adam and Eve's fall, it is only the first one, found on page 20, that follows the Biblical account by depicting the fallen angel as a snake when he addresses Eve; in the others he is in human form, albeit in the one in the lower register of page 31 he has a clearly visible tail. That Eve finds her interlocutor's appearance unremarkable and that she later tells Adam that the visitor's garments signify that 'he is ærendsecg uncres herran / hefoncyninges' (658–59a) [he is a messenger of our lord, of the king of heaven] suggest that he did not come to her as a snake; only after the narrative of *Genesis A* resumes does Eve identify the tempter both as a 'nædre' (897a) [snake] and as a 'fah wyrm' (899a) [accursed – and perhaps variegated – serpent].

The possibility that the fallen angel reverted to a more angelic form before approaching Eve complicates the poet's apparently straightforward explanation of why the tempter succeeds with her after having failed with Adam: 'hæfde hire wacran hige / metod gemearcod' (590b–91a) [the lord had appointed to her a weaker mind]. The extreme otherness of the talking snake allows Adam, with unassailable logic, to reject it as being unlike any angel he had ever seen. But the tempter may well appear angelic to Eve's eyes because, like the Satan of *Paradise Lost*, he may have 'not yet lost / All [his] original brightness' (Hughes, I.591–92). Adam's unreflective obedience and myopia effectively shield him from the tempter's arguments, but one wonders what result might have obtained had the tempter chosen a form that more closely approximated that which Adam expects angels to possess. The phrase 'wacran hige' is also problematic. Even allowing for its overt misogynism, the phrase proves to be rather slippery since its comparand is never articulated. Is Eve's mind weaker than God's, Adam's, the tempter's? There is no Biblical basis for so characterizing Eve's mind, but as the narrative of the fall developed over the centuries, Eve's weakness came to bear more and more weight for the events that transpired in Eden. And in a somewhat paradoxical vein, the poet will later explain that Eve did what she did 'þurh holdne hyge' (708a) [with a loyal, gracious mind].

Genesis B's treatment of the fall of Adam and Eve contains several other unique aspects: following her eating of the apple, the tempter makes good on his promise and grants Eve the ability to see beyond the limits of her human perception so that heaven and earth seem 'hwitre' (603b) [brighter] to her and all the world 'wlitigre' (604a) [more beautiful]. The poet, who in the metacommentary he sprinkles throughout the episode never strays from the doctrinal point of view, is careful to note that Eve is able to do this through a 'laðan læn' (601a) [hateful gift]. When Eve goes to tempt Adam, she does not do so alone, but in the company of the tempter, who stays for the duration of Adam's temptation, a temptation that takes place over the course of an entire day. And finally, once Adam eats the apple, the tempter returns to Satan, who remains chained in hell throughout this episode, to report on his success.

Further Reading

Dockray-Miller, Mary. 'Breasts and babies: the maternal body of Eve in the Junius *Genesis*'. In *Naked before God: Uncovering the Body in Anglo-Saxon England*, ed. Benjamin C. Withers and Jonathan Wilcox, 221–56. Morgantown: West Virginia University Press, 2003.

Jager, Eric. 'Tempter as rhetoric teacher: the fall of language in the Old English *Genesis B*'. In *The Poems of MS Junius 11: Basic Readings*, ed. Roy M. Liuzza, 99–118. Basic Readings in Anglo-Saxon England 8. London: Routledge, 2002.

Karkov, Catherine E. 'The Anglo-Saxon *Genesis*: text, illustration, and audience'. In *The Old English Hexateuch: Aspects and Approaches*, ed. Rebecca Barnhouse and Benjamin C. Withers, 201–37. Publications of the Rawlinson Center 2. Kalamazoo: Medieval Institute Publications, 2000.

Mintz, Susannah B. 'Words devilish and divine: Eve as speaker in *Genesis B*'. *Neophilologus* 81 (1997): 609–23.

Orchard, Andy. 'Intoxication, fornication, and multiplication: the burgeoning text of *Genesis A*'. In *Text, Image, Interpretation: Studies in Anglo-Saxon Literature and Its Insular Context in Honour of Éamon Ó Carragáin*, ed. A.J. Minnis and Jane Roberts, 333–54. Studies in the Early Middle Ages 18. Turnhout: Brepols, 2007.

Remley, Paul G. 'The Biblical sources of *Genesis A* and *B*'. In his *Old English Biblical Verse: Studies in 'Genesis', 'Exodus' and 'Daniel'*, 94–167. Cambridge: Cambridge University Press, 1996.

Renoir, Alain. 'Eve's I.Q. rating: two sexist views of *Genesis B*'. In *New Readings on Women in Old English Literature*, ed. Helen Damico and Alexandra Hennessey Olsen, 262–72. Bloomington: Indiana University Press, 1990.

Wright, Charles D. '*Genesis A* ad litteram'. In *Old English Literature and the Old Testament*, ed. Michael Fox and Manish Sharma, 121–71. Toronto Anglo-Saxon Series 10. Toronto: University of Toronto Press, 2012.

Exodus

Survives uniquely in Oxford, Bodleian Library, MS Junius 11, pp. 143–71. There are two lacunae in the text, caused by the loss of perhaps as many as six manuscript pages.

Exodus follows *Genesis* in Junius 11, just as it does in the Bible. Written by the same scribe responsible for the poems that respectively precede and follow it, *Genesis* and *Daniel*, *Exodus* is laid out according to the same plan they are. Unlike the partially illuminated *Genesis*, *Exodus* contains only one zoomorphic capital, the *h* of 'hwæt,' the poem's first word. The poem was laid out with space left blank to accommodate other zoomorphic capitals that were never added. Beginning with the capital on page 156 and continuing for the remainder of the poem, the capitals are simply enlarged versions of regular letters. Whether the scribe who wrote the text or a later hand added the simple capitals is not clear, and it is also not clear why whoever added them failed to do so in the spaces left for capitals on pages 146, 148, and 149. No illustrations accompany the poem, but as is the case with *Genesis* and *Daniel*, *Exodus* contains numerous spaces and some seven whole pages that apparently were meant to contain illuminations.

Exodus covers only a small portion of the material contained in its Biblical source. Drawing mostly from Exodus 12–15, the poem touches briefly on only one of the plagues of Egypt before recounting the Israelites' flight from Egypt, their crossing of the Red Sea, and the destruction of the Pharaoh and his army. While *Exodus* follows the events of the Biblical narrative, the poem is not a straightforward paraphrase in the manner of *Genesis A*; rather, the *Exodus*-poet crafts the Biblical material into a work of verbal art that everywhere bears the impress of his own extraordinary artistic sensibility. His treatments of the tenth plague and the pillars of cloud and fire that lead and protect the Israelites during their flight out of Egypt well illustrate how he freely reshapes his inherited material. The death of the Egyptians' first-born sons is the last of ten plagues visited upon Egypt, and it is the event that enables the Israelites to escape from captivity and begin their journey to the land that God had promised would be theirs. The Biblical narrative focuses heavily on the instructions the Israelites were given to place a sign on their door frames so that their first-born would be spared, but the *Exodus*-poet omits this entirely. The death of the first-born, in contrast, is related vividly by the poet, who labels the angel who kills them a 'leodhata' (40a) [tyrant; persecutor] and a 'bana' (39b) [slayer] and who tells us that for the Egyptians, 'heaf wæs geniwad, / swæfon seledreamas' (35b–36a) [lamentation was renewed, the joys of the hall died] as the 'land drysmyde / deadra hræwum' (40b–41a) [land was choked with the corpses of the dead]. In the Bible, Pharaoh and his officials take up the pursuit of the Israelites because they wish to return them to servitude but in the hands of the *Exodus*-poet, the Egyptians' pursuit is put rather into terms that the Anglo-Saxon audience would have understood deeply and immediately: vengeance. The Egyptian forces in *Exodus* pursue the Israelites eagerly and relentlessly not to recapture escaping slaves but to kill the Israelites 'on hyra broðorgyld' (199a) [as repayment for slain brothers]. What makes this moment even more revealing of the *Exodus*-poet's artistry is that the term 'broðorgyld' is a *hapax legomenon*, a lexeme that occurs only one time in the written records that have survived from Anglo-Saxon England. Not only does the poet recast the episode so that it conforms to his and his audience's cultural world, he coins a compound that speaks to the heart of the matter: no longer slave masters who belatedly realize that freeing their captives was a mistake, the Egyptians are driven by the desire to avenge the death of their kinsmen with blood, a desire central to the feud cultures of the early Germanic world.

The pillars of cloud and fire that appear in Exodus also play an important role in the narrative of *Exodus*, but as with the tenth plague, the poet uses the Biblical account not as a model to be slavishly followed but rather as a springboard for his imagination. The Bible tells us that God sends a pillar of cloud to lead the Israelites by day and a pillar of fire to lead them by night.

In addition, when the Israelites are trapped between the Red Sea and the advancing Egyptian army, the pillar of cloud moves between the two forces and keeps them separate throughout the night. While the *Exodus*-poet follows his source in this instance, he develops these fantastic pillars to a greater extent than does the Bible. The pillar of cloud is sent not just to guide the people during the day, but to protect them from the 'byrnendne heofon' (73b) [burning sky] and the 'hate heofontorht' (78a) [heaven-bright heat] that threatens to destroy them as they move across the desert. In an extended metaphorical passage (itself a rarity in OE poetry), the cloud is variously described as a 'bælce' (73a) [canopy; covering], a 'halgan nette' (74a) [holy net], and a 'segle' (81b) [a sail]. And in a manoeuvre that displays the poet's sense of narrative balance and his talent for crafting unique compounds, the pillar of fire's functions parallel those of the pillar of cloud: it guides the Israelites by night and protects them from being slain by 'westengryre' (117b) [terror inspired by the wilderness].

One of the poem's most notable features is the degree to which its Biblical narrative material is articulated within the vernacular heroic tradition. This tradition's presence is announced in the poem's first word, the interjection 'Hwæt'. Elsewhere, the scene in which the Egyptian army approaches the Israelites camped on the shore of the Red Sea, stressing as it does the forest of spears and banners they bear, the shields glinting in the sun, and the noise of trumpets, relies heavily on compositional elements drawn directly from the heroic tradition. Not only are the Israelites thrown into despair by the sight of the approaching army, but the presence of 'herefugolas' (162a) [battle-birds] who are greedy for the fight and wolves who sing their 'atol æfenleoð' (165a) [terrible evening song] in expectation of the feast they will enjoy following the battle further intensifies the scene's affective dynamics because they point, economically and powerfully, to imminent bloodshed. Other scenes similarly are articulated within the register of traditional oral poetics, as for example, when Moses is introduced not only as the wise and prudent elder dear to God, but as the 'leoda aldor' (12b) [chief of the people], the 'herges wisa' (13b) [leader of the army], and the 'freom folctoga' (14a) [bold leader of the people], terms more appropriate to a warrior than a holy man. In a similar vein, the Israelites are not depicted as a defenceless band, but are described as a 'wiglic werod' (233a) [a war-like host]. Moses commands trumpets to be sounded to gather the people and the soldiers among them to put on their coats of mail and set their minds on courageous deeds. Before he begins the speech in which he will exhort his troops, Moses, the 'hildecalla' (252b) [battle-herald], 'bord up ahof' (253b) [raised up his shield].

As happens elsewhere in the corpus of OE vernacular poetry, articulating events from sacred history within the tradition of heroic verse on occasion leads to incongruous narrative moments: if the image of Moses raising his shield and addressing his troops as if they were Germanic warriors preparing to face a deadly foe is not jarring enough, we can always contemplate the way in which the force at the front of the assembled Israelites, those warriors hardened in hand-to-hand combat, the brave warriors unafraid of the carnage created by weapons or bloody sword wounds proudly and courageously lead the Israelites *away* from, not towards, an armed engagement with the Egyptians. But while these and similar moments may seem decidedly odd to our narrative sensibilities, they may have been received very differently by the poem's intended audience, one steeped in the expressive economy of oral poetics in ways that we can never be.

Narratively, *Exodus* everywhere bears the stamp of the intriguing and highly individualistic poetic mind responsible for its creation. Even on the level of the poem's language, we can see ample evidence of the poet's artistry since the poem contains an unusually high percentage of words and compounds that are recorded nowhere else in OE poetry or prose. In addition to filtering his inherited Biblical material through the lens of the Anglo-Saxon heroic ethos, the *Exodus*-poet also sharply diverges from the Biblical narrative by inserting into the story of the exodus a passage of nearly 100 lines in which he touches briefly on Noah and then offers a somewhat full account of the Abraham and Isaac story. The shift away from the exodus out of Egypt is rather abrupt, but just because such a shift strikes our narrative sensibilities as odd, there is little reason to assume that the stories of Noah and Abraham and Isaac are interpolations. In stressing as they do the covenants God makes – and keeps – with the Israelites, the narratives of Noah and Abraham link thematically with the larger narrative of the exodus.

The narrative structure of *Exodus*'s closing sections has, like the Noah and Abraham sections, been viewed as problematic, so much so that some of its editors have proposed rearranging its sections, despite there being no evidence in the manuscript to suggest that the concluding lines (516 to 590) were corrupted either when they were copied or when the gatherings were bound together to form the current codex. On the fifth line of page 169, the text moves without interruption from a standard phrase condemning the Egyptians for being God's enemies ('Hie wið god wunnon') (515b) [they fought against God] to the 'halige spræce, / deop ærende' (518b–19a) [holy speech, the deep message] Moses offers the Israelites once they have safely traversed the Red Sea. As with the shift to the stories of Noah and Abraham, the narrative here moves abruptly from the destruction of the Pharoah and his forces, a destruction that is rendered in sharp and powerfully articulated detail, to the generalized homiletic observations Moses offers on the transitory nature of the joys of this life and the everlasting ones that await the righteous.

We need not, however, reach far to justify this turn in the narrative, since it seems entirely fitting for Moses to temper the joy the Israelites must feel at the destruction of Pharaoh and his forces with a firm reminder of this world's ephemerality. Moses then continues in a different vein and assures the Israelites that if they follow the path of righteousness, God will keep his covenant with them and will enable them to overrun each of their enemies and inhabit the 'sigerice' (563a) [victorious realm] they had been promised.

In themselves, the homiletic passages are not puzzling; rather it is their apparent disruption of the narrative's flow that has led them to be so viewed because rather than concluding with them, as we might expect, the poem instead returns to the jubiliation of the Israelites, who are once again described with a military term, 'werod' (565b) [army], and who celebrate by uttering 'hildespelle' (574a) [war-like speech] and singing a 'fyrdleoð' (578b) [war-song], before concluding with the Israelites plundering the corpses of the Egyptians that have washed up on the shore. As he has done throughout, the poet here deploys the expressive economy of heroic poetry (the celebration is accompanied by the noise of trumpets and the raising of banners), the register with which the entire poem is so deeply infused. The starkness and immediacy of the striking final images are also in line with the images the poet employs throughout the narrative. While we must acknowledge that the poem may have been mistakenly or faultily copied on the pages of the Junius 11, the poem as it survives may also reflect the *Exodus*-poet's artistic vision for his retelling of the Biblical narrative. If the latter is the case, then the 'problem' lies not with the poem, but with our contemporary interpretive strategies.

Further Reading

Earl, James W. 'Christian tradition in the Old English *Exodus*'. In *The Poems of MS Junius 11: Basic Readings*, ed. Roy M. Liuzza, 137–72. Basic Readings in Anglo-Saxon England 8. New York: Routledge, 2002.

Lapidge, Michael. 'Versifying the Bible in the Middle Ages'. In *The Text in the Community: Essays on Medieval Works, Manuscripts, Authors and Readers*, ed. Jill Mann and Maura Nolan, 11–40. Notre Dame: University of Notre Dame Press, 2006.

Portnoy, Phyllis, 'Ring composition and the digressions of *Exodus*: the "Legacy" of the "Remnant"'. *ES* 82 (2001): 289–307.

Remley, Paul G. '*Exodus* and the liturgy of baptism'. In his *Old English Biblical Verse: Studies in 'Genesis', 'Exodus', and 'Daniel'*, 168–230. Cambridge: Cambridge University Press, 1996.

Savage, Anne. 'The Old English *Exodus* and the colonization of the Promised Land'. *New Medieval Literatures* 4 (2001): 39–60.

Daniel

Survives in a unique copy in Oxford, Bodleian Libarary, MS Junius 11, pp. 173–212.

From its numerous blank spaces and pages, more than thirty in all, it is apparent that *Daniel* was intended to be the third illustrated poem in the Junius 11 codex. There are no zoomorphic capitals in *Daniel* and no space is left blank for them: the capitals that appear in the manuscript are the sort of simple, enlarged ones that begin to appear part way through *Genesis* and that appear exclusively in *Exodus*, with the exception of the zoomorphic capital with which that poem begins. There is a lacuna in *Daniel* caused by the loss of a single manuscript page, although whether the poem is complete as we have it or ends where and how it does because the manuscript is missing a leaf or perhaps several leaves following page 212, remains an open question.

Like the two poems that precede it, *Daniel* utilizes only a portion of its Biblical source, in this case the first five books of Daniel, which treat the Israelites' falling into sin, their conquest by the Babylonians, and the reigns – and deaths – of the Babylonian kings Nebuchadnezzar and his son, Belshazzar. The *Daniel*-poet makes no attempt to present all the episodes contained in the first five books of Daniel, choosing rather to concentrate heavily on Book 3, in which Daniel does not even figure. So far as its treatment of its source material is concerned, *Daniel* occupies a position somewhere between that of *Genesis A*, a very close paraphrase, and of *Exodus*, a freely supplemented account. Although the first three poems in Junius 11 are devoted to recounting and so aiding the spread of Christian doctrine, *Daniel* is perhaps the most overtly didactic of them: the sinful behaviour it details is always corrected swiftly, harshly, and on occasion, fatally. For example, the Israelites turn away from the teachings of God and shortly thereafter Nebuchadnezzar attacks Jerusalem, plunders the temple of Solomon, and takes the Israelites to Babylon where he forces them into captivity. The poem's didacticism has an immediacy that the other two Old Testament poems in Junius 11 lack because on several occasions the poet employs the first-person singular pronoun 'ic' [I] in order to exploit the affective dynamics attendant upon moments when a speaker directly addresses his or her listening audience. He employs this strategy effectively in the prayer for divine assistance Azarias utters from within a furnace and in the song of celebration he and the other two youths offer following their rescue from the furnace by an angel.

Although he follows his Biblical source closely in many instances, the *Daniel*-poet often reshapes rather than paraphrases his inherited material.

This is especially apparent in the first half of the poem, where he greatly reduces the role that Daniel plays, elides the details of Nebuchadnezzar's first dream, and dilates the scene in which an angelic protector arrives to save three wise Israelites – Azarias, Ananias, and Misahel – from the flames of the furnace into which Nebuchadnezzar has them thrown after they refuse to worship a golden idol. The *Daniel*-poet draws upon the Biblical account for the episode's salient details, which include the king's anger, his commanding that the fire be far greater than a normal fire, the death of many Babylonians when the fire spills out of the furnace, the presence of an angel sent by God to protect the three youths, and their stepping unharmed out of the flames. But even when he works closely with the narrative framework of his source, he nevertheless leaves his own imprint upon the material. We can see his hand in the deployment of the term 'bolgenmod' [enraged; swollen with anger] – a component of the expressive economy of Anglo-Saxon oral poetics that points to an imminent slaughterous encounter – to characterize the king's excessive anger and, further, in the attention he gives both to the fire that is built and to the sudden and terrible deaths of the Babylonian servants who stoke the furnace's flames.

As is true of *Exodus*, *Daniel* contains several significant narrative incongruities, including most importantly the rescue of the three youths from the furnace, an episode which takes up a disproportionately large percentage of the poem's 774 lines. The episode does have some puzzling features, containing as it does two long homiletic passages that are stylistically disjunct from the surrounding narrative and a repetition of the youths' rescue from the furnace. Additionally, the prayer Azarias offers requesting God to deliver them from the peril of the furnace is uttered *after* they have already been saved. While granting that the narrative trajectory of *Daniel* is unusual in this episode, especially when the youths are rescued and then immediately resuced again, there are several reasons for attributing the passage to the *Daniel*-poet and not to the hand of an interpolator. Deriving perhaps from the Vulgate, which contains both the Prayer of Azarias and the Song of the Three Youths, as the homiletic lyrics that appear in the poem are known, the homiletic passages stand as logical extensions of the poem's didacticism. Both the Prayer of Azarias, which has many points of contact with the Exeter Book poem *Azarias*, and the Song of the Three Youths afford the *Daniel*-poet the opportunity to impart highly devotional material directly to his audience in the voice of a cleric addressing a congregation. He may figuratively grind his gears somewhat here by departing from his usual practice of allowing his message to get across without any meta-textual commentary, but the step from delivering an implicitly devotional message, as when he condemns the drunken and disrepectful behaviour of Nebuchadnezzar's son Belshazzar, to offering an explicit one is small indeed.

We cannot know for certain which version of the Bible the poet used as his source, but the Vulgate, to which he may have had access, provides some clues to the poem's puzzling narrative trajectory since in it the youths are also spared twice, first by divine grace and then, following the Prayer of Azarias, by angelic intervention. The first appearance of the angel in *Daniel*, for which there is no precedent in the source, remains problematic, but it is a problem that ultimately may be rooted in an unrecoverable aesthetic decision of the poet's. The placement of Azarias's prayer after the youths' rescue may also be attributable to the source. In the Vulgate, God acts, unbidden, to protect the youths the moment they are thrown, tightly bound, into the furnace by having the flames surge over them and onto the Babylonians who stoke it; the Anglo-Saxon poet follows this pattern but for some reason has the angel initially intervene, not God. Acknowledging and accepting the poet's hand in the narrative's construction at this point does not, of course, explain the repetition or remove any of its awkwardness, and since we know so little about the composition and transmission of OE vernacular verse, we are left with, among others, the following unanswerable questions: Should the repetition be attributed to an error or some sort of aesthetic failure on the poet's part? What role, if any, do the affective dynamics of the scenes in which the heroes are twice rescued and their foes twice put to grisly deaths play? Was the scene repeated in the version that the copyist used? And, finally, how great was the Biblical source's influence and was that source the Vulgate?

The ending of *Daniel* poses a further problem since it is not clear whether the poem comes to its planned conclusion or ends defectively owing to the loss of its final page or pages. The poem's final episode, in which an angelic hand appears and writes on the wall of King Belshazzar's hall 'worda gerynu / baswe bocstafas' (722b–723a) [the mystery of words in enigmatic crimson characters] that no one but Daniel can understand, may be complete as we have it: Daniel doesn't reveal either the meanings of the words or the king's fate, but the narrative context for this episode, a drunken feast in which the Babylonians scandalously misuse the 'huslfatu halegu' (704a) [holy sacrificial vessels] they aquired when they pillaged Jerusalem by drinking toasts to devils, strongly suggests that Belshazzar will be punished severely for his prideful, blasphemous behaviour, just as his father Nebuchadnezzar was before finally seeing the light and converting. The poem may also end where it does because a page or more of it has gone missing. An audience familiar with the stories of the Babylonian kings from the book of Daniel or elsewhere would know that Daniel goes on to reveal that the cryptic words of the angel announce that Belshazzar has been found wanting in God's sight, that his kingdom's days have reached their end, and that his land will be divided. But given the poet's earlier practice of carefully balancing sinful behaviour with that behaviour's correction, the story of Daniel and Belshazzar as we have it seems truncated, especially when we consider the much fuller treatment that it receives in the Bible, where the words the angelic hand writes on the wall are not just alluded to, as in *Daniel*, but are reported and carefully explained by the prophet. The abruptness of the poem's ending, the implicit, rather than explicit, nature of its message, the omission of the cryptic words central to the episode, and the failure to present both Daniel's interpretation of the words and the death of the king all point towards the poem's incomplete state. But as we noted earlier, whether the poem concludes or simply stops on page 212 remains an open question, one that, barring the discovery of new evidence, seems likely to remain unresolved.

Further Reading

Anderson, Earl R. 'Style and theme in the Old English *Daniel*'. ES 68 (1987): 1–23.
Bugge, John, 'Virginity and prophecy in the Old English *Daniel*'. ES 87 (2006): 127–47.
George, J.-A. '"Hwalas þec herigað": creation, closure and the *Hapax Legomena* of the OE *Daniel*'. In *Lexis and Texts in Early English: Studies Presented to Jane Roberts*, ed. Christian J. Kay and Louise M. Sylvester, 105–16. Costerus ns 133. Amsterdam: Rodopi, 2001.
Lerer, Seth. 'Poet of the *boceras*: literacy and power in the Old English *Daniel*'. In his *Literacy and Power in Anglo-Saxon Literature*, 126–57. Lincoln: University of Nebraska Press, 1991.
Remley, Paul G. '*Daniel* and Greek scriptural tradition'. In his *Old English Biblical Verse: Studies in Genesis, Exodus, and Daniel*, 231–33. Cambridge: Cambridge University Press, 1996.

Christ and Satan

Survives uniquely in Oxford, Bodleian Library, MS Junius 11, pp. 213–29.

Christ and Satan, the name given to the final poem in the Junius Manuscript, has little in common with the three poems that precede it in Junius 11 beyond its focus on Christian doctrine. *Genesis*, *Exodus*, and *Daniel* are all the product of a single scribal hand, and although these poems were produced by poets with very different artistic sensibilities and capabilities, they are all based, sometimes very closely, on material found in the Old

Testament. Further, all three poems share the same design features as they were meant to be illustrated in the way that the first half of *Genesis*, the only poem with accompanying illustrations, is. *Christ and Satan*, in contrast appears to have been a later addition to the codex: it is the work of three other scribal hands; no source, Biblical or otherwise, has yet been discovered for it; and its format suggests that it was not intended to be extensively illustrated. *Christ and Satan* has only two pages that are not filled entirely by text: the last one, page 229, and page 225. The space below the poem's conclusion is left blank, but since the bottom third of page 225 is filled not with an illustration but rather with a line drawing of a geometric pattern that may be a design for the codex's original cover, we cannot say for certain that either space was meant to accommodate a drawing. *Christ and Satan* also contains, with one exception, modestly sized and simple capital letters that do not have as much space dedicated to them as do the decorative capitals in the first three poems (they are only slightly larger than the rest of the lettering and they are fitted into small indentations). The only decorative touch in the poem is a single zoomorphic capital that appears near the end of the poem, on the bottom of page 226.

Unlike the other poems in the codex, *Christ and Satan* is not a close or free paraphrase of Biblical material, but rather treats in what appear to be discrete, if unmarked, sections three moments from sacred history. The poem opens with a very brief account of the creation and the fall of the rebel angels before devoting the majority of its first, and longest section to the lamentations of Satan in hell. The second section recounts the harrowing of hell, in part from the perspective of the fallen angels. In the third and shortest section, the poet offers a somewhat idiosyncratic treatment of Christ's temptation in the desert by Satan. Although non-Biblical, the matter of *Christ and Satan* fits well with the subject matter of the other Junius 11 poems, completing as it does the thematic cycle begun by *Genesis* by presenting another version of the fall followed by Christ's harrowing of hell. *Christ and Satan* further complements (and perhaps complicates) the thematics of the other Junius poems by linking the Old Testament material to that of the New Testament through the figure of Christ, who figures directly not just in the narrative of the harrowing of hell but, somewhat surprisingly, in the narrative of the fallen angel's expulsion. The narrator ascribes to Christ the expulsion of the fallen angels, and although the narrator and Satan acknowledge God's presence, both several times place Christ, not his father, at the centre of power, as Satan does when he credits the son with 'alles gewald' (117b) [power over all] and when he later notes that in heaven the son was surrounded by 'eadige bearn ealle' (143) [all the blessed children]. *Christ and Satan*'s many formal and narrative departures from the other poems in Junius 11, along with the comment, 'Finit Liber II. Amen' [here ends book II. Amen], appended after the poem's final verse, serve to distinguish it further from the first three poems in Junius 11 which in the scribe's eyes may have comprised Liber I.

Christ and Satan's moral compass is both conventional and predictable: 'oferhygd' [pride] is the cause of the angels' fall from heaven and unlike the Satan of *Genesis B*, who wishes only to establish a separate realm for himself, the Satan of *Christ and Satan*, who painfully speaks in an 'eisegan stefne' (36a) [a horrible voice], more conventionally desires to 'towerpan' (85a) [overthrow] the son and take control for himself of 'burga ... / eall' (86b–87a) [all the cities]. The poem also contains numerous passages in which the poet underscores the moral lessons he is imparting by directly exhorting the poem's reading and/or listening audience to live their lives according to Christian principles, as he does, for example, at lines 200b and following:

> Gemunan we þone halgan drihten,
> ecne in wuldre mid alra gescefta ealdre;
> ceosan us eard in wuldre mid ealra cyninga cyninge,
> se is Crist genemned.

[Let us bear in mind the holy lord, eternal in glory with the author of all creation; let us choose a glorious dwelling with the king of all kings, who is named Christ.]

The poem may treat the creation and the fall of the angels rather reductively and it may offer us fallen angels who lack the depth and complexity of their counterparts in *Genesis B*, but it renders the horrors of hell, to which the narrative returns in several passages, powerfully and effectively. The inhabitants of hell are 'earme æglecan' (73a) [wretched awe-inspiring ones] who 'hwilum nacode ... / winnað ymb wyrmas' (134b–35a) [at times struggle, naked, among serpents]. Further, as Satan observes in his first speech (81–124), the doors of hell are eternally guarded by fire-breathing dragons and hell itself is a woeful home, full of punishment and inhabited by snakes. What little light there is emanates 'geond þæt atole scræf attre geblonden' (128) [throughout that horrible pit, mixed with venom] from the fires that torture the fallen angels.

The poet heightens the affective dynamics of his depiction of hell and the suffering of the fallen angels by drawing upon the traditional themes of exile and of joy in the hall. Sounding like an exiled warrior, Satan several times laments that because he has been banished he must now tread the 'wræclastas' [paths of exile]. He also laments that he has led his followers to this 'atola

ham / fyre onæled' (95b–96a) [terrible dwelling, consumed with fire]. The
pains of hell are sharpened by their expression in a negative instantiation of
the theme of joy in the hall. The hall the fallen angels occupy is filled not
with the joyous noise of human voices or the harp, but with 'nædran swæg'
(101b) [the noise of serpents], and rather than being the site of activities
that celebrate and strengthen community, it is, in contrast, a windy hall,
alternately hot and cold, where naked men fight among (and perhaps with)
serpents. Although the poet consistently condemns Satan for his rebellion,
Satan does emerge, albeit temporarily, as a sympathetic character in an
apostrophe in which he movingly laments what his actions have cost him:

> Eala drihtenes þrym! Eala duguða helm!
> Eala meotodes miht! Eala middaneard!
> Eala dæg leohta! Eala dream godes!
> Eala engla þreat! Eala upheofen!
>
> (163–66)

[Alas, the glory of the lord. Alas, the protector of retainers. Alas the might of
the creator. Alas the middle-earth. Alas the day's brightness. Alas the joy of
God. Alas the troop of angels. Alas the sky.]

But unlike John Milton, who in *Paradise Lost* creates a Satan who wins –
and holds – the sympathy of many readers, the poet of *Christ and Satan*
quickly re-establishes his Satan as 'godes andsaca' (189a) [God's enemy], a
phrase that is twice used of the demon Grendel in *Beowulf*. The poem's
first section comes to a close with two long passages in which yet more of
hell's horrors are catalogued, but this time they are contrasted with a list
of heaven's joys.

The second section, which focuses on the harrowing of hell, opens with
another brief recapitulation of Satan's rebellion. In a narrative move that
displays the poet's skill, he renders Christ's approach to hell from the
perspective of the fallen angels, a strategy that lends an immediacy to the
terror and panic that runs through their ranks as Christ comes to punish
them. Not only do the fallen angels dread the physical torments that await
them, they also know that they will be forever humiliated by Christ's freeing
of the souls trapped in hell. The poet returns at the section's conclusion to
one of his favourite topics, the horrors of hell, but, like an effective preacher,
he shifts his focus this time from the pain of the hell-bound demons to the
torments that await those who reject the path of righteousness. This section
also contains two noteworthy speeches: one in which Eve acknowledges to
Christ her sinful role in causing the fall before asking that she and all her kin
be taken from hell and brought into the glory of God and one in which

Christ briefly, simply, and poignantly maps the trajectory of his life on earth from his birth, to his persecution, and finally to his crucifixion and ressurection.

As is true of the second section, the third's beginning is not in any way indicated in the text. It may begin as early as line 597 with the poet's brief recapitulation of the last judgement, or it may begin as late as line 663, when the poet turns from his depiction of the joyous praise God receives to the figure of Christ, 'se drihten, seðe deað for us / geþrowode þeoden engla' (663–64a) [the lord, the one who suffered death for us, the prince of angels]. By far the shortest section of the poem, Christ's temptation departs freely from the versions contained in the gospels of Matthew and Luke. The poem treats only two of the temptations – Satan's request that Christ prove his divinity by turning stones into bread and Satan's offer of sovereignty over all the kingdoms and peoples of earth –, but since the manuscript appears to be defective at line 675 (both the syntax and sense break down between lines 675 and 676 although there is no physical damage to the page or disruption to the text's copying), we cannot be sure that the text did not also include the third temptation, one in which Satan suggests Christ cast himself from the top of the temple in order to prove that angels will protect him from so much as dashing his foot against a stone. The poet does flesh out the rather sparse details of the gospel accounts by giving both Satan and Christ longer speeches, by having Satan dramatically seize Christ 'mid hondum' (679b) [with his hands], and by referring to Satan as 'atol' (680a) [horrible one], 'bealowes gast' (681a) [evil spirit], and 'awyrgda' (674a) [the cursed one] (this last is a label Christ several times applies to Satan). The poet also adds an emphasis to the episode that it lacks in the gospel accounts by using Christ's denunciation of Satan to return to the torments that Satan experiences in hell, one of the poem's central themes. These torments include Satan's having to measure the height and depth of hell with his hands, a punishment not earlier mentioned. The narrative concludes with Satan, who is filled with a terrible fear, standing at the very bottom of hell where he is cursed one final time, in this instance by the the other damned spirits who inhabit hell: 'La, þus beo nu on yfele! Noldæs ær teala' (729) [Lo, you are now in an evil situation. You did not earlier desire good].

Further Reading

Buchelt, Lisabeth C. 'All about Eve: memory and re-collection in Junius 11's epic poems *Genesis* and *Christ and Satan*'. In *Women and Medieval Epic*, ed. Sara S. Poor and Jana K. Schulman, 137–58. New York: Palgrave Macmillan, 2007.

Ericksen, Janet Schrunk, 'The wisdom poem at the end of MS Junius 11'. In *The Poems of MS Junius 11: Basic Readings*, ed. Roy M. Liuzza, 302–26. Basic Readings in Anglo-Saxon England 8. New York: Routledge, 2002.

Morey, James H. 'Adam and Judas in the Old English *Christ and Satan*'. *SP* 87 (1990): 397–409.

Wehlau, Ruth. 'The power of knowledge and the location of the reader in *Christ and Satan*'. *JEGP* 97 (1998): 1–12.

The Poems of the Vercelli Book

Vercelli, Biblioteca Capitolare, CXVII.

Commonly known as the Vercelli Book, Vercelli, Biblioteca Capitolare, CXVII, is comprised of twenty-three prose homilies (on which see Part 2) among which are interspersed six poems: *Andreas* and *Fates of the Apostles* between Homilies V and VI; *Soul and Body I*, *Homiletic Fragment I*, and *The Dream of the Rood* between Homilies XVIII and XIX; and, finally, *Elene* between Homilies XXII and XXIII. Generally assigned a date in the mid to late tenth century, the manuscript is missing numerous leaves and has others that are stained, but is otherwise relatively intact.

The Vercelli Book appears to be the product of a single scribal hand and, while its design features are not nearly so elaborate as those of Junius 11, attention has been given to the presentation of its texts. Some texts begin at the top of a new page, even if doing so means leaving a considerable blank space following the end of the preceding text. Homilies I–V and *Andreas* all are so formatted, but thereafter the scribe's practice varies: some texts are placed at the top of a new folio, but others, such as *Fates of the Apostles*, begin in mid-page after just a small gap. While the codex's design results in blank spaces in the manuscript, there is no evidence that either the homilies or the poems were meant to be illuminated, and the only 'illustration' in the manuscript, that of a running dog in the bottom margin of fol. 49^v, may be nothing more than a doodle produced either by the scribe or a later hand. All the texts, with the exception of the acephalic *Homiletic Fragment I*, begin with a large, plain capital letter which in somes cases is followed either by several smaller capitals or a full line of them. There is one zoomorphic capital, on fol. 49^r near the end of *Andreas*, and two more

The Anglo-Saxon Literature Handbook, First Edition. Mark C. Amodio.
© 2014 Mark C. Amodio. Published 2014 by John Wiley & Sons, Ltd.

quasi-zoomorphic ones (each of which has the face of an animal with something like branches forming the rest of the capital letter – an *m* – that it represents). Two other spaces have been left blank: one is for a capital that was never added and the other appears to have been set aside for a quasi-zoomorphic *m* that was never added, although a large, plain *m* was.

Just how the Vercelli Book, a text produced in Anglo-Saxon England containing OE prose and poetry, found its way to Italy is one of the enduring puzzles of Anglo-Saxon literary history. To raise but two of many possible scenarios, might a traveler (to Rome?) have left it there, accidently or on purpose, or might it perhaps have been purchased by or given as a gift to someone living in Vercelli or elsewhere in Italy? To date, no incontrovertible evidence regarding the manuscript's place of production or its history prior to its arrival in Vercelli has been uncovered.

Further Reading

Treharne, Elaine. 'The form and function of the Vercelli Book'. In *Text, Image, Interpretation: Studies in Anglo-Saxon Literature and Its Insular Context in Honour of Éamon Ó Carragáin*, ed. A.J. Minnis and Jane Roberts, 253–66. Studies in the Early Middle Ages 18. Turnhout: Brepols, 2007.

Andreas

The unique copy of the poem survives in Vercelli, Biblioteca Capitolare, CXVII, fols 29ᵛ–52ᵛ. The poem has only one lacuna caused by the absence of a leaf between the currently numbered pages 42 and 43.

In keeping with the Vercelli Book's homiletic and didactic focus, the first poem in it recounts the missions of St Matthew (briefly) and St Andrew (at much greater length) to Mermedonia, a land inhabited by cannibals who prey on all foreigners who venture there. No direct source for the poem has yet to be discovered, but a number of versions of the saint's life survive in Greek and Latin, and two prose versions survive in OE, both of which are, like *Andreas*, housed in collections of homilies. Because it cannot be linked definitively to any one of the surviving Greek versions of the apocryphal *Acts of Andrew and Matthew in the Land of the Cannibals*, the poem is generally believed to have been based upon a now-lost Latin recension of the Greek text. Both its broad narrative contours and many of its narrative specifics, including virtually all of its many fantastic elements (which include the reanimation of the corpses of Abraham, Isaac, and Jacob; a stone carving of an angel that moves and talks; the melting of the Mermedonians' swords;

the deadly and devastating flood that wells forth from a stone pillar; and the enormous abyss that Andrew causes to open up when he puts a stop to the flood) can be traced to the surviving narratives of the *Acts*, such as the version preserved in the Latin *Recensio Casanatensius*.

Despite being heavily indebted to its source(s) for many of its narrative features, *Andreas* is not a simple paraphrase but everywhere reveals the poet's hand and artistry. He frequently exploits fully the didactic possibilities of his source material, as when he greatly expands the scene in which Christ, disguised as a helmsman, questions Andrew's knowledge of his life on earth. The poet also increases his material's affective dynamics by, for example, presenting in oftentimes gruesome detail such things as the tortures Matthew and Andrew suffer, the grisly culinary practices of the Mermedonians, and the bloody death suffered by the Mermedonian prison guards. In articulating his inherited narrative material within the expressive economy of Anglo-Saxon oral poetics, the *Andreas*-poet taps directly, and often effectively, into the specialized ways of meaning that discourse affords him, as when he invokes the theme of the beasts of battle during a terrifying storm at sea or when he describes the Mermedonians' anger using the powerfully metonymic word 'gebolgen' [swollen with anger].

The poem opens with a brief rehearsal of the mission of St Matthew to the Mermedonians, a savage, cannibalistic people who seize, bind, and blind all foreigners who come to their land before forcing them to drink a potion that robs them of their wits. After thirty days, the Mermedonians kill and eat their captives. God visits Matthew in the Mermedonian prison and urges him to suffer his tortures patiently before announcing that Andrew will rescue him. When Andrew learns God's plan, he does not immediately accept it, suggesting instead to God that an angel could make the journey more easily. In what may be a last-ditch effort to avoid undertaking what must appear to him to be a suicide mission, Andrew reveals that he cannot undertake the mission because he knows neither the 'hæleða gehygdo' (200a) [thoughts of the warriors] nor the path 'ofer cald wæter' (201a) [over cold water] that will lead him to Mermedonia. There is no trace of the saint's resistance in the *Acts*, where he replies to God with a simple 'I am ready, Lord' (Calder and Allen, 17), but in adding it to his narrative the *Andreas*-poet does more than simply supplement his source material; he injects a degree of psychological reality into a genre known more for its emphasis on pious, patient obedience to God's will.

After acceding to God's request, Andrew gathers his men and sails for Mermedonia, a journey remarkable both for the terrible storm they encounter along the way and for the long conversation Andrew has with the helmsman, who turns out to be Christ in disguise. The storm at sea well exemplifies the poem's didacticism in that it tests Andrew and his men in order to reinforce to them (and by extension to the poem's audience) the value of patiently putting their faith in Christ, for the helmsman suggests to Andrew that he seek to allay his men's fear by relating the mysteries ('gerynu' [419a]) of Christ's teaching since 'God eaðe mæg / heaðoliðendum helpe gefremman' (425b–26a) [God easily may help journeying warriors]. After reassuring the men that Christ will never abandon them if they remain steadfast, the seas subside and Andrew and the disguised Christ begin their conversation, shortly after the start of which Andrew's men fall into a peaceful sleep. Christ directs this discourse, which extends throughout an entire day, by posing a series of simple questions, the answers to which allow Andrew to relate some scriptural miracles – and a non-scriptural one – as he 'ondlangne dæg / herede hleoðorcwidum haliges lare' (818b–19) [throughout the day praised with words the doctrine of the holy one]. As in the *Acts*, the scriptural miracles, including Christ's turning water into wine and his feeding a crowd from just two fish and five loaves of bread, are passed over in a brief, almost perfunctory, fashion, while the non-scriptural miracle, which involves first Christ's commanding a stone carving of an angel to come down from the wall to preach to non-believers and then his commanding it to raise Abraham, Isaac, and Joseph from the dead so that they may also go out and preach receives fuller, more dramatic treatment.

At the conversation's conclusion, Andrew is transported by Christ to just outside the gates of Mermedonia, where he awakens next to his companions, who have been taken there by angels, although the men report that they dreamt eagles brought them there. Andrew enters the city alone and frees Matthew and all the other prisoners, who Matthew leads safely to freedom with the assistance of clouds that cover them and so prevent the Mermedonians from noticing their escape. Andrew remains behind and prevents the cannibalistic Mermedonians, who are gripped by fear of famine now that their prison is empty, from killing one of their own children by melting the swords they wield. The devil suddenly appears in their midst, reveals Andrew's presence, and urges the Mermedonians to capture and torture him, which they dutifully do, subjecting him to both physical and psychological ordeals designed to break him body and spirit. He bears his torments admirably, and in a passage that directly links the life of this *miles Christi* with that of Christ himself, he asks if God has forsaken him: 'forlætest ðu me?' (1413b) [have you abandoned me?]. God assures him that what he suffers is not too severe for him to bear, but it is not until the fourth round of the graphically depicted tortures is about to begin that Andrew is released from his suffering.

The final portion of the poem finds Andrew still in Mermedonia where, serving as a conduit for divine speech, he releases from a stone pillar a flood that will cleanse the city. The waters dramatically surge forth from the pillar and drown many of the still-sleeping Mermedonians as an angel prevents others from escaping by encircling the city with a wall of fire. This deluge exacts a high and deadly toll until Andrew commands it to halt, after which he performs several more miracles: he causes an abyss to open up into which the waters drain, and after the people profess their faith in the Christian God, Andrew restores to life all the young men who had died in the flood (except the fourteen worst). Having already gone through something of a forced, and terrifying baptism, the Mermedonians convert, following which Andrew departs, much to their sorrow, and journeys back to Achaia, where he receives the palm of martyrdom.

The degree to which the poet emphasises the *miles* at the seeming expense of the devotional by situating the saint and his companions firmly within the secular heroic tradition distinguishes *Andreas* from other saints' lives, even those of other *miles Christi*. From its opening line, 'Hwæt! We gefrunan on fyrndagum' (1) [Lo, we have heard in days of old] – a line that closely echoes *Beowulf*'s ('Hwæt we Gar-Dena in geardagum' [1] [Lo, we of the spear Danes in days of old] –, the poem points us toward the distant, pagan past. The introduction of the main characters, who are described as 'tireadige hæleð' (2b) [glorious warriors], 'frome folctogan' (8a) [bold chiefs], 'fyrdhwate' (8b) [bold in battle], and 'rofe rincas' (9a) [valiant warriors] who readily raise 'rond ond hand' (9b) [shield and hand] 'on meotudwange' (11a) [on the battlefield], further locates us within the traditional world of Germanic heroic narrative. The poem offers hints that these figures are not wholly anchored in the pagan, heroic world (there are, after all, twelve of them and we are told that their lord sends them on separate journeys, details that a Christian audience would immediately associate with the apostles and their individual missions), but given the degree to which the poem's opening is articulated in the traditional heroic register, the first character named might just as easily have been one from the early Germanic pagan world.

Situating first the twelve apostles and then more specifically Matthew, Andrew, and Andrew's followers within the Germanic warrior ethos does, however, lead to some occasional narrative incongruities. To take one instance, as soon as he enters the city, Matthew is captured, bound, blinded, and forced to drink a magical, dehumanizing potion (although the potion fails to affect the saint's mind, which remains focused on God's glory and power). While in captivity, this 'beadurofne' (145a) [battle-brave one] engages in no martial activity but rather suffers his torments patiently while waiting to learn what God has planned for him. Filtering his narrative through the heroic ethos may seem a questionable narrative strategy, but the disjunction that arises here from describing a necessarily passive Christian hero such as Matthew with a term that seems better suited to an active, secular hero such as Beowulf, may be more apparent to modern audiences than to the poem's intended one. The *Andreas*-poet is far from alone in treating his material in this fashion; we need not look far to discover other Christian characters in OE poetry who are similarly described. In fact, one of the other poems in the Vercelli Book, *The Dream of the Rood*, depicts as a Germanic warrior another figure from sacred history known for his passivity and patient suffering, not his martial prowess: Christ.

Elsewhere, however, the traditional expressive economy merges only imperfectly with the poet's inherited material, as is apparent in the brief scene in which Andrew confronts the guards outside the prison's gates. In the *Acts*, the guards die but only after the saint first looks up to heaven and prays. He then stretches 'his right hand towards the prison' and makes 'the sign of the Holy Cross', whereupon the guards fall down and die (bloodlessly) and the prison door opens because its 'iron melted' (Calder and Allen, 25). In the OE poem, the saint observes the guards and in the next moment the 'Deaðræs forfeng / hæleð heorodreorige' (995b–96a) [rush of death seized the blood-soaked warriors]. Andrew does pray before the presumably locked door of the prison, which then miraculously opens at his touch, but when he first arrives, he merely looks the guards' way and suddenly their corpses lie strewn on the ground, where they 'deaðwang rudon' (1003b) [redden the death-plain]. While this decidedly abrupt and puzzling turn of events may be the result of an authorial or scribal error, it may simply evidence an imperfect seam within the text's poetics. Bloody conflicts are common in secular heroic poetry and gore is certainly present in many Anglo-Saxon saints' lives, but it usually comes from, and is not precipitated by, the saints, as in *Andreas* where pieces of Andrew's flesh and tufts of his hair dot the landscape through which he is dragged by his captors. The scene before the prison gates in Mermedonia may best be understood as a not wholly successful attempt to articulate material through an expressive economy that cannot, in this instance, easily or fluidly accommodate the demands the source material places on it because the affective dynamics of the heroic tradition demands that the guards die a bloody death, however narratively incongruous such a death may be. Because the character poised to cause this bloody death is not a warrior, but rather a saint whose life of patient suffering is meant to model Christ's, he proves to be not a fitting agent of the type of death the tradition demands and that the audience expects. The resultant disjunction arises here from the tension between the heroic ethos within which the poem is articulated and the poet's inherited Christian material, a tension that, this instance at least, the *Andreas*-poet could not overcome or even address, either directly or indirectly.

Although contemporary audiences may be puzzled by the *Andreas*-poet's presentation of Andrew's companions as 'beornas beadurofe' (848b) [battle-brave warriors] and although the fabric of the narrative is rough in places, elsewhere the poet deploys the expressive economy of Anglo-Saxon oral poetics seamlessly and skilfully, as when he uses the traditional thematics of the beasts of battle to focus and heighten the terror that Andrew and his men experience during the storm at sea. The *Andreas*-poet's treatment of this theme is unique in that he substitutes sea creatures for the wolves and carrion birds that are elsewhere found in this well-attested theme, but the scene retains its traditional affective dynamics as the 'hornfisc' (370b) [pike] and 'græga mæw' (371b) exult in their expectation of soon feasting on the corpses of the apostle and his comrades. No deaths occur since the storm is a divinely sent test for Andrew, but the presence of the theme significantly points the emotional, affective pitch of the terror that grips the men by tapping into the theme's inherent, traditional meaning. Earlier the poet even more idiosyncratically reveals how fluid and adaptable the traditional expressive economy is when he turns the Mermedonians themselves into carrion beasts. When they capture Matthew, the Mermedonians are described as being first 'wælgrædige' (135a) [greedy for slaughter/corpses], a uniquely occurring compound that closely echoes the *wæl*-compounds that occur in other instantiations of the beasts of battle. Following this description, the poet explicitly links the Mermedonians to the beasts of battle when he describes them as 'wælwulfas' (149a) [slaughter wolves]. And although Matthew is not put to death by his captors, the graphic accounts of what the Mermedonians plan to do to him (break apart his joints and distribute his body parts to young and old warriors who will feast upon them), which is followed closely by an equally graphic description of the way in which they rip apart their captives' flesh 'blodigum ceaflum' (159a) [with bloody jaws] substitute effectively within the scene's affective dynamics for the actual death towards which the theme traditionally points.

One of the most enduring, interesting, and perhaps insoluble critical questions concerning *Andreas* has to do with its many connections to another OE poem: the secular and heroic *Beowulf*. Space does not permit a full consideration of this matter, so here we must consider it briefly and selectively. On the narrative level, both poems have as a central figure a young hero who, accompanied by a group of warriors, journeys over water in order to confront an enemy known for his/their brutal, cannibalistic ways. They both triumph over their foes before returning to their homelands, where they eventually meet their deaths. Although the enemy Beowulf encounters seems more monster than man while the ones Andrew meets seem more men than monsters, Grendel and the Mermedonians are closely linked, not just culinarily but thematically and linguistically. Grendel eats thirty Danes a night and the Mermedonians regularly wait thirty days before devouring all the strangers they capture. When they do devour people, both do so in a spectacularly gory fashion, although while we witness Grendel kill and eat someone, the Mermedonians' actions are only reported. Both Grendel and the Mermedonians are described as being 'bolgenmod' [swollen with anger] and as 'aglæcan' [awe-inspiring ones], and finally, both suffer bloody deaths: Grendel has his arm and shoulder wrenched off in Heorot and the Mermedonian prison guards meet a bloody end. Linguistically, many of *Andreas*'s phrases and half-lines find close, oftentimes exact, parallels in *Beowulf*, including 'heah ond horngeap' (*And* 668a and *Bwf* 82a) [high and wide-gabled] and 'fugole gelicost' (*And* 497b and *Bwf* 218b) [most like a bird]. The points of contact between the poems may be signs of direct literary, intertextual borrowing, with *Beowulf*, because of its greater artistry, generally thought to be the source text, although any argument that rests on such subjective criteria must necessarily remain tenuous. Alternatively, the poems' similarities may be traced to the traditional expressive economy of Anglo-Saxon oral poetics, a specialized way of speaking comprised of inherited, widely shared, oftentimes formulaic verbal collocations and larger narrative units.

Considerable evidence can be easily adduced for both positions, but we will focus here only on one pair of related lexemes and on one thematically resonant phrase. The uniquely occurring and much discussed compound 'meoduscerwan' (1526) [serving of mead] in *Andreas* is generally taken as a metaphor for the panic and terror that the Mermedonians experience when Andrew calls forth a flood, the waters of which sweep through their city. This compound is related to another uniquely occurring one, *Beowulf*'s 'ealuscerwen' (769a), a word whose meaning has not been fully uncovered, but that may mean 'dispensing of (bitter) ale'. Although frequently taken to be the derivative text, *Andreas* situates the word in a seemingly more appropriate context than does *Beowulf*. In the former, the metaphor of drink is applied logically enough to flood waters while in the latter the bitter drink referred to is not a liquid, but synesthetically, a sound: the noise of Heorot straining under the actions of the fierce duo grappling within its walls. Did the *Andreas*-poet borrow from *Beowulf* in this instance and in the process of borrowing the compound did he improve it, or is there a resonance to 'ealuscerwen' that neither he – nor we – can fully hear? Further complicating matters, both poets may have independently created their compounds.

Andreas and *Beowulf* do share verbal expressions, but many of these are also found elsewhere in the corpus of OE vernacular poetry, which reduces the likelihood that the correspondences between the two poems are wholly intertextual. For example, the phrase 'atol aglæca' [terrible awe-inspiring one], which occurs three times in Beowulf (592a, 732a, and 816a), occurs once in Andreas (1312a) and once in Christ and Satan (160a). The way this phrase is used in Andreas reveals that the poet's understanding of it stems from its metonymic, greater-than-textual meaning rather than from its surface meaning in Beowulf's narrative, and that he came to it not through the process of direct intertextual borrowing, but rather through traditional Anglo-Saxon oral poetics. 'Aglæca' is a very slippery term, since it applies both to monstrous characters such as the Mermedonians, Satan, Grendel, Grendel's mother, and the dragon, as well as to heroic ones such as Beowulf and Sigemund. But when 'atol' is attached to it, the adjective serves to disambiguate the noun considerably by restricting its range of meaning to characters who are clearly monstrous. For example, in Christ and Satan and Andreas, the devil is described not just as an 'aglæca' but as an 'atol aglæca'. 'Aglæca' by itself can, and frequently does, similarly refer to monstrous characters, but it also describes heroic characters, including most notably Beowulf, who straddle the border between human and other-than-human behaviour. When applied to such characters, the noun is never accompanied by 'atol'. In Andreas, the poet uses 'aglæca' to refer to St Andrew, a character who would seem not to share any traits with the far darker and far more problematic non-monstrous characters who also fall under the term's umbrella. While we may be tempted to see the poet's application of the term to the saint as a sign of his distance from the traditional expressive economy in which this metonym resonates so effectively and consistently, when we consider the context within which the term is used and who uses it, we see instead that the Andreas-poet employs the term both uniquely and traditionally, for it is the devil who labels the saint an 'aglæcan' (1359a). So labelling the saint is rather understandable since from the demonic perspective, a man who can so patiently endure so much physical and mental torture, and who has other powers as well (Andrew causes the Mermedonians' swords to melt at one point and he may well have played some role in the deaths of the prison guards), must certainly appear to be an 'aglæca'. We may never be able to settle the question of Andreas's relationship to Beowulf, but this should not prevent us from appreciating both the artistry and accomplishment of the Andreas-poet.

Further Reading

Blurton, Heather. 'Self-eaters: the cannibal narrative of Andreas'. In her Cannibalism in High Medieval Literature, 15–34. Basingstoke: Palgrave Macmillan, 2007.

Foley, John Miles. 'Indexed translation: the poet's self-interruption in the Old English *Andreas*'. In his *Singer of Tales in Performance*, 181–207. Bloomington: Indiana University Press, 1995.

Frank, Roberta. 'North Sea soundings in *Andreas*'. In *Early Medieval English Texts and Interpretations: Studies Presented to Donald G. Scragg*, ed. Elaine Treharne and Susan Rosser, 1–11. MRTS 252. Tempe: ACMRS, 2002.

Garner, Lori Ann. 'The Old English *Andreas* and the Mermedonian cityscape'. *Essays in Medieval Culture* 24 (2007): 53–63.

Godlove, Shannon N. 'Bodies as borders: cannibalism and conversion in the Old English *Andreas*'. *SP* 106 (2009): 137–60.

Wilcox, Jonathan. 'Eating people is wrong: funny style in *Andreas* and its analogues'. In *Anglo-Saxon Styles*, ed. Catherine Karkov and George H. Brown, 201–22. SUNY Series in Medieval Studies. Albany: State University of New York Press, 2003.

Fates of the Apostles

Survives in a unique copy in the Vercelli Book on fols 52^v–54^r.

Fates of the Apostles is the first text in the Vercelli Book, whether in prose or verse, that does not begin at the top of a new page. Instead, it begins about halfway down the folio on which *Andreas* concludes, following *Andreas* after only a small gap, a practice that the scribe engages in elsewhere, although not with absolute consistency. A blank space has been left at the beginning of the poem's first line for an initial ornamental 'h' that was never inserted, and the four other letters of the first word, 'wæt', appear in small capitals. This short poem ends about three-quarters of the way down fol. 54^r, and after the poem's final word, 'FINIT', which is also in small capitals, the rest of the folio is left blank, with the following text, Homily VI, beginning at the top of a new page on fol. 55^v. The scribe who copied *Fates of the Apostles* appears to be the same one who copied the other prose and poetic texts contained in the Vercelli Book.

Fates of the Apostles is a brief verse martyrology for which no single source has been discovered. A Latin source is often postulated since the names of the apostles are all given in their Latin form, but not much weight can be placed on this given that the Latin names of the saints were widely used in texts, the liturgy, and elsewhere. The intensely personal opening and closing of the poem, along with the author's naming himself and including a request for his readers' prayers near the poem's conclusion, suggest that we need look no further for the source of *Fates* than the artistic imagination of the poet whose runic 'signature' is found cryptically encoded in the text: Cynewulf.

The narrative of *Fates* offers capsule accounts of the martyrdoms of Christ's twelve disciples after he sent them out to spread his word throughout the world. The entry for St Andrew, presented here in its entirety, is representative of the telegraphic way in which the poem proceeds:

> Swylce Andreas in Achagia
> for Egias aldre geneðde.
> Ne þreodode he fore þrymme ðeodcyninges,
> æniges on eorðan, ac him ece geceas
> langsumre lif, leoht unhwilen,
> syþþan hildeheard, heriges byrhtme,
> æfter guðplegan gealgan þehte.

(16–22)

[Likewise Andrew in Achaia risked his life before Ægeas. He did not hesitate before the glory of any king on earth, but chose for himself eternal, long-enduring life, eternal light after the battle-brave one, to the tumult of the host, was stretched out on the cross after the battle-play.]

This and the other very brief recitations that comprise the poem may reveal its metonymic, and perhaps mnemonic, function and purpose. If read privately, the short narratives become the sites for extended reflection on the apostles' missions and the grim fates they met in discharging their divinely appointed tasks. Since *Fates* is contained in a codex that may have served as the basis for both private reflection on and public articulation of Christian principles, the narratives that comprise it may also function as metonymic pathways to all the details of the apostles' lives and deaths.

The strongly devotional focus of *Fates* is of a piece with that of the other prose and verse texts found in the Vercelli Book. Additionally, as do several of the codex's other poems, most notably *Andreas*, *Dream of the Rood*, and *Elene*, *Fates* describes its characters in terms that seem far more appropriate to Germanic warriors than to the companions of Christ. We are told at the poem's beginning that its subject will be 'hu þa æðelingas ellen cyðdon' (3) [how the noblemen made known their courage], a line that, with one minor variation, is the same as *Beowulf*'s third line: 'hu þa æþelingas ellen fremedon' [how the noblemen peformed courageous deeds]. Just like the Germanic warriors who appear in heroic verse, the twelve are, we learn, 'dædum domfæste, dryhtne gecorene' (5) [powerful, illustrious in deeds, chosen by the lord]. In many ways the opening of *Fates* sounds like a compressed version of *Beowulf*'s highly traditional, heroic, and secular opening lines, lines that recount the glories of a line of accomplished warrior kings and briefly articulates the characteristics of good kings. The presence of the 'I heard' formula, an important component of traditional oral poetics, similarly points us towards the heroic ethos, but just as the *Andreas*-poet adapts and redirects the elements of the tradition's expressive economy that he employs, so, too, in *Fates* is the 'I heard' formula used traditionally to give decidedly heroic overtones to the Christian past being celebrated, but it is also used non-traditionally in two instances because instead of functioning, as it does in *Beowulf* and elsewhere, as a pathway to the richly associative world of the oral tradition, in *Fates* the formula directs us to the literate, Christian tradition. The call to attention signalled by 'hwæt' leads not to the distant, oral past, but to the works of 'æglæawe menn' (24a) [men skilled in the law] and 'halige bec' (63b) [holy books], while the 'I heard formula' points to the story of Jacob. The only one of the four occurrences of 'hwæt' in the poem that aligns with its traditional use is the one that opens the poem: following the interjection, the poet mentions not a written or literate source but rather the 'sang' (1a) [song] he is going to relate. But even in this instance the poet once again adapts and redirects the traditional expressive economy by grounding his song in his own mind, not in the traditional, oral past (as the *Beowulf*-poet does), for he tells us that his song emanates not from the shared communal storehouse that is the oral tradition but is rather one that he 'siðgeomor fand / on seocum sefan' [weary of life found in (his) sick mind].

The poet announces his presence in the poem in several ways: through his initial address to his audience, through his closing call to be remembered in his readers'/listeners' prayers, and through the visual puzzle he sets those 'foreþances gleaw' (96b) [shrewd of deliberation] in the form of a series of runes on fol. 54ʳ, a page that is, unfortunately, heavily damaged by a stain of some kind that obscures many letters and words. The runes appear in the sequence ᚠ ᚹ ᚢ ᚱ ᚳ ᛗ ᚾ [F, W, U, L, C, Y, N] and when this sequence is unscrambled the runes reveal what may be the poet's name: Cynwulf, a variant spelling of Cynewulf. Although he and Cædmon are the only two Anglo-Saxon poets we can confidently name, we know very little about Cynewulf other than that he appears to have authored *Fates* and the three other poems mentioned above. We do not know where or when he lived, or even whether he was an actual, historical figure or simply one created by the author(s) of what we have come to know as the Cynewulf canon. But given how little we know about Cynewulf himself, the evidence of the runic signatures, the intensely self-focused contexts in which they appear, and the poems' linguistic and stylistic similarities point strongly to their being the product of a single artistic sensibility.

The narrative portion of *Fates* is framed by Cynewulf's self-presentation as someone who is acutely aware of the approaching end of his own days and of the necessary voyage he will soon have to undertake, alone, when his soul and body separate. He gives this theme, one that is taken up at greater length in another Vercelli Book poem, *Soul and Body I*, moving expression when he acknowledges that his soul must soon journey 'of þisse worulde' (111b–12a) [from this world] into the unknown while his body will seek the grave, the 'langne ham, / eardwic uncuð' (92b–93a) [long home, the unknown abode] where his 'lic, eorðan dæl, / ... wunigean weormum to hroðre' (94b–95) [body, this portion of earth, ... shall remain behind to the pleasure of worms]. Whether these comments, which are echoed in the other passages in which he runically encodes his name, reveal anything about Cynewulf's age and health at the time he commited them to the page is an intriguing but ultimately unanswerable question: the author may have been ailing in mind and body, as he says, or he may just have been adopting a fictional persona that is consonant with and reinforces the didactic and devotional purposes of his verbal art.

Further Reading

Kowalik, Barbara. 'The motif of journey in Cynewulf's *Fates of the Apostles*'. In *Þe comoun peplis language*, ed. Marcin Krygier and Liliana Sikorska, 99–111. Medieval English Mirror 6. New York: Peter Lang, 2010.

McBrine, Patrick. 'The journey motif in the poems of the Vercelli Book'. In *New Readings in the Vercelli Book*, ed. Samantha Zacher and Andy Orchard, 298–317. Toronto Anglo-Saxon Series 4. Toronto: University of Toronto Press, 2009.

McCulloh, John M. 'Did Cynewulf use a martyrology? Reconsidering the sources of *The Fates of the Apostles*'. *ASE* 29 (2000): 67–83.

Soul and Body I (and *II*)

Survives in the Vercelli Book, fols 101^v–4^r. A closely related poem, *Soul and Body II*, survives in the Exeter Book, fols 98^r–100^r.

The subject of *SB I*, a dialogue between a departed soul and its dead body, was a popular one in the Middle Ages. Although no single source for this poem has yet to be identified, a number of prose analogues in both Latin and the vernacular exist from the Anglo-Saxon period and earlier. The Latin analogues include several Pseudo-Augustine sermons and some anonymous homilies, and the vernacular ones include two poems found in the Exeter Book, *SB II* and Riddle 43, as well as passages in the Vercelli Book's Homily IV and Homily XXII. *SB I* articulates, often quite dramatically – and graphically – common ideas about the effects of the sinful practices many engage in during their time in the world. Although the two Anglo-Saxon soul and body poems differ in a number of ways (the Exeter version is shorter, omitting the address of the blessed soul to the body found in Vercelli; Exeter omits a number of lines found in Vercelli; and there are numerous instances in which different words are used as well as several passages that are arranged differently in the two texts), the points of contact between them, including the only two occurrences in recorded Anglo-Saxon of the past participle 'bicowen/becowen' [to chew through], suggest that they either had a common, now-lost source, or that one version is a copy of the other, although if this is the case we still cannot determine which of the two served as the source for the other.

Soul and Body I (*SB I*) breaks up into several narrative sections. The poem opens with a brief admonitory statement from the poet in which he makes explicit the poem's didactic focus as he urges all men to be mindful of the necessary, and possibly terrible, journey that awaits the soul after its inevitable separation from the body, a journey that will lead the soul to either 'wite' [torments] or 'wuldor' (7a) [glory]. The poem then turns to the diatribe of a soul suffering eternal punishment that is compelled to visit its body weekly. As in other soul and body texts, where the soul is often given a one-day respite from its confinement either in heaven or hell, the soul visits its body weekly, not out of a desire to do so, but because it is compelled to do so. At the conclusion of the damned soul's speech, the poem turns, in graphic detail to the body, which is trapped in the grave, is being devoured by worms, and is falling to pieces. The final section of the poem is devoted to the speech of a saved soul, but owing to the probable loss of a manuscript page between the folios currently numbered 103 and 104, this speech and the poem breaks off in mid-sentence. *SB I* is followed in the manuscript by the aptly named *Homiletic Fragment I*, the beginning of which is lost. The Exeter Book poem, *Soul and Body II* (*SB II*), does not include the saved soul section, but rather concludes about one-third of the way down on fol. 100^r after describing the decaying body. Since *SB II* is marked by the Exeter scribe with the punctuation he typically uses to indicate the completion of a text, or section, and since the poem is immediately followed after a blank space of about a line by the next poem in the collection, *Deor*, the poet or scribe either did not wish to copy the saved soul's speech or the exemplar from which he worked lacked it. Either way, it is clear from the poem's *mise-en-page* in its codex that *SB II* was deemed complete as it stands.

The message the damned soul conveys, that the body's sinful behaviour while alive resulted in the soul's consignment to an afterlife of punishment and that things would have been far different for the soul if the body had only followed the proper, Christian path, is entirely conventional and consonant with the overall focus of the Vercelli Book, but the poet gives the soul a resonant and pointed voice, one that is described as being 'cearful' [anxious] and 'cealdan' (15) [cold]. The lot of the damned soul even while it resided in the body was one of pain and suffering, as the body's 'fyrenlustas' (34b) [sinful desires] oppress the soul trapped within it: 'Ne meahte ic ðe of cuman' (33b) [I was not able to come out of you], it tells the body. So difficult was its time in the body that it 'þuhte ful oft / þæt hit wære XXX þusend wintra / to þinum deaðdæge' (35b–37a) [often seemed that it would be thirty thousand years to the day of your death]. The soul condemns the body for keeping itself 'wines sæd' (39b) [sated with wine] while the soul 'ofþrysted wæs / godes lichoman, gastes dryncess' (40b–41a) [was very thirsty for the body of God, the drink of the spirit]. After excoriating the body for being 'eorðan fulnes' (18a) [foulness of the earth], a 'weriga' (22a) [wretch], and 'wyrma gyfl' (22b) [food for worms], the soul reminds the body that it is now 'dumb ond deaf' [dumb and deaf] and that its joys 'ne synt … awhit' (65) [are not … anything]. But despite the fact that the body will have to answer for its sinfulness at the day of judgement, the fate of the soul is inextricably intertwined with the fate of the body, for as the soul says: 'Ac hwæt do wyt unc?' (100b) [But what can we two do ourselves?]. The iteration in the soul's final words of the dual personal pronoun, a pronoun that bespeaks a close connection between the two to whom it refers, here stresses the body and soul's finally inescapable interconnectedness: 'Sculon wit þonne eft æftsomne siððan brucan / swylcra yrmða, swa ðu unc her ær scrife' (101–2) [The two of us must afterwards endure such miseries as you here earlier fixed as our lot].

Following the departure of the damned soul, the poem offers a graphic, rather grisly depiction of the body decaying in the grave. The 'dust' lies where it is, incapable of answering its 'geomrum gaste' [sad spirit] or offering 'geoce oððe frofre' (107) [help or consolation] because worms have dragged its tongue away in ten pieces. And in a passage that would find a fit home in the most fiery of eschatological homilies, the poet casts a brutally unflinching eye on the body's decomposed state:

> Bið þæt heafod tohliden, handa toliðode,
> geaglas toginene, goman toslitene,
> sina beoð asocene, swyra becowen,
> fingras tohrorene.

> (108–11a)

[That head is split asunder, the hands disjointed, the jaws distended, the palate torn asunder, the sinews are chewed through, the fingers destroyed.]

The poet doesn't stop here, but drives his point home by telling us, among other things, that the worm 'gifer' [the greedy one] bores through the teeth and eats through the eyes as he makes his way down from the top of the skull, clearing a path for the other worms to the feast.

As does the damned soul, the saved soul still visits the body but it seeks out its former abode 'gefean' (130b) [with joy] and 'lustum' (131a) [with pleasure]. Rather than scolding the body for the sins it committed while alive, the saved soul 'gode word sprecað' (132b) [speaks good words] that are wise, triumphant, and true. The body is the saved soul's 'Wine leofesta' (135a) [dearest friend], and while the body's state in the grave is no different from that of the damned soul's body – 'wyrmas gyt / gifre gretaþ' (135b–36a) [worms still eagerly attack] it – the soul avoids offering any details and seeks to comfort the body by informing it that the soul wishes it could take the body back to the 'fæder rice' (137b) [the father's kingdom] where 'wyt englas ealle gesawon' (140) [we two could see all the angels]. Echoing the rhetoric of the damned soul, the saved soul notes that because the good body went hungry while alive, the body 'gefyldest me / godes lichoman, gastes drynces' (143) [filled me with God's body, the soul's drink]. The saved soul continues in this vein and lists the ways in which the good body's Christian practices paved the way for the soul's blissful afterlife, although it notes that even the good body is destined to be humiliated after death since it was God's wish that all living creatures must 'laðlic legerbed cure' (155) [choose a loathsome grave]. The saved soul also promises that it and its body will be reunited at the day of judgement, as the damned soul did, but unlike the former pair, for whom there will be no end of punishment, the saved soul and its body have no reason to dread the final judgement since the body need not be ashamed of its earthly actions. The poem breaks off in mid-sentence where a leaf has been lost, but not very much appears to be missing.

The damned soul's shrill, often nearly hysterical voice and the poet's rather conventional approach to his subject matter have not won it many admirers, but situated within the broader homiletic context of the Vercelli Book or read as an isolated rumination on the effects of living a sinful life, its message comes across in a lively, sometimes discomfiting fashion, and if it were to be given voice by a talented reader/performer, one can imagine that its impact might be significant.

Further Reading

Davis, Glenn. 'Corporeal anxiety in *Soul and Body II*'. *PQ* 87 (2008): 33–50.
Matto, Michael. 'The Old English *Soul and Body I* and *Soul and Body II*: ending the rivalry'. *In Geardagum* 18 (1997): 39–58.
Zacher, Samantha. 'The "body and soul" of the Vercelli Book: the heart of the corpus'. In her *Preaching the Converted: The Style and Rhetoric of the Vercelli Book Homilies*, 140–78. Toronto Anglo-Saxon Series 1. Toronto: University of Toronto Press, 2009.

Homiletic Fragment I

Survives uniquely in the Vercelli Book, fols 104^r–4^v.

Homiletic Fragment I is an acephalous poem of fewer than fifty lines that warns its readers to be on guard against hypocrites while alive and to choose the better path, one that that will result in their sharing 'heofones leoht' (44b) [heaven's light] 'mid englum' (45a) [with the angels] once God puts an end to their earthly existence. Because the leaf containing its beginning (and most likely the ending of the preceding poem, *Soul and Body I*) is missing from the manuscript, *HF I* begins in mid-sentence on the top of fol. 104^r. The poet warns his readers that while a deceiver may 'fæger word / utan ætywe' (17b–18a) [show fair words on the outside], his mind is 'synnum fah' (16a) [stained with sins], and in one of this slender poem's more memorable moments he compares such deceitful men with bees who have 'hunig on muðe' (21b) [honey in the mouth] but have behind them an 'ætterne tægel' (20b) [posionous tail] with which they 'wundiaþ / sare mid stinge' (22b–23a) [wound sorely with a sting] when the opportunity arises.

Further Reading

Pulsiano, Phillip. 'Bees and backbiters in the Old English *Homiletic Fragment I*'. *ELN* 25 (1987): 1–6.

Randle, Jonathan T. 'The "homiletics" of the Vercelli Book poems: the case of *Homiletic Fragment I*'. In *New Readings in the Vercelli Book*, ed. Samantha Zacher and Andy Orchard, 185–224. Toronto Anglo-Saxon Series 4. Toronto: University of Toronto Press, 2009.

The Dream of the Rood

Survives in the Vercelli Book, fols 104^v–106^r. Several sections of the poem are also inscribed using the runic alphabet on the Ruthwell Cross, a stone monument in Dumfriesshire, Scotland.

The Dream of the Rood (DR) is the earliest dream vision to survive from Anglo-Saxon England. No source has been discovered for the poem, and although the Cross is the subject of numerous Latin sermons and even some riddles, so far as we can determine the poem is solely the product of its author's talented and inventive mind. The cult of the Cross, whose origins have been traced to the Emperor Constantine's conversion in the fourth century, was well established in Anglo-Saxon England and may have been of particular interest or importance to the compiler of the Vercelli Book since in addition to *DR*, the manuscript contains another poem, *Elene*, that traces the search Helena undertakes for the true Cross.

Unlike the majority of the extant OE poetic corpus, *DR* exists in two versions. In addition to the version found in the Vercelli Book, sections of the poem were carved into a stone monument, the Ruthwell Cross. This cross, which is itself an important archaeological remain, thus preserves part of *DR* in a medium (stone) and in an alphabet (the futhorc) that were only very rarely used for the encoding of vernacular verse in Anglo-Saxon England. Additionally, the cross preserves the poem in the Northumbrian dialect, not West Saxon, the 'standard' dialect in which the great majority of the vernacular written records survive. The existence of two versions separated by a century or more raises a great many questions not only about the poem's date and place of composition, but also more generally about the circulation of texts in the Anglo-Saxon period.

The poem opens with the dreamer announcing that he is going to reveal not just a dream, but 'swefna cyst' (1a) [the best of dreams], the object of which is first somewhat cryptically introduced as a 'syllicre treow' (4b) [marvellous tree] that is suspended in the air, wound about with light, and 'begoten mid golde' (6a) [sprinkled with gold]. The nature of this fantastic tree, which is so large that it seems to stretch to the four corners of the horizon, comes more fully into focus when we learn that there are five gems upon its 'eaxlegespanne' (9a) [shoulder-span] and that it is the object to which 'halige gastas, / men ofer moldan, ond eall þeos mære gesceaft' (11b–12) [holy spirits, men throughout the earth and all this glorious creation] direct their gaze. But while this object, which is revealed as the Cross when the dreamer identifies it as the 'sigebeam' (13a) [victory-tree], is dazzlingly beautiful, covered as it is with gems and gold, its almost overwhelming ornamentation does not prevent the dreamer from also perceiving the 'earmra ærgewin' (19a) [old strife of the wretched ones] once the tree begins 'swætan on þa swiðran healfe' (20a) [to bleed on the right side]. The fundamentally paradoxical nature of the Cross – it is both an object of great beauty and the locus of unimaginable, if necessary, suffering –, is powerfully articulated when the dreamer reveals that as he gazed upon the Cross, 'hwilum hit wæs mid wætan bestemed, / beswyled mid swates gange, hwilum mid since gegyrwed' (22b–23) [at times it was wet with blood, soaked with the flow of blood; at times it was adorned with treasure]. The sight of the tree fills the dreamer with sorrow and fear, and he realizes that he is 'synnum fah' (13b) [stained with sins] and 'forwunded mid wommum' (14a) [badly wounded with sins].

One of the remarkable features of the rood is that it does not simply bear mute, symbolic witness to one of Christianity's central events, the Crucifixion of Christ, as we would expect, but rather speaks directly to the dreamer, and by extension, the poem's audience. Although talking objects are a staple of both Latin and vernacular riddles (and in some Latin riddles the Cross itself is the speaker), it is only in *DR* that the Cross relates its history and enables us to consider the Crucifixion from its uniquely participatory perspective. Because it is by chance located at the edge of a wood, the tree is seized by 'strange feondas' (30b) [strong enemies], hewn into a cross, and set upon a hill. The transformation from tree to the spectacle of the rood somehow invests it with enormous power – 'Ealle ic mihte / feondas gefyllan' (37b–38a) [I could have felled all the enemies] – even before its intimate association with Christ begins, but it resists the impulse to act several times, and instead 'fæste stod' (38b) [stood firmly] as the terrible events of the Crucifixion unfold. Its steadfast obedience models that to which all good Christians should aspire, but its behaviour here also recalls the obedience and loyalty that members of a lord's comitatus were expected to display. Because the rood has the ability to wreak violence on its lord's enemies, it throws into sharp relief the very different foundations of the Christian and heroic ethoi: adherence to the lord's will is paramount to both, but engaging in violence in the lord's service is a critical component of the latter that has no place in the former. The combination of what from our perspective appear to be not only different, but mutually exclusive, ethoi is not unique to *DR*, but in it the Christian and the heroic are melded in a way that is as paradoxical as it is striking for the rood offers a very non-orthodox account of the Crucifixion in which Christ is not a passive sufferer but an active participant in his own death.

When Christ first appears in the poem, he is described as a 'geong hæleð' (39a) [young warrior], a term that locates us firmly in the heroic world. This young warrior is, further, 'strang and stiðmod' (40a) [strong and resolute] and 'modig on manigra gesyhðe' (41a) [courageous in the sight of many], as all good Germanic warriors should be. And finally, this warrior is not led passively to his cross but instead actively mounts the 'gealgan heanne' (40b) [the high gallows]. That the poet uses the b-verse of line 39 to inform us that the 'young warrior' 'wæs god ælmihtig' [was God almighty] may reveal both how deeply rooted in the secular, heroic world are the phrases he uses here, and how unusual his depicting Christ as a warrior is since we might well think that an audience accustomed to hearing Christ described in such terms would not need the explicit qualification offered in 40b. To better understand the presentation of Christ, we need look no further than early Germanic secular culture, one that does not celebrate, or perhaps much value, patient, passive self-sacrifice. By creating a Christ who models the sort of heroic self-sacrifice we see in a secular hero such as Beowulf, the poet makes Christ's sacrifice more culturally understandable and acceptable. As Christ readies himself for his ordeal, the poet employs the contextually appropriate verb *ongirwan* [divest; strip] that echoes, semantically and phonologically, the verb *gegyrwan* [to arm, to gird oneself with weapons], a verb that often appears in martial contexts.

In creating an active, heroic Christ, though, the poet also creates a problem, since while he stretches the narrative's fabric by allowing his Christ to climb willingly and vigorously up onto the cross, having him or the rood exercise their immense power would irreparably rend a narrative whose contours cannot be altered. The poet avoids showing Christ passively bearing the insult of being nailed to the Cross – something antithetical to the culture within which the poem was produced – by transferring it to the rood: in an extraordinary bit of narrative legerdemain, the 'deorcum næglum' (46a) [dark nails] are 'Þurhdrifan' (46a) [driven through] not the body of Christ but 'me' (46a) [me], that is, the rood, and it is on the rood, not Christ's body, that 'syndon þa dolg gesiene, / opene inwidhlemmas' (46b–47a) [the wounds are visible, the open malicious wounds]. Christ's physical suffering, which is a foundational part of the Christian devotional paradigm, is curiously absent in the rood's account of the event. The rood uses the dual pronoun 'unc' when relating that 'the two of us both together' were mocked at the Crucifixion, but it returns its focus to itself and uses the first-person-singular pronoun *ic* when recounting that 'Eall ic wæs mid blode bestemed' (48b) [I was entirely soaked with blood] that comes, it notes almost in passing, 'of þæs guman sidan' (49a) [from the side of that man]. In a beautifully understated and simple line, one that explicitly reveals the identity both of the warrior who is put to death and of the object upon which he dies – 'Crist wæs on rode' (56b) [Christ was on the Cross] –, Christ comes back into focus as the centre of the awful event the rood narrates, but in the six lines that follow, the rood's first-person-singular pronoun appears six times as it beholds the events that unfold following the Crucifixion, including the sky's darkening, the arrival of those who take down and care for the 'limwerigne' (63a) [limb-weary] corpse of Christ as it, growing cold, 'hwile reste' (64b) [rests for a time]. Although the physical suffering of Christ comes to an end with his death, the death he suffers, as the poet stresses, is only temporary. Christ ascends to heaven shortly after the Crucifixion, but another painful and humiliating ordeal awaits the rood: it is felled a second time, and with the other crosses is thrown into a deep, dark pit, where it remains until it is recovered by the lord's friends and 'gyredon' [adorned; girded] with 'golde ond seolfre' (77) [gold and silver].

After concluding its narrative of the Crucifixion, the Cross makes explicit its central position within Christian doctrine, both by paralleling its position to that of Mary's (as she is the best of women, so it is the best of trees) and by revealing that although it once had been 'geworden wita heardost' (87) [made the harshest of torments], it is now an object to be feared and venerated, because at the day of judgement it will lead those who carried it in their hearts while they were in the world into the kingdom of heaven. The final voice in the poem, the dreamer's, brings the narrative back to where it began – the human world –, but now the dreamer speaks not from a sense of ignorant wonder but rather from one of deep-seated understanding. He knows that he, and perhaps all men, are in the world 'ana ... / mæte werede' (123b–24a) [alone ... with a little troop], as was Christ after his body was taken down from the Cross. But by keeping to the path of righteousness, which the dreamer accomplishes by adhering to the words of the Cross, he and all who follow a similar path are destined to do as Christ did 'þa he mid manigeo com, / gasta weorode, on godes rice' (151b–52) [when he came with a multitude, a troop of spirits, into God's kingdom]. The final two sections of the poem, one spoken by the Cross and the other by the dreamer, have a didactic, homiletic focus that aligns them with many of the texts in the Vercelli Book. If they sound rather flat to our ears it may only be because what precedes them allows us to witness and perhaps even feel the events of the Crucifixion with an intimacy that no other narrative account of it achieves.

Soul and Body I, Homiletic Fragment I, and The Dream of the Rood are sometimes taken as a sort of verse booklet within the larger plan of the Vercelli Book but because we know so little about the principles underlying the compilation of the codex, we cannot know for certain if this grouping is the result of the scribe's or compiler's agency or simply the result of happenstance. Some thematic links do exist among these texts, but DR seems more closely aligned with Elene, a poem that is not part of the 'booklet', than with either of the other two. Given the paucity of evidence regarding the manuscript's compilation, we should perhaps not search too long or hard for the reason they appear in succession since that reason may simply be that they were to hand when the compiler reached this point in his copying.

Further Reading

Earl, James W. 'Trinitarian language: Augustine, The Dream of the Rood and Ælfric'. In Source of Wisdom: Old English and Early Medieval Latin Studies in Honour of Thomas D. Hill, ed. Charles D. Wright, Frederick M. Biggs, and Thomas N. Hall, 63–79. Toronto: University of Toronto Press, 2007.
Hall, Thomas N. 'Prophetic vision in The Dream of the Rood'. In Poetry, Place, and Gender: Studies in Medieval Culture in Honor of Helen Damico, ed. Catherine E. Karkov, 60–74. Kalamazoo: Medieval Institute Publications, 2009.

Kendall, Calvin B. 'From sign to vision: the Ruthwell Cross and the *Dream of the Rood*'. In *The Place of the Cross*, ed. Catherine Karkov, Sarah Larratt Keefer, and Karen Louise Jolly, 129–44. Woodbridge: Boydell Press, 2006.

Ó Carragáin, Éamon. *Ritual and the Rood: Liturgical Images and the Old English Poems of the 'Dream of the Rood' Tradition*. British Library Studies in Medieval Culture. London and Toronto: The British Library and University of Toronto Press, 2005.

Ó Carragáin, Éamon, and Richard North. 'The *Dream of the Rood* and Anglo-Saxon Northumbria'. In *'Beowulf' and Other Stories: A New Introduction to Old English, Old Icelandic, and Anglo-Norman Literatures*, ed. Richard North and Joe Allard, 160–88. 2007. 2nd edn. New York: Pearson/Longman, 2012.

Orchard, Andy. '*The Dream of the Rood*: Cross-references'. In *New Readings in the Vercelli Book*, ed. Samantha Zacher and Andy Orchard, 225–53. Toronto Anglo-Saxon Series 4. Toronto: University of Toronto Press, 2009.

Raw, Barbara. 'The cross in *The Dream of the Rood*: martyr, patron, and image of Christ'. *LSE* ns 38 (2007): 1–15.

Roberts, Jane. 'Some relationships between the *Dream of the Rood* and the cross at Ruthwell'. *Studies in Medieval English Language and Literature* (Tokyo) 15 (2000): 1–25.

Elene

Survives uniquely in the Vercelli Book, fols 121^r–33^v.

Elene is the final poem to appear in the Vercelli Book and it is one of two poems in the codex to bear the runic 'signature' of Cynewulf. By far the longest of the poems attributed to Cynewulf, *Elene* is one of the final texts in the Vercelli collection, falling as it does between Homily XXII and the final piece in the collection, Homily XXIII. Following the conclusion of Homily XXII, which ends about midway down on fol. 120^v, *Elene* begins at the top of a new folio, 121^r, with an enlarged but not ornate capital Ƿ. There are no obvious physical lacunae in the poem, but in two places, following lines 438 and 1043, syntactic breakdowns suggest that something, probably not very much, has been lost, likely through a copying error. The only physical damage to the poem occurs on fol. 121^r, where the text field has been stained, perhaps through the application of reagent, but no words are obscured. The poem was copied by the same scribe responsible for copying the other prose and poetic texts contained in the Vercelli Book.

Elene relates an important piece of Biblical apocrypha, the story of the Invention, or discovery, of the Cross by Helen, the mother of the Roman emperor Constantine. As attested by the numerous surviving Greek and Latin versions of this story, it was a popular topic in the late antique and early medieval worlds. We cannot know for certain which version(s)

Cynewulf may have utilized, but the similarities between his narrative and that contained in *The Acts of St Cyriacus* point to it as *Elene*'s source. As Anglo-Saxon authors were wont to do, Cynewulf adheres to his source material but freely expands upon it, as he does in the account of the dream that Constantine, the Roman emperor, has the night before taking the field against the numerically superior Huns. Whereas the *Acts* simply mentions that Constantine becomes frightened when he sees the enemy's vast forces, Cynewulf presents their approach in more detail and articulates it through the affectively charged thematics of Anglo-Saxon oral poetics: in *Elene*, spears and mail-coats gleam, the battle standard is raised with a shout, trumpets sound, and horses paw the ground. Furthermore, the wolf and the raven, carrion-eaters who are integral parts of the traditional thematics of the beasts of battle, make not just one, but several appearances in close succession. Similarly, where the *Acts* treats the ensuing battle between the Roman and Hunnish in a few short sentences, Cynewulf provides a full – and stirring – account as shields crack, swords chop, and fated men fall under the shower of arrows and the flight of spears, cruel 'hildenædran' (119b) [battle-serpents].

Following his rout of the Huns, Constantine learns both the source and meaning of the 'sigores tacen' (85a) [sign of victory] that came to him in his dream and converts to Christianity. Shortly thereafter he delegates his mother to undertake the search for the Cross and puts her in command of a multitude of men. The preparations for her expedition and the sea voyage itself are articulated in highly traditional terms: troops eagerly arrive at the shore of the Mediterranean and the ships, the 'Fearoðhengestas' (226b) [sea-horses], the 'wæghengestas' (236b) [wave-horses], are loaded, appropriately enough, with 'bordum ond ordum' (235a) [shields and swords]. Despite its highly traditional nature, this martial expedition is unique on two accounts: women accompany the warriors on the sea voyage and the entire force is under the command of a 'guðcwen' (254a) [war-queen]. The poem's narrator calls attention to the unusual nature of this situation when he remarks 'Ne hyrde ic sið ne ær / on egstreame idese lædan, / on merestræte, mægen fægerre' (240b–42) [I have never heard, afterwards or before, of a woman leading on the sea, on the sea-road, a fairer host]. That the compound 'guðcwen' is recorded only twice in OE, both times in *Elene*, allows us further to gauge the uniqueness of this situation. Having a woman head an army is so novel a situation that Cynewulf must resort to using an otherwise unattested, and perhaps newly coined, compound, 'guðcwen', to describe Helen's position. Despite being dubbed a 'guðcwen', Helen's power may not be all that it seems: even though she is accompanied by a mighty troop, one that both protects her and poses a real threat to the inhabitants of Jerusalem once she enters the city, she exercises her power only once, when she commands that the wise man Judas be thrown into a pit. Aside from this, she does nothing other than threaten a group of wise men with death by fire, and she never carries out the threat. Helen is, finally, not a true warrior-woman as, say, Grendel's mother and the Biblical heroine Judith are. Possessing only the trappings of masculine military power, her actions are limited to spreading the doctrine of Christianity, as she does when she lectures, often quite pointedly, the Jewish wise men on the virtues of Christianity and the sinful nature of their practices.

In both the *Acts* and *Elene*, the Jews resist aiding Helen in her search because they believe revealing the Cross's whereabouts will threaten the survival of their culture and result in the diminution of their power. As Judas's father tells him, they must keep the Cross's hiding place secret 'þy læs towor-pen sien / frod fyrngewritu ond þa fæderlican / lare forleten' (430b–32a) [lest the wise ancient writings be thrown over and our ancestral teaching be abandoned] following its recovery. Judas holds out for as long as he can, but after suffering physical and mental privation for the seven days he is chained to the bottom of a pit, he capitulates and, in a detail that is shared between the *Acts* and the poem, prays 'on Ebrisc' (724b) [in Hebrew] that the hiding place of the Cross, which his starvation has caused him to forget, be revealed through a divine sign. When in immediate response to his protracted prayer a plume of smoke arises from where the Cross has been buried, Judas forsakes his past and resolves to convert to Christianity. He proves his loyalty to his newly adopted faith by engaging in a verbal duel with the devil in a scene reminiscient of Christ's dialogue with the devil in *Christ and Satan*.

Judas, who takes the name Cyriacus following his baptism, is put into service by Helen one final time when she requests his help in finding the nails used in Christ's crucifixion. Another miracle reveals their location and they shine forth from the pit where they were hidden 'swylce heofonsteorran / oððe goldgimmas' (1112b–13a) [as if they were stars of heaven, or golden gems], images that echo those we find at the opening of another poem in the Vercelli Book that also meditates on the nature and power of the Cross, *The Dream of the Rood*. The uncovering of the nails and the revelation of their power (incorporated into the emperor's bridle as a bit, the nails will enable him to 'oferswiðan ... / feonda gehwylcne' [1177b–78a] [overcome ... each of his enemies] in battle) returns the narrative to the theme – the power of the Cross – with which it opened, a theme that drives *DR* as well. The shared focus of these two poems reveals that the Cross was important enough to the Vercelli Book's compiler for him to include two poems devoted to it in the collection, but whether this reflects the Cross's larger cultural importance or is mere happenstance cannot be determined.

The poem's conclusion is marked definitively in the manuscript by the word 'finit', but following this the poet, about whom we know nothing more than his name, Cynewulf, appends what appears to be an autobiographical passage. Marked off, as are the poem's other sections, by a Roman numeral (the final section is number XV) and further distinguished from the rest of the poem by virtue of its heavy use of internal rhyme, this section contains another of Cynewulf's runic 'signatures', the second one in the Vercelli Book. Although the sections the poet adds at the end of the four poems attributed to him are all somewhat autobiographical, Cynewulf is more highly confessional in the section appended to *Elene* than he is in the others as he comments not only on his advanced age, physical infirmity, and sinful past, but also on his conversion in his old age, something that occurs once God 'bancofan onband, breostlocan onwand' (1249) [unbound his body, opened his heart]. Before accepting what he says as shedding light on his life, however, we need to situate these comments within the larger context of the poem to which they are appended and note that while they may well be autobiographical (we have no way of assessing either their accuracy or veracity), he may have constructed these details to fit into the thematics of the preceding poem, one in which conversions figure prominently and in which the unconverted attempt to keep their secrets and their minds closed from the wisdom of God. When the poet credits his meditation on the Cross with enabling him to recall the miracle of its Invention, he models the type of behaviour the poem seeks to instill in its readers/listeners, and when he concludes by sketching the fates that await men at Judgement Day, he sounds, in keeping with the homiletic tone of the final passage, very much like a cleric offering a sermon.

Cynewulf's comments in this addendum are also important because he touches briefly on his compositional practices and the source of his artistry, topics of great interest to us but on which Anglo-Saxon authors are, unfortunately, nearly universally silent. The picture Cynewulf presents of his compositional practices is remarkably contemporary and further reveals just how little some things have changed from the Anglo-Saxon period to the present day since he 'wordcræftum wæf ond wundrum læs, / þragum þreodude ond geþanc reodode / nihtes nearwe' (1237–39a) [composed poetry and collected wonders, deliberated for a time and arranged my thoughts anxiously by night]. And in a comment that recalls a salient detail in Bede's story of the poet Cædmon, Cynewulf further explains that his artistry is a gift from God, one he received when God instilled grace in his mind and 'leoðucræft onleac. Þæs ic lustum breac, / willum in worlde' (1250–51a) [unlocked the art of poetry. I have used it joyfully and in accordance with my desire in the world]. As to what exactly this desire is,

Cynewulf is silent, but the focus of his poems and the homiletic nature of the comments he appends to *Elene* suggest that they were of a piece with those of the person or persons responsible for compiling the Vercelli Book, a rich, complex collection of highly devotional texts.

Further Reading

Erussard, Laurence. 'Language, power and holiness in Cynewulf's *Elene*'. *Medievalia et Humanistica* ns 34 (2008): 23–41.

Klein, Stacy S. 'Crossing queens, pleasing hierarchies'. In her *Ruling Women: Queenship and Gender in Anglo-Saxon Literature*, 53–85. Notre Dame: University of Notre Dame Press, 2006.

Heckman, Christina. 'Things in doubt: inventio, dialectic, and Jewish secrets in Cynewulf's *Elene*'. *JEGP* 108 (2009): 449–80.

Johnson, David F. 'Hagiographical demon or liturgical devil? Demonology and baptismal imagery in Cynewulf's *Elene*'. *LSE* ns 37 (2006): 9–30.

Sharma, Manish. 'The reburial of the cross in the Old English *Elene*'. In *New Readings in the Vercelli Book*, ed. Samantha Zacher and Andy Orchard, 280–97. Toronto Anglo-Saxon Series 4. Toronto: University of Toronto Press, 2009.

Zollinger, Cynthia Wittman. 'Cynewulf's *Elene* and the patterns of the past'. *JEGP* 103 (2004): 180–96.

The Exeter Book

Exeter, Cathedral Library, Dean and Chapter MS 3501, fols 8^r–130^v.

Held in the library of Exeter Cathedral, Exeter, Dean & Chapter MS 3501, known less formally as the Exeter Book, preserves more than thirty poems on a variety of religious and secular topics, and no other manuscript from the period contains as many individual vernacular poems. The product of a single scribal hand, the Exeter Book is by far the most eclectic vernacular poetic codex to survive from Anglo-Saxon England, containing as it does several poetic genres, including riddles and the so-called elegies, not elsewhere attested in the written records of Anglo-Saxon England. Although we cannot be certain, the Exeter Book is generally identifed as the 'ı mycel englisc boc be gehwilcum þingum on leoðwisan gewhorht' (fol. 1^v) [one large English book on various things composed in poetry] mentioned in the list of more than fifty books Leofric, the Bishop of Exeter (d. 1072) who established the see there in 1050, bequeathed to the cathedral chapter. The principles behind its compilation are especially murky and it may be best to accept Bishop Leofric's description and to leave the matter there.

The codex itself has suffered considerable damage over the centuries. Fol. 8^r is marred by a circular stain caused when something – a glue pot, perhaps, or maybe a beer mug – was apparently set on the manuscript. The larger stain on fols 8^r–10^v may have resulted from the spilling of the container's contents, and we are fortunate that much of the text remains legible under the stain. Finally, cuts on some of the first folios suggest that the codex may have been used as a cutting board. Fols 119^r–30^v have more extensive damage caused, it appears, by a hot object having been placed on the manuscript. While it was not always treated carefully, as the stains, burn damage, and

The Anglo-Saxon Literature Handbook, First Edition. Mark C. Amodio.
© 2014 Mark C. Amodio. Published 2014 by John Wiley & Sons, Ltd.

cuts all witness, its layout was carefully planned and the texts are written in a clear, consistent hand. The manuscript's formatting is also consistent: the beginnings of texts (and of sectional divisions within some individual poems) are indicated by capitals, some of which are rather small and plain and others of which are large and comparatively more decorative. Not very ornate, the capitals in the Exeter Book nevertheless are generally not as plain as the non-zoomorphic ones in Junius 11 or the capitals found in the Vercelli Book (excepting a few) or in Cotton Vitellius A.xv, the *Beowulf* manuscript. In a number of instances, following the initial capital, the whole first word is written out in small capitals and sometimes the first few words of a poem are. Texts are generally separated from one another by a blank line or, in some cases, by several blank lines, and some initial capitals extend down for several lines and out into the left-hand margin.

The first poem in the Exeter Book is either a discrete series of lyrical poems based on the Latin 'Great O' antiphons celebrating the wonder and mystery of Christ's conception and birth, or it is the first section of a longer poem celebrating three critical moments in Christ's history: his Advent, Ascension, and Final Judgement. These poems are often given the names *Christ I, II*, and *III*, but because the issue of *Christ*'s unity remains a vexed and open one, and because they may be three separate poems that owe their position in the Exeter Book to the codex's complier, we will follow the practice of the their most recent editor and refer to them as *The Advent Lyrics, The Ascension*, and *Christ in Judgement*. However, since most editions number the lines of these poems as if they were a single entity, we will, for ease of reference, adopt this practice when citing them below.

Further Reading

Conner, Patrick W. *Anglo-Saxon Exeter: A Tenth-Century Cultural History*. Studies in Anglo-Saxon History 4. Woodbridge: Boydell Press, 1993.

The Advent Lyrics

The unique copy of this poem, which is frequently designated *Christ I*, survives in the Exeter Book, fols 8ʳ–14ʳ.

The antiphons upon which nine of the twelve *Advent Lyrics* (*AL*) are based are part of the pre-Christmas-week liturgy. The sources of two of the remaining poems, 7 and 10, are antiphons not connected to the Advent celebration; to date, no source has been identified for poem 11, although several analogues have been suggested. Recited at Vespers, the antiphons, all of which begin with the exclamation 'O', celebrate such things as the approach of Christ's birth, the miracle of the Virgin Birth, and the Holy Trinity. The first of the OE *AL* is defective, owing to the loss of at least one manuscript leaf, but since the rest of the poems all begin with an OE equivalent to the Latin 'O', 'Eala', we may cautiously surmise that the first one did as well. The OE poems are closely related to their sources, as we can see in poem 1 where the Latin phrase 'lapisque angularis' [corner stone] becomes OE 'weallstan' (2a) [cornerstone]. Ranging as they do from seventeen to seventy-three lines, the OE poems are far more than the brief, devotional utterances that the antiphons are: in the hands of the Anglo-Saxon poet they become sites of extended devotional, almost homiletic meditation and instruction as well, as the poet expands his source material in ways both predictable and surprising. For example, while he employs the architectural imagery central to the antiphon 'O Rex gentium' in poem 1, the poet does not just reveal Christ to be the 'weallstan' as the antiphon does, but also that he is a cornerstone that was rejected by earlier builders. Picking up the theme of Christ's saving mercy that runs through many of the poems, the poet assures us that even though this 'weallstan' was earlier 'wiðwurpon' (3a) [thrown aside], it will nonetheless serve as the 'hea-fod … healle mærre / ond gesomnige side weallas / fæste gefoge, flint unbræcne' (4–6) [head(stone) of the glorious hall, an unbroken flint, one that will unite the broad walls with a secure joint]. Architectural metaphors are also employed in poem 9, one of those that focuses on the mystery of the Virgin Birth. In this poem, Mary is the 'wealldor' (328a) [gateway] through which Christ crosses into the human world. Because Mary is also a pathway to salvation, the poet notes that Christ locked the gateway behind him, ensuring that Mary was 'eft unmæle ælces þinges' (333) [afterwards spotless in all things]. The architectural metaphor is articulated again in poem 9, when the poet literalizes, perhaps somewhat disturbingly, Christ's role as 'clavis David', the 'key of David' (the phrase is from the Latin antiphon that is the source of poem 2), by revealing that Christ locks the gateway through which he passes with the 'liþucægan' (334a) [key of his body; literally limb-key]. He is 'se þe locan healdeð' (19a) [the one who holds the lock] and it is his body that will once again open the lock following the Crucifixion.

The mystery of the Virgin Birth is the subject of poem 7, one of the lyrics not based on an Advent antiphon and one that is further distinguished from the rest of the poems that comprise *AL* by virtue of its being presented almost entirely in direct discourse. The lyric, which at fifty lines is the third longest, contains only one line of narration; the rest is spoken in the voices of Joseph and Mary, whose identities emerge only through their speeches and not by any discourse markers such as 'cwæð Maria' [said Mary]. After opening with the familiar 'Eala' that begins all the poems except the acephalous first one, the voice of poem 7 quickly reveals itself as Mary's:

> Eala Ioseph min, Iacobes bearn,
> mæg Dauides, mæran cyninges,
> nu þu freode scealt fæste gedælan,
> alætan lufan mine.
>
> (164–67a)

[O my Joseph, son of Jacob and kinsman of David, the renowned king, now you must firmly sunder my friendship, forsake my love.]

Joseph's doubts are part of the tradition surrounding the birth of Christ that developed in apocryphal writings, and in presenting these doubts in an exchange between Joseph and Mary, the poet offers what may be one of the earliest examples of drama in English literary history as Joseph movingly reveals that he has endured 'worn ... / sidra sorga' (169b–70a) [a great many ... of broad sorrows], 'sarcwida' (170b) [bitter words], 'hosp' (171b) [contempt], and 'tornworda fela' (172a) [many scornful words] on account of his supposedly adulterous young bride, and that he must shed 'tearas' (172b) [tears] on her behalf.

Joseph is not the only one who suffers; Mary, too, has 'þæs byrdscypes bealwa onfongen' (182) [endured harms as a result of this pregnancy]. In his final speech before Mary reveals that she became pregnant not 'þurh gemæcscipe monnes ower, / ænges on eorðan' (199–200a) [not through sexual intercourse ever with any man on earth], Joseph reveals just how difficult his situation is because 'Me nawþer deag, / secge ne swige' (189b–90a) [neither speech nor silence profits (him)]:

> Gif ic soð sprece,
> þonne sceal Dauides dohtor sweltan
> stanum astyrfed. Gen strengre is
> þæt ic morþor hele; scyle manswara
> laþ leoda gehwam lifgan siþþan
> fracoð in folcum.
>
> (190b–95a)

[If I speak the truth, then must David's daughter die, killed by stones. Yet it is harder that I conceal a mortal sin; the perjurer must afterward live hateful to all people, despised among the folk.]

Comparing just this passage with the antiphonal source of poem 7, which is cited below in its entirety, allows us to gauge just how radically the poet of *AL* departs from his source: 'O Joseph, why did you believe what before you feared? Why indeed? The One whom Gabriel announced would be the coming Christ is begotten in her by the Holy Spirit' (Calder and Allen, 73). Aside from its being almost wholly direct discourse, poem 7 typifies the poet's relationship to the sources of *AL* in other ways: the Latin antiphons provide him with little more than each poem's broad thematic contours, which he then fleshes out in poems that remain true to the antiphons' devotional purposes even as they draw their readers and/or listeners into sometimes complex considerations of and engagements with sacred history.

Further Reading

Farina, Lara. 'Before affection: *Christ I* and the social erotic'. In her *Erotic Discourse and Early English Religious Writing*, 15–33. The New Middle Ages. New York: Palgrave Macmillan, 2006.

Hill, Thomas D. 'Literary history and Old English poetry: the case of *Christ I, II*, and *III'*. In *Sources of Anglo-Saxon Culture*, ed. Paul E. Szarmach and Virginia D. Oggins, 3–22. Kalamazoo: Medieval Institute Publications, 1986.

Irving, Edward B. 'The advent of poetry: *Christ I'*. ASE 25 (1996): 123–34.

Salvador, Mercedes. 'Architectural metaphors and Christological imagery in the *Advent Lyrics*: Benedictine propaganda in the Exeter Book?' In *Conversion and Colonization in Anglo-Saxon England*, ed. Catherine E. Karkov and Nicholas Howe, 169–211. MRTS 318. Essays in Anglo-Saxon Studies 2. Tempe: ACMRS, 2006.

The Ascension

Also known as *Christ II*, a unique copy survives in the Exeter Book, fols 14ʳ–20ᵛ. There is a lacuna in the manuscript following line 117 where a leaf has gone missing from the codex.

The second poem in the Exeter Book takes as its central theme another moment of great importance in Christian sacred history, the Ascension of Christ forty days after the Crucifixion. More overtly homiletic and reflective than *The Advent Lyrics*, *The Ascension* is one of the four OE poems that bear the runic 'signature' of Cynewulf. While he drew upon a fairly wide variety of scriptural texts in composing *The Ascension*, Cynewulf's heaviest debts are to the final few sections of Gregory the Great's Homily 29, the 'Ascension Homily', and to passages of the Venerable Bede's *Ascension Hymn*. Despite its broadly homiletic tone, *The Ascension* opens not with an address to many men, as homiletic writings very frequently do, but rather to a 'mon se mæra'

(441a) [an illustrious man] whom Cynewulf encourages 'geornlice gæstgerynum, / … modcræfte sec / þurh sefan snyttro' (440a–43a) [eagerly to explore spiritual mysteries through the skill of the mind, through sagacious understanding]. This otherwise unidentified man may have been Cynewulf's patron, or he may simply stand for all those who read or hear the poem since Cynewulf announces near its conclusion that he 'leofra gehwone læran wille' (815) [desires to teach each of the beloved ones], and not just a single man.

As in his other poems, in *The Ascension* Cynewulf transposes the expressive economy of the vernacular heroic tradition to a Christian key, but the language and thematics of the heroic tradition are not woven as thoroughly into *The Ascension*'s fabric as they are in other of the poems attributed to him. Christ is described early on in terms that are frequently applied to secular rulers: he is a 'þeoden þrymfæst' (457a) [a glorious prince], a 'sincgiefan' (460a) [dispenser of treasure] who is 'sigehremig' (531a) [exultant in victory], 'meahtum strang' (647a) [strong in his might], and, twice, 'modig' (647a; 746a) [courageous]. The terms for the companions who attend him are similarly drawn from the heroic register and are used more commonly of warriors than angels or disciples: 'þegna gedryht' (457b) [troop of thanes], 'leof weorud' (458a) [beloved troop], 'hæleð' (461a) [warriors], 'Þegnas' (470b) [thanes], 'hæleð hygerofe' (534a) [brave-mined warriors], 'þegnas þrymfulle' (541a) [glorious thanes]. Aside from its lexicon, however, the poem is not heavily indebted to the heroic register as Cynewulf for the most part remains firmly within that of the Christian tradition.

In focusing on the faithfulness of the angelic host that attends Christ at his death and in the days preceding the Ascension, on the intense sorrow of the men who witness the event, and on the 'folces unrim' (569b) [countless number of people] Christ frees from hell, Cynewulf uses the Ascension as a way of pointing the continued importance of sacred history in the daily life of every Christian. Christ himself stresses this when he tells his disciples that even though he is returning to heaven, 'Næfre ic from hweorfe' (476b) [I will never depart from you]. The dynamism and presentness that characterize Cynewulf's conception of the Ascension are reflected both in the poem's structure (the event is reported several times in the narrative) and in its language (the verb *astigan*, which occurs six times in the poem, means both 'to ascend' *and* 'to descend'). In an image that comes from Gregory, Cynewulf likens Christ to a 'fæla fugel' (645a) [beloved bird] who flies to heaven and then returns 'hwilum … to eorþan' (648a) [at times … to the earth] after having been for a time in the 'engla eard' (646a) [dwelling of angels]. And as does Gregory, who expands upon a single statement in Solomon's Canticle of Canticles (2.8), Cynewulf presents Christ's mission on earth as a series of 'leaps' (six for Cynewulf and five for Gregory) over difficulties, leaps that model behaviour Cynewulf exhorts Christians to emulate daily:

> Þus her on grundum godes ece bearn
> ofer heahhleoþu hlypum stylde,
> modig ofer muntum. Swa we men sculon
> heortan gehygdum hlypum styllan
> of mægene in mægen.
>
> (744–48a)

[Thus here in the world the eternal son of God sprang in leaps over the high hills, brave across the mountains. So we men must in our hearts' thoughts spring in leaps from strength to strength.]

The poem's final sections meditate upon one of Christ's 'leaps', the Final Judgement. As he does throughout the poem, Cynewulf stresses how important this event is to each Christian. Perhaps as a way of increasing this point's affective impact, he offers himself as an object lesson: because he has 'ne heold teala þæt me hælend min / on bocum bibead' (353b–54a) [not held well what my lord commanded me in books] he knows that he will 'þæs brogan ... / geseon synwræce' (354b–55a) [look upon this terror, the punishment of sin] when he stands 'fore onsyne eces deman' (357b) [before the face of the eternal judge]. Cynewulf characteristically inserts himself near his poems' conclusions both as a figure in the poem and by means of a runically encoded 'signature', and while he does so in *The Ascension*, the poem ends on a note that is broadly eschatological, not autobiographical. In *The Ascension*, the poet's persona serves a largely, and perhaps exclusively, didactic function: far from revealing much of anything about Cynewulf himself, the *ic* [I] in the poem stands as a rather flat and curiously impersonal figure, especially in contrast to the *ic* that emerges at the conclusions of his other 'signed' poems, in which we hear, among other things, of his advanced age, physical infirmities, and nearness to death. After calling attention to the punishments that await him and after calling further attention to himself, in an admittedly oblique fashion by weaving the runes that spell his name into a passage detailing some of the great many terrors that await the sinful following death, Cynewulf shifts his focus back to the poem's intended audience, namely 'gumena gehwylc' (820b) [each man] who must 'georne biþencan' (821b) [eagerly think about] the lessons of Christ's life and the Ascension. In returning to 'each man' Cynewulf brings his poem – which opened with the exhortation to a single man that he should through 'modcræfte sec / ... sefan snyttro' (441b–42a) [mental skill seek ... wisdom of the mind] so that he might know for himself the truth of Christ's incarnate mission – full circle. And in briefly touching upon three central moments of

Christ's mission – the Nativity, Ascension, and Final Judgement –, he not only maps the trajectory of his own poem but provides a strong thematic bridge between the poems that precede and follow them in the Exeter Book. Whether this bridge is authorial or whether we owe *The Ascension*'s placement in the manuscript to a decision of the codex's compiler is a question that has not yet been definitively answered, and that may never be.

Further Reading

Bjork, Robert E. 'The symbolic use of Job in Ælfric's Homily on Job, *Christ II*, and the *Phoenix*'. In *Latin Learning and English Lore: Studies in Anglo-Saxon Literature for Michael Lapidge*, ed. Katherine O'Brien O'Keeffe and Andy Orchard, vol. II, 315–30. Toronto Old English Series 14. 2 vols. Toronto: University of Toronto Press, 2005.

Chase, Colin. 'God's presence through grace as the theme of Cynewulf's *Christ II* and the relationship of this theme to *Christ I* and *Christ III*'. *ASE* 3 (1974): 87–101.

Marchand, James W. 'The leaps of Christ and *The Dream of the Rood*'. In *Source of Wisdom: Old English and Early Medieval Latin Studies in Honour of Thomas D. Hill*, ed. Charles D. Wright, Frederick M. Biggs, and Thomas N. Hall, 80–89. Toronto Old English Series 16. Toronto: University of Toronto Press, 2007.

Wright, Charles D. 'Old English homilies and Latin sources'. In *The Old English Homily: Precedent, Practice, and Appropriation*, ed. Aaron J. Kleist, 15–66. Studies in the Early Middle Ages 17. Turnhout: Brepols, 2007.

Wright, Charles D. 'The persecuted church and the *Mysterium Lunae*: Cynewulf's *Ascension*, lines 252b–272 (*Christ II*, lines 691b–711)'. In *Latin Learning and English Lore: Studies in Anglo-Saxon Literature for Michael Lapidge*, ed. Katherine O'Brien O'Keeffe and Andy Orchard, vol. II, 293–314. Toronto Old English Series 14. 2 vols. Toronto: University of Toronto Press, 2005.

Christ in Judgement

The unique copy of this poem survives in the Exeter Book, fols 20^v–32^r, and is also known as *Christ III*.

The third poem in the Exeter Book, *Christ in Judgement* (*CJ*), complements the manuscript's first two texts and brings the course of sacred history begun in the *Advent Lyrics* and continued in *The Ascension* to its logical – and chronological – close. While it is reminiscent of Cynewulf's 'signed' poems, it cannot be securely attributed it to him, as it had been in the past. Situated in the tradition of eschatological writing, the poem addresses a topic of great interest to Anglo-Saxon authors and, presumably, their audiences. No source has been discovered for *CJ*, and it is unlikely that the poet relied on a single one. Portions of the poem are derived from the Bible, especially Revelations and sections of Isaiah, Mark, and Luke, but the poet is selective in what he draws upon and seems to rely to a large extent on nothing other than his own imagination. A number of patristic texts have been put forth as analogues to the poem and while we cannot know for certain that the *CJ*-poet knew any of them, the analogues testify to the subject matter's broad appeal and to the widespread nature of many of the themes and images that Anglo-Saxon authors and audiences associated with the Day of Judgement.

Given that the poet draws upon a number of different sources, we might expect the poem to be a loosely knit pastiche of eschatological material, but it proves to be a well-crafted piece of devotional poetry, one full of vivid and dynamic images. The poem announces its subject and reveals its didactic focus from the outset as it opens on a highly emotional, affective note, one that it will sustain throughout, warning as it does that Judgement Day will 'mid fere foldbuende / ... / æt midre niht mægne bihlameð' (867–69) [resound over the throng of earth dwellers with sudden terror at midnight] and that just as a thief takes his 'slæpe gebundne' (873b) [sleep-bound] victims by surprise, so too will Judgement Day 'eorlas ungearwe yfles genægeð' (874) [assault with evil unprepared men]. With the zeal and effectiveness of a preacher addressing a congregation, the poet renders the turmoil of doomsday through a series of powerful images, first noting that the trumpets that will sound will blow so loudly that 'Beofað middangeard, / hruse under hæleþum' (881b–82a) [middle-earth will tremble, the earth under men]. Howling winds will arise and the combined noise of trumpets and winds will 'fyllað mid fere foldan gesceafte' (952) [fill with fear the creatures of the earth]. To this already overwhelming tumult will be added a 'heard gebrec, hlud, unmæte, / swar ond swiðlic, swegdynna mæst / ældum egeslic' (953–55a) [harsh crashing sound, loud, immense, painful, and violent, the greatest of resounding dins, terrifying to men]. The sun will shine 'on blodes hiw' (935a) [in the colour of blood], the moon will 'niþer gehreoseð' (938b) [fall down], and the stars 'stredað of heofone' (939b) [will scatter from heaven]. A fire that will scorch the 'sæs mid hyra fiscum, / eorþan mid hire beorgum, ond upheofon / torhtne mid his tunglum' (966b–68a) [seas with their fish, the earth with its mountains, and heaven with its stars] announces God's wrath, which is so great that even the 'heagengla mægen, / for ðære onsyne beoð egsan afyrhte' (1018b–19) [host of archangels were frightened in terror].

Because at doomsday all will have to be judged, the shock and surprise of the day's advent will descend equally upon the evil and the good, who will stand 'gemengde' (894b) [mixed together] at the initial assembly, although they will shortly thereafter be permanently divided into two groups since 'him is ham sceapen / ungelice, englum ond deoflum' (897b–98a) [for them is a different home prepared, for angels and for devils]. The separation of the saved and the damned, the sheep and the goats, is a fundamental part of the rhetoric of doomsday, but in *CJ* it becomes an important structural component as well, as the poet carefully balances the sections cataloguing the joys that await the saved and those that detail the horrors the sinful will face. For example, the 'þreo tacen somod' (1235a) [three tokens together] that will mark the saved are balanced by the three great pains that the damned will suffer. The saved will 'fore leodum leohte bicaþ' (1238) [shine brightly before mankind]; they will 'him in wuldre witon waldendes giefe' (1243) [themselves know in glory the grace of the ruler]; and they are able to see the damned 'sar þrowian, … / weallendne lig, ond wyrma slite, / bitrum ceaflum, byrnendra scole' (1249–51) [sorely suffer … the surging flame, the bite of serpents with fierce jaws, the multitude of burning people]. In contrast, the damned will first see the 'grim helle fyr' (1269a) [grim hell fire] that they must endure forever. They must also endure 'scoma mæste' (1273b) [the greatest of shames], namely that not only the lord, but also 'heofonengla here, ond hæleþa bearn, / ealle eorðbuend ond atol deofol' (1277–78) [the troop of angels, the sons of men, all earth-dwellers, and the terrible devil] will be able to see through their bodies to their sinful souls. Finally, for all eternity the damned will have to 'Geseoð … þa betran blæde scinan' (1291) [look upon … those better ones shine in heavenly splendour]. A similar sense of rhetorical balance marks the catalogues with which the poem ends, although the poet switches his usual order of presentation and offers first the punishments that await the sinful before concluding on a positive note with the comforts the 'gecorene' (1223a) [the chosen] will enjoy.

As in many doomsday narratives, Christ speaks directly in *CJ*, and while he often speaks in the register of high orthodoxy, especially when he is talking to the saved about their rewards or remonstrating the damned for their sinful behaviour, he adopts here a far less elevated, more personal register as he recounts, among other things, his humilation at being wrapped in 'wonnum claþum' (1423a) [dusty clothes] and being placed 'on heardum stane' (1424b) [on hard stone] when he was born, helpless (this is another source of humilation to him), into the world of man, as well as the physical torments he endured, including the 'hearmslege' (1434a) [grievous blows] his head suffered, the 'spatl' (1435b) [spittle] his face 'of muðe onfeng, manfremmendra' (1436) [received from the mouth of evil-doers], the flogging he received 'sweopum' (1441a) [with whips], and the 'hwæsne beag' (1443b) [sharp crown] that was 'þream biþrycton' (1445a) [painfully pressed] onto his head. Christ's voice in *CJ* is more individuated and distinctive than the voice he's given even in texts as closely analaguous to *CJ* as Vercelli Homily VIII. For example, to the series of questions he asks the damned, questions also found in Vercelli Homily VIII, the *CJ*-poet adds one that is moving in its plaintiveness: 'For hwon ahenge þu mec hefgor on þinra honda rode / þonne iu hongade?' (1487–88a) [Why do you hang me more painfully on the cross of your hands than I formerly was hung?].

In keeping with the poem's highly pitched affective dynamics, the poet foregrounds the physical suffering of Christ at several points in the narrative. So central is Christ's suffering to the narrative that even when the poet focuses on the Cross and its important function at doomsday (1061 ff.), Christ's wounded body is nevertheless made manifest both indirectly through the blood he shed during the Crucifixion (the Cross is 'blode bistemed' (1085b) [moistened with blood]), and directly when the 'reade rod' (1101) [reddened Cross] upon which the damned will stare forces them to confront their own 'bealwe' (1105a) [destruction] and, somewhat abruptly, the body of Christ. Upon his body are visible both 'þa ealdan wunde on þa openan dolg' (1107) [the old wounds and the open wounds] caused when evil men 'mid næglum þurhdrifan' (1109a) [pierced with nails] his 'hwitan honda ond þa halgan fet' (1110) [white hands and holy feet], and the 'blod ond wæter' (112a) [blood and water] that flow from his side.

Further Reading

Arner, Timothy D. and Paul D. Stegner. '"Of þam him aweaxeð wynsum gefea": the voyeuristic appeal of *Christ III*'. *JEGP* 106 (2007): 428–46.

Biggs, Frederick M. 'The fourfold division of souls: the Old English *Christ III* and the insular homiletic tradition'. *Traditio* 45 (1989–90): 35–51.

Shimomura, Sachi. 'Visualizing judgment in Anglo-Saxon England: illumination, metaphor, and *Christ III*'. In her *Odd Bodies and Visible Ends in Medieval Literature*, 13–38. The New Middle Ages. New York: Palgrave Macmillan, 2006.

The Life of St Guthlac

The Exeter Book contains two poems on the life of Guthlac of Crowland, *Guthlac A* on fols 32ᵛ–44ᵛ and *Guthlac B* on fols 44ᵛ–52ᵛ. Both poems are incomplete: there is a lacuna in *Guthlac A* following line 368 owing to the loss of at least one folio, and near the conclusion of *Guthlac B* a strip which might have contained four or five lines of verse has been cut from the top of fol. 53, although an entire folio may have been lost between the current fols 52 and 53.

Guthlac is a historical figure who was born into a noble Mercian family sometime in the late seventh century. He spent several years as a soldier fighting the British along the Mercian borders, but in his early twenties he renounced his goods and position, gave up secular life, and entered the monastery at Repton. He remained in the monastery only a few years before choosing a more severely ascetic path by embracing the ermetic life, spending the final fifteen or so years of his life as an anchorite in the desolate fens of Crowland. A popular figure among Anglo-Saxon authors and audiences, Guthlac is the subject of no fewer than three separate vernacular texts and his death is mentioned in a fourth: the Exeter Book contains two poetic treatments of his life, *Guthlac A* and *Guthlac B*; his life is the subject of Vercelli Homily XXIII; and, finally, his death is recorded in the Anglo-Saxon Chronicle (see Part 2), where in the majority of texts it stands alone as the entry for 714, as it does in the C-text: 'Her forðferde Guþlac se halga' (O'Brien O'Keeffe, Anglo-Saxon Chronicle, 43) [At this time Guthlac the holy passed away]. Guthlac is also the subject of Felix's *Vita Sancti Guthlaci*, and Chapter 50 of Felix's text – a lengthy Latin prose account commissioned by King Ælfwald that may have been written within living memory of the saint – is generally accepted as being the source for many of the details contained in *Guthlac B*, a poem that treats the saint's final days and his hagiographic death. The relationship of *Guthlac A* to Felix's text remains vexed, and to date no demonstrable source for the OE poem has been discovered.

Guthlac A

The Exeter Book scribe marks the beginning of *Guthlac A* in the same way he does the other long poems in the manuscript: the first letter is written in a large initial capital and the rest of the line is written in small capitals. That the presentation of the poem thus accords with the scribe's usual practice is noteworthy only because its first twenty-nine lines are sometimes thought to belong to the preceding poem, *Christ in Judgement*. While the comment written by a much later hand in the upper margin of the folio on which *Guthlac A* begins, 'of the joyes prepared for them that serve God and keep his commandments', is connected with the beginning of *Guthlac A*, it also applies equally well to the end of *CJ*. However, the evidence of the poem's *mise-en-page* seems sufficient to establish that the scribe had no difficulty understanding the connection between the first twenty-nine lines of the poem and the narrative saints' life that follows it, because he does not in any way separate the 'prologue' to *Guthlac A* from the beginning of the poem. The scribe marks the beginning of the poem's second section on the bottom of fol. 33ᵛ, the point at which the narrative finally turns explicitly to Guthlac, and so we should perhaps consider the entire first ninety-two lines of the poem a 'prologue' of sorts since after opening with a brief discussion on the joys that await the 'soðfæstra' (22a) [those firm in truth] the poet reminds us that holiness manifests itself in many ways in the world before celebrating the particular type of piety Guthlac embodies, that of saints who patiently endure hardship and derision and who 'to heofonum hyge staþeliað' (66) [steadfastly fix their minds on heaven].

As is frequently the case in the vernacular religious poetry that survives from the Anglo-Saxon period, the patience of these saints is cast in a courageous light, and they are situated within the secular heroic tradition by being labeled 'gecostan cempan' (91) [proved warriors], members, as it were, of a divine 'duguð' [troop of tried warriors]. Articulating the actions of saints within the register of the vernacular heroic tradition can, and often does, lead to narrative disruptions in OE poetry. But in the case of Guthlac, referring to him as 'Cristes cempa' (153a) [Christ's soldier] or as 'eadig oretta, ondwiges heard' (176) [blessed warrior, firm in resistance] is wholly appropriate since the poet tells us that early in life the saint 'gelufade / frecnessa fela' (109b–10a) [loved many physical dangers] before putting aside worldly concerns for pious ones.

The spectre of violence hangs over much of the poem, as it does in Guthlac's multiple encounters with legions of demons after he decides to establish his dwelling in the fens of Crowland in a spot to which the demons liked to retire 'æfter tintergum … / ðonne hy of waþum werge cwoman / restan ryneþragum, rowe gefegon' (211–13) [after their torments … when they rested for a space of time glad for the quiet]. Despite Guthlac's martial experience and the poem's engagement of the heroic register, the struggles over this locale prove to be anything but physical as both the saint and his demonic tormentors suffer only spiritually. During his encounters with the demons, Guthlac is threatened with a variety of bodily torments, including destruction by fire (several times) and being rent apart and having his body scattered 'blodgum lastum' (289a) [on the bloody tracks], but no harm befalls the saint.

The demons are not the only ones, though, who raise the spectre of physical punishment without ever resorting to it: Guthlac does so as well. However, since the poem celebrates the saint's Christian, not secular, life and heroism, Guthlac raises the spectre of physical violence only negatively when he explains to the demons what he will *not* do to them: 'No ic eow sweord ongean / mid gebolgne hond oðberan þence / worulde wæpen, ne sceal þes wong gode / þurh blodgyte gebuen weorðan' (302b–5) [I will not, with an enraged hand, think to bear a sword against you, a weapon in the world, nor ought this place be turned to God through bloodshed]. Guthlac offers, in short, a negative instantiation of the heroic ethos, one he paradoxically articulates through the highly affective and richly associative expressive economy of Anglo-Saxon oral poetics.

The poem may celebrate the type of patient, physically passive heroism valued by the Christian tradition, but the roots of this heroism are nonetheless firmly planted in the secular tradition, making Guthlac a Christian hero unlike any other in the extant literature, for he embraced the martial life and possessed the very 'eorðwela' (62a) [earthly wealth] that the poet warns is the focus of far too many who 'þæs hades hlisan willað / wegan on wordum ond þa weorc ne doð' (60–61) [desire the reputation of a (holy) state and carry it in their words but do not perfom (holy) works]. The heroism which the poem explores, a heroism which results in Guthlac ultimately driving the devils away from what becomes a 'grena wong' (746a) [green place], is aptly summed up near the poem's conclusion when the poet celebrates Guthlac, and those who tread a similar path, because they

> habbað wisne geþoht,
> fusne on forðweg to fæder eðle,
> gearwaþ gæstes hus, on mid gleawnesse
> feond oferfeohtað ond firenlustas
> forberað in breostum.
>
> (800b–4a)

[have a wise, eager thought for the journey forth to the father's homeland, make ready the dwelling place of the spirit, and with prudence conquer the fiend and restrain wicked desires in their breasts.]

The poet knows that the temptations in life are many and that the need for constant vigilance is perhaps most acutely felt by those who, like Guthlac – whose name can be translated 'battle-play' – have experienced them first hand before discovering the path of the 'soðfæste'. *Guthlac A* may not achieve the descriptive or rhetorical heights that other OE homiletic poetry routinely does, but the poet makes his point with considerable artistry, and at times, felicity.

Guthlac B

Guthlac A concludes about halfway down fol. 44ᵛ of the Exeter Book, and after a blank space equivalent to several lines (into which a much later hand has added 'Of the creacion of man & of his falle'), the scribe marks the beginning of a new poem, known to us as *Guthlac B*, in his usual manner: a large initial capital is followed by a series of small capitals that extends all the way across the manuscript page (although the final two letters, pE, are slightly smaller for reasons of space). On linguistic and stylistic grounds, this second poem on the life of St Guthlac is generally considered to be the product of someone other than the poet of *Guthlac A*, and accordingly the poems are most often viewed as discrete pieces of verbal art. Despite being two distinct poems that share only a common subject, they have traditionally been lineated as a single entity when they have been edited, a practice we will follow when citing *Guthlac B*.

Although both *Guthlac A* and *Guthlac B* take as their subject the life of St Guthlac of Crowland, there is surprisingly little narrative overlap between them, which may explain their sequential placement in the codex. After opening with a short account of the fall and of the many miracles Guthlac performed in healing those who came seeking his assistance, *Guthlac B* dwells briefly on the saint's tribulations with the demons he must displace in order to build his abode in the fens, the topic to which *Guthlac A* is chiefly devoted. The *Guthlac B*-poet adds some dramatic details to his account, including the fact that 'hwilum brugdon eft / awyrgde wærlogan on wyrmes bleo, / earme adloman attre spiowdon' (910b–12) [at times the accursed covenant breakers again turned into the shape of a snake; the wretched fire-maimed cripples spewed venom], but neither the attacks themselves nor Guthlac's patient endurance of them receive much attention. Regarding Guthlac's steadfastness in the face of his demonic adversaries, a topic the *Guthlac A*-poet dilates, the poet of *Guthlac B* says simply that Guthlac was always 'þonces gleawne' (914a) [prudent of thought] and that 'He geþyldum bad, / þeah him feonda hloð feorhcwealm bude' (914b–15) [he patiently endured, even though the troop of fiends threatened him with mortal destruction].

Unlike *Guthlac A*, for which no single source has been discovered, the narrative of *Guthlac B* draws heavily on the material contained in the fiftieth chapter of Felix's Latin life, a chapter that includes the sudden onset of Guthlac's illness and his certain knowledge that a 'wiga wælgifre' (999a) [slaughter-greedy warrior], death, 'nealæceð' (1033b) [draws near], as well as the saint's death and the voyage of his attendant to find Guthlac's sister. While many of the poem's narrative details can be traced to Felix, including the sweet fragrance that emanates from Guthlac's mouth and the bright light that envelopes his dwelling from 'midnight till dawn' (Calder and Allen, 111) just prior to his death, the poet frequently, if selectively, expands them. Further, while the Anglo-Saxon poet remains indebted to the structure of Felix's narrative, he articulates his poem within his native tradition's expressive economy, as we can see in the poet's handling of Guthlac's attendant's journey to find the saint's sister. All Felix says is that his attendant 'took a boat, left the haven and started on the journey' (Calder and Allen, 112). The Anglo-Saxon poet, in contrast, does not simply mention the boat but uses several metaphors to describe it, including 'wæghengest'

(1329a) [wave-horse], 'brimwudu' (1331b) [sea-wood], 'lagumearg' (1332b) [sea-steed], and 'hærnflota' (1333b) [wave-floater]. He also includes in his account the attendant's boarding, the boat's launching, its speedy progress, its 'sundplegan' (1334a) [play in the water (rough passage?)], and its safe arrival. What he does, in short, is use the components of a traditional and widely occurring Anglo-Saxon theme, that of the sea voyage, to flesh out Felix's spare narrative of the journey.

While Felix's chapter is devoted exclusively to Guthlac's death, the Anglo-Saxon poet, betraying his perhaps parochial interest in promoting the saint's cult, adds some details not found in the Latin text, including that hungry birds would fly to Guthlac's hands, 'þær hy feorhnere / witude fundon ond hine weorðedon / meaglum steafnum' (917b–19a) [where they found appointed life-sustaining nourishment and honoured him with earnest voices], and that all those suffering from physical and spiritual afflictions who sought him out in the fens departed 'hælde bu tu / lic ond sawle' (928b–29a) [healed both in body and soul]. The poet, curiously, also omits certain details contained in Felix's life, most notably the name of the saint's attendant and that of his sister. And unlike the *Guthlac A*-poet, who claims to have acquired information about Guthlac from those who held the saint in living memory, the *Guthlac B*-poet explicitly notes that his sources are written: 'Us secgað bec / hu Guðlac wearð þurh Godes willan / eadig on Engle' (878b–80a) [books tell us how Guthlac became, through God's will, favoured with divine blessing among the English].

When faced with the terrible physical suffering that descends upon him seven days before his death (which occurs shortly after Easter), Guthlac retains his characteristic patience which is, as in *Guthlac A*, presented in heroic terms: 'ða wæs Guðlace on þa geocran tid / mægen gemeðgad, mod siwþe heard, / elnes anhydig' (976–78a) [then in that grievous time was Guthlac's strength exhausted, but his spirit was strong, resolute in its courage]. As death stealthily approaches, 'strong and hreðe' (1140b) [strong and savage], Guthlac 'on elne bad' (1136a) [awaited courageously]. Even though he is wracked with pain and barely able to speak near the end, he remains 'eorl ellenheard' (1165a) [a warrior firm in courage]. But unlike *Guthlac A*, where the saint responds in kind to the demon's threats – even surpassing them, according to the demons – in *Guthlac B* he is the model of patient passivity: 'Dryhtnes cempa, / from folctoga, feonda þreatum / wiðstod stronglice' (901b–3a) [the warrior of the lord, the brave leader of the people, firmly withstood the troops of fiends]. Guthlac's activity in the poem, if we can even label it that, is limited to his spirit's eagerness to depart on the 'forðsið' [onward journey; death], a point that the poet stresses several times in the narrative and one that becomes literalized at the moment of the saint's death when he 'his gæst onsende / weorcum wlitigne in wuldres dream' (1303b–4) [sent forth his soul, beautiful in its works, into the joy of glory].

Despite his past as an active military man, Guthlac's heroism is of a singularly Christian type and as is true of much other OE Christian poetry, many of the heroic traits celebrated in the secular poetry, including steadfastness in the face of adversity and fealty to one's lord, are simply transposed into a wholly Christian key. In *Guthlac B*, this transposition takes on a strikingly individual dimension as the poet details Guthlac's heroic struggle not against legions of demons, but against the illness that ravages him, making it difficult for him to talk or even draw breath. After telling his servant, 'Nu ic swiðe eom / weorce gewergad' (1268b–69a) [now I am wearied with suffering], the saint 'to þam wage gesag, / heafelan onhylde, hyrde þa gena / ellen on innan, oroð stundum teah / mægne modig' (1269b–72a) [sagged against the wall and bowed his head; he then still obeyed his courage within, and drew breath from time to time, the brave man, through an exercise of effort]. What Guthlac does, in short, is offer a model to the wider Christian community of the sort of 'heroic' behaviour available to those facing death.

The poem concludes with Guthlac's attendant's poignant address to the saint's sister (unnamed in the poem but identified by Felix as Pega). In this passage we can once again witness an Anglo-Saxon poet's negotiation of his inherited tradition as the attendant (also unnamed in the poem but known, again from Felix, as Beccel) bemoans the loss of Guthlac in terms that recall yet another frequently occurring Anglo-Saxon theme, that of exile: 'Ellen bið selast þam þe oftost sceal / dreogan dryhtenbealu, deope behycgan / þroht, þeodengedal þonne seo þrag cymeð, / wefen wyrdstafum' (1348–51a) [Courage is best to the one who most often must endure his lord's destruction, deeply think about hardship, parting from his lord when the time fixed by fate's decrees comes].

Further Reading

Biggs, Frederick M. '*The Dream of the Rood* and *Guthlac B* as a literary context for the monsters in *Beowulf*'. In *Text, Image, Interpretation: Studies in Anglo-Saxon Literature and Its Insular Context in Honour of Éamon Ó Carragáin*, ed. A.J. Minnis and Jane Roberts, 289–301. Studies in the Early Middle Ages 18. Turnhout: Brepols, 2007.

Calder, Daniel G. '*Guthlac A* and *Guthlac B*: some discriminations'. In *Anglo-Saxon Poetry: Essays in Appreciation for John C. McGalliard*, ed. Lewis E. Nicholson and Dolores Warwick Frese, 65–80. Notre Dame: University of Notre Dame Press, 1975.

Hall, Alaric. 'Constructing Anglo-Saxon sanctity: tradition, innovation and Saint Guthlac'. In *Images of Medieval Sanctity: Essays in Honour of Gary Dickson*, ed. Debra Higgs Strickland, 207–35. Visualising the Middle Ages 1. Leiden: Brill, 2007.

Johnson, David F. 'Spiritual combat and the Land of Canaan in *Guthlac A*'. In *Intertexts: Studies in Anglo-Saxon Culture Presented to Paul E. Szarmach*, ed. Virginia Blanton and Helene Scheck, 307–17. MRTS 334. Arizona Studies in the Middle Ages and the Renaissance 24. Tempe: ACMRS, 2008.

Olsen, Alexandra Hennessey. '*Guthlac B* and the cycle of history'. In her *Guthlac of Croyland: A Study of Heroic Hagiography*, 69–109. Washington: University Press of America, 1981.

Olsen, Alexandra Hennessey. 'The return of the hero-saint: a reconsideration of *Guthlac A*'. In her *Guthlac of Croyland: A Study of Heroic Hagiography*, 15–67. Washington: University Press of America, 1981.

Powell, Stephen D. 'The journey forth: elegiac consolation in *Guthlac B*'. ES 79 (1998): 489–500.

Roberts, Jane. '*Guthlac A*: sources and source hunting'. In *Medieval English Studies Presented to George Kane*, ed. Edward Donald Kennedy, Ronald Watson, and Joseph S. Wittig, 1–18. Suffolk: D.S. Brewer, 1988.

Sharma, Manish. 'A reconsideration of the structure of *Guthlac A*: the extremes of saintliness'. *JEGP* 101 (2002): 185–200.

Azarias

The unique copy survives in the Exeter Book, fols 53^r–55^v.

Azarias is also known as the *Canticles of the Three Youths*, a title that reflects the poem's contents with greater accuracy than does *Azarias* since the poem contains two hymns, one by Azariah and a longer one by him Hananiah, and Mishael. The top of fol. 53^r has been cut away, resulting in the loss of three or perhaps four lines of writing (the corresponding lacuna on fol. 53^v occurs between lines 28a and 29b in edited versions of the poem). Just what and how much has been lost is unclear: the presence of a descender just above the capital 'h' in *Azarias*'s first word, 'him', witnesses the presence of text on the now-missing portion of the folio, and since the ending of the preceding poem, *Guthlac B*, is also wanting, the manuscript may be missing an entire folio or folios, which may have contained the ending of *Guthlac B*, the beginning of *Azarias*, and perhaps other texts. The fuller narrative context of the episode in both the Bible and *Daniel* suggests that *Azarias* is acephalous since the poem begins with Azarias already in the oven.

The source for *Azarias* is the third chapter of the Old Testament book of Daniel, which was also the primary source for *Daniel*, one of the poems contained in the Junius Manuscript, and as might be expected there are a great many points of contact between the first seventy or so lines of *Azarias* and the section of *Daniel* (lines 279–439) that details the trials to which the Babylonian king Nebuchadnezzar subjects the three youths. The beginning of *Azarias* and the corresponding section in *Daniel* are so closely related that one might have been used as the source of the other. The two poets may have worked from a common, now lost exemplar, but the poems may also owe their close similarity to each poet's negotiation of the traditional expressive economy through which all OE poetry was articulated, an economy predicated upon a flexible system of metrical, lexical, and thematic substitution (within limits), not verbatim repetition. After its first seventy lines, *Azarias* begins to depart in its specifics both from *Daniel* and the Vulgate, but it remains true to them in its tone, general focus, and narrative trajectory: after being cast into the oven as punishment, the three youths are visited by an angel who offers them God's protection and ensures that they emerge from the fiery trial unscathed.

Less narratively driven than its related section in *Daniel*, *Azarias* is more explicitly devotional. The following succinctly captures the poem's thrust and tone:

> Wis bið se þe con
> ongytan þone geocend, þe us eall good syleð
> þe we habbað þenden we her beoð
> ond us milde meotod mare gehateð,
> gif we geearniað, elne willað,
> ðonne feran sceal þurh frean hæse
> sundor anra gehwæs sawl of lice.
>
> (87b–93)

[Wise is he who can perceive/understand the preserver, who gives us all the good things that we have while we are here and the mild lord promises us more, if we earn it, courageously desire it when, through the lord's command, the soul of each and every one is sundered from the body.]

With its focus on the kindness of God and his willingness to help those whose devotion to him leads them into adversity, *Azarias* thematically complements the Guthlac poems that precede it. That both poems literalize the assistance God offers his followers in the form of an angelic visitor (for the youths, one that arrives when they are in the fire, and for Guthlac, one who visits him every night of the fifteen years he spends in the fens) is yet another intriguing point of contact between them.

Azarias contains a half-line in Latin, 100b ('lux et tenebre' [light and darkness]), something that happens only rarely in Anglo-Saxon vernacular poetry.

But, as in *The Phoenix*, a poem whose final lines are written in macaronic Latin and OE verse, in *Azarias* the Latin conforms to Anglo-Saxon metrical principles. The scribe further testifies to the easy intersection of these expressive economies by using the standard insular abbreviation for 'ond', 7, instead of the Latin 'et' (which the poem's editors generally supply).

Further Reading

Farrell, R.T. 'The unity of Old English *Daniel*'. *RES* ns 18 (1967): 117–35.
Kirkland, James W. and Charles E. Modlin. 'The art of *Azarias*'. *MÆ* 41 (1972): 9–15.

The Phoenix

Unique copy survives in the Exeter Book, fols 55ᵛ–65ᵛ.

The Phoenix is another of the Christian poems found at the beginning of the Exeter Book. Although there are a number of unclear and/or disputed readings in the poem, the folios that contain it are largely free from defects. The poem is divided into eight sections in the manuscript, with each section being marked in the Exeter Book scribe's usual fashion: a capital smaller than the modestly ornamental one found at the poem's beginning is followed by a string of smaller capitals that reach nearly to the right margin. The narrative breaks roughly into two parts: the first reworks and expands a Latin text attributed to Lactantius, *Carmen de Ave Phoenice* [Song concerning the Bird Phoenix] and the second offers a careful and detailed explication of the material presented in the first part. The division of the poem into two parts is clear from a narrative perspective (the poet announces his purpose at the outset of the poem's second part) even though it is not reflected in the poem's layout: the second part begins on fol. 61ʳ in the middle of the fifth section, three lines up from the bottom (line 381 in the edited version), with nothing on the manuscript page indicating that a new section has begun.

As is the case with most Anglo-Saxon poets who worked from known sources, the *Phoenix*-poet follows Lactantius closely in some regards but less closely in others. On occasion he adds narrative details, as he does in his account of the Phoenix's rebirth. About this mythical creature Lactantius tells us only that out of the ashes of the fire that consumes the aged Phoenix emerges a 'limbless creature, a worm' (Calder and Allen, 116). The *Phoenix*-poet informs us first that 'of þam ade æples gelicnes / on þære ascan bið eft gemeted' (230–31) [from that pyre the likeness of an apple is afterwards discovered] and that the worm emerges from this apple-shaped object. He also adds that the worm 'ærest bið swylce earnes brid' (235) [at first is like an eagle's chick]. More generally, the poet simply expands the material he finds in his sources, as when he fleshes out Lactantius's somewhat terse descriptions of the paradisiacal land the Phoenix inhabits or when he adds to the poem's second part a section from the book of Job in which Job likens his hoped for resurrection to that which 'se fugel fenix' (558a) [the bird phoenix] undergoes. The poet not only significantly dilates his source but occasionally infuses his description of the beautiful sights, lovely sounds, and delightful smells of this landscape with a lyricism rarely encountered in the extant corpus of OE poetry: 'Wlitig is se wong eall, wynnum geblissad / mid þam fægrestum foldan stencum' (7–8) [Beautiful is all that place, blessed in joys with the fairest fragrance on earth]. More frequently, however, the glories of the landscape emerge through rather lengthy lists of what is exluded from it:

> Nis þær on þam londe laðgeniðla,
> ne wop ne wracu, weatacen nan,
> yldu ne yrmðu ne se enga deað,
> ne lifes lyre, ne laþes cyme,
> ...
> ne wintergeweorp, ne wedra gebregd,
> hreoh under heofonum, ne se hearda forst,
> caldum cylegicelum, cnyseð ænigne.
>
> (50–59)

[There is in that land no persecutor, no weeping, no misery, nor sign of woe, no old age nor wretchedness, no painful death, no loss of life, no arrival of evil … no winter tempest, nor sudden change of weather, fierce under the heavens, nor does severe frost, in cold icicles, strike anyone.]

The myth of the Phoenix was widespread and popular in the ancient world, and the OE version, which is here briefly summarized, touches on virtually all of its major points: after living for many centuries, a bird beautiful beyond description leaves its homeland and seeks out a place where no people live. In this place it gathers the most fragrant herbs and flowers to build its nest in a tall tree. Warmed by the hot summer sun, the fragrant nest bursts into flames that consume the bird's aged body. After a time, a worm-like creature emerges from the ashes, a creature that in a short space of time grows into a Phoenix. Once fully grown, the Phoenix gathers up the residue of the fire, including all the bone fragments, and after carefully wrapping them in herbs, grasps them in his claws and flies back to his homeland where he enjoys a life of bliss.

When it is time, once again, for him to die, he does not mourn his approaching death, but rather 'siteð siþes fus' (208a) [eagerly awaits the journey hence] because he knows that 'æfter ligþræce lif edniwe, / feorh æfter fylle' (370–71a) [after the fire has spent its force, life is renewed, life after death].

Even though *The Phoenix* is a Christian poem, there is little in the first section that reveals it as such beyond its epithets for God (and even these need not refer in many cases solely to the Christian God) and the brief and rather general statements in his praise that the poet sprinkles into the narrative. The landscape which the Phoenix inhabits, while paradisiacal, does not specifically recall or reflect that of Eden. Similarly, the sole indication that the Phoenix's daily adoration of the sun, one of the many details the Anglo-Saxon poet found in Lactantius, is a Christian and not pagan activity in the source where the Phoenix explicitly worships Phoebus, comes from the poet's labelling the sun 'godes condelle' (91b) [God's candle], the 'torht tacen godes' (96a) [bright token of God]. The bird's other daily activities, including its flights, its baths, and its singing are either not situated within a Christian context or are, once again, given what amounts to a rather slight Christian colouring. The bird's voice is more beautiful 'þonne æfre byre monnes / hyrde under heofonum, siþþan heahcyning, / wuldres wyrhta, woruld staþelode' (128b–30) [then ever a child of man heard under the heavens since the high-king, the creator of glory, established the world], and it spends its days 'sælum geblissad' (140b) [joyously elated], but there is no indication that the subject of its song or the source of its joy is rooted in Christianity. The poet even refrains from Christianizing the main theme of the poem's first part, that of the bird's death and rebirth, despite the centrality of the resurrection myth to Judaeo-Christian belief. To take but one example, after the reborn Phoenix reaches maturity and is 'feþrum gefrætwad' (239a) [adorned with feathers], the poet simply notes that 'Þonne bræd weorþeð / eal edniwe eft acenned, / synnum asundrad' (240b–41a) [then the flesh refined by fire becomes entirely new, born again sundered from sins].

If the myth's points of contact with Christian belief are underplayed in the poem's first part in which the poet treats the myth's Christian resonances in a subtle and restrained fashion – when, that is, he mentions them at all –, in the second he misses no opportunity to explicate the myth through the lens of Christian belief by interpreting it first in connection with the Resurrection (lines 381–588) and then with Christ (589–677). The beginning of the poem's second part is signalled not formally but tonally. The shift in tone is apparent at the beginning of part two when, after briefly recapitulating the Phoenix's life, death, and rebirth cycle, the poet links this cycle directly to the existence of those good Christians who choose 'æfter sarwræce ... / þurh deorcne deað ... geofona neotan / on sindreamum' (383a) [after sore misery ...

through dark death ... to enjoy (God's) gifts in everlasting joy]. Taking no chances that the message will not be received, the poet, as is typical of his practice in the poem's second part, immediately articulates his point as explicitly as possible: 'Þisses fugles gecynd fela gelices / bi þam gecornum Cristes þegnum' (387–88) [this bird's nature is very like that of the chosen thanes of Christ] who through God's assistance hold onto joys during the 'frecnan tid' (390b) [terrible time] they spend on earth and who, as a result of their faith, 'heanne blæd / in þam uplican eðle gestrynaþ' (392b) [acquire high glory in that celestial homeland].

The second section follows the general structure of the first as the poet returns to and carefully explains many of the earlier section's details, always viewing them in the second section from a Christian perspective. To cite but two examples, the loss of Eden is equated ('Is þon gelicast' (424a) [that is most like]) to the journey of the Phoenix when it 'ofgiefeð / eard ond eþel' (426b–27a) [abandons its dwelling-place and its own country]. Near the end of the second part, the poet situates the rebirth of the Phoenix within sacred history by noting that the bird represents Christ because 'Swa se hælend us helpe gefremede / þurh his lices gedal' (650–51a) [as the Saviour helped us through his body's parting at death], so the Phoenix fills his two wings with delightful plants and with beautiful fruits of the earth when it 'afysed bið' (654b) [is eager to go hence].

The poem ends with a short passage composed in macaronic Latin and OE verse, one of a small handful of such passages in the extant OE poetic corpus: 'Hafað us alyfed lucis auctor / þæt we motun her merueri / goddædum begietan gaudia in celo' (667–69) [The author of light has granted us that we may here obtain and get through good deeds joy in heaven]. As we can see even from this short sample, the Latin verses conform, metrically and syntactically, to the expressive economy through which Anglo-Saxon poets always articulated poetry, something that witnesses both the flexibility of that economy and the cultural diglossia of those who composed vernacular verse. What is perhaps most surprising about the macaronic verses that bring *The Phoenix* to a close is that there is not more of them, both in this poem and elsewhere in the Anglo-Saxon poetic records especially when, as is the case with *The Phoenix*, an OE poem is demonstrably based on a known Latin source.

Further Reading

Anderson, Earl R. 'Old English poetic texts and their Latin sources: iconicity in *Cædmon's Hymn* and *The Phoenix*'. In *The Motivated Sign: Iconicity in Language and Literature* 2, ed. Olga Fischer and Max Nänny, 109–32. Philadelphia: John Benjamins, 2000.

Bjork, Robert E. 'N.F.S. Grundtvig's 1840 Edition of the Old English *Phoenix*: A Vision of a Vision of Paradise'. In *Unlocking the Wordhord: Anglo-Saxon Studies in Memory of Edward B. Irving, Jr.*, ed. Mark C. Amodio and Katherine O'Brien O'Keeffe, 217–39. Toronto: University of Toronto Press, 2003.

Bjork, Robert E. 'The symbolic use of Job in Ælfric's Homily on Job, *Christ II*, and the *Phoenix*'. In *Latin Learning and English Lore: Studies in Anglo-Saxon Literature for Michael Lapidge, ed.* Katherine O'Brien O'Keeffe and Andy Orchard, vol. II, 315–30. Toronto Old English Series 14. 2 vols. Toronto: University of Toronto Press, 2005.

Faraci, Dora. 'Sources and cultural background: the example of the Old English *Phoenix*'. *Rivista di cultura classica e medioevale* 42 (2000): 225–39.

Petersen, Helle Falcher. 'The Phoenix: the art of literary recycling'. *NM* 101 (2000): 375–86.

Steen, Janie. 'The figure of *The Phoenix*'. In her *Verse and Virtuosity: The Adaptation of Latin Rhetoric in Old English Verse*, 35–70. Toronto Old English Series 18. Toronto: University of Toronto Press, 2008.

Juliana

Survives uniquely in the Exeter Book, fols 65^v–76^r. The poem suffers from two lacunae caused by the loss of at least a single leaf, and possibly several leaves, between the current fols 69^v and 70^r and between fols 73^v and 74^r.

Juliana is the last of the Christian poems clustered at the beginning of the Exeter Book. Whether this grouping of devotional pieces reflects the scribe's or compiler's desires and design for the manuscript or whether it is an *ad hoc* arrangement that simply witnesses the availability of certain texts at the early stages of the codex's construction are matters that we cannot satisfactorily determine. Along with three other poems, *Elene* and *Fates of the Apostles* in the Vercelli Book and another poem in the Exeter Book, *The Ascension* (also known as *Christ II*), *Juliana* is generally acknowledged to be the work of a poet named Cynewulf. The four poems attributed to him all share certain syntactic, thematic, and lexical characteristics and all bear a runic 'signature' that spells out the poet's name. These signatures appear near the end of each poem and are found in passages in which the poet offers some general, apparently autobiographical information and, further, asks the readers of the poems to offer their prayers for him.

Juliana is a saint's life, a genre popular among poets and prose writers during and after the Anglo-Saxon period. The poem details the physical tortures, spiritual steadfastness, and ultimate martyrdom by beheading of St Juliana, who is wed against her will to the pagan senator Eleusius. As he does in the other poems attributed to him, Cynewulf draws his material from a Latin source, in this instance the *Passio S. Iuliane*. Cynewulf adheres closely to his Latin text, relying upon it for the poem's general narrative trajectory, including Juliana's piety and her insistence on preserving her virginity until such time as Eleusius renounces his gods and accepts the Christian God. He derives from his source both the tortures she suffers at Eleusius's hands, which include her being stripped naked and beaten with whips and hung by her hair for six hours, and her seizing of and protracted conversation with a demon who, in the guise of an angel, visits her in prison. Yet Cynewulf, as Anglo-Saxon authors working from known texts habitually do, also omits much as well, notably the simultaneous beheading of the 130 Nicomedian men and women who convert to Christianity after hearing the captive Juliana offer an extended prayer. He also freely adds details not found in the source, as, for example, when he reports that 'micle mægne' (690a) [a great troop] and 'sidfolc micel' (692a) [a great multitude] accompany the saint's body to its grave, a matter on which the source is silent.

Throughout the poem, Juliana remains a model of 'soðfæstnesse' [faithfulness], a virtue celebrated throughout Anglo-Saxon Christian literature and one stressed in several other of the Exeter Book's Christian poems, most notably *Guthlac A* and *B*. Although *Juliana* remains firmly focused on the saint's trials and martyrdom, the poem's heroine remains throughout a rather static figure: she never wavers in her devotion to her lord, she does not suffer any anxiety or apprehension about the torments that await her, and the devil who assumes an angelic form and visits her while she is imprisoned causes her neither emotional nor physical discomfort. In contrast, the poem's other characters are more fully developed. Even though Eleusius falls prey to the sort of excessive anger that is frequently associated with tyrants, he is drawn to Juliana not simply because she is a Christian virgin he can defile but because 'his mod ongon / fæmnan lufian ... / Iulianan' (26b–28a) [his heart began to love the virgin ... Juliana]. His desire for her is coded negatively for us – 'hine fyrwet bræc' (27b) [desire pressed him] –, but the syntactic awkwardness of this phrase, which many editors mark as an aside by placing it within parentheses, suggests that it may have been inserted to counterbalance the unambiguously positive statement regarding Eleusius's desire that precedes it.

The devil who visits Juliana while she is imprisoned is perhaps the most fully developed character in the poem. Under the physical restraint Juliana imposes on him when she, following divine orders, seizes him, the devil delivers in a series of lengthy speeches what amounts to little more than a litany of the usual distress demons inflict or threaten to inflict upon those who do not remain steadfast in their faith. But during this discourse, the devil not only asks why the saint continues to demand that he rehearse his evil deeds ('Hwæt sceal ic ma riman / yfel endeleas?' (505b–6a) [Why must I recount more endless evil?]), but he also bemoans his imprisonment, casting it as 'þreat ormæte' (465a) [excessive ill-treatment] and claiming that the saint 'þreades / þurh sarslege' (546b–47a) [tortured him through a painful blow]. He speaks also about the painful punishments that await devils who fail in their missions once they return to hell, and as Juliana drags him, fettered, towards an audience with Eleusius, the demon pleads with her, asking 'fore godes sibbum / þæt þu furþur me fraceþu ne wyrce, / edwit for eorlum' (540b–42a) [for the sake of God's kindness that [she] do [him] no further insults, disgrace before the earls]. After finally convincing Juliana to release him, he promptly disappears, only to reappear later in the narrative when he 'hearmleoð agol, / earm ond unlæd' [sang a song of grief, wretched and miserable] in which he urges that she be repaid 'mid gyrne' [with affliction] because 'heo goda ussa / meaht forhogde' (619–20a) [she scorned the power of our gods]. But when Juliana does nothing more than look towards him, the devil beats a retreat that is hasty and perhaps somewhat comic: 'Wa me forworhtum. Nu is wen micel / þæt heo mec eft wille earmne gehynan / yflum yrmþum, swa heo mec ær dyde' (632–34) [Woe is me, condemned by sins to hell. Now I greatly expect that she will again humiliate me, the wretched one, with evil miseries, as she previously did]. This devil is not of the order of *Paradise Lost*'s Satan or *Genesis B*'s tempter, but here and elsewhere, he proves engaging and interesting, and perhaps even earns our sympathy.

The expressive economy of oral poetics is part of the very fabric of *Juliana*, as it is for all the vernacular poems that survive from the Anglo-Saxon period, but on the thematic level it does not loom as large as it does in some of the other poems attributed to Cynewulf or in other Christian poems derived from Latin sources, such as *Andreas* and *Exodus*, even though *Juliana*, like the one that precedes it in the Exeter Book, opens with the highly traditional and resonant 'I heard' formula. Space does not permit a full consideration of how Cynewulf negotiates the traditional expressive economy in the poem, so a single example will have to suffice. The term 'aglæca' [awesome opponent, ferocious fighter], which is used to describe only a surprisingly limited set of characters, is a powerfully metonymic term in Anglo-Saxon oral poetics and is part of a constellation of lexical and thematic narrative elements that points to imminent slaughterous encounters. The characters to whom it applies (sometimes as a simplex and sometimes as part of a compound) are often easily identified as monstrous; among this group we find Grendel, the dragon, and Grendel's mother in *Beowulf*. It is also applied to characters who are not monstrous but who are, nevertheless, complex and troubling, a group that includes Beowulf and Sigemund in *Beowulf* and titular figure in *Andreas*. As he is three times identified as an *aglæca*, the devil in *Juliana* must be placed in this group, but despite the seeming appropriateness of including him with other monstrous or quasi-monstrous figures, he shares little, if anything, with the other *aglæcan*. He spends the majority of his time in the poem locked in the saint's firm grip; he is dragged along, rather like a recalcitrant schoolboy, by the saint when she goes to meet Eleusius; and he, perhaps with a great sense of relief, apparently simply disappears once she releases him (a defect in the manuscript caused by a missing leaf or leaves prevents us from knowing precisely what happens when he is set free). He mentions cruel torments and evil deeds under the saint's grip, but otherwise his demonic pedigree is all that establishes him as an *aglæca*. And, significantly, the term is not, as it is elsewhere in OE poetry, an important part of the thematics of slaughter within the poem: in fact, it is used only of the devil who visits her, and is used neither of Eleusius nor of those who torture the saint. Being a demon certainly makes *Juliana*'s devil a formidable figure and thus the term retains some of its traditional, associative resonances, but what is perhaps most important about Cynewulf's deployment of *aglæca* in this poem is that it witnesses the flexibility and adaptability of oral poetics: while the constituents of this specialized expressive economy function most powerfully when situated fully within that economy, they can also be used outside it, where they will continue to function, albeit with diminished effectiveness.

Juliana concludes with the poet seeking the prayers of his readers in a passage that contains some apparently biographical details as well as a so-called runic 'signature' that spells the poet's name. As is true of the other passages in which the name Cynewulf is written in runes, the poet speaks in his own voice directly to his audience, but the passage that concludes *Juliana* is different from the other three in that it is less detailed, less personal, and more cryptic than the others. He recalls all the 'synna wunde' (710a) [wounds of sin] he committed upon himself and is aware that he will need the saint to intercede on his behalf because he was slow to acknowledge his shame 'þenden gæst ond lic geador siþedan / onsund on earde' (714–15a) [while spirit and body together journeyed without injury in the world], but the voice in the passage seems less intimate and less engaging than it is in the other passages. The poem's final passage runs to the end of the manuscript page and so its rather uninspired (and uninspiring) nature may simply be the result of the poet (or the scribe responsible for copying *Juliana*) adding what amounts to filler on fol. 76^r so that he could follow his usual practice and begin the next poem at the top of a page.

Further Reading

Dendle, Peter. 'How naked is Juliana?' *PQ* 83 (2004): 355–70.
Frantzen, Allen J. 'Drama and dialogue in Old English poetry: the scene of Cynewulf's *Juliana*'. *Theatre Survey: the Journal of the American Society for Theatre Research* 46 (2007): 99–119.
Harbus, Antonina. 'Articulate contact in *Juliana*'. In *Verbal Encounters: Anglo-Saxon and Old Norse Studies for Roberta Frank*, ed. Antonia Harbus and Russell Poole, 183–200. Toronto Old English Series 13. Toronto: University of Toronto Press, 2005.
Lapidge, Michael. 'Cynewulf and the *Passio S. Iulianae*'. In *Unlocking the Wordhord: Anglo-Saxon Studies in Memory of Edward B. Irving, Jr.*, ed. Mark C. Amodio and Katherine O'Brien O'Keeffe, 147–71. Toronto: University of Toronto Press, 2003.
Olsen, Alexandra Hennessey. 'Cynewulf's autonomous women: a reconsideration of Juliana and Elene'. In *New Readings on Women in Old English Literature*, ed. Alexandra Hennessey Olsen and Helen Damico, 222–34. Bloomington: Indiana University Press, 1990.

The Wanderer

The unique copy of this poem is found on fols 76ᵛ to 78ʳ of the Exeter Book.

The Wanderer is the first of nine (or by some counts ten) relatively short poems contained in the Exeter Book that, because of certain similarities in tone, subject matter, and worldview have long been grouped together under the rubric 'elegy'. Just how appropriate this generic classification is remains open to question (no universally accepted definition of the genre has to date been put forth), but since the term 'elegy' allows us to establish broad ideational links among the poems so designated (these are, in order of their appearance in the manuscript, *The Wanderer*, *The Seafarer*, *The Rhyming Poem*, *Deor*, *Wulf and Eadwacer*, *The Wife's Lament*, *Resignation A* [and perhaps *B*], *The Husband's Message*, and *The Ruin*), it remains useful, so long as we remain aware that in employing it we are placing these poems within a taxonomy that was developed long after the cultural moment in which the poems were produced, and that what to our eyes look like defining generic features may or may not have been recognized as such by the poems' intended audiences.

The poem is undamaged in the Exeter Book and begins with a moderately oversized capital 'o', one that is more similar to the small capitals used to mark internal section divisions in the poem that precedes it, *Juliana*, than to the larger, modestly ornamental ones found at the beginning of many other poems in the codex. From its very first words, 'Oft him anhaga' (1a) [Often the solitary being], the poem establishes its subject's isolation from his culture's community, a theme central to all the other OE elegies as well. The reasons for his exile are never detailed; rather the poem focuses on the the acute physical and mental suffering that defines the exile's existence: 'mod-cearig' (2b) [troubled in thought], an exile 'longe sceolde / hreran mid hondum hrimcealde sæ' (3b–4) [must for a long time stir with his hands the icy-cold sea], all the while remaining 'earfeþa gemyndig' (6b) [mindful of the afflictions of earthly life]. As is the case with the other so-called elegies, the suffering detailed in *The Wanderer* is all the more acute for its being reported directly by the very character who is experiencing it. The presence of the first-person pronoun 'ic' (8a) [I] powerfully concretizes and localizes the details that are being related: rather than hearing second hand about a character's suffering, as, for example, we do of Grendel's misery early in *Beowulf*, the Wanderer relates his in his own voice starting at line 8: 'Oft ic sceolde ana uhtna gehwylce / mine ceare cwiþan' (8–9a) [Often I must alone, in the hour before each daybreak, lament my sorrows]. The distress is present and continuous, and the harshness of the speaker's physical reality acutely reflects the pain caused by his exclusion from the social and political worlds.

This exclusion and the hardships that attend it remain the twin focuses of the Wanderer, whose voice enters the narrative at line 8. He begins by offering what amounts to a précis of successful aristocratic behaviour, one based, perhaps, on his own hard experience in the world: 'Ic to soþe wat' (11) [I know too truly] that an earl must 'his ferðlocan fæste binde, / healde his hordcofan, hycge swa he wille' (13–14) [bind fast his mind, hold his heart, though he think as he wishes]. The 'werig mod' (15a) [weary mind] and 'se hreo hyge' (16a) [the troubled mind] cannot withstand the vicissitudes of fate or afford comfort, especially for him because there 'Nis nu cwicra nan' (9b) [is now not anyone alive] with whom he dares share his thoughts. He offers an especially poignant and almost paradigmatic articulation of the exile's plight in lines 17–29. Among other things, he reveals that he is 'earmcearig' (20a) [wretched], 'eðle bidæled' (20b) [deprived of his homeland], 'freomægum feor' (21a) [far from his noble kinsmen], and 'feterum sælan' (21b) [bound in fetters]. A few lines later he reveals that the death of his lord has forced him to go 'wintercearig ofer waþema gebind' (24) [desolate as winter over the expanse of the waves] in search of another 'sinces bryttan' (25b) [distributor of treasure] who 'in meoduhealle min mine wisse, / oþþe mec freondleasne frefran wolde' (27–28) [in the mead-hall might know of my (origins), or who might comfort me, friendless]. His recollection of the joys he once experienced makes his journey on the 'wræclast' (32a) [exile-path] even more distressful; far from attenuating his sorrow, the memories of what he once had and lost increase it. While asleep, the 'earmne anhogan' (40a) [wretched solitary one] thinks that he once again embraces and kisses his dear lord and lays his hands and head upon his lord's knee in an intimate gesture that is all the more moving for its simplicity. But when he awakens, what the 'anhaga' saw while asleep proves illusory as the stark reality that greets him contains nothing but barren waves, bathing sea-birds, and 'hrim ond snaw hagle gemenged' (48) [frost and snow (falling) mixed with hail]. That the Wanderer employs the present indicative upon waking, and not the present subjunctive as he did when relating what he dreamt, throws his present wretchedness into even sharper relief.

The juxtaposition between his recollected joys and his present woes makes the wounds of his heart (49) even heavier and leads him to ponder first why 'modsefa min ne gesweorce / þonne ic eorla lif eal geondþence, / hu hi færlice flet ofgeafon' (59–61) [my mind does not grow dark when I contemplate the lives of earls, how they suddenly abandoned the hall], and then to note resignedly that 'þes middangeard / ealra dogra gehwam dreoseð ond fealleþ' (62b–63) [this middle-earth perishes and decays every day]. In shifting his attention away from his own state, the Wanderer adopts for the first time a more general focus, as he offers advice on those behaviours a wise man should avoid (which include not being 'to wanhydig, / ne to forht ne to fægen' [67b–68a] [too reckless, nor too timid, nor too contented), before briefly cataloguing some of the many fates to which men must ultimately fall prey:

> Sume wig fornom,
> ferede in forðwege, sumne fugel oþbær
> ofer heanne holm, sumne se hara wulf
> deaðe gedælde, sumne dreorighleor
> in eorðscræfe eorl gehydde.
>
> (80b–84)

[War carried off one man, brought him on the journey hence; another the bird bore over the high sea; another the grey wolf took a share of in death; another a grief-stricken man hid in a grave.]

The references to war, the bird, and the wolf are constituents of a well-attested traditional scene known as the beasts of battle. That the *Wanderer*-poet employs these narrative elements outside the context in which they most frequently occur, one in which the appearance or mention of the carrion eaters usually signals an imminent slaughterous encounter, witnesses the fluidity and flexibility of the traditional expressive economy since its elements' affective dynamics continue to resonate even when deployed in a non-traditional context. *The Wanderer* also contains a compact and very effective articulation of the *ubi sunt* motif in which the poet laments the loss of those objects, animals, and people which were all part of 'seledreamas' (93b) [hall-joys]: gone, he tells us, are horses, kins-men, treasure-giver, seats at the feast, bright cups, armour-clad warriors, and the glory of the prince. After noting that 'Eall is earfoðlic eorþan rice' (106a) [the kingdom of earth is entirely full of hardship], The Wanderer concludes with a simple yet moving statement that well captures the fleet-ing quality of human existence: 'Her bið feoh læne, her bið freond læne, / her bið mon læne, her bið mæg læne, / eal þis eorþan gesteal idel weorþeð' (108–10) [Here wealth is transitory, here a friend is temporary, here a man is temporary, here a kinsman is ephemeral; everything in this world becomes useless].

These are the final words the Wanderer utters but they do not conclude the poem: another voice, perhaps the same one which speaks the poem's first seven lines, reveals that the entirety of the Wanderer's speech was 'cwæð … on mode' (111a) [spoken … in his mind] as he 'gesæt him sundor æt rune' (111b) [sat apart consulting with himself]. This final detail, that the Wanderer is within, yet apart from, some sort of social group poignantly complicates his situation by suggesting that he remains somehow exiled from the culture within which he currently finds himself. The voice which closes the poem also works to direct the poem away from the wholly secular concerns of the Wanderer to more explicitly Christian ones by reminding his readers/listen-ers of the value of seeking honour and 'frofre to fæder on heofonum' (115a) [consolation from the father in heaven]. While this message does not conflict with the one the Wanderer offers, neither does it meld as seamlessly with it as Christian passages in other poems frequently do. However, the Christian didacticism of the poem's final few lines is of a piece with that of several of the poems found near *The Wanderer* in the Exeter Book, especially the three that immediately follow it.

Further Reading

Hill, Thomas D. 'The unchanging hero: a stoic maxim in *The Wanderer* and its contexts'. *SP* 101 (2004): 233–49.

Irvine, Susan. 'Speaking one's mind in *The Wanderer*'. In *Inside Old English: Essays in Honour of Bruce Mitchell*, ed. John Walmsley, 117–33. Oxford: Blackwell, 2006.

Langeslad, Paul S. 'Boethian similitude in *Deor* and *The Wanderer*'. *NM* 109 (2008): 205–22.

Liuzza, Roy M. 'The Tower of Babel: *The Wanderer* and the ruins of history'. *Studies in the Literary Imagination* 36 (2003): 1–35.

Low, Anthony. 'Exile in the tenth century: alienation and subjectivity in *The Wanderer*'. In his *Aspects of Subjectivity: Society and Individuality from the*

Middle Ages to Shakespeare and Milton, 1–21. Pittsburgh: Duquesne University Press, 2003.

Orchard, Andy. 'Re-reading *The Wanderer*: the value of cross-references'. In *Via Crucis: Essays on Early Medieval Sources and Ideas in Memory of J.E. Cross*, ed. Thomas N. Hall, Thomas D. Hill, and Charles D. Wright, 1–26. Medieval European Studies 1. Morgantown: West Virginia University Press, 2002.

Wolfe, Melissa J. '"Swa cwæð snottor on mode": four issues in *The Wanderer*'. *Neophilologus* 92 (2008): 559–65.

The Gifts of Men

The unique copy of this poem is found on fols 78ʳ to 80ʳ of the Exeter Book.

To date, no source has been identified for the short poem known as *The Gifts of Men*, which is perhaps to be expected given the universality of its message that God does not concentrate his manifold gifts in a single man but spreads them out among individuals in order to prevent men from falling prey to '*wlenco*' [pride]. The majority of the poem is given over to cataloguing the various divine gifts of which man is the beneficiary, almost all of which are introduced with the phrase 'sum bið' [one is]: 'Sum biþ woðbora, / giedda giffæst. Sum biþ gearuwyrdig' (35b–36) [One is a poet gifted with songs. One is eloquent]. The list contains a great many gifts and/or skills that are wholly secular, including harp-playing, running, piloting a ship, swimming, wine-tasting, and being quick with dice. But while much of the poem concentrates on secular skills, they are situated firmly within a Christian context. And towards the end of the poem, its emphasis shifts away from gifts measureable in practical, worldly terms to more religious ones: 'Sum bið deormod deofles gewinnes ... Sum cræft hafað circnytta fela, / mæg on lofsongum lifes waldend / hlude hergan' (89–93a) [one is brave in battling the devil ... one has skill in many offices of the church, and can in hymns loudly praise the ruler of life]. The poem concludes by stressing once again that God grants men a single gift each for their own benefit, completing the overtly Christian framework with which it began:

> he missenlice monna cynne
> gielpes styreð ond his giefe bryttað,
> sumum on cystum, sumum on cræftum,
> sumum on wlite.

(104–7a)

[he variously steers the race of man from pride and bestows his gifts: to one virtues, to one skills, to one beauty].

Further Reading

Cross, J.E. 'The Old English poetic theme of "The Gifts of Men"'. *Neophilologus* 46 (1962): 66–70.

Russom, Geoffrey R. 'A Germanic concept of nobility in *The Gifts of Men* and *Beowulf*. *Speculum* 53 (1978): 1–15.

Precepts

The unique version of this poem is found on fols 80ʳ–81ʳ of the Exeter Book. There are several small holes on these pages but no loss of text.

Precepts is a ninety-four-line poem in the admonitory tradition. In it a father, who is identified as an experienced, wise, and mature man, offers his son advice on a variety of mostly secular topics. The poem has no known source, but its structure may derive from the Mosaic deuteronomy of *Exodus* 20.1–17. The wisdom imparted in each of the poem's ten 'sections' is largely general in its nature, and is occasionally proverbial and/or gnomic. Despite, or perhaps because of, the universality of the advice imparted, the poet rarely rises above the platitudinous in his advice, as when, for example, he urges his son in the second section never to tolerate sin in a friend or kinsman 'þy læs þec meotud oncunne, / þæt þu sy wommes gewita' (18b–19a) [lest the lord accuse you of being an accessory to the sin]. The poem is Christian and didactic, framing as it does a clear and uncomplicated division between following the path of God and following that of the fiend. Despite the poem's Christian impulse and the explicitly moral nature of some of its advice, the father's focus tends to be mostly secular and practical: 'Druncen beorg þe ond dollic word, / man on mode ond in muþe lyge, / yrre ond æfeste ond idese lufan' (34–36) [Guard yourself against drunkenness and foolish words, wickedness in the mind and lying in the mouth, anger and malice – and the love of women]. Although not matching the aesthetic accomplishment of the verse that surrounds it in the Exeter Book, *Precepts* offers advice that would resonates with, for example, *The Wanderer*'s 'anhaga' (1a) [solitary being, lonely being], whose exile may in part be attributable to his inability to navigate successfully his culture's social and political waters and his failure to be 'a giedda wis, / wær wið willan, worda hyrde' (41b–42) [ever wise in speech, on guard against desires, cautious of words]. Despite the apparent banality of the father's recommendation that the son 'beo leofwende, leoht on gehygdum / ber breostcofan' (92–93a) [be amiable, light in thoughts, and keep his spirit up], the scribe or compiler responsible for ordering, and perhaps even selecting, the texts in the Exeter Book may well have found *Precepts* a fitting companion to a far more artistically accomplished poem such as *The Wanderer*, whose admonitory passages have strong thematic links to *Precepts*.

Further Reading

Hansen, Elaine Tuttle. 'Parental instruction in Old English poetry: *Precepts* and Hrothgar's "Sermon"'. In her *The Solomon Complex: Reading Wisdom in Old English Poetry*, 126–52. McMaster Old English Studies and Texts 5. Toronto: University of Toronto Press, 1988.
McEntire, Sandra. 'The monastic context of Old English "Precepts"'. *NM* 91 (1990): 243–49.
Jacobs, Christina. '*Precepts* and the Exeter Book of vernacular instructive poetry'. In *Varieties and Consequences of Literacy and Orality*, ed. Ursula Schaefer and Edda Spielmann, 33–48. Tübingen: G. Narr, 2001.

The Seafarer

The unique copy of *The Seafarer* occupies fols 81^v–84^v of the Exeter Book. The leaves on which the poem is written are undamaged, but the text itself appears defective in several places, perhaps owing to scribal errors or corruptions in his exemplar.

The Seafarer is part of a small group of poems found in the Exeter Book that are designated as elegies. One of the distinguishing characteristics of these poems is that they typically take the form of a first-person narrative in which the speaker directly addresses his (or, more rarely, her) reading/listening audience and reveals that he is, for reasons that are often only sketched out or simply left undisclosed, physically isolated from human society and the pleasures and comforts it affords. As is true of the other elegies, there are no known sources for *The Seafarer*, although a number of possible analogues for several of its passages have so far been adduced in writings from several traditions, including the Welsh and the Latin Christian. The universality of the concerns and anxieties which the elegies voice may help explain why this small group of poems spoken by unidentified speakers in uncertain circumstances continues to resonate so powerfully with contemporary readers.

Like his counterparts in poems such as *The Wanderer* and *The Wife's Lament*, the speaker in *The Seafarer* lives a daily existence that is defined by its extreme physical hardship and psychological privation. Acutely aware of his isolation and the harshness of his surroundings, he views the sea not as a place of escape or refuge, for on it he suffers 'bitre breostceare' (4a) [bitter innermost anxiety] on the decks of what he, in a uniquely occuring – and still rather puzzling – compound, calls 'cearselda fela' (5b) [many abodes of sorrow]. His pain is powerfully localized and effectively, if simply, detailed: during the 'nearo nihtwaco' (7a) [anxious night-watch] it is often his duty to hold, 'Calde geþrungen / wæron mine fet, forste gebunden' (8b–9) [my feet were pinched with cold, fettered with extreme cold]. In his isolation, the Seafarer, who reveals he is 'winemægum bidroren' (16a) [deprived of loving kinsmen], takes the cries of sea-birds 'fore hleahtor wera' (21b) [for the laughter of men]. The Seafarer's situation is very reminiscent of the Wanderer's, but while the Wanderer appears to have been forced unwillingly into exile, the Seafarer seems rather to have chosen the hard life he lives 'in brimlade' (30a) [on the sea-path] since he ventures on the 'hean streamas' (34b) [deep seas] because 'cnyssað … / heorte geþohtas' [the thoughts of (his) heart insistently urge] him towards the sea and away from the joys of the human world. His rejection of worldly joys, the contrast he draws between himself and comfortable, affluent land dwellers who do not understand 'hwæt þa sume dreogað / þe þa wræclasts widost lecgað' (56b–57) [what the ones who tread the farthest paths of exile endure], and the frequently homiletic tone of the poem, especially in what is often taken as its second half, underscore *The Seafarer*'s Christian didactic focus.

Even though it is more explicitly Christian than the other elegies, *The Seafarer* falls short of being solely homiletic because it blends its religious message with ones that are more secular in nature. To take one example, shortly after explaining – in language that would resonate powerfully from the pulpit – that he chose his lone path on the sea 'Forþon me hatran sind / dryhtnes dreamas þonne þis deade lif, / læne on londe' (64b–66a) [because to me warmer are the joys of the lord than this dead, transitory life on land], the Seafarer articulates a sentiment that would fit comfortably into the secular, heroic ethos of *Beowulf*: a man should do good deeds while alive so that so that he will earn the the praise of those 'æftercweþendra' (72b) [speaking after a man's death], which the Seafarer acknowledges is 'lastworda betst' (73b) [the best reputation]. In detailing both the perils that will lay low each man – 'adl oþþe yldo oþþe ecghete' (70) [illness, or old age, or sword hate] – and the decayed state of the world – 'næron nu cyngingas ne caseras / ne goldegiefan swylce iu wæron' (82–83) [there are not now kings, nor emperors, nor gold-givers as there formerly were] –, the poem similarly draws upon the register of the secular, heroic ethos, doing so explicitly in line 70, which echoes the language of Hrothgar's so-called sermon in *Beowulf*.

Although the poem gives considerable attention throughout to secular matters, it concludes on a series of Christian notes: men may wish to honour their departed brothers by heaping their graves with treasure, but the

Seafarer recognizes the futility of doing so since 'ne mæg þære sawle þe bið synna ful / gold to geoce for godes egsan' (100–1) [gold may not help the soul that is sinful before the terror of God]. Similarly, although the world, like the surface of the sea, is in constant flux, the devout have no need to worry since God made its foundations steadfast. Still, it falls to the righteous man to chart, as the Seafarer does, his own course through the turbulent swirl of quotidian life by keeping his attention focused 'on staþelum' (109b) [fixed positions] as he 'Stieran ... strongum mode' (109a) [steers ... (his) wilful mind] away from temptations, despite the physical and pyschological hardships he must daily endure.

Further Reading

Dyas, Dee. '*The Wanderer* and *The Seafarer* reconsidered'. In her *Pilgrimage in Medieval English Literature, 700–1500*, 105–23. Woodbridge: D.S. Brewer, 2001.

Magennis, Hugh. 'The solitary journey: aloneness and community in *The Seafarer*'. In *Text, Image, Interpretation: Studies in Anglo-Saxon Literature and Its Insular Context in Honour of Éamon Ó Carragáin*, ed. A.J. Minnis and Jane Roberts, 303–18. Studies in the Early Middle Ages 18. Turnhout: Brepols, 2007.

Matto, Michael. 'True confessions: "The Seafarer" and technologies of the "Sylf"'. *JEGP* 103 (2004): 156–79.

Orton, Peter. 'The form and structure of *The Seafarer*'. In *Old English Literature: Critical Essays*, ed. Roy M. Liuzza, 353–81. New Haven: Yale University Press, 2002.

Sobecki, Sebastian I. 'The interpretation of *The Seafarer* – a re-examination of the pilgrimage theory'. *Neophilologus* 92 (2008): 127–39.

Vainglory

The unique copy of this poem occupies fols 83^r–84^v in the Exeter Book.

Vainglory is another of the short, instructional poems found in the Exeter Book. Its speaker invokes several unidentified authorities, including a 'frod wita' (1a) [wise counsellor] who is 'boca gleaw' (4a) [learned in books] and a 'witga' (50b) [prophet] whose song is related later in the poem. No source or analogue for it has so far been discovered, and the prophet whose song appears in the poem remains unidentified. Although not generally numbered among the masterpieces of OE poetry, *Vainglory* is noteworthy for its high concentration of uniquely occurring or rare words and compounds: it contains, in its eighty-four lines, more than twenty such terms, including the *hapax legomena* 'ærcwide' [utterance of old, ancient speech] and 'æscstede' [battlefield], and the rare 'wigsmiþas' [war-smith] (four occurrences) and 'soþgied' [true tale] (two occurrences), as well as uniquely occurring variants of other terms. The text itself is clean and the folios are undamaged, but it contains several syntactical knots that have yet to be satisfactorily untangled and that do not seem to be the results of faulty transmission or a flawed exemplar.

The poem itself is rather straightforward. After announcing at the outset that he has been instructed by the 'bodan ærcwide' (4b) [the ancient speech of God's messenger], the poem's speaker relates both the behaviour he wishes to warn his readers against – drunken boasting – and the fate that awaits those who fall prey to it (they will become 'wyrmum beþrungen' [56b] [oppressed by worms]). He approaches his topic in a conventional and largely undistinguished fashion, the poem never rising to the level of many of the other poetic and prose texts devoted to detailing sinful behaviours and their punishments. There is some effective rhetorical balancing in the poem as the poet several times contrasts 'godes agen bearn' (6b) [God's own son] (meaning here a devout man, not Christ) with both 'þone wacran' (7b) [a weaker man] and 'feondes bearn' (47b) [the fiend's son]. The poet also several times notes that the actions of the vainglorious are rooted in 'oferhygd' [excessive pride], and by using this same term to explain the root of the fallen angels' rebellion he creates a clear, if perhaps banal, link between the two groups. Similarly, the poem's doctrinal purpose finds effective, if not especially inspired, expression in a statement with gnomic overtones: 'Se þe hine sylfne in þa sliþan tid / þurh oferhygda up ahlæneð, / ahefeð heahmodne, se sceal hean wesan' (52–54) [the one who in an evil time raises himself up through pride, exalts his haughty self, shall be abased]. And finally, one may well wonder why any Christian would need to be informed either that a drunken, querulous boaster 'biþ feondes bearn / flæsce bifongen' (47b–48a) [is the fiend's son clothed in flesh] or that 'godes agen bearn' (80b) [God's own son] (here probably Christ) is the constant companion of every 'eaðmodne eorl' (78) [humble man] one encounters.

The *Vainglory*-poet's treatment of his subject may not scale any doctrinal heights, but in depicting this behaviour in the way that he does, he sheds a very different, and perhaps corrective, light on behaviour – drinking and boasting – foundational to the heroic ethos celebrated in a wide number of poems. To the eyes of the *Vainglory*-poet, there is nothing noble, elevated, or ennobling about boasting. The scene of boasting the poet presents, containing as it does many traditional thematic elements, including drinking, feasting, and noise, recalls those found in heroic poetry. In *Vainglory*, however, these activities are criticized, not praised, as the poet warns explicitly against drunkeness and presents the boasters, perhaps with some irony, as 'wlonce wigsmiþas' (14a) [proud war-smiths] who can be found not on battlefields but in 'winburgum' (14b) [towns where wine is drunk]. Words take the place of actions for them as they 'wordum wrixlað' (16a) [exchange words] while sitting around composing 'soðgied' (15b) [true tales]. Once 'win hweteð' (18b) [wine incites] them, they seek strife not against external enemies but rather threaten to rend the social fabric by attempting to discover 'hwylc æscstede inne in ræcede / mid werum wunige' (17b–18a) [which battlefield may dwell among men within the hall]. The noise that is central to the traditional thematics of joy in the hall is present in *Vainglory* as well, but here it is presented not as a positive sign of the human, heroic community, but rather as a roaring, and confusing, cacophony in which voices compete with each other. The most telling detail the *Vainglory*-poet includes comes when, after reporting on the potentially violent behaviour of men who engage in drunken boasting, he resignedly comments that 'sindan to monige þæt' (25b) [there are too many of that type], an observation that may derive from his first-hand experience. But just as we must avoid falling into the trap of thinking that the society depicted in narrative poetry accurately represents the culture in which it was produced, so, too, must we approach the apparent social critique discovered in an instructional poem such as *Vainglory* with a tempered, critical eye.

Although we still do not understand the principle (if there was one) of compilation underlying the construction of the Exeter Book, *Vainglory*'s positioning immediately following *The Seafarer* raises some intriguing issues, one of which is whether we can, or should, read the poems as in some way 'speaking to' each other. If approached in this light, one may possibly discern a broad ideational link between these texts because the actions detailed in *Vainglory* may well be among those that led the Seafarer to turn his back on society in favour of the solitary path that he chooses, a path frequently trod by those religious who reject this world and concentrate solely on their salvation in the next.

Further Reading

McKinnell, John. 'A farewell to Old English elegy: the case of *Vainglory*'. *Parergon* ns 9 (1991): 67–89.

Roberts, Jane. 'A man *boca gleaw* and his musings'. In *Intertexts: Studies in Anglo-Saxon Culture Presented to Paul E. Szarmach*, ed. Virginia Blanton and Helene Scheck, 119–37. MRTS 334. Arizona Studies in the Middle Ages and the Renaissance 24. Tempe: ACMRS, 2008.

Widsið

Widsið survives uniquely in the Exeter Book, fols 84ᵛ–87ʳ. The poem begins about halfway down fol. 84ᵛ with a decorative initial that is significantly larger than all but one other in the codex.

Widsið purports to be an account, presented almost entirely in the first person, of the career of a professional singer/oral poet named Widsith. His name, which may be translated as 'one who has travelled widely', is apt since he claims to have journeyed throughout much of the known world. Although the figure of the Anglo-Saxon oral poet, or *scop*, looms large both in some of the period's texts – especially *Beowulf* – and in some contemporary criticism – especially oral theory –, we know very little about what they did and how they did it, and we cannot even be entirely certain that they actually existed. In addition to Cædmon, the non-literate cowherd turned oral poet of Bede's *Ecclesiastical History* (see Part 2), we can put names to only two others, Widsith and Deor, neither of whom can claim even the quasi-historical status of Cædmon but who are rather wholly fictional. Along with Bede's account of Cædmon, *Widsið* is one of the few Anglo-Saxon texts that touches, directly or indirectly, upon the compositional and/or performative practices of *scopas* or the roles they played within Anglo-Saxon culture. While the poem is an important source of information regarding them and while its form may witness an earlier, more fully oral stage in the culture's development, the evidence it offers must be approached with caution because the poem is not the equivalent of anthropological field notes but is rather a fictionalized, and perhaps idealized, representation of oral poets and their practices.

Widsið, for which there is no known source or analogue, opens with a brief introduction in which an unidentified speaker reveals that, true to his name, Widsith has travelled widely throughout the earth and that he often 'on flette geþah / mynelicne maþþum' (3b–4a) [in the hall received desirable treasure]. In his own voice, Widsith offers two lists, one in which the *scop* names many early Germanic rulers and the tribes they governed, and another in which he names those in whose courts he has served as a singer. The simple, paratactic syntax and the additive nature of this list – 'Ætla weold Hunum, Eormanric Gotum, / Becca Baningum, Burgendum Gifica' (18–19) [Attila ruled the Huns, Eormanic the Goths, Becca the Banings, Gifica the Burgundians] – may cause us to wonder what its attraction is, especially when, as is the case in *Widsið*, many of the names mentioned are unknown to us, but within oral cultures, lists of this sort function as a *paideia*, or cultural encyclopaedia. What seem to those of us outside the culture to be empty markers (the names of unknown characters) function metonymically via the channels of traditional referentiality for those within the culture and so reverberate for them in ways that outsiders cannot fully understand.

But the lists in *Widsið* also serve a purpose that is as apprehensible to us as it is to the poem's intended audience: the list of rulers illustrates how important it is that each 'eorl æfter oþrum eðle rædan' (12) [earl rule nobly one after another]. The list of those whom Widsith has served also affords the poet the opportunity to articulate, and so model, the transactive economy upon which singers depended. The voice that introduces the singer initially raises the topic of compensation in a passing remark about what Widsith has received for his services, and Widsith himself broaches the subject several times when he cites some of the rich goods that were bestowed upon him, including a 'beag' (90a) [circular ornament] that was made of 'siex hund ... smætes goldes' (91) [six hundred pieces of pure gold]. But it is in the lines that close the poem, which come after the apparent conclusion of Widsith's comments and are generally attributed to the same voice that opens the poem, that the transactive, reciprocal nature of the relationship between singers and the lords they serve is acknowledged and explicitly articulated. Put simply, those who desire to have their deeds and repute disseminated and so preserved by the singers must be willing to reward the singers' efforts. For their part, the 'gleomen' (136a) [performers/entertainers] who criss-cross the world 'þearfe secgað, þoncword sprecaþ' (137) [voice their need, and speak words of thanks], knowing they will always meet one who is able to judge songs well (whether because they are aesthetically pleasing works of verbal art or because they effectively trumpet the subjects' accomplishments is not clear). The singers also know that they will be generously rewarded by the one who 'fore duguþe wile dom aræran, / eorlscipe æfnan, oþþæt eal scæceð / leoht ond lif somod' (140–42a) [before the troop wishes to raise up his fame, to perform heroic deeds, until everything passes away, light and life together].

The meagre nature of the evidence concerning the Anglo-Saxon *scop* makes that offered by *Widsið* all the more important, as modest and opaque as it may be. *Deor* offers us a glimpse of what happens when a *scop* no longer finds support, *Beowulf* may offer us moments of scopic performance, *The Fortunes of Men* makes brief mention of a *scop* who is monetarily rewarded by his lord, and, of course, Bede gives us his cowherd, Cædmon, but beyond this we know very little about Anglo-Saxon oral poets and their practices.

Further Reading

Klausner, David N. 'Petitionary poetry in Old English and Early Welsh: *Deor*, *Widsið*, *Dadolwch Urien*'. In *Poetry, Place, and Gender: Studies in Medieval Culture in*

Honor of Helen Damico, ed. Catherine E. Karkov, 197–210. Kalamazoo: Medieval Institute Publications, 2009.

Niles, John D. '*Widsið*, the Goths, and the anthropology of the past'. In his *Old English Heroic Poems and the Social Life of Texts*, 73–109. Studies in the Early Middle Ages 20. Turnhout: Brepols, 2007.

Rollman, David A. '*Widsith* as an Anglo-Saxon defense of poetry'. *Neophilologus* 66 (1982): 431–39.

Znojemská, Helena. 'A *scop* among scribes: a reading in the manuscript context of *Widsið*'. *Litteraria Pragensia* 31 (2006): 36–64.

The Fortunes of Men

Survives uniquely in the Exeter Book on fols 87ʳ–88ᵛ. A small stain on fol. 87ᵛ covers but does not obscure a few letters.

The Fortunes of Men is another of the short, so-called wisdom or catalogue poems included in the Exeter Book. Although these poems, for which no sources have been identified, are not grouped together according to any discernable plan, that they are found loosely clustered in the same section of the manuscript in which the elegies appear may bespeak some sort of connection between these genres, at least in the eyes of the manuscript's scribe or compiler. Like the other poems of its type, including *The Gifts of Men* and *Vainglory*, *Fortunes* is a Christian, didactic work, the purpose of which the poet articulates about two-thirds of the way through: 'Swa missenlice meahtig dryhten / geond eorþan sceat eallum dæleð, / scyreþ ond scrifeð ond gesceapo healdeð, / sumum eadwelan, sumum earfeþa dæl' (64–67) [so variously mighty God deals out to all throughout the region of the earth, ordains and allots and governs fates: to some prosperity, to some affliction]. Although Christian in its outlook, the poem neither explicitly ties the many different sorts of grim fates that await men to their sinful behaviour nor gives special emphasis to the redemptive powers of faith. For better or worse, everything happens through divine decree since 'God ana wat / hwæt ... winter bringað' (8b–9) [God alone knows what ... the years will bring]. Nor would it matter if men knew their fate, since altering or avoiding it 'Ne bið ... monnes geweald' (14b) [is not ... in man's power].

Despite the poem's conventional subject matter, *Fortunes* stands somewhat apart from the other poems of its type because of its strongly humanistic focus, something that adds an unusual degree of poignancy to what could easily have been simply yet another list of sinful and righteous behaviours. After noting that it is through God's grace that parents are able to bear, foster, clothe, and guide their children, the poet not only begins to list the grim fates in store for some of their children, including being devoured young by a wolf and being consumed by fire, but he also twice (in connection with these same two fates) turns his attention away from those who suffer these fates to the mother of each. And in the latter case, which contains a still unsolved textual crux and in which it is further unclear if the consuming fire is a funereal one or is perhaps being used as a means of execution, the mother does not just mourn the demise of her child in the flames; she 'gesihð' (47b) [sees] it in all its terrible sadness and, perhaps, horror. Several other similarly poignant moments stand out in the poem: in one, the corpse of a man 'riding' on the gallows will suffer terrible indignities from a carrion eater, in this instance the raven, which 'nimeþ heafodsyne, / sliteð ... sawelleasne' (36–37a) [will take his eye, rend ... his lifeless body]. While this is a more detailed, explicit, and realistic account than we get in other gallows scenes, what makes it truly striking is that the corpse in *Fortunes* cannot use his hands to drive away his avian tormentor but must helplessly suffer brutal indignities from its claws and beak. Elsewhere, a man who dies after tumbling from a tree is described, mid-fall, as being 'on fliht' (22b) [in flight], despite being 'fiþer-leas' (22a) [wingless]. The final example we will mention here, overindulgence in alcohol, is one commonly found in poems of this type. As in *Vainglory*, drunkenness on 'meadubence' (48b) [the mead-bench] can lead to violence and death. But in *Fortunes*, one who fails to 'gemearcian his muþe mode sine' (53a) [set bounds for his mouth with his mind] is bound 'dreogan dryhtenbealo' (55a) [to endure the loss of a lord] in addition to dying. And if exile and death were not punishment enough for the drunken man, after his death men will remember him as a 'sylfcwale' (56a) [suicide].

God is also the source of the good fortune that falls upon some, but just as he does with ill fortune, the *Fortunes*-poet does not tie the reception of good fortune to a man's behaviour, rather presenting it as if it were allotted by chance. The poet begins his list of good fortunes by citing one who in his youth 'his earfoðsiþ ealne forspildan' (59) [will put an end to all his time of hardship] before going on to live a prosperous, happy life with his family, in whose midst he joyfully drinks mead and enjoys his treasure. Although such a trajectory is often employed by authors of redemption narratives, the *Fortunes*-poet resists freighting it with any moral or religious overtones, something that holds for everything he mentions in his rather eclectic list of good fortunes, one that includes becoming a scholar, being skilled in games of chance, training hawks, and being rewarded for singing to the harp before a lord. Perhaps the surest indicator of the poet's non-moralizing perspective is that drinking – responsibly, and not to excess – figures prominently in the list of good fortunes as well, being mentioned not once but twice. The poem ends on a devout note, with the poet reminding his readers/listeners that they owe thanks to God for that which he 'fore his miltsum monnum scrifeð' (98) [on account of his mercies assigns]. While this is appropriate, its perfunctoriness belies the poet's greater concern, which is simply to have his audience accept that what will happen in this world will happen.

Further Reading

Deskis, Susan E. 'Exploring text and discourse in the Old English gnomic poems: the problem of narrative'. *JEGP* 104 (2005): 326–44.

DiNapoli, Robert. 'Close to the edge: *The Fortunes of Men* and the limits of wisdom literature'. In *Text and Transmission in Medieval Europe*, ed. Chris Bishop, 127–47. Newcastle upon Tyne: Cambridge Scholars Publishing, 2007.

Jurasinski, Stefan. 'Caring for the dead in *The Fortunes of Men*'. *PQ* 86 (2007): 343–63.

Maxims (I)

The unique copy of this poem survives in the Exeter Book, fols 88ᵛ–92ᵛ. A similar but much shorter poem, known as *Maxims II*, survives in London, BL, MS Cotton Tiberius B.i., fols 115ʳ–15ᵛ. The following focuses only on the Exeter Book poem.

Maxims, another of the Exeter Book's wisdom poems, is comprised wholly of gnomic statements – brief articulations of general, uncontested truths in the forms of maxims, aphorisms, or proverbs – strung together with no apparent focus or overarching purpose. So opaque is its organizing principle, if there is one, that we cannot be certain if the poem we label *Maxims* is a single entity with three separate sections, as is generally accepted, or is instead three separate poems the compiler/scribe of the Exeter Book placed consecutively in the manuscript. Formally, the layout of *Maxims* and of the poems that precede and follow it, *The Fortunes of Men* and *The Order of the World*, departs from the scribe's usual practice as each section/poem begins with a large decorative letter, with only the remainder of the first word written in smaller capitals. Further complicating this issue, the scribe adopts the same format for the poems clustered around *Maxims* and the poems/sections that constitute *Maxims* that he elsewhere employs for sections of a longer text such as *Juliana*. The subject matter of the various sections of *Maxims* provides no clues as to whether it is one poem or three since it is all very much of a piece: the order of the maxims could easily be shifted with no discernable loss, or gain, in meaning and coherence.

The sentiment behind the poem is Christian, as the poet early on announces: 'God sceal mon ærest hergan / fægre, fæder userne, forþon þe he us æt frymþe geteode / lif ond lænne willan' (4b–6a) [one must at first fittingly praise God, our father, because he from the beginning gave us life and impermanent desire]. Although other Christian sentiments are articulated elsewhere in the poem and although the poet devotes several lines of verse near the poem's conclusion to the story of Cain and Abel, as much weight – and perhaps more – is given to general truths of human nature and the natural world as to Christian ones, and there may even be a streak of pagan thought running through the poem. The range of the poem's subject matter and the universal applicability of its maxims suggest that the audience for whom it was intended was concerned not only with contemplating Christian truths, but with more general ones as well. Similarly, the poem's moralizing is frequently couched within a lay, and not a religious, context: for example, women must keep their promises to their men and not spend time with others when their men are away; and unhappy, friendless men who take wolves as friends very often suffer for it. While the morals of these and other statements are clear, those of many others are not. Such maxims as 'Seoc se biþ þe to seldan ieteð' (111) [he who seldom eats will be sick] and 'werig scealc wiþ winde roweþ' (185a) [a man who rows against the wind will be weary] may have specific, or general, cultural, social, and/or political applications, but to function effectively as gnomic statements, which they do, they need not be tied to a specific moral but must only speak to a general truth.

Maxims, with its compact statements and abrupt shifts in focus stands as one of the more inaccessible pieces of Anglo-Saxon verbal art, and its appeal is further limited by its modest aesthetic accomplishments and metrically defective lines. However, wisdom literature is a well-attested genre, one that may have greatly appealed to the Exeter Book's compiler since the codex contains several other examples of it.

Further Reading

Cavill, Paul. 'The Old English *Maxims*'. In his *Maxims in Old English Poetry*, 156–83. Cambridge: D.S. Brewer, 1999.

Deskis, Susan E. 'Exploring text and discourse in the Old English gnomic poems: the problem of narrative'. *JEGP* 104 (2005): 326–44.

O'Camb, Brian. 'Bishop Æthelwold and the shaping of the Old English Exeter *Maxims*'. *ES* 90 (2008): 253–73.

Wright, Charles D. 'The blood of Abel and the branches of sin: *Genesis A*, *Maxims I* and Aldhelm's *Carmen de uirginitate*'. *ASE* 25 (1996): 7–19.

The Order of the World

Unique copy survives in the Exeter Book, fols 92ᵛ–94ʳ.

The Order of the World belongs to the genre of wisdom literature, a genre popular in Anglo-Saxon England and one which is well represented in the Exeter Book, where several wisdom poems are clustered together. An explicitly Christian poem that is carefully constructed and highly didactic, *The Order of the World* sets forth and extols the virtues of God and his glory as creator in a fashion that is as methodical as it is focused, something that sets it apart from the many wisdom poems whose gnomic statements appear in a seemingly random fashion with accompanying commentary. Unlike the poets of other wisdom poems, who seem content to have their gnomic statements serve as springboards for each reader's/listener's own contemplation and interpretation, the *Order*-poet carefully and insistently guides his audience towards the Christian truths he wishes them to understand. Where the *Maxims*-poet, for example, simply offers observations that are oftentimes cryptic, oblique, and open to a wide variety of interpretations, the *Order*-poet opts to spell his message out: in speaking of the sun's setting, for example, he explains that 'scir gescyndeð in gesceaft godes / under foldan fæþm, farende tungol' (74–75) [the journeying bright star hastens by God's decree under the earth's embrace]. In this same vein, he elsewhere attributes the balance of the world to the 'stiþe stefnbyrd' (45a) [unyielding direction] of God, 'se steora' (45b) [the steerer/helmsman].

The rhetorical structure of the poem reflects and reinforces the poet's focus on both the divine basis of the world's orderliness and the necessity for men to be properly instructed by a 'wisne woðboran' (2a) [wise orator/philosopher/poet] in order to better understand the workings of the world's 'searoruna gespon' (16b) [web of mysteries]. Adopting rhetoric reminiscent of a preacher's, the poet employs the imperative mood to exhort his audience on several occasions, telling them first 'Leorna þas lare' (23a) [learn this teaching] and later 'Gehyr nu þis herespel ond þinne hyge gefæstna' (37) [hear this noble discourse and make constant your mind]. The poet himself aptly sums up his purpose in the poem's closing lines:

> Forþon scyle mon gehycgan þæt he meotude hyre;
> æghwylc ælda bearna forlæte idle lustas,
> læne lifes wynne, fundige him to lissa blisse,
> ...
> fere him to þam sellan rice.

[Therefore should one resolve that he will be a servant to the Lord; each son of man must leave behind idle pleasure, the transitory joy of life, aspire to the delight of bliss ... journey to the good realm.]

Further Reading

DiNapoli, Robert. 'The heart of the visionary experience: *The Order of the World* and its place in the Old English canon'. *ES* 79 (1998): 97–108.

Borysławski, Rafał. 'Wordhordes craeft: confusion and the order of the wor(l)d in Old English gnomes'. In *The Propur Langage of Englische Men*, ed. Marcin Krygier and Liliana Sikorska, 119–31. Medieval English Mirror 4. New York: Peter Lang, 2008.

Hansen, Elaine Tuttle. 'Beyond the father's voice'. In her *The Solomon Complex: Reading Wisdom in Old English Poetry*, 68–99. McMaster Old English Studies and Texts 5. Toronto: University of Toronto Press, 1988.

Wehlau, Ruth. 'Rumination and re-creation: poetic instruction in *The Order of the World*'. *Florilegium* 13 (1994): 65–77.

The Rhyming Poem

Survives uniquely in the Exeter Book, fols 94^r–95^v.

With generic and thematic affiliations to the so-called elegies, wisdom poetry, and perhaps even riddles, *The Rhyming Poem (RP)* is one of the more difficult OE poems to categorize. Further complicating matters is that no other poem in the surviving corpus of Anglo-Saxon poetry employs rhyme as a central feature of its versification. In addition to its rhymes, which occur internally between the final words of each half-line as well as between the final words of full lines, the poem also has several other unusual metrical features. It does not display the range of metrical verse types found in OE poetry but rather has a very high concentration of a single type, known as the A-verse, in which a stressed syllable is followed by an unstressed one. Its alliteration is also consistently heavier than is normal because while typically only the initial consonant clusters *sc-*, *st-*, and *sp-* alliterate, *RP* contains a number of others, including *fr-*, *bl-*, and *dr-*, that do as well. Why *RP* has the metrical idiosyncrasies it does is a question we cannot take up here, but it may well be that it is something of a metrical experiment, one that for unknown reasons was not repeated elsewhere.

RP does not fit securely into any one genre, but since the poem follows the general contours of the other elegies in that it is spoken by a first-person narrator who has experienced a serious loss, the precise nature and causes of which are never revealed, it is frequently classified with the so-called elegies. As do the elegies, *RP* stresses the mutable and frequently painful nature of human existence as the speaker, who had once been 'Glæd ... gliwum' (3a) [happy in joys], now is 'hreoh' (43a) [troubled] in his breast and 'nydbysgum neah' (44a) [near distress]. The adverb 'nu' (43a) [now], which marks a shift in the speaker's focus from the joys that life holds to its pain and hardships, links him with the speakers of the other elegies. But unlike the elegies, which derive much of their power from the sharp, painful contrast of joys recalled in the midst of present sorrows, in *RP*, the happy memories never intrude upon the speaker's sorrow but remain segregated from it, a segregation reflected in the poem's structure. Until the poem's mid-point, the speaker focuses solely on the many joys he, a man of 'heanne had' (15a) [high rank], finds in the world, and only after that point does he turn from the blissful to the painful. His comments in the first half amount to a veritable index of what Anglo-Saxon culture prizes and celebrates, including, to cite but a few examples, feasts, visits from guests, the possession of estates, the sound of harps, and the presence of a band of household retainers who serve and protect their lord. While many of the joys he cites pertain specifically to him and his situation, others are more general in nature and are articulated via broad, gnomic statements that sound, as in the following, as if they come from a wisdom poem rather than an elegy: 'ellen eacnade, ead beacnade, / ... / mod mægnade, mine fægnade' (31–33) [courage increased, riches beckoned, ... mind gained might, love rejoiced].

The second half of the poem complements and balances the first by offering a litany not of the world's joys but of the sorrows and hardships that arise when evil flourishes. And as in the first half, these sentiments are articulated in mostly general, gnomic terms: 'Wercyn gewiteð, wælgar sliteð, / flahmah fliteð, flan mon hwiteð' (61–62) [Mankind goes hence, the deadly spear slits, the hostilely determined one is contentious, crime polishes the arrow]. Even when the speaker discusses digging his own grave, his tone is curiously general: 'Me þæt wyrd gewæf, ond gewyrht forgeaf, / þæt ic grofe græf, ond þæt grimme græf / flean flæsce ne mæg, þonne flanhred dæg / nydgrapum nimeþ' (70–73a) [fate wove that for me, and bestowed that work, that I dug an open grave, and that cruel grave the flesh cannot escape, when the arrow-swift day seizes with a violent grasp]. The poem concludes on a Christian note, as the speaker, utilizing the rhetoric of a homilist, urges his audience, 'Uton nu halgum gelice / scyldum biscyrede scyndan generede, / wommum biwerede' (83b–85a) [Let us now hasten, like the saints cut off from sins, defended from moral stains] to seek the 'soðne god' (87a) [true God].

Although the leaves on which *RP* appears are undamaged and even though the poem appears to have been copied with the same care that the Exeter Book scribe elsewhere exhibits, it nonetheless presents difficulties in terms of its sense (it contains a number of rare or uniquely occurring lexemes and compounds), its metre (there are a number of defective or absent rhymes), and its grammar and syntax (which are especially knotty in places). Sounding at times like an elegy, at others like a wisdom poem, and at others like a riddle, and possessing a metre that is both traditional and non-traditional, it remains very much *sui generis* in the corpus of OE verse.

Further Reading

Abram, Christopher. 'The errors in *The Rhyming Poem*'. *RES* 58 (2007): 1–9.

Klinck, Anne L. '*The Riming Poem*: design and interpretation'. *NM* 89 (1988): 266–79.

Olsen, Alexandra Hennessey. 'Subtractive rectification and the Old English *Riming Poem*'. *In Geardagum* 24 (2003): 57–66.

Wentersdorf, Karl P. 'The Old English *Rhyming Poem*: a ruler's lament'. *SP* 82 (1985): 265–94.

The Panther, The Whale, The Partridge (*The Old English Physiologus*)

The Panther survives on fols 95^v–96^v and *The Whale* on fols 96^v–97^v of the Exeter Book. A single line of text, comprising one and a half lines of a poem known as *The Partridge* survives at the bottom of fol. 97^v. The text found at the top of fol. 98^r may be the conclusion of *The Partridge*, but as at least one leaf of the manuscript is missing between between 97^v and 98^r, this cannot be known for sure. The fragment is sometimes treated as a separate poem, *Homiletic Fragment III*.

Two short poems, *The Panther* and *The Whale*, along with a fragment of a third known as the *The Partridge*, comprise what is generally known as *The Old English Physiologus*, or bestiary, although this may be something of a misnomer since no other version of *The Old English Physiologus* contains so few poems. With roots in ancient Greece, *The Old English Physiologus* was a popular text throughout the Middle Ages and beyond. Which Latin manuscript served as the source for this group of animal poems in the Exeter Book has so far not been determined. As Anglo-Saxon poets typically do, the poet draws heavily from his source, but, as is also typical, he freely departs from it as well. For example, in both the Latin and Anglo-Saxon versions of *The Whale*, seafarers frequently mistake the sleeping whale for an island, anchor their ships in the 'sand', and go 'ashore', only to drown when the whale awakens and immediately dives below the surface, taking the sailors and their boats with it. In the Latin version, the heat from the fires the sailors build while camping on its back causes it to awaken and then dive, but in the OE version the whale is more nefarious, consciously waiting until the men are relaxed and resting before suddenly submerging and dragging them to a watery grave. A break in sense following line 81a of *The Whale* suggests that one verse or more has been lost, but the poems are otherwise undamaged in the manuscript.

The Panther and *The Whale* are exercises in Christian allegory that complement each other well. The panther is a Christ figure that sleeps for three days and then rises stronger than before, and he 'is æghwam freond, / duguða estig, butan dracan anum' (15b–16) [is a friend to everyone, bounteous of blessings, except to the dragon (i.e. Satan) alone]. Its voice is 'woþa wynsumast' (43a) [the most pleasant of noises], and after it speaks a 'stenc ut cymeð … swettra ond swiþra swæcca gehwylcum' (44b–46) [an odour comes out … sweeter and stronger than every scent]. The voice and pleasant scent draw throngs of people and animals alike to the panther. To make certain that his allegory will not be misinterpreted or go undetected, he carefully parallels the panther with Christ, who on 'þy þriddan dæge / of digle aras' (61a–62b) [the third day arose from the secret place] and who is kind to all, 'butan dracan anum, / attres ordfruman. Þæt is se ealda feond' (57b–58) [except to the dragon alone, the chief of wickedness. That is the old fiend]. A 'swete stenc' (64) [sweet odour] also spreads throughout the world following Christ's resurrection that, along with his voice, brings throngs of 'soðfæste men' (66b) [true men] to him.

The poems follow the formatting of those that immediately precede them: each begins with a large initial capital, with only the remaining letters of the first word being copied in small capitals, and they are generally treated as separate texts. However, the opening lines of *The Whale*, 'Nu ic fitte gen ymb fisca cynn / wille woðcræfte wordum cyþan / þurh modgemynd bi þam miclan hwale' (1–3) [Now I in a section will further make known in words through the art of poetry/song, my thoughts concerning the great whale], bespeak the close connection between the poems. This connection is also reflected on the narrative level as well for the whale represents Satan as explicitly as the panther does Christ. The whale is initially described simply in terms of its ferociousness (it is 'frecne ond ferðgrim' [5a] [voracious and savage]), but after detailing how it drags ships and sailors into a watery 'deaðsele' (30a) [hall of death], the poet places its actions in a Christian, moral context, condemning them as being not simply accidentally dangerous (as in the Latin *Physiologus*) but rather as consciously evil: 'Swa bið scinna þeaw, / deofla wise' (31b–32a) [Such is the custom of evil spirits, the way of devils].

The panther and whale share one characteristic: they both produce a sweet smell that draws throngs of others to them, but the parallel ends there. The panther's emanates from its mouth and is closely associated with its voice and, by extension, Christ's; the whale's, in contrast, stems from its 'innoþe' (55a) [stomach] and is produced when the creature is hungry and wishes to attract its prey. Those who respond to the panther's 'æþele stenc' (74b) [noble scent] find themselves among the elect, while those who respond to the whale's 'wynsum stenc' (54b) [pleasant scent] find themselves trapped in the whale's jaws and devoured. Maintaining the pattern he earlier establishes, the *Whale*-poet explicitly equates the whale's actions with the devil's, once more adopting rather homiletic rhetoric:

> Swa biþ gumena gehwam,
>
> ...
> læteð hine beswican þurh swetne stenc,
> leasne willan, þæt he biþ leahtrum fah
> wið wuldorcyning.
>
> (62b–67a)

[So it is for every man ... [who] allows himself to be ensnared through a sweet fragrance, a false pleasure, so that he is stained with sins against the king of glory].

The poem that follows *The Whale* is generally identified as *The Partridge* based on this bird's appearance in *The Physiologus* but since only one and a half verse lines survive, this identification must necessarily remain tentative. The apparent loss of a leaf or leaves prevents us from knowing whether *The OE Physiologus* contained more than the three poems that survive and the same loss prevents us from determining whether the verse fragment that occupies the top half of fol. 98ʳ is the conclusion of *The Partridge*, of another, now lost poem in the *Physiologus*, or of an entirely different text. Being for the most part a general exhortation to Christian living – 'Uton we þy geornor gode oliccan' (12) [Let us the more eagerly be submissive to God] in order to dwell in the 'eardwica cyst' (15b) [the best of dwellings (i.e., paradise)] – there is little in this fragment to connect it with the *Physiologus*, and so it is frequently designated *Homiletic Fragment III*. While acephalous, there is no doubt that what we have is its conclusion, since the word *Finit* is written between two of the marks, :- and :₇ typically employed by Anglo-Saxon scribes to signal a section's or a text's conclusion.

Why this is the only of the Exeter Book's texts so marked is another question to which no satisfactory answer has yet emerged.

Further Reading

Biggs, Frederick M. 'The eschatological conclusion of the Old English *Physiologus*'. *MÆ* 58 (1989): 286–97.

McFadden, Brian. 'Sweet odors and interpretive authority in the Exeter Book *Physiologus* and *Phoenix*'. *Papers on Language and Literature* 42 (2006): 181–209.

Znojemská, Helena, 'Sailing the dangerous waters: images of land and sea in *The Seafarer*, *The Panther and The Whale*'. *Prague Studies in English* 24 (2005): 87–105.

Soul and Body II (and *I*)

Versions of this poem survive both in the Exeter Book, fols 98[r]–100[r] and in the Vercelli Book, fols 101[v]–4[r].

One of the very few Anglo-Saxon poems to survive in more than a single version, *SB II* is a shorter version of a poem found in the Vercelli Book, *SB I*. There is no way of determining whether *SB II* is a contraction of *SB I*, whether *I* is an expansion of *II*, or whether they were both copied from the same exemplar and owe their differences solely to the idiosyncrasies of the scribes who copied them. The versions exhibit some variation in word choice and some brief passages are ordered differently, but the major narrative difference is that *SB II* omits the incomplete speech of the soul to the body with which, owing to a manuscript lacuna, the fragmentary Vercelli Book version concludes. While *SB II*'s tone is at times reminiscent of a shrill homily and while its images are more explictly gruesome than is typical of the texts included in the Exeter Book, its Christian didactic focus is shared by many of them.

Further Reading

Davis, Glenn. 'Corporeal anxiety in *Soul and Body II*'. *PQ* 87 (2008): 33–50.

Matto, Michael. 'The Old English *Soul and Body I* and *Soul and Body II*: ending the rivalry'. *In Geardagum* 18 (1997): 39–58.

Zacher, Samantha. 'The "body and soul" of the Vercelli Book: the heart of the corpus'. In her *Preaching the Converted: The Style and Rhetoric of the Vercelli Book Homilies*, 140–78. Toronto Anglo-Saxon Series 1. Toronto: University of Toronto Press, 2009.

Deor

The unique version of this poem is found in the Exeter Book, fols 100^{r-v}.

Deor is a short, eponymous poem ostensibly spoken by a poet, or *scop*, and it is one of the few prose or poetic texts in the surviving corpus that sheds light, however sketchily and problematically, on the role of the poet in Anglo-Saxon culture. The poem's narrative is straightforward: Deor briefly, and very elliptically, mentions the difficulties faced by a number of figures from Germanic history and legend – some of whom are known and some of whom have yet to be positively identified – before he turns to the difficulties he faces after apparently losing his position at court to another *scop*, Heorrenda. Generally classified among the elegies, *Deor* fits this genre only marginally because much about it is *sui generis*. Of all the first-person speakers in the elegies, only Deor is named (although as is the case with many Anglo-Saxon names, *deor* could be a noun, meaning 'animal', 'beast', or an adjective, meaning 'fierce', 'bold'). In addition, that the situation causing Deor's distress is spelled out far more clearly than is typical of the elegies, that he focuses on the hardships of others and not exclusively his own, and that the poem has a consolatory, even hopeful, tone set it apart from the elegies and even from the 'elegiac' passages frequently encountered in OE verse. A number of *Deor*'s formal features are similarly unique to it: presented in strophes and employing one of the only refrains found in the entire corpus – 'Þæs oferode, þisses swa mæg' [that came to an end, so may this] –, in form and content it is perhaps the closest that OE verse comes to the lyric, a genre whose popularity explodes in the later Middle Ages.

The narratives related in each of the short strophes are all brief and cryptic. In some cases they are inscrutably allusive, as in the fourth strophe, presented here in its entirety: 'Ðeodric ahte þritig wintra / Mæringa burg; þæt wæs monegum cuþ' (19–21) [Theodoric ruled the stronghold of the Merovingians for thirty winters; this was known to many]. Depending on the recipient's view of Theodoric, this can be taken in any number of ways. Other of the strophes are linked by suffering, but in some the strophe's subject is the one who suffers and in others he is the cause of distress. Weland, the smith of Germanic legend, 'hæfde him to gesiþþe sorge ond longaþ, / wintercealde wræce' (3–4a) [had as his companion sorrow and longing, wintry-cold suffering], especially after he falls under the power of Nithhad. Beadohild suffers the death of her brother and becomes pregnant after being raped. In contrast, the subject of the fifth strophe, Eormanric, who possesses 'wylfenne geþoht' (22a) [a wolfish mind], was a 'grim cyning'

(23b) [cruel king]. The many he 'sorgum gebunden' (24b) [bound in sorrows], can only frequently wish 'þæt þæs cynerices ofercumen wære' (26) [that the kingdom would be overcome]. The last strophe before Deor turns to his own plight differs from those that precede it in that it is the most general: an unnamed man who 'Siteð sorgcearig, sælum bidæled, / on sefan sweorceð' (28–29a) [sits oppressed with anxiety, deprived of good fortune, becomes troubled in his mind]. His anonymity and the severe – and undetailed – nature of his plight (it seems to him that 'endeleas earfoða dæl' (30) [endless is his portion of hardships]) align this figure very closely to those we encounter in the other elegies, although he, unlike them, never gives voice to his own pain.

Deor saves his own troubles for last: he was for a time 'Heodeninga scop' (36b) [the poet of the Heodeningas] but has lost his position to Heorrenda, a 'leoðucræftig monn' (40a) [a man skilled in poetry]. Not only does Deor lose his social position to Heorrenda, he loses the rewards and rights that postion bestowed upon him since Heorrenda, Deor informs us, now receives 'londryht ... / þæt me eorla hleo ær gesealde' (40b–41) [the landright ... that the protector of earls earlier gave to me].

While the tone of most of the strophes is elegiac, the refrain that closes each one alters the dynamics of the narratives and shifts the poem's tone and our attention: where the other elegies leave us with a sense of the inescapable nature of the suffering the speakers experience, *Deor* holds forth the promise of better that will be reached through patient understanding and acceptance of the world's mutability: 'Þæs ofereode, þisses swa mæg' is really just another way to say 'this, too, shall pass'.

The poem's unusual qualities extend as well to its *mise-en-page*. Its opening is formatted following one of the scribe's usual practices in this section of the manuscript (only the first two letters of the first word are capitalized, the initial one as a large capital and the following one as a small capital), but each strophe begins at the left margin with a single large capital and each one ends with the mark that the scribe typically uses to indicate the end of a poem or the conclusion of a section within a long poem. And since, with the exception of the final one, the strophes do not end at the right margin, the blank space that occurs after each of the first five connect *Deor*, visually, if perhaps incidentally, with the format for physically encoding poetry that arises shortly after the close of the Anglo-Saxon period. As with *The Rhyming Poem*, it is impossible to know both why *Deor* has the unique formal features it does and why virtually no traces of its formal features are found elsewhere: is it perhaps an idiosyncratic experiment or simply the only poem of its type to survive? Its situation in the Exeter Book, along with the manuscript's other formally or generically idiosyncratic texts raises some interesting, but ultimately unanswerable, questions about the codex itself.

Further Reading

Foley, John Miles. 'Afterword: "Deor" and Anglo-Saxon *Sêmata*'. In his *Homer's Traditional Art*, 263–70. University Park: Pennsylvania State University Press, 1999.

Harris, Joseph. '*Deor* and its refrain: preliminaries to an interpretation'. *Traditio* 43 (1987): 23–53.

Klausner, David N. 'Petitionary poetry in Old English and Early Welsh: *Deor*, *Widsið*, *Dadolwch Urien*'. In *Poetry, Place, and Gender: Studies in Medieval Culture in Honor of Helen Damico*, ed. Catherine E. Karkov, 197–210. Kalamazoo: Medieval Institute Publications, 2009.

Niles, John D. 'Excursus: the refrain in *Deor*'. In his *Old English Heroic Poems and the Social Life of Texts*, 289–93. Studies in the Early Middle Ages 20. Turnhout: Brepols, 2007.

Trilling, Renée R. 'Ruins in the realms of thoughts: reading as constellation in Anglo-Saxon Poetry'. *JEGP* 108 (2009): 141–67.

Wulf and Eadwacer

Survives uniquely in the Exeter Book, fols 100^v–1^r.

The nineteen-line poem given the title *Wulf and Eadwacer* is one of the most allusive pieces of verbal art to have survived from Anglo-Saxon England. Generally classified as an elegy, in it a speaker who is revealed by the poem's grammar to be a woman, laments the difficult situation in which she finds herself. While clearly related to the OE elegies, its *mise-en-page* and narrative elusiveness also connect it to the OE riddles, the first group of which immediately follow it in the Exeter Book. Rather than follow his usual practice when beginning a new poem, the scribe rather adopts the format he uses for the strophes of the poem that precedes it and for the the fifty-nine riddles that follow: only the first letter of the first word is capitalized, with the remainder of the poem written in the scribe's square Anglo-Saxon miniscule. *Wulf* also contains what appears to be a refrain – 'Ungelic is us' [it is different for us] (3, 8) – something only rarely encountered in OE verse, and several of its lines are very short and so appear to be metrically deficient, although in each case the sense of the 'defective' line is complete. The poem, as is typical of OE verse texts, is not formatted as poetry but is written out continuously from the manuscript's left to right margins and so, unlike *Deor*, the refrains and the possible strophes they mark are in no way distinguished visually. And finally, unlike elegies such as *The Seafarer* and *The Wanderer*, there is no explicit or discernable Christian element to *Wulf*: it remains a wholly secular piece, one of the few such to be found in the Exeter Book, whose contents, while extremely varied, tend to be Christian and didactic.

The narrative of *Wulf* is one of the most cryptic to survive from the period. If it is a riddle, it is one that has so far remained unsolved, as none of the various solutions put forth have gained much acceptance. Its elegiac qualities are readily apparent even though its narrative thread is knottier and more indeterminate than that of any other elegy: its speaker bemoans, in order, her separation from her lover/husband (Wulf?), his difficult/dangerous situation, her conflicted feelings regarding her relationship with another man, and the apparent loss of her child, which is taken either by one of the men (or another one) or by a wolf. We know that she is physically separated from someone she identifies as Wulf ('Wulf is on iege, ic on oþerre' [4] [Wulf is on an island, I on another]), that Wulf's island is surrounded by fens and inhabited by 'wælreowe weras' [6] [blood-thirsty men]), and that if he were to return 'on þreat' (2b, 7b) [in a troop] her people 'willað … hine aþecgan' (2a, 7a) [will … kill him], but these details raise as many questions as they answer. Is Wulf an outlaw or has he been unjustly exiled? Are the fierce men who occupy the island he also currently inhabits his allies or is he in danger from them? And to what does the refrain that punctuates the narrative of her and Wulf's situations – 'Ungelic is us' (3, 8) [it is different for us] – refer?

The air of uncertainty that hangs over the poem's narrative complicates all attempts at interpreting it definitively, but its indeterminate, almost riddling nature does not diminish or dilute its affective dynamics. The speaker's anguish is everywhere evident, whether she's detailing the way her environment reflects her mental state ('hit wæs renig weder ond ic reotugu sæt' (10) [the weather was rainy and I sat tearful], describing her internal conflict over what may or may not be a forced sexual relationship with another man ('wæs me wyn to þon, wæs me hwæþre eac lað' (12) [it was to me a joy; it was however also hateful), or explaining how her yearning for Wulf's visits (which she tellingly describes as 'seldcymas' (14b) [rare comings]) makes her not only anxious and sad, but physically ill. That perhaps the most moving situation in the poem – the apparent abduction of the speaker's child by either a man (Wulf? Eadwacer? someone else?) or by a wolf ('Uncerne ear[m]ne hwelp / bireð wulf to wuda' [16b–17a] [Wulf/a wolf carries our wretched whelp/child to the woods]) – is also the most impenetrably mysterious one is somehow wholly appropriate. The enigmatic nature of this work extends even to the gnomic-sounding lines with which it closes: 'Þæt mon eaþe tosliteð þætte næfre gesomnad wæs, / uncer giedd geador' (18–19) [One may easily tear asunder that which was never joined, the song/riddle of us together].

As do the other OE elegies, *Wulf* leaves us knowing little about its speaker and about what has transpired in her life, but the suffering she experiences in her isolated and vulnerable state continues to move us despite the enormous gulf separating Anglo-Saxon England from the present day.

Further Reading

Belanoff, Patricia A. 'Women's songs, women's language: *Wulf and Eadwacer* and *The Wife's Lament*'. In *New Readings on Women in Old English Literature*, ed. Helen Damico and Alexandra Hennessey Olsen, 193–203. Bloomington: Indiana University Press, 1990.

Chance, Jane. 'The errant woman as *scop* in *Wulf and Eadwacer* and *The Wife's Lament*'. In her *Woman as Hero in Old English Literature*, 81–94. Syracuse: Syracuse University Press, 1986.

Gameson, Fiona, and Richard Gameson. '*Wulf and Eadwacer, The Wife's Lament*, and the discovery of the individual in Old English verse'. In *Studies in English Language and Literature. 'Doubt Wisely': Papers in Honour of E.G. Stanley*, ed. M.J. Toswell and E.M. Tyler, 457–74. London: Routledge, 1996.

Klinck, Anne L. 'Poetic markers of gender in medieval "woman's song": Was anonymous a woman?' *Neophilologus* 87 (2003): 339–59.

Renoir, Alain. '*Wulf and Eadwacer*: a noninterpretation'. In *Franciplegius: Medieval and Linguistic Studies in Honor of Francis Peabody Magoun, Jr.*, ed. Jess B. Bessinger and Robert P. Creed, 147–63. New York: New York University Press, 1965.

The Exeter Book Riddles

The Exeter Book riddles survive uniquely in three groups: Riddles 1–59 on fols 101^r–14^v, Riddles 30b and 60 on fol. 122^v, and Riddles 61–95 on fols 124^v–30^v. Many of the riddles, especially those on fols 124^v–30^v, are incomplete as a result of the damage the final folios of the manuscript suffered when some sort of hot object was placed on it.

The Exeter Book riddles, of which there are more than ninety, are a unique and eclectic collection that defies easy or simple characterization, but from the surviving evidence we can adduce that the Anglo-Saxons had a fondness for descriptive, literary riddles that frequently turn on metaphorical word-play. We do not know whether the riddles in the Exeter Book are the work of a single author/translator, or several, and we similarly do not know if they owe their order in the codex to the Exeter scribe or if it derives from whatever exemplar he might have used.

Unlike the Latin riddles produced in Anglo-Saxon England by Aldhelm, Tatwine, and Eusebius, all of which tend to be rather short (the majority of Aldhelm's are ten lines or fewer), those in the Exeter Book are of varying lengths. Some are as brief as one or two lines and the longest, Riddle 40, which is a reworking of Aldhelm's Riddle 100, breaks off at line 108 on fol. 111ᵛ. Since a leaf has gone missing between the manuscript's current fols 111ᵛ and 112ʳ, there is no way of determining how much longer it originally was. In many of the vernacular riddles, the object that is the riddle's subject directly addresses the reading/listening audience, and after offering clues to its identity ('Neb wæs min on nearwe' [Riddle 10, 1a] [My face was in confinement] or 'Ic þurh muþ sprece mongum reordum' [Riddle 8, 1] [I through my mouth speak with many voices]), the object frequently commands its audience to 'Saga hwæt ic hatte' (Riddle 10, 11b) [Say what I am called]. Others, including the charming and well-known Riddle 47, are presented as straightforward metaphorical puzzles. While many of the riddles have clear, or at least generally agreed-upon solutions, a number have multiple solutions and others remain unsolved. In some cases, damage to the manuscript has rendered the riddles fragmentary and virtually incomprehensible; this is especially true of the final large group of riddles with which the manuscript closes since the last few folios in the manuscript suffered severe burn damage. A number of riddles, including the runic riddles and the sole Latin riddle (90), remain unsolved because they are simply too opaque. The solution for one of the runic riddles, Riddle 75, could be piss, hound, elk, or Christ, depending on how one chooses to read the four runes that make up line 2a of this one-and-a-half-line riddle.

The subjects of the riddles are largely quotidian and include, among others, such objects as dough (45), oven (or bookcase) (49), fire (50), tree (30a), rake (34), and onion (65). More abstract subjects also appear, including creation (40, 66, and 94), soul and body (43), and the month of December (22). Other, more unusual objects also make an appearance, including icebergs (33 and 68). Several of the riddles touch on Christian subjects, including battering ram, cross (53), chalice (48 and 59), and Bible (26 and 67). The collection, however, is not dominated by a Christian ethos and the riddles are largely secular. A small handful turn on double-entendres, some of which are subtle, others of which are blatant. Only Riddle 37, one of the seven inescapably erotic riddles (the others are 25, 44, 45, 54, 61, 62), has a Latin source or analogue, Symphosius's Riddle 73, but the erotic dimensions of the Exeter Book riddle are wholly the creation of the Anglo-Saxon author. Symphosius's bellows describes itself as one who does 'not die immediately when the breath leaves, for it returns continually; although it often departs again too' (Calder and Allen, 167). Compare the Anglo-Saxon, which reads in part: 'Ic þa wihte geseah; womb wæs on hindan / þriþum aþrunten. Þegn folgade, / mægenrofa man, … / Ne swylteð he symle, þonne he syllan sceal / innað þam oþrum, ac him eft cymeð / bot in bosme, blæd biþ aræred' (1–7a) [I saw a creature; its belly was in the rear greatly swollen. A retainer of great power went along as a follower … He doesn't always die when he must give the inner part to others, but he comes again, restored within: breath is raised up]. The erotic riddles all have other, non-erotic solutions, but how these riddles found their way into the Exeter Book remains an enduring mystery. We should be grateful to whoever decided to include them not just for continuing to amuse us so many centuries after they were committed to the page, but more importantly because without them our understanding of Anglo-Saxon culture would be even more limited than it is. Finally, in what may be nothing more than a fortuitous coincidence, the last words of Riddle 95, which are also the last words penned by the Exeter Book scribe, offer intriguing and still pertinent commentary on the entire collection of riddles and on the organizing principles at work over the final sections of the codex:

> Þeah nu ælda bearn
> londbuendra lastas mine
> swiþe secað, ic swaþe hwilum
> mine bemiþe monna gehwylcum.
>
> (10b–13)

[Even though the sons of men, land-dwellers, now eagerly seek my tracks, I at times conceal my footsteps from each of men.]

Further Reading

Bitterli, Dieter. *Say What I Am Called: The Old English Riddles of the Exeter Book and Anglo-Latin Riddle Tradition.* Toronto: University of Toronto Press, 2009.

Murphy, Patrick J. *Unriddling the Exeter Riddles.* University Park: Pennsylvania State University Press, 2011.

Orchard, Andy. 'Enigma variations: the Anglo-Saxon riddle-tradition'. In *Latin Learning and English Lore: Studies in Anglo-Saxon Literature for Michael Lapidge,* ed. Katherine O'Brien O'Keeffe and Andy Orchard, vol. I, 284–304. Toronto Old English Series 14. 2 vols. Toronto: University of Toronto Press, 2005.

Wilcox, Jonathan. '"Tell me what I am": the Old English riddles'. In *Readings in Medieval Texts: Interpreting Old and Middle English Literature,* ed. David Johnson and Elaine Treharne, 46–59. Oxford: Oxford University Press, 2005.

The Wife's Lament

The unique copy of this poem survives in the Exeter Book, fols 115^{r-v}.

The Wife's Lament (WL), for which no source has yet been discovered, is a powerful articulation of the physical and psychological hardships an isolated individual suffers. It is one of only two elegies spoken by a woman, *Wulf and Eadwacer* being the other, and like *Wulf*, its focus remains entirely secular throughout. While all the elegies are enigmatic, WL and *Wulf*, are rather more cryptic than the rest. Both *Wulf*, which immediately precedes Riddles 1–59 in the manuscript, and WL, which immediately follows Riddle 59, have been taken as riddles, a view that finds considerable support in both the poems' cryptic narratives and in the way their beginnings are laid out on the page. Departing from his usual practice, the scribe begins *Wulf* with a single small capital, the same practice he employs in the strophes of *Deor*. In WL, he continues the format he uses for the riddles, perhaps in part because the poem begins with the first-person pronoun *ic* [I], a pronoun that begins some fifty-one of the Exeter Book's ninety-five riddles. In what is an intriguing coincidence, the narrator of the first of the two especially cryptic poems that bookend the first group of riddles uses the multivalent term 'gydd', whose meanings include 'song', 'poem', 'riddle', and 'tale', at the end of her narrative and the narrator of the second of these poems uses it in her first line. We cannot be sure, but the fundamentally riddling nature of both these poems may have been what led the scribe to bookend Riddles 1–59 with *Wulf* and WL.

WL is spoken in the first person by a narrator who finds herself in a physically and psychologically difficult situation, one made all the more difficult for her having been forced into it. As is true of the other elegies, the powerful emotions that form the affective foundations of WL are clearly articulated (the poem opens with its speaker, who, through the grammar is identified as a woman, announcing that she will relate a 'giedd … bi me ful geomorre' [1] [a poem/tale/ riddle … concerning myself, full sad]) but the details of why and how she ended up in this situation are only sketchily presented. We know little other than that the narrator has been separated from her husband/lover and that this separation leads directly to all her difficulties. Since her lord doesn't seem to have been exiled, the reasons for his departure are murkier than they are even in *Wulf*. After he leaves, she is exposed to the malice of his kinsmen, who for unknown reasons plot 'þurh dyrne geþoht, … todælan unc' (12) [through hidden thoughts … to separate the two of us]. Her situation is further complicated by her lord's nature. He is 'ful gemæcne' (18a) [fully equal] to her and they both happily vow that only death will separate them, but he is 'heardsæligne, hygegeomorne, / mod miþendne, morþor hycgendne' (19–20) [unfortunate, sorrowful, concealing his thoughts, thinking of murder]. For reasons she doesn't reveal, she suffers his enmity and, further, is commanded by him to live 'on wuda bearwe, / under actreo in þam eorðscræfe' (27b–28) [in a grove of trees under an oak tree in an earth-cave].

The narrator establishes a bleak emotional context for the poem early on by referring twice to her sorrow (1b and 17b), to herself as a 'wineleas wræcca' (10a) [friendless wretched person], to her longing (14b), and to the punishments she suffers on what she labels her 'wræcsiþa' (5b) [exile journey], but it is only in the poem's second half that she reveals the grievous, daily, and inescapable nature of her physical and emotional suffering. In doing so, she fully aligns the affective dynamics of her 'giedd' with that of the other elegies. The place she is forced to inhabit, with its 'dena dimme' (30a) [dark valleys], 'duna uphea' (30b) [high mountains], and 'bitre burgtunas brerum beweaxne' (31) [bitter enclosures overgrown with briars] is truly a 'wic wynna leas' (32) [joyless place]. Her mental state is of a piece with the landscape as the memory of her lord's 'fromsiþ' (33a) [absence on a journey] cruelly seizes her. Instead of contrasting her current situation with joyful memories of her past pleasure, she heightens our sense of her extreme discomfort by contrasting it instead with the situation of those who are together in their beds 'þonne ic on uhtan ana gonge / under actreo ... þær ic sittan mot sumorlangne dæg, / þær ic wepan mæg mine wræcsiþas, / earfoþa fela' (35–39a) [when I in the time before dawn go alone under the oak tree... There I must sit for a summer-long day, there I weep over my exile journeys, my many afflictions]. For her, however, there is neither respite nor escape:

> forþon ic æfre ne mæg
> þære modceare minre gerestan,
> ne ealles þæs longaþes þe mec on þissum life begeat.
>
> (39b–41)

[therefore I can never have rest from my grief, nor at all from the weariness that has seized me in this life.]

In its final section, the poem follows the trajectory of several of the other elegies as the narrator shifts her gaze from her immediate troubles, but in so doing she retains her wholly secular focus and so ends on a secular and gnomic, rather than homiletic, note as she announces that a young man must be sorrowful and stern of heart because despite the 'breostceare' (44b) [innermost anxiety] and 'sinsorgna' (45a) [continual troubles] he will experience he must also nonetheless keep a happy demeanour. In what may be the narrator's sole act of resistance, she closes by offering what amounts to a curse: she wishes her 'freond' (47b) [friend] should find himself sitting alone 'under stanhliþe storme behrimed' (48) [under a rocky slope covered with hoar-frost by a storm], in a 'dreorsele' (50a) [horrid dwelling], enduring what she daily suffers – 'micle modceare' (51a) [great grief] – all the while recalling 'to oft / wynlicran wic' (51b–60a) [too often a more delightful dwelling place].

Wulf and *WL* may be the only examples of a genre otherwise unattested in OE, the women's song, but given the slenderness of the evidence this designation may not warranted. Both poems do explore the vulnerability of unattached women in Anglo-Saxon culture, and the harsh and untenable situations that they face may offer a glimpse, partial and imperfect though it be, into the world of Anglo-Saxon domestic relations, a rare topic in the poetic corpus.

Further Reading

Frese, Dolores Warwick. 'Sexing political tropes of conquest: *The Wife's Lament* and Laȝamon's *Brut*'. In *Sex and Sexuality in Anglo-Saxon England: Essays in Memory of Daniel Gillmore Calder*, ed. Carol Braun Pasternack and Lisa M.C. Weston, 203–33. MRTS 277. Tempe: ACMRS, 2004.

Horner, Shari. 'En/closed subjects: *The Wife's Lament* and the culture of early medieval female monasticism'. *Æstel* 2 (1994): 45–61.

Kinch, Ashby. 'The ethical agency of the female lyric voice: *The Wife's Lament* and Catullus 64'. *SP* 103 (2006): 121–52.

Klein, Stacy S. 'Gender and the nature of exile in Old English elegies'. In *A Place to Believe In: Locating Medieval Landscapes*, ed. Clare A. Lees and Gillian Overing, 113–31. University Park: Pennsylvania State University Press, 2006.

Renoir, Alain. 'A reading of *The Wife's Lament*'. *ES* 58 (1977): 4–19.

Shimomura, Sachi. 'Remembering in circles: *The Wife's Lament*, *conversatio*, and the community of memory'. In *Source of Wisdom: Old English and Early Medieval Latin Studies in Honour of Thomas D. Hill*, ed. Charles D. Wright, Frederick M. Biggs, and Thomas N. Hall, 113–29. Toronto Old English Series 16. Toronto: University of Toronto Press, 2007.

Judgement Day I

The unique copy of this poem survives in the Exeter Book, fols 115ᵛ–17ᵛ.

Judgement Day I is one of three Christian eschatological poems in the extant corpus of OE vernacular verse, with *Christ in Judgement* and *Judgement*

Day II being the others. *JD I*'s theme is explored in passages of other poems and is a frequent topic among prose authors, especially the homilists, but unlike the poems and most of the prose texts that focus on the end of the world, *JD I* does not draw upon any of the many Latin or vernacular texts devoted to this topic. The poem is homiletic in its tone and focus, and the poet privileges the emotional over the intellectual, contemplative, and philosophical throughout as he contrasts, in a manner at times helter-skelter, the current poor state of the world with the final reckoning to which all Christians, righteous and sinful alike, will be subjected at the end of the world. The poem is repetitive and overtly didactic, but when placed within what may be its proper context – that of the pulpit – its author emerges as an effective rhetorician who succeeds in getting his message across to his listening/reading audience affectively and effectively.

The immediacy of poem's tone recalls that of many homilists, and the urgency of its opening lines, 'Ðæt gelimpan sceal, þætte lagu floweð, / flod ofer foldan; feores bið æt ende / anra gehwylcum' (1–3a) [That must come to pass, that the sea will flow as a flood over the earth; life will then end for everyone], recalls that of Wulfstan's well-known *Sermo Lupi ad Anglos* [Sermon of the Wolf to the English] (see Part 2). After asserting that the path to salvation lies within each one who is willing 'soþ geþencan' (4b) [to reflect upon the truth], the poet launches into the first of several descriptions of the destruction that will precede the final call to judgement, one in which fire, which he mentions multiple times, figures prominently. Those whose sinfulness results in their being consigned to hell will find themselves in a world where 'næfre dæg scineð' (19b) [day never shines] and where fire and 'brogna hyhst' (23b) [the worst of terrors] await them 'butan ende' (27a) [without end]. Although hell's fires burn eternally, once the divinely sent fires of judgement cool, neither 'ban ne blod' (40a) [bone nor blood] will remain 'her' (40a) [here], and nothing will be heard 'nymþe wætres sweg' (38b) [except the sound of water].

Before returning to the fiery end of the world and before touching upon the rewards awaiting the faithful, the poet interrupts himself to articulate his purpose for his reading/listening audience: 'Forþon ic a wille / leode læran þæt hi lof godes / hergan on heahþu ... / ond a lufan dryhtnes / wyrcan in þisse worulde' (46b–50a) [therefore I ever will teach the people that they the glory of God praise on high ... and ever attain the love of the lord in this world]. From a rhetorical perspective, this move seems ill advised since at the very least it deflects the audience's attention away from the very matters the poet wants them to contemplate. However, situated within the immediate, almost interactive dynamic the poet establishes throughout (by, among other things, using the adverb 'her' and the first-person-plural pronoun 'we' in the lines cited immediately above), this direct address emerges not as a rhetorical blunder but as a device that allows him to connect closely with his audience. After returning to his subject, this time with more of an emphasis on the rewards that await the one who 'swa geomor wearð / sarig fore his synnum' (87b–88a) [was so sorrowful, afflicted with grief on account of his sins], the poet concludes on a subtly effective note. Rather than leave his audience to contemplate on their own the poem's final, and arresting, image, that of the word of the Lord emanating from the heavens as a trumpet blast so powerful that it will make the 'wongas beofiað / for þam ærende þat he to us eallum wat' (112b–13) [fields tremble on account of that message that he will make known to us all], the poet engages them in what amounts to a call and response in which the voice of each reader/listener participates. Employing the imperative mood, the poet first instructs his audience to 'Oncweþ nu þisne cwide' (114a) [Speak now this utterance] and then provides the 'cwide', one that succinctly articulates the major points he has made throughout his poetic homily:

> cuþ sceal geweorþan
> þæt ic gewægan ne mæg wyrd under heofonum
> ac hit þus gelimpan sceal leoda gehwylcum
> ofer eall beorht gesetu, byrnende lig.
> Siþþan æfter þam lige lif bið gestaþelad,
> welan ah in wuldre se nu wel þenceð.

(114b–19)

[what I cannot frustrate must be clearly known, the fate beneath the heavens, but it must come to pass to all people upon their houses, the burning flame. Then after that flame will life be restored; he will have prosperity in glory, the one who now thinks properly.]

In returning to the language employed in the poem's opening, this final utterance draws this admittedly minor, but nonetheless well-conceived and well-crafted piece to a successful close, one entirely consistent with its affective dynamics and emotional focus.

Further Reading

Lochrie, Karma. 'The structure and wisdom of *Judgment Day I*'. NM 87 (1986): 201–10.

Lochrie, Karma. 'Wyrd and the limits of human understanding: a thematic sequence in the "Exeter Book"'. *JEGP* 85 (1986): 323–31.

Menner, Robert J. 'The vocabulary of the Old English poems on Judgment Day'. *PMLA* 62 (1947): 583–97.

Resignation (A and B)

Unique version is found in the Exeter Book, fols 117ᵛ–19ᵛ.

Although we know little about the organizing principles that account for the selection and ordering of the various poems that comprise the Exeter Book, *Resignation* and the poem that precedes it in the manuscript, *Judgement Day I*, may well have been placed sequentially because the scribe or compiler viewed them as companion pieces. The first part of *Resignation*, which is often designated *Resignation A*, takes the form of a penitential prayer of the sort that one might surmise the poet of *JD I* would hope to inspire in his readers/listeners. As does the speaker of *JD I*, the speaker of *Resignation* also uses the first-person pronoun to good rhetorical effect, both in the poem's homiletic first half and in its elegiac second half. The closing of *Resignation* also aligns itself seamlessly with the preceding poem as its speaker accepts that his divinely determined fate is inevitable, the point with which the speaker of *JD I* frames his poem. There is no known source or analogue for *Resignation*, but the subject matter of its first half – the speaker's continued sinfulness and God's beneficient mercy – is common to many homilies and sermons, and its second half shares enough thematic and linguistic affinities with the so-called elegies found in the Exeter Book that it is generally, although not universally, numbered among them. *Resignation* is also the first poem in the Exeter Book to display damage from the hot object that was placed on the back of the manuscript. From fol. 118ᵛ, where only a few letters have been lost in the right margin about halfway down the page, to the end of the manuscript, the size of the burn increases steadily and, as a result, the amount of text lost to the burn increases in the final folios.

The prayerful qualities of *Resignation*'s first section are established from the poem's opening lines (the first of which is metrically deficient): 'Age mec se ælmihta god, / helpe min se halga drhyten' (1–2a) [May almighty God hold me in his keeping, may the holy lord be my help]. Acutely aware that he is complicit in his sinfulness since he has 'ma fremede / grimra gylta þonne me god lyfde' (27b–28) [committed more of terrible transgressions than God allowed me], the speaker also 'bote gemon' (20b) [remembers the reward of eternal life] and tells the 'cyninga wuldor' (21a) [king of glory] that he will 'cume to, gif ic mot' (21b) [come to it, if I may]. The prayer-like first half of the poem ends with the speaker acknowledging that 'God ic hæbbe / abolgen' (78b–79a) [I have made God swollen with anger] and that as a result he must 'martirdom / deopne adreoge' (81b–82a) [endure an onerous martyrdom]. Following this, the poem's second part, known as *Resignation B*, turns away from the penitential and devotional towards the secular and elegiac. The speaker adopts the tone and language shared by the small group of OE elegies in which a first-person speaker, who is usually an 'anhoga' (89b) [solitary being, lonely being], reveals the present, often extreme hardships he or she endures. The speaker of *Resignation* does suffer, admitting that he is 'fus on ferþe' (84a) [eager in mind to die], that 'him bið a sefa geomor, / mod morgenseoc' (95b–96a) [for him ever is his heart sad, his spirit sick in the morning], and that he has been 'afysed ... / earm of ... eþle' (88b–89a) [driven away, a wretched one, from (his) homeland]. So severe are the torments of exile that 'Ne mæg þæs anhoga, / leodwynna leas, leng drohtian, / wineleas wræcca' (89b–91a) [the solitary being, deprived of the joy that comes from being among one's own people, cannot long live, a friendless exile].

But unlike the speakers of the other elegies, the speaker of *Resignation* reveals the cause, or perhaps one of the causes, of his woe: 'on frymðe gelomp / yrmþu ofer eorþan' (84b–85a) [from the beginning of life poverty befell (him) throughout the earth]. He returns to this issue several times before the close of the poem, as when he reveals that he cannot embark upon the sea journey he desires to take because 'nah ic fela goldes / ne huru þæs freondes, þe me gefylste / to þam siðfate' (101b–3a) [I do not have much of gold, nor indeed friends who can help me on that journey]. Although the poverty at the centre of *Resignation*'s second half is a weighty problem, in so articulating the cause of his misery, the poem's speaker also somewhat diminishes it since it has a clear (if perhaps for him unattainable) solution. This contrasts sharply with the other elegies, in which the speakers find themselves trapped within far more complex, intractable situations. Whereas the other elegies come to rather open-ended, indeterminate conclusions, *Resignation* ends on a soundly didactic note – 'Giet biþ þæt selast, þonne mon him sylf ne mæg / wyrd onwendan, þæt he þonne wel þolige' (117–18) [Yet is that best, when a man may not himself change his fate, that he then endures it well] – that may increase its effectiveness from a doctrinal perspective but surely limits and diminishes it from an artistic one.

Further Reading

Deskis, Susan E. 'Jonah and genre in *Resignation B*'. *MÆ* 67 (1998): 189–200.
Gretsch, Mechthild. 'A Context for *Resignation A?*' In *Intertexts: Studies in Anglo-Saxon Culture Presented to Paul E. Szarmach*, ed. Virginia Blanton and Helene Scheck, 103–17. MRTS 334. Arizona Studies in the Middle Ages and the Renaissance 24. Tempe: ACMRS, 2008.
Pulsiano, Phillip. 'Spiritual despair in *Resignation B*'. *Neophilologus* 79 (1995): 155–62.

The Descent into Hell

The unique copy of this text is found in the Exeter Book, fols 119ᵛ–21ᵛ.

The poem we know as *The Descent into Hell* is neither a full nor systematic engagement with one of the most popular topics of the Middle Ages, the Harrowing of Hell. In addition to *Descent*, this theme appears in the poetry in *Christ*, *Christ and Satan*, *The Dream of the Rood*, and *Judgement Day II*, as well as in numerous prose texts. Traces of various theological writings have been detected in the poem, including, among a number of others, the Gospel of Matthew and the apocryphal Gospel of Nicodemus, but no single source has yet been discovered for it. There seems little likelihood of a single source turning up because the poet, if he worked from sources and did not just rely on his own knowledge of his subject, used his source material even more loosely than is typical of Anglo-Saxon authors in his idiosyncratic and at times peculiar and confusing poem. His treatment of the descent into hell, for example, bears only passing resemblence to the apocryphal Gospel of Nicodemus, the text that may have served as the source for lines 23b–76. The poet, however, uses only a fraction of the gospel account, leaving out a number of dramatic conversations (including ones between hell and Satan and Satan and Christ), the character of Satan, and even the Harrowing itself.

Although there are no formal divisions in the manuscript, the poem itself has a tripartite structure. The lack of connections between the sections and the abrupt shifts that accompany the transition from one to the next make it difficult to decipher the poem's organizational structure. Opening with the visit of the two Marys to the empty tomb of Christ, the poem then touches briefly and generally upon the Resurrection before turning in the final part to Christ's descent into hell. Comprising fully one-half of the poem, the final section takes the form of a homiletic speech of joyful thanks to Christ, the 'wilcuman' (58a) [welcome one] for coming to free those who 'on þissum bendum bidan' (62) [wait in these bonds].

But even though the poem presents its subject matter idiosyncratically (for example, in the first section's narrative chronology Christ descends to hell after, not before, the resurrection), it nevertheless contains a number of intriguing and effective narrative moments, including the description of the joy felt in hell at Christ's coming. This is a startling moment because the patriarchs who experience the joy are at first identified using a term, 'helwaran' (21a) [the inhabitants of hell], associated more with hell's infernal and damned occupants than with those who will be freed as a result of the Harrowing. The poet employs the topos of the *miles Christi* to good effect in the long speech beginning on line 59 with the speaker, who sounds very much like a secular hero, recalling the 'sweord ond byrnan / helm ond heorosceorp' (72b–73a) [sword and coat of mail, helmet and war-like dress] he received from the Lord, objects that the speaker has at the ready since he has continued to hold onto them 'nu giet' (73b) [up to now]. Christ's destruction of the gates of hell, which he accomplishes not with the assistance of 'helmberendra' (37b) [helmeted warriors] or 'byrnwigend' (38a) [armour-clad warriors], whom he 'rohte' [cared] not to lead 'to þære hilde' (37a) [to that battle], is presented with an admirably simple efficiency that mirrors the effortlessness of Christ's actions: at his appearance before the gates, 'þa locu feollan, / clustor of þam ceastrum' (39b–40a) [the locks dropped off, the bars from that fortified settlement]. The same is true of the poet's description of hell's gates as seen by John the Baptist after Christ's arrival: 'Geseah he helle duru hædre scinan, / þa þe longe ær bilocen wæron, / beþeahte mid þystre' (53–55a) [Saw he the doors of hell shine brightly, the ones that long before were locked, covered with darkness].

The text of *Descent* was substantially damaged by the hot object that burned all the folios from 118ᵛ to 130ᵛ, the final folio with writing in the codex. Numerous attempts have been made to fill in the textual lacunae in *Descent* and the other affected poems, but because the damage is so extensive, all the recreated readings must remain highly speculative.

Further Reading

Brantley, Jessica. 'The iconography of the Utrecht Psalter and the Old English *Descent into Hell*'. *ASE* 28 (1999): 43–63.

Hall, Thomas N. 'The armaments of John the Baptist in *Blickling Homily 14* and the Exeter Book *Descent into Hell*'. In *Intertexts: Studies in Anglo-Saxon Culture Presented to Paul E. Szarmach*, ed. Virginia Blanton and Helene Scheck, 289–306. MRTS 334. Arizona Studies in the Middle Ages and the Renaissance 24. Tempe: ACMRS, 2008.

Rambaran-Olm, M.R. 'Is the title of the Old English poem *The Descent into Hell* suitable?' *SELIM: Journal of the Spanish Society for Medieval English Language and Literature* 13 (2005–6): 73–85.

Tamburr, Karl. 'Providential view and penitential mode in the Old English harrowing of hell'. In his *The Harrowing of Hell in Medieval England*, 44–83. Cambridge: D.S. Brewer, 2007.

Almsgiving

Unique copy found in the Exeter Book on fols 121ᵛ–22ʳ.

Almsgiving, an eight-line poem extolling the virtues of charity, is part of a small group of short miscellaneous poems on religious and moral topics that the scribe or compiler chose to group together in the Exeter Book. The poem begins on the bottom-most line of fol. 121ᵛ and concludes on the top of fol. 122ʳ two lines above the burn mark, making it the only undamaged member of its eclectic group. *Almsgiving* begins by asserting that 'Wel bið þam eorle, þe him on innan hafað, / reþehygdig wer, rume heortan' (1–2) [It is well for that man, a right-minded man, who has within him a liberal heart]. The poet equates the giving of alms with the water used to put out the flames that threaten cities, and concludes that by the giving of alms, 'he … ealle toscufeð / synna wunde sawla lacnað' (7b–8a) [entirely removes the wounds of sin and heals souls]. These final lines underscore the various benefits to be derived from charity, as the pronoun 'he' can possibly refer to almsgivers, the recipients of their largesse, and/or God. No source has been uncovered for the poem, but its subject is one that was addressed, in passing or at length, by numerous ancient and medieval authors.

Further Reading

Berkhout, Carl T. 'Some notes on the Old English *Almsgiving*'. *ELN* 10 (1972–73): 81–85.

Pharaoh

Unique copy survives in the Exeter Book, fol. 122ʳ.

No poetic parallels to *Pharaoh*, which takes the form of a question-and-answer dialogue, survive in the OE poetic corpus, but verse and prose dialogues, including *Solomon and Saturn*, do. The eight-line *Pharaoh* begins 'Saga me hwæt þær weorudes wære ealles / on Farones fyrde' (1–2a) [Say to me what was the number of all the people in Pharaoh's army], and not only provides an answer to the question ('siex hun[… … .]a searohæbbendra] (6) [six hundred [thousand] warriors]), but also apparently mentions the army's destruction: 'þæt eal fornam yþ[… …]' (7) [the wave that all destroyed]. Although its last few lines have been damaged by the burn, as these two quotations reveal, the poem nevertheless appears to be complete since the final word, which is undamaged, is followed by the punctuation mark the scribe typically uses at the end of a text.

Further Reading

Trahern, Joseph B. 'The *Ioca Monachorum* and the Old English *Pharaoh*'. *ELN* 7 (1970–71): 165–8.

The Lord's Prayer I

Survives in the Exeter Book on fol. 123[r].

The Exeter Book contains one of three poetic articulations of the Lord's Prayer found in the OE poetic corpus (*II* is found in CCCC, MS 201 and *III* in Oxford, Bodleian Library, MS Junius 121). *Lord's Prayer I*, at 11 lines, is by far the shortest of the three (*II* runs to 123 lines and *III* to 37 lines) and it is also the only one that does not offer a full line-by-line translation of the prayer's Latin text. The text of *I* is more a paraphrase of the Latin than a translation of it, and of only a portion of the original at that. The closing lines of the prayer are representative of the way in which the poet who crafted *Lord's Prayer I* handles the original:

> Ne læt usic costunga cnyssan to swiðe,
> ac þu us freodom gief, folca waldend,
> from yfla gehwam, a to widan feore.

(9–11)

[Do not allow temptations to disturb us exceedingly but you should give to us freedom, ruler of the people, from each of evils, for evermore.]

Part of the first line of the poem has been lost to burn damage: only a small portion of the ascender of the initial capital with which the poem begins remains visible in the left margin, and there is space between it and the damaged, partial letters (the first of which appears to have been '*g*') for perhaps as many as five or six letters.

Further Reading

Gretsch, Mechthild. 'A Context for *Resignation A*?' In *Intertexts: Studies in Anglo-Saxon Culture Presented to Paul E. Szarmach*, ed. Virginia Blanton and Helene Scheck, 103–17. MRTS 334. Arizona Studies in the Middle Ages and the Renaissance 24. Tempe: ACMRS, 2008.

Keefer, Sarah Larratt. 'Respect for the book: a reconsideration of "form", "content" and "context" in two vernacular poems'. In *New Approaches to Editing Old English Verse*, ed. Sarah Larratt Keefer and Katherine O'Brien O'Keeffe, 21–44. Rochester: D.S. Brewer, 1998.

Homiletic Fragment II

Unique version of this text survives in the Exeter Book, fols 122[r-v].

The twenty-line poem that begins on the last two lines of the Exeter Book's fol. 122ʳ is generally labelled a fragment because its themes are believed to be somehow incomplete or underdeveloped, but the evidence of the manuscript suggests that it may be complete as it stands. A portion of the poem that was written on fol. 122ᵛ has been lost to the burn, but the final word, 'leohtes' is clearly visible, as is one of the two points and part of the descender of the punctuation mark the scribe regularly uses to mark the end of poems.

In the face of the many uncertainties with which life presents them ('Monig biþ uncuþ ... waciaþ wordbeot; swa þeos woruld fareð, / scurum scyndeð' [4b–7a] [Much is unknown ... promises become weak; so this world goes, hurries onward in storms]), the poem's readers/listeners are exhorted to 'þinne dom arær' (2b) [achieve glory for yourself] by keeping their focus on the unchanging and unified nature of God: 'An is geleafa, an lifgende, / an is fulwiht, an fæder ece, / an is folces fruma, se þas foldan gesceop, duguðe ond dreamas' (8–11a) [There is one faith, one living God, one baptism, one eternal father, one Lord of the people who shaped this earth, its riches and joys]. The poet invokes the Nativity at the poem's conclusion as the event that helped bring light back to the world, drawing back the 'heolstre' (13a) [darkness] under which the world's glory had been concealed. Whether complete as we have it or fragmentary, the poem's homiletic tone and focus never vary and its message is delivered with a straightforward, effective simplicity.

Further Reading

Wittig, Joseph S. '"Homiletic Fragment II" and the Epistle to the Ephesians'. *Traditio* 25 (1969): 358–63.

The Husband's Message

Unique copy survives in the Exeter Book, fols 123ʳ⁻ᵛ.

Because of burn damage to the Exeter Book, the text of *The Husband's Message* (*HM*) is damaged in two places, at the poem's beginning and about two-thirds of the way through. The damage is so extensive as to thwart all attempts at even a partial reconstruction of the missing lines. Although the poem does not exhibit the intensity of feeling characteristic of the OE elegies, *HM* is generally classified among them. Like the two other elegies devoted to human love relationships, *Wulf and Eadwacer* and

The Wife's Lament, HM remains focused throughout on wholly secular matters. Narratively, it shares certain features with the other elegies, including a romantically linked couple (it is not clear that they are married) who are separated from each other because the man has been driven into exile as the result of a feud. As is typical of the elegies as a whole, the poem is also short on explanatory details. The couple's past life together, one that was happy and marked by the 'wordbeotunga' (15b) [promises] the two of them 'on ærdagum oft gespræcon' (16) [in earlier days often spoke], is mentioned, but not only are the past joys they experienced not contrasted with any present miseries, their present situations are not especially wretched for either of the poem's central figures. They may be physically separated but neither is trapped within a difficult and perhaps dangerous situation as are some characters in the other elegies; accordingly, the tone of *HM* is rather upbeat as it looks forward to a soon-to-be realized happier time, not to past joys.

Troubles do beset the couple in the poem in that a feud 'adraf / sigeþeode' (19b–20a) [drove (the man) away from the victorious people] and forced him, 'nyde gebæded' (40a) [compelled by necessity] and 'forðsiþes georn' (42b) [eager to depart], to 'faran on flotweg' (42a) [journey on the sea-way], but rather than focus on the fraught causes of his exile, the difficulties that attended the journey he was compelled to undertake, or the pain and suffering their separation causes either him or the 'sinchroden' (14a) [treasure adorned] woman he left behind, the poem rather focuses on the prosperity he has achieved in his exile. Far from an intensely personal, emotionally wrought rumination on the plight of an isolated, exiled figure powerless to effect any change in his or her situation, *HM* is an invitation from a man who has found success abroad (he now 'genoh hafað / fædan gold' [35b–36a] [has enough adorned gold]) to the woman he left behind asking her to follow his path, quite literally, by voluntarily boarding a boat and joining him so that they can resume the happy life they at one time enjoyed when they 'an lond bugan' (18b) [dwelled in one land] in 'freondscype' (19a) [friendship].

Like the other elegies, *HM* is delivered in the first person, but the voice that speaks in the poem does not, as we might expect, belong to someone directly involved in the situation; rather, it belongs to an inanimate object, the rune-stick charged with delivering the message the man 'agrof' (13b) [carved] upon it. Talking objects are encountered very frequently in the OE riddles and this, along with the still-undeciphered series of runes at the poem's conclusion, suggest that *HM* may share more affinity with the riddles than the elegies. Space does not permit a full consideration of the poem's enigmatic qualities, but it does directly follow Riddle 60 in the manuscript and since one of the solutions proposed for Riddle 60 is rune staff, there are good narrative and formal reasons for connecting *HM* to the riddle because the text of *HM* may be read as constituting the 'ærendspræce' (Riddle 60, 15b) [verbal message] the speaking object of Riddle 60 promises to 'abeo-dan bealdlice' (Riddle 60, 16a) [boldly announce] at the riddle's conclusion. The first line of *HM*, 'Nu ic onsundran þe secgan wille' (1) [Now I privately will say to you], can then be seen as marking not the beginning of a new poem, but a new section of Riddle 60, a view supported both by the narra-tive and formal evidence of the manuscript (*HM* is broken into three sec-tions in the manuscript, each of which is indicated by the presence of an initial capital). These poems may also be independent of each other and might appear together because they both contain talking rune staves or they may owe their place in the codex simply to happenstance.

Further Reading

Bragg, Lois. 'Runes and readers: in and around "The Husband's Message"'. *SN* 71 (1999): 34–50.

Niles, John D. 'The trick of the runes in *The Husband's Message*'. In his *Old English Enigmatic Poems and the Play of the Texts*, 213–50. Studies in the Early Middle Ages 13. Turnhout: Brepols, 2006.

Renoir, Alain. 'The least elegiac of the elegies: a contextual glance at *The Husband's Message*'. *SN* 53 (1981): 69–76.

The Ruin

Unique copy survives in the Exeter Book on fols 123ᵛ–24ᵛ.

Although often numbered among the OE elegies, *The Ruin*, which is more dispassionately ruminative than intensely emotional, does not share much with the other elegies, almost all of which are uttered in the first person by a speaker who directly relates to the reading/listening audience the extraor-dinary pain she or he is currently experiencing, usually as the result of exile. The tone of *The Ruin* is closer to that of the so-called lone survivor's speech in *Beowulf* (2247–66), but unlike the lone survivor, who hides within the earth objects that metonymically, and painfully, recall for him the now past joys and glory of his own people, the speaker of *The Ruin* gazes with what may be best characterized as an air of detached wonder upon the 'enta gewe-orc' (2b) [ancient work of giants], noting their decayed state: 'Hrofas sind gehrorene, hreorge torras' (3) [the roofs are fallen, the towers ruinous]. As his thoughts travel from the ruins to those who created them in the distant past, he observes that while a wall that is 'ræghar ond readfah rice æfter oþrum, / ofstonden under stormum' (10–11a) [grey with lichen and stained with red had remained standing under storms, from one reign to another], now it is decrepit and its builders are in 'heardgripe hrusan' (8a) [the cruel grip of the earth]. His tone throughout is one of resignation to the inevitable forces that will ultimately destroy all human creations, but it is not a resignation that is tinged with the sort of strong emotions we encounter in the OE elegies.

The poet appreciates the accomplishments of the builders – 'Beorht wæron burgræced, burnsele monige, / heah horngestreon' (21–22a) [bright were the buildings in the town, many bathhouses, an abundance of high pinnacles] – but notes that while they were 'dreama full' (23b) [full of joys], builders and structures alike fell prey to 'wyrd seo swiþe' (24b) [powerful fate]. He also observes that 'Crungon walo wide, cwoman woldagas, / swylt eall fornom secgrofra wera' (25a) [those slain in battle fell dead far and wide, days of pestilence arrived, death carried off the host of men], and that 'Betend crungon / hergas to hrusan' (28b–29a) [the restorers fell dead, armies to the earth], but he neither dwells on the causes or the inevitablity of the devastation the ruins witness nor attempts to draw either an implicit or explicit moral from the scene. He does imagine how 'þær iu beorn monig / glædmod ond goldbeorht gleoma gefrætwed, / wlonc ond wingal wighyrstum scan' (32b–34) [there formerly many a man, glad and bright with gold, adorned with splendours, proud and flushed with wine shone in his war trappings], and so seems to be on the verge of articulating one of the sharp contrasts between present woes (or in this case destruction) and past joys that are characteristic of the OE elegies; however, he turns his attention instead to a description of the ruins' engineering, focusing on the way the natural hot springs are channelled into a central hot bath, a feat that elicits a very appreciative comment: 'Þæt wæs hyðelic' (41b) [that was convenient]. Much of the last few lines of the poem have been lost to the burn damage, but the comment at line 41b brings the poem's readers/listeners right back to the poem's opening line: 'Wrætlic is þes wealstan' (1a) [Wondrous is this masonry].

Despite its loose, and partial, tonal associations with the elegies, we might perhaps best think of *The Ruin* as being *sui generis*. It does not explore the suffering experienced and reported in the first person by the isolated exiles we encounter in the elegies and neither does it fit into the category of didactic literature, either religious or secular. Parts of it seem to point towards the theme of *sic transit gloria mundi*, but the poet never fully develops that line of thinking. If it is meant to be a moral poem – and it is far from certain that it is –, the *Ruin*-poet is unusual among his contemporaries in that he does not explicitly articulate one for his readers/listeners, but rather leaves them to draw their own moral(s). The poem's manuscript context may offer some clues as to why the poet might have left his moral (if, that is, he wanted to point one) unarticulated: *The Ruin* is the last of the small group of poems that separate the first set of riddles from the set with which the manuscript concludes and so it might be seen as mimicking the rhetoric of the riddles, in which solutions are never offered but are left to the audience to decipher. Finally, the poem does not fit into the category of the *encomium urbis*, in which a city is celebrated, as in *Durham*, but rather offers a stark counterpoint to that genre by focusing on a fallen, decrepit city.

The Ruin might not fit comfortably into the categories that our contemporary interpretive strategies have established for the reception of Anglo-Saxon verbal art, but its *mise-en-page* reveals that it was considered complete as copied, and the number of rare and unique terms that it contains, as well as the careful architectural descriptions and compact and effective renderings of the forces that brought both the city and its builders to ruin, witness the author's aesthetic sensibilities and artistic accomplishment.

Further Reading

Dailey, Patricia. 'Questions of dwelling in Anglo-Saxon poetry and medieval mysticism: inhabiting landscape, body, and mind'. *NML* 8 (2006): 175–214.

Orchard, Andy. 'Reconstructing *The Ruin*'. In *Intertexts: Studies in Anglo-Saxon Culture Presented to Paul E. Szarmach*, ed. Virginia Blanton and Helene Scheck, 45–68. MRTS 334. Arizona Studies in the Middle Ages and the Renaissance 24. Tempe: ACMRS, 2008.

Trilling, Renée R. 'Ruins in the realms of thoughts: reading as constellation in Anglo-Saxon Poetry'. *JEGP* 108 (2009): 141–67.

The Poems of Cotton Vitellius A.xv

London, BL, Cotton Vitellius A.xv, one of several Anglo-Saxon manuscripts containing significant amounts of OE poetry, suffered only relatively minor damage, mostly to the edges of pages, in the fire at Ashburnham House in October of 1731. In an attempt to halt the deterioration of the pages singed in the fire, paper edging was added to each folio in the nineteenth century before the manuscript was re-bound. This method stabilized the crumbling edges of the manuscript, but at a cost: in many places the newly added edging obscured letters.

Vitellius A.xv is a composite manuscript, comprised of, respectively, the Southwick codex and the Nowell codex. Dated to the middle of the twelfth century and written in a single hand, the Southwick codex contains a version of St Augustine's *Soliloquies*, *The Gospel of Nicodemus*, *The Debate of Solomon and Saturn*, and a few lines of a homily on St Quintin. The Nowell codex, which dates to the tenth or eleventh century, contains a mix of prose and poetic texts written by two scribes. The first three of its works, all of which are in the first scribe's hand, are prose compositions: the acephalous *Life of St Christopher*, *The Wonders of the East*, and Alexander's *Letter to Aristotle* (on all three see Part 2). These are followed in turn by two poetic texts, *Beowulf* and *Judith*. In addition to copying the three prose works in the codex, the first scribe copied *Beowulf* from its inception to line 1939, ending with the word 'scyran', which in the manuscript is the final word on the third line from the top of fol. 172ᵛ. The second scribe, whose hand is contemporary with that of the first scribe, takes up the text at the now damaged beginning of the next line in mid-sentence (the first few letters he wrote

The Anglo-Saxon Literature Handbook, First Edition. Mark C. Amodio.
© 2014 Mark C. Amodio. Published 2014 by John Wiley & Sons, Ltd.

are lost) and it is in his hand that the remainder of *Beowulf* and what survives of the fragmentary *Judith* are written. Why the first scribe's stint ends where, and how it does, remains a mystery.

Further Reading

Kiernan, Kevin. '*Beowulf*' *and the Beowulf Manuscript*. 1981. Rev. edn., Ann Arbor: University of Michigan Press, 1996.

Beowulf

Survives in London, BL, Cotton Vitellius A.xv, fols 132^r–201^v.

Among OE poetry, only *Genesis* at just under 3,000 lines approaches *Beowulf*'s length (3,182 lines), and even then it does so only if we include the slightly more than 500 lines of *Genesis B*. But it is not only *Beowulf*'s length that sets it apart from the remainder of the extant vernacular poetic corpus; it is one of the few works of OE secular heroic poetry to survive intact and it is arguably more sophisticated and more complex than any other surviving OE poem. The poem, which has no lacunae caused by loss of a leaf or leaves, is divided into sections marked imperfectly by Roman numerals running from I to XLIII, with XXIII having been mistakenly omitted by the first scribe. Each new section begins with a large, modestly ornamental capital, although in some cases, as in sections II, IIII and XVIIII, damage to the manuscript has left no, or only partial, traces of the capitals. The logic behind these section divisions has yet to be fully understood, and it remains unclear if they are scribal or authorial. The final folio of the poem, 201^v, shows non-fire related damage, as does fol. 182^r. The damage on both folios – many letters have been rubbed away – is consistent with what would happen were gatherings circulated without any sort of protective cover.

As is the case with the few other surviving examples of the secular heroic tradition, no known source or analogue has yet been uncovered for *Beowulf*, and even its Christian elements cannot be traced to specific texts. Does this then mean that we ought to view the poem as wholly the product of the *Beowulf*-poet's own, at times perhaps idiosyncratic, imaginative faculties? To answer this question fully, or even partially, would require more space than is available here, so for our purposes we will simply answer with a qualified 'yes': the poem is the product of the poet's uniquely talented artistic sensibility, but it is also deeply and inextricably rooted in the Anglo-Saxon poetic tradition. The *Beowulf*-poet's accomplishment is nothing short of extraordinary: working wholly within the expressive economy that is Anglo-Saxon oral poetics and working with that economy's highly traditional – and specialized – metrics, lexicon, thematics, and story-patterns, he creates a work of verbal art that, paradoxically, is our best and most important witness to the vernacular heroic tradition at the same time that it points to often deep fissures within that tradition.

While the poem contains many examples of the way in which the *Beowulf*-poet habitually negotiates (and perhaps reshapes) the tradition within which he articulates his verbal art, space will permit us only to consider briefly one: his treatment of the war-band, or comitatus. The importance of this group in Germanic culture has been noted since at least the first century CE, when Tacitus, in the fourteenth chapter of his *Germania*, famously observes that 'infamy and lifelong scandal await the man who outlives his leader by retreating from the battle-line: to defend their chief and guard him, to ascribe to his glory their own brave deeds, is their foremost oath. The leader fights for victory, the retainers for their leader' (Rives, 83). In the prose records from the Anglo-Saxon period, the complex nexus of interwoven – and bi-directional – obligations foundational to the comitatus finds perhaps its fullest articulation in the Anglo-Saxon Chronicle entry for 755. The comitatus also figures importantly in several OE poems, most notably *Brunanburh*, *Maldon*, and *Finnsburh*, where its treatment echoes that which it receives in the *Germania* and the Chronicle. But whereas the other heroic poems in which the comitatus figures offer uniform and consistently positive depictions of it, *Beowulf* problematizes it, revealing it to be an unobtainable – and perhaps outdated – ideal rather than the viable, functioning paradigm for heroic conduct it is elsewhere presented to be.

The *Beowulf*-poet does not directly critique the idea of the comitatus, but his criticism of it is no less sharp – or apparent – for being oblique. When the young Geatish hero Beowulf decides to journey across the water to assist the Danes in their struggle against the monstrous Grendel, he does so accompanied by his comitatus, none of whom expects to return alive. The comitatus awaits Grendel in Heorot, the royal hall of the Danish King Hrothgar, alongside Beowulf and one of them falls victim to the ravager in the moments after Grendel first enters the hall, but the fight itself takes place entirely between Beowulf and Grendel: the comitatus, relegated to the sidelines throughout, plays no role in it whatsoever. Even before the battle, there are signs that point to the comitatus's problematic role in the poem. Upon his arrival at Heorot, Beowulf initally requests that he alone be permitted to defeat Grendel, but with his next breath he includes his men – and perhaps even the Danes – in the impending martial encounter. The grammar of the lines in question, 431–32, has proved somewhat difficult to parse because Beowulf appears to contradict himself and because it lacks coordinating conjunctions, but the first part of his request – 'þæt ic mote ana' (431a) [that I might alone] – presents no interpretive problems. Whether we read it as a slip of the tongue, as a revealing glimpse into his psyche, or as evidence of the comitatus's waning cultural importance, this half line, in which Beowulf allots no meaningful role to his men in the coming struggle, points the comitatus's uneasy situation within the poem's narrative contours.

The poet's second critique of the comitatus is both more apparent and more dramatic: when he goes to face a dragon late in his life, Beowulf is once again accompanied by a group of hand-picked warriors. When the group arrives at the dragon's barrow and Beowulf and the dragon first clash, the comitatus flees to the relative safety of the woods. The flight of the comitatus to the woods reveals not only that the lord-retainer bond rests on rather unstable footing for the warriors, but also that it is tenuous for Beowulf as well: rather than relying on his men in the battle, in his final speech before going to face the dragon he undercuts the entire institution of the comitatus by explicitly instructing his men to remain out of the fray, saying that it is fitting only for him to face the creature:

> Nis þæt eower sið,
> ne gemet mannes nef(ne) min anes,
> þæt he wið aglæcean eofoðo dæle,
> eorlscype efne.
>
> (2532b–35a)

[this is not your undertaking, nor is it fitting for any man except me alone that he fight, perform heroic action.]

The failure of the comitatus bond is thus bi-directional: Beowulf fails his warriors (in ordering his men not to join in the fight he rejects/ignores the very principle of mutual need/obligation upon which the comitatus is founded) just as surely as they fail him by retreating to the woods in his hour of need.

If *Beowulf* were our only source of evidence regarding the comitatus in early Germanic culture, we would have little choice but to see it as a fracturing component of a heroic culture that was itself perhaps already vestigial at the time the poem was composed and not as the powerfully determinative and culturally central one it is depicted to be elsewhere. But while *Beowulf* undoubtedly opens an important window onto the practices and function of the comitatus within early Germanic culture, we are as yet unable to determine whether the *Beowulf*-poet's treatment of it is as idiosyncratic, innovative, and perhaps even non-traditional as it appears to be, or if it simply reflects an otherwise unattested brachiation of the poetic tradition, one in which the comitatus was not viewed through an idealized lens as, say, it is in *Maldon*, but rather through a more critical one. The *Beowulf*-poet's treatment of the comitatus is emblematic of his approach in general: the poem he creates is our most important witness to and source of information on the Anglo-Saxon vernacular heroic tradition, but it is also one that often steps outside of (and in so doing possibly redefines) the tradition as its narrative moves into and out of unexpected and, from the perspective of the tradition, previously unexplored territory.

Beowulf's narrative opens with a brief account of the genealogy of the Danish royal line from its founding by the quasi-mythic figure Scyld Scefing down to Hrothgar, the king who occupies the throne during the years of Grendel's attacks. Providing more than Hrothgar's ancestry, the genealogy also serves as the vehicle through which the poet economically and effectively sets out both the traits that a king must possess as well as the practices in which he must engage to become a successful leader in the early Germanic world. With Scyld as the paradigm, we learn that a 'god cyning' (11b) [good king] is one who is both obeyed by 'æghwylc þara ymbsittendra / ofer hronrade' (9–10a) [each of the neighbouring peoples over the ocean] and one who receives from these peoples 'gomban' (11a) [tribute]. In addition to exerting his martial superiority over the tribes within his political ambit and receiving tribute from them, a good king must also necessarily be generous and distribute a portion of the treasure he acquires to the warriors who swear loyalty to him as a way of ensuring that in his old age, 'þonne wig cume' (23b) [when war should come] his 'wilgesiþas' (23a) [desired companions] will 'leode gelæsten' (24a) [stand by the people].

Hrothgar proves to be a successful king, and as a result his 'geogoð geweox / magodriht micel' (66b–67a) [troop of untried warriors grew into a mighty band of young retainers]. To celebrate his people's prosperity and prowess, he commands that a great hall be built. This hall, which is named Heorot upon its completion, serves as an important locus of community, a centre where human culture is collectively, and often noisily, celebrated through rituals such as feasting, the singing of songs, the dispensing of treasure, and the circulation of a communal drinking cup. Heorot, though, is more than an emblem of the Danes' success and a locus for human celebration; it also proves to be the site of great social and cultural distress for shortly after it is constructed it becomes the target of Grendel, a creature who emerges from the moors and visits death upon the hall nightly for twelve years, killing thirty warriors at a time. Grendel's attacks put great stress on the hall, whose name translates to 'hart; male deer', and the culture centred in it. Although these attacks virtually paralyze Danish society, they have little lasting effect on either the hall itself or the culture it emblematizes. Heorot will be severely damaged when the two outsiders Beowulf and Grendel fight within it, but afterwards it will quickly be repaired and restored to its former glory. What it will not survive is an internal threat, for it will be burnt to the ground during an internecine conflict that erupts between 'aþumsweorum' (84) [son-in-law and father-in-law].

Grendel, the creature who poses the most immediate threat to the stability of Heorot during the twelve years he attacks it nightly, proves to be a rather complex figure, one to whom the label 'monster' applies only partially and imperfectly. He dwells in darkness on the borders of human society, in close enough proximity to Heorot that he is able to hear the 'dream' (88b) [joy] that daily emantes from the hall, but beyond this, Grendel remains something of a cypher. Neither his relationship to the human world nor his motives for attacking Heorot with the frequency and ferocity that he does are ever made explicit. Even his physical attributes remain vague as they are never detailed. A wide variety of terms are used to describe him, some of which point to his monstrosity (for example, 'grimma gæst' [102a] [grim guest, visitor; or grim evil spirit, demon], 'mære mearcstapa' [103a] [well known wanderer in the waste borderland], and 'Wiht unhælo' [120b] [misfortunate creature]) and some of which complicate it (for example 'rinc siðian' [720b] [journeying warrior], 'healðegn' [142a] [hall retainer], and 'wonsæli wer' [105a] [unblessed man]). Perhaps most importantly, he is several times described as an 'aglæca' [awesome opponent, fearsome fighter], a term used of several other characters in the poem, including Grendel's mother, the dragon, and, perhaps somewhat surprisingly, Beowulf. The cloud of indeterminacy that hovers over Grendel extends to his mode of locomotion (which is several times described by the verb 'scriðan' [to glide]) and even to his name, for which a number of possible etymologies have been proposed, although none has so far gained universal acceptance. The indeterminacy that attends Grendel plays an important part in the poem's affective dynamics because it forces its audience to flesh him out in ways that are all the more terrifying for being highly idiosyncratic.

From the outset, Grendel is established as an 'atol angengea' (165a) [horrible lone-going one] who dwells 'earfoðlice ... in ðystrum' (86b–87b) [grievously/bitterly/painfully ... in darkness]. Since the culture celebrated in the poem prizes collectivity and distrusts and frequently demonizes lone-goers, Grendel's solitariness emerges immediately as one of his most troubling characteristics: as the so-called elegies contained in the Exeter Book eloquently articulate, being exiled from one's homeland and/or tribe ranks as one of the most painful fates a member of Anglo-Saxon society could suffer. Yet while Grendel stands as the paradigmatic outsider and while the poem itself endorses its human culture's strongly negative view of those who do not fit within its ambit, two of its central characters, Scyld Scefing and Beowulf, paradoxically have much in common with the outsiders the culture fears and distrusts. Scyld arrives Moses-like as an infant, his ancestry remaining forever unknown. Although Beowulf's lineage is known, there is still much about him that witnesses his status as an other, including, his physical attributes and his arrival in Denmark from a foreign land, unannounced and uninvited, to offer his assistance to Hrothgar (who so far as we know has not broadcast any appeals for external help). The Danish coast-guard who rides up to confront and assess the possible threat posed by Beowulf and his armed troop as they come ashore in Denmark immediately singles Beowulf out, tellingly observing that Beowulf possesses an 'ænlic ansyn' (251a) [unique/peerless appearance]. While referring to Beowulf's unmatched size (the coast-guard confesses that he has never seen a man as large as Beowulf), this phrase also speaks directly to Beowulf's status as an other. Both compounds are built on the same element 'an', the pertinent meaning of which in this context is 'one particular person, thing, occasion, event, etc. out of many' (DOE, s.v.), and so a more literal translation of the phrase would render something along these lines: 'one-like singular-sight'. While such a translation is far from elegant, it does help clarify the underlying sense of the coast-guard's comment, something that becomes even more apparent when we consider that of the nearly ninety times in which the adjective 'ænlic' occurs in OE prose and poetry, only in this instance is it coupled with the partially redundant compound 'ansyn'.

The many parallels that exist between Beowulf and the monstrous Grendel also signal Beowulf's otherness. To cite only some of the more important ones, Beowulf has the strength of thirty men in his arm and Grendel kills thirty Danes a night; Grendel does not use weapons, relying instead on his main might, and prior to their fight Beowulf disarms, stripping off his byrnie and perhaps even the remainder of his clothing; Grendel's rapacity is matched – if not surpassed – by Beowulf's raw brutality (during the fight he tears off Grendel's arm and shoulder); and except for the 'wop' (785b) [lamentation] and 'gyreleoð' (786a) [song of terror] that Grendel emits, their struggle remains outside the realm of the verbal as they fight in silence. They are also connected lexically, as the same adjective, 'gebolgen' [swollen with rage], and the same noun, 'aglæca' [awesome opponent, ferocious fighter] are used to describe them, and syntactically for at times during their fight it is nearly impossible to determine who is doing what to whom. The correspondences between Beowulf and Grendel result in a decided blurring, at times even to the point of elision, of their differences, something that complicates our reception and understanding of them and of their uneasy situation in the very different worlds (human and monstrous) we expect them to inhabit. Space will not permit a full exploration of this issue, so we will briefly take up only one example: Beowulf's decision to fight Grendel without sword or chain-mail, without, that is, either the offensive or defensive technology human culture has developed.

Grendel's reliance on the killing power of his bare hands is one of the many things that signal his status as a societal outsider, and in eschewing sword and byrnie Beowulf moves himself significantly closer to the position Grendel occupies. Framed in the context of levelling the playing field, Beowulf's decision to forego weapons may well be one of the chief reasons he is able to succeed against Grendel when so many before him have fatally failed. Against human foes, the technology of weapons and armour proves beneficial to those who employ it, but it also constrains them as much as it protects and aids them. Literally freed of byrnie and sword, objects that define as much as protect him, and figuratively freed of the culture these objects symbolize, Beowulf is able to do something that no other man can: displaying a raw and terrifying ferocity, he becomes Grendel-like in order to defeat Grendel. We do not know enough about the fight in Heorot to surmise whether Beowulf achieves some sort of transcendent, berserker-like mental state during it (although we do know that he is 'bolgenmod' [709a] [swollen with anger] as he awaits Grendel), but he does enter a liminal space between the human and the monstrous. Following Beowulf's defeat of Grendel, Hrothgar works carefully to reel him back from this space by lavishing gifts on him and promising that he will 'for sunu ... / freogan on ferhþe' (947b–48a) [as a son ... love (him) in (his) heart].

Shortly after he dispatches Grendel, Beowulf must again confront another monstrous outsider, Grendel's mother. She poses a threat very different from that posed by her son, most obviously in her gender, but in other ways as well. Several things differentiate Grendel's mother's attack from those of her son: unlike Grendel who attacks nightly for many years and kills in that span an enormous number of men, she attacks once and kills only one man, and whereas Grendel effectively wrests control of the hall from the Danes every evening, her attack is more of a smash-and-grab raid in that she enters stealthily, seizes one warrior, and hastily returns to her dwelling. From one of the rare glimpses into Grendel's mind that the poem offers, it seems that he enjoys his slaughterous visits: as he stands in the doorway surveying the sleeping Geatish warriors, Grendel's 'mod ahlog' (730b) [mind laughed/exulted]. His mother, in contrast, embarks on her sole visit to Heorot 'galg-mod' (1277a) [sad, gloomy, fierce, stern]. The first element in this compound is closely related to the noun 'gealga' [gallows], and so a more literal rendering of it would be 'gallows-minded', a phrase that suggests Grendel's mother is aware that she may not survive her attempt to avenge her son's death. Her attack also differs from Grendel's in that it is clearly and singularly motivated – she wishes her 'sunu deoð wrecan' (1278b) [son's death to avenge] – and, finally, where Grendel effectively paralyzes human culture by nightly establishing a monstrous world order, his mother's actions strongly suggest that she seeks nothing more than redress for her son's death. This last issue is especially important as it points to what may perhaps be the most significant difference between Grendel and Grendel's mother – one that is entirely overlooked by both the Danes and the Geats in the aftermath of her attack – namely that her actions fit seamlessly within the code of conduct that developed in early Germanic culture regarding feuds. Unlike her son, who is either ignorant of or wilfully ignores this code (Grendel will not 'fea þingian' [156b] [settle by payment] and so no one should 'wenan ... / beorhtre bote to banan folmum' [157b–58] [expect ... bright compensation at the slayer's hands]), his mother's course of action is not only acceptable within human culture, but expected and, perhaps, demanded by the heroic culture the poem depicts: the death of a family member at the hands of another demands action, be it in the form of economic recompense, 'wergild' [man-payment], or blood.

Aside from her participation in feud culture, there are other signs in the poem that signal her complex and problematic connection to the human social world and to the poem's heroic ethos. Her dwelling, although located at the bottom of a mere, is described in human terms – it is a 'hrofsele' (1515a) [roofed hall] and a 'niðsele' (1513a) [a hall lower down, perhaps in an abyss; a hall where one is exposed to the hatred of a foe] – and it is perhaps unexpectedly lighted by a fire. Her hall also contains the body of Grendel and a store of treasure. While there is no evidence to suggest that the former is displayed ritually and the latter decoratively, as they might be in a human hall, their presence leaves open the possibility, however tentatively and incompletely, that she may be more than a monstrous 'brimwylf' (1506a) [female sea-wolf] or 'grundwyrgenne' (1518b) [female outcast of the deep].

From the terms used to describe her, a number of which (including the two cited immediately above) are unique, we can gauge just how difficult it is for the poet to situate her within the poem's heroic ethos, something that we may illustrate by briefly considering the recent translation for yet another *hapax legomenon* used of her, 'aglæcwif' (1259a), found in the glossary of the fourth edition of Klaeber's *Beowulf*. A decided improvement over Klaeber's earlier 'wretch, or monster, of a woman', the fourth edition's 'troublemaker, female adversary' is not itself wholly satisfactory as it fails adequately to reflect the meaning of the compound's initial element: an *aglæca* is not merely someone who is troublesome but rather someone who inspires awe, terror, and dread, potentially in allies as much as in enemies. The complete half-line in which the compound 'aglæcwif' occurs, 'ides aglæcwif', is also rather telling in this regard. A literal translation, which would yield something more along the lines of 'woman/lady, awe-inspiring woman', raises the issue of why the poet doubly marks Grendel's mother's gender, a gender about which there is apparently no confusion, especially since in seven of the eight times the word 'modor' occurs in the poem, it refers to Grendel's mother. A related phrase found in *Judith*, where the poet early on describes the poem's eponymous heroine as 'ides ælfscinu' (*Judith* 14a) [a woman radiant as an elf/delusive as an elf/divinely inspired], may shed some light here. Even though the redundancy is not as evident in *Judith*, the adjective 'ælfscinu' is grammatically marked as feminine. In both cases, the redundancy may be evidence of the poets' attempts to find apt language to describe threatening female characters whose actions, especially the killing of men, place them in a very select group within the poetic corpus: aside from Grendel's mother and Judith, killing is solely the provenance of men in Anglo-Saxon literature. The radically transgressive nature of Grendel's mother's behaviour may further help explain why the poet on some six occasions unambiguously refers to her using either masculine pronouns or masculinely inflected adjectives: as we might expect in a culture in which blood feuds are so important, there is a rich and varied lexicon that can be used of an avenger, but only when the avenging figure is male, not female.

The narrative context for Beowulf's fight with Grendel's mother is also more complex than that of his fight with Grendel. Whereas Beowulf apparently decides to fight Grendel out of some vague sense of obligation to the Danes and his largely unarticulated desire to make a heroic name for himself, he takes up the fight with Grendel's mother after Hrothgar effectively appoints him as champion of the Danes, telling the Geatish warrior 'Nu is se ræd gelang / eft æt þe anum' (1376b–77a) [Now is help dependent once more upon you alone]. That the Danes do not place the death of Æschere, the man she snatches and kills during her attack on Heorot, within the tradition of the blood-feud, where it could, and perhaps should, be seen as balancing out the death of Grendel further complicates matters. She is motivated by the desire for revenge, and although we cannot know whether she would have returned to Heorot had Beowulf not killed her on the following day, the narrative points to her attack being a singular, not recurring, event. However understandable the humans' inability to so contextualize her actions might be, especially in the face of Grendel's recurring attacks, in seeking her out in her dwelling Beowulf not only continues the feud but he also behaves as first Grendel and then his mother heretofore have: he becomes the same sort of aggressive, uninvited, and deadly outsider that they have been, an other who invades and threatens (and in this instance utterly destroys) the stability of an established social order.

As he prepares to fight Grendel's mother, Beowulf does not discard the defensive and offensive technologies of helmet, byrnie, and sword as he did prior to his engagement with Grendel; rather, he carefully arms himself before journeying into Grendel's mother's territory, a territory that is clearly inhospitable to humans, located as it is at the bottom of a mere populated with 'wyrmcynnes fela' (1425b) [many a serpent], 'sellice sæd-racan' (1426a) [strange sea snakes], and 'nicras' (1427b) [water-mon-sters]. He even bears with him a named sword, Hrunting, that is 'ahyrded heaþoswate' (1460a) [hardened in blood shed in battle]. The technology he bears and upon which he depends functions only partially as desired: his defensive garb – his byrnie – twice keeps him from harm, once from Grendel's mother's claws during his descent through the mere and once from the point of the 'seax' [1545b] [knife] she wields during their fight, but his offensive weapon, the special, named sword he bears fails, a fail-ure that points yet again the limits of humanity's power and also the limits of human culture's ability to suppress a monstrous other who threatens its stability.

After encountering considerable difficulty in the fight with Grendel's mother (at one point he falls to the floor, whereupon she sits on him and attempts to stab him with her 'seax'), Beowulf prevails, but only through the agency of an 'ealdsweord eotenisc' (1558a) [ancient sword made by giants] that he discovers among the treasure in her hall. With this sword he decapitates Grendel's mother and then her son's corpse, but his use of this found object is problematic because it is only Beowulf's more-than-human attributes that permit him to wield this sword since it, being 'giganta geweorc' (1562b) [the work of giants] is 'mare ðonne ænig mon oðer / to beadulace ætberan meahte' (1560–61) [greater than any other man to battle might bear]. By reaching into the world of the giants Beowulf once again trangresses the limits of humanity and he once again temporarily occupies, as he does during the fight with Grendel, a liminal space between the human and the monstrous. The extraordinary nature of both his foe (as was the case with Grendel, some sort of spell or charm apparently keeps man-made weapons from harming Grendel's mother) and the sword he uses is reinforced when, after decapitating Grendel's corpse, the sword's blade melts, leaving Beowulf with only its hilt.

Despite their differences, the threats that Grendel and his mother pose are fundamentally similar in that both seek not so much to destroy the human social order as to redefine and reshape it. Formidable as the Grendelkin are, they and their threats pale in comparison to that of the third, and final, monstrous other Beowulf encounters: 'se wyrm' (2287a) [the dragon]. After returning home from Denmark, Beowulf in due course ascends the Geatish throne. He prospers as king, remarking shortly before he dies that during his reign 'næs se folccyning, / ymbesittendra ænig ðara / þe mec guðwinum gretan dorste, / egesan ðeon' (2733b–36a) [there was not a folk-king, any of those neighbouring tribes, who dared to greet me with comrades-in-arms or terribly threaten me]. The dragon, who has been guarding its treasure hoard for some 300 winters, is roused by the theft of a single cup, a cup that shortly thereafter comes into Beowulf's possession. Damage to the surface of fol. 182^r, which appears to be a palimpsest, prevents us from knowing anything definitive about the one who takes the cup since only the first letter, þ, of the lexeme that describes him is legible. 'Þeof' [thief], 'þeo(w)' [servant/slave], and 'þegn' [nobleman] have all been proposed as emendations.

The dragon soon discovers the loss and responds with unparalleled – almost unimaginable – intensity and ferocity. Unlike Grendel who targets only Heorot during his nightly attacks, and unlike Grendel's mother who kills but a single man, the dragon seeks nothing less than the eradication of every living creature: 'no ðær aht cwices / lað lyftfloga læfan wolde' (2314b–15) [the hated air-flyer desired to leave nothing alive there]. As terrifying as the killing power of the Grendelkin is, that of the fifty-foot-long, flying, poisonous, fire-breathing dragon is incalculably greater. In its first foray following the theft of the cup, the dragon wreaks a wide swath of destruction across the Geatish countryside, burning down Beowulf's hall in the process. It retires at dawn to its barrow, a 'dryhtsele dyrnne' (2320a) [secret noble hall], and its diminished treasure hoard. Whether its rampage is over at this point or merely suspended until evening falls once again cannot be determined since before it can reemerge Beowulf seeks out its barrow and, standing alone in front of its entrance, looses a verbal fusillade – 'word ut faran, / stearcheort styrmde' (2551b–52a) [words journeyed out, the stout-hearted one stormed] – to which the dragon responds by attacking.

Although Grendel and his mother are strange and formidable foes, their actions are nevertheless understandable from the human perspective. We may not be able to explain why Grendel attacks Heorot with such frequency and ferocity, but whether prompted by something as simple as hunger alone, or in combination with more complicated (and unarticulated) matters such as anger at being excluded from human society or the desire to rule in Hrothgar's stead, his actions – aside from his culinary predilections – nevertheless fit comfortably into the human social paradigm. The same is true of Grendel's mother, whose actions, as we saw above, conform closely to what human society proscribes for men involved in a blood feud. Even in death, Grendel remains connected to human culture, as his body parts (first his arm and shoulder and later his head) are displayed in Heorot. In gazing upon them, the Danes, and by extension all of human culture, assert their social system's superiority over the one Grendel imposed upon them. Their gaze and the display of Grendel's body parts, however, do even more: they establish a safe, controlled, and contained space within human culture for the threatening otherness that Grendel embodies.

Given the degree to which Grendel's body parts are fetishized by human culture and the importance placed on their public display, we might expect the bodies of Grendel's mother and the dragon to be treated similarly, but they are not: after beheading Grendel's mother, Beowulf does not give her corpse another thought, and following the dragon's death, his comitatus 'ofostlic(e)' (3130a) [hurriedly] 'scufun' (3131b) [shove] the dragon's corpse 'ofer weallclif, leton weg niman / flod fæðmian frætwa hyrde' (3132–33) [over the cliff; they let the waves engulf the guardian of the treasure]. Although narratively inconsequential, Beowulf's inattention to Grendel's mother's corpse and the unceremonious tipping of the dead dragon into the water reveal the unsettling and incomprehensible alterity of these two monstrous foes. We can perhaps best understand why there is space in Heorot for Grendel's body parts, but not for those of a female avenger or of an 'atol inwitgæst' (2670a) [horrible malicious foe] such as the dragon by recognizing that there are no cultural categories into which the latter two can be placed. Monstrous others with human (and male) attributes are knowable in ways that monstrous others who are female and wholly non-human foes are not. These latter two types remain so threatening even in death that human culture has no space, literally and figuratively, for them, preferring instead to relegate them to marginalized, inaccessible places. Danes come from far and wide to publically – and collectively – vent their frustration by hacking at Grendel's arm and shoulder with their swords when his body parts are first displayed in Heorot, but they are afforded no such opportunity to do the same to the more threatening, ultimately unknowable bodies of Grendel's mother and the dragon.

Just as the dragon is a monstrous foe very different from the other two that Beowulf faces in the poem, so, too, is his encounter with the dragon very different from his encounters with Grendel and Grendel's mother. Structurally, the dragon fight, which is comprised of three distinct engagements, is far more complex than either of the two preceding fights. As soon as Beowulf grasps Grendel's arm, Grendel seeks to flee since he knows he is in the grip of a foe more powerful than any he had ever faced before. In the fight against Grendel's mother, Beowulf is first seized on his way to her hall at the bottom of the mere, but suffers no harm because his byrnie protects him. During his struggle with her, Beowulf falls, but he makes short work of her as soon as he regains his feet, killing her with a stroke to the neck that breaks her 'banhringas' (1567a) [vertebrae].

The dragon fight, in contrast, is comprised of three separate engagements, the first of which Beowulf initiates. Standing in front of the dragon's barrow, from which he has vowed he will not 'forfleon fotes trem' (2525a) [flee the space of a foot], he 'Let ða of breostum ða he gebolgen wæs, ... word ut faran, / stearcheort styrmde' (2550–52a) [Let then from his breast, when he was swollen with anger ... words journey out; the stout-hearted one stormed]. What Beowulf says is, tellingly, not reported, and from the verb 'styrman' [storm; shout], a word that occurs only rarely in the poetic corpus, it seems likely that Beowulf does not so much utter a coherent statement as simply let loose an inarticulate shout. Their first meeting, which immediately follows Beowulf's shout, proves inconclusive, as Beowulf's man-made sword fails to harm the dragon and the dragon's fiery breath is similarly unable to injure Beowulf who is protected by his shield. After a short respite, the combatants meet once more and Beowulf again proves unable to injure the dragon, even though during this meeting he thrusts his sword, Nægling, into the dragon's head. Not only does this stroke have little effect upon the dragon, the blade fails, shattering into pieces. Wiglaf, a member of Beowulf's comitatus who is also his kinsman, joins him during the second encounter but does not engage in the fight as he instead is forced to seek protection behind Beowulf's shield after the dragon's fire consumes his wooden one. The third and final time they meet, Beowulf faces the dragon armed only with a 'wællseaxe' (2703b) [battle-knife]. In this encounter, the dragon fatally wounds Beowulf and is wounded by Wiglaf who, unlike Beowulf, avoids its head and instead 'nioðor hwene sloh' (2699b) [struck it a little downward]. While perhaps less heroic a strategy than Beowulf's, Wiglaf's proves more successful: as a result of his stroke, the dragon's 'fyr ongon / sweðrian syððan' (2701b–02a) [fire began afterwards to subside]. Beowulf rouses himself sufficiently to cut the dragon through the middle, although whether his or Wiglaf's proves the killing blow is unclear.

In addition to being the longest and most narratively complex of the monster fights, the dragon fight also reveals more about Beowulf's mental state than the earlier ones. As he does when he faces Grendel's mother, Beowulf relies on human technology when engaging the dragon: this time, however, he not only bears his own 'iren ærgod' (2586a) [hitherto excellent sword] Nægling and wears a byrnie, but he also orders the construction of a 'wig-bord wrætlic' (2339a) [wondrous battle-shield], one that is 'ealle irenne' (2338a) [entirely iron]. However, Beowulf commissions this special shield only after announcing that he would, if he could, meet the dragon unarmed as he did when he fought Grendel in Heorot: 'Nolde ic sweord beran ... swa ic gio wið Grendle dyde' (2518b–21b) [I would not bear a sword ... as I formerly against Grendel did]. While witnessing the extraordinary depth of Beowulf's courage, this statement also, and somewhat troublingly, reveals that even at this late stage in his life he has not fully reconciled his heroic impulses with his kingly obligations. His disarming before the Grendel fight can easily be cast in a positive light by placing it within the context of Beowulf's youthful desire to further his heroic reputation by not just killing Grendel, but by doing so on equal terms. As commendable as his impulse towards fair play may be, his wish that he could similarly grapple unarmed with the dragon strikes a note more problematic than heroic.

What is perhaps most disconcerting about Beowulf's speeches prior to the dragon fight is that in them he neither acknowledges that the dragon is a foe unlike any other he has ever faced, nor that a king's death has more far-reaching consequences than a hero's, for while the death of a hero may leave a significant hole in the social fabric, that of a king necessarily rends it. As a young hero, Beowulf is acutely aware that the consequences of his death will be more local than global: in a speech tinged with grimly humorous over-tones, he announces before his fight with Grendel that should Grendel defeat him, the Danes will not have to worry about attending to his corpse given Grendel's habit of devouring his victims. In contrast, Beowulf neither reflects upon his death (indeed, he never mentions it) in any of the speeches he makes preceding the dragon fight, nor does he voice any concern regard-ing the succession of the Geatish crown, a succession complicated by his failure to leave behind a son. He speaks of his death only after receiving a fatal wound, and then it is only to leave instructions regarding the disposi-tion of his corpse and the placement of his barrow.

Beowulf leaves behind him not a legacy of success, but one of failure: the poem does not detail the fate of the Geats following Beowulf's demise, but an unnamed messenger announces that their future will be one rife with hardships and warfare once word of Beowulf's death spreads. As it turns out, the future of the Geats proves even bleaker than the messenger paints it, culminating in short order in nothing less than the tribe's dispersal and disappearance. It is within the context of the tribe's grim future that Wiglaf, the young hero Beowulf designates as his successor following their defeat of the dragon, offers one of the few criticisms of Beowulf explicitly articulated in the poem: 'Oft sceall eorl monig anes willan / wræc adreogan, swa us geworden is' (3077–78) [Often must many an earl suffer distress for the will of one, as has befallen us]. This criticism, while warranted, nonetheless points to one of the poem's enduring puzzles and perhaps the largest of the cultural fissures that the poet uncovers: throughout his life, Beowulf faithfully fulfils his roles as hero and a king, yet his actions lead directly to his people's extinction. Wiglaf may blame Beowulf for the Geats' problems, but the fault lies rather in the heroic ethos which the *Beowulf*-poet celebrates and questions.

The Christianity that is anachronistically threaded through the narrative is another of the poem's enduring puzzles: even though all the characters in *Beowulf* are pagan, the poem contains many epithets that may well refer to the Christian deity. In addition, the poem's thematics on occasion reveal Christian influence, as when the poet locates Grendel among 'Caines cynne' (107a) [Cain's race] and goes on to note that the 'ece drihten' (108a) [eternal lord] avenged Abel's death. Given that throughout the Anglo-Saxon period the technology of writing resided firmly in the hands of Christian clerics, those who, in short, had direct access to the early medieval world's wealth of Christian texts, and given that the expressive economy of oral poetics itself also proved an accommodating and successful vehicle for the presentation of Biblical and other Christian material, we might well expect Christian elements to seep into much of the period's verbal art, as they everywhere do. What is striking about the Christian element in *Beowulf* is that it is not more prevalent than it is: aside from the epithets, many of which may not, in fact, point so directly to the Christian God, there is not much explicit Christian thought or doctrine found in the poem. The Danes are condemned for turning to pagan practices in an attempt to halt Grendel's attacks, but even at this moment the poem's Christianity remains rather muted as the poet pauses only to observe first that the Danes behave as they do because 'ne wiston hie drihten God' (181b) [they did not know the lord God], and second that one who 'sawle bescufan / in fyres fæþm' (184b–85a) [shoves (his) soul in the fire's embrace] will fare worse than the one who 'æfter deaðdæge drihten secean' (187) [after (his) death-day seeks the lord].

Although they surface only occasionally and are never more than momentarily the poem's focus, *Beowulf*'s Christian elements are not crude or clumsy additions to its narrative, but are threaded into the very fabric of this secular heroic poem, something that suggests that they were either original components of the narrative or that, more likely, they were introduced into it early enough in its existence so that by the time the poem came to be physically encoded on the page they had become completely melded into its originally non-Christian framework. Except in the one instance cited above, the poet does not privilege one system of beliefs over the other; rather he presents them, without comment or criticism, as complementary, not competing, components of the poem's cultural matrix. On occasion, these two belief systems are juxtaposed in the narrative, as, for example, when Beowulf approvingly mentions the 'beorht beacen Godes' (570a) [bright beacon of God] and in the next breath asserts that 'Wyrd oft nereð / unfægne eorl, þonne his ellen deah!' (572b–73) [Fate often spares the undoomed man when his courage suffices], or when the monstrous Grendel is situated within Biblical history as a member of 'Caines cynne'. Jarring though they may be to us, these moments cause no disruption in the surface of the narrative. In terms of sheer bulk, the Christian elements substantially outweigh the overtly pagan ones, but the poem's ethos remains far more heavily oriented towards the pagan rather than the Christian world, especially in the poem's second half, which is dominated by an elegiac tone, accounts of intractable human blood feuds, and Beowulf's heroic reflections and actions.

The elegiac tone of the second half is given its sharpest articulation in the so-called lay of the lone survivor (2247–70a), a moving passage in which the sole remaining member of an unidentified tribe consigns to the earth his people's treasures now that 'Bealocwealm' (2265b) [violent slaughter] has siezed all but him. Like much of the poem's second half, this passage, the thematics of which link it with the OE elegies, is devoid of Christian reference or sentiment and focuses entirely on matters secular and heroic as its speaker recounts the many joys of human culture that are now closed off to him as he awaits his death. The poem's final scenes are also deeply elegiac and wholly secular. As Beowulf's body is consumed by the flames of his pyre, an unidentified woman keens, mourning his loss and lamenting the misery and humiliation that awaits his tribe. After his barrow, into which is placed the decrepit hoard removed from the dragon's barrow, is constructed, twelve riders circle it speaking of their king and perhaps their sorrow (damage to the manuscript precludes our knowing this for certain). They also utter a 'wordgyd' (3172a) [song; eulogy] in which they lament their 'hlafordes hryre' (3179a) [lord's fall] and praise him for being 'wyruldcyninga / manna mildust and monðwærust, / leodum liðost ond lofgeornost' (3180b–82) [of world kings, the mildest of men and the most gentle, most gracious to the people, and the most eager for fame].

The end of the poem does more, though, than knit up the narrative of Beowulf's life and offer another glimpse into Anglo-Saxon funerary practices (the others include the ship burial of Scyld Scefing described in the poem's opening lines and the ritual immolations that occur in the Finnsburh episode); it again foregrounds the oral culture the poem invokes at its inception through its call to attention, 'Hwæt' (1a) [So; lo], and its use of the 'I heard' formula ('we … gefrunon' [1–2] [we … have heard]). In an oral culture – and the one depicted in the poem is largely oral, even if the poem as we have it is undoubtedly the product of literate culture – one's name and the deeds upon which it rests can survive only so long as they are retained, either in living memory or in song. Songs are an especially important component of the cultural encyclopaedia that is oral tradition since they transmit and preserve cultural practices, social mores, and heroic deeds, and they figure in *Beowulf* in a number of ways. Some are performed within the poem's narrative frame, as during the Finn episode and perhaps after the creation of Heorot, while others are only reported as being performed, as is the case with those sung during the celebration that follows Grendel's defeat or at the poem's conclusion. And, of course, the poem itself is a song, one that indexes the tradition from which it emerged in the richest and most complex of fashions. We can never know the content of the song that is sung at Beowulf's barrow or whether the warriors who sing it engage the performative poetics Bede depicts in his story of the cowherd Cædmon, but given that its purpose is to commemorate the deeds and so keep alive the name of the Geatish hero and king, it may have been very similar to another work of verbal art, one that has kept Beowulf's name alive for more than a millennium: the eponymous poem we know as *Beowulf*.

Further Reading

Amodio, Mark C. 'Affective criticism, oral poetics, and Beowulf's fight with the dragon'. *OT* 10 (1995): 54–90.

Foley, John Miles. '*Beowulf* and the Old English poetic tradition'. In his *Immanent Art: From Structure to Meaning in Traditional Oral Epic*. Bloomington: Indiana University Press, 1991.

Georgianna, Linda. 'King Hrethel's sorrow and the limits of heroic action in *Beowulf*'. *Speculum* 62 (1987): 829–50.

Harris, Joseph. '*Beowulf* as epic'. *OT* 15 (2000): 159–69.

Hill, John M. *The Narrative Pulse of 'Beowulf': Arrivals and Departures*. Toronto Old English Series 17. Toronto: University of Toronto Press, 2008.

Irving, Edward B. *Rereading 'Beowulf'*. 1989. Rpt. Philadelphia: University of Pennsylvania Press, 1992.

Jones, Chris. 'Where now the harp? Listening for the sounds of Old English verse, from *Beowulf* to the twentieth century'. *OT* 24 (2009): 485–502.

Lapidge, Michael. '*Beowulf* and the psychology of terror'. In *Heroic Poetry in the Anglo-Saxon Period: Studies in Honor of Jess B. Bessinger, Jr.*, ed. Helen Damico and John Leyerle, 373–402. Studies in Medieval Culture 32. Kalamazoo: Medieval Institute Publications, 1993.

Lerer, Seth. '"On fagne flor": The postcolonial *Beowulf*, from Heorot to Heaney'. In *Postcolonial Approaches to the European Middle Ages: Translating Cultures*, ed. Ananya Jahanara Kabir and Deanne Williams, 77–102. Cambridge Studies in Medieval Literature 54. Cambridge: Cambridge University Press, 2005.

Lockett, Leslie. 'The role of Grendel's arm in feud, law, and the narrative strategy of *Beowulf*. In *Latin Learning and English Lore: Studies in Anglo-Saxon Literature for Michael Lapidge*, ed. Katherine O'Brien O'Keeffe and Andy Orchard, vol. I, 368–88. Toronto Old English Series 14. 2 vols. Toronto: University of Toronto Press, 2005.

Momma, Haruko. 'The education of Beowulf and the affair of the leisure class'. In *Verbal Encounters: Anglo-Saxon and Old Norse Studies for Roberta Frank*, ed. Antonia Harbus and Russell Poole, 163–82. Toronto Old English Series 13. Toronto: University of Toronto Press, 2005.

Niles, John D. 'Locating *Beowulf* in literary history'. In his *Old English Heroic Poems and the Social Life of Texts*, 13–58. Studies in the Early Middle Ages 20. Turnhout: Brepols, 2007.

Orchard, Andy. 'Beowulf and other battlers: an introduction to *Beowulf*'. In *'Beowulf' & Other Stories: A New Introduction to Old English, Old Icelandic and Anglo-Norman Literatures*, ed. Richard North and Joe Allard, 63–94. 2007. 2nd edn. New York: Pearson/Longman, 2012.

Orchard, Andy. *A Critical Companion to 'Beowulf'*. Cambridge: D.S. Brewer, 2003.

Renoir, Alain. 'Introduction'. In *A Readable 'Beowulf': The Old English Epic Newly Translated*, by Stanley B. Greenfield, 1–26. Carbondale: Southern Illinois University Press, 1982.

Renoir, Alain. 'Point of view and design for terror in *Beowulf*'. NM 63 (1962): 154–67.

Scheil, Andrew. 'The historiographic dimensions of *Beowulf*'. JEGP 107 (2008): 281–302.

Thormann, Janet. 'Enjoyment of violence and desire for history in *Beowulf*'. In *The Postmodern 'Beowulf': A Critical Casebook*, ed. Eileen A. Joy and Mary K. Ramsey, 287–318. Morgantown: West Virginia University Press, 2006.

Judith

Survives uniquely in London, BL, Cotton Vitellius A.xv, fols 202^r–9^v.

Judith is the fifth and final item in what is known as the Nowell codex, a manuscript written in two scribal hands that contains three prose texts, *The Life of St Christopher*, *The Wonders of the East*, and Alexander's *Letter to Aristotle* (see Part 2), as well as an additional verse text, *Beowulf*. A composite manuscript, Vitellius A.xv is comprised of the Nowell codex, which dates to the tenth or eleventh century and the Southwick codex, which dates to the middle of the twelfth. Written entirely in the hand of the second of the two Nowell codex scribes, *Judith* wants both its beginning and its ending. We cannot determine with any certainty whether the poem is nearly complete as we have it or if it is but a small piece of a much longer work, but the section divisions found on fols 205ʳ (XI) and 207ᵛ (XII) suggest that a substantial amount of the poem may be missing. Although part of the Cottonian collection housed in Ashburnham House, *Judith* suffered only minimal damage in the fire that swept through the building in October of 1731. We are able to ascertain with some confidence that the leaves wanting from the text went missing prior to the fire because the transcription Franciscus Junius made in the mid seventeenth century is comprised only of the material contained in the extant manuscript.

Based on the apocryphal Book of Judith, chiefly Chapters xii–xvi, *Judith* adheres only loosely to the Vulgate account. Among his other changes, the *Judith*-poet significantly reduces the number of characters and he does not include the long canticle of Judith that comprises the Vulgate's sixteenth book, although whether this is by the poet's design or the result of manuscript loss cannot be determined. Despite being highly selective in terms of the episodes he includes, the poet remains faithful to the Vulgate's narrative trajectory: Judith visits the Assyrian camp and after several days is brought to the tent of Holofernes, who has been inflamed with desire for her since her arrival and who intends to force himself upon her in the privacy of his tent. Holofernes, though, becomes so drunk that he passes out, providing Judith the opportunity to decapitate him. She returns to the Hebrew camp, displays the Assyrian's severed head before her assembled people, and incites them to attack the Assyrians, who are routed in the subsequent battle. As do the other Anglo-Saxon poets who take as their subjects Christian heroes, the *Judith*-poet firmly situates both the narrative and his heroine within the Anglo-Saxon heroic ethos.

Judith remains faithful to the two traditions – the Christian and the vernacular heroic – that drive it, but the poet's individual genius sets it apart from other Christian heroic poems because he does not just invoke or utilize his traditional, inherited patterns; rather, he alters them, in ways both subtle and overt. To take but one example, the surviving portion of the poem opens on the fourth day of Judith's visit to Holofernes, a day on which Holofernes calls to a magnificent feast 'ealle ða yldestan ðegnas' (10a) [all the most senior noblemen]. Scenes of feasting are common in OE poetry and constitute an important part of the thematics of the traditional narrative structure known as joy in the hall, but what sets Holofernes's feast apart from others in the corpus is that while it fits the traditional narrative template, from the outset the poet points the feast's negative qualities. The feast is described initially as a 'winhatan' (8a), a *hapax legomenon* for which the meanings 'feast' and 'invitation to wine' have been proposed. A less elegant rendering of this term, but one that more accurately reflects the sense of enforced joviality that infuses the scene, would be 'summons to wine-drinking'. Those who attend the feast are described by the rare word 'weagesiðas' (16b) [companions in misery], which occurs in the poetry only here and an additional three times in prose homilies. A great many cups and bowls are carried to those attending the feast, as we might expect, but before they can be served, we ominously learn that their recipients are 'fæge' (19b) [doomed to die]. Finally, another *hapax legomenon*, 'gytesalum' (22b), describes Holofernes's 'joy at the pouring out of wine'. Any host might be expected to experience something akin to this since feasts are occasions of communal celebration, but whatever positive sense might attend this word quickly dissipates as we learn that the 'inwidda' (28a) [wicked one] didn't just offer his men wine, but that he 'drencte' (29b) [drenched] them with it 'oðþæt hie on swiman lagon' (30b) [until they lay unconscious].

The poet's treatment of his heroine is marked by a similar adherence to and departure from tradition. Our sense of Judith is complicated from the outset by the poet's employment of the rare word 'ælfscinu' (14a) to describe her, a term that occurs only twice elsewhere in the Anglo-Saxon poetic corpus, both times in connection with the seductive, and hence dangerous and perhaps problematic but not violent Sarah in *Genesis A* (1827a and 2713a). *Ælfscinu*'s semantic range is broad as the following meanings are all attached to it: 'radiant or fair as an elf, beautiful; delusive as an elf; divinely inspired'. All of these apply to Judith: her otherworldly beauty plays an important role in the incapacitation of Holofernes (along with the copious quantity of wine he imbibes), she is 'gleaw' (13b) [shrewd], and she asks for, and receives, divine inspiration prior to beheading Holofernes. Judith's actions also complicate our understanding of her as she is the only non-monstrous female figure in the extant poetic corpus to wield a weapon or kill anyone, let alone a powerful and accomplished warrior such as Holofernes. Her resolve needs stiffening before she kills him, but after praying for God's help she successfully decapitates him.

That she receives his 'sweord ond swatigne helm, swylce eac side byrnan / gerenode readum golde' (337–38a) [sword and bloody helmet, likewise also his broad byrnie ardorned with red gold] along with his personal wealth, including rings, as reward for the role she plays in liberating her people from the oppression of the Assyrians, further witnesses her unique situation within the corpus. Unlike other female figures, such as those who at the end of *Judith* and of *Exodus* acquire treasure by plundering dead warriors, Judith participates actively in the exchange economy that is such an important component of the heroic culture depicted in the poetic corpus. She is, notably, the only woman to do so: the usual recipients of this economy's most common coin – war-gear in the form of rings, swords, helmets, and byrnies – are males who are part of a lord's comitatus. The lexeme 'gearuþoncol' (341a) [ready-witted, wise, resourceful] may usefully and compactly index both Judith's unique position among Anglo-Saxon vernacular heroes and the tradition's difficulty situating her within an otherwise exclusively male heroic universe, but because the term is a *hapax legomenon*, it must be treated with due caution.

If the *Judith*-poet pushes on and extends the boundaries of his inherited traditional expressive economy in establishing his heroine as an active female participant in the otherwise exclusively male Anglo-Saxon heroic universe, he also works successfully within that expressive economy's confines. His battle scenes, for example, stand as memorable articulations of the tradition's heroic ethos: as the Hebrews initially descend on the Assyrian forces, the poet focuses in quick succession upon the noise that signals the onset of the martial engagement ('Dynedan scildas, / hlude hlummon' [204a] [the shields clashed, loudly resounded]), upon the expectation that the carrion-eating beasts of battle have of gorging upon the fallen, and finally upon the unremitting advance of the Hebrews ('Stopon heaðorincas, / beornas to beadowe' [212b–13a] [Warriors stepped forward, men to the battle]). The Assyrian forces offer resistance at first, but are soon swept away by the tide of the advancing Hebrews, who 'nanne ne sparedon / þæs herefolces, heanne ne ricne, / cwicera manna þe hie ofercuman mihton' (233b–35) [spared none of the people forming the army, the low or the high, of those living men that they might overcome]. But even within this otherwise highly traditional battle scene, the poet's individual talent shines forth: as the rout progresses and as the battle line moves ever closer to the Assyrian camp, the Assyrian chiefs gather outside the tent where, they believe, Holofernes remains with Judith. Despite the direness of the situation, the men are loath to enter the tent uninvited for fear of interrupting Holofernes and inciting his wrath, and so in a moment that is poignantly telling – and perhaps even tinged with comedy – they gather outside the tent and 'ða somod ealle / ongunnon cohhetan' (269b–70a) [then all together began to cough to gain his attention]. When the poet shifts his attention from the despair Holofernes's death engenders among the Assyrian chiefs back to the battle, we discover that the expectations of the beasts of battle have been fulfilled, as the greatest part of the Assyrian forces lie 'on ðam sigewonge, sweordum geheawen, / wulfum to willan ond eac wælgifrum / fuglum to frofre' (294–96a) [on that field of victory, hewn down by swords, to the pleasure of wolves and also as a joy to the slaughter-greedy birds]. The rout is so complete that of the Assyrian forces, only 'Lythwon becom / cwicera to cyððe' (310b–11a) [few came alive to their homeland].

Although *Judith* remains faithful to the trajectory of the Biblical narrative, the poem often seems to celebrate the heroic as much as, if not more than, it celebrates the Christian tradition, and as a result, *Judith* may be the least didactic and least dogmatic example of OE Christian-heroic poetry. Its Christian message often seems to be pushed to the side, especially during the battle scenes, and when it does occupy the poet's attention, it does so in but a few narrative moments, including Judith's prayer to God for assistance in strengthing her resolve before she decapitates Holofernes ('Forgif me, swegles ealdor, / sigor and soðne geleafan, þæt ic mid þys sweorde mote / geheawan þysne morðres bryttan' [88b–90a] [Give me, lord of heaven, victory and true faith so that I with this sword might cut down this giver/ perpetrator of death]; the poet's assurance that it was God who granted her the victory over Holofernes; Judith's informing the Hebrews at the beginning of her speech to them that God is 'bliðe' (154b) [joyful] on their behalf, and the conclusion of this speech in which she tells them that they will have 'tir æt tohtan, swa eow getacnod hafað / mihtig dryhten þurh mine hand' (197–98) [glory at battle, as the mighty lord has signified to you through my hand]. In the final portion of the poem written in the hand of the scribe, whose stint ends with 'sigorlean' in line 344a on fol. 209ᵛ, the poet notes that Judith ascribes to God all the fame and honour she received on earth. What follows is praise for God's glory that, for the *Judith*-poet, is uncharacteristically broad:

> Ðæs sy ðam leofan drihtne
> wuldor to widan aldre, þe geceop wind ond lyfte,
> roderas ond rume grundas, swylce eac reðe streamas
> ond swegles dreamas, ðurh his sylfes miltse.
>
> (346b–50)

[Of this let there be glory forever to the dear lord, who shaped the wind and the air, the heavens and the spacious grounds, likewise also the fierce streams and the joys of heaven through his own mercy.]

Aside from the disjunction in narrative tone and style between these lines and the several hundred that precede them, our reception of them is further complicated by the fact that they are written not in the scribe's hand, but in one dated to about 1600. Junius's seventeenth-century transcription ends with these lines, but even though he accepts them as the work of the *Judith*-poet, questions remain as to their provenance and authenticity: were they copied from a now lost final leaf or leaves? If so, do they represent all the lost material or did the the seventeenth-century copyist simply fit what he could into the space provided by the bottom margin of fol. 209ᵛ? And finally, were they also composed by the person who added them? Barring the discovery of the putative lost leaf (or leaves), these and other questions regarding this fragmentary text must remain unanswered.

Further Reading

Chickering, Howell D. Jr. 'Poetic exuberance in the Old English *Judith*'. *SP* 106 (2009): 119–36.

Garner, Lori Ann. 'The art of translation in the Old English *Judith*'. *SN* 73 (2001): 171–83.

Hartman, Megan E. 'A drawn-out beheading: style, theme, and hypermetricity in the Old English *Judith*'. *JEGP* 110 (2011): 421–40.

Magennis, Hugh. 'Gender and heroism in the Old English *Judith*'. In *Writing Gender and Genre in Medieval Literature: Approaches to Old and Middle English Texts*, ed. Elaine M. Treharne, 5–18. Cambridge: Cambridge University Press, 2002.

Mullally, Erin. 'The cross-gendered gift: weaponry in the Old English *Judith*'. *Exemplaria* 17 (2005): 255–84.

Thijs, Christine. 'Feminine heroism in the Old English *Judith*'. *LSE* ns 37 (2006): 41–62.

Poems from Various Manuscripts

The *Metres of Boethius*

Survives in London, BL, Cotton Otho A.vi, fols 1–129. The verses alone
of this manuscript's prosimetrical version of Boethius's *Consolation of
Philosophy* were transcribed in the late seventeenth century by Franciscus
Junius in what is now designated as Oxford, Bodleian Library, Junius 12.

The text that has long been known as the *Metres of Boethius* is not strictly
speaking a poetic text in its own right, despite its presentation as such in the
ASPR and in editions stretching back to the seventeenth century. The *Metres*
as we know it is, rather, the construction of generations of editors who have
habitually, and puzzlingly, divorced the OE verse equivalents of Boethius's
Latin poems from the prose sections among which they are interspersed in
Cotton Otho A.vi, typically relegating them to appendices in both original-
language editions and modern English translations of the OE *Consolation*.
Malcolm Godden and Susan Irvine, the most recent editors of the OE
Consolation, are the first ones to restore the text to the prosimetrical form
preserved in Cotton Otho A.vi, although for the sake of consistency with
long-established practice, we will here continue to refer to the verses in
Cotton Otho as the *Metres*.

Cotton Otho A.vi was one of the manuscripts that suffered especially
heavy and irreparable damage in the fire that swept through Ashburnham
House in October of 1731. Ten leaves have been lost, and many of the
pages that survive, especially among the first sixty folios, are severely damaged and difficult to read. Were it not for the transcriptions Franciscus
Junius made in the late seventeenth century of the metrical passages in

The Anglo-Saxon Literature Handbook, First Edition. Mark C. Amodio.
© 2014 Mark C. Amodio. Published 2014 by John Wiley & Sons, Ltd.

Otho A.vi (which were written on separate pieces of paper that have been pasted in to his transcription of the prose version of the OE *Consolation* found in Oxford, Bodleian Library, Bodley 180 [see Part 2]), our knowledge of the prosimetrical version would be greatly diminished since Junius's transcription provides the only witness not only to the presence of the verse preface but also to Metres 1–4, as the surviving portion of Otho A.vi commences in the midst of Prose 4. Additionally, the Junius 12 transcription preserves a great many words and letters that are now no longer legible, or are simply wanting, owing to the damaged, and in many instances fragmentary, state of the prosimetrical manuscript's leaves. Despite the poor general condition of Otho A.vi, the layout of the text can still readily be discerned: as is typical of the way in which vernacular poetry is encoded on the manuscript page throughout the Anglo-Saxon period, the versified portions of the text are written out in continuous blocks of prose. The individual poems begin on new lines and space has been left at the beginning of each section for large, perhaps ornamental, capitals that were never added.

The authorship of the prosimetrical version remains a contested and unsettled issue, although it has, by a tradition that stretches back to its prose and verse prefaces, been widely attributed to King Alfred. Whether he authored this version remains unclear, however, and it is far from certain that the prosimetrical version is even the product of a single author as the poems it contains strike some as the work of a separate versifier. The version in Bodley 180, which renders both the prose and metrical passages of the Latin original in OE prose, is generally accepted as being the source for the prose and verse sections of the prosimetrical version, a view based in part on the evidence of the prose preface, which claims that after King Alfred 'þas boc hæfde geleornode ond of Lædene to Engliscum spelle gewende, þa geworhte he hi eft to leoðe swa swa heo nu gedon is' (Godden and Irvine, I, 383) [had learned this book and turned it from Latin into an English account, then he made it again in verse, just as it now is done]. Additionally, because the verses of the *Metres* correspond far more closely to the prose paraphrases of Boethius's poems found in Bodley 180 than they do to the Latin poems themselves, it is generally believed that the *Metres*-poet worked from the vernacular paraphrases and not the Latin poems.

The demonstrably close connection of the poems that comprise the *Metres* to their corresponding prose paraphrases has led them to be viewed unfavourably, and in some cases to their being summarily dismissed by some commentators as inferior examples of OE poetry. His habits of taking his subject matter from a known and demonstrable source, the prose paraphrases of Bodley 180, and of importing words and phrases directly from his source, including many that are usually only found in prose, including 'aþeostrian' (M6.4) [grow dim], 'weorðscipe' (M19.44) [dignity], and 'mettrymnes' (M26.112) [weakness], help establish for many the *Metres*-poet as more a marginally talented and uninspired versifier than a poet. The opening lines of Metre 13 provide a clear indication of how the *Metres*-poet typically operates, as the verses

> Ic wille mid giddum get gecyðan
> hu se ælmightga [ealla] gesceafta
> bryrð mid his bridlum, begð ðider he wile
> mid his anwalde, ge endebyrd
> wundorlice wel gemetgað

(Godden and Irvine, I, 439. 1–5)

[I will with songs yet make known how the almighty all creation guides with his bridle, bends it where he wishes with his power, and the divinely appointed order of the universe he wonderfully well regulates]

closely echo the corresponding prose paraphrase of Bodley 180: 'Ic wille nu mid giddum gecyðan hu wundorlice drihten welt eallra gesceafta mid þam bridlum his anwealdes, and mid hwilcere endebyrdnesse he gestaðolað and gemetgað ealle gescefta' (Godden and Irvine, I, 293.2–4) [I will now with songs make known how wonderfully the lord all creation rules through the power of his bridle, and with what divine ordering he makes steadfast and regulates all creation]. Far from an isolated incidence, close correspondences of this kind occur throughout.

That the *Metres*-poet does not work directly from Boethius's Latin poems but rather the OE prose paraphrases of them is beyond dispute, but the reasons he does so are far from clear. To some, this practice suggests Alfredian authorship, since the verses of the Latin original would pose some difficulties to one with Alfred's apparently modest grasp of Latin, both in terms of the complex narrative uses to which they are put and in terms of the varied array of different metrical types (which number nearly twenty) Boethius deploys.

Boethius's Latin *Consolation* contains thirty-nine poems, of which all but seven are paraphrased in Bodley 180. The *Metres*-poet in turn versifies all but three of these, most likely because, as is generally accepted, the three he does not versify are the only ones not clearly marked in Bodley 180 by phrases very similar to that found at the end of Chapter 36: 'Ða se wisdom þa þis spell areht hæfde, þa ongan he eft singan and þus cwæð' (Godden and Irvine, I, 347.223–24) [When Wisdom this narrative had recounted, then began he again to sing and thus said]. In turning the prose paraphrases into vernacular poems, the *Metres*-poet for the most part adheres closely to his source, adding to them mostly words and phrases that are seen largely as window-dressing in that they seem to do little more than fulfil the demands of Anglo-Saxon metrics. But as is true of Anglo-Saxon translators in general, the *Metres*-poet produces what is more a free adaptation of his source, rather than a word-for-word translation of it, as he often cuts or reorders the material of his source and in a few instances significantly supplements it through additions that stem from the *Metres*-poet himself, and not from any known sources. And although he certainly does not navigate the traditional expressive economy of Anglo-Saxon oral poetics with the skill, fluidity, creativity, or success of many other poets, the *Metres*-poet nonetheless effectively employs the specialized language of Anglo-Saxon poetry as witnessed by the great many lexemes and formulaic verbal collocations found throughout the *Metres* that are components of this specialized language, including 'soðcwidas' (M6.2a) [true sayings], 'lungre' (M7.19b) [quickly], 'eorla' (M9.59b), 'metodes' (M11.25b) [God's], and the phrases 'wordhord onleac' (M6.1b) [word-hoard unlocked] and 'lænan gesceaft' (M20.157b) [loaned creation]. The former of these phrases is found twice in *Andreas* (316b and 601b), and once each in *Beowulf* (259b) and *Widsið* (1b), and the latter appears in *The Ascension* (*Christ II*) (842b), *Guthlac A* (371b), *Homiletic Fragment II* (12a), and *Beowulf* (1622b). Examples of other such words and formulas abound in the *Metres*, as well as traces of oral-traditional themes, including storm at sea (M6) and the beasts of battle (M1).

Although the *Metres*-poet generally proceeds by making relatively minor additons to his source, on occasion he departs entirely from it, as he does perhaps most notably in Metre 1, a versification of the historical material, for which there is no precedent in the Latin *Consolation*, presented in prose in Bodley 180's Chapter 1 and neatly summarized in the list of chapters: 'Ærest hu Gotan gewunnon Romana rice and hu Boetius hi wolde eft berædan and Ðeodric þa þæt anfunde and hine het on carcerne gebringan' (Godden and Irvine, I, 239.1–3) [First how the Goths conquered the kingdom of the Romans and how Boethius would dispossess them of it and then Theoderic discovered that and commanded him to be brought to prison]. In the course of the eighty-four-line Metre 1, the *Metres*-poet adds significant details to his source by relating, for example, not simply that Theoderic executed Pope John, but how he did it ('Het Iohannes, godne papan, / heafde beheawon' [M1.42–43a] [He commanded that the head of John, the good pope, be cut off]), or by reporting the Romans' reaction to Theoderic's baptism ('Fægnodon ealle / Romwara bearn' [34b–35] [All the children of the Romans rejoiced]). While the prose account presents many of its details in a somewhat subdued, almost annalistic fashion as when he comments of Theoderic's failure to hold to a promise that 'he þa gehat swiðe yfele gelæste and swiðe wraðe geendode mid manegum mane' (Godden and Irvine, I, 243.9–10) [he fulfilled that promise very badly and very evilly ended with many a crime], the *Metres*-poet reveals himself to be less restrained and more explicitly judgemental: after relaying the substance of the promise Theoderic made to the Romans regarding their right to hold onto their 'ealdrihta' (36a) [ancient rights], the poet pointedly informs us that Theoderic 'þæt eall aleag' (39b) [lied about all that]. About Theoderic's beheading of the pope the poet offers the equally blunt assertion that 'næs ðæt hærlic dæd' (43b) [that was not a noble deed].

The most widely known, and perhaps the most significant, of the additions the *Metres*-poet makes occurs in M20, when he supplements his source's account of God's positioning of the earth in the universe, 'heo ne helt on nane healfe, ne on nanum eorðlicum þinge ne stent, ne nanwuht eorðlices hio ne healt þæt hi ne sige' (Godden and Irvine, I, 317.211–13) [nothing holds it on either side, nor on any earthly things does it stand, nor does anything earthly hold it so that it does not sink], by likening the earth to an egg:

> Hwæt, hi þeah eorðlices auht ne haldeð
> is þeah efneðe up and ofdune
> to feallanne foldan ðisse,
> þæm anlicost þe on æge bið
> gioleca on middan, glideð hwæðre
> æg ymbutan. Swa stent eall weoruld
> stille on tille, streamas ymbutan,
> lagufloda gelac, lyfte and tungla,
> and sio scire scell scriðeð ymbutan
> dogora gehwilce, dyde lange swa.
>
> (Godden and Irvine, I, 467–68.166–75)

[So, although nothing earthly holds it, it is however equally easy for this earth to fall up and down like the yolk that is in the middle of an egg, and the egg, however, glides around it. So stands all the world still in place, the streams around it, the motion of the sea, the air and stars, and the bright shell glides around each of days, as it has long done so.]

In its somewhat odd and confusing attempt to explain a natural phenomenon, this passages reveals, albeit in a flash, the *Metres*-poet's independence and ability, as he comes close to positing a theory of the earth's rotation and effectively describes the earth's ineffable and subtle movement by employing the same verb, 'scriðan', that the *Beowulf*-poet uses to describe the equally unknowable mode of the 'sceadugenga' (703a) [shadow-goer] Grendel's locomotion during his approach to Heorot. That this passage also contains one of the few *hapax legomena* in the *Metres*, 'efneðe' (167a) further suggests that the poet, when striking out wholly on his own, is capable of some modest accomplishments, although three other *hapax legomena* constructed on the same root, 'efnbehefu' (M12.7b) [equally necessary], 'efnlica' (20.19b) [an equal], 'efnmærne' (M10.32a) [equally famous], as well as five more 'efen-' compounds in the *Metres* admittedly point more to the poet's limitations than skill.

The criticism levelled at the *Metres*-poet may finally be warranted since his verse rarely reaches any sort of aesthetic heights, but we must remember that not all Anglo-Saxon vernacular verbal art was produced by artists whose capabilities approach those of, say, the *Beowulf*-poet or the *Exodus*-poet, and that, accordingly, there is much to be learned even from poets of modest abilities, for even the least skilled Anglo-Saxon poet had a deeper, more immediate connection to his tradition and its poetics than any contemporary student could ever possess. Despite its many pedestrian qualities, the *Metres* nonetheless remains an important source of still largely unmined information regarding poetic making in the Anglo-Saxon period thanks to the unparalleled connection between it and its source.

Further Reading

Anlezark, Daniel. 'Three notes on the Old English *Metres of Boethius*'. *N&Q* ns 51 (2004): 10–15.

Irvine, Susan. 'Fragments of Boethius: the reconstruction of the Cotton manuscript of the Alfredian text'. *ASE* 34 (2005): 169–81.

Kiernan, Kevin. 'Alfred the Great's burnt *Boethius*'. In *The Iconic Page in Manuscript, Print, and Digital Culture*, ed. George Bornstein and Theresa Tinkle, 7–32. Ann Arbor: University of Michigan Press, 1998.

Szarmach, Paul E. 'An apologia for the *Metres of Boethius*'. In *Naked Wordes in English*, ed. Marcin Krygier and Liliana Sikorska, 107–34. Frankfurt: Peter Lang, 2005.

The *Metrical Psalms* of the Paris Psalter

Vernacular verse translations of Psalms 51–150 survive on fols 64^r–175^v of Paris, Bibliothèque Nationale, Fonds Latin 8824, a manuscript known as the Paris Psalter that apparently was owned at one point by John, Duke of Berry. Fragments of quotations from twenty-five metrical psalms, many of which correspond closely with the prose and metrical psalms of the Paris Psalter, survive in Oxford, Bodleian Library, Junius 121.

The manuscript known as the Paris Psalter is a remarkable and complex document, preserving as it does Latin and OE versions of 150 psalms presented side by side in double columns on the manuscript's unusually long and narrow pages. The manuscript, in which only a single scribal hand is evident, is generally well preserved, although there are numerous textual lacunae brought about by the removal of fourteen leaves, many of which are thought to have been illuminated. The first fifty psalms are translated into prose (see Part 2), and the Latin and OE texts are preceded by brief vernacular introductions as well as brief arguments in Latin. For reasons that remain unknown, no vernacular introductions accompany the final 100 psalms, although the Latin arguments continue throughout. Beginning with the acephalic Psalm 51, all the remaining psalms are translated into OE verse, not prose. Because one of the manuscript's lacunae claims the end of Psalm 50 and the beginning of Psalm 51, we have no way of knowing if the shift from prose to poetry was remarked upon or passed over silently, although given the general practices of scribes and compilers in the Anglo-Saxon period, it seems most likely that this change went unremarked. The change from prose to verse is also not signalled by any alteration in the manuscript's layout since throughout the Anglo-Saxon period prose and verse texts are both written out as continous blocks of prose. The Prose Psalms are generally thought to be the work of King Alfred the Great, but the author of the metrical translations has yet to be identified. The text of the *Metrical Psalms* runs to just over 5,000 lines, making it by far the longest verse text in the Anglo-Saxon vernacular corpus, although for reasons that may have to do in part with the nature of its subject matter and in part with the quality of its verse, it has attracted very little critical attention.

Unlike the many Anglo-Saxon translators who depart frequently and freely from their source texts, the translator of the *Metrical Psalms* offers in many instances what amount to word-for-word renderings of his Latin text, with some occasional, and mostly minor, additions. For example, Psalm 62.4 ('Quia melior est misericordia tua super vitam: labia mea laudabunt te' [Thorpe, *Libri Psalmorum*, 155] [Because your mercy is better than life: my lips will praise you]) appears in OE as 'Ys þin milde mod micele betere / þonne þis læne lif þe we lifiað on; / weleras ðe mine wynnum heriað' [Your mild spirit is much better than this loaned life in which we live; my lips joyfully praise you]. The OE words that find no counterpart in the Latin, læne [loaned] and wynnum [joyfully], reveal, however, that the translator nonetheless situates his creations within the Anglo-Saxon verse and prose traditions. Læne, often joined with words such as 'lif' [life], as here, or 'gesceaft' [creation], is found throughout the verse and prose records where it points powerfully and succinctly to the transitory nature of all earthly things. In using wynnum, which in this form occurs only in poetry, the translator draws upon the specialized expressive economy of oral poetics in which Anglo-Saxon vernacular poetry is articulated. Psalm 107.2 affords another glimpse into the translator's approach to his task. The Latin, which reads 'Ex[s]urge, Gloria mea, ex[s]urge psalterium et cithara; ex[s]urgam diluculo' (Thorpe, *Libri Psalmorum*, 313) [Arise, my Glory, arise psalter and harp; I will arise at daybreak], is translated into OE as follows: 'Aris nu, wuldur min, þæt ic wynlice / on psalterio þe singan mote, / and ic ðe on hleoðre hearpan swylce / on ærmergen eac gecweme' [Arise now, my glory, so that I joyfully might sing the psalter to you, and I in the voice of the harp in like manner will please you through singing in the early morning]. These sorts of minor additions can be found throughout the verse translations in the Paris Psalter and along with, for example, the translator's occasional difficulties in understanding his Latin text, contribute to his being viewed as a poet of modest talents. Despite the shortcomings of the *Metrical Psalms*, though, it consistently reveals the depth of the translator's devotion. While works of genius understandably attract considerable attention, more pedestrian, even workmanlike endeavours such as the *Metrical Psalms* or the *Metres of Boethius* can frequently teach us just as much, if not more, about the Anglo-Saxon poetic tradition and about the process of producing verbal art during the period.

Further Reading

Diamond, Robert E. *The Diction of the Anglo-Saxon Metrical Psalms*. The Hague: Mouton and Co., 1963.

Griffith, M.S. 'Poetic language and the Paris Psalter: the decay of the Old English tradition'. *ASE* 20 (1991): 167–86.

Orchard, Andy. 'The word made flesh: Christianity and oral culture in Anglo-Saxon Verse'. *OT* 24 (2009): 293–318.

Solomon and Saturn I and *II*

Solomon and Saturn I survives in two manuscripts, CCCC 41, pp. 196–98 and CCCC 422, pp. 1–6. The version in CCCC 41 is fragmentary, breaking off in line 94, while the version in CCCC 422 runs to 169 lines. In CCCC 422, Solomon and Saturn engage in a prose dialogue on pages 6–12. This dialogue breaks off in mid sentence owing to the loss of a leaf or leaves, and the currently numbered p. 13 begins with a brief verse fragment that may be the misplaced conclusion to *Solomon and Saturn II*. The poem is incomplete owing to loss and concludes imperfectly on p. 26. A second version of the prose dialogue is found in the twelfth-century Southwick codex that forms the first part of London, BL, Cotton Vitellius A.xv, fols 86^v–93^v.

Solomon and Saturn I (*SS I*) is one of a very small number of Anglo-Saxon poems to survive in multiple copies. The issue is too complex to take up here, but the multiple copies of *SS I* are important witnesses to the ways in which Anglo-Saxon poets negotiate their traditional expressive economy and to the ways in which Anglo-Saxon scribes actively recompose the texts they copy.

Only the first ninety-four lines of *SS I* are preserved in CCCC 41, where they are written in the top, side, and bottom margins of three pages in a hand very similar to the one that copied the manuscript's main text, a vernacular version of Bede's *Ecclesiastical History of the English People*. How and why the poem came to be inscribed in this fashion are unknown. Another version of the poem is found in CCCC 422, but the application of a reagent to this manuscript has resulted in severe staining which has rendered the beginning of the text virtually unreadable. In addition to the damage from the reagent, the CCCC 422 version also has several textual lacunae: the second page is a palimpsest in which the text of the poem has been scraped off and replaced by a Latin excommunication, and elsewhere several leaves have apparently gone wanting. CCCC 422 also contains one of the two surviving prose dialogues between Solomon and Saturn, with the other being found in Cotton Vitellius A.xv. The CCCC 422 scribe abruptly, and without any alteration to the poem's *mise-en-page*, begins the prose text in the middle of the page, following the poem's line 169, which suggests that the poem may be complete as we have it. Since at least a leaf is missing after page 12, we cannot know if the scribe, when he switched back to verse at some point on the now lost page(s), did so in the same seamless fashion.

The poem is nominally a dialogue – a genre popular in many cultures from Antiquity onward –, but Saturn asks only three questions (one of which is lost along with the rest of the opening of the poem) about 'se gepalmtwigoda Pater Noster' (12) [the palm-twigged Pater Noster] in *SS I*; from line 63 onward the remainder of the poem is given over to Solomon's detailed explanation of the Pater Noster's power and the purposes to which it may be put. Solomon begins his exposition by reifying the Pater Noster in terms reminiscent of the Rood in *The Dream of the Rood*: 'Gylden is se godes cwide, gimmum astæned, / hafað sylfren leaf' (63–64a) [God's utterance is made of gold, adorned with precious stones; it has silver leaves]. Talking objects occur with some frequency in OE poetry, especially in *DR* and the riddles, but the *SS I*-poet goes far beyond this and thoroughly anthropomorphizes the Pater Noster, which, if it were to be 'mid fiftigum / clusum beclemme' (70b–71a) [bound with fifty locks], would easily 'ealle toslited' (72b) [cut them all in pieces]. Among the many of its powers Solomon enumerates are the following: it 'Hungor ... ahieded' (73a) [destroys hunger], 'helle gestruded' (73b) [despoils hell], and 'wuldor getimbred' (74b) [builds glory]. In addition, it is 'Lamena ... læce' (77a) [a physician to the lame], 'deafra duru' (78a) [a door to the deaf], 'folces ner-igend' (80b) [the saviour of people], and, perhaps somewhat surprisingly, 'yða yrfeweard, earmra fisca' (81) [the guardian of the waves, of the wretched fish]. After explaining that the Pater Noster enables those who 'godes cwide / singan soðlice' (84b–85a) [truly sing God's utterance] to put the devil to flight, Solomon personifies many of the prayer's letters and explains how each combats the devil, often in graphic detail. Some seven-teen of the prayer's letters are personified, with all but a few written in both the runic and Latin alphabets, starting with the '*p*', (runic ᛈ) in 'pater', which has a 'gyldene gade' (91a) [golden goad] with which he scourges and pursues 'þone grymman feond' (91b) [the grim fiend]. The letter '*t*', (runic ᛏ) 'hine teswað and hine on ða tungan sticað, / wræsted him ðæt woddor, and him ða wongan brieced' (94–95) [injures him and pierces his tounge, twists his mouth and breaks his cheek]. '*R*', (runic ᚱ) angrily shakes the devil by his hair and uses flint to break his leg, and '*s*', (runic ᛋ) scatters his teeth 'geond helle heap' (115a) [throughout the troop of hell]. Because the runic letters are not a part of the poem's metrics they offer an intriguing, but opaque clue, as to the readerly skills of the poem's intended audience.

Although *Solomon and Saturn II (SS II)* purports to be a dialogue between the same two participants, there is little that connects it thematically, generi-cally, or artistically to *SS I*. At times a confused – and confusing – poem, *SS II* is set up from its outset as a contest, with the voice of an observer report-ing 'Hwæt ic flitan gefrægn on fyrndagum / modgleawe men' (1a) [Lo, I heard contend in days of old two men wise in mind]. Although one figure is from the Old Testament and the other from the pagan past, they are pre-sented, somewhat surprisingly in the case of Saturn, without bias: both are 'middangeardes ræswan' (2b) [leaders of middle-earth]. While Solomon is acknowledged as being more famous, Saturn's pursuit of knowledge has led him to travel extensively and to acquire the keys to books in which learning has been locked, although damage to the manuscript makes it impossible to know this for certain. Damage to the manuscript also prevents us from knowing precisely what the terms of the contest were, but from a partial reply of Solomon's we know that if he cannot answer one of Saturn's ques-tions he will remain quiet, something he admits will then permit Saturn to return home where he will 'gilpan ðæt ðu hæbbe gumena bearn / forcumen and forcyðded' (206–7a) [boast that you have overcome and found fault with the sons of men]. Yet although the dialogue is framed as a contest, it is one with little or no evidence of conflict or drama; indeed, at one point Solomon seems downright solicitous of Saturn's fate when, after commenting briefly on the evil men to whose race Saturn belongs, he urges him to distance himself from them: 'Ne beyrn ðu in ða inwitgecyndo' (331b) [Do not involve yourself in that evil nature].

Their discussion covers a wide range of topics, among which are the power of books, the deeds of the sea-traveller 'weallende Wulf' (213a) [surging Wulf], the nature of the fantastic bird Vasa mortis, the rebellion in heaven, free will, and the success of evil men. The questions themselves range from Saturn's straightforward 'Ac hwa demeð ðonne dryhtne Criste / on domes dæge, ðonne he demeð eallum gesceaftum?' (337–38) [But who will then judge the lord Christ on judgement day, when he judges all creation?], to the riddling one he poses at lines 230–37 that explicity evokes the rhetoric of the OE riddles in its final line ('Saga hwæt ic mæne' [237b] [Say what I mean]), to ones that continue to be obscure (cf. lines 248–53). The responses are equally varied, with some being direct replies, 'Hwa dear ðonne dryhtne deman, ðe us of duste geworhte' (338) [Who dares to judge the lord who created us from the dust], and with some being answered obliquely or not at all.

The context for the dialogue is a thoroughly Christian one, but the understated approach to promulgating Christian doctrine seen in line 338 is evident throughout. The discussion encompasses a number of topics that would have been of interest to non-Christians in the early Germanic world as well, including the feats of the dragon-slayer 'weallende Wulf' (213a) [surging Wulf] who kills twenty-five dragons before dying himself, the terrible effects of old age, and the unfathomable and unchangeable workings of fate. Solomon draws some, but not all, of these exchanges into the ambit of Christian thought, as he does when, after noting in an utterance with gnomic overtones, one moreover tinged perhaps with some resignation, that 'Wyrd bið wended hearde, wealleð swiðe geneahhe' (437) [Fate is with difficulty altered; it is frequently zealous], he concludes that a wise man can nevertheless weather the vicissitudes of fate if seeks help from his friends and 'ðeh hwæðre godcundes gæstes brucan' (443) [moreover enjoys the Holy Spirit].

SS I and *II* are two of the more obscure and difficult pieces of verbal art to have survived from the Anglo-Saxon period, and many questions regarding their generic affiliations and artistic accomplishment remain unanswered. To date no known sources for either poem have been discovered, although an array of Biblical and patristic passages have been proposed as analogues for various portions of both. However, whether these poems owe any debt to written sources or are solely the product of the learned, if idiosyncratically manifested intellect(s) responsible for their creation remains unsettled.

Further Reading

Anlezark, Daniel. 'The fall of the angels in *Solomon and Saturn II*'. In *Apocryphal Texts and Traditions*, ed. Kathryn Powell and Donald Scragg, 121–33. Publications of the Manchester Centre for Anglo-Saxon Studies 2. Cambridge: D.S. Brewer, 2003.

Hansen, Elaine Tuttle. 'Asking and answering: riddles, charms, and *Solomon and Saturn II*'. In her *The Solomon Complex: Reading Wisdom in Old English Poetry*, 41–67. McMaster Old English Studies and Texts 5. Toronto: University of Toronto Press, 1988.

O'Brien O'Keeffe, Katherine. 'Source, method, theory, practice: on reading two Old English verse texts'. In *Textual and Material Culture in Anglo-Saxon England: Thomas Northcote Toller and the Toller Memorial Lectures*, ed. Donald Scragg, 161–81. Publications of the Manchester Centre for Anglo-Saxon Studies 1. Cambridge: D.S. Brewer, 2003.

Powell, Kathryn. 'Orientalist fantasy in the poetic dialogues of *Solomon and Saturn*'. *ASE* 34 (2005): 117–43.

The Menologium

Survives uniquely in London, BL, Cotton Tiberius B.i, fols 112^r–14^v.

The Menologium is one of two relatively short poems found between a long prose text, the *Orosius*, and the C-text of the Anglo-Saxon Chronicle (see Part 2) in London, BL, Cotton Tiberius B.i. The first three texts in this codex, *The Menologium*, *Maxims II*, and the C-text of the Chronicle up to the entry for AD 490 on fol. 118^v are all written in the same scribal hand. As is the case with most Anglo-Saxon codices, the principles of selection underlying the compilation of the texts that comprise Tiberius B.i are far from clear. *The Menologium* and the C-text of the Chronicle share a certain calendrical focus, but they are far more different than alike. The Chronicle offers terse prose summaries of events believed to have occurred in specific years, while *The Menologium* offers instruction, perhaps in a mnemonic fashion, on the beginning of each of the year's seasons and on some thirty of the liturgically important days that occur each year. Some of the days highlighted, including the Nativity, the Annunciation, and the Assumption of the Virgin Mary are of obvious importance, but the poet's reasons for selecting the other events and days he does, including the feast of the Circumcision, and the days for saints such as Laurence, Augustine of Canterbury, and Bartholomew, are more obscure.

The poem specifies no dates, but offers touchstones by which those of specific feasts could be calculated. For example, we are told that the feast of the Circumcision occurs 'on þy eahteoðan dæg' (3b) [on the eighth day] after 'Crist wæs acennyd' (1a) [Christ was born], a birth that occurs 'on midne winter' (2a) [on mid-winter (Christmas)]. The date of the Invention of the Cross is calculated thusly from the first day of May: 'And þæs embe twa niht þætte tæhte god / Elenan eadigre æþelust beama, / on þam þrowode þeoden engla' (83–85a) [And then about two nights it is that God showed the more blessed Elena the most noble of trees on which the prince of angels suffered]. The dates of movable feasts such as Easter and the Ascension (which is celebrated on the fortieth day after Easter) fall outside the poet's system of reckoning, but while he acknowledges that these dates cannot 'be getale healdan / dagena rimes' (63b–64a) [by a reckoning of the number of days be grasped], he is confident nevertheless that 'sceal wintrum frod / on circule cræfte findan / halige dagas' (66b–68a) [those wise in winters shall find through skill the holy days in the cycle (of the church year)]. This comment may well point to the purpose of the poem: although often taken as a mnenomic, it seems to be more a flexible instructional tool, one that enables those who follow its system to calculate many dates in the liturgical year if they are familiar with some well-known calendrical signposts, including the beginning of seasons or months, or a major, fixed religious feast such as Christmas, since other dates can then be worked out according to the system the poet models.

Why the scribe responsible for copying the beginning of the Chronicle begins his stint by including two short poems is something of a mystery, especially since there is not much by way of an ideational link among these rather diverse texts, one of which obliquely presents selected dates from the liturgical calendar, one of which is comprised of brief gnomic statements strung together according to no discernable organizing principle, and one of which is comprised of brief notices of selected historical events. All three are meant to be instructional in their respective ways, and so this may account for their grouping in the manuscript, but this only takes us so far in understanding why they were included in the codex.

Further Reading

Hansen, Elaine Tuttle. 'Wisdom for Christians'. In her *The Solomon Complex: Reading Wisdom in Old English Poetry*, 100–25. McMaster Old English Studies and Texts 5. Toronto: University of Toronto Press, 1988.

Head, Pauline. 'Perpetual history in the Old English *Menologium*'. In *The Medieval Chronicle: Proceedings of the 1st International Conference on the Medieval*

Chronicle, ed. Erik Kooper, 155–162. Costerus ns 120. Amsterdam: Rodopi, 1999.

Stanley, Eric G. 'The prose *Menologium* and the verse *Menologium*'. In *Text and Language in Medieval English Prose*, ed. Akio Oizumi, Jacek Fisiak, and John Scahill, 255–67. New York: Peter Lang, 2005.

Toswell, M.J. 'The Metrical Psalter and *The Menologium*: some observations'. *NM* 94 (1993): 249–57.

The Rune Poem

Survives only in a version printed by George Hickes in 1705, in Vol. I of his *Linguarum Veterum Septentrionalium Thesaurus Grammatico-Criticus et Archæologicus*.

The Rune Poem (RuP) is one of a few OE poems that survive only because transcriptions were made before the manuscripts that contained them were lost or destroyed (*The Battle of Maldon* is another). The transmission history of *RuP* is especially complex since not only was the poem's manucript – London, BL Cotton Otho B.x – destroyed in the fire at Ashburnham House in 1731, but the transcription George Hickes used as the basis of his printed edition of the poem has been lost as well. As a result, the text as we know it may have gone through a certain, perhaps high, degree of editorial filtering at a very early stage in its critical history. Although unlikely, Hickes may have worked from a transcription that was the equivalent of a hand-written photocopy, but there is no way of knowing whether the transcription was accurate or flawed and whether it faithfully represented both the text and the layout of the manuscript's pages. We cannot, for example, determine if Hickes's presentation, which echoes that of the Exeter Book riddles, is of Hickes's design or reflects the *mise-en-page* of the lost Tiberius B.x. Hickes begins each stanza at the left margin and marks the beginning of each stanza in the left margin with an alphabetic transcription of each rune in Anglo-Saxon miniscule followed by the runic symbols themselves. This design might replicate the layout of the now lost transcription or it might have been dictated by the technology that was available to him at the time of his volume's printing since the runes, along with their Anglo-Saxon counterparts and names were printed from two separate copper plates and only exist in combination with the text of the poem on Hickes's printed page.

RuP illustrates the characters of the futhorc, an alphabet that was used in the early Germanic world chiefly for inscriptions. Deriving its name from the first six of its characters, the Anglo-Saxon futhorc contained some twenty-eight characters. Several of these, æsc (æ), wynn (ρ), thorn (þ), and eth (ð), were incorporated by the Anglo-Saxons into the Roman alphabet where they continued to function, as they did in the futhorc, as either, or both, letters or words. It is this latter function that provides *RuP* with its organization since the poet proceeds in order through all the symbols as he offers brief comments, some of which have decidedly gnomic and/or riddling overtones, on each of the futhorc's characters. Most of the entries are three lines long, but some are two or four and the final one is five. The entries are generally metrically regular, although several of them are hypermetric. All the entries begin the same way, with a runic symbol followed by 'byþ' [is], as in the following: '[ᚱ] (rad) byþ on recyde rinca gehylcum / sefte, and swiþhwæt ðam ðe sitteþ on ufan / meare mægenheardum ofer milpaþas' (13–15) [(riding) is easy for each of the warriors in the hall and very strenuous for the one who sits upon a very powerful horse over the miles]. The sentiment expressed here, with its witty and thinly veiled, if still rather vague, social criticism, is nevertheless somewhat more pointed and specific than gnomic utterances typically are. Despite its apparent affiliations to wisdom poems and riddles, *RuP* finally fits comfortably into neither category.

If the poem was meant to instruct by having its readers/listeners work out the name of the rune from its short stanzas, beginning each stanza with the runic solution seems a self-defeating strategy and would, further, make it a verbal puzzle of a type unlike any other that survives from Anglo-Saxon England. In addition to its possibly gnomic and/or riddling stanzas, others are purely descriptive and may serve as mnemonics for the rune's name: '[ᛁ] (is) byþ oferceald, ungemetum slidor, / glisnaþ glæshluttur, gimmum gelicust, / flor forste geworuht, fæger ansyne' (29–31) [Ice is excessively cold, immensely slippery, it glistens clear as glass, most like to precious stones, a floor wrought by extreme cold, a fair sight]. The names that were traditionally associated with the runes limited the poet's choices throughout, but despite being an artist of modest artistic talent, the *RuP*-poet nevertheless on occasion exceeds his poem's formal limitations.

Further Reading

Niles, John D. 'Runic hermeneutics in *The Rune Poem*'. In his *Old English Enigmatic Poems and the Play of the Texts*, 251–79. Studies in the Early Middle Ages 13. Turnhout: Brepols, 2006.

Trilling, Renée R. 'Ruins in the realms of thoughts: reading as constellation in Anglo-Saxon Poetry'. *JEGP* 108 (2009): 141–67.

DiNapoli, Robert. 'Odd characters: runes in Old English poetry'. In *Verbal Encounters: Anglo-Saxon and Old Norse Studies for Roberta Frank*, ed. Antonia

Harbus and Russell Poole, 145–61. Toronto Old English Series 13. Toronto: University of Toronto Press, 2005.

Millar, Angel. 'The Old English Rune Poem – semantics, structure, and symmetry'. *Journal of Indo-European Studies* 34 (2006): 419–36.

The Poems of the Anglo-Saxon Chronicle

See Part 2 for details of the Chronicle's multiple manuscripts.

Comprised for the most part of the brief, telegraphic prose annals typified by the entry in MS C for the year 101, 'Her Clemens papa forðferde' (O'Brien, O'Keeffe, *Anglo-Saxon Chronicle*, 18) [Here Pope Clement passed away], the Anglo-Saxon Chronicle also contains a number of more discursive prose entries as well as several entries that are generally considered to be poetic. As is the case with all OE poetry, the presence of the metrical, lexical, and syntactic patterns of the traditional expressive economy is what primarily distinguishes prose from poetry: since both types of discourse are physically encoded on the manuscript page in the same fashion, that is as blocks of *scriptio continua* written from the left margin to the right, there is nothing that formally distinguishes OE prose from OE poetry.

Six entries in the Chronicle are generally considered to be poems: 937 (*The Battle of Brunanburh*), 942 (*The Capture of the Five Boroughs*), 973 (*The Coronation of Edgar*), 975 (*The Death of Edgar*), 1036 (*The Death of Alfred*), and 1065 (*The Death of Edward*). There are a number of other potentially poetic passages (for example, 1086) found in MS E, the so-called Peterborough Continuation, but they will not be considered here because they belong more properly to early Middle English than to Anglo-Saxon literary history. With the exception of *Brunanburh*, which will be treated separately below, the Chronicle-poems are frequently seen as little more than aesthetically wanting treatments commemorating a few moments of importance in the island's history: two focus on English victories (*Brunanburh* and *Five Boroughs*), two on the deaths of nobles (*Alfred* and *Edward*), and one on a coronation that took place fourteen years after the king's ascension. The final one, *The Death of Edgar*, might be profitably viewed as a poetic compilation of the year 975's important events, which happen to include Edgar's death.

While not among the most accomplished poems to have survived from the period, the ones found in the Chronicle are not artless creations but attest to the continued vibrancy of the traditional expressive economy of oral poetics. For example, of the ten half-lines found in lines 24–28 of *The Death of Edgar*, eight find direct parallels in *Beowulf*, *The Seafarer*, *Andreas*, and

The Fight at Finnsburh. If we were to consider the context of each half-line in more detail, which space does not permit, we would find that the poet responsible for the Chronicle poem draws as effectively upon the phrases as the poets of the other, more highly regarded poems do. The opening lines of *The Death of Edgar* well illustrate the poet's fine aesthetic sensibilities:

> Her geendode eorðan dreamas
> Eadgar, Engla cyning, ceas him oðer leoht,
> wlitig, and wynsum, and þis wace forlet,
> lif þis læne.

(1–4a)

[Here Edgar ended earthly joys; the king of the English chose another light, beautiful and joyous, and this weak life abandoned, this transitory life.]

Why only a small number of the Chronicle's entries are articulated in verse remains a mystery: there is nothing that distinguishes the deeds and events catalogued in the poems from those that are expressed only in prose. We might well expect that the martial victories recounted in *Brunanburh* and *Five Boroughs* should be articulated via the pathways of the heroic tradition's expressive economy, but the same does not hold for the other poems. Adding further to the mystery, not all the poems appear in all the versions of the Chronicle. *The Death of Edgar*, for example, is found in three manuscripts, but in two others the same topic is treated in prose entries, and in another the king's death warrants only a one-sentence entry of the type encountered with great frequency in all the versions of the Chronicle: 'Her Eadgar cing forþferde' (Baker, *Anglo-Saxon Chronicle*, 84) [here King Edgar died].

Further Reading

Carroll, Jayne. '*Engla Waldend, Rex Admirabilis*: poetic representations of King Edgar'. *RES* ns 58 (2007): 113–32.

Salvador-Bello, Mercedes. 'The Edgar panegyrics in the Anglo-Saxon Chronicle'. In *Edgar, King of the English, 959–975: New Interpretations*, ed. Donald Scragg, 252–72. Publications of the Manchester Centre for Anglo-Saxon Studies 8. Woodbridge: Boydell Press, 2008.

Thormann, Janet. 'The *Anglo-Saxon Chronicle* poems and the making of the English nation'. In *Anglo-Saxonism and the Construction of Social Identity*, ed. Allen J. Frantzen and John D. Niles, 60–85. Gainesville: University Press of Florida, 1997.

Trilling, Renée R. 'Poetic memory: the canonical verse of the Anglo-Saxon Chronicle'. In her *The Aesthetics of Nostalgia: Historical Representation in Old English Verse*, 175–213. Toronto Anglo-Saxon Series 3. Toronto: University of Toronto Press, 2009.

The Battle of Brunanburh

Found under the entry for the year 937 in MSS A, B, C, and D of the Anglo-Saxon Chronicle; MS E mentions the battle in a single sentence and MS F offers a very brief prose account.

Generally considered to be the most poetic of the Chronicle poems, *The Battle of Brunanburh*, at seventy-three lines, is also twice as long as the next longest one. As with the other five Chronicle poems, *Brunanburh*'s *mise-en-page* in no way differentiates it from the prose entries that surround it. But like the others *Brunanburh* is also linked to the prose by more than its layout since it opens with the same word, 'Her' [Here], typically employed in the Chronicle to mark the beginnings of a new prose entry. 'Her' appears frequently in the poetry, as we might expect, but nowhere except in the Chronicle is it a poem's first word. The sixth Chronicle poem, *The Death of Alfred*, also begins with 'her', but it begins as prose, not as poetry, switching over to something approaching regular poetic metre in line 5. Because it is the first, longest, and most aesthetically accomplished of the Chronicle poems, *Brunanburh* is sometimes seen as a vestige of an earlier stage of poetic composition, but we should resist adopting this view since it rests upon the false assumption that the earlier a poem's putative date of composition, the more traditional it must be.

Brunanburh's subject is the resounding military victory a force from Wessex led by King Athelstan and his brother Edmund earned over an army comprised of Norsemen, Irishmen, Scots, and Britons led by Anlaf (who is most likely Olaf Guthfrithson), the Norse king of Dublin. Although we know the year in which the battle took place, and although the poem memorializes the name of the town near where the battle took place (Brunanburh) and that of the body of water (Dingesmere) over which Olaf and the Northmen fled in disarray back to Ireland, the precise locale has yet to be unequivocally identified. That the battle's location is lost to us does nothing, however, to diminish the energy or accomplishment of the poem, one in which the poet draws upon a number of traditional elements in detailing the martial feats of 'afaran Eadweardes' (7a) [Edward's sons].

The martial, traditional nature of the poem is made evident from the outset when we learn that Athelstan and Edmund 'Bordweal clufan, / heowan heaþolinde hamora lafan' (5b–6) [split the shield-wall, hewed war-shields with the leavings of hammers], and so earned 'ealdorlangne tir' (3b) [lifelong glory]. The forces opposing the English suffer terrible losses: 'Hettend crungun, / Sceotta leoda and scipflotan / fæge feollan, feld dennede / secga swate' (10b–13a) [the enemy perished, men of the Scots and sailors fell fated to die; the field resounded with the blood of men], and they leave behind not just 'unrim heriges / flotan and Sceotta' (31b–32a) [a countless number of that predatory host of seamen and Scots], but also 'Fife … / cyningas giunge, / sweordum aswefede, swilce seofene eac / eorlas Anlafes' (28b–31a) [five young kings who had been put to sleep by the sword, likewise also seven of Anlaf's earls]. We can get a sense of the poet's artistry from even these few lines, containing as they do one word, 'bordweal', that occurs elsewhere in the extant corpus only three times, once each in *Beowulf*, *Maldon*, and *Riddle 33*; another, 'ealdorlangne', that is a *hapax legomenon*; and another uniquely occurring one, 'dænnede', the meaning of which remains unknown. We can see further signs of the poet's skill in his economic and effective deployment of the traditional theme of the beasts of battle (60–65a), and in the rhetorical balancing through which he sharply contrasts the defeated Constantine, who 'hreman ne þorfte / mæca gemanan' (39b–40a) [had no need to exult in the meeting of swords], with the brothers, who return to Wessex 'wiges hremige' (59b) [exulting in the battle].

But while *Brunanburh* rightly deserves its position among the great articulations of martial deeds in OE poetry, it is removed from them not just because of its immediate context in the almost wholly prose Chronicle and because it is based on a purportedly historical event, but because it closes with a direct acknowledgment of the existence of written sources, something that does not occur in the other secular, heroic poetry that survives from the period:

> Ne wearð wæl mare
> on þis eiglande æfre gieta
> folces gefylled beforan þissum
> sweordes ecgum, þæs þe us secgað bec,
> ealde uðwitan.
>
> (65b–69a)

[Not ever yet before this has there been a greater slaughter on this island of people felled by the edges of swords, as books tell us, the old historians.]

Further Reading

Bredehoft, Thomas A. *The Battle of Brunanburh* in Old English Studies. In *The Battle of Brunanburh: A Casebook*, ed. Michael Livingston, 285–94. Exeter Medieval Texts and Studies. Exeter: University of Exeter Press, 2011.

Cavill, Paul. 'The site of the *Battle of Brunanburh*: manuscripts and maps, grammar and geography'. In *A Commodity of Good Names: Essays in Honour of*

Poems from Various Manuscripts

Margaret Gelling, ed. O.J. Padel and David N. Parsons, 303–19. Donington: Shaun Tyas, 2008.

Foot, Sarah. 'Where English becomes British: rethinking contexts for Brunanburh'. In Myth, Rulership, Church and Charters: Essays in Honour of Nicholas Brooks, ed. Julia Barrow and Andrew Wareham, 127–44. Aldershot: Ashgate, 2008.

Hill, John M. 'The Battle of Brunanburh and the construction of mythological lordship'. In his The Anglo-Saxon Warrior Ethic: Reconstructing Lordship in Early English Literature, 93–110. Gainesville: University Press of Florida, 2000.

Scragg, Donald G. 'A reading of Brunanburh'. In Unlocking the Wordhord: Anglo-Saxon Studies in Memory of Edward B. Irving, Jr., ed. Mark C. Amodio and Katherine O'Brien O'Keeffe, 109–22. Toronto: University of Toronto Press, 2003.

The Battle of Maldon

Survives only in an eighteenth-century transcription made before the manuscript that contained it, London, BL, Cotton Otho A.xii, was lost in the Cottonian fire of 1731.

Because the folios on which the unique copy of The Battle of Maldon in Cotton Otho A.xii were destroyed in the fire at Ashburnham House in 1731, our knowledge of the poem derives solely from a transcription made by David Casley. Casley's transcription, which until 1985 had been mistakenly attributed to John Elphinston, survives in Oxford, Bodleian Library, Rawlinson B 203, fols 7^r–12^v. The opening and the closing of Maldon are defective owing to the loss of perhaps several leaves, although just how much of the poem has been lost remains a matter of speculation. Given that Casley titled his transcription a 'fragment' ['Fragmentum quoddam historicum de Eadrico, etc.'], it seems likely that the manuscript was already damaged at the time of his copying.

Maldon relates a crushing defeat Byrhtnoth, ealdorman of Essex, and his men suffered at the hands of Viking raiders in August of 991. That this particular event should be commemorated is something of a puzzle, especially since the battle turns on a serious tactical error made by Byrhtnoth. Despite being greatly outnumbered, the English still held the advantage because the forces were separated by the tidal waters of the River Blackwater, with the Viking raiders located on an island from which the mainland could be reached solely via a narrow causeway that appeared only at low tide. Given the tactical advantage their position afforded them, the English were able to hold the Vikings at bay until Byrhtnoth, in response to requests from the raiders, granted the invaders safe passage over the causeway: as a result, the Vikings soon won the day, killing Byrhtnoth and many other Englishmen in the process. The battle itself is of little military or historical significance, and if the poem had not survived, we likely would know nothing of the events it memorializes.

Because Byrhtnoth is a historical figure and because the poem itself is rather specific regarding, among other things, the topography of the spot where the battle took place and the tactics employed by the English, the poem may be the product of an eye-witness to, or participant in, the battle or of someone with close second-hand knowledge of the fight and its particulars. Were evidence to be discovered that establishes that the poet had, say, participated in or witnessed the battle, the poem could lay strong claim to being one of the most important documents to survive from Anglo-Saxon England, but since no such evidence has to date been adduced, we ought to treat the poem as we would any other work of verbal art from the period, and so should view it as the creation of a unique and idiosyncratic artistic temperament and not as the early medieval equivalent of a newspaper account of the fight.

Whatever its relationship to the actual events that took place on the banks of the Blackwater more than a thousand years ago, *Maldon* nevertheless offers perhaps the fullest and most focused articulation of the Anglo-Saxon heroic ethos found anywhere in the literature extant from the period. To take but a few examples, before his death, Byrhtnoth urges his troops to fight courageously and even instructs them in the defensive formation they should employ. After riding through his ranks, he alights among his comitatus, 'mid leodon þær him leofost wæs, / þær he his heorðwerod holdost wiste' (23–24) [among the people where it was most pleasing to him, where he knew his hearth-companions to be most faithful]. In a speech meant to instill confidence in his men while simultaneously denigrating his enemies, he ridicules the Vikings' suggestion that bloodshed could be avoided if the English were to pay tribute, telling them that instead of gold, his men 'willað eow to gafole garas syllan, / ættrynne ord and ealde swurd, / þa heregeatu þe eow æt hilde ne deah' (46–48) [will give you spears as tribute, the poisoned point and tried swords, war-equipment that will not be of use to you in battle]. Byrhtnoth kills several Vikings during the battle, striking one so hard 'þæt seo byrne tobærst' (144a) [that the coat of mail burst apart], after which the ealdorman 'hloh' (147a) [laughed contemptuously]. And despite sustaining several serious and debilitating wounds which make it impossible for him to remain steady on his feet, Byrhtnoth 'hyssas bylde, / bæd gangan forð gode geferan' (169b–70) [emboldened his warriors and bid his good men to advance in battle] before being hacked to death by several Vikings.

The words and actions of his men mirror Byrhtnoth's as they embark upon what prove to be their final acts after vowing either to repulse the invaders or to die in the attempt, as Leofsunu memorably does in a statement that echoes one made by the aged king Beowulf:

> Ic þæt gehate, þæt ic heonon nelle
> fleon fotes trym, ac will furðor gan,
> wrecan on gewinne minne winedrihten.
>
> (246–48)

[This I vow, that I will not flee a foot's length hence, but I will proceed to avenge my gracious lord in the battle.]

Other characters echo these sentiments, including Dunnere, an 'unorne ceorl' (256a) [simple peasant] who is one of the few non-noble characters to appear, let alone speak, in the heroic poetry, and Offa, who had vowed to ride back home alongside his lord or fall in the fight. In death he fulfils the ideal of the comitatus, since his corpse 'læg ðegenlice ðeodne gehende' (294) [lay manfully close to his lord]. The heroism of the English so moves a Northumbrian hostage, Æscferth, that he gets swept up in the moment as well and 'ongan geornlice fylstan' (265) [began eagerly to help] the English 'þa hwile ðe he wæpna wealdan moste' (272) [as long as he might wield weapons] until he, too, is slaughtered. Similar moments could easily be adduced in the poem, but space will permit us to consider just one more, a statement by Byrhtwold that perhaps more than any other admirably and succinctly captures the spirit of the heroic ethos with which the poem is so thoroughly infused:

> Hige sceal þe heardra, heorte þe cenre,
> mod sceal þe mare, þe ure mægen lytlað.
> Her lið ure ealdor eall forheawen,
> god on greote. A mæg gnornian
> se ðe nu fram þis wigplegan wendan þenceð.
> Ic eom frod feores; fram ic ne wille,
> ac ic me be healfe minum hlaforde,
> be swa leofan men, licgan þence.
>
> (312–19)

[The mind must be sterner, the heart bolder, the spirit must be greater as our might dwindles. Here lies our chief, slaughtered by many blows, the good man on the sand. The one who thinks now to turn from the game of war will ever have cause to mourn. I am advanced in years; I will not depart, but I by the side of my lord, beside the well loved man, intend to lie.]

While the poem idealizes the heroism of the English, the heroic ethos it celebrates ultimately emerges as a flawed and perhaps fractured – or fracturing – cultural institution. Two moments in particular are especially telling in this regard for the sobering counterpoint they offer to the poem's otherwise uniformly positive, and uniformly inflated (or idealized) depiction of the English force's heroism. The first is Byrhtnoth's ceding the superiority of his position by allowing the numerically superior raiders to cross the causeway unharmed, a decision that stems from his 'ofermode' (89b) [pride, arrogance, over confidence]. There is a decidedly pejorative overtone to this word in the poem, especially in light of the later description of Byrhtnoth as a 'modi man' (147a) [an arrogant man] who laughs derisively at a fallen foe. His offering the Vikings safe passage across the Blackwater may reveal that he has fallen victim to his own heroic rhetoric, but we ought to refrain from placing too much weight on either a poor tactical decision by the English leader or the terms used to describe him since warriors, and in particular the leaders of warriors, need to be confident in their abilities and battlefield decisions.

The second moment that may reveal a fissure in the poem's heroic foundations, the Englishman Godric's fleeing upon the deceased Byrhtnoth's horse, points more directly to possible fissures in the heroic ethos. His flight in itself is not very consequential since the presence of one man more or less at the fight would have had little bearing on the outcome. However, because he flees on Byrhtnoth's horse accompanied by his brothers, Godric and his companions are mistaken by many in the English force for Byrhtnoth and his comitatus, his hand-picked band of warriors. Believing that their leader is retreating, many among the English follow suit and abandon the fight. The resulting depletion of the English ranks throws the heroism of those who remain into sharper relief, but the departure of what the poet tells us is 'manna ma þonne hit ænig mæð wære' (195) [many more than was at all right] also raises the possibility that the warriors who remain behind and who so dramatically articulate the tenets of the heroic code are very much in the minority. So contextualized, it becomes clear that the out-sized, almost inflated heroic speeches that comprise the bulk of the poem's 325 lines perhaps ought to be seen not as reflections of current social or cultural praxis, but rather as attempts to palliate what might have been a particularly galling defeat by nostalgically situating it and its English participants within the heroic ethos, within, that is, a system of behaviour that reflects not current practices but rather those of the distant, idealized past.

The poet's depiction of the English force's heroism does, however, witness the extent to which that ethos – from whatever source – was still present, at least as a literary construct. Despite being a demonstrably late composition (the event it commemorates occurred in 991), the poem is articulated fully within the expressive economy of oral poetics, as the highly traditional nature of its lexemes and thematics reveal. Its metrics are irregular on occasion, but whether this is evidence that the poem was composed at a time when the traditional expressive economy was beginning to weaken, or simply of errors on the poet's (or copyist's) part cannot be determined. Surmising that the poem witnesses the continued presence of some sort of active oral poetics and thus that the poet is not so far removed from his predecessors is tempting, but the poem may also be the product of someone consciously attempting to recall a glorified and idealized heroic past as he attempts to wrest something positive out of the military disaster that befell the English on the banks of the River Blackwater.

Further Reading

Bately, Janet M. 'Bravery and the vocabulary of bravery in *Beowulf* and the *Battle of Maldon*'. In *Unlocking the Wordhord: Anglo-Saxon Studies in Memory of Edward B. Irving, Jr.*, ed. Mark C. Amodio and Katherine O'Brien O'Keeffe, 274–301. Toronto: University of Toronto Press, 2003.

Hill, John M. 'Triumphant lordship and new retainership in *The Battle of Maldon*'. In his *The Anglo-Saxon Warrior Ethic: Reconstructing Lordship in Early English Literature*, 111–28. Gainesville: University Press of Florida, 2000.

Matto, Michael. 'A war of containment: the heroic image in *The Battle of Maldon*'. *SN* 74 (2002): 60–75.

Niles, John D. '*Maldon* and mythopoesis'. In his *Old English Heroic Poems and the Social Life of Texts*, 203–36. Studies in the Early Middle Ages 20. Turnhout: Brepols, 2007.

Trilling, Renée R. 'Verse memorials and the Viking Conquest'. In her *The Aesthetics of Nostalgia: Historical Representation in Old English Verse*, 125–74. Toronto Anglo-Saxon Series 3. Toronto: University of Toronto Press, 2009.

The Fight at Finnsburh

A fragment of this poem survives only in the version George Hickes printed in his *Linguarum Veterum Septentrionalium Thesaurus Grammatico-Criticus et Archæologicus*.

The Fight at Finnsburh is a fragmentary poem of nearly forty-eight lines that survives only in the version George Hickes printed from a manuscript leaf that was itself apparently defective. The leaf – now lost – is generally believed to have been part of London, Lambeth Palace 487. Hickes's version, while valuable because it is our only record of the poem, is not especially authoritative since it contains numerous errors, some of which appear to be the results of his miscomprehension of the original, some of which appear to be errors in transcription, and some of which may be scribal. As a result, any investigation of the poem's language, metrics, and syntax must be undertaken with even greater than usual care since there is no satisfactory way of determining just how and where Hickes's text deviates from what was on the manuscript leaf. Hickes seems to have printed as much of the poem as the leaf contained, but just how much of the poem is missing remains a question that we cannot answer.

Despite the problems and questions that attend it, *Finnsburh* occupies an important position within the corpus of extant OE verse because it provides us with one of our only glimpses into a genre that is, perhaps somewhat surprisingly, not well attested: heroic verse that is not tinged with either Christian sentiment or Christian references, but is rather wholly secular in its orientation, outlook, and articulation. While *Deor* and *Widsið* are both candidates for inclusion in this genre, each contains at least one reference to what is usually taken to be the Christian God, unlike *Finnsburh* which contains none. Too much weight, however, cannot not be placed upon *Finnsburh*'s secular nature because there is no way finally of determining what the poem's missing sections might have touched upon.

Finnsburh also stands apart from most of the surviving corpus in that it is one of the only surviving pieces of Anglo-Saxon poetry to offer an independent account of events related in another poem. The disastrous visit made by Hnæf and his band of Jutes that the fragment relates is also the subject of the so-called Finn episode found in *Beowulf* at lines 1063–1160a. Because they focus on the same events, these texts speak to each other in ways that few other OE poems do, or can do. The fragment and episode do not descend from a common ancestor but rather are independent treatments of Hnæf's ill-fated visit to Finn offered from very different perspectives. How each poet handles the martial engagements that are at the centre of each narrative throws the differences between the poem and the episode into sharp relief: the *Beowulf*-poet treats the fighting that breaks out twice only in the most general of terms, while in the portion of *Finnsburh* that survives, the poet places his audience right in the thick of the battle as the Danes in their hall see light reflecting off the armour and weapons of the attacking Frisians. Perhaps owing to generic affliliations (the poem is often considered to be a heroic lay while the episode is part of a heroic epic), the two pieces proceed along different stylistic trajectories, with the author of the fragment relying heavily on direct discourse to create a sense of dramatic immediacy that is entirely lacking in the episode, which the *Beowulf*-poet relates in the third person. While we are fortunate to have in this instance two unrelated treatments of the same event, the allusive nature of both pieces prevent them from shedding much light on each other. For example, from the poem we may infer that Hnæf, who is described in a uniquely occurring epithet as being 'heaþogeong' (2b) [war-young], was at the time of the visit a young leader whose political inexperience may well have contributed to the initial outbreak of violence – in which he loses his life – that erupts between the visitors and their Frisian hosts. The *Beowulf*-poet, in contrast, touches on neither Hnæf's age nor his martial or political experience (or lack thereof) in the episode. And it is from the episode alone that we learn that Hildeburh and Finn have a son old enough to participate in the initial fighting (during which he is also killed). Finally, while the fight depicted in *Finnsburh* appears to be the first of the two that are mentioned in *Beowulf*, we cannot be wholly certain of this for in the poem the fighting goes on for five days, while in the episode it is concluded over the space of a single night.

Taken on its own, the fragment stands as a compact articulation of the Anglo-Saxon heroic ethos. The surviving portion of the poem begins with Hnæf stating that the unusual light one of his men has seen outside the hall is 'ne dagað eastan, ne her draca fleogeð, / ne her ðisse healle hornas ne byrnað' (3–4) [not the day dawning in the east, nor flies a dragon here, nor burn here the gables of this hall], but is, rather, the reflection emanating from the armor and weapons of an approaching hostile troop. As the force nears, Hnæf, in a speech that weaves together several strands of the expressive economy's thematics of battle (which has already been partly invoked by the shining objects), notes that 'fugelas singað, / gylleð græghama, guðwudu hlynneð, / scyld scefte oncwyð' (5b–7a) [the carrion birds will sing, the grey-coated one will howl, the battle-wood will resound, the shield will echo from the shaft]. Following Hnæf's call to awaken, in the hall 'Ða aras mænig goldhladen ðegn' (14a) [Then arose many a gold-adorned warrior] who gird themselves with their swords and move to defend the doors of their hall from the approaching Frisians. The heroic mindset and determination of those within the hall is eloquently articulated by a member of the Secgan tribe, Sigeferth, who fights alongside the Jutes and who from his position in a doorway announces to the Frisians that he is a 'wreccea wide cuð; fæla ... weana gebad, / hearda hilda. Ðe is gyt her witod / swæþer ðu sylf to me secean wylle' (25–27) [widely known hero (who has) survived many woes, many hard battles. To you is yet here appointed whichever of two things you yourself will seek from me].

The hall soon resounds with 'wælslihta gehlyn' (28b) [the din of slaughter strokes], and as the fighting begins the poet acknowledges that 'sceolde cellod bord cenum on handa, / banhelm berstan (buruhðelu dynede)' (29–30) [the beaked shield in the hands of the brave ones and the bone-helmet must shatter; the fortress floor resounded]. Even though we cannot confidently assess the artistic ability of the *Finnsburh*-poet because the sample of his work that has survived is so limited, the poem does contain a rather high number of *hapax legomena*, as well as several arresting images. To take but one example, so intense is the fighting that the 'swurdleoma' (35b) [sword-light; light from the flashing (?) swords] makes it appear 'swylce eal Finnsburuh fyrenu wære' (36) [as if all Finnsburh were afire]. In recalling the bright objects Hnæf mentions at the fragment's beginning, the poet taps once more into the traditional thematics of battle and, further, points to the devastation that will befall Finnsburh, and to the funeral pyres that will, as we know from the episode, consume the corpses of the dead warriors once the fighting ceases. The image with which the fragment concludes offers yet another tantalizing, if brief, glimpse of the range and depth of the poet's artistry, as an unnamed and wounded warrior reports 'þæt his byrne abro-cen wære, / heresceorp unhror, and eac wæs his helm ðyrel' (44–45) [that his mail-coat was broken into pieces, the war-dress useless, and also his helmet was pierced]. Because the poem abruptly breaks off shortly after this, we have no way of knowing whether the survivor is a Dane or a Frisian but in this instance the narrative's indeterminacy, even though it owes its existence to happenstance, actually imparts a greater resonance to the image of the survivor than it would otherwise possess: because he is not identifed as a member of either side, he thus speaks to the terrible toll the battle takes on both sides.

Further Reading

Fry, Donald K. 'The hero on the beach in *Finnsburh*'. NM 67 (1966): 27–31.

Staples, Martha Jane. 'Lingering phonemes: the vocabulary of the Finnsburg Fragment'. *Medieval Perspectives* 17 (2003): 162–74.

Watson, Jonathan. 'The *Finnsburh* Skald: kennings and cruces in the Anglo-Saxon Fragment'. *JEGP* 101 (2002): 497–519.

Waugh, Robin. 'The characteristic moment as a motif in *The Finnsburg Fragment* and *Deor*'. *English Studies in Canada* 23 (1997): 249–61.

Waldere

The surviving two leaves of this poem are in the Royal Library, Copenhagen catalogued under the designation Ny kgl. sam. 167b (4ó).

The sole piece of OE poetry to treat the story of Walter of Aquitaine, *Waldere* survives uniquely in two apparently discontinuous leaves that are the sole survivors of an otherwise lost manuscript housed in the Royal Library, Copenhagen. The leaves both have small portions of their originally conjugate leaves attached, on which now only a few whole or partial letters can be made out. As the materials treating the legend of Walter in Latin, Icelandic, and Middle High German attest, his story was popular in the early Germanic world. The narrative preserved in the OE poem accords, in some ways, with those of the *Waltharius*, a ninth- or tenth-century Latin poem that had long been attributed to Ekkehard, a monk of St Gallen, but no source or analogue has to date been discovered for the OE text. The leaves containing *Waldere* are written in a single scribal hand, but aside from this nothing is known about the provenance of the fragments, and little can be ascertained about what must have been the originally much longer heroic poem to which they tantalizingly bear witness. Damage to the surface of the manuscript (the letters on the right-hand margins on fols 1^r and 2^v have been partially rubbed away) and to the manuscript itself (there is a small hole in the middle of fol. 2) has rendered a number of letters largely illegible and editors have, accordingly, had to resort to informed reconstruction.

In Fragment I, so designated because the narrative moment it preserves is widely, but not universally, thought to be anterior to the one preserved in Fragment II, an unnamed female speaker, who is generally taken to be Waldere's betrothed, Hildegyth, encourages Waldere to face the Frankish king Guthhere (who pursues them when their flight from Attila's court takes them and the substantial amount of treasure they are carrying into Guthhere's lands) in single combat. In Fragment II, Waldere addresses Guthhere before the combat which, we know from other sources, ends with each seriously, but not fatally, wounded. As does most of the other surviving heroic poetry from the period, *Waldere* effortlessly melds elements of both the pagan and Christian worlds. Hildegyth, for example, begins her speech by reminding Waldere that through his sword, Mimming, a work of Weland's, 'Oft æt hilde gedreas / swatfag and sweordwund secg æfter oðrum' (I, 4b–5) [often at battle perished blood-stained and sword-wounded, one warrior after another], and that he, as befits his position as 'Ætlan ordwyga' (I, 6a) [Attila's point-warrior], should allow neither his 'ellen' (I, 6b) [courage] nor his 'dryhtscype' (I, 7b) [valor] to 'gedreosan to dæge' (I, 7a) [perish today]. Shortly before Fragment I breaks off, she switches her focus from these and other secular concerns and reminds him to honour 'ðe selfne / godum dædum, ðenden ðin god recce' (I, 22b–23) [your self through good deeds, while God cares for you], a Christian sentiment that Waldere echoes just before Fragment II breaks off: 'Se ðe him to ðam halgan helpe gelifeð / to gode gioce, he þær gearo findeð' (II, 27–28) [he who entrusts himself to the holy one for help, to God for divine help, will readily find it there].

Hildegyth stands somewhat apart from the few other women encountered in the heroic poetry in that she takes a more direct and active role in urging Waldere not to lose his resolve in the fight by reminding him that he has never been known 'ðurh edwitscipe' (I, 14) [ignominiously]

> wig forbugan oððe on weal fleon,
> lice beorgan, ðeah þe laðra fela
> ðinne byrnhomon billum heowun.
>
> (I, 15–17)

[to evade battle or flee to the wall to protect (his) body, even though many hateful ones hewed (his) coat of mail with swords.]

Continuing in this vein, she tells him 'Ne murn ðu for ði mece; ðe wearð maðma cyst / gifeðe to geoce' (I, 24–25a) [do not be anxious about your sword; the best of treasures was given to you as an aid]. Were they to come from the mouth of one of the many women who populate Old Norse literature, Hildegyth's comments would not be in the least unusual since women in the Norse tradition commonly 'hvetja' [make keen; encourage; sharpen] their men. However, coming from the mouth of a female character in the Anglo-Saxon tradition they are noteworthy in large part because they are so unusual; women typically are situated in the background of OE heroic narratives and even when they enter the foreground, as the Danish queen Wealhtheow does on several occasions in *Beowulf*, they remain well removed from the world of martial activity to which Hildegyth so directly speaks. Wealhtheow's contention in *Beowulf* that 'druncne dryhtguman doð swa ic bidde' (1231) [drunken warriors do as I bid] may perhaps indicate that she, too, verbally spurs warriors to act heroically, but since neither she nor anyone else elaborates on her oblique and qualified statement (do only 'druncne dryhtguman' obey her, and in what social, political, or military context?), just how it should be taken remains unresolved.

As is true of Fragment I, the narrative details of Fragment II are somewhat murky: set in the moments before two warriors engage in single combat, it may contain two speeches, one by an unnamed speaker and the second by Waldere – who is identified in the text –, but both speeches may also be Waldere's. Opening in the midst of a speech that focuses on a sword, which may be Mimming or perhaps one that belongs to Guthhere, Fragment II touches in its few lines directly on a number of issues central to the heroic economy within which the combatants participate, especially the importance that inheres in war gear. The sword mentioned at the fragment's beginning was given by Theodoric, along with 'sinc micel' (II, 5b) [many treasures], as a 'iulean' (II, 7b) [reward for something done long ago] to Widia, a warrior in his service. In his speech, Waldere first calls Guthhere's attention to the coat of mail he wears, 'Ælfheres laf, / god and geapneb, golde geweorðod' (II, 18b–19) [Alfhere's legacy, good and with a curving front, ennobled with gold], before challenging him to come and 'Feta, gyf ðu dyrre, / æt ðus heaðuwerigan hare byrnan' (II, 16b–17) [Fetch, if you dare, the grey byrnie from this battle-weary one]. Waldere, wearing his father's chain-mail and standing as he does gripping his 'hildefrofre' (12b) [battle-consolation/battle-help], strikes as paradigmatically heroic a figure as we encounter anywhere in the extant poetry, and we can only regret that not more of the poem survives. Although we cannot know for certain from the surviving portions of *Waldere* if the complete poem would have approached the length, narrative complexity, and artistic accomplishment of *Beowulf*, the pacing and scope of the surviving material suggest that it might well have.

Further Reading

Andersson, Theodore M. 'The speeches in the *Waldere* fragments'. In *De Gustibus: Essays for Alain Renoir*, ed. John Miles Foley, 21–29. Albert Bates Lord Studies in Oral Tradition 11. New York: Garland, 1992.

Himes, Jonathan. *The Old English Epic of 'Waldere'*. Newcastle upon Tyne: Cambridge Scholars Publishing, 2009.

Tyler, Lee Edgar. 'The heroic oath of Hildebrand'. In *De Gustibus: Essays for Alain Renoir*, ed. John Miles Foley, 551–85. Albert Bates Lord Studies in Oral Tradition 11. New York: Garland, 1992.

Durham

Survives in Cambridge, CUL, Ff.i.27, fol. 101ᵛ, and in Hickes's *Linguarum Veterum Septentrionalium Thesaurus Grammatico-Criticus et Archæologicus.*, a text based on the now severely damaged London, BL, Cotton Vitellius D.xx.

Two copies of *Durham* survived from the Anglo-Saxon period, one now housed in the collection of Cambridge University and one that was part of the Cottonian collection. The folio containing *Durham* is not among the few pages of Cotton Vitellius D.xx that survived the fire of 1731, but before it was lost, George Hickes used it as the basis of the text he printed in his *Thesaurus*. The surviving manuscript, CUL, FF.i.27, is a miscellaneous collection of texts pertaining to Durham, including most notably Symeon of Durham's *Historia Dunelmensis ecclesiase* [*History of the Church of Durham*] and the *Historia de sancto Cuthberto* [*History of St Cuthbert*]. There is no know source for *Durham*, and although it shares some points of contact with a Latin text generally thought to be a continuation of Symeon's chronicle, the *Capitula de miraculis et translationibus sancti Cuthberti* [*Chapters concerning the miracles and translations of St Cuthbert*], the nature of the relationship, if there is one, between the texts remains unclear.

Unlike the majority of poems from the period, whose dates of composition cannot be determined with anything approaching precision, *Durham*, because it mentions an event that occurred in 1104 – the translation of St Cuthbert's remains to a newly constructed cathedral in the city – has a clear *terminus post quem*. The poem's language provides further evidence of its late date, showing signs of being in transition, as, for example, in the accusative plural ending in -*s*, not -*an*, in 'geferes' (13b), but its metre conforms more rather than less to classical Anglo-Saxon metre. On the whole, *Durham* should be situated among our surviving Anglo-Saxon texts and not among the transitional texts that have survived, including the Peterborough Continuation of the Anglo-Saxon Chronicle, because transitional texts evidence to a far greater degree the changes large and small that swept through and radically altered the language during the post-Conquest period. Although the poem's *mise-en-page* follows that of the other extant OE poems in that it is written in a continuous block of prose and not lineated as poetry, it is far more heavily pointed than any other piece of OE poetry, with *punctūs* marking most clausal boundaries and sometimes coming before and after individual words. While its pointing may simply evidence the scribe's or copyist's idiosyncratic practice or his equally idiosyncratic – and highly unusual – extension of the pointing system he used in the preceding Latin text to a vernacular one, it may also be an early sign of the transition in the ways in which vernacular texts were physically encoded on the page that was to begin after the period's close.

Comprised of two sections – one that describes Durham's environs and another that lists the names of some of the notables whose relics are housed there – *Durham* has long been considered the sole surviving OE example of a well-attested Latin genre, the *encomium urbis*. Given its thematic focus and its points of contact with Latin examples of the genre, there is no reason to dispute its generic classification, although there is no evidence that the poem is modelled upon any surviving Latin text. The poem opens with brief descriptions of the steep, rocky slopes upon which the city was established and of the river, the Wear, that flows by it, a river in which 'wunað / feola fisca kyn' (4b–5a) [many kinds of fish dwell]. The fecundity of life below the river's waters are matched by that found within the 'wudafæstern micel' (6b) [great sheltering wood] which grows by the city, in whose deep dales 'wuniad … wilda deor monige, / … deora ungerim' (7b–8b) [dwelt … many wild beasts, … a countless number of beasts]. The poem then abruptly shifts gears and becomes little more than a list of some of the great and holy men whose relics are housed in the city, among which are counted the bodies of St Cuthbert and the venerable Bede, and the head of King Oswald. The bishops Aidan and Æthelwold, the abbot, Boisil, who taught the young Cuthbert, and the 'æðele geferes' (13b) [noble companions] Eadberch and Eadfrith also earn mentions. The poem ends by gesturing towards the 'unarimeda reliquia' (19) [unnumbered relics] that are found alongside these men in the city where 'monia wundrum gewurðað, ðes ðe writ seggeð / midd ðene drihnes wer domes bideð' (20–21) [many wonders come to pass, as the writing says, where the man of God awaits judgement]. The final two-and-a-half lines of the poem appear to have been rubbed out, although if the poem as it survives is fragmentary, it nevertheless comes to a satisfactory conclusion.

Further Reading

Blurton, Heather. '*Reliquia*: writing relics in Anglo-Norman Durham'. In *Cultural Diversity in the British Middle Ages: Archipelago, Island, England*, ed. Jeffrey Jerome Cohen, 39–56. New Middle Ages. New York: Palgrave Macmillan, 2008.

Grossi, Joseph. 'Preserving the future in the Old English *Durham*'. *JEGP* 111 (2012): 42–73.

Howe, Nicholas. 'Conclusion: by way of *Durham*'. In his *Writing the Map of Anglo-Saxon England: Essays in Cultural Geography*, 225–31. New Haven: Yale University Press, 2008.

Part 4

Critical Approaches

The Alterity of Anglo-Saxon Literature

The prose and poetry that survives from the Anglo-Saxon period is markedly different from the verbal art produced in all subsequent periods of English literary history, and before we begin this brief survey of some of the interpretive strategies/critical approaches that have been employed to help us understand the literary remains of the period, we must first address the alterity of Anglo-Saxon literature. Produced in what is chronologically the most remote period in English literary history, Anglo-Saxon literature is also linguistically inaccessible to contemporary English speakers who do not have special training in the language, known as Old English (OE), that was spoken during the period. Because Chaucer writes in a Middle English (ME) dialect that is the direct ancestor of Modern English (NE) – East Midlands –, speakers of NE can read his fourteenth-century prose and poetry without much difficulty; Chaucer's present-tense verbs, which end in -th instead of -s, along with such things as the inconsistent spellings preserved in non-normalized editions of his work and some unusual (or now obsolete) lexemes may give contemporary readers momentary pause, but because his language's grammar and syntax are similar to that of NE, his works remain readily available to us in the original ME, even though they were written over 600 years ago, and even though, as he observantly notes in Book II of *Troilus and Criseyde*, 'in forme of speche is chaunge' (22). Other ME dialects, especially that of the West Midlands, pose more of a hurdle to the modern reader than does Chaucer's, but modern readers are for the most part able to negotiate ME texts without too much difficulty, especially when the texts are presented in glossed and normalized editions.

The Anglo-Saxon Literature Handbook, First Edition. Mark C. Amodio.
© 2014 Mark C. Amodio. Published 2014 by John Wiley & Sons, Ltd.

In contrast, the original-language versions of texts written in OE are not readily accessible to most modern readers because they are written in what is for NE speakers now the equivalent of a foreign language. As a result, most modern readers must rely on NE translations of OE texts. Although the English language exists along an unbroken continuum that extends from Anglo-Saxon England to the present day, it has undergone a series of major changes in its syntax, grammar, lexicon, orthography, and pronunciation that all but obscure the many connections that continue to exist between OE and NE. Some of these changes were already in progress during the Anglo-Saxon period, but others either began in or accelerated during the post-Conquest period, the period in which the English language underwent the most dramatic and most far-reaching transitions to date in its history.

The great cultural divide that separates the earliest period of English history from the present day also contributes to Anglo-Saxon literature's alterity. The contours of English culture begin to take shape with the arrival of the Germanic tribes in the middle of the fifth century, but England does not become a unified nation in the modern sense of the term until sometime well after the close of the Anglo-Saxon period. While for convenience we talk about Anglo-Saxon England as if it were a coherent, well-defined cultural, social, racial, religious, and political entity almost from the moment the continental tribes began to arrive to that fateful day in October of 1066 when Harold II was killed at Hastings, the reality is far more complex and far less easy to categorize. To take but one example, the conversion of the island's inhabitants to Christianity, a process generally accepted as beginning with the arrival in Kent of the Augustinian mission in 597 does not proceed in a steady, systematic, and orderly fashion because while in some areas the new religion was readily embraced, in others pagan practices persisted. And even after an area had been converted, there was no guarantee that it would remain Christian after a new ruler came to power. Similarly, while the overwhelmingly Christian nature of the period's surviving literary records signals the religion's widespread presence and importance in Anglo-Saxon England, we need to recall that throughout the period the technology of literacy remained firmly – and exclusively – in the hands of Christian clerics who may have had little interest in preserving in writing any non-Christian material, material with which they further may well have had very limited contact since it chiefly circulated via non-written channels. From the surviving literary records we are able to surmise that there was an audience, perhaps quite a large one, for Christian material, but other segments of the population could have been either unaware of or wholly uninterested in Christian vernacular prose and poetry.

Another factor contributing to the alterity of Anglo-Saxon literature is that with few exceptions we do not know when, where, or by whom a given piece of literature was composed, and we also generally cannot know with any certainty when or where or by whom the extant texts, which in many cases are themselves copies of copies, were first committed to the page. Even if we were able to date and geographically situate the extant texts with more precision, we would remain unable to contextualize them further because we know so little about the historical moments in which they were created and even less about the authors who created them. While we know, for example, that Ælfric of Eynsham, who lived in the late tenth and early eleventh centuries, authored two series of Catholic homilies as well as numerous other prose texts, this knowledge takes us only so far because the details of Ælfric's life are largely unrecorded. So far as the Anglo-Saxon poetic records are concerned, the situation is even more complex: whereas we can confidently attribute some of the prose texts to named authors and so can therefore tentatively assign likely dates of composition to some texts, we know the names of only four poets, three of whom, Cædmon, Deor, and Widsith, are most likely fictitious. Cynewulf is the generally agreed upon name of the fourth poet, but of him we know nothing other than that his name is runically encoded (once in a scrambled order) in what are generally taken to be autobiographical verses that conclude two poems found in the Vercelli Book and two found in the Exeter Book. While stylistic and syntactic evidence suggests a single author created the four works attributed to Cynewulf, the strongest evidence for his authorship – the presence of his name in each of them – is also, and unfortunately, rather circular.

Despite the inherent alterity of Anglo-Saxon literature, the recalibrations contemporary readers need to undertake in order to understand it are not so different from those we must engage when encountering the verbal art produced in any other period of English literary history. OE poetry requires us to make a few more conscious adjustments than we must make when reading Chaucer, Milton, or Shakespeare, but once we come to understand, for example, that OE poetry frequently proceeds in a non-linear fashion, that it is often highly allusive, that it relies heavily on repetition (with variation), and that it utilizes repeated, formulaic verbal and thematic collocations, we are well on the way to becoming responsible readers of OE verse. If we do not adjust our interpretive strategies to take into account Anglo-Saxon literature's far-ranging alterities, we run the risk of misunderstanding it and as a result may ask of it questions that are either (or both) inappropriate and impertinent. To take but one example: because it does not progress linearly, *Beowulf*'s narrative was famously criticized by an influential early-twentieth-century editor, Frederich Klaeber, for its 'lack of steady advance', and he further criticized the *Beowulf*-poet for being someone who 'does not hesitate to wander from the subject' (Klaeber, lvii). These are criticisms that, we might add, were levelled (and in some quarters are still levelled) at the narrator of Laurence Sterne's great eighteenth-century comic novel, *Tristram Shandy*, a work in which Sterne gleefully plays with and interrogates the very foundations of narrative, and of the authorial practices that continue to dominate to this day, in much the way that post-modernists do. From a contemporary perspective, Klaeber's views on *Beowulf* are both accurate and warranted: the poem's narrative does not always advance steadily and linearly, and a great deal of material that does not bear directly on the poem's action is threaded into its narrative, especially in the account of Beowulf's fatal encounter with the dragon that constitutes the poem's so-called second half. But to note these attributes is simply to note that *Beowulf* is a work of art produced in a very different period from ours and that its stylistics, poetics, and aesthetics differ in significant ways from those that have, since the close of the Anglo-Saxon period, shaped English literary history.

Despite the inherent otherness of Anglo-Saxon literature, a wide variety of critical approaches have been successfully applied to it, including philological, rhetorical, exegetical, historical, linguistic, textual, cultural, psychological, folkloric, new critical, post-modern, and oral-traditional ones, to offer but a highly selective list. The boundaries between these – and all – critical approaches are, of course, not nearly so absolute as they appear when they are put into a list and are neatly, if artificially, categorized and separated from each other; rather, they are extremely fluid, and in practice, most criticism typically winds up drawing from and combining several schools of thought, sometimes in expected, sometimes in unpredictable ways. Because anything like a complete – or even relatively full – treatment of the history of Anglo-Saxon literary criticism falls well beyond the scope of this discussion, it is to a necessarily brief and highly selective consideration of some of these approaches that we now turn.

Source Studies

Because a great many of the prose and poetic texts extant from the period
are translations of earlier texts, source studies have long been foundational
to Anglo-Saxon literary criticism. As Donald G. Scragg comments more generally about this critical approach, 'The study of a writer's sources has for
two centuries been a widely accepted means of understanding the workings
of his or her mind, for in selecting, reorganizing and modifying ideas from
earlier writers, authors display their own particular cast of thought' ('Source
Study', 39). Since authors in the Anglo-Saxon period rarely, if ever, translate
texts word for word, even though we frequently know the sources upon
which much of the surviving prose and poetry from the period is based,
we typically cannot pinpoint the precise redactions used by Anglo-Saxon
authors in creating their texts and translations. For example, many Christian
poems, including *Genesis A*, *Daniel*, and *Exodus*, are clearly based on sections of Biblical books, but we do not know which version(s) of the Bible the
Anglo-Saxon authors may have had to hand, and we further do not know
which extant Biblical manuscripts these authors may have consulted. As a
result, even in cases where there is an indisputable link between a known
source and an Anglo-Saxon text, those who engage in source studies must
proceed with caution, as Michael Lapidge does in arguing that 'a manuscript
copy of the *Passio S. Iulianae* very similar to, and possibly identical with, the
exemplar that underlies Cynewulf's *Juliana*, is extant in Paris, Bibliothèque
Nationale de France, lat. 10861' ('Cynewulf and the *Passio S. Iuliane*', 147).
Samantha Zacher astutely speaks to what we may gain from source studies
in her recent discussion of the source she discovered for Vercelli Homily VII.
Although her comments are directed specifically at the text, author, and
intended audience of this particular Vercelli Book prose homily, they apply

The Anglo-Saxon Literature Handbook, First Edition. Mark C. Amodio.
© 2014 Mark C. Amodio. Published 2014 by John Wiley & Sons, Ltd.

equally well to source studies in general: comparing a source text to its OE adaptation/translation enables us not only to elucidate or correct 'corruptions in the Old English text' (and perhaps even to determine whether they are scribal or authorial), but also to gain a clear sense of the OE author's 'method of adaptation' and of his 'target audience' by carefully considering the 'textual omissions, additions, and changes' evident in the OE text ('The source of Vercelli VII', 104).

To cite but one example, in comparing the Latin version of Boethius's *Consolation of Philosophy* with the OE translation attributed to King Alfred the Great, Alfred emerges as a translator who tends to simplify his source material, either because his own grasp of the original Latin is not entirely secure or because he wished to make his vernacular version more accessible to his target audience, something Ælfric of Eynsham, the author of two series of Catholic homilies and a series of saints' lives, among other texts, seems to have done on a regular basis. Another Anglo-Saxon translator, the anonymous one responsible for producing the OE version of Bede's *Ecclesiastical History* makes more overt, and to many, more systematic changes in his source material. Among other things, he omits a substantial amount of material, including 'most of the Roman history and Easter controversy .... [and] Bede's detailed account of the Pelagian heresy and St. Germanius's battle against it' (Rowley, 4), and he also rearranges much of the original's material. To many critics, this OE translator's handling of his source material bespeaks not only his intellectual limitations but more importantly his failure to understand Bede's vision for the *EH* and the methodology foundational to it. When we situate Alfred's and the Anglo-Saxon translator of Bede's practices alongside those of their fellow Anglo-Saxon translators, we discover that virtually all of them handle their source material in ways that strike our modern sensibilities as being rather free, if not downright fast and loose. Sources are usually left unidentified by the translator, something seen clearly in the practice of the translator of the *Old English Martyrology* who, in compiling his text, appears to have consulted 'more than two hundred' sources (Cross, 'On the library', 249), many of which have been confidently identified but many of which 'remain unidentified' (Cross, 'On the library', 248). However, once we adjust our critical expectations and acknowledge that the principle of strict fidelity to the source text and the desire to reproduce it as accurately as possible, both of which are important to our contemporary sensibilities, did not weigh heavily, if at all, upon Anglo-Saxon translators, we can better consider and appreciate the ways in which Anglo-Saxon translators (and authors) routinely, and with varying degrees of success, 'appropriated the past, translating history ... into new political and cultural contexts' (Rowley, 5).

Finally, because Anglo-Saxon poets articulate their verbal art via the channels of the specialized, dedicated register of oral poetics, those extant poems based on known sources afford us the opportunity to examine the different ways poets utilize the 'unique significative capabilities' (Foley, *Singer of Tales*, 181) of their native poetic tradition's expressive economy as they produce what John Miles Foley has aptly, and usefully, labelled 'indexed translations' (*Singer of Tales*, 184). We will consider the nature of this expressive economy more fully below when we touch upon the school of criticism known as oral theory, but for now it is important to recall that the presence of this expressive economy, be it realized in a traditional lexical metonym, such as 'gebolgen' [swollen with anger, enraged] as in *Juliana*, *Andreas*, *Genesis A* and elsewhere (see Amodio, *Writing the Oral Tradition*, 59–66), in a verbal formula such as the 'I heard' collocation that begins *Exodus* and is found in other source-based poems (see Parks, 'The traditional narrator'), or in a traditional theme such as the beasts of battle found in *Andreas* and elsewhere (see Olsen, *Speech, Song, and Poetic Craft*, 45–50), sheds a great deal of light on the processes (both individual and collective) by which Anglo-Saxon authors turned their Latin prose sources into vernacular poems. Because source studies generally, and logically, proceed by cataloguing and assessing similarities, divergences, and absences, they provide an important point of departure for other, more theoretically oriented approaches. But before turning to some of these approaches, we will first consider ones that are similarly also grounded in matters more material than theoretical, such as manuscript, palaeographic, and syntactic/grammatical studies.

Manuscript Studies

Because they are rare and very often unique components of Anglo-Saxon material culture, the extant manuscripts from the period have long been the objects of critical attention. Many have suffered damage over the centuries of their existence, and so considering any given manuscript's physical condition is a crucial first step in understanding the text(s) it preserves. Critical editions of Anglo-Saxon prose and poetic texts routinely include detailed descriptions of the manuscripts' physical characteristics such as the size of the page, the number of gatherings, and the style and size of the script, because the rarity and fragility of the manuscripts severely – and understandably – limits direct access to them. Although published more than fifty years ago, N.R. Ker's *Catalogue of Manuscripts containing Anglo-Saxon* remains an indispensible source of information on the physical details and likely dates of composition of manuscripts containing vernacular texts. Helmut Gneuss's *Handlist of Anglo-Saxon Manuscripts: A List of Manuscripts and Manuscript Fragments Written or Owned in England up to 1100* serves as a welcome and necessary companion to Ker because it strives to be 'a complete inventory of *all* surviving manuscripts and fragments of the period, including those exclusively in Latin' (Gneuss, 1; his emphasis). Palaeography, an integral component of manuscript studies, provides important clues regarding the dates at which manuscripts were written and often the locales in which they were produced.

The Anglo-Saxon Literature Handbook, First Edition. Mark C. Amodio.
© 2014 Mark C. Amodio. Published 2014 by John Wiley & Sons, Ltd.

Grammatical and Syntactic Studies

Grammatical and syntactic studies have long been important components of Anglo-Saxon studies, and while grammars are among the works extant from Anglo-Saxon England, they are all devoted to explaining Latin, not vernacular grammar. Only a small handful, including ones by Bede (*De orthographia*), Alcuin (*Ars grammatica*), and Ælfric of Eynsham (*Grammar*) survive (whether more were written and lost is impossible to determine), and with the exception of Ælfric's, which he wrote in a mixture of the vernacular and Latin, they are entirely in Latin. It is not until OE texts become the objects of concerted critical interest in the nineteenth century that comprehensive examinations of the language begin appearing, culminating in Bruce Mitchell's magisterial two-volume *Old English Syntax*. Scholars continue to explore the language's grammar, syntax, and lexicon not only to further our understanding of how such things as, say, the negative indefinites (Mitchell, *Old English Syntax*, I. 176–79, §436–46) or clauses of purpose and result (Mitchell, *Old English Syntax*, II. 414–522, §2802–3006) function, but also to help situate texts more fully within their temporal moments and geographical locations (see Amos). In addition, an examination of texts' syntax and grammar can often further our understanding of their generic affiliations and traits, and, perhaps most intriguingly and most importantly, texts' grammatical and syntactic stylistics can shed light on the identity of Anglo-Saxon authors, most of whom, as we have seen in Parts 2 and 3 above, remain unknown to us. As Daniel Donoghue demonstrates in *Style in Old English Poetry: The Test of the Auxiliary*, approaching the poems of Cynewulf, one of the few named Anglo-Saxon poets, with an eye towards their grammatical and syntactic stylistics helps to support, and also to question, the 'common authorship already assumed' (106) of the four

The Anglo-Saxon Literature Handbook, First Edition. Mark C. Amodio.
© 2014 Mark C. Amodio. Published 2014 by John Wiley & Sons, Ltd.

poems that are routinely attributed to him largely because they bear Cynewulf's runic 'signature'. There are many features of Anglo-Saxon literature that prevent us from deploying with the same degree of success the type of literary forensics Don Foster has developed and so brilliantly applied in *Author Unknown* to a temporally and generically broad range of texts, but since our extant OE texts best preserve the linguistic footprints of their unknown authors (even if in many cases undoubtedly filtered through those of the unknown scribes and copyists who participated directly in the process of textual production and dissemination), the grammar, syntax, punctuation, and general *mise-en-page* of our OE texts rank as among the most important, and most concrete evidence that survives from the period.

Theoretical Perspectives

As is true for the literature produced in all subsequent periods of English literary history, OE prose and verse texts are now routinely explored by scholars working within (and often among) a wide variety of theoretical schools, but such was not always the case. In the not-too-distant past, the study of medieval England's earliest texts was largely seen as the purview of those who, in Dr Johnson's memorable words, wandered into the 'dusty deserts of barren philology' (*A Dictionary of the English Language*, vii). Anglo-Saxon literary criticism is rooted in the largely philological enquiries undertaken by nineteenth-century continental scholars and for a long time philological concerns dominated the field, but beginning around the middle of the last century a wide number of critical approaches have been applied to OE prose and verse texts with results that are oftentimes as productive as they are intriguing. Not every approach has found complete – or easy – acceptance as there are still those within and without the field who question the validity of applying to OE texts critical approaches that were initially developed for and/or applied to texts from more contemporary periods in English literary history. Indeed, as the editors of the recent critical casebook, *The Postmodern Beowulf*, note in their preface, Anglo-Saxonists who 'engage contemporary, poststructuralist criticism often find themselves "challenged as intruders, as strangers on the beach, not unlike the way Beowulf and his retainers rouse the coastguard's suspicion as they arrive in Denmark"' (Joy and Ramsey, xiii; citing Frantzen, 'Who do these Anglo-Saxon(ist)s think they are', 4). While contemporary theories and their attendant methodologies are regularly trumpeted by their adherents (and derided by their detractors), it is, oddly, chiefly (and perhaps only) among Anglo-Saxonists that we discover an almost apologetic defensiveness about

The Anglo-Saxon Literature Handbook, First Edition. Mark C. Amodio.
© 2014 Mark C. Amodio. Published 2014 by John Wiley & Sons, Ltd.

the whole enterprise of bringing contemporary theory to OE texts. Even Allen Frantzen, in a spirited and wide-ranging defence of his own *Desires for Origin*, a methodologically innovative work heavily criticized by Joyce Hill (among others), is careful to establish his grounding in what he labels the more 'traditional' modes of approaching Anglo-Saxon literature and the 'knowledge of languages, history, literature, and culture ... that medieval scholarship requires' ('Who do these Anglo-Saxon(ist)s think they are', 3). That those who seek to expand the critical focus of the field do so with a certain amount of defensiveness is understandable because, as Joy and Ramsey, striking a note similar to one sounded by Frantzen and others, observe, 'within the field of Old English ..., the resistance to theory, in general, has been strong, and occasionally mean-spirited' (xiii). While we do not have the space to explore further the issues of this internecine conflict, it is important to recall that in and of themselves, theoretical approaches are neither valid nor invalid; what matters, of course, is how responsibly they are applied because while theories of all kinds can and frequently do open up important windows onto the workings of Anglo-Saxon literature, they can also function as a meat-grinder does in that whatever combination of raw materials is fed into it emerges from the other end in a form that was predetermined at the start of the process. The key to being a responsible interpreter, of whatever critical persuasion, is to approach each text on its own terms instead of attempting to force it into a preconceived and often ill-fitting interpretive scheme.

Space does not permit a full treatment of the many and varied critical perspectives that are routinely used to further our understanding of Anglo-Saxon literature, so what follows will necessarily be a cursory and highly selective glance at just a few of them, and at only a small fraction of the intriguing and enlightening critical work that has been produced in each field.

Christianity

Given both the important cultural position Christianity comes to acquire in England during the Anglo-Saxon period and given the heavily Christian focus and subject matter of much of the prose and poetry extant from the period – the great majority of which was both created and physically encoded on the page by Christian clerics –, it is not surprising that the Christian sources, contexts, and focus of much Anglo-Saxon literature have all attracted considerable attention. Scholars have approached the issue from perspectives that run the gamut from the biblical exegesis of Margaret

Goldsmith and Alvin Lee to Paul Remley's rather more nuanced and sensitive attempts to contextualize the four Christian poems in the Junius manuscript by carefully tracking down and considering the possible Biblical sources of each, to Edward B. Irving Jr's equally subtle and even-handed reading of the nature of Christianity in *Beowulf*. The different approaches advocated by these scholars each have many adherents and the broad perspectives within which they operate can be summarized as follows: the first two are interested in demonstrating the degree to which individual OE texts can be seen as reflecting and articulating a Christian worldview, while the latter two resist placing the argumentative cart before the textual horse, choosing rather to assess carefully the texts before attempting to situate them within the larger context of Christian writings and thinking. At the outset of her study, Goldsmith makes her aims clear when she announces that '*Beowulf* is a Christian allegory of the life of man' (4). From this point of departure, she works to support her reading of what is arguably one of the most wholly secular pieces of literature to survive from the period. In a similar vein, Lee bases his study on the premise that 'the total argument of [*Guest Hall*] is an attempt to demonstrate how the extant Old English poetic corpus has as its major function in Anglo-Saxon England the re-creation, in poetic terms, of the biblical vision of human life' (6) because, in his view, 'most Old English poetry reflects ... an imaginative unity ... that is at once heroic, Germanic, didactic, *and* Christian' (6; emphasis his). The contrast between Goldsmith's and Lee's comments and, say, Remley's contention that 'when we attempt to make sense of the heterogeneous contents of Junius 11, ... it remains necessary to maintain a distinction between the received text of the sequence of biblical poetry in the manuscript and the literary content and meaning of the verse itself' (4) or Irving's more pointed assertion that although 'the early Middle Ages provided an ample supply of patristic material, to argue ... that it must have been put to use – that no vernacular poet could have fought off the urge to wrap any plain tale he had to tell in rich folds of typology, allegory and deeper meanings' ('Nature of Christianity', 7) is indefensible both speak directly to and usefully illuminate just how disparate the interpretive strategies used to investigate the Christian elements of OE prose and poetry can be. There are, of course, a great many studies that fall between the extremes cited above, including, to take but one example, Thomas D. Hill's nuanced and convincing reading of Elene as *Ecclesia* in his 'Sapiential structure and figural narrative in the Old English *Elene*', that put the Christian elements in Anglo-Saxon literature into profitable conversation with everything from late-antique patristic writings, to Freudian psychoanalysis, to Biblical exegesis, to contemporary popular culture.

Germanic legend

Although elements of Germanic legend are neither so deeply imbued nor so widespread in Anglo-Saxon literature, especially in the prose, as are Christian ones, they nevertheless are present, in a small number of texts – including *Beowulf*, *The Finnsburh Fragment*, *Deor*, *Widsið*, *Waldere*, Anglo-Saxon genealogies, and some versions of the Anglo-Saxon Chronicle – if usually only in an oblique, allusive, and possibly fractured fashion. Unlike the legendary material that survives from early medieval Iceland, a closely related Germanic culture whose literary remains post-date the Anglo-Saxon era, the legendary foundations of OE poetry and prose, which have always loomed much larger in the critical imagination than on the manuscript page, are neither well nor fully preserved. This situation has not, however, in Roberta Frank's insightful and witty view, kept this particular 'cabbage-patch' from being 'well trampled' ('Germanic legend', 89), especially by earlier generations of scholars, many of whom operated under the assumption that the traces of Germanic legend found in Anglo-Saxon literature were evidence of the earliest and purest stage of English literary history, a stage that existed before the literature and the pagan culture it was believed to preserve were forever altered under the pens of Christianizing monks. Writing on a closely related topic, that of the search for Anglo-Saxon paganism, E.G. Stanley discovers that many of those who were convinced that the literary records afforded ample evidence of Germanic paganism usually, and unsurprisingly, found what they 'were looking for' (*Search*, 83), a comment that also applies equally well to much of the early work done on the role of Germanic legend in Anglo-Saxon literature.

A considerable proportion of the legendary material that survives does so in two poems, *Deor* and *Widsið*, that present it in catalogue-like form, much as Homer does in the well-known, and lengthy, catalogue of ships found in Book II (579–905) of the *Iliad*. In all three poems, the legendary material offered amounts to little more than the recitation of the hero's name, which is supplemented, for the Anglo-Saxon heroes, by mention of their tribal affiliations in some cases, and, for the Greek heroes, by mention of their native cities and the number of ships that accompanied each of them. Aside from this sparsely presented information, there is very little elaboration. Even in the rare instances when an Anglo-Saxon author elaborates on legendary material, as when the *Beowulf*-poet uses a few broad strokes to sketch the entirety of Scyld Scefing's life at the poem's beginning, the compressed and highly allusive fashion in which legendary material is presented suggests its intended audiences' deep familiarity with the narratives of what to contemporary audiences are in many instances figures about whom we know nothing beyond their names. To borrow Foley's formulation, these names function as traditional metonyms that bring to the surface of the narrative present in which they occur 'a wealth of associations' (*Immanent Art*, 11) now largely lost to us but readily available to the poems' intended audiences, audiences, that is, that were steeped in the traditions in which the poems are situated.

Just how resonant these associations were remains unmeasureable. On the one hand, the lack of legendary material may have been the result of a conscious program of excision on the part of the Christian clerics/scribes from whose pens most, and perhaps all, of our surviving Anglo-Saxon texts derive, but, on the other hand, it may stem from entirely other causes. The question Alcuin, the great eighth-century cleric, poses with obvious disapproval in a letter to a bishop he identifies as 'Speratus', 'Quid Hinieldus cum Christo?' (Dümmler, 183) [What has Hinield (Ingeld) to do with Christ?], is often thought to witness both the presence of non-Christian material within a Christian community and Alcuin's understandably dim view of it. Both of these surmises may be correct, but J.A. Bullough's observation that 'Nowhere else in the substantial corpus of his letters does Alcuin name a known figure in early Germanic legend and literature – the Ingeld of *Beowulf* and *Widsith* – or refer specifically to the vernacular literature of his home country' (93), casts matters in a somewhat different light, and suggests that the metonymic referentiality of the named legendary figures in Anglo-Saxon literature is less powerful than often supposed. If this were the case, it would help to explain why, in part, there is very little cross-referencing of traditional figures in the extant literature. Were it not, to take but one example, for the survival of the Cotton Vitellius A.xv manuscript, we would know nothing of the eponymous hero of *Beowulf* since no mention of him survives outside the borders of the poem. Several of the poem's other figures are mentioned elsewhere in the period's surviving literary record, most notably Hnæf, Offa, and Hrothgar (all in *Widsið*), but no external reference to its central figure, Beowulf, is found in any OE prose or poetic text. It may well be, as Craig R. Davis suggests, that 'the few extant tales of pagan times survived in part because of their relatively low cultural profile' (9). Whether the few non-Christian works to come down to us from Anglo-Saxon England had a low profile is, of course, open to debate, and even if it could be established that they did, we would remain unable to determine whether such a profile helped preserve them from Christian clerics/scribes who routinely eradicated traces of the pagan past, or whether it witnessed the place of the distant, pagan, legendary past in 'an increasingly hostile, or perhaps merely preoccupied, intellectual culture' (C. Davis, 162). This aspect of Anglo-Saxon culture has received, and will continue to receive, considerable scrutiny from contemporary students of the period, but it may well be that the Anglo-Saxons themselves spent more time living in the present moment, anticipating and contemplating the future than gazing backward.

Gender

Although gender studies and, more specifically, those that focus on feminist matters and concerns, are well-established components of the contemporary critical landscape, they were until fairly recently not common in Anglo-Saxon studies. In fact, as the co-editors of *New Readings on Women in Old English Literature*, Helen Damico and Alexandra Hennessey Olsen, observe, at the time of its publication in 1990 their volume of 'critical studies on women in Old English literature' was 'the first and only one of its kind' (*New Readings*, vii). Most of the essays Damico and Olsen include had been previously published, something that attests to the considerable interest in gender studies prior to the volume's publication, but in putting together this collection the editors called attention to these studies and to the need for more like them. In one of the essays that appeared in print for the first time in the volume, Alain Renoir challenges what he sees as 'a fundamental dogma of the twentieth century', namely 'that the Middle Ages had nothing but contempt for the intelligence of women' ('Eve's I.Q. rating', 262). After carefully reassessing Eve's role in the fall as presented by the *Genesis B*-poet, Renoir concludes his argument, which he labels as 'obviously female sexist' in opposition to the prevailing 'male sexist' readings of the poem, with a lengthy comment that, because of its insightfulness and continued relevance, is cited here in full:

> the very fact that one can mount some kind of argument in defense of Eve's intelligence suggests a perfectly outrageous and futile hypothesis which I cannot refrain from formulating here: If mediaeval English studies had been initiated by female scholars nurtured on the Germanic tradition rather than by male scholars nurtured on the French and monastic traditions, our fundamental dogma today might conceivably be that the Middle Ages unexceptionally assumed the intellectual superiority of women.
>
> (Renoir, 'Eve's I.Q. rating', 271)

In an early, important book that approached Anglo-Saxon literature from the perspective of gender studies/feminist criticism, *Woman as Hero in Old English Literature*, Jane Chance posits that 'There were ... two archetypes of women that ordered the Anglo-Saxon social world', both of which 'were drawn from the Bible': Eve, the 'overly-aggressive retainer', and Mary, 'the perfect maiden, wife, mother – and heroic and militant Ecclesia figure' (xvii). While the sharply bifurcated view she adopts proves somewhat restrictive and over-determined in practice, it does allow Chance to discuss a wide range of the female characters who populate OE poetry and prose, and throughout her discussion she not only focuses attention on what had been long-neglected subject matter, but she demonstrates that the female characters of Anglo-Saxon literature should occupy a central, not peripheral, position in the critical conversation. In an essay that appeared several years after Chance's book, Karma Lochrie takes a similar, but somewhat more nuanced and flexible approach, one that well illustrates how powerful and appropriate a tool feminist criticism can be in the interpretation of Anglo-Saxon literature. Focusing her attention on the poem *Judith*, Lochrie explores what she sees as the poem's crisis inducing intersection of the categories 'of gender and social rank' ('Gender', 5), an intersection that leads directly to a stunning cultural inversion in Judith's appropriation of 'the masculine fantasies of rape and violence in her decapitation of Holofernes and her subsequent exhortation to battle' (14). As Lochrie compellingly argues, 'The twin categories of the masculine and the feminine undergird the larger structures of rank (leader/subordinate) and of war (victors/conquered and sexual violence/military violence). When these categories are crossed or undone, as they are when Judith decapitates Holofernes, a crisis of individual and collective identity ensues' (16). The rarity of the actions that give rise to this crisis witness its depth and unsettling nature: women are far more frequently subjected to violence, as, for example, is Juliana in the eponymous poem in which she appears and, although Anglo-Saxon literature fairly swarms with examples of male violence (enacted alike upon males and females, as well as demons and monsters), Judith stands with Grendel's mother as one of the only female figures who directly engage in violence. And even then, the *Beowulf*-poet's insistence on Grendel's mother's otherness, her monstrosity, places her in a more liminal category than Judith occupies since Judith remains an indisputably human figure, albeit one situated by her gender, race, religion, and actions at the very edges of the poet's expressive economy.

Although medieval gender studies, like their more contemporarily focused counterparts, continue to be dominated by feminist concerns and approaches, the problematics of medieval masculinity and the field of men's studies have begun to attract critical attention because, as Thelma Fenster puts it in her preface to *Medieval Masculinities: Regarding Men in the Middle Ages*, 'While apotheosizing its perceivedly important men, historical discourse effaced the perceivedly unimportant ones – the millions of men who were only men' (x). In an essay in the same collection, Clare A. Lees turns her attention specifically to the Anglo-Saxon cultural world and focuses on *Beowulf*'s 're-presentation of patriarchy and of masculine values' as a way of understanding 'just what kind of perspective on men in what kinds of institutions *Beowulf* offers' ('Men and *Beowulf*', 141). As she argues in her conclusion, it is only by looking afresh at and questioning the poem's 'ideologies of patriarchy and masculinism' (146) – ideologies that long ago took on the air of received truths – that students of the poem can avoid the trap of 'falling into glib and easy statements' about both 'its apparent celebration of male violence' (146) and its masculinist focus and aims.

Psychological

One of the general characteristics of Anglo-Saxon literature is that it does not frequently, or in any real depth, explore the interiority of its characters, and, perhaps as a result, psychological and psychoanalytical approaches have to date been only occasionally adopted. The *Beowulf*-poet, for example, rarely exposes the inner workings of his characters' minds, and in the majority of the instances when he does so, he only reports on the characters' anger. Just before the final – and mutually fatal – meeting between Beowulf and the dragon we learn that the 'wyrm' [dragon] is 'yrre' (2669b) [angry], and just before the fight begins we learn that Beowulf is 'gebolgen' (2550b) [swollen with anger] (2550b) as he stands in front of the dragon's barrow and utters what may be some sort of battle-cry. Beyond these and the several other reports of characters' anger contained in the poem, the poet only rarely offers glimpses of his characters' thoughts, and on the very few occasions when he chooses to do so, he does so briefly and cryptically. For example, when, after crashing in the doors of Heorot, Grendel stands surveying the sleeping Danes upon whom he expects to feast, we learn that 'Þa his mod ahlog' [then his mind laughed] (730b). Similarly, Beowulf's 'breost innan weoll, / þeostrum geþoncum, swa him geþywe ne wæs' (2331b–32) [breast welled within with dark thoughts, as was not customary for him], after he learns that the dragon has destroyed his hall.

Despite Anglo-Saxon literature's focus chiefly on external, rather than internal matters, a number of intriguing and interesting psychological and psychoanalytical studies have been produced, including articles by Renoir and Michael Lapidge that explore the psychology of *Beowulf* largely via the pathway of the poem's affective dynamics, and a book by James W. Earl that remains one of the few to view Anglo-Saxon literature through the lens of psychoanalytical theory. In 'Point of view and design for terror in *Beowulf*', Alain

Renoir argues that 'the *Beowulf* poet masterfully succeeds not only in selecting immediately effective details but also in presenting them from such points of view as are likely to arouse the most appropriate emotional reactions in the audience' (158). To illustrate Renoir's point – and the poet's technique – we need look no further than Grendel's eyes, the 'one detail that is most symbolic of the mysteriously destructive force which [the poet] wishes to suggest' (166). Grendel's eyes are mentioned only once in the poem, as he stands in the doorway of Heorot gazing upon the Geats sleeping before him, and even though 'we cannot see the monster himself, the sight of his eyes gives us the distressing sensation that *he* can see us' (166; his emphasis). The sudden, and unannounced, shift in point of view that accompanies the detail of Grendel's eyes uncomfortably aligns the audience with the Geats he anticipates devouring in what Renoir rightly asserts is 'one of the most effective presentations of terror in English literature' (167). In '*Beowulf* and the psychology of terror', Lapidge first establishes the ways in which *Beowulf* is 'permeated' with terror before exploring why 'the *Beowulf*-poet was so interested in the representation' (386) of it. After briefly surveying the work of some early psychoanalysts, including Freud, on nightmares and establishing that 'there are close similarities between the *Beowulf*-poet's description of Grendel and the monsters of nightmares as known to modern psychologists' (391), Lapidge concludes that the poet's 'presentation of Grendel … betrays his fascination with the workings of the human mind and the mechanism of fear' (394).

Earl devotes fully the second half of his *Thinking about 'Beowulf'* 'to issues of individual consciousness, creativity, and reader response' (viii), and, as he states at the beginning of Chapter 4, '*Beowulf* and the Men's Hall', he is deeply interested in 'testing the usefulness of psychoanalytic anthropology as an approach to *Beowulf*' (100). Contending that the 'role of psychoanalysis in critical thinking today … is to reassert the value and legitimacy of the individual (whether the author or the reader) as a focus of critical attention and the importance of the unconscious and the irrational in interpretation – and in mental life generally' (164–65), Earl argues finally that 'the poem functions as a screen for our projections, which can be manipulated by the plot and predictably drawn toward resolution' (173). His approach, which is predicated heavily both on 'Freud's theory of identification' (101) and on his examination of the workings of his own subconsciousness (he analyses several of his own dreams), differs sharply from those adopted by Renoir and Lapidge, but in their own way all three – and the other psychologically and psychoanalytically oriented studies that have to date been produced – help to bridge what is often mistakenly assumed to be the enormous and insurmountable gulf that separates the culture and literature of Anglo-Saxon England from those of the present day.

Oral-traditional

The final critical approach we will consider is one that focuses on the medieval English oral tradition and the role it played in shaping the literature extant from Anglo-Saxon England. Perhaps more so than any other critical school, oral theory has generated considerable – and in some quarters continuing – controversy since it was applied in its earliest incarnations to OE poetry beginning in the 1950s. The reasons for oral theory's complex and at times hostile reception cannot be delved into here, but for our purposes it will suffice to say that the insistence of early oralists on both the mutual exclusivity of the oral and the literate and on the 'orality' of the surviving texts (all of which are indisputably written products) were important contributing factors to what threatened to develop into a critical impasse in the late 1970s, as was an at times marked unwillingness (and/or inability) on the part of non-oralists to accept a new and admittedly radical paradigm for the composition and dissemination of works of verbal art. By the end of the following decade, however, the work of scholars such as Katherine O'Brien O'Keeffe, Alain Renoir, and especially John Miles Foley began to move the field of oral studies beyond the heavily, almost exclusively, structuralist focus it inherited from the theory of oral-formulaic composition (which is also known as the Parry-Lord theory after its two chief architects, Milman Parry and Albert B. Lord), the school of thought that determined the field's contours for close to three decades.

What was, and for some still is, unsettling about oral theory is that it is not centred on the technology of literacy and the literate habits of mind it engenders, but instead proposes a very different model for the composition and dissemination of verbal art, one in which composition takes place only in public via the tongue instead of in private via the pen (or nowadays the computer keyboard). Further, oral texts, because they exist only in the moments they are articulated, have neither the fixity nor the physicality that literate texts, by virtue of their being encoded on the page, possess. Since until fairly recently only one technology – writing – was available for the recording of verbal art, our understanding of the medieval English oral tradition is destined to remain both imperfect and highly speculative as no unequivocably oral and non-written evidence of the medieval English oral tradition survives. This, however, does not mean that we must remain completely in the dark regarding it. Thanks to the work of oral theorists we now possess a firm understanding of how oral literature could be composed and disseminated before (and even during) the rise of literacy, and, in the oral poetics that are everywhere evidenced in the written poetic records (and at times in the surviving prose), we can discover evidence of the oral tradition's nature and functionality.

One of the most important advances in the development of oral theory was the recognition that not only does traditional oral verbal art differ from literate verbal art in the manner in which it is composed and disseminated, but its aesthetics and mode of transmitting meaning differ as well. While from its earliest days oral theory focused on understanding the former, it paid scant, if any, attention to the latter until the late 1980s when a number of scholars independently began exploring the aesthetics and affective dynamics of traditional oral verbal art, two areas of enquiry that did not fit comfortably, if at all, within the narrow and strict structuralist confines of oral-formulaic criticism because it posited that oral poets were not conscious artists who leave their unique impress on every line of the texts they create, but rather were mere facilitators who simply reassembled inherited, pre-fabricated elements and patterns (lexical, thematic, and narrative) into recognizable, and hence acceptable, forms. Some fifty years ago, Eric Havelock memorably summed up the view of the oral poet that would come to dominate oral theory for several decades: the oral poet is, Havelock tells us, best thought of as a 'man living in a large house crowded with furniture, both necessary and elaborate. His task is to thread his way through the house, touching and feeling the furniture as he goes and reporting its shape and texture.' While acknowledging that 'The route he chooses will have its own design', Havelock contends that this is the sole contribution the oral-traditional poet makes to the works of verbal art he fashions because since 'This house, these rooms, and the furniture he did not himself fashion', he can only 'recall them to us' (*Preface to Plato*, 88–89).

That thinkers such as Lord, Havelock, and the many who followed them failed to recognize or acknowledge the aesthetics of traditional verbal art points not to shortcomings on their part, but rather to just how deeply and thoroughly ingrained literate practices and habits of mind were at the time of the theory's early application to medieval English literature, and to how deeply ingrained they still are. The formulaic lexical and narrative collocations upon which oralists focused received the attention they did precisely because they so clearly index compositional strategies and habits of mind very different from the ones that came to dominate soon after the Norman Conquest, and that continue to dominate today.

Whereas in contemporary discourse 'formulaic' carries a mostly derogatory sense (as in 'I found that film formulaic'), in the context of early medieval English literature 'formulaic' is a neutral term used to describe one of OE poetry's most salient features: the repeated phrasal (and larger) narrative collocations found throughout the corpus. The verbal and thematic formulas in OE verse most likely developed, along with the singular metrical system in which verse was always articulated in Anglo-Saxon England, as an aid to oral poets, for whom composition and public performance were simultaneous and necessarily interdependent actions. That formulas play such an important role in shaping the verse extant from Anglo-Saxon England – all of which is unquestionably written – witnesses not the continued presence of a functioning oral tradition throughout the period, but rather the degree to which that tradition continued to influence the compositional strategies and practices of literate poets who, even though they composed pen-in-hand, continued to engage the expressive economy of medieval English oral poetics. And, as recent work by Samantha Zacher (*Preaching the Converted*) and Tiffany Beechy (*The Poetics of Old English*) has demonstrated, evidence of oral poetics is also found in the prose records.

While numerous studies contributed to the re-imagining and re-vivifying of oral theory, we will close with the briefest of glances at two works by Foley, *Traditional Oral Epic* and *Immanent Art*, and one by Renoir, *A Key to Old Poems*, because in the first one Foley offers what remains one of the most important explorations of the structural workings of traditional verbal art and because in the other two Foley and Renoir establish important and productive theoretical frameworks for understanding the aesthetics and affective dynamics of traditional verbal art. *Traditional Oral Epic*, as Foley states at its outset, focuses nearly exclusively on structural matters and 'attempts to outline a comparative context for studies of phraseology and narrative pattern in various traditions of oral epic' (x). Rather than working from the assumption, as many had, that all oral traditions function similarly, Foley advocates a '"tradition-dependent" perspective – a point of view that understands oral traditions (and oral-derived texts) as individual expressions of an enormously large and complex phenomenon' (ix). Although this may appear to be somewhat of a given, it was a revolutionary insight at the time it was first articulated because for decades oral traditions had been treated as if all their particulars could be subsumed under a one-size-fits-all model of Oral Tradition. Many oral traditions do have features that connect them to each other (such as composition in performance, reliance on formulaic expressions, and a specialized, dedicated lexicon and metrics), but each tradition nonetheless instantiates these features in unique, often idiosyncratic ways. Failing to take this into account, as for many years was the case, led to many impertinent and inappropriate questions being asked, as well as to conclusions that were at times forced and inaccurate since the expressive economies through which different cultures articulate their oral traditions are 'formed in symbiosis with [the traditions'] various meters and general prosodies' (*Traditional Oral Epic*, 389).

The final two works we will glance at were among the first to expand oral theory's focus beyond the structural to the aesthetic, as Renoir's title (*A Key to Old Poems*) and Foley's subtitle to *Immanent Art* (*From Structure to Meaning in Traditional Oral Epic*) both announce. These two works, perhaps more than any others, helped direct the field of oral studies towards the productive ground it continues to occupy today. Both studies acknowledge the necessity of being well grounded in the structural principles of any given tradition as a necessary first step in analysing oral-traditional verbal art, and each goes on to explore the specialized ways in which this verbal art transmits meaning. For Renoir, awareness of the rhetorical contexts in which any given piece of verbal art, oral or written, was composed and within which it was intended to be received, is a crucial pre-condition to responsible interpretation 'because an understanding of a given rhetorical system is necessary to grasp certain aspects of works composed within that system' (*Key to Old Poems*, 132). Once armed with such understanding, interpreters must still learn to 'take the text on its own terms and to base our interpretation on such rhetorical tradition or traditions as we find clearly represented there ... [because] [i]n doing so, we spare ourselves the frustration of looking for things that are not there while overlooking those that are' ('Oral-formulaic rhetoric', 135). By concentrating on the affective dynamics of texts drawn from a variety of different time periods and composed within different rhetorical traditions, Renoir both establishes the effectiveness of his approach and works to establish an interpretive framework within which to situate the aesthetics of traditional verbal art.

Foley's *Immanent Art* follows the same trajectory as Renoir's in that its focus is on aesthetic and interpretive matters, rather than performative and structural ones. While both offer careful close readings of texts rooted in different oral traditions and while both approach the question of traditional oral aesthetics from a largely Receptionalist perspective, Foley's *Immanent Art* also looks more globally at oral traditional aesthetics and offers the first in-depth model for understanding not just how traditional verbal art is constructed, but how it means as well. Similarly, Renoir, in a discussion of the different kinds of contexts in which texts from oral and written traditions are situated importantly distinguishes between a text's '*intrinsic context*', which he defines as 'the context provided by the text proper' and its '*extrinsic context*', or 'the context drawn from outside'

(*Key to Old Poems*, 18; his emphasis) the text proper, that is, the context supplied by the text's recipient. In drawing a distinction between the way meaning is encoded in the verbal art produced within oral and literate traditions, Foley proposes a related set of terms: 'conferred' and 'inherent' meaning. As Foley explains, 'In the modern literary work of art we place the highest priority on a writer's personal manipulation of original or inherited material' and a text within a literate tradition 'is praised for the finesse with which an author (not a tradition) *confers* meaning on his or her creation' (*Immanent Art*, 8; his emphasis). In contrast, because the expressive economy within which a traditional work is expressed is 'metonymic' and summons 'conventional connotations to conventional structures', the 'meaning it conveys is principally *inherent*' and 'depends primarily on elements and strategies that were in place long before the execution of the present version of the text' (8; his emphasis).

The distinction Foley draws between 'inherent' and 'conferred' meaning is analogous to the one Renoir draws between 'intrinsic' and 'extrinsic' contexts: were we to combine these two useful sets of terms, we would say that individual poets working within an active, performative oral tradition and those working within a literate, non-performative tradition in which oral poetics continues to shape the form and guide the reception of works of verbal art negotiate *extrinsic* pathways of *inherent* meaning at the same time that they *intrinsically confer* meaning (which may be traditional or idiosyncratic and hence post-traditional or some combination of the two) upon the works of verbal art they create. While these modes of meaning are very different, it is important to note, as both Renoir and Foley do, that their relationship is symbiotic, not competitive. Although, for example, the heavily formulaic nature of medieval English oral poetics led many early investigators mistakenly to believe that the poets who engaged it were somehow imprisoned by it, the expressive economy of which oral poetics is such an important component is no more imprisoning than is that of modern English: expressive economies may differ in many, if not most, of their salient details, but at the base communicative level each one uniquely licenses and enables the fluent expression of simple or complex ideas. As anyone who has ever learned a foreign language, especially an inflected or non-Indo-European one knows, modes of expression different from one's native mode often seem impenetrable, as the meaning and etymology of the word 'barbarian' bears out. The ancient Greeks used the word to identify 'all those who are not Greek', and the word itself appears to be an echoic approximation/ recreation of what, to the Greeks' ears, were the unintelligible sounds uttered by foreigners.

But while the 'foreignness' of the constitutive elements of Anglo-Saxon oral poetics (such as its formulaic expressions and lexical and thematic systems) contributed to their being easily identified, that of their aesthetics had just the opposite effect: because it was so different from that with which investigators were familiar, the aesthetics of texts composed within the expressive economy of oral poetics proved more, rather than less, difficult to see and understand. Further compounding the situation, the very interpretive strategies that were routinely brought to bear on texts composed within the expressive economy of oral poetics were poorly suited to the task because they were developed as ways of understanding the literate poetics that spreads inexorably in the post-Conquest period, not the oral poetics through which verbal art had to be articulated throughout the Anglo-Saxon period. In treating texts composed within oral poetics as if they had been composed within the very different confines of a literate poetics, investigators could not help but ask questions that frequently led to unproductive and even mistaken answers. The reason for this is as simple as it was long in arriving: the literate habits and practices of mind that took root during the Anglo-Saxon period and began to flower and spread during the post-Conquest period came over several centuries to be so powerfully ingrained that scholars simply assumed that they had existed throughout the entirety of English literary history and that, therefore, the aesthetics of all English literature could profitably be viewed through a single perspective. Whatever did not conform to the literate aesthetic paradigm was judged to be, among other things, artistically deficient, mechanical, barbaric, or worse. The work done by Renoir, Foley, and others, including most notably O'Brien O'Keeffe in her *Visible Song: Transitional Literacy in Old English Verse*, is valuable not just for the insights into the mechanics and aesthetics of oral poetics found within it, but also because it helped bring to light a number of the unacknowledged, unquestioned, and closely held critical assumptions that had greatly impeded scholars' ability to recognize, let alone begin to interrogate, the ways in which meaning is encoded in the expressive economy of the medieval English oral tradition.

Despite their apparent stolidity and physicality, texts are infinitely malleable and, at times, extremely slippery. Texts are also remarkably responsive, something borne out by the valuable and wide-ranging criticism produced both by the few scholars who could be cited by name in this brief chapter as well as by the legions of others who have contributed, and who continue to contribute, to our ever-growing understanding of the literature extant from the earliest period of English literary history. But no matter which perspective one adopts, or, to be more precise, which perspectives one chooses to draw upon in formulating one's own, it is important to remember that criticism can, to return to the metaphor Renoir employs in the title of his 1989 book, serve as a key that unlocks and clarifies texts, but it can, if applied irresponsibly, frequently do neither.

Part 5

Themes

Anglo-Saxon Thematics

In the final section of this *Handbook*, we turn to consider a few of the major and minor themes that percolate through the poetry and prose extant from the Anglo-Saxon period. But before we can undertake even the sort of brief and cursory survey that follows, a few words of caution and explanation are in order since Anglo-Saxon thematics has some qualities that distinguish it in important ways from the thematics of other periods in English literary history. First the caution: as is equally true of much else that survives from the Anglo-Saxon period, if we were to approach the thematics of OE prose, and especially of OE verse, as if it were precisely analogous to the thematics of later literary periods, we would end up looking fruitlessly for things that are not there while overlooking what is, and we would further run the risk of asking unproductive questions. The need for this caution can be traced in part to the period's inescapable alterity; as we saw in the preceding chapter, when approaching Anglo-Saxon literature we need to be especially conscious of the interpretive strategies we bring to bear on it and we must be ready – and willing – to monitor them and to recalibrate them as necessary when, as is often the case, they prove inadequate to the task at hand. While the sort of critical self-awareness advocated here is, in general, a sound practice to follow, it is especially important when dealing with OE verse and prose because the thematics found in this literature is sharply bifurcated in a way that the thematics of no other period of English literary history is, for in the literary remains of Anglo-Saxon England we discover both a literate-based thematics that is very familiar to us because it functions as does contemporary thematics and a thematics that is very unfamiliar because it derives from the expres-

The Anglo-Saxon Literature Handbook, First Edition. Mark C. Amodio.
© 2014 Mark C. Amodio. Published 2014 by John Wiley & Sons, Ltd.

sive economy of oral poetics. That the former behaves and responds in familiar and expected ways points the at times deep connectivity that exists between the earliest period of English literary history and all subsequent ones: for example, the metaphor Alfred employs in the preface to his translation of St Augustine's *Soliloquies* to explain his compositional practices, namely that he constructs his edifice (his text) out of the works of various patristic writers (the woods from which he harvests the raw materials for his edifice), remains as clear and effective today as when he first composed it since the model of intertextuality he so eloquently invokes remains firmly in place, more than a thousand years after Alfred wrote. The latter, in contrast, requires that we adjust our interpretive strategies before it can be profitably approached, something that points the at times large gulf that separates the Anglo-Saxon period from the ones that follow it: for example, the word 'hwæt' with which the OE poem *Exodus* begins, far from being simply an introductory interjection, is a traditional metonym freighted with meaning (what John Miles Foley would label inherent meaning and with what Alain Renoir would label extrinsic meaning) that signals, in conjunction with the other elements of the 'I heard' formula of which it is part, the onset of a particular type of narrative. This latter type of thematics is a major component of the poetic records but as some recent work by, among others, Samantha Zacher and Tiffany Beechy has shown, it is also present in some prose works as well, something that suggests that the border between the genres of poetry and prose were more porous in the Anglo-Saxon period than they have subsequently become.

In what follows, we will variously consider both broad thematic elements such as the heroic or the eschatological, and focused and specific ones, such as the beasts of battle and the transitory nature of human existence. Some themes run through both the prose and poetic records while others appear most fully, or exclusively, in the latter. Similarly, some are found in both Christian and secular texts, while others appear in one or the other. Finally, some of them will primarily bear the meaning that their authors confer on them and so will function much as themes do in contemporary literate thematics, while others will primarily bear inherent, traditional meaning(s) derived from the expressive economy of oral poetics. The following discussion makes no attempt to be exhaustive but rather aims only to illustrate, and briefly at that, a small portion of the myriad themes found in OE prose and poetry. The groupings and divisions set forth below are admittedly arbitrary, and the themes upon which we will touch could easily have been presented in any number of other combinations. Additionally, the number of themes addressed could have been easily – and greatly – expanded.

Heroism

The Anglo-Saxon theme of heroism is familiar to contemporary audiences, both because many of its features continue to be reflected in its modern instantiations and because it looms large in *Beowulf*, perhaps the most-studied and most widely known text to survive from Anglo-Saxon England. But as is true of so much else regarding OE poetry and prose, some clarification is required because the type of heroism that informs texts such as *Beowulf*, *The Battle of Maldon*, *The Battle of Brunanburh*, *The Finnsburh Fragment*, and *Waldere*, and that has received by far the bulk of critical and popular attention, comprises only one of this theme's strands. Along with the secular heroism depicted in the poems listed above, other poetic (and prose) texts explore and celebrate a more particular, if to contemporary audiences less familiar, type of Christian heroism. Although surviving to the present day, this type of heroism is now found almost exclusively in verbal art produced for a niche audience rather than for the culture at large. Perhaps because their aesthetics speaks more directly to the expectations of contemporary readers, the poems dominated by the theme of secular heroism are generally judged to be artistically and narratively superior to those that explore and celebrate Christian heroism. When, however, we take a quantitative, rather than subjectively qualitative, view of the surviving literary records, a rather different picture emerges because those works devoted to Christian heroism far outnumber their secular heroic counterparts. In fact, the above-cited list of heroic poems is not illustrative, but rather includes virtually all the secular heroic poems that have survived, and among the prose texts there is also not very much in the secular heroic vein. By way of contrast, there are any number of poems devoted to the theme of Christian heroism, and when we turn to the prose, the number increases

The Anglo-Saxon Literature Handbook, First Edition. Mark C. Amodio.
© 2014 Mark C. Amodio. Published 2014 by John Wiley & Sons, Ltd.

dramatically, especially if we were to count as individual examples all the saints' lives recounted in texts such as Bede's *Ecclesiastical History*, Ælfric's *Lives of Saints*, or elsewhere. While the reasons for this disparity are intriguing and important, consideration of them lies well beyond the present discussion. For our purposes, we will note only that the surviving verbal art from Anglo-Saxon England in which the theme of heroism figures prominently tilts far more heavily towards Christian rather than secular heroism.

Although the primary strands of this theme diverge in significant ways, there are also many points of contact between them, including, among a host of others, bravery in the face of dire physical danger, the public articulation of one's heroic intents via the significative pathway of the 'beot', and what may be the theme's single most important element, loyalty to one's lord. As may be expected, *Beowulf* offers numerous instantiations of all these thematic components: in his 'beot' before meeting the dragon he announces that he will not flee 'fotes trem' (2525a) [the space of a foot] from the monstrous foe; during the dragon fight, he gets close enough to his foe's head to drive his sword, Nægling, into its skull, shattering the weapon in the process; and, following the destruction of Nægling, he faces the fifty-foot-long monster armed only with a 'wællsæx' (2703b) [battle-knife], a weapon with a blade about twelve inches long. Among the poem's many depictions of loyalty, we cite here only one that is especially poignant: mistakenly convinced that the blood and gore that boils to the surface of the mere Beowulf has entered in search of Grendel's mother signals the Geatish hero's demise, the Danes who accompanied him to the mere's edge return sadly home. In contrast, even though the band of Geats who journeyed with Beowulf to Denmark read the signs in the mere in a similar fashion, they nonetheless loyally remain at the water's edge, staring, perhaps despondently, into the roiling, gore-filled water.

Despite the limited size of the corpus in which secular heroism functions as a controlling theme, many other equally dramatic, or even more dramatic, examples of loyalty could be easily adduced, among which the grim resolve of the combatants in *Waldere* and *The Finnsburg Fragment*, the moving speech Byrhtnoth gives to his doomed troops in *The Battle of Maldon*, the decision, also in *Maldon*, made by a Northumbrian hostage to fight – and die – alongside his captors, and the vivid depiction of martial activity in *The Battle of Brunanburh* are but a few.

The theme's Christian strand shares many features with the secular one, and, if anything, may even stress the concept of loyalty even more strongly. A divine, not earthly, leader is the focus of the Christian heroes' loyalty, however, and the manner in which loyalty most often manifests itself differs in each strand as well, with a character's obedience to divine will replacing publically articulated vows of fealty to an earthly leader and passive martyrdom replacing death on the battlefield in a lord's or king's service. On occasion, as in *Andreas*, a character may gently question, or even overtly resist, a divine imperative, but in the end loyalty in the Christian sphere finds expression exclusively through obedience and submission to the divine will, be it by undertaking what has all the airs of a suicide mission to cannibalistic Mermedonia (*Andreas*), withstanding grievous physical torture before receiving the palm of martyrdom (as in, among many other poetic and prose accounts, *Juliana* and *Andreas*), or simply following other divine commands (as in Bede's story of the cowherd Cædmon or in any number of the prose saints' lives), given either directly or indirectly.

At times the secular and Christian strands come together within a single narrative, with results that sometime appear jarring to our contemporary narrative sensibilities. This is often the case for much of the surviving Christian heroic poetry, where the ideal of Christian heroism (which centres on absolute obedience to divine will and passive endurance of physical and/ or psychological humiliation and pain) is blended with elements of the secular heroic ethos (which centres on loyalty to an earthly lord or king and active participation in martial encounters) to produce moments that range from the powerfully effective (as when Guthlac withstands the horrors he gazes upon after being physically transported to the mouth of hell by demons who wish to shatter the faith to which he resolutely clings in *Guthlac A*), to the puzzlingly incongruous (as when the group that accompanies Andreas on the voyage to rescue Matthew from the Mermedonians is presented as a martial comitatus in *Andreas*), to the sublimely moving (as when Christ, who has been described as a young warrior, actively ascends his cross in *The Dream of the Rood*). Although this mixture of the secular and the heroic may frequently strike us as odd and puzzling, the extant evidence suggests that Christian heroism was very popular among those who produced and consumed OE verse and prose texts since it survives in a far greater number of them than does secular heroism. The discrepancy in survival rates may perhaps be most safely ascribed to the vicissitudes of fate since we have no way of knowing how much more literature was produced and then lost, but we cannot rule out other factors, including that the tastes of the Anglo-Saxons ran decidedly to the Christian and to the Christian heroic (a genre that has since largely disappeared from English literary history) and that heroic texts may have simply been produced in far smaller numbers or may have been destroyed because they did not serve any explicit Christian purpose, for the answer to the question Alcuin famously posed in one of his letters, 'Quid Hinieldus cum Christo?' (Dümmler, 183) [What has Hinield (Ingeld) to do with Christ?], is 'not much'.

The End of the World

Eschatological matters find frequent, eloquent, and dramatic articulation in the prose records, including in well-known homilies from the Vercelli and Blickling collections, and they also figure in the poetic records, as in the *Soul and Body* poems, the *Judgement Day* poems, and elsewhere. That many Anglo-Saxon authors chose to ruminate upon the constellation of themes associated with Christian eschatology, which include, among others, the transitory nature of human life (often expressed via the *ubi sunt* topos), the decayed state of the world, the separation of the soul from the body, the release of souls from hell, the return of the lord, the eternal punishments of the wicked, and the joyous judgement of the righteous, is not surprising given both the stress Christian theological thought places on such matters and the often didactic aims of many OE verse and prose texts. The narrative drama inherent in virtually all the thematic threads that run through eschatological matters may also help explain their prevalence and their popularity, for in addition to their obvious dogmatic value, they may also have resonated aesthetically with the authors who produced them, with the clerics who utilized them in their preaching, and with those who received them, either through reading or hearing them read aloud. Moments akin to Guthlac's witnessing from the mouth of hell the 'grimman gryre' (*Guthlac A*, 571a) [cruel terror] that awaits those trapped there, to the bones of a dead man calling out to him 'Forhwon come þu hider us to sceawigenne?' (Blickling Homily X, 113) [Why have you come hither to gaze upon us?], and to St Paul's seeing 'manige swearte saula be heora handum gebundne' [many black souls with their hands bound] hanging from a cliff where 'fynd þara on nicra onlicnesse heora gripende wæron, swa swa grædig wulf' (Blickling Homily XV [XVI], 209–11) [fiends in the likeness of water-

The Anglo-Saxon Literature Handbook, First Edition. Mark C. Amodio.
© 2014 Mark C. Amodio. Published 2014 by John Wiley & Sons, Ltd.

monsters were seizing them like greedy wolves], abound in eschatological writings, where their narrative power and affective dynamics are not diluted despite their frequency of occurrence. Among the many eschatological writings to survive, Blickling Homily X (given the title 'þisses middangeardes ende neah is' [the end of this world is near] by an early editor) and Vercelli Homily IV stand out as especially noteworthy.

Eschatological themes are most often employed in the service of authors' doctrinal purposes, but they are also put to other purposes as well. On occasion they are used to underscore the severity of current social and political conditions, and they also find their way into narratives focused on more secular topics. Bishop Wulfstan famously contextualizes his searing observations on the political plight of the English and the grave moral decay of English society in the late tenth and early eleventh centuries within the rhetoric of eschatology when he begins his *Sermo Lupi ad Anglos* [Sermon of the Wolf to the English] by announcing that 'þeos woruld is on ofste, and hit nealæcð þam ende, þy hit is on worolde aa swa leng swa wyrse' (Bethurum, 267) [this world is in haste and it draws near to the end; and therefore it is in the world ever the worse the longer the world exists]. The anonymous author of Vercelli Homily XI adopts a similar tactic when, to cite but one example, he asserts 'þætte ure ealra ende swiðe mislice toweard nealæceð. Nu syndon þa Godes cyrican beareafode and þa wiofeda toworpene þurh hæðenra manna gehresp and gestrodu, and þa weallas syndon tobrocene and toslitene' (Scragg, *Vercelli Homilies*, 225.89–92) [that the end of us all approaches near in diverse ways. Now are God's churches plundered and the altars destroyed through the pillaging and plundering of heathen men, and the walls are shattered and torn asunder]. Eschatological threads are also woven into the narrative tapestry of some largely secular works. To cite only a few well-known examples found in *Beowulf*, the description of the mere in which Grendel's mother dwells shares a number of features with the horrid pool St Paul gazes upon in Blickling Homily XV [XVI]; hell seizes Grendel's soul, and Beowulf's soul departs his body 'secean soðfæstra dom' (2820) [to seek the judgement of the righteous]. Whether these moments are conscious evocations of eschatological themes or analogues to them remains impossible to determine, especially as Christianity is not the sole belief system in which the end of days figures prominently.

The Transitory Nature of Life

In addition to the sort of large, broadly-defined, and mostly amorphous themes we have considered so far, of which the heroic and the eschatological are among the most pervasive, a great number of other, more tightly focused themes are found in Anglo-Saxon literature, but because even a brief survey of them is beyond the scope of the present discussion, we must limit our discussion to only a very few of them. As even a passing acquaintance with OE poetry and prose makes clear, the Anglo-Saxons possessed a keen awareness of, and perhaps appreciation for, the transitory nature of human existence. In the poetic records, the phrase 'lænan gesceaft' [loaned, transitory creation] and others closely related to it such as 'lænan life' [loaned, transitory life] and 'lænan tid' [loaned, transitory time] succinctly and powerfully capture the essence of this theme, one that finds its most frequent expression not only in Christian poems such as *Guthlac* and *The Phoenix* but that is also found within in more secular texts as well. The *Wanderer*-poet briefly, yet effectively, ruminates anaphorically on this theme over the course of several lines: 'Her bið feoh læne, her bið freond læne, / her bið mon læne, her bið mæg læne, / eal þis eorþan gesteal idel weorþeð' (108–10) [here is wealth transitory, here is a friend transitory, here is a man transitory, here is a kinsman transitory; all this earth's frame shall become destitute]. In the prose, the theme of life's ephemerality finds perhaps its most well known expression in the story Bede relates in the second book of his *Ecclesiastical History* of a sparrow that momentarily escapes wintry weather by flying through an open door of a hall that is lighted and warmed by a fire before exiting back into the storm via another door. As the unnamed counsellor of Eadwine who relates the story aptly observes, 'Swa þonne þis monna lif to medmiclum fæce ætyweð; hwæt þær foregange, oððe hwæt þær æfterfylige, we ne

The Anglo-Saxon Literature Handbook, First Edition. Mark C. Amodio.
© 2014 Mark C. Amodio. Published 2014 by John Wiley & Sons, Ltd.

cunnun' (Miller, 136.5–6) [So then this life of men appears for a brief space of time; what precedes it, or what follows it, we do not know]. The fullest expression of this theme in the poetry is perhaps also its most poignant: following Beowulf's defeat of Grendel's mother, the aged King Hrothgar offers some practical advice to the young, ascendant Geatish hero in a speech that has the overtones of a sermon and that ends with the king listing some of the many means by which 'deað oferswyðeð' (1768b) [death overpowers] us, including 'gripe meces, oððe gares fliht, / oððe atol yldo' (1765–66a) [the attack of a sword, or the flight of an arrow, or terrible old age].

Fate

The degree to which the course of human events is determined by a powerful and controlling force is another favorite theme of Anglo-Saxon authors. Central to many articulations of this theme is the concept of 'wyrd', a term whose overtones allow it to be used in both Christian (divine will, providence, etc.) and secular (fate, fortune, chance) contexts. In Christian prose and poetic writings, characters obediently follow the path their faith, and sometimes God or Christ themselves, sets for them. To the example of Guthlac, who early in his life rejects the secular world for an ermetic existence, we can add legions of other characters who similarly follow internally directed devotional paths. Sometimes, though, as in *Andreas* and Bede's story of the cowherd Cædmon in the *Ecclesiastical History*, divine commands are given directly and clearly, while at other times they are given more cryptically, as when an angelic hand appears and enigmatically writes on the walls of King Balshazzar's hall in *Daniel* or when Constantine has a vision of the Cross prior to a decisive battle in *Elene*. 'Wyrd' is an important component of the world depicted in *Beowulf*, and even though it would be a mistake to view this (or any) OE text as holding a mirror up to the beliefs and practices of Anglo-Saxon culture and society, the prominent place accorded fate in the poem may reflect something of its importance in the culture's secular thought. That 'wyrd' appears in the poem several times in gnomic statements – compact, aphoristic utterances that are frequently proverbial in their import – suggests just how widespread are the sentiments underlying such statements as Beowulf's 'Gæð a wyrd swa hio scel' (455b) [Goes ever fate as it must] and 'Wyrd oft nereð / unfægne eorl, þonne his ellen deah!' (572b–73) [Fate often saves the undoomed man, when his courage is strong]. In Christian prose and poetry, where 'wyrd' occurs most fre-

The Anglo-Saxon Literature Handbook, First Edition. Mark C. Amodio.
© 2014 Mark C. Amodio. Published 2014 by John Wiley & Sons, Ltd.

quently, it generally carries the meaning 'divine providence', but even in a text with strong Christian inflections such as *The Wanderer*, it retains its more secular overtones in some instances, as it does when the speaker of that poem's first few lines gnomically concludes that 'Wyrd bið ful aræd!' (5b) [fate is entirely inexorable!]. In *Beowulf*, the word's meaning is non-Christian, but its being employed on several occasions in close proximity to references to the Christian God (or to his power) suggests that the *Beowulf*-poet, at least – and perhaps his audience – saw them as being complementary, or parallel, and not competing references to the unknowable power(s) that determine the course of human existence.

Wisdom

Wisdom is a theme that threads its way through much OE prose and verse. In the prose records, the OE translations of Boethius's *Consolation of Philosophy* and of Pope Gregory the Great's *Pastoral Care*, both of which are generally attributed to King Alfred the Great, seek to instruct readers in matters both practical and esoteric. The same can also be said of the many homilies, sermons, and other Christian didactic prose texts that survive. Wisdom figures prominently in a number of poetic texts, especially *Maxims I* and *II*, and *Vainglory*, although they tend to focus more on the theme's secular than religious dimensions and applications. And in *Beowulf*, wisdom is accorded an important place in several narrative moments, including the Danish king Hrothgar's so-called sermon, and, perhaps most famously, in the Danish coast-guards gnomically tinged statement that 'Æeghwæþres sceal / scearp scyldwiga gescad witan, / worda ond worca, se þe wel þenceð' (287b–89) [A sharp shield-warrior must know the distinction between each of two things, words and works, he who thinks rightly.]

Equally important is the related theme of the lack of knowledge, one that appears frequently in Christian and secular texts. As we might expect, eschatological texts tend to draw heavily on this theme, devoted as they are to subjects – the last days of the world and what comes after them – that are destined forever to remain outside the realm of man's experience. The properties of the divine as they manifest themselves in the world, both physically in a phenomenon such as the movement of the sun across the sky and metaphysically in, to cite but one example, the workings of divine providence, are frequently addressed via the theme of man's lack of understanding, for the divine lies well beyond man's comprehension. As is true of the theme of wisdom, the theme of mankind's limited knowledge also figures promi-

The Anglo-Saxon Literature Handbook, First Edition. Mark C. Amodio.
© 2014 Mark C. Amodio. Published 2014 by John Wiley & Sons, Ltd.

nently in many texts that are more secularly focused. In some instances, as in the so-called poetic elegies found in the Exeter Book, a general, undefined air of unknowing permeates the narratives, as their speakers, who remain anonymous, never reveal what brought them to the dire, lonely, painful, and sometimes dangerous situations in which they find themselves. In *Beowulf*, the theme of mankind's limited knowledge is pervasive. It brackets the entire narrative, which begins with the arrival from parts unknown of Scyld Scefing – the progenitor of the Danish royal line that includes Hrothgar –, and concludes with the Geats, Beowulf's tribe, facing a grim, unsettled, and unknown future. Elsewhere in the narrative, explicit articulations of this theme can be found in the poet's comments on such things as the final destination of the ship bearing Scyld's corpse and Grendel's movements following his nightly attacks on Heorot, the Danish royal hall. The theme also runs implicitly through many sections of the narrative, as even a brief glance at the little that is known about Grendel reveals. Grendel's physicality is famously not detailed by the poet (until, that is, Beowulf wrenches off Grendel's arm and shoulder and later decapitates his corpse), his motives for attacking Heorot are never articulated, where he lives is both inaccessible to men and shrouded in mystery, and even his mode of locomotion remains largely unknown.

Otherness

Distrust or even fear of otherness is another frequently occurring theme in the literature that survives from Anglo-Saxon England. The threat of invasion was a very real one throughout much of the period, and as a result the Danes often figure prominently in this theme's expression. At times they are directly portrayed as a divine scourge sent to punish the English for their sinful wickedness, as they are in the homilies, especially those of Wulfstan. At other times, their savagery and otherness is expressed less directly, but no less effectively, as when, for example, the *Maldon*-poet describes them as 'wælwulfas' (96a) [slaughter-wolves]. It is not difficult to map the fear of outsiders and/or the attendant fear of invasion onto any number of poetic or prose texts, with Grendel again standing as something of a poster-boy for this theme since his desire to replace human society with one of his own devising poses a much greater threat than either his bloody nightly attacks upon Heorot or his grisly culinary predilections. Alterity is also explicitly foregrounded in two of the texts found along with *Beowulf* and *Judith* in Cotton Vitellius A.xv, the *Letter of Alexander to Aristotle* and *The Wonders of the East,* and it may well be that the texts gathered in the codex were selected precisely because they all focus on others and otherness. While many of the wondrous beings and creatures encountered in *Alexander's Letter* and *Wonders* are dangerous, the latter also depicts a number of creatures that are strange but benign, such as a race of people who grow to fifteen feet and who have large heads and ears the size of fans, or the inhabitants of an island whose eyes shine like lanterns on a dark night, a physical trait they share with the ravenous Grendel. Others are, however, typically anything but benign in Anglo-Saxon literature, and they are far more likely to be depicted as real and frequently very present menaces than as exotic, distant, and non-threatening curiosities.

The Anglo-Saxon Literature Handbook, First Edition. Mark C. Amodio.
© 2014 Mark C. Amodio. Published 2014 by John Wiley & Sons, Ltd.

In addition to the type of explicitly foregrounded alterity of characters such as Grendel, the Danish invaders in *The Battle of Maldon*, the demons in *Guthlac A*, or the many found in *Wonders* and the *Letter of Alexander*, to cite but a few examples, we do not have to look far to discover other types of alterity that are more subtle but that nonetheless produce considerable anxiety. Some of the terms used to describe Grendel's mother and the Biblical heroine Judith in, respectively, *Beowulf* and *Judith*, not only insistently point their otherness but also reveal the ways in which the dominant masculinist discourse within which the poems were composed fails to locate these transgressively active female figures within the confines of the masculine, martial cultural worlds the poems depict. While we might well expect characters such as Grendel's mother and Judith to be marked by a certain degree of alterity, a troubling and decentring whiff of it can also be detected in characters who appear to be firmly, and positively grounded in the their texts' worlds, including perhaps most notably the heroes Beowulf and Sigemund in *Beowulf*, both of whose heroism is complicated, and to a large extent even defined, by their otherness.

Oral-Traditional Themes

While themes are by definition flexible, fungible components of all verbal art, in Anglo-Saxon England many of them also serve more specialized purposes because they function as meaning-bearing units within the expressive economy of oral poetics. These themes were among the earliest features of the traditional expressive economy to be identified and investigated, and they function both narratively and affectively by summoning to the narrative's surface a world of interconnected associations. For example, the much-studied theme of the hero on the beach is often expressed through some combination of the following constellation of narrative moments: a hero who journeys from afar in the company of an armed troop stands at or straddles the border of two worlds in the presence of a flashing light. When deployed within the expressive economy of traditional oral poetics, these constituent elements signals an approaching slaughterous encounter. This theme is present in a number of poems, including *Andreas*, *Exodus*, *Judith*, and *Guthlac B*. *Beowulf* offers several instantiations of it, including what is probably its most-studied occurrence: the Geatish hero's arrival on the shores of Denmark to offer the Danes his help against Grendel. The slaughter to which the theme points does not occur immediately after Beowulf and his men land in Denmark or when they are approached and questioned by the Danish coast-guard (although the potential for violence is certainly present), but rather only after several hundred lines of the narrative have elapsed. The theme's affective dynamics, however, is kept present and active during this stretch through the appearance of numerous shining objects, the most startling and terrifying of which – Grendel's eyes – are mentioned only moments before the bloody and brutal fight which brings the theme to its culmination begins. In the oral-traditional theme of the beasts of battle, one found

The Anglo-Saxon Literature Handbook, First Edition. Mark C. Amodio.
© 2014 Mark C. Amodio. Published 2014 by John Wiley & Sons, Ltd.

in *Beowulf*, *Andreas*, *Elene*, and elsewhere, the appearance of carrion eat-ers, often a wolf, raven, and eagle, serves to cue the audience to an approaching scene of carnage. Frequently described as 'grædig' [greedy], the beasts sing their terrible war-songs in expectation of feasting on the dead, and in one instance an anthropomorphized raven is reported as telling the eagle 'hu him æte speow' (*Beowulf*, 3026b) [how he succeeded at the meal].

In addition to the two cited above, the list of oral-traditional themes found in OE poetry include, among others, exile, sleep after feasting, scourging, the cliff of death, sea voyage, gift-giving, approach to battle, battle, joy in the hall, and speaking wood. While these have been identified and catego-rized via specific constellations of salient narrative details, they are neither fixed nor unvarying because like virtually all the constituent elements of oral poetics, traditional oral themes are protean multiforms that exhibit variation within limits. As a result, even though, for example, the carrion eaters of the beasts of battle theme usually include among their numbers a wolf and an eagle or raven, the *Andreas*-poet's substitution of a 'horn-fisc' (370b) [pike] and a 'græga mæw' (371b) [grey gull] who are 'wælgifre' (372a) [eager to prey on the slaughtered] neither diminishes the theme's nar-rative effectiveness nor alters its affective dynamics. Similarly, while the theme points to the impending carnage of a martial engagement, such a scene is not required. Andreas and his men get caught in a frightening storm on their sea voyage but even though no harm befalls them (thanks to the presence of Christ who is disguised as the boat's pilot) the theme nevertheless retains its full traditional referentiality and emotional impact. The same is true of the theme's final occurrence in *Beowulf*: while the carnage to which it points is left unexpressed, the theme nonetheless powerfully and effec-tively signals the grim and violent fate awaiting the Geats – they will be dispersed and disappear from the historical record – following the death of Beowulf, the king who ruled and protected them for more than fifty years.

There are, of course, a great many more themes in Anglo-Saxon literature than the few that have been sketched briefly above. While some seem to have a certain structural integrity (this is especially true of those deployed within the expressive economy of oral poetics), it is important to remember that they are not the fixed, quantifiable entities that they sometimes appear to be when they are brought under the microscope of critical analysis, but rather remain flexible, protean expressions of their creators' aesthetic impulses, which are as varied and diffuse as are the authors themselves. We would do well to keep this in mind anytime we find ourselves wandering through the rich landscape of Anglo-Saxon themes. We must also keep in mind that the Anglo-Saxons themselves may have had a very different sense of their literature's themes and that, accordingly, they may well have seen and responded to patterns and connections that as yet remain undetected by our contemporary critical sensibilities. Additionally, many of the patterns and connections established by contemporary criticism may well have gone unnoticed by the Anglo-Saxons, for although contemporary culture exists on a continuum that stretches back to Anglo-Saxon England – and beyond – there is at best a strange likeness, to borrow a phrase via Chris Jones from Geoffrey Hill's *Mercian Hymns*, between the 'heom' [them] of Anglo-Saxon England and the 'us' [us] of the contemporary world.

Bibliography

Abram, Christopher. 'The errors in *The Rhyming Poem*'. *RES* 58 (2007): 1–9.

Amodio, Mark C. 'Affective criticism, oral poetics, and Beowulf's fight with the dragon'. *OT* 10 (1995): 54–90.

Amodio, Mark C. *Writing the Oral Tradition: Oral Poetics and Literate Culture in Medieval England*. Poetics of Orality and Literacy 1. Notre Dame: University of Notre Dame Press, 2004.

Amos, Ashley Crandell. *The Linguistic Means of Determining the Dates of Old English Literary Texts*. Cambridge: Medieval Academy of America, 1980.

Anderson, Earl R. 'Old English poetic texts and their Latin sources: iconicity in *Cædmon's Hymn* and *The Phoenix*'. In *The Motivated Sign: Iconicity in Language and Literature 2*, ed. Olga Fischer and Max Nänny, 109–32. Philadelphia: John Benjamins, 2000.

Anderson, Earl R. 'Style and theme in the Old English *Daniel*'. *ES* 68 (1987): 1–23.

Andersson, Theodore M. 'The speeches in the *Waldere* fragments'. In *De Gustibus: Essays for Alain Renoir*, ed. John Miles Foley, 21–29. Albert Bates Lord Studies in Oral Tradition 11. New York: Garland, 1992.

Anlezark, Daniel. 'The fall of the angels in *Solomon and Saturn II*'. In *Apocryphal Texts and Traditions*, ed. Kathryn Powell and Donald Scragg, 121–33. Publications of the Manchester Centre for Anglo-Saxon Studies 2. Cambridge: D.S. Brewer, 2003.

Anlezark, Daniel, ed. and trans. *The Old English Dialogues of Solomon and Saturn*. Woodbridge: Boydell and Brewer, 2009.

Anlezark, Daniel. 'Three notes on the Old English *Metres of Boethius*'. *N&Q* ns 51 (2004): 10–15.

Archibald, Elizabeth. *Apollonius of Tyre: Medieval and Renaissance Themes and Variations, Including the Text of the 'Historia Apollonii Regis Tyri' with an English Translation*. Cambridge: D.S. Brewer, 1991.

Arner, Timothy D. and Paul D. Stegner. '"Of þam him aweaxeð wynsum gefea": the voyeuristic appeal of *Christ III*'. *JEGP* 106 (2007): 428–46.

Aronstam, Robin Ann. 'The *Blickling Homilies*: a reflection of popular Anglo-Saxon belief'. In *Law, Church, and Society: Essays in Honor of Stephan Kuttner*, ed. Kenneth Pennington and Robert Somerville, 271–80. Philadelphia: University of Pennsylvania Press, 1977.

Austin, Greta. 'Marvelous people or marvelous races? Race and the Anglo-Saxon *Wonders of the East*'. In *Marvels, Monsters and Miracles: Studies in the Medieval and Early Modern Imaginations*, ed. Timothy S. Jones and David A. Sprunger, 25–51. Studies in Medieval Culture 42. Kalamazoo: Medieval Institute Publications, 2002.

The Anglo-Saxon Literature Handbook, First Edition. Mark C. Amodio.
© 2014 Mark C. Amodio. Published 2014 by John Wiley & Sons, Ltd.

Baker, Peter S. *The Anglo-Saxon Chronicle: A Collaborative Edition*. Vol. 8: *MS F*. Cambridge: D.S. Brewer, 2000.

Baker, Peter S. *Introduction to Old English*. 3rd edn. Oxford: Wiley-Blackwell, 2012.

Baker, Peter S., and Michael Lapidge, eds. *Byrhtferth's 'Enchiridion'*. EETS ss 15. Oxford: Oxford University Press, 1995.

Barlow, Frank. *The English Church 1000–1066: A History of the Later Anglo-Saxon Church*. 1963. 2nd edn. London: Longman, 1979.

Barrow, Julia and Nicholas Brooks, eds. *St. Wulfstan and His World*. Burlington: Ashgate, 2005.

Bately, Janet M. 'The Alfredian canon revisited: one hundred years on'. In *Alfred the Great: Papers from the Eleventh-Centenary Conference*, ed. Timothy Reuter, 107–20. Burlington, VT: Ashgate, 2003.

Bately, Janet M. *The Anglo-Saxon Chronicle: A Collaborative Edition*. Vol. 3: *MS A*. Cambridge: D.S. Brewer, 1986.

Bately, Janet M. 'Boethius and King Alfred'. In *Platonism and the English Imagination*, ed. Anna Baldwin and Sarah Hutton, 38–44. Cambridge: Cambridge University Press, 1994.

Bately, Janet M. 'Bravery and the vocabulary of bravery in *Beowulf* and the *Battle of Maldon*'. In *Unlocking the Wordhord: Anglo-Saxon Studies in Memory of Edward B. Irving, Jr.*, ed. Mark C. Amodio and Katherine O'Brien O'Keeffe, 274–301. Toronto: University of Toronto Press, 2003.

Bately, Janet M. 'The classical additions in the Old English *Orosius*'. In *England before the Conquest: Studies in Primary Sources Presented to Dorothy Whitelock*, ed. Peter Clemoes and Kathleen Hughes, 237–51. Cambridge: Cambridge University Press, 1971.

Bately, Janet M. 'Did King Alfred actually translate anything? The integrity of the Alfredian canon revisited'. *MÆ* 78 (2009): 189–215.

Bately, Janet M. 'Lexical evidence for the authorship of the prose psalms in the Paris Psalter'. *ASE* 10 (1982): 69–95.

Bately, Janet M., ed. *The Old English Orosius*. EETS ss 6. London: Oxford University Press, 1980.

Bately, Janet M. 'Old English prose before and during the reign of King Alfred'. *ASE* 17 (1988): 93–138.

Bately, Janet M., Michelle Brown, and Jane Roberts, eds. *A Palaeographer's View: The Selected Writings of Julian Brown*. London: Harvey Miller Publishers, 1993.

Beechy, Tiffany. *The Poetics of Old English*. Burlington: Ashgate, 2010.

Belanoff, Patricia A. 'Women's songs, women's language: *Wulf and Eadwacer* and *The Wife's Lament*'. In *New Readings on Women in Old English Literature*, ed. Helen Damico and Alexandra Hennessey Olsen, 193–203. Bloomington: Indiana University Press, 1990.

Benson, Larry D. gen. ed. *The Riverside Chaucer*. 3rd edn. Boston: Houghton Mifflin, 1987.

Berkhout, Carl T. 'Some notes on the Old English *Almsgiving*'. *ELN* 10 (1972–73): 81–85.

Bethurum, Dorothy, ed. *The Homilies of Wulfstan*. 1957. Rpt. Oxford: Clarendon Press, 1998.

Biggs, Frederick M. '*The Dream of the Rood* and *Guthlac B* as a literary context for the monsters in *Beowulf*'. In *Text, Image, Interpretation: Studies in Anglo-Saxon Literature and Its Insular Context in Honour of Éamon Ó Carragáin*, ed. A.J. Minnis and Jane Roberts, 289–301. Studies in the Early Middle Ages 18. Turnhout: Brepols, 2007.

Biggs, Frederick M. 'The eschatological conclusion of the Old English *Physiologus*'. *MÆ* 58 (1989): 286–97.

Biggs, Frederick M. 'The fourfold division of souls: the Old English *Christ III* and the insular homiletic tradition'. *Traditio* 45 (1989–90): 35–51.

Bitterli, Dieter. *Say What I Am Called: The Old English Riddles of the Exeter Book and Anglo-Latin Riddle Tradition*. Toronto: University of Toronto Press, 2009.

Bjork, Robert E. 'N.F.S. Grundtvig's 1840 Edition of the Old English *Phoenix*: a vision of a vision of paradise'. In *Unlocking the Wordhord: Anglo-Saxon Studies in Memory of Edward B. Irving, Jr.*, ed. Mark C. Amodio and Katherine O'Brien O'Keeffe, 217–39. Toronto: University of Toronto Press, 2003.

Bjork, Robert E. 'The symbolic use of Job in Ælfric's Homily on Job, *Christ II*, and the *Phoenix*'. In *Latin Learning and English Lore: Studies in Anglo-Saxon Literature for Michael Lapidge*, ed. Katherine O'Brien O'Keeffe and Andy Orchard, vol. II, 315–30. Toronto Old English series 14. 2 vols. Toronto: University of Toronto Press, 2005.

Bjork, Robert E., and John D. Niles, eds. *A 'Beowulf' Handbook*. Lincoln: University of Nebraska Press, 1998.

Bjork, Robert E., and Anita Obermeir. 'Date, provenance, author, audiences'. In *A 'Beowulf' Handbook*, ed. Robert E. Bjork and John D. Niles, 13–34. Lincoln: University of Nebraska Press, 1998.

Blair, John. *The Church in Anglo-Saxon Society*. Oxford: Oxford University Press, 2005.

Blair, Peter Hunter. *An Introduction to Anglo-Saxon England*. 1956. 3rd edn. Cambridge: Cambridge University Press, 2003.

Blair, Peter Hunter. *The World of Bede*. New York: St Martin's, 1971.

Blurton, Heather. *Cannibalism in High Medieval Literature*. Basingstoke: Palgrave Macmillan, 2007.

Blurton, Heather. '*Reliquia*: writing relics in Anglo-Norman Durham'. In *Cultural Diversity in the British Middle Ages: Archipelago, Island, England*, ed. Jeffrey Jerome Cohen, 39–56. New Middle Ages. New York: Palgrave Macmillan, 2008.

Bolton, Whitney F. 'How Boethian is Alfred's *Boethius?*' In *Studies in Earlier Old English Prose*, ed. Paul E. Szarmach, 153–68. Albany: State University of New York Press, 1986.

Borysławski, Rafał. 'Wordhordes craeft: confusion and the order of the wor(l)d in Old English gnomes'. In *The Propur Langage of Englische Men*, ed. Marcin Krygier and Liliana Sikorska, 119–31. Medieval English Mirror 4. New York: Peter Lang, 2008.

Bosworth, Joseph, and T. Northcote Toller, eds. *An Anglo-Saxon Dictionary Based on the Manuscript Collections of the Late Joseph Bosworth*. 1898. Rpt. London: Oxford University Press, 1998.

Bragg, Lois. 'Runes and readers: in and around "The Husband's Message"'. *SN* 71 (1999): 34–50.

Brantley, Jessica. 'The iconography of the Utrecht Psalter and the Old English *Descent into Hell*'. *ASE* 28 (1999): 43–63.

Bredehoft, Thomas A. '*The Battle of Brunanburh* in Old English Studies'. In *The Battle of Brunanburh: A Casebook*, ed. Michael Livingston, 285–94. Exeter Medieval Texts and Studies. Exeter: University of Exeter Press, 2011.

Bredehoft, Thomas A. *Textual Histories: Readings in the Anglo-Saxon Chronicle*. Toronto: University of Toronto Press, 2001.

Buchelt, Lisabeth C. 'All about Eve: memory and re-collection in Junius 11's epic poems *Genesis* and *Christ and Satan*'. In *Women and Medieval Epic*, ed. Sara S. Poor and Jana K. Schulman, 137–58. New York: Palgrave Macmillan, 2007.

Buck, R.A. 'Women and language in the Anglo-Saxon *Leechbooks*'. *Women and Language* 23 (2000): 41–50.

Bugge, John, 'Virginity and prophecy in the Old English *Daniel*'. *ES* 87 (2006): 127–47.

Bullough, J.A. 'What has Ingeld to do with Lindisfarne?' *ASE* 22 (1993): 93–125.

Calder, Daniel G. '*Guthlac A* and *Guthlac B*: some discriminations'. In *Anglo-Saxon Poetry: Essays in Appreciation for John C. McGalliard*, ed. Lewis E. Nicholson and Dolores Warwick Frese, 65–80. Notre Dame: University of Notre Dame Press, 1975.

Calder, Daniel G., and Michael J. B. Allen, trans. *Sources and Analogues of Old English Poetry. The Major Latin Texts in Translation*. Totowa: Rowman and Littlefield, 1976.

Cameron, Angus, Ashley Crandell Amos, and Antonette diPaolo Healey, eds. *Dictionary of Old English. Fascicle G and Fascicles A to F (with revisions)*. Toronto: Pontifical Institute of Mediaeval Studies, 2008.

Cameron, M.L. *Anglo-Saxon Medicine*. CSASE 7. Cambridge: Cambridge University Press, 1993.

Campbell, James. *The Anglo-Saxon State*. 2000. Rpt. London: Hambledon Continuum, 2003.

Campbell, James, Eric John, and Patrick Wormald, eds. *The Anglo-Saxons*. 1982. Rpt. London: Penguin, 1991.

Carnicelli, Thomas A. ed. *King Alfred's Version of St. Augustine's Soliloquies*. Cambridge: Harvard University Press, 1969.

Carroll, Jayne. '*Engla Waldend, Rex Admirabilis*: poetic representations of King Edgar'. *RES* ns 58 (2007): 113–32.

Carver, Martin. *Sutton Hoo: Burial Ground of Kings?* Philadelphia: University of Pennsylvania Press, 1998.

Cavill, Paul. *Maxims in Old English Poetry*. Cambridge: D.S. Brewer, 1999.

Cavill, Paul. 'The site of the *Battle of Brunanburh*: manuscripts and maps, grammar and geography'. In *A Commodity of Good Names: Essays in Honour of Margaret Gelling*, ed. O.J. Padel and David N. Parsons, 303–19. Donington: Shaun Tyas, 2008.

Chance, Jane. *Woman as Hero in Old English Literature*. Syracuse: Syracuse University Press, 1986.

Chase, Colin. 'God's presence through grace as the theme of Cynewulf's *Christ II* and the relationship of this theme to *Christ I* and *Christ III*'. *ASE* 3 (1974): 87–101.

Chenard, Marianne Malo. 'King Oswald's holy hands: metonymy and the making of a saint in Bede's *Ecclesiastical History*'. *Exemplaria* 17 (2005): 33–56.

Chickering, Howell D., Jr. 'Poetic exuberance in the Old English *Judith*'. *SP* 106 (2009): 119–36.

Chickering, Howell D., Jr. 'Some contexts for Bede's *Death-Song*'. *PMLA* 91 (1976): 91–100.

Clark, Cecily. 'The narrative mode of the Anglo-Saxon Chronicle before the Conquest'. In *England before the Conquest: Studies in Primary Sources Presented to Dorothy Whitelock*, ed. Peter Clemoes and Kathleen Hughes, 215–35. Cambridge: Cambridge University Press, 1971.

Clayton, Mary. 'Homiliaries and preaching in Anglo-Saxon England'. *Peritia* 4 (1985): 207–42.

Clement, Richard W. 'The production of the *Pastoral Care*: King Alfred and his helpers'. In *Studies in Earlier Old English Prose*, ed. Paul E. Szarmach, 129–52. Albany: State University of New York Press, 1986.

Clemoes, Peter, ed. *Ælfric's Catholic Homilies: The First Series*. EETS ss 17. Oxford: Oxford University Press, 1997.

Cockayne, Thomas Oswald, ed. and trans. *Leechdoms, Wortcunning, and Starcraft of Early England*. Vol. II. London: Longman, Green, Longman, Roberts, and Green, 1865.

Cohen, Jeffrey J. *Medieval Identity Machines*. Medieval Cultures 35. Minneapolis: University of Minnesota Press, 2003.

Colgrave, Bertram, and R.A.B. Mynors, ed. and trans. *Bede's Ecclesiastical History of the English People*. 1969. Rpt. Oxford: Clarendon Press, 1992.

Conner, Patrick W. *Anglo-Saxon Exeter: A Tenth-Century Cultural History*. Studies in Anglo-Saxon History 4. Woodbridge: Boydell Press, 1993.

Cross, J.E. 'The Old English poetic theme of "The Gifts of Men"'. *Neophilologus* 46 (1962): 66–70.

Cross, J.E. 'On the library of the Old English martyrologist'. In *Learning and Literature in Anglo-Saxon England: Studies Presented to Peter Clemoes on the Occasion of his Sixty-fifth Birthday*, ed. Michael Lapidge and Helmut Gneuss, 227–49. Cambridge: Cambridge University Press, 1981.

Cubbin, G.P. *The Anglo-Saxon Chronicle: A Collaborative Edition*. Vol. 6: *MS D*. Cambridge: D.S. Brewer, 1996.

Dailey, Patricia. 'Questions of dwelling in Anglo-Saxon poetry and medieval mysticism: inhabiting landscape, body, and mind'. *NML* 8 (2006): 175–214.

Damico, Helen, and Alexandra Hennessey Olsen, eds. *New Readings on Women in Old English Literature*. Bloomington: Indiana University Press, 1990.

Davis, Craig R. *Beowulf and the Demise of Germanic Legend in England*. New York: Garland, 1996.

Davis, Glenn. 'Corporeal anxiety in *Soul and Body II*'. *PQ* 87 (2008): 33–50.

Dendle, Peter. 'How naked is Juliana?' *PQ* 83 (2004): 355–70.

Deskis, Susan E. 'Exploring text and discourse in the Old English gnomic poems: the problem of narrative'. *JEGP* 104 (2005): 326–44.

Deskis, Susan E. 'Jonah and genre in *Resignation B*'. *MÆ* 67 (1998): 189–200.

Diamond, Robert E. *The Diction of the Anglo-Saxon Metrical Psalms*. The Hague: Mouton and Co. 1963.

DiNapoli, Robert. 'Close to the edge: *The Fortunes of Men* and the limits of wisdom literature'. In *Text and Transmission in Medieval Europe*, ed. Chris Bishop, 127–47. Newcastle upon Tyne: Cambridge Scholars Publishing, 2007.

DiNapoli, Robert. 'The heart of the visionary experience: *The Order of the World* and its place in the Old English canon'. *ES* 79 (1998): 97–108.

DiNapoli, Robert. 'Odd characters: runes in Old English poetry'. In *Verbal Encounters: Anglo-Saxon and Old Norse Studies for Roberta Frank*, ed. Antonia Harbus and Russell Poole, 145–61. Toronto Old English Series 13. Toronto: University of Toronto Press, 2005.

Discenza, Nicole Guenther. *The King's English: Strategies of Translation in the Old English 'Boethius'*. Albany: State University of New York Press, 2005.

Discenza, Nicole Guenther. 'The Old English *Bede* and the construction of Anglo-Saxon authority'. *ASE* 31 (2002): 69–80.

Dockray-Miller, Mary. 'Breasts and babies: the maternal body of Eve in the Junius *Genesis*'. In *Naked before God: Uncovering the Body in Anglo-Saxon England*, ed. Benjamin C. Withers and Jonathan Wilcox, 221–56. Morgantown: West Virginia University Press, 2003.

Dockray-Miller, Mary. 'Female devotion and the Vercelli Book'. *PQ* 83 (2004): 337–54.

Dobbie, Elliot Van Kirk, ed. *The Anglo-Saxon Minor Poems*. ASPR 6. 1942. Rpt. New York: Columbia University Press, 1985.

Dobbie, Elliot Van Kirk, ed. *Beowulf and Judith*. ASPR 4. 1953. Rpt. New York: Columbia University Press, 2003.

Donoghue, Daniel. *Style in Old English Poetry: The Test of the Auxiliary*. New Haven: Yale University Press, 1987.

Downey, Sarah. 'Too much of too little: Guthlac and the temptation of excessive fasting'. *Traditio* 63 (2008): 89–127.

Dümmler, Ernst, ed. *Alcuini Epistolae*. MGH, Epistolae Aevi Karolini 4.2. Berlin: MGH, 1895.

Dumville, David, ed. *The Anglo-Saxon Chronicle: A Collaborative Edition*. Vol. 1: *MS F*. Cambridge: D.S. Brewer, 2001.

Dyas, Dee. *Pilgrimage in Medieval English Literature, 700–1500*. Woodbridge: D.S. Brewer, 2001.

Earl, James W. 'Christian tradition in the Old English *Exodus*'. In *The Poems of MS Junius 11: Basic Readings*, ed. Roy M. Liuzza, 137–72. Basic Readings in Anglo-Saxon England 8. New York: Routledge, 2002.

Earl, James W. *Thinking about 'Beowulf'*. Stanford: Stanford University Press, 1994.

Earl, James W. 'Trinitarian language: Augustine, *The Dream of the Rood*, and Ælfric'. In *Source of Wisdom: Old English and Early Medieval Latin Studies in Honour of Thomas D. Hill*, ed. Charles D. Wright, Frederick M. Biggs, and Thomas N. Hall, 63–79. Toronto: University of Toronto Press, 2007.

Ericksen, Janet Schrunk. 'The wisdom poem at the end of MS Junius 11'. In *The Poems of MS Junius 11: Basic Readings*, ed. Roy M. Liuzza, 302–26. Basic Readings in Anglo-Saxon England 8. New York: Routledge, 2002.

Erussard, Laurence. 'Language, power and holiness in Cynewulf's *Elene*'. *Medievalia et Humanistica* ns 34 (2008): 23–41.

Faraci, Dora. 'Sources and cultural background: the example of the Old English *Phoenix*'. *Rivista di cultura classica e medioevale* 42 (2000): 225–39.

Bibliography

Farina, Lara. *Erotic Discourse and Early English Religious Writing*. The New Middle Ages. New York: Palgrave Macmillan, 2006.

Farrell, R.T. 'The unity of Old English *Daniel*'. *RES* ns 18 (1967): 117–35.

Foley, John Miles. *Homer's Traditional Art*. University Park: Pennsylvania State University Press, 1999.

Foley, John Miles. *Immanent Art: From Structure to Meaning in Traditional Oral Epic*. Bloomington: Indiana University Press, 1991.

Foley, John Miles. *Pathways of the Mind: Oral Tradition and the Internet*. Urbana: University of Illinois Press, 2012.

Foley, John Miles. *The Singer of Tales in Performance*. Bloomington: Indiana University Press, 1995.

Foley, John Miles. *Traditional Oral Epic: 'The Odyssey', 'Beowulf' and the Serbo-Croatian Return Song*. Berkeley and Los Angeles: University of California Press, 1990.

Foot, Sarah. 'Where English becomes British: rethinking contexts for *Brunanburh*'. In *Myth, Rulership, Church and Charters: Essays in Honour of Nicholas Brooks*, ed. Julia Barrow and Andrew Wareham, 127–44. Aldershot: Ashgate, 2008.

Foster, Don. *Author Unknown: On the Trail of Anonymous*. New York: Henry Holt and Co., 2000.

Frank, Roberta. 'Germanic legend in Old English literature'. In *The Cambridge Companion to Old English Literature*, ed. Malcolm Godden and Michael Lapidge, 88–106. Cambridge: Cambridge University Press, 1991.

Frank, Roberta. 'North Sea soundings in *Andreas*'. In *Early Medieval English Texts and Interpretations: Studies Presented to Donald G. Scragg*, ed. Elaine Treharne and Susan Rosser, 1–11. MRTS 252. Tempe: ACMRS, 2002.

Frantzen, Allen J. 'Drama and dialogue in Old English poetry: the scene of Cynewulf's *Juliana*'. *Theatre Survey: the Journal of the American Society for Theatre Research* 46 (2007): 99–119.

Frantzen, Allen J. 'Who do these Anglo-Saxon(ist)s think they are, anyway?' *Æstel* 2 (1994): 1–43.

Frese, Dolores Warwick. 'Sexing political tropes of conquest: *The Wife's Lament* and Laȝamon's *Brut*'. In *Sex and Sexuality in Anglo-Saxon England: Essays in Memory of Daniel Gillmore Calder*, ed. Carol Braun Pasternack and Lisa M.C. Weston, 203–33. MRTS 277. Tempe: ACMRS, 2004.

Friedman, John Block. 'The marvels-of-the-east tradition in Anglo-Saxon art'. In *Sources of Anglo-Saxon Culture*, ed. Paul E. Szarmach with the assistance of Virginia Darrow Oggins, 319–41. Studies in Medieval Culture 20. Kalamazoo: Medieval Institute Publications, 1986.

Fry, Donald K., ed. *Finnsburh Fragment and Episode*. London: Methuen, 1974.

Fry, Donald K. 'The hero on the beach in *Finnsburh*'. *NM* 67 (1966): 27–31.

Fulk, R.D., ed. and trans. *The 'Beowulf' Manuscript*. Dumbarton Oaks Medieval Library 3. Cambridge: Harvard University Press, 2010.

Fulk, R.D., Robert E. Bjork, and John D. Niles, eds. *Klaeber's 'Beowulf'*. 4th edn. Toronto: University of Toronto Press, 2008.

Gameson, Fiona, and Richard Gameson. '*Wulf and Eadwacer*, *The Wife's Lament*, and the discovery of the individual in Old English verse'. In *Studies in English Language and Literature. 'Doubt Wisely': Papers in Honour of E.G. Stanley*, ed. M.J. Toswell and E.M. Tyler, 457–74. London: Routledge, 1996.

Garmonsway, G.N. *Ælfric's Colloquy*. London: Methuen, 1939.

Garner, Lori Ann. 'The art of translation in the Old English *Judith*'. *SN* 73 (2001): 171–83.

Garner, Lori Ann. 'The Old English *Andreas* and the Mermedonian cityscape'. *Essays in Medieval Culture* 24 (2007): 53–63.

Gatch, Milton McC. 'King Alfred's version of Augustine's *Soliloquia*: some suggestions on its rationale and unity'. In *Old English Prose: Basic Readings*, ed. Paul E. Szarmach, with the assistance of Deborah A. Oosterhouse, 199–236. Basic Readings in Anglo-Saxon England 5. New York: Garland, 2000.

Gatch, Milton McC. *Preaching and Theology in Anglo-Saxon England: Ælfric and Wulfstan.* Toronto: University of Toronto Press, 1977.

George, J.-A. "'Hwalas þec herigað": creation, closure and the *Hapax Legomena* of the OE *Daniel*'. In *Lexis and Texts in Early English: Studies Presented to Jane Roberts*, ed. Christian J. Kay and Louise M. Sylvester, 105–16. Costerus ns 133. Amsterdam: Rodopi, 2001.

Georgianna, Linda. 'King Hrethel's sorrow and the limits of heroic action in *Beowulf*'. *Speculum* 62 (1987): 829–50.

Gilligan, Thomas F., trans. *The Soliloquies of Saint Augustine.* New York: Cosmopolitan Science & Art, 1943.

Gneuss, Helmut. *Handlist of Anglo-Saxon Manuscripts. A List of Manuscripts and Manuscript Fragments Written or Owned in England up to 1100.* MRTS 241. Tempe: ACMRS, 2001.

Godden, Malcolm, ed. *Ælfric's Catholic Homilies: Introduction, Commentary, and Glossary.* EETS ss 18. Oxford: Oxford University Press, 2000.

Godden, Malcolm, ed. *Ælfric's Catholic Homilies: The Second Series.* EETS ss 5. London: Oxford University Press, 1979.

Godden, Malcolm. 'Apocalypse and invasion in late Anglo-Saxon England'. In *From Anglo-Saxon to Early Middle English: Studies Presented to E.G. Stanley*, ed. Malcolm Godden, Douglas Gray, and Terry Hoad, 130–62. Oxford: Clarendon Press, 1994.

Godden, Malcolm. 'Did King Alfred write anything?' *MÆ* 76 (2007): 1–23.

Godden, Malcolm. 'Text and eschatology in Book III of the Old English *Soliloquies*'. *Anglia* 121 (2003): 177–209.

Godden, Malcolm, and Susan Irvine, eds. *The Old English Boethius: An Edition of the Old English Versions of Boethius's 'De Consolatione Philosophiae'.* 2 vols. Oxford: Oxford University Press, 2009.

Godden, Malcolm, and Michael Lapidge, eds. *The Cambridge Companion to Old English Literature.* Cambridge: Cambridge University Press, 1991.

Godlove, Shannon N. 'Bodies as borders: cannibalism and conversion in the Old English *Andreas*'. *SP* 106 (2009): 137–60.

Goldsmith, Margaret E. *The Mode and Meaning of 'Beowulf'.* London: Athlone, 1970.

Gonser, Paul, ed. *Das angelsächsische Prose-Leben des hl. Guthlac.* Heidelberg, Carl Winter's Universitätsbuchhandlung, 1909.

Goolden, Peter, ed. *The Old English Apollonius of Tyre.* Oxford: Oxford University Press, 1958.

Green, Richard H., trans. *The Consolation of Philosophy.* Indianapolis: Bobbs-Merrill, 1962.

Gretsch, Mechthild. *Ælfric and the Cult of the Saints in Late Anglo-Saxon England.* CSASE 34. Cambridge: Cambridge University Press, 2005.

Gretsch, Mechthild. 'A Context for *Resignation A*?' In *Intertexts: Studies in Anglo-Saxon Culture Presented to Paul E. Szarmach*, ed. Virginia Blanton and Helene Scheck, 103–17. MRTS 334. Arizona Studies in the Middle Ages and the Renaissance 24. Tempe: ACMRS, 2008.

Griffith, M.S. 'Poetic language and the Paris Psalter: the decay of the Old English tradition'. *ASE* 20 (1991): 167–86.

Grossi, Joseph. 'Preserving the future in the Old English *Durham*'. *JEGP* 111 (2012): 42–73.

Gwara, Scott. '*Forht* and *fægen* in *The Wanderer* and related literary contexts of Anglo-Saxon warrior wisdom'. *MS* 69 (2008): 255–98.

Hall, Alaric. 'Constructing Anglo-Saxon sanctity: tradition, innovation and Saint Guthlac'. In *Images of Medieval Sanctity: Essays in Honour of Gary Dickson*, ed. Debra Higgs Strickland, 207–35. Visualising the Middle Ages 1. Leiden: Brill, 2007.

Hall, J.R. 'The Old English epic of redemption: the theological unity of MS Junius 11'. In *The Poems of MS Junius 11: Basic Readings*, ed. Roy M. Liuzza, 20–68. Basic Readings in Anglo-Saxon England 8. New York: Routledge, 2002.

Hall, Thomas N. 'The armaments of John the Baptist in *Blickling Homily 14* and the Exeter Book *Descent into Hell*'. In *Intertexts: Studies in Anglo-Saxon Culture Presented to Paul E. Szarmach*, ed. Virginia Blanton and Helene Scheck, 289–306. MRTS 334. Arizona Studies in the Middle Ages and the Renaissance 24. Tempe: ACMRS, 2008.

Hall, Thomas N. 'Prophetic vision in *The Dream of the Rood*'. In *Poetry, Place, and Gender: Studies in Medieval Culture in Honor of Helen Damico*, ed. Catherine E. Karkov, 60–74. Kalamazoo: Medieval Institute Publications, 2009.

Halsall, Maureen. *The Rune Poem: A Critical Edition*. McMaster Old English Studies and Texts 2. Toronto: University of Toronto Press, 1981.

Hamerow, Helena, David Alban Hinton, and Sally Crawford, eds. *The Oxford Handbook of Anglo-Saxon Archaeology*. Oxford: Oxford University Press, 2011.

Hansen, Elaine Tuttle. *The Solomon Complex: Reading Wisdom in Old English Poetry*. McMaster Old English Studies and Texts 5. Toronto: University of Toronto Press, 1988.

Harbus, Antonina. 'Articulate contact in *Juliana*'. In *Verbal Encounters: Anglo-Saxon and Old Norse Studies for Roberta Frank*, ed. Antonia Harbus and Russell Poole, 183–200. Toronto Old English Series 13. Toronto: University of Toronto Press, 2005.

Hargrove, Henry Lee, trans. *King Alfred's Old English Version of St. Augustine's Soliloquies Turned into Modern English*. New York: H. Holt and Co., 1904.

Harris, Joseph. 'Beasts of battle, south and north'. In *Source of Wisdom: Old English and Early Medieval Latin Studies in Honour of Thomas D. Hill*, ed. Charles D. Wright, Frederick M. Biggs, and Thomas N. Hall, 3–25. Toronto Old English Series 16. Toronto: University of Toronto Press, 2007.

Harris, Joseph. '*Beowulf* as epic'. *OT* 15 (2000): 159–69.

Harris, Joseph. '*Deor* and its refrain: preliminaries to an interpretation'. *Traditio* 43 (1987): 23–53.

Harris, Stephen J. 'The liturgical context of Ælfric's homilies for rogation'. In *The Old English Homily: Precedent, Practice, and Appropriation*, ed. Aaron J. Kleist, 143–69. Studies in the Early Middle Ages 17. Turnhout: Brepols, 2007.

Harris, Stephen J. *Race and Ethnicity in Anglo-Saxon Literature*. Medieval History and Culture 24. New York: Routledge, 2003.

Hartman, Megan E. 'A drawn-out beheading: style, theme, and hypermetricity in the Old English *Judith*'. *JEGP* 110 (2011): 421–40.

Havelock, Eric. *Preface to Plato*. 1963. Rpt. Cambridge: Harvard University Press, 1982.

Head, Pauline. 'Perpetual history in the Old English *Menologium*'. In *The Medieval Chronicle: Proceedings of the 1st International Conference on the Medieval Chronicle*, ed. Erik Kooper, 155–162. Costerus ns 120. Amsterdam: Rodopi, 1999.

Hecht, Hans, ed. *Bischof Wærferths von Worcester Übersetzung der Dialoge Gregors des Grossen*. Leipzig, 1900–07. Rpt. Darmstadt: Wissenschaftliche Buchgesellschaft, 1965.

Heckman, Christina. 'Things in doubt: inventio, dialectic, and Jewish secrets in Cynewulf's *Elene*'. *JEGP* 108 (2009): 449–80.

Herzfeld, George, ed. and trans. *An Old English Martyrology*. EETS os 116. 1900. Rpt. London: Boydell and Brewer, 2005.

Heuchan, Valerie. 'God's co-workers and powerful tools: a study of the sources of Alfred's building metaphor in his Old English translation of Augustine's *Soliloquies*'. *NQ* ns 54 (2007): 1–11.

Heyworth, Melanie. '*Apollonius of Tyre* in its manuscript context: an issue of marriage'. *PQ* 86 (2007): 1–26.

Hickes, George. *Linguarum veterum septentrionalium thesaurus grammatico-criticus et archæologicus*. 1703–05. Rpt. 2 vols. in 1, New York: George Olms, 1970.

Higham, N.J. *(Re-)reading Bede: the 'Ecclesiastical History' in Context*. New York: Routledge, 2006.

Hill, David. *An Atlas of Anglo-Saxon England*. 1981. 2nd edn. Oxford: Blackwell, 2002.

Hill, John M. *The Anglo-Saxon Warrior Ethic: Reconstructing Lordship in Early English Literature*. Gainesville: University Press of Florida, 2000.

Hill, John M. *The Narrative Pulse of 'Beowulf': Arrivals and Departures*. Toronto Old English Series 17. Toronto: University of Toronto Press, 2008.

Hill, Thomas D. 'Literary history and Old English poetry: the case of *Christ I, II,* and *III*'. In *Sources of Anglo-Saxon Culture*, ed. Paul E. Szarmach and Virginia D. Oggins, 3–22. Kalamazoo: Medieval Institute Publications, 1986.

Hill, Thomas D. 'The *Passio Andreae* and *The Dream of the Rood*'. *ASE* 38 (2009): 1–10.

Hill, Thomas D. 'Sapiential structure and figural narrative in the Old English *Elene*'. *Traditio* 27 (1971): 159–77.

Hill, Thomas D. 'The unchanging hero: a stoic maxim in *The Wanderer* and its contexts'. *SP* 101 (2004): 233–49.

Himes, Jonathan. *The Old English Epic of 'Waldere'*. Newcastle upon Tyne: Cambridge Scholars Publishing, 2009.

Hitch, Susan. 'Alfred's cræft: imagery in Alfred's version of Augustine's *Soliloquies*'. *Journal of the Department of English* (University of Calcutta) 22 (1986–87): 130–47.

Holsinger, Bruce. 'The parable of Caedmon's *Hymn*: liturgical invention and literary tradition'. *JEGP* 106 (2007): 149–75.

Homer. *The Iliad*. Trans. Robert Fitzgerald. New York: Doubleday, 1989.

Horner, Shari. 'En/closed subjects: *The Wife's Lament* and the culture of early medieval female monasticism'. *Æstel* 2 (1994): 45–61.

Howe, Nicholas. 'Falling into place: dislocation in the Junius Book'. In *Unlocking the Wordhord: Anglo-Saxon Studies in Memory of Edward B. Irving, Jr.*, ed. Mark C. Amodio and Katherine O'Brien O'Keeffe, 14–37. Toronto: University of Toronto Press, 2003.

Howe, Nicholas. *Writing the Map of Anglo-Saxon England: Essays in Cultural Geography* New Haven: Yale University Press, 2008.

Hughes, Merritt Y., ed. *John Milton: Complete Poems and Major Prose*. 1957. Rpt. Indianapolis: Odyssey Press, 1975.

Irvine, Susan, ed. *The Anglo-Saxon Chronicle: A Collaborative Edition*. Vol. 7: MS E. Cambridge: D.S. Brewer, 2004.

Irvine, Susan. 'Fragments of Boethius: the reconstruction of the Cotton manuscript of the Alfredian text'. *ASE* 34 (2005): 169–81.

Irvine, Susan. 'Speaking one's mind in *The Wanderer*'. In *Inside Old English: Essays in Honour of Bruce Mitchell*, ed. John Walmsley, 117–33. Oxford: Blackwell, 2006.

Irving, Edward B., Jr. 'The advent of poetry: *Christ I*'. *ASE* 25 (1996): 123–34.

Irving, Edward B., Jr. 'The nature of Christianity in *Beowulf*'. *ASE* 13 (1984): 7–21.

Irving, Edward B., Jr. *Rereading 'Beowulf'*. 1989. Rpt. Philadelphia: University of Pennsylvania Press, 1992.

Jacobs, Christina. '*Precepts* and the Exeter Book of vernacular instructive poetry'. In *Varieties and Consequences of Literacy and Orality*, ed. Ursula Schaefer and Edda Spielmann, 33–48. Tübingen: G. Narr, 2001.

Jager, Eric. 'Tempter as rhetoric teacher: the fall of language in the Old English *Genesis B*'. In *The Poems of MS Junius 11: Basic Readings*, ed. Roy M. Liuzza, 99–118. Basic Readings in Anglo-Saxon England 8. London: Routledge, 2002.

Jeffrey, J. Elizabeth. *Blickling Spirituality and the Old English Vernacular Homily: A Textual Analysis*. Studies in Mediaeval Literature 1. Lewiston: Edwin Mellen Press, 1989.

Johnson, David F. 'Hagiographical demon or liturgical devil? Demonology and baptismal imagery in Cynewulf's *Elene*'. *LSE* ns 37 (2006): 9–30.

Johnson, David F. 'Spiritual combat and the Land of Canaan in *Guthlac A*'. In *Intertexts: Studies in Anglo-Saxon Culture Presented to Paul E. Szarmach*, ed. Virginia Blanton and Helene Scheck, 307–17. MRTS 334. Arizona Studies in the Middle Ages 24. Tempe: ACMRS, 2008.

Johnson, Samuel. *A Dictionary of the English Language*. 2 vols. London: W. Strahan, 1755.

Jolly, Karen. 'Cross-referencing Anglo-Saxon liturgy and remedies: the sign of the cross as ritual protection'. In *The Liturgy of the Late Anglo-Saxon Church*, ed. Helen Gittos and M. Bradford Bedingfield, 213–43. Woodbridge: Boydell Press, 2005.

Jones, Chris. *Strange Likeness: The Use of Old English in Twentieth-Century Poetry*. Oxford: Oxford University Press, 2006.

Jones, Chris. 'Where now the harp? Listening for the sounds of Old English verse, from *Beowulf* to the twentieth century'. *OT* 24 (2009): 485–502.

Joy, Eileen A. and Mary K. Ramsey, eds. with the assistance of Bruce D. Gilchrist. *The Postmodern 'Beowulf': A Critical Casebook*. Morgantown: West Virginia University Press, 2006.

Jurasinski, Stefan. 'Caring for the dead in *The Fortunes of Men*'. *PQ* 86 (2007): 343–63.

Karkov, Catherine E. 'The Anglo-Saxon *Genesis*: text, illustration, and audience'. In *The Old English Hexateuch: Aspects and Approaches*, ed. Rebecca Barnhouse and Benjamin C. Withers, 201–37. Publications of the Rawlinson Center 2. Kalamazoo: Medieval Institute Publications, 2000.

Keefer, Sarah Larratt. 'Respect for the book: a reconsideration of "form", "content" and "context" in two vernacular poems'. In *New Approaches to Editing Old English Verse*, ed. Sarah Larratt Keefer and Katherine O'Brien O'Keeffe, 21–44. Rochester: D.S. Brewer, 1998.

Kendall, Calvin B. 'From sign to vision: the Ruthwell Cross and the *Dream of the Rood*'. In *The Place of the Cross*, ed. Catherine Karkov, Sarah Larratt Keefer, and Karen Louise Jolly, 129–44. Woodbridge: Boydell Press, 2006.

Ker, N.R., ed. *Catalogue of Manuscripts Containing Anglo-Saxon*. 1957. Rpt. Oxford: Clarendon Press, 1990.

Ker, N.R., ed. *The Pastoral Care: King Alfred's Translation of St. Gregory's Regula Pastoralis. MS. Hatton 20 in the Bodleian Library at Oxford, MS. Cotton Tiberius B.XI in the British Museum, MS. Anhang 19 in the Landesbibliothek at Kassel*. EEMF 6. Copenhagen: Rosenkilde and Bagger, 1956.

Keynes, Simon. 'The cult of King Alfred the Great'. *ASE* 28 (1999): 225–356.

Keynes, Simon, and Michael Lapidge, trans. *Alfred the Great. Asser's Life of King Alfred and Other Contemporary Sources*. London: Penguin Books, 1983.

Kiernan, Kevin. 'Alfred the Great's burnt *Boethius*'. In *The Iconic Page in Manuscript, Print, and Digital Culture*, ed. George Bornstein and Theresa Tinkle, 7–32. Ann Arbor: University of Michigan Press, 1998.

Kiernan, Kevin. *'Beowulf' and the Beowulf Manuscript*. 1981. Rev. edn. Ann Arbor: University of Michigan Press, 1996.

Kiernan, Kevin. 'Reading Cædmon's "Hymn" with someone else's glosses'. *Representations* 32 (1990): 157–74.

Kim, Susan M. '"If one who is loved is not present, a letter may be embraced instead": Death and the *Letter of Alexander to Aristotle*'. *JEGP* 109 (2010): 33–51.

Kinch, Ashby. 'The ethical agency of the female lyric voice: *The Wife's Lament* and Catullus 64'. *SP* 103 (2006): 121–52.

Kirkland, James W. and Charles E. Modlin. 'The art of *Azarias*'. *MÆ* 41 (1972): 9–15.

Klaeber, Frederick, ed. *'Beowulf' and the 'Fight at Finnsburg'*. 1922. 3rd edn. Lexington: D.C. Heath and Co., 1950.

Klausner, David N. 'Petitionary poetry in Old English and Early Welsh: *Deor, Widsið, Dadolwch Urien*'. In *Poetry, Place, and Gender: Studies in Medieval Culture in Honor of Helen Damico*, ed. Catherine E. Karkov, 197–210. Kalamazoo: Medieval Institute Publications, 2009.

Klein, Stacy S. 'Gender and the nature of exile in Old English elegies'. In *A Place to Believe In: Locating Medieval Landscapes*, ed. Clare A. Lees and Gillian Overing, 113–31. University Park: Pennsylvania State University Press, 2006.

Klein, Stacy S. *Ruling Women: Queenship and Gender in Anglo-Saxon Literature*. Notre Dame: University of Notre Dame Press, 2006.

Klinck, Anne L. *The Old English Elegies: A Critical Edition and Genre Study*. Montreal and Kingston: McGill–Queen's University Press, 1992.

Klinck, Anne L. 'Poetic markers of gender in medieval "woman's song": was anonymous a woman?' *Neophilologus* 87 (2003): 339–59.

Klinck, Anne L. '*The Riming Poem*: design and interpretation'. *NM* 89 (1988): 266–79.

Kowalik, Barbara. 'The motif of journey in Cynewulf's *Fates of the Apostles*'. In *Þe comoun peplis language*, ed. Marcin Krygier and Liliana Sikorska, 99–111. Medieval English Mirror 6. New York: Peter Lang, 2010.

Kotzor, Günter. 'The Latin tradition of martyrologies and the *Old English Martyrology*'. In *Studies in Earlier Old English Prose*, ed. Paul E. Szarmach, 301–33. Albany: State University of New York Press, 1986.

Krapp, George Philip, ed. *The Junius Manuscript*. ASPR 1. 1931. Rpt. New York: Columbia University Press, 2003.

Krapp, George Philip, ed. *The Paris Psalter and the Meters of Boethius*. ASPR 5. 1932. Rpt. New York: Columbia University Press, 2004.

Krapp, George Philip, ed. *The Vercelli Book*. ASPR 2. 1932. Rpt. New York: Columbia University Press, 2004.

Krapp, George Philip, and Elliott Van Kirk Dobbie, eds. *The Exeter Book*. ASPR 3. 1936. Rpt. New York: Columbia University Press, 2004.

Langeslad, Paul S. 'Boethian similitude in *Deor* and *The Wanderer*'. *NM* 109 (2008): 205–22.

Lapidge, Michael. '*Beowulf* and the psychology of terror'. In *Heroic Poetry in the Anglo-Saxon Period: Studies in Honor of Jess B. Bessinger, Jr.*, ed. Helen Damico and John Leyerle, 373–402. Studies in Medieval Culture 32. Kalamazoo: Medieval Institute Publications, 1993.

Lapidge, Michael. 'The career of Aldhelm'. *ASE* 36 (2007): 15–69.

Lapidge, Michael. 'Cynewulf and the *Passio S. Iulianae*'. In *Unlocking the Wordhord: Anglo-Saxon Studies in Memory of Edward B. Irving, Jr.*, ed. Mark C. Amodio and Katherine O'Brien O'Keeffe, 147–71. Toronto: University of Toronto Press, 2003.

Lapidge, Michael. 'Versifying the Bible in the Middle Ages'. In *The Text in the Community: Essays on Medieval Works, Manuscripts, Authors, and Readers*, ed. Jill Mann and Maura Nolan, 11–40. Notre Dame: University of Notre Dame Press, 2006.

Lapidge, Michael, John Blair, Simon Keynes, and Donald Scragg, eds. *The Blackwell Encyclopaedia of Anglo-Saxon England*. 1999. Rpt. Oxford: Blackwell, 2004.

Lee, Alvin A. *The Guest-Hall of Eden: Four Essays on the Design of Old English Poetry*. New Haven: Yale University Press, 1972.

Lees, Clare A. 'Men and *Beowulf*'. In *Medieval Masculinities: Regarding Men in the Middle Ages*, ed. Clare A. Lees, 129–48. Medieval Cultures 7. Minneapolis: University of Minnesota Press, 1994.

Lees, Clare A. ed., with the assistance of Thelma Fenster and Jo Ann McNamara. *Medieval Masculinities: Regarding Men in the Middle Ages*. Medieval Cultures 7. Minneapolis: University of Minnesota Press, 1994.

Lerer, Seth. '"On fagne flor": The postcolonial *Beowulf*, from Heorot to Heaney'. In *Postcolonial Approaches to the European Middle Ages: Translating Cultures*, ed. Ananya Jahanara Kabir and Deanne Williams, 77–102. Cambridge Studies in Medieval Literature 54. Cambridge: Cambridge University Press, 2005.

Lerer, Seth. *Literacy and Power in Anglo-Saxon Literature*, Lincoln: University of Nebraska Press, 1991.

Langeslag, Paul S. 'Boethian similitude in *Deor* and *The Wanderer*'. *NM* 109 (2008): 205–22.

Liggins, Elizabeth M. 'The authorship of the Old English *Orosius*'. *Anglia* 88 (1970): 290–322.

Lionarons, Joyce Tally. 'From monster to martyr: the Old English legend of Saint Christopher'. In *Marvels, Monsters, and Miracles: Studies in the Medieval and Early Modern Imaginations*, ed. Timothy S. Jones and David A. Sprunger, 167–82. Studies in Medieval Culture 42. Kalamazoo: Medieval Institute Publications, 2002.

Liuzza, Roy M. 'The Tower of Babel: *The Wanderer* and the ruins of history'. *Studies in the Literary Imagination* 36 (2003): 1–35.

Lochrie, Karma. 'Gender, sexual violence, and the politics of war in the Old English *Judith*'. In *Class and Gender in Early English Literature: Intersections*, ed. Britton J. Harwood and Gillian R. Overing, 1–20. Bloomington: Indiana University Press, 1994.

Lochrie, Karma. 'The structure and wisdom of *Judgment Day I*'. *NM* 87 (1986): 201–10.

Lochrie, Karma. 'Wyrd and the limits of human understanding: a thematic sequence in the "Exeter Book"'. *JEGP* 85 (1986): 323–31.

Lockett, Leslie. 'An integrated re-examination of the dating of Oxford, Bodleian, Library Junius 11'. *ASE* 31 (2002): 141–73.

Lockett, Leslie. 'The role of Grendel's arm in feud, law, and the narrative strategy of *Beowulf*'. In *Latin Learning and English Lore: Studies in Anglo-Saxon Literature for Michael Lapidge*, ed. Katherine O'Brien O'Keeffe and Andy Orchard, vol. I, 368–88. Toronto Old English Series 14. 2 vols. Toronto: University of Toronto Press, 2005.

Lord, Albert Bates. 'Cædmon revisited'. In *Heroic Poetry in the Anglo-Saxon Period: Studies in Honor of Jess B. Bessinger, Jr.*, ed. Helen Damico and John Leyerle, 121–37. Studies in Medieval Culture 32. Kalamazoo: Medieval Institute Publications, 1993.

Low, Anthony. *Aspects of Subjectivity: Society and Individuality from the Middle Ages to Shakespeare and Milton*. Pittsburgh: Duquesne University Press, 2003.

Magennis, Hugh. 'Ælfric and heroic literature'. In *The Power of Words: Anglo-Saxon Studies Presented to Donald G. Scragg on his Seventieth Birthday*, ed. Hugh Magennis and Jonathan Wilcox, 31–60. Morgantown: West Virginia University Press, 2006.

Magennis, Hugh. 'Gender and heroism in the Old English *Judith*'. In *Writing Gender and Genre in Medieval Literature: Approaches to Old and Middle English Texts*, ed. Elaine M. Treharne, 5–18. Cambridge: Cambridge University Press, 2002.

Magennis, Hugh. 'The solitary journey: aloneness and community in *The Seafarer*'. In *Text, Image, Interpretation: Studies in Anglo-Saxon Literature and Its Insular Context in Honour of Éamon Ó Carragáin*, ed. A.J. Minnis and Jane Roberts, 303–18. Studies in the Early Middle Ages 18. Turnhout: Brepols, 2007.

Magennis, Hugh. 'Warrior saints, warfare, and the hagiography of Ælfric of Eynsham'. *Traditio* 56 (2001): 27–51.

Magennis, Hugh, and Mary Swan, eds. *A Companion to Ælfric*. Brill's Companions to the Christian Tradition 18. Leiden: Brill, 2009.

Marchand, James W. 'The leaps of Christ and *The Dream of the Rood*'. In *Source of Wisdom: Old English and Early Medieval Latin Studies in Honour of Thomas D. Hill*, ed. Charles D. Wright, Frederick M. Biggs, and Thomas N. Hall, 80–89. Toronto Old English Series 16. Toronto: University of Toronto Press, 2007.

Matto, Michael. 'The Old English *Soul and Body I* and *Soul and Body II*: ending the rivalry'. *In Geardagum* 18 (1997): 39–58.

Matto, Michael. 'True confessions: "The Seafarer" and technologies of the "Sylf"'. *JEGP* 103 (2004): 156–79.

Matto, Michael. 'A war of containment: the heroic image in *The Battle of Maldon*'. *SN* 74 (2002): 60–75.

Mayr-Harting, Henry. *The Coming of Christianity to Anglo-Saxon England*. 1972. 3rd edn. University Park: Pennsylvania State University Press, 1991.

McBrine, Patrick. 'The journey motif in the poems of the Vercelli Book'. In *New Readings in the Vercelli Book*, ed. Samantha Zacher and Andy Orchard, 298–317. Toronto Anglo-Saxon Series 4. Toronto: University of Toronto Press, 2009.

McCulloh, John M. 'Did Cynewulf use a martyrology? Reconsidering the sources of *The Fates of the Apostles*'. *ASE* 29 (2000): 67–83.

McEntire, Sandra. 'The monastic context of Old English "Precepts"'. *NM* 91 (1990): 243–49.

McFadden, Brian. 'The social context of narrative disruption in *The Letter of Alexander to Aristotle*'. *ASE* 30 (2001): 91–114.

McFadden, Brian. 'Sweet odors and interpretive authority in the Exeter Book *Physiologus* and *Phoenix*'. *Papers on Language and Literature* 42 (2006): 181–209.

McKinnell, John. 'A farewell to Old English elegy: the case of *Vainglory*'. *Parergon* ns 9 (1991): 67–89.

Menner, Robert J., ed. *The Poetical Dialogues of Solomon and Saturn*. New York: MLA, 1941.

Menner, Robert J. 'The vocabulary of the Old English poems on Judgment Day'. *PMLA* 62 (1947): 583–97.

Millar, Angel. '*The Old English Rune Poem* – semantics, structure, and symmetry'. *Journal of Indo-European Studies* 34 (2006): 419–36.

Miller, Thomas, ed. and trans. *The Old English Version of Bede's Ecclesiastical History of the English People*. EETS os 95–96. 1890. Rpt. Woodbridge: Boydell and Brewer, 2007.

Mitchell, Bruce. *A Critical Bibliography of Old English Syntax to the End of 1984*. Oxford: Blackwell, 1990.

Mitchell, Bruce. *Old English Syntax*. 2 vols. Oxford: Clarendon Press, 1985.

Mitchell, Bruce, and Fred C. Robinson, eds. 1982. *A Guide to Old English*. 8th edn. Oxford: Wiley-Blackwell, 2012.

Mitchell, Bruce, and Fred C. Robinson, eds. *Old English Verse Texts from Many Sources: A Comprehensive Collection*. EEMF 23. Copenhagen: Rosenkilde and Bagger, 1991.

Mintz, Susannah B. 'Words devilish and divine: Eve as speaker in *Genesis B*'. *Neophilologus* 81 (1997): 609–23.

Mittman, Asa Simon. *Maps and Monsters in Medieval England*. Studies in Medieval History and Culture. New York: Routledge, 2006.

Molyneaux, George. 'The *Old English Bede*: English ideology or Christian instruction?' *EHR* 124 (2009): 1289–1323.

Momma, Haruko. 'The education of Beowulf and the affair of the leisure class'. In *Verbal Encounters: Anglo-Saxon and Old Norse Studies for Roberta Frank*, ed. Antonia Harbus and Russell Poole, 163–82. Toronto Old English Series 13. Toronto: University of Toronto Press, 2005.

Morey, James H. 'Adam and Judas in the Old English *Christ and Satan*'. *SP* 87 (1990): 397–409.

Morris, Richard, ed. and trans. *The Blickling Homilies of the Tenth Century*. EETS os 58, 63, and 73. 1874. Rpt. Woodbridge: Boydell and Brewer, 1997.

Mullally, Erin. 'The cross-gendered gift: weaponry in the Old English *Judith*'. *Exemplaria* 17 (2005): 255–84.

Murphy, Patrick J. *Unriddling the Exeter Riddles*. University Park: Pennsylvania State University Press, 2011.

Niles, John D. *Old English Enigmatic Poems and the Play of the Texts*. Studies in the Early Middle Ages 13. Turnhout: Brepols, 2006.

Niles, John D. *Old English Heroic Poems and the Social Life of Texts*. Studies in the Early Middle Ages 20. Turnhout: Brepols, 2007.

Nokes, Richard Scott. 'The several compilers of Bald's *Leechbook*'. *ASE* 33 (2004): 51–76.

O'Brien O'Keeffe, Katherine, ed. *The Anglo-Saxon Chronicle: A Collaborative Edition*. Vol. 5: *MS C*. Cambridge: D.S. Brewer, 2001.

O'Brien O'Keeffe, Katherine. 'Inside, outside, conduct and judgment: King Alfred reads the *Regula Pastoralis*'. In '*Un serto di fiori in man recando': Scritti in onore di Maria Amalia D'Aronco*, ed. Silvana Serafin and Patrizia Lendinara, 333–45. 2 vols. Undine: Forum, 2007.

O'Brien O'Keeffe, Katherine. 'Source, method, theory, practice: on reading two Old English verse texts'. In *Textual and Material Culture in Anglo-Saxon England: Thomas Northcote Toller and the Toller Memorial Lectures*, ed. Donald Scragg, 161–81. Publications of the Manchester Centre for Anglo-Saxon Studies 1. Cambridge: D.S. Brewer, 2003.

O'Brien O'Keeffe, Katherine. *Visible Song: Transitional Literacy in Old English Verse*. CSASE 4. Cambridge: Cambridge University Press, 1990.

O'Camb, Brian. 'Bishop Æthelwold and the shaping of the Old English Exeter *Maxims*'. *ES* 90 (2008): 253–73.

Ó Carragáin, Éamon. *Ritual and the Rood: Liturgical Images and the Old English Poems of the 'Dream of the Rood' Tradition*. British Library Studies in Medieval Culture. London and Toronto: The British Library and University of Toronto Press, 2005.

Ó Carragáin, Éamon, and Richard North. 'The *Dream of the Rood* and Anglo-Saxon Northumbria'. In '*Beowulf*' and Other Stories: A New Introduction to Old English, Old Icelandic, and Anglo-Norman Literatures*, ed. Richard North and Joe Allard, 160–88. 2007. 2nd edn. New York: Pearson/Longman, 2012.

O'Donnell, Daniel P. *Cædmon's Hymn: A Multimedia Study, Edition, and Archive*. Cambridge: D.S. Brewer in association with SEENET and The Medieval Academy, 2005.

Ogawa, Hiroshi. 'Stylistic features of the Old English *Apollonius of Tyre*'. *Poetica* (Tokyo) 34 (1991): 57–74.

Olsen, Alexandra Hennessey. 'Cynewulf's autonomous women: a reconsideration of Juliana and Elene'. In *New Readings on Women in Old English Literature*, ed. Helen Damico and Alexandra Hennessey Olsen, 222–34. Bloomington: Indiana University Press, 1990.

Olsen, Alexandra Hennessey. *Guthlac of Croyland: A Study of Heroic Hagiography*. Washington: University Press of America, 1981.

Olsen, Alexandra Hennessey. *Speech, Song, and Poetic Craft: The Artistry of the Cynewulf Canon*. New York: Peter Lang, 1984.

Olsen, Alexandra Hennessey. 'Subtractive rectification and the Old English *Riming Poem*'. *In Geardagum* 24 (2003): 57–66.

O'Neill, Patrick P. *King Alfred's Old English Prose Translations of the First Fifty Psalms*. Cambridge: Medieval Academy of America, 2001.

O'Neill, Patrick P. 'The Old English introductions to the prose psalms of the Paris Psalter: sources, structure, and composition'. *SP* 78 (1981): 20–38.

Orchard, Andy. 'Beowulf and other battlers: an introduction to *Beowulf*'. In '*Beowulf*' and Other Stories: A New Introduction to Old English, Old Icelandic and Anglo-Norman Literatures*, ed. Richard North and Joe Allard, 63–94. 2007. 2nd edn. New York: Pearson/Longman, 2012.

Orchard, Andy. *A Critical Companion to 'Beowulf'*. Cambridge: D.S. Brewer, 2003.

Orchard, Andy. 'The *Dream of the Rood*: Cross-references'. In *New Readings in the Vercelli Book*, ed. Samantha Zacher and Andy Orchard, 225–53. Toronto Anglo-Saxon Series 4. Toronto: University of Toronto Press, 2009.

Orchard, Andy. 'Enigma variations: the Anglo-Saxon riddle-tradition'. In *Latin Learning and English Lore: Studies in Anglo-Saxon Literature for Michael Lapidge*, ed. Katherine O'Brien O'Keeffe and Andy Orchard, vol. I, 284–304. Toronto Old English Series 14. 2 vols. Toronto: University of Toronto Press, 2005.

Orchard, Andy. 'Intoxication, fornication, and multiplication: the burgeoning text of *Genesis A*'. In *Text, Image, Interpretation: Studies in Anglo-Saxon Literature and Its Insular Context in Honour of Éamon Ó Carragáin*, ed. A.J. Minnis and Jane Roberts, 333–54. Studies in the Early Middle Ages 18. Turnhout: Brepols, 2007.

Orchard, Andy. 'Poetic inspiration and prosaic translation: the making of *Cædmon's Hymn*'. In *Studies in English Language and Literature. 'Doubt Wisely': Papers in Honour of E.G. Stanley*, ed. M.J. Toswell and E.M. Tyler, 402–22. London: Routledge, 1996.

Orchard, Andy. *Pride and Prodigies: Studies in the Monsters of the 'Beowulf' Manuscript*. 1985. Rev. edn. Toronto: University of Toronto Press, 1995.

Orchard, Andy. 'Reconstructing *The Ruin*'. In *Intertexts: Studies in Anglo-Saxon Culture Presented to Paul E. Szarmach*, ed. Virginia Blanton and Helene Scheck, 45–68. MRTS 334. Arizona Studies in the Middle Ages and the Renaissance 24. Tempe: ACMRS, 2008.

Orchard, Andy. 'Re-reading *The Wanderer*: the value of cross-references'. In *Via Crucis: Essays on Early Medieval Sources and Ideas in Memory of J.E. Cross*, ed. Thomas N. Hall,

Thomas D. Hill, and Charles D. Wright, 1–26. Medieval European Studies 1. Morgantown: West Virginia University Press, 2002.

Orchard, Andy. 'The word made flesh: Christianity and oral culture in Anglo-Saxon verse'. *OT* 24 (2009): 293–318.

Orchard, Andy. 'Wulfstan as reader, writer, and rewriter'. In *The Old English Homily: Precedent, Practice, and Appropriation*, ed. Aaron J. Kleist, 157–82. Studies in the Early Middle Ages 17. Turnhout: Brepols, 2007.

Orton, Peter. 'The form and structure of *The Seafarer*'. In *Old English Literature: Critical Essays*, ed. Roy M. Liuzza, 353–81. New Haven: Yale University Press, 2002.

Parkes, M.B. *Pause and Effect: An Introduction to the History of Punctuation in the West.* Berkeley and Los Angeles: University of California Press, 1993.

Parkes, M.B. *Scribes, Scripts, and Readers: Studies in the Communication, Presentation, and Dissemination of Medieval Texts.* London: Hambledon Press, 1991.

Parks, Ward. 'The traditional narrator and the "I heard" formulas in Old English poetry'. *ASE* 16 (1987): 45–66.

Pelteret, David, ed. *Anglo-Saxon History: Basic Readings.* Basic Readings in Anglo-Saxon England 6. New York: Garland, 2000.

Peck, Russell, ed., with Latin translations by Andrew Galloway. *Confessio Amantis.* 2000. 3 vols. Vol. 1. Middle English Texts. 2nd edn. Kalamazoo: Medieval Institute Publications, 2006.

Petersen, Helle Falcher. '*The Phoenix*: the art of literary recycling'. *NM* 101 (2000): 375–86.

Plummer, Charles, ed. *Two of the Saxon Chronicles Parallel.* 2 vols. 1892 and 1899. Rpt. Oxford: Clarendon Press, 2000.

Pope, John C., ed. *Homilies of Ælfric: A Supplementary Collection.* 2 vols. EETS 259 and 260. Oxford: Oxford University Press, 1967 and 1968.

Portnoy, Phyllis. 'Ring composition and the digressions of *Exodus*: the "Legacy" of the "Remnant"'. *ES* 82 (2001): 289–307.

Powell, Kathryn. 'Orientalist fantasy in the poetic dialogues of *Solomon and Saturn*'. *ASE* 34 (2005): 117–43.

Powell, Stephen D. 'The journey forth: elegiac consolation in *Guthlac B*'. *ES* 79 (1998): 489–500.

Pratt, David. *The Political Thought of King Alfred the Great.* Cambridge: Cambridge University Press, 2010.

Pratt, David. 'Problems of authorship and audience in the writings of Alfred the Great'. In *Lay Intellectuals in the Carolingian World*, ed. Patrick Wormald and Janet L. Nelson, 162–91. Cambridge: Cambridge University Press, 2007.

Pulsiano, Phillip. 'Bees and backbiters in the Old English *Homiletic Fragment I*'. *ELN* 25 (1987): 1–6.

Pulsiano, Phillip. 'Spiritual despair in *Resignation B*'. *Neophilologus* 79 (1995): 155–62.

Rambaran-Olm, M.R. 'Is the title of the Old English poem *The Descent into Hell* suitable?' *SELIM: Journal of the Spanish Society for Medieval English Language and Literature* 13 (2005–6): 73–85.

Randle, Jonathan T. 'The "homiletics" of the Vercelli Book poems: the Case of *Homiletic Fragment I*'. In *New Readings in the Vercelli Book*, ed. Samantha Zacher and Andy Orchard, 185–224. Toronto Anglo-Saxon Series 4. Toronto: University of Toronto Press, 2009.

Rauer, Christine. 'Usage of the *Old English Martyrology*'. *Foundations of Learning: The Transfer of Encyclopaedic Knowledge in the Early Middle Ages*, ed. Rolf H. Bremmer, Jr. and Kees Dekker, 125–46. Storehouses of Wholesome Learning 1. Dudley: Peeters, 2007.

Raw, Barbara. 'The cross in *The Dream of the Rood*: martyr, patron, and image of Christ'. *LSE* ns 38 (2007): 1–15.

Raymond, Irving W., trans. *Seven Books of History against the Pagans.* New York: Columbia University Press, 1936.

Reichardt, Paul F. 'Bede on death and a neglected Old English lyric'. *Kentucky Philological Review* 12 (1997): 55–60.

Remley, Paul G. *Old English Biblical Verse: Studies in Genesis, Exodus, and Daniel*, 94–167. Cambridge: Cambridge University Press, 1996.

Renoir, Alain. 'Eve's I.Q. rating: two sexist views of *Genesis B*'. In *New Readings on Women in Old English Literature*, ed. Helen Damico and Alexandra Hennessey Olsen, 262–72. Bloomington: Indiana University Press, 1990.

Renoir, Alain. 'Introduction'. In *A Readable 'Beowulf': The Old English Epic Newly Translated*, trans. Stanley B. Greenfield, 1–26. Carbondale: Southern Illinois University Press, 1982.

Renoir, Alain. *A Key to Old Poems: The Oral-Formulaic Approach to the Interpretation of West-Germanic Verse*. University Park: Pennsylvania University Press, 1988.

Renoir, Alain. 'The least elegiac of the elegies: a contextual glance at *The Husband's Message*'. *SN* 53 (1981): 69–76.

Renoir, Alain. 'Oral-formulaic rhetoric and the interpretation of written texts'. In *Oral Tradition in Literature: Interpretation in Context*, ed. John Miles Foley, 103–135. Columbia: University of Missouri Press, 1986.

Renoir, Alain. 'Point of view and design for terror in *Beowulf*'. *NM* 63 (1962): 154–67.

Renoir, Alain. 'A reading of *The Wife's Lament*'. *ES* 58 (1977): 4–19.

Renoir, Alain. '*Wulf and Eadwacer*: a noninterpretation'. In *Franciplegius: Medieval and Linguistic Studies in Honor of Francis Peabody Magoun, Jr.*, ed. Jess B. Bessinger and Robert P. Creed, 147–63. New York: New York University Press, 1965.

Riedinger, Anita R. 'The Englishing of Arcestrate: woman in *Apollonius of Tyre*'. In *New Readings on Women in Old English Literature*, ed. Helen Damico and Alexandra Hennessey Olsen, 292–306. Bloomington: Indiana University Press, 1990.

Rives, J.B., trans. *Germania by Tacitus*. Oxford: Clarendon Press, 1999.

Roberts, Jane. '*Guthlac A*: sources and source hunting'. In *Medieval English Studies Presented to George Kane*, ed. Edward Donald Kennedy, Ronald Watson, and Joseph S. Wittig, 1–18. Suffolk: D.S. Brewer, 1988.

Roberts, Jane. 'A man *boca gleaw* and his musings'. In *Intertexts: Studies in Anglo-Saxon Culture Presented to Paul E. Szarmach*, ed. Virginia Blanton and Helene Scheck, 119–37. MRTS 334. Arizona Studies in the Middle Ages and the Renaissance 24. Tempe: ACMRS, 2008.

Roberts, Jane. 'The Old English prose translation of Felix's *Vita sancti Guthlaci*'. In *Studies in Earlier Old English Prose*, ed. Paul E. Szarmach, 363–79. Albany: State University of New York Press, 1986.

Roberts, Jane. 'Some relationships between the *Dream of the Rood* and the cross at Ruthwell'. *Studies in Medieval English Language and Literature* (Tokyo) 15 (2000): 1–25.

Rollman, David A. '*Widsith* as an Anglo-Saxon defense of poetry'. *Neophilologus* 66 (1982): 431–39.

Rosenthal, Joel T. 'Bede's *Ecclesiastical History*: numbers, hard data, and longevity'. In *Intertexts: Studies in Anglo-Saxon Culture Presented to Paul E. Szarmach*, ed. Virginia Blanton and Helene Scheck, 91–102. MRTS 334. Arizona Studies in the Middle Ages and the Renaissance 24. Tempe: ACMRS, 2008.

Rosenthal, Joel T. 'Bede's use of miracles in *The Ecclesiastical History*'. *Traditio* 31 (1975): 328–35.

Rowley, Sharon M. *The Old English Version of Bede's Historia Ecclesiastica*. London: D.S. Brewer, 2011.

Rumble, Alexander, ed. *Leaders of the Anglo-Saxon Church: From Bede to Stigland*. Woodbridge: Boydell Press, 2012.

Russom, Geoffrey R. 'A Germanic concept of nobility in *The Gifts of Men* and *Beowulf*'. *Speculum* 53 (1978): 1–15.

Rypins, Stanley, ed. *Three Old English Prose Texts in MS Cotton Vitellius A xv*. EETS os 161. 1924 (for 1921). Rpt. Woodbridge: Boydell and Brewer, 1998.

Salvador, Mercedes. 'Architectural metaphors and Christological imagery in the *Advent Lyrics*: Benedictine propaganda in the Exeter Book?' In *Conversion and Colonization in Anglo-Saxon England*, ed. Catherine E. Karkov and Nicholas Howe, 169–211. MRTS 318. Essays in Anglo-Saxon Studies 2. Tempe: ACMRS, 2006.

Salvador-Bello, Mercedes. 'The Edgar panegyrics in the Anglo-Saxon Chronicle'. In *Edgar, King of the English, 959–975: New Interpretations*, ed. Donald Scragg, 252–72. Publications of the Manchester Centre for Anglo-Saxon Studies 8. Woodbridge: Boydell Press, 2008.

Savage, Anne. 'The Old English *Exodus* and the colonization of the Promised Land'. *New Medieval Literatures* 4 (2001): 39–60.

Scheil, Andrew. 'The historiographic dimensions of *Beowulf*'. *JEGP* 107 (2008): 281–302.

Scragg, Donald G. 'A reading of *Brunanburh*'. In *Unlocking the Wordhord: Anglo-Saxon Studies in Memory of Edward B. Irving, Jr.*, ed. Mark C. Amodio and Katherine O'Brien O'Keeffe, 109–22. Toronto: University of Toronto Press, 2003.

Scragg, Donald G. 'The significance of the Vercelli Book among Anglo-Saxon vernacular writings'. In *Vercelli tra Oriente ed Occidente tra Tarda Antichita e Medioevo*, ed. Vittoria Dolcetti Corazza, 35–43. Vercelli: Edizioni dell'Orso, 1997.

Scragg, Donald G. 'Source study'. In *Reading Old English Texts*, ed. Katherine O'Brien O'Keeffe, 39–58. Cambridge: Cambridge University Press, 1997.

Scragg, Donald G., ed. *The Vercelli Homilies and Related Texts*. EETS os 300. Oxford: Oxford University Press, 1992.

Schreiber, Carolyn. *King Alfred's Old English Translation of Pope Gregory the Great's 'Regula Pastoralis' and Its Cultural Context*. Münchener Universitätsschriften 25. Bern: Peter Lang, 2002.

Sharma, Manish. 'The reburial of the cross in the Old English *Elene*'. In *New Readings in the Vercelli Book*, ed. Samantha Zacher and Andy Orchard, 280–97. Toronto Anglo-Saxon Series 4. Toronto: University of Toronto Press, 2009.

Sharma, Manish. 'A reconsideration of the structure of *Guthlac A*: the extremes of saintliness'. *JEGP* 101 (2002): 185–200.

Sheppard, Alice. 'A word to the wise: thinking, knowledge and wisdom in *The Wanderer*'. In *Source of Wisdom: Old English and Early Medieval Latin Studies in Honour of Thomas D. Hill*, ed. Charles D. Wright, Frederick M. Biggs, and Thomas N. Hall, 130–44. Toronto Old English Series 16. Toronto: University of Toronto Press, 2007.

Sheppard, Alice. *Families of the King: Writing Identity in the 'Anglo-Saxon Chronicle'*. Toronto Old English Series 12. Toronto: University of Toronto Press, 2004.

Shimomura, Sachi. *Odd Bodies and Visible Ends in Medieval Literature*. The New Middle Ages. New York: Palgrave Macmillan, 2006.

Shimomura, Sachi. 'Remembering in circles: *The Wife's Lament*, *conversatio*, and the community of memory'. In *Source of Wisdom: Old English and Early Medieval Latin Studies in Honour of Thomas D. Hill*, ed. Charles D. Wright, Frederick M. Biggs, and Thomas N. Hall, 113–29. Toronto Old English Series 16. Toronto: University of Toronto Press, 2007.

Shippey, Thomas A. 'Wealth and wisdom in King Alfred's *Preface* to the Old English *Pastoral Care*'. *EHR* 94 (1979): 346–55.

Skeat, Walter W., ed. and trans. *Ælfric's Lives of Saints*. 2 vols. EETS os 76 and 114. 1881 and 1900. Rpt. Woodbridge: Boydell and Brewer, 2003.

Smyth, Alfred P. *King Alfred the Great*. Oxford: Oxford University Press, 1995.

Squires, Ann, ed. *The Old English Physiologus*. Durham Medieval Texts 5. Durham: Durham Medieval Texts, 1988.

Sobecki, Sebastian I. 'The interpretation of *The Seafarer* – a re-examination of the pilgrimage theory'. *Neophilologus* 92 (2008): 127–39.

Stafford, Pauline. 'The Anglo-Saxon Chronicles, identity and the making of England'. *Haskins Society Journal* 19 (2007): 28–50.

Stanley, Eric G. 'The prose *Menologium* and the verse *Menologium*'. In *Text and Language in Medieval English Prose*, ed. Akio Oizumi, Jacek Fisiak, and John Scahill, 255–67. New York: Peter Lang, 2005.

Stanley, Eric G. *The Search for Anglo-Saxon Paganism. NQ* 209–10 (1964–65). Rpt. Cambridge: D.S. Brewer, 1975.

Stanley, Eric G. 'Wulfstan and Ælfric: "The true difference between the Law and the Gospel"'. In *Wulfstan, Archbishop of York: the Proceedings of the Second Alcuin Conference*, ed. Matthew Townend, 429–41. Studies in the Early Middle Ages 10. Turnhout: Brepols, 2004.

Staples, Martha Jane. 'Lingering phonemes: the vocabulary of the Finnsburg Fragment'. *Medieval Perspectives* 17 (2003): 162–74.

Steen, Janie. *Verse and Virtuosity: The Adaptation of Latin Rhetoric in Old English Verse*. Toronto Old English Series 18. Toronto: University of Toronto Press, 2008.

Stenton, F.M. *Anglo-Saxon England*. 1943. 3rd edn. 1971. Reissue Oxford: Oxford University Press, 2001.

Sterne, Laurence. *Tristram Shandy*, ed. Howard Anderson. New York: W.W. Norton, 1980.

Stock, Brian. *Listening for the Text: On the Uses of the Past*. Parallax: Re-Visions of Culture and Society. Baltimore: Johns Hopkins University Press, 1990.

Stodnick, Jacqueline. 'What (and where) is the *Anglo-Saxon Chronicle* about?: spatial history.' *BJRL* 86 (2004): 87–104.

Swanton, Michael, ed. and trans. *Anglo-Saxon Prose*. London: Dent, 1975.

Sweet, Henry, ed. and trans. *King Alfred's West-Saxon Version of Gregory's Pastoral Care*. EETS os 45. 1871–1872. Rpt. Woodbridge: Boydell and Brewer, 2007.

Szarmach, Paul E. 'Ælfric revises: the lives of Martin and the idea of the author'. In *Unlocking the Wordhord: Anglo-Saxon Studies in Memory of Edward B. Irving, Jr.*, ed. Mark C. Amodio and Katherine O'Brien O'Keeffe, 38–61. Toronto: University of Toronto Press, 2003.

Szarmach, Paul E. 'Alfred's *Boethius* and the four cardinal virtues'. In *Alfred the Wise: Studies in Honour of Janet Bately on the Occasion of Her Sixty-Fifth Birthday*, ed. Jane Roberts, Janet L. Nelson, and Malcolm Godden, 223–35. Cambridge: D.S. Brewer, 1997.

Szarmach, Paul E. 'An apologia for the *Metres of Boethius*'. In *Naked Wordes in English*, ed. Marcin Krygier and Liliana Sikorska, 107–34. Frankfurt: Peter Lang, 2005.

Szarmach, Paul E. 'The meaning of Alfred's *Preface* to the *Pastoral Care*'. *Mediaevalia* 6 (1982 for 1980): 57–86.

Szarmach, Paul E. 'The "poetic turn of mind" of the translator of the OE *Bede*'. In *Anglo-Saxons: Studies Presented to Cyril Roy Hart*, ed. Simon Keynes and Alfred P. Smyth, 54–68. Dublin: Four Courts Press, 2006.

Szarmach, Paul E. 'The Vercelli Homilies: style and structure'. In *The Old English Homily and its Backgrounds*, ed. Paul E. Szarmach and Bernard F. Huppé, 241–67. Albany: State University of New York Press, 1978.

Szarmach, Paul E. 'The Vercelli prose and Anglo-Saxon literary history'. In *New Readings in the Vercelli Book*, ed. Samantha Zacher and Andy Orchard, 12–40. Toronto Anglo-Saxon Series 4. Toronto: University of Toronto Press, 2009.

Tamburr, Karl. *The Harrowing of Hell in Medieval England*. Cambridge: D.S. Brewer, 2007.

Thijs, Christine. 'Feminine heroism in the Old English *Judith*'. *LSE* ns 37 (2006): 41–62.

Thormann, Janet. 'The *Anglo-Saxon Chronicle* poems and the making of the English nation'. In *Anglo-Saxonism and the Construction of Social Identity*, ed. Allen J. Frantzen and John D. Niles, 60–85. Gainesville: University Press of Florida, 1997.

Thormann, Janet. 'Enjoyment of violence and desire for history in *Beowulf*'. In *The Postmodern 'Beowulf': A Critical Casebook*, ed. Eileen A. Joy and Mary K. Ramsey, 287–318. Morgantown: West Virginia University Press, 2006.

Thorpe, Benjamin, ed. and trans. *Ancient Laws and Institutes of England*. 2 vols. London: G. Eyre and A. Spottiswoode, 1840.

Thorpe, Benjamin, ed. *Libri Psalmorum: Versio Antiqua Latina cum Paraphrasi Anglo-Saxonica.* Oxford: E Typographeo Academico, 1835.

Toller, T. Northcote, and Alistair Campbell, eds. *An Anglo-Saxon Dictionary Based on the Manuscript Collections of Joseph Bosworth: Supplement.* 1921. *Enlarged Addenda and Corrigenda to the Supplement by T. Northcote Toller to An Anglo-Saxon Dictionary Based on the Manuscript Collections of Joseph Bosworth* by Alistair Campbell. Oxford: Oxford University Press, 1972.

Toswell, M.J. 'The Metrical Psalter and *The Menologium*: some observations'. *NM* 94 (1993): 249–57.

Townend, Matthew, ed. *Wulfstan, Archbishop of York: The Proceedings of the Second Alcuin Conference.* Studies in the Early Middle Ages 10. Turnhout: Brepols, 2004.

Trahern, Joseph B. 'The *Ioca Monachorum* and the Old English *Pharaoh*'. *ELN* 7 (1970–71): 165–8.

Treharne, Elaine. 'The form and function of the Vercelli Book'. In *Text, Image, Interpretation: Studies in Anglo-Saxon Literature and Its Insular Context in Honour of Éamon Ó Carragáin*, ed. A.J. Minnis and Jane Roberts, 253–66. Studies in the Early Middle Ages 18. Turnhout: Brepols, 2007.

Trilling, Renée R. *The Aesthetics of Nostalgia: Historical Representation in Old English Verse.* Toronto Anglo-Saxon Series 3. Toronto: University of Toronto Press, 2009.

Trilling, Renée R. 'Ruins in the realms of thoughts: reading as constellation in Anglo-Saxon Poetry'. *JEGP* 108 (2009): 141–67.

Tyler, Lee Edgar. 'The heroic oath of Hildebrand'. In *De Gustibus: Essays for Alain Renoir*, ed. John Miles Foley, 551–85. Albert Bates Lord Studies in Oral Tradition 11. New York: Garland, 1992.

VanderBilt, Deborah. 'Translation and orality in the Old English *Orosius*'. *OT* 13 (1998): 377–97.

Wallace-Hadrill, J.M. *Bede's Ecclesiastical History of the English People: A Historical Commentary.* Oxford: Clarendon Press, 1988.

Watson, Jonathan. 'The *Finnsburh* Skald: kennings and cruces in the Anglo-Saxon Fragment'. *JEGP* 101 (2002): 497–519.

Waugh, Robin. 'The blindness curse and nonmiracles in the Old English prose *Life of Saint Guthlac*'. *MP* 106 (2009): 399–426.

Waugh, Robin. 'The characteristic moment as a motif in *The Finnsburg Fragment* and *Deor*'. *English Studies in Canada* 23 (1997): 249–61.

Wehlau, Ruth. 'The power of knowledge and the location of the reader in *Christ and Satan*'. *JEGP* 97 (1998): 1–12.

Wehlau, Ruth. 'Rumination and re-creation: poetic instruction in *The Order of the World*'. *Florilegium* 13 (1994): 65–77.

Wentersdorf, Karl P. 'The Old English *Rhyming Poem*: a ruler's lament'. *SP* 82 (1985): 265–94.

Whatley, E. Gordon. 'Hagiography and violence: military men in Ælfric's *Lives of Saints*'. In *Source of Wisdom: Old English and Early Medieval Latin Studies in Honour of Thomas D. Hill*, ed. Charles D. Wright, Frederick M. Biggs, and Thomas N. Hall, 217–38. Toronto Old English Series 16. Toronto: University of Toronto Press, 2007.

Whitelock, Dorothy, ed. and trans. *The Anglo-Saxon Chronicle. A Revised Translation.* 1961. Rpt. Westport: Greenwood Press, 1986 Norwich: Jarrold and Sons, 1961.

Whitelock, Dorothy, ed. and trans. *English Historical Documents.* Vol. I: *c. 500–1040.* 1955. 2nd edn. Rpt. New York: Routledge, 1996.

Wilcox, Jonathan, ed. and trans. *Ælfric's Prefaces.* Durham: Durham Medieval Texts, 1994.

Wilcox, Jonathan. 'Eating people is wrong: funny style in *Andreas* and its analogues'. In *Anglo-Saxon Styles*, ed. Catherine Karkov and George H. Brown, 201–22. SUNY Series in Medieval Studies. Albany: State University of New York Press, 2003.

Wilcox, Jonathan. '"Tell me what I am": the Old English riddles'. In *Readings in Medieval Texts: Interpreting Old and Middle English Literature*, ed. David Johnson and Elaine Treharne, 46–59. Oxford: Oxford University Press, 2005.

Wilcox, Jonathan. 'The wolf on the shepherds: Wulfstan, bishops, and the context of the *Sermo Lupi ad Anglos*'. In *Old English Prose: Basic Readings*, ed. Paul E. Szarmach, with the assistance of Deborah A. Oosterhouse, 395–418. Basic Readings in Anglo-Saxon England 5. New York: Garland, 2000.

Wittig, Joseph S. '"Homiletic Fragment II" and the Epistle to the Ephesians'. *Traditio* 25 (1969): 358–63.

Wolfe, Melissa J. '"Swa cwæð snottor on mode": four issues in *The Wanderer*'. *Neophilologus* 92 (2008): 559–65.

Wright, Charles D. 'The blood of Abel and the branches of sin: *Genesis A*, *Maxims I* and Aldhelm's *Carmen de uirginitate*'. *ASE* 25 (1996): 7–19.

Wright, Charles D. '*Genesis A ad litteram*'. In *Old English Literature and the Old Testament*, ed. Michael Fox and Manish Sharma, 121–71. Toronto Anglo-Saxon Series 10. Toronto: University of Toronto Press, 2012.

Wright, Charles D. 'Old English homilies and Latin sources'. In *The Old English Homily: Precedent, Practice, and Appropriation*, ed. Aaron J. Kleist, 15–66. Studies in the Early Middle Ages 17. Turnhout: Brepols, 2007.

Wright, Charles D. 'The persecuted church and the *Mysterium Lunae*: Cynewulf's *Ascension*, lines 252b–272 (*Christ II*, lines 691b–711)'. In *Latin Learning and English Lore: Studies in Anglo-Saxon Literature for Michael Lapidge*, ed. Katherine O'Brien O'Keeffe and Andy Orchard, vol. II, 293–314. Toronto Old English series 14. 2 vols. Toronto: University of Toronto Press, 2005.

Wright, Cyril E., ed. *Bald's Leechbook. British [Library] Royal Manuscript 12 D. xvii*. EEMF 5. Copenhagen, Rosenkilde and Bagger, 1955.

Yerkes, David. *Syntax and Style in Old English. A Comparison of the Two Versions of Wærferth's Translation of Gregory's Dialogues*. Binghamton: MRTS, 1982.

Yerkes, David. *The Two Versions of Wærferth's Translation of Gregory's Dialogues: An Old English Thesaurus*. Toronto: University of Toronto Press, 1979.

Yorke, Barbara. *The Conversion of Britain: Religion, Politics, and Society in Britain c. 600–800*. New York: Pearson/Longman, 2006.

Zacher, Samantha. *Preaching the Converted: The Style and Rhetoric of the Vercelli Book Homilies*. Toronto Anglo-Saxon Series 1. Toronto: University of Toronto Press, 2009.

Zacher, Samantha. 'The source of Vercelli VII: an address to women'. In *New Readings on the Vercelli Book*, ed. Samantha Zacher and Andy Orchard, 98–127. Toronto Anglo-Saxon Series 4. Toronto: University of Toronto Press, 2009.

Znojemská, Helena. 'Sailing the dangerous waters: images of land and sea in *The Seafarer*, *The Panther and The Whale*'. *Prague Studies in English* 24 (2005): 87–105.

Znojemská, Helena. 'A *scop* among scribes: a reading in the manuscript context of *Widsið*'. *Litteraria Pragensia* 31 (2006): 36–64.

Zollinger, Cynthia Wittman. 'Cynewulf's *Elene* and the patterns of the past'. *JEGP* 103 (2004): 180–96.

Index

Index of Manuscripts

The Anglo-Saxon Literature Handbook, First Edition. Mark C. Amodio.
© 2014 Mark C. Amodio. Published 2014 by John Wiley & Sons, Ltd.